fundamentals of organizational behaviour

key concepts, skills & best practices

First Canadian Edition

Robert Kreitner
Arizona
State University

Angelo Kinicki
Arizona
State University

Nina Cole
Ryerson
University

McGraw-Hill Ryerson

Toronto   Montréal   Boston   Burr Ridge, IL   Dubuque, IA   Madison, WI   New York
San Francisco   St. Louis   Bangkok   Bogotá   Caracas   Kuala Lumpur   Lisbon   London
Madrid   Mexico City   Milan   New Delhi   Santiago   Seoul   Singapore   Sydney   Taipei

McGraw-Hill
Ryerson Limited

A Subsidiary of The McGraw·Hill Companies

Fundamentals of Organizational Behaviour
Key Concepts, Skills and Best Practices
First Canadian Edition

ISBN: 0-07-091091-X

1 2 3 4 5 6 7 8 9 10   RRD   0 9 8 7 6 5 4 3

Printed and bound in the U.S.A.

Vice President, Editorial and Media Technology: *Patrick Ferrier*
Sponsoring Editor: *Lenore Gray Spence*
Managing Editor, Development: *Kim Brewster*
Director of Marketing: *Jeff MacLean*
Marketing Manager: *Kelly Smyth*
Supervising Editor: *Anne Nellis*
Production Coordinator: *Kelly Selleck*
Composition: *Bookman Typesetting Co. Inc.*
Cover Image: *National Geographic/Joel Sartore*
Cover Design: *Greg Devitt*
Interior Design: *Maureen McCutcheon/Greg Devitt*
Printer: *RR Donnelley Receivables, Inc.*

National Library of Canada Cataloguing in Publication

Kinicki, Angelo
  Organizational behaviour : key concepts, skills and best practices /
Angelo Kinicki, Robert Kreitner, Nina Cole. — 1st Canadian ed.

Includes bibliographical references and index.
ISBN 0-07-091091-X

1. Organizational behavior.   I. Kreitner, Robert   II. Cole, Nina D. (Nina Dawn)   III. Title.

HD58.7.K49 2002   658   C2002-904727-7

Angelo Kinicki is a Professor and Dean's Council of 100 Distinguished Scholar at Arizona State University. He joined the faculty in 1982, the year he received his doctorate in business administration from Kent State University. His specialty is Organizational Behaviour.

Angelo is recognized for both his research and teaching. He has published over 60 articles in a variety of leading academic and professional journals devoted to organizational behaviour. Angelo's outstanding teaching performance resulted in his selection as the Graduate Teacher of the Year and the Undergraduate Teacher of the Year in the College of Business at Arizona State University. He also was acknowledged as the Instructor of the Year for Executive Education from the Center for Executive Development at Arizona State University.

Angelo also is a busy consultant and speaker with companies around the world. His clients are many of the Fortune 500 companies as well as a variety of entrepreneurial firms.

Robert Kreitner, PhD is an Emeritus Professor of Management at Arizona State University. Prior to joining ASU in 1975, Bob taught at Western Illinois University. He also has taught organizational behaviour at the American Graduate School of International Management (Thunderbird). Bob is a popular speaker, consultant, and executive developer who has addressed a diverse array of audiences worldwide on management topics. Bob has authored articles for many respected journals and also is the co-author (with Fred Luthans) of the award-winning book *Organizational Behavior Modification and Beyond: An Operant and Social Learning Approach,* and the author of *Management,* 8th edition, a best-selling introductory management text.

In 1981–82 he served as Chairman of the Academy of Management's Management Education and Development Division. Bob spent six months teaching management courses for the University in Micronesia, and in 1996, he taught two courses in Albania's first-ever MBA program. He taught a summer leadership program in Switzerland from 1995 to 1998.

Nina Cole is Associate Professor of Organizational Behaviour and Human Resources Management at Ryerson University in Toronto.

Prior to her academic career, she spent 12 years in the business world— eight years as a human resources management consultant, and four years as a human resources manager. The last 13 years have been spent as an academic, teaching and conducting research in human resources management and organizational behaviour.

Nina has published articles in both academic journals and industry publications, and has led seminars to assist managers in these challenging areas. She has spoken and written on these topics on numerous occasions and has also co-authored textbooks on human resources management.

Active Learning

Robert Kreitner, Angelo Kinicki, and Nina Cole have developed this text to provide lean and efficient coverage of topics such as diversity in organizations, ethics, and globalization, which are recommended by AACSB International—the Association to Advance Collegiate Schools of Business. Timely chapter-opening cases, learning outcomes, a wealth of skill-building experiential end-of-chapter material, four-colour presentation, lively writing style, and real-world in-text examples are all used to enhance this overall educational package.

This successful author team has designed this text to facilitate active learning by relying on the following:

PERCEPTIONS ABOUT WOMEN AND THE NEW ECONOMY: EBAY'S LORNA BORENSTEIN

Perceptions about women in the workplace are slowly changing. Ask Lorna Borenstein how women are faring in the New Economy, and the general manager of eBay Canada Ltd. says:

"I can walk into a room now and no one is going to mistake me for an assistant. That hasn't always been the case. I've been asked to get the coffee more than once."

Ms. Borenstein, a lawyer who also has an MBA, started out in the legal profession, then moved to Hewlett-Packard and ran her own Internet consulting firm. In her mid-thirties, she says New Economy companies are an ideal place for women, or anyone, to prove themselves because people do not generally use stereotypes to make assumptions about your ability.

Nevertheless, the leadership of major Internet firms is still mostly male. One exception is eBay itself, with female CEO Meg Whitman and other women like Borenstein leading eBay operations in other countries. She pre-

dicts that as the industry matures and recovers from its recent meltdown, the eBay example will become the norm.

Borenstein attributes her own self-esteem to the confidence of her mother, who became a superior court judge in Quebec and never doubted that women should be able to have the same success as men. That's a belief she hopes to pass on to her own three children and especially her two young daughters.

But Borenstein worries that lack of career-related self-efficacy may deter many women from promoting themselves as much as they should. Borenstein's own moves from law through industry and now to management of an internet firm were the result of a series of careful decisions—indicating her internal locus of control—but she also acknowledges the involvement of an external force called luck!

Lorna Borenstein, general manager of eBay Canada Ltd.

Source: Adapted from E Church, "EBay executive sees level field," *Globe & Mail*, March 29, 2001, p B17.

Brief Chapter Opening Cases—

For some real-world context, these cases use topics that are timely and relevant to actual life situations.

OB in Action Case: Christine Carmichael
(applicable to Chapter 3: Motivation)

Christine Carmichael

Tony Dunlop, the new president of Roselawn Manufacturing Ltd., was very concerned. He had been hired to "turn the company around" and reverse the declining customer service levels and profitability which had resulted from the disastrous implementation of new enterprise resource software, which integrated all of the company's existing systems and used one underlying data base. Roselawn Manufacturing was 30 years old, had 35 employees at its Scarborough headquarters, and just over 200 manufacturing workers at its plant in Oshawa.

The board of directors had suspected for some time that employee morale was a major problem. These suspicions had been confirmed last week when a group of employees went to the Ontario Human Rights Commission and accused Tony's predecessor, John Morgan, of creating a "poisoned environment" for employees, particularly females. Tony had just finished a long discussion with Christine Carmichael, a recently departed employee, and now was convinced that changes had to be made in the way employees were treated. He decided to review what Christine had told him about how her motivation had been destroyed during the year she worked at Roselawn Manufacturing and try to identify specific problems that needed to be addressed.

Great Expectations

Upon completing her university degree in Business Administration, Christine Carmichael applied for numerous positions she found on the Internet, in the local newspaper, and at her university's career service department. She knew it would be difficult to land her "dream job" in human resources management, as she was just starting out and had a limited network of contacts in that profession. In August, Christine applied for a management trainee position at a local company, Roselawn Manufacturing Ltd. This position appealed to her because a large component of the work was training staff on the new enterprise resource software that the company was about to implement. Also, Christine was to be groomed for a management position once one became available. Although the position had relatively low pay for a university graduate, Christine wanted to gain experience and hoped that with hard work, she would be compensated equitably.

Christine started working the first week of September, during the pilot project for the new system. Her boss, Mel, was the Accounting Supervisor. Mel was friendly and helpful, but very busy. During her first week, she was present for all training sessions on the new software, which was expected to go live on November 1. Suddenly, it was decided that the software would not be implemented until the following summer. This dramatically changed the position for which Christine was hired. Optimistically, she hoped to learn more about Roselawn Manufacturing and more about the software, and them help to train other employees before they started using it.

Christine spent the next few weeks assisting in the preparation for the new software by converting data from the old system to the new. She was given conflicting instructions by her boss (Mel), the general manager (Bill), and the Vice President of Finance (Andy). She found it difficult to complete tasks because each person acted as though they were in charge. This confusion continued through the entire duration of the project. Christine started to wonder if the delays were a result of this method of organization.

The Staff Party

Christine noticed that many of the staff seemed afraid of the new software. They seemed to have adopted the opinion that if they avoid it, they could prolong the time until they would have to start using it. Perhaps as a result of the other employees' discomfort with the idea of learning new software, Christine found it very hard to fit in at her new job. People did not welcome her because they did not welcome the purpose for which she was hired. She was ignored in the social atmosphere and looked down upon by those who feared change. Two weeks after she began her new job, the company had its annual staff party, and she was not invited. It was the talk of the office both before and after the party, which added insult to injury and made Christine feels like an outsider.

Reality Bites

After all the data conversion was completed, Christine began working for the general manager, Bill. She worked hard and frequently stayed late in order to learn the business. About

OB In Action Cases—

An Appendix containing supplementary cases: "OB In Action" is included after chapter 13. Great for more in-depth individual study or group assignments.

Active Learning

Mentoring—Part of Diversity Management at Rogers

Phillip Francis, Manager, Corporate Diversity at Rogers, says that commitment to diversity is "about attracting and retaining the best employees we can. It's about changing circumstances for employees and being responsible for employees' individual needs. It makes good business sense to us."

Mentoring is one way to provide feedback to employees. In 2000, Rogers successfully completed a diversity mentoring program pilot project and rolled it out nation-wide. Rather than having one-on-one mentoring, they opted for a team-based mentoring program to provide broader feedback to employees. The pilot program was made available to 25 Toronto employees with 22 participating mentors at the director or vice president level.

The mentors and employees were split into five teams, and flexibility allowed individuals to approach other teams for guidance and feedback in areas of interest that may not have been covered by their own mentors. Each team was composed of a diverse group of people, with mentors from many areas within the company, who were able to support the employees' goals. Employees receive a minimum of two hours per month with their mentors, and the teams are responsible for deciding how best to use their time.

Rogers conducted a survey of the pilot ~~program~~ start, but some one-on-one time should ~~be~~ relationship building, more time and effo

Another ongoing component of Rogers' ~~program~~ which call centre training is provided to ~~people on~~ unemployment, are not eligible for empl~~oyment~~

"The reason we are involved is because ~~we are committed~~ to diversity and recognized in the comm~~unity~~

Since becoming participants some two a~~nd a half years ago~~ the Goodwill program, A follow-up surve~~y found that employ-~~ ees have zero turnover—all are still wit~~h the company.~~ That's performance management!

Source: Adapted from L. Young, "Mentoring Program is ~~…~~

How to Win Clients and Influence People

Brian Mulroney's habit of helping out his pals hurt him when he was prime minister, but ~~now that he's~~ become a private sector operator, the same schmoozy approach is making him—and his ~~clients—very~~ rich. Mulroney has been able to parlay his background into a global lobbying business. Y~~ou can~~ find him zig-zagging the globe, lobbying foreign governments on behalf of big-name client~~s.~~

Mulroney sits on the boards of several carefully selected companies, including Barrick Go~~ld. Before~~ he took his place on the board, Mulroney had a chance to show his stuff. Barrick had bo~~ught sev-~~ erals of Toronto, which operated gold mines in Chile. But one of its main deposits ran a~~cross the bor-~~ der into Argentina. Since relations between the two countries were quite strained, Bar~~rick could-~~ n't see how it could go about mining the deposit. So Mulroney was asked to smooth th~~ings over.~~

His technique was very straightforward. "I met with the two heads of state separately," ~~he says. "Then~~ I talked to their ministers, as well as representatives from the private sector." Result: tw~~o months later,~~ Chile and Argentina had signed a new mining agreement. Now, everything needed to ope~~rate the mine~~ can flow freely from one side of the Andes to the other. How do you convince two hea~~ds of state to~~ change their legislation? "It's all in the way you present things," explains Mulroney. "P~~eople respect~~ their own concerns, constraints, and agendas. I know what they are and how to satisfy ~~them. I am on~~ an equal footing with these leaders. I have credibility. The solutions I propose are reali~~stic."~~

Source: D Bérard, "How to Win Clients and Influence People," Canadian Business, April 30, 1999, pp 42–45.

Monkey See, Monkey Do

A study by researchers from Canada and the United Sates of 187 work group members from 20 different organizations uncovered a "monkey see, monkey do" effect relative to antisocial behaviour. Employees who observed their coworkers engaging in antisocial conduct at work tended to exhibit the same bad behaviour. Antisocial behaviour, as measured in this study, included the following acts:

—damaging company property
—saying hurtful things to coworkers
—doing poor work; working slowly
—complaining with coworkers
—bending or breaking rules
—criticizing coworkers
—doing something harmful to boss or employer
—starting an argument with a coworker
—saying rude things about the boss or organization.

According to the researchers, "The message for managers seems clear—antisocial groups encourage antisocial individual behaviour. It is crucial to nip behaviours deemed harmful in the bud so as to avoid a social influence effect. Managers who expect that isolating or ignoring antisocial groups will encourage them to change are probably mistaken."

You Decide . . .

Are these antisocial behaviours also unethical? As a manager, how would you handle these behaviours if they occurred in your work group?

Source: ~~Qu~~oted and adapted from S L Robinson and A M ~~O'Lear~~y-Kelly, "Monkey See, Monkey Do: The Influence of ~~Work Gro~~ups on the Antisocial Behavior of Employees," ~~Academy of~~ Management Journal, December 1998, pp 658–72.

Special Boxed Features—

Each chapter contains boxed features on Focus on Diversity, International OB, and Ethics At Work to highlight examples of real companies, personalities, and issues to offer students practical experience.

---

summary of key concepts

- *Name five "soft" and four "hard" influence tactics, and summarize the practical lessons from influence research.* Five soft influence tactics are rational persuasion, inspirational appeals, consultation, ingratiation, and personal appeals. They are more friendly and less coercive than the four hard influence tactics: exchange, coalition tactics, pressure, and legitimating tactics. According to research, soft tactics are better for generating commitment and are perceived as more fair than hard tactics.

- *Identify and briefly describe French and Raven's five bases of power.* French and Raven's five bases of power are reward power (rewarding compliance), coercive power (punishing noncompliance), legitimate power (relying on formal authority), expert power (providing needed information), and referent power (relying on personal attraction)

- *Define organizational politics, explain what triggers it, and specify the three levels of political action in organizations.* Organizational politics is defined as intentional acts of influence to enhance or protect the self-interests of individuals or groups. Uncertainty triggers most politicking in organizations. Political action occurs at individual, coalition, and network levels. Coalitions are informal, temporary, and single-issue alliances.

- *Distinguish between favourable and unfavourable impression management tactics.* Favourable upward impression management can be job-focused (manipulating information about one's job performance), supervisor-focused (praising or doing favours for the boss), or self-focused (being polite and nice). Unfavourable upward impression management tactics include decreasing performance, not

---

Summary of Key Concepts—

This section includes responses to the learning objectives in each chapter making it a handy review tool for all users.

Active Learning

Key Terms—
Key Terms are bolded within the text and defined in the margins for easy reference.

key terms

centralized decision making, 281	line managers, 272	organizational ecology, 275
closed system, 272	mechanistic organizations, 280	span of control, 271
contingency approach, 278	open system, 272	staff managers, 272
decentralized decision making, 281	organic organizations, 280	strategic constituency, 278
differentiation, 279	organization, 270	unity of command principle, 270
integration, 279	organization chart, 270	

discussion questions

1. How many organizations directly affect your life today? List as many as you can.

2. What would an organization chart of your current (or last) place of employment look like? Does the chart you have drawn reveal the hierarchy (chain of command), division of labour, span of control, and line-staff distinctions? Does it reveal anything else? Explain.

3. How would you respond to a manager who claimed that the only way to measure a business's effectiveness is in terms of how much profit it makes?

4. In a nutshell, what does contingency organizational design entail?

5. If organic organizations are popular with most employees, why can't all organizations be structured in an organic fashion?

6. Which of the three new organizational configurations probably will be most prevalent 10 to 15 years from now? Why?

Discussion Questions—
These sets of review questions cover key concepts of the chapter and can be used to generate classroom discussion or for individual review.

internet exercises

www.queendom.com

1. Relationships and Communications Skills Testing

Managers, who are responsible for getting things accomplished with and through others, simply cannot be effective if they are unable to interact skillfully in social settings. As with any skill development program, you need to know *where you are* before constructing a learning agenda for *where you want to be.* Go to Body-Mind Queen-Dom (**www.queendom.com**), and select the category "Tests & Profiles." (Note: Our use of this site is for instructional purposes only and does not constitute an endorsement of any products that may or may not suit your needs. There is no obligation to buy anything.) Next, choose "Relationships" and select the "Communication Skills Test," read the brief instructions, complete all 34 items, and

ones: Arguing Style Test; Assertiveness Test; and Conflict Management Test.

QUESTIONS

1. How did you score? Are you pleasantly (or unpleasantly) surprised by your score?
2. What is your strongest social/communication skill?
3. Reviewing the questionnaire item by item, can you find obvious weak spots in your social/communication skills? For instance, are you a poor listener? Do you interrupt too often? Do you need to be more aware of others, both verbally and nonverbally? Do you have a hard time tuning

Internet Exercises—
Detailed and challenging, these exercises (two per chapter) are found at the end of each chapter. This resource helps students understand how to use the Internet as a powerful resource in business practice.

Active Learning

experiential exercises

1. Anger Control Role Play

Objectives

1. To demonstrate that emotions can be managed.
2. To develop your interpersonal skills for managing both your own and someone else's anger.

Introduction

Personal experience and research tell us that anger begets anger. People do not make their best decisions when angry. Angry outbursts often inflict unintentional interpersonal damage by triggering other emotions (e.g., disgust in observers and subsequent guilt and shame in the angry person). Effective managers know how to break the cycle of negative emotions by defusing anger in themselves and

ROLE 1: THE ANGRY (OUT-OF-CONTROL) SHIFT SUPERVISOR

You work for a leading electronics company that makes computer chips and other computer-related equipment. Your factory is responsible for assembling and testing the company's most profitable line of computer microprocessors. Business has been good, so your factory is working three shifts. The day shift, which you are now on, is the most desirable one. The night shift, from 11 P.M. to 7:30 A.M. is the least desirable and least productive. In fact, the night shift is such a mess that your boss, the factory manager, wants you to move to the night shift next week. Your boss just broke this bad news as the two of you are having lunch in the company cafeteria. You are shocked

Experiential Exercises—

These additional exercises (two per chapter) are designed to sharpen users' skills by either recommending how to apply a concept, theory, or model, or by giving an exemplary corporate application. Students will benefit from real-world experiences and direct skill-building opportunities.

Personal Awareness and Growth Exercises—

These exercises (two per chapter) are included to help readers personalize and expand upon key concepts as they are presented in the text. These exercises encourage active and thoughtful interaction rather than passive reading.

personal awareness and growth exercises

1. How Ready Are You to Assume the Leadership Role?

Objectives

1. To assess your readiness for the leadership role.
2. To consider the implications of the gap between your career goals and your readiness to lead.

Introduction

Leaders assume multiple roles. Roles represent the expectations that others have of occupants of a position. It is important for potential leaders to consider whether they are ready for the leadership role because mismatches in expectations or skills can derail a leader's effectiveness. This exercise assesses your readiness to assume the leadership role.

Instructions

For each statement, indicate the extent to which you agree

9. I would enjoy coaching other members of the team.	1 — 2 — 3 — 4 — 5
10. It is important to me to recognize others for their accomplishments.	1 — 2 — 3 — 4 — 5
11. I would enjoy entertaining visitors to my firm even if it interfered with my completing a report.	1 — 2 — 3 — 4 — 5
12. It would be fun for me to represent my team at gatherings outside our department.	1 — 2 — 3 — 4 — 5
13. The problems of my teammates are my problems too	1 — 2 — 3 — 4 — 5

CBC video case

Gap Adventures

Gap Adventures sells a hot holiday product—adventure travel and eco-tourism in Central and South America. The company has been very successful, growing from two employees to 70, with $12 million in sales, as well as winning awards for its ethical practices. Their corporate culture has been family-oriented, with all employees having input into decision making. At this point, owner Bruce Poon Tip sees himself as better at building businesses than at maintaining them and wants to move on to new challenges in expanding and diversifying Gap's operations.

So Bruce has hired Dave Bowen, a marketing expert from the company's largest US competitor, to shake up the Gap Adventures organization, which he sees as a bit too complacent, and

Dave's new approach to management results in a new reservation system and a new phone system, both of which have serious bugs to be worked out. He also establishes a number of new company policies, which are taking some time to get through to employees out in the field. Employees are working longer hours, and dealing with increased stress. Overall, as Bruce leaves for the Amazon to get married, he sees the culture as more serious, more controlled, more corporate and less relaxed than it was before.

QUESTIONS FOR DISCUSSION

1. What corporate values have changed at Gap Adventures since the arrival of Dave Bowen?
2. Explain how the culture change at Gap Adventures has

CBC Video Cases—

A CBC video case is included with each chapter. This resource offers the opportunity for situational analysis in the classroom, or individual viewing through video streaming through our Online Learning Centre at **www.mcgrawhill.ca/ college/kreitner**.

Instructor
supplements

This incredible new book also uses some exciting and useful supplements for instructors and students.

Bridge to the Next Chapter

Chapter 3 presents the process motivational theory where the individual makes his or her mind up using what Charles Handy calls a motivational calculus. It discusses the issue of inequity, expectancy theory and its practical application, five practical implications of goal-setting theory, and some special issues when implementing motivational programs.

You might have your students discuss in small group the process they go through when they decide how hard to study for an exam or a final. What are the factors? Does their major make a difference? Whether they want to go to graduate school? Is it their own self-image that spurs them on? What others will think of them? Do they care? What might motivate them to care if they do not? How important is motivation in Canada? Is it overrated?

Current Event

In January 2002, GM and Ford announced expected layoffs of at least 15,000 if not 20,000. Both of these car companies have struggled with quality issues. Ford has been recently hit with the Ford 'Exploder' issue and the tire problems. It fired its CEO in the last months of 2001 and Bill Ford, great grandson of the founder, Henry Ford was appointed to chair the board and be CEO. Ford is an environmentalist, has worked for Ford quietly for many years, and says he never wanted to head the company. In college, he never told people he was from "that" Ford family. He cares about employees and the image of Ford.

However, after 9/11 and even prior to that, the economy was heading into a recession and car manufactures were in trouble. To try to help they offered 0% financing for a few months in order to boost sales. This appears to have worked, but did not make money. The new lines are in and Ford has a winner in its new Mustang. That is good news, but clearly there are lots of problems still to be tackled. Ford will cut at least 10,000 jobs as part of a major restructuring plan and it may be as high as 20,000.

The questions now are: how do you motivate the remaining employees? What new motivation techniques might you employ? What can be done when morale is low and motivation is not high? Does fear of losing one's job motivate? What can Bill Ford do to motivate all workers towards the goal of making Ford a better and more prosperous car company?

Internet Exercise

The purpose of the exercise is for the student to identify motivational techniques or programs that are being used at different companies. They are go to The Foundation for Enterprise Development at www.fed.org/library/index.html. To begin their search they are to select the resource library and follow up by choosing to view the library by subject. They will be given a variety of categories to choose from. They are to use the categories of "Case Studies" of private companies or "Case Studies of Public Companies" and then pick one company that they would like to analyze.

BROWNSTONE RESEARCH GROUP

Instructor's Resource Guide
ISBN 007091095-2

The Instructor's Manual is a creative guide to understanding organizational behaviour. It includes the traditional elements of chapter outlines, learning outcomes, and opening case introductions, as well as discussion guides regarding the International OB boxes, Focus on Diversity boxes, and Ethics At Work boxes; OB in Action Cases; and a guide to maximizing effective use of the Personal Awareness and Growth Exercises, the Experiential Exercises, the Internet Exercises, and the CBC Video Cases. This resource guide also includes additional review and discussion questions and answers, critical thinking exercises and solutions, and research insights for class discussion. Each element will assist the instructor and students in maximizing the ideas, issues, concepts and important management approaches included in each chapter.

Instructor's Presentation CD-ROM (including Computerized Test Bank and Powerpoint® Presentations)
ISBN 007091094-4

This CD-ROM allows professors to easily create their own custom presentation. They can pull from resources on the CD, like the Test Bank and PowerPoint® Presentation, or from their own PowerPoint® slides or Web screen shots.

Computerized Test Bank

The Test Bank is designed using easy-to-use Brownstone Computerized Test Bank software and contains approximately 1,200 questions, with a mix of true/false, multiple-choice, and essay questions. Multiple-choice questions are ranked (easy, medium, or hard) to help the instructor provide the proper mix of questions. This enhanced-feature test generator allows you to add and edit questions, save and reload multiple tests, select questions based on type, difficulty, keyword, and more.

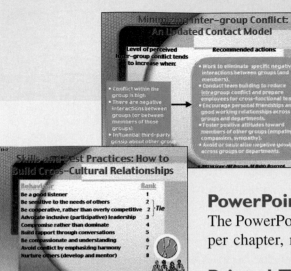

PowerPoint®

The PowerPoint® Presentations feature approximately 20 slides per chapter, making notetaking easier for all your students.

Printed Test Bank
ISBN 007091092-8

CBC Videos
ISBN 007091093-6

A complete set of CBC videos, including segments from *Venture* and *The Fifth Estate* offers instructors the opportunity to highlight such topics as Negotiation, Conflict Management, Self-Management/ Etiquette-Diversity, Listening, and Teamwork—all for situational analysis in the classroom. Video cases for the students can be found in the text. And for instructors there is a video guide in the Instructor's Resource Guide that is also downloadable from the Online Learning Centre.

Online Learning Centre
ISBN 007091096-0
www.mcgrawhill.ca/college/kreitner

The Online Learning Centre (OLC) is a Web site that follows the text chapter-by-chapter, with additional materials and quizzing that enhances the text and/or classroom experience. As students read the book, they can go online to take self-grading quizzes, review material, or work through interactive exercises. OLCs can be delivered multiple ways—professors and students can access them directly through the textbook Web site, through PageOut, or within a course management system (e.g. WebCT or Blackboard).

Instructor supplements

PageOut

McGraw-Hill's unique point-and click course Web site tool, enables users to create a full-featured, professional quality course Web site without knowing HTML coding. With PageOut you can post your syllabus online, assign McGraw-Hill Online Learning Centre content, add links to important off-site resources, and maintain student results in the online grade book. You can send class announcements, copy your course site to share with colleagues, and upload original files. PageOut is free for every McGraw-Hill Ryerson user and, if you're short on time, we even have a team ready to help you create your site!

Primis Online

You can customize this text by using McGraw-Hill's Primis Online digital database. This feature offers you the flexibility to customize your course to include material from the largest online collection of textbooks, readings, and cases. Primis leads the way in customized eBooks with hundreds of titles available at prices that save your students money off bookstore prices. Additional information is available from your local McGraw-Hill sales representative.

WebCT/BlackBoard

This textbook is available in two of the most popular course-delivery platforms—WebCT and BlackBoard—for more user-friendliness and enhanced features. Contact your local McGraw-Hill sales representative for more information.

i-Learning Sales Specialist

Your *Integrated Learning Sales Specialist* is a McGraw-Hill Ryerson representative who has the experience, product knowledge, training, and support to help you assess and integrate any of the below-noted products, technology, and services into your course for optimum teaching and learning performance. Whether it's how to use our test bank software, helping your students improve their grades, or how to put your entire course on-line, your i-Learning Sales Specialist is there to help. Contact your local i-Learning Specialist today to learn how to maximize all McGraw-Hill Ryerson resources!

Student CD-ROM

All copies of this text are packaged with a special Student CD-ROM. This added-value feature includes:

- Interactive modules that encourage hands-on learning about such topics as Motivation, Leadership, and Organizational Communication
- Chapter outlines
- Interactive chapter quizzes
- Videos of real-world companies
- Exercises and quizzes to enhance videos

McGraw-Hill's PowerWeb

Harness the assets of the Web by keeping current with PowerWeb! This online resource provides high quality, peer-reviewed content including up-to-date articles from leading periodicals and journals, current news, weekly updates, interactive exercises, Web research guide, study tips, and much more! http://www.dushkin.com/powerweb

preface

We know of no documented case of a student saying, "I want a longer, more expensive textbook with more chapters." We got the message! Indeed, there is a desire for shorter and less expensive textbooks in today's fast-paced world where work overload and tight budgets are a way of life. Within the field of organizational behaviour ("OB"), so-called "essentials" texts have attempted to satisfy this need. Too often however, brevity has been achieved at the expense of up-to-date examples, artful layout, and learning enhancements. We believe "brief" does not have to mean outdated and boring.

A New Standard

Kreitner, Kinicki, and Cole's *Fundamentals of Organizational Behaviour: Key Concepts, Skills and Best Practices* represents a new standard in OB essentials textbooks. The following guiding philosophy inspired our quest for this new standard: "Create a short, up-to-date, practical, user-friendly, interesting, and engaging introduction to the field of organizational behaviour." Thus, in this book,

you will find lean and efficient coverage of topics recommended by AACSB International conveyed with pedagogical features found in full-length OB textbooks. Among those pedagogical enhancements are timely chapter-opening cases, a rich array of contemporary in-text examples, an appealing four-colour presentation, interesting captioned photos, instructive chapter summaries, special boxed features (on international OB, managing diversity, and business ethics), and three types of exercises at the end of each chapter—Experiential Exercises, Personal Awareness and Growth Exercises, and Internet Exercises—in addition to CBC Video Cases and Discussion Questions.

Efficient and Flexible Structure

The 13 chapters in this text are readily adaptable to traditional 12- or 13-week academic terms, summer and intersessions, management development seminars, and distance learning programs via the Internet. Following highlighted coverage of important topics—including business

ethics, international OB, and managing diversity—the topical flow of this text goes from micro (individuals) to meso (groups and teams) to macro (organizations). Mixing and matching chapters (and topics within each chapter) in various combinations is not only possible, but strongly encouraged to create optimum teaching/learning experiences.

Engaging Pedagogy

We have a passion for teaching organizational behaviour in the classroom and via textbooks because it deals with the intriguing realities of working in modern organizations. Puzzling questions, insights, and surprises hide around every corner. Seeking useful insights about how and why people behave as they do in the workplace is a provocative, interesting, and oftentimes fun activity. After all, to know more about organizational behaviour is to know more about both ourselves and life in general. We have designed this text to facilitate active learning by relying on the following learning enhancements:

- several Learning Outcomes at the start of each chapter to focus attention on key topics, themes, and objectives

- brief Chapter Opening Cases to provide a real-world context for the topics at hand

- an efficient get-right-down-to-business writing style

- numerous up-to-date examples from the real world weaved into textual discussions to bring them to life for the reader

- special boxed features: International OB, Focus on Diversity, and Ethics At Work

- OB In Action Cases are a group of supplementary cases that allow for further individual study or group projects

- Chapter Summaries of Key Concepts related to each of the learning outcomes for handy review

- Key Terms with handy page references and Discussion Questions to cover key concepts from the chapter

- two Personal Awareness and Growth Exercises following each chapter to help the reader personalize and expand upon key concepts

- two Experiential Exercises following each chapter that require thoughtful interaction in order to gain hands-on experience with the concepts in the chapter

- two detailed and challenging Internet Exercises following each chapter to tap the immense poten-tial of the Internet as a learning resource

- a CBC video case is included with each chapter, offering the opportunity to highlight key concepts for situational analysis in the class-room or individual study

Complete Teaching/Learning Package

- *Instructor's Resource Guide*—the Instructor's Resource Guide is a creative guide to understanding organizational behaviour. It includes the traditional elements of chapter outlines, learning outcomes, and opening case introductions; as well as discussion guides regarding the International OB boxes, the Focus on Diversity boxes, and the Ethics At Work boxes; OB in Action Case Studies, and a guide to maximizing effective use of the Personal Awareness and Growth Exercises, the Experiential Exercises, the Internet Exercises, and the CBC Video Cases. It also includes additional review and discussion questions and answers, critical thinking exercises and solutions, and research insights for class discussion. Each element will assist the instructor and students in maximizing the ideas, issues, concepts, and important management approaches included in each chapter.

- *Test Bank*—consists of approximately 20 true/false, 40–50 multiple choice, and five essay questions per chapter. A Brown-stone computerized version is also available.

- *Power Point® Presentations*—approximately 15–20 slides per chapter.

- *CBC Videos*—one CBC video segment (from *Venture* or *The Fifth Estate*) is included with each chapter.

- *Instructor's Presentation CD-ROM*—This CD-ROM contains all of the text's visually oriented supplement items in one presentation management system. By collecting many features of the Power Point® presentations, Computerized Test Bank, and lecture material in an electronic format, this CD offers a comprehensive and convenient tool that allows instructors to customize their lectures and presentation.

- *Online Learning Centre* (www.mcgrawhill.ca/college/kreitner)—

  - *Instructor Resource Centre*—A secured Instructor Resource Centre stores essential course materials and saves prep time before class. This area also stores the Instructor's Resource Guide, Power Point® presentations, CBC video material, and additional readings and exercises.

  - *Student Resource Centre*—This is the perfect solution for Internet-based content. This Web site follows the textbook chapter by chapter and contains text pedagogy and supplementary material. As students read through their book, they can refer to the OLC for learning outcomes, chapter summaries, CBC video streaming and exercises, sample test questions, interactive glossary, and more.

Grateful Appreciation

Many people have assisted us with their helpful comments, recommendations, and suggestions for this first Canadian edition. We extend special appreciation to the following instructors who provided valuable feedback during the writing process:

Ron Burke, *York University*
Joan Condie, *Sheridan College*
Ike Hall, *British Columbia Institute of Technology*
Anne Harpur, *Humber College*
Jack Ito, *University of Regina*
Joanne Leck, *University of Ottawa*
Beverly Linnell, *Saskatchewan Applied Institute of Technology*
Lisa Phillips, *Douglas College*
Shirley Richards, *Humber College*

For this first Canadian edition, we also extend recognition and appreciation to the following U.S. instructors whose feedback contributed to the success of the Kreitner fifth edition and Kinicki first edition:

Joe S. Anderson, *Northern Arizona State University*
Anthony F. Chelte, *Western New England College*
Pamela L. Cox, *SUNY–Oswego*
Robert Culpepper, *Stephen F. Austin State University*
Scott Douglas, *Florida State University*
Janice M. Feldbauer, *Austin Community College*

Jean Hanebury, *St. Leo's University*
Barbara L. Hassell, *Indiana University–Purdue University, Indianapolis*
Peter L. Henderson, *Faulkner University*
Eileen Hogan, *Kutztown University*
Gabriel Jaskolka, *Tiffin University*
Katryna Johnson, *Concordia University–Saint Paul*
Thomas J. Keefe, *Indiana University Southeast*
Andrew Klein, *Keller Graduate School*
Joseph F. Kornfeind, *Muhlenberg College*
Robert C. Liden, *University of Illinois at Chicago*
Hany H. Makhlouf, *University of the District of Columbia*
Barbara G. McCain, *Oklahoma City University*
Thomas McFarland, *Mt. San Antonio College*
Janice S. Miller, *University of Wisconsin–Milwaukee*
Clark Molstad, *California State University, San Bernardino*
Gordon A. Morse, *George Mason University*
Audrey Murrell, *University of Pittsburgh*
Stefanie Naumann, *Louisiana State University*
Linda L. Neider, *University of Miami*
Isaac Owolabi, *Montreat College*
Mark W. Phillips, *University of Texas–San Antonio*
Sandra Powell, *Weber State University*
Brooke Quigg, *Pierce College*

Randall G. Sleeth, *Virginia Commonwealth University*
Susan M. Smith, *Finger Lakes Community College*
B. Kay Snavely, *Miami University*
Kenneth C. Solano, *Northeastern University*
Raymond T. Sparrowe, *Cleveland State University*
Leigh Stelzer, *Seton Hall University*
Susan Stites-Doe, *SUNY College at Brockport*
Nell Tabor Hartley, *Robert Morris College*
Sandy J. Wayne, *University of Illinois at Chicago*
Alan R. Zeiber, *Portland State University*

Sincere thanks must be expressed to the McGraw-Hill Ryerson Limited team: Sponsoring Editor, Lenore Gray Spence; Managing Editor, Development, Kim Brewster; Supervising Editor, Anne Nellis; and Copy Editor, Erin Moore.

On a personal note, we dedicate this book to our family members and friends as a gesture of thanks for providing the moral support and encouragement that was instrumental throughout the writing of this textbook. You lifted our tired spirits when needed and encouraged us at every stage.

This project has been a joy from start to finish. We enjoyed reading and learning more about the latest developments within the field of organizational behaviour. To the students who use this book—we hope you enjoy it. Best wishes for success!

This text has been approved by the Human Resources Professional Association of Ontario and is listed as a recommended text in the HRPAO's "Curriculum Summary."

brief contents

contents

Part One
Managing People 2

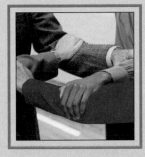

Part Two
Managing Individuals 24

Part Four
Managing Organizational Processes 194

Part Five
Managing Evolving Organizations 268

chapter

one

Introduction to Organizational Behaviour

LEARNING OUTCOMES

After reading the material in this chapter, you should be able to:

- Define organizational behaviour and explain why it is important for managers.

- Identify at least four people-centred practices in successful companies.

- Contrast McGregor's Theory X and Theory Y assumptions about employees.

- Identify the four principles of total quality management (TQM).

- Define the term *E-business*, and specify five ways the Internet is affecting the management of people at work.

- Describe the four layers of diversity in an organization's workforce. Explain three general diversity management practices.

MANAGERS CRUCIAL TO CURBING TURNOVER

"People leave managers. They don't leave organizations," says Keith Bowman, Director of Human Resources at Ernst & Young. "For the last five years, people have had an incredible number of work opportunities. They are more likely to look for other jobs and leave. The role of the manager is absolutely fundamental to keeping people from leaving."

Ernst & Young conducted a confidential employee poll to gather opinions on how well managers fostered a positive work environment and helped employees grow. The results were used to help its management become more effective in reducing turnover.

This approach comes at a time when the working world is under siege by an employee retention crisis—one that observers say will only get more severe in the years to come as an impending labour shortage of almost one million workers is expected across all industries in Canada. As a result, organizations are desperate to understand how to keep top talent from job-hopping.

Their desperation is well-founded, given that one in three workers will resign from his or her job in the next two years, according to a new survey by the Hay Group. Ineffective managers are a major factor in the increasing rates of departure, says the research company, which interviewed over one million employees in 330 organizations around the world.

"Poor managers have a huge impact on employee turnover. Management's inability to adapt to the times will continue to contribute dramatically to sustaining high levels of turnover," says Ron Grey, Managing Director of the Hay Group Canada. "We have seen significant problems with senior managers who have not recognized the changing relationship with workers and continue to operate using historical methods," he says.

As the workplace becomes more team-based and virtual, the role of managers must also change, Mr. Bowman says. "More work is team-based. More work is done from home. Managers should look for results and output, not whether their people are in the office at 9 a.m."

Ron Grey, managing director, Hay Group Canada.

Source: Adapted from N Southworth, "Managers crucial to curbing turnover," *Globe & Mail*, May 20, 2001, p M1. See also A Tomlinson, "Top talent a flight risk in tough times," *Canadian HR Reporter*, February 25, 2002, pp 1, 11.

Managers Get Results with and through Others

How important are people for organizational effectiveness in the 21st century? Stanford University's Jeffrey Pfeffer and his colleagues recently drew this conclusion:

> There is a substantial and rapidly expanding body of evidence, some of it quite methodologically sophisticated, that speaks to the strong connection between how firms manage their people and the economic results achieved.[1]

Thus there has been a growing awareness that the study of human behaviour in organizations is important. Specifically, effective management of organizations requires the ability to understand, predict, and influence behaviour. **Organizational behaviour**, commonly referred to as OB, is a field of study dedicated to better understanding and managing people at work, both individually and in groups. OB involves the study of what people think and feel and the resulting effect on individual and group behaviour within organizations. OB researchers investigate unanswered questions relating to effective management of behaviour in organizations, and the results are intended to be used by managers and other employees to improve workplace effectiveness.

> **Organizational behaviour**
>
> A field of study dedicated to better understanding and managing people at work, both individually and in groups.

Research evidence indicates that *people-centred practices* are strongly associated with much higher profits and significantly lower employee turnover. In order for any team of managers and other employees to contribute to organizational goals and objectives, they must all work together and reinforce people-centred practices. The following seven people-centred practices have been identified in successful companies:

1. Job security (to eliminate fear of layoffs).
2. Careful hiring (emphasizing a good fit with the company culture).
3. Power to the people (via decentralization and self-managed teams).
4. Generous pay for performance.
5. Lots of training.
6. Less emphasis on status (to build a "we" feeling).
7. Trust building (through the sharing of critical information).[2]

Importantly, these factors are a *package* deal, meaning they need to be installed in a coordinated and systematic manner—not in bits and pieces.

Sadly, too many managers tend to act counter to their declarations that people are their most important asset. For example, undue emphasis on short-term profit precludes long-term efforts to nurture human resources. Also, excessive layoffs, when managers view people as a cost rather than an asset, erode trust, commitment, and loyalty.[3] *Only 12 percent of today's organizations have the systematic approaches and persistence to qualify as true people-centred organizations, thus giving them a competitive advantage.*[4]

The purpose of this first chapter is to explore the manager's job, define and examine organizational behaviour and its evolution, and look at important current issues affecting organizational behaviour today.

For better or for worse, managers touch our lives in many ways. Schools, hospitals, government agencies, and large and small businesses all require systematic management. Formally defined, **management** is

> **Management**
>
> Process of working with and through others to achieve organizational objectives efficiently and ethically.

the process of working with and through others to achieve organizational objectives in an efficient and ethical manner. From the standpoint of organizational behaviour, the central feature of this definition is "working with and through others."

Managers play a constantly evolving role. Today's successful managers are no longer the I've-got-everything-under-control order givers of yesteryear. Rather, they need to creatively envision and actively sell bold new directions in an ethical and sensitive manner. Effective managers are team players empowered by the willing and active support of others who are driven by conflicting self-interests. Each of us has a huge stake in how well managers carry out their evolving role. Henry Mintzberg, a respected management scholar at McGill University, observed: "No job is more vital to our society than that of the manager. It is the manager who determines whether our social institutions serve us well or whether they squander our talents and resources."[5]

Extending our managerial thrust, let us take a closer look at the skills managers need to perform, the evolving relationship between employer and employee, and the future direction of management.

A Skills Profile for Managers

Observational studies by Mintzberg and others have found the typical manager's day to be a fragmented collection of brief episodes.[6] Interruptions are commonplace, while large blocks of time for planning and reflective thinking are not. Specific skills that effective managers perform during their hectic and fragmented workdays include:[7]

- Clarifies goals and objectives for everyone involved.
- Encourages participation, upward communication, and suggestions.
- Plans and organizes for an orderly work flow.
- Has technical and administrative expertise to answer organization-related questions.
- Facilitates work through team building, training, coaching, and support.
- Provides feedback honestly and constructively.
- Keeps things moving by relying on schedules, deadlines, and helpful reminders.
- Controls details without being overbearing.
- Applies reasonable pressure for goal accomplishment.
- Empowers and delegates key duties to others while maintaining goal clarity and commitment.
- Recognizes good performance with rewards and positive reinforcement.

Managerial skills research yields three useful lessons:

1. Dealing effectively with *people* is what management is all about. Thus, knowledge about OB is critical for management success.
2. Managers with high people skills mastery tend to have better business unit performance and employee morale than managers with low people skills mastery.[8]
3. *Effective* female and male managers *do not* have significantly different skill profiles,[9] contrary to claims in the popular business press in recent years.[10]

Companies Undervaluing Skills Learned During Relocation

As the global economy continues to expand, companies need people who can efficiently conduct business in foreign markets—people who possess what are in effect a whole new set of cross-cultural competencies that have become essential for doing business in international settings. Working in other countries is valuable for teaching people to work successfully in often radically different settings.

These skills include an awareness of different communication styles, the ability to give and receive feedback in a culturally sensitive manner, and the ability to function within more traditional settings where hierarchies are still important. Levi Strauss managers in Malaysia had to figure out if the company would extend its benefit package to the children of all four of an employee's wives. Another manager in Indonesia helped people escape from riots that had ravaged the city. Such experiences open people up to new ways of thinking and different ways of doing things.

However, poor management of relocation is frustrating many ambitious employees who would otherwise be anxious to take on international assignments. Such assignments have long been considered a beneficial experience, giving the employee a varied perspective on different ways of doing things. In fact, expatriate experience (a native of one country working in another) has become a virtual necessity for anyone hoping to reach senior ranks in many organizations. Some companies have added cross-cultural competencies to their performance evaluations, but many others still don't fully appreciate the value of competencies acquired while abroad. Thus many employees considering a potential international posting are concerned that the assignment may be a career-limiting rather than a career-enhancing move. It's a common problem that causes many people to leave their company soon after returning home from an international assignment.

Source: Adapted from D Brown, "Companies undervaluing skills learned during relocation," *Canadian HR Reporter*, February 28, 2000, pp 15, 21.

21st-Century Managers

Today's workplace is indeed undergoing immense and permanent changes.[11] Organizations are being "reengineered" for greater speed, efficiency, and flexibility.[12] Entrepreneurial spirit is needed in both small and large businesses. Teams are pushing aside the individual as the primary building block of organizations.[13] Costs are being managed by use of contract workers. Command-and-control management is giving way to participative management and empowerment.[14] Ego-centred leaders are being replaced by customer-centred leaders. Employees increasingly are being viewed as internal customers. All this creates a mandate for a new kind of manager in the 21st century. Table 1–1 contrasts the characteristics of past and future managers. As the balance of this book will demonstrate, the managerial shift in Table 1–1 is not just a good idea, it is an absolute necessity in the new workplace.

The Field of Organizational Behaviour: Past and Present

OB is not an everyday job category such as accounting, marketing, or finance. Students of OB typically do not get jobs in organizational behaviour, per se. This reality in no way lessens the importance of OB in effective organizational management. OB is a *horizontal* discipline that cuts across virtually every job category, business function, and professional specialty. Anyone who plans to make a living in a large or small, public or private, organization needs to study organizational behaviour.

Evolution of the 21st-Century Manager **TABLE 1–1**

	Past Managers	Future Managers
Primary role	Order giver, privileged elite, manipulator, controller	Facilitator, team member, teacher, advocate, sponsor, coach
Learning and knowledge	Periodic learning, narrow specialist	Continuous life-long learning, generalist with multiple specialties
Compensation criteria	Time, effort, rank	Skills, results
Cultural orientation	Monocultural, monolingual	Multicultural, multilingual
Primary source of influence	Formal authority	Knowledge (technical and interpersonal)
View of people	Potential problem	Primary resource
Primary communication pattern	Vertical	Multidirectional
Decision-making style	Limited input for individual decisions	Broad-based input for joint decisions
Ethical considerations	Afterthought	Forethought
Nature of interpersonal relationships	Competitive (win–lose)	Cooperative (win–win)
Handling of power and key information	Hoard and restrict access	Share and broaden access
Approach to change	Resist	Facilitate

In order to understand behaviour in organizations, it is necessary to draw upon a diverse array of disciplines, including psychology, management, sociology, organization theory, social psychology, statistics, anthropology, general systems theory, economics, information technology, political science, vocational counselling, human stress management, psychometrics, ergonomics, decision theory, and ethics. This rich heritage has spawned many competing perspectives and theories about human work behaviour.

A historical perspective of the study of people at work helps in studying organizational behaviour. In other words, we can better understand where the field of OB is today and where it appears to be headed by appreciating where it has been. Let us examine four significant landmarks in the evolution of understanding and managing people:

1. The human relations movement.
2. The total quality management movement.
3. The Internet revolution.
4. Workforce diversity.

The Human Relations Movement

A unique combination of factors during the 1930s fostered the human relations movement. First, following legalization of union–management collective bargaining in North America in the early 20th century, management began looking for new ways of handling employees. Second, behavioural scientists conducting on-the-job research started calling for more attention to the "human" factor. Managers who had lost the battle to keep unions out of their factories heeded the call for better human relations and improved working conditions.

The human relations movement gathered momentum through the 1950s, as academics and managers alike made stirring claims about the powerful effect that individual needs, supportive supervision, and group dynamics apparently had on job performance.

The Writings of Mayo and Follett   Essential to the human relations movement were the writings of Elton Mayo and Mary Parker Follett. Australian-born Mayo advised managers to attend to employees' emotional needs in his 1933 classic, *The Human Problems of an Industrial Civilization*. Follett was a true pioneer, not only as a woman management consultant in the male-dominated industrial world of the 1920s, but also as a writer who saw employees as complex combinations of attitudes, beliefs, and needs. Mary Parker Follett was way ahead of her time in telling managers to motivate job performance instead of merely demanding it, a "pull" rather than "push" strategy. She also built a logical bridge between political democracy and a cooperative spirit in the workplace.[15]

McGregor's Theory Y   In 1960, Douglas McGregor wrote a book entitled *The Human Side of Enterprise*, which has become an important philosophical base for the modern view of people at work.[16] Drawing upon his experience as a management consultant, McGregor formulated two sharply contrasting sets of assumptions about human nature (see Table 1–2). His **Theory X** assumptions were pessimistic and negative and, according to McGregor's interpretation, typical of how managers traditionally perceived employees. To help managers break with this negative tradition, McGregor formulated his **Theory Y**, a modern and positive set of assumptions about people. McGregor believed managers could accomplish more through others by viewing them as self-energized, committed, responsible, and creative beings.

Theory X

Negative, pessimistic assumptions about human nature and its effect on productivity.

Theory Y

Positive assumptions about employees being responsible and creative.

TABLE 1–2   McGregor's Theory X and Theory Y

Outdated (Theory X) Assumptions about People at Work	Modern (Theory Y) Assumptions about People at Work
1. Most people dislike work; they avoid it when they can.	1. Work is a natural activity, like play or rest.
2. Most people must be coerced and threatened with punishment before they will work. People require close direction when they are working.	2. People are capable of self-direction and self-control if they are committed to objectives.
3. Most people actually prefer to be directed. They tend to avoid responsibility and exhibit little ambition. They are interested only in security.	3. People generally become committed to organizational objectives if they are rewarded for doing so.
	4. The typical employee can learn to accept and seek responsibility.
	5. The typical member of the general population has imagination, ingenuity, and creativity.

Source: Adapted from D McGregor, *The Human Side of Enterprise* (New York: McGraw-Hill, 1960), Ch 4.

New Assumptions about Human Nature   However, modern research methods have shown that the human relationists embraced some naive and misleading conclusions. Despite its shortcomings, the human relations movement opened the door to more progressive thinking about human nature. Rather than continuing to view employees as passive economic beings, managers began to see them as active social beings and took steps to create more humane work environments.

In today's world, three important features of the business landscape affecting OB are total quality management, the Internet revolution, and workforce diversity. Each of these will be discussed briefly, and their relevance to the following chapters in this book will be noted.

The Total Quality Management Movement

Thanks to the concept of **total quality management** (TQM), the quality of much of what we buy today is significantly better than in the past. The underlying principles of TQM are more important than ever given the growth of both E-business on the Internet[17] and the overall service economy.

> **Total quality management**
>
> An organizational culture dedicated to training, continuous improvement, and customer satisfaction.

In a recent survey of 1,797 managers from 36 countries, "customer service" and "quality" ranked as the corporate world's top two concerns.[18] TQM principles have profound practical implications for managing people today.[19]

TQM means that an organization's culture is focused on the constant attainment of customer satisfaction. This involves the continuous improvement of organizational processes, resulting in high-quality products and services.[20] TQM is necessarily employee driven because product/service quality cannot be continuously improved without the active learning and participation of *every* employee. Thus, in successful quality improvement programs, TQM principles are embedded in the organization's culture.[21]

The Deming Legacy   TQM is firmly established today thanks in large part to the pioneering work of W Edwards Deming.[22] Ironically, the mathematician credited with Japan's post–World War II quality revolution rarely talked in terms of quality. He instead preferred to discuss "good management" during the hard-hitting seminars he delivered right up until his death at age 93 in 1993.[23] Although Deming's passion was the statistical measurement and reduction of variations in industrial processes, he had much to say about how employees should be treated. Regarding the human side of quality improvement, Deming called for the following:

- Formal training in statistical process control techniques and teamwork.
- Helpful leadership, rather than order giving and punishment.
- Elimination of fear so employees will feel free to ask questions.
- Emphasis on continuous process improvements rather than on numerical quotas.
- Teamwork.
- Elimination of barriers to good workmanship.[24]

One of Deming's most enduring lessons for managers is his 85–15 rule.[25] Specifically, when things go wrong, there is roughly an 85% chance the *system* (including management, machinery, and rules) is at fault. Only about 15% of the time is the individual employee at fault. Unfortunately, as Deming observed, the typical manager spends most of his or her time wrongly blaming and punishing individuals for system failures. Statistical analysis is required to uncover system failures.

Principles of TQM   Despite variations in the language and scope of TQM programs, it is possible to identify four common TQM principles:

1. Do it right the first time to eliminate costly rework.
2. Listen to and learn from customers and employees.
3. Make continuous improvement an everyday matter.
4. Build teamwork, trust, and mutual respect.[26]

Deming's influence is clearly evident in this list.[27] Once again, as with the human relations movement, we see people as the key factor in organizational success.

In summary, TQM advocates have made a valuable contribution to the field of OB by providing a *practical* context for managing people. When people are managed according to TQM principles, everyone is more likely to get the employment opportunities and high-quality goods and services they demand.[28]

The Internet Revolution

We can be forgiven if the Internet revolution has left us a bit dizzy. In just a few short years, dot-coms exploded onto the scene, with promises of *everything* for sale *cheap* on the Internet. Then, just as suddenly, many dot-coms truly did explode, leaving their overworked employees jobless and their founders telling bizarre riches-to-rags stories.[29] Strange and unforeseen things happened. For example, Pets.com, with a popular and expensive advertising campaign, went broke trying to sell $10 bags of dog food. Meanwhile, General Electric, a "bricks-and-mortar" stalwart, had great success selling $65,000 medical software packages over the Internet.[30]

As we continue to analyze the 2000–2001 dot-com crash looking for winning formulas, one thing is very clear. The Internet—the global network of computers, software, cables, servers, switches, and routers—is here to stay as a business tool.[31] In fact, while dot-coms were going out of business in droves in 2000, the overall Internet economy mushroomed 58% from the year before to $830 billion.[32]

The purpose of this section is to define *E-business* and identify significant OB implications in the ongoing Internet revolution (as signs of what lies ahead).

E-Business Is Much More than E-Commerce   Experts on the subject draw an important distinction between *E-commerce* (buying and selling goods and services over the Internet) and **E-business**, using the Internet to facilitate *every* aspect of running a business.[33] Intel, as a case in point, is striving to become an E-corporation, one that relies primarily on the Internet to not only buy and sell things, but to facilitate all business functions, exchange knowledge among its employees, and build partnerships with outsiders as well. Why? Consider this recent survey finding: "firms that embraced the Internet averaged a 13.4% jump in productivity . . . [in 2000], compared with 4.9% for those that did not."[34] E-business has significant implications for managing people at work because it eventually will seep into every corner of life both on and off the job.

E-business

Running the *entire* business via the Internet.

E-Business Implications for OB   The following list is intended to suggest some of the implications of E-business relating to OB issues:

- *E-management.* 21st-century managers, profiled earlier in Table 1–1, are needed in the fast-paced Internet age. They are able to create, motivate, and lead teams of far-flung specialists linked by Internet E-mail and project management software and by fax and phone. Networking skills, applied both inside and outside the organization, are essential today. (See Chapters 3, 10, and 11.)

- *E-communication.* E-mail has become one of the most used and abused forms of organizational communication. Today's managers need to be masters of concise, powerful E-mail and voice-mail messages. Communicating via the Internet's World Wide Web is fast and efficient for those who know how to fully exploit it. Additionally, employees who "telecommute" from home via the Internet present their managers with unique motivational and performance measurement problems. For their part, telecommuters must strike a productive balance between independence and feelings of isolation. (See Chapter 9.)

- *Goal setting and feedback.* Abundant research evidence supports the coupling of clear and challenging goals with timely and constructive feedback for keeping employees headed in the right direction. Thanks to Web-based software, managers can efficiently create, align, and track their employee's goals.[35] (See Chapter 4.)

- *Organizational structure.* The Internet and modern telecommunications technology have given rise to "virtual teams" and "virtual organizations." Time zones, facilities, and location no longer are hard constraints on getting things accomplished. Got a great product idea but don't have the time to build a factory? No problem, just connect with someone via the Internet who can get the job done. This virtual workplace, with less face-to-face interaction, requires managers and employees who are flexible and adaptable and not bound by slow and rigid bureaucratic communication and methods. (See Chapter 11.)

- *Job design.* The *work itself* is a powerful motivator for many employees today, especially those in information technology. Boring and unchallenging and/or dead-end jobs will repel rather than attract top talent in the Internet age (see Chapter 3).

- *Decision making.* Things indeed are moving faster and faster in the Internet age. Just ask the typical overloaded manager who reports making more decisions in less time than he or she used to.[36] Adding to the pressure, databases linked to the

Telecommuters need to strike a productive balance between independence and feelings of isolation.

Internet give today's decision makers unprecedented amounts of both relevant and irrelevant data. Moreover, decision makers cannot ignore the trend away from command-and-control tactics and toward employee empowerment and participation. In short, there is more "we" than "me" for Internet-age decision makers. (See Chapter 6.)

- *Speed, conflict, and stress.* Unfortunately, conflict and stress are unavoidable by-products of strategic and operational speed. The good news is that conflict and stress can be managed. (See Chapters 5 and 8.)

- *Change and resistance to change.* As "old economy" companies race to become E-corporations, employees are being asked to digest huge doses of change in every aspect of their worklives. (See Chapter 13.)

- *Ethics.* Internet-centred organizations are littered with ethical landmines needing to be addressed humanely and responsibly. Among them are around-the-clock work binges, exaggerated promises about rewards, electronic monitoring, repetitive-motion injuries from excessive keyboarding, unfair treatment of part-timers, and privacy issues.[37] (See Chapter 6.)

Overall, it is easy to see why the Internet revolution represents a significant new era for understanding and managing people at work. The problems, challenges, and opportunities are immense. Hang on tight; it promises to be an exciting ride!

Workforce Diversity

Diversity

The host of individual differences that make people different from and similar to each other.

Workforce diversity management is one of the most important issues facing organizations today. As Canada's population continues to become more diverse, so will its workforce. **Diversity** represents the multitude of individual differences and similarities that exist among people.[38] There are many different dimensions or components of diversity that make all of us unique and different from others. Figure 1–1 shows the "diversity wheel" and its four layers. Personality is at the centre of the diversity wheel because it represents a stable set of characteristics that is responsible for a person's individual identity. The dimensions of personality are discussed further in Chapter 2.

The next layer of diversity consists of a set of internal dimensions such as age, race, and gender that are referred to as the primary dimensions of diversity.[39] These dimensions, for the most part, are not within our control, but strongly influence our attitudes, expectations, and assumptions about others, which in turn influence our behaviour.

The next layer of diversity is composed of external, or secondary, dimensions such as religion and marital status. They represent individual differences that we have a greater ability to influence or control. These dimensions also exert a significant influence on our perceptions, behaviour, and attitudes. The final layer of diversity includes organizational dimensions such as job title, union affiliation, and seniority. The Royal Bank of Canada encourages this aspect of diversity by encouraging staff mobility within the bank. Each year, 25 percent of employees assume new work roles.[40]

Glass ceiling

Invisible barrier blocking qualified women and minorities from top management positions.

One of the most well-known problems faced by women and visible minorities in the workplace is the **glass ceiling**. The glass ceiling represents an invisible barrier that blocks certain workers, primarily qualified women and visible minorities, from advancing into top management positions. It can be particularly de-motivating because employees can look up and see coveted top management positions through the transparent ceiling but are unable to obtain them. One study found that the barrier is much greater for minorities, and called it a "concrete ceiling."[41]

In Canada, legislation covering federal workers and those in some provinces requires employers to actively pursue **employment equity**. Employment equity involves working to increase the number of workers from groups that have historically been underrepresented in an organization's workforce. In particular, the legislation requires that steps be taken to increase the representation of qualified women, visible minorities, Aboriginal people, and persons with disabilities at all levels of an organization.

Managing Diversity

Managing diversity involves activities aimed at managing individual differences in order to enable people to perform up to their maximum potential, including but not limited to those required for employment equity. It focuses on changing an organization's culture, policies, and procedures such that employees can perform at their highest level of productivity. To attract and retain the best workers, companies need to adopt policies and programs that meet the needs of a diverse group of workers. Programs such as daycare, eldercare, flexible work schedules, less rigid relocation policies, and mentoring programs are likely to assist workers from all backgrounds to perform their job duties at an optimal level.

Organizations encounter a variety of barriers when attempting to implement diversity initiatives. It is thus important for present and future managers to consider these barriers before rolling out a diversity program. The following is a list of the most common barriers to implementing successful diversity programs:[42]

1. *Inaccurate stereotypes and prejudice.* This barrier manifests itself in the belief that differences are viewed as weaknesses. In turn, this promotes the view that diversity hiring will mean sacrificing competence and quality.

2. *Ethnocentrism.* The ethnocentrism barrier represents the feeling that one's cultural rules and norms are superior or more appropriate than the rules and norms of another culture.

3. *Poor career planning.* This barrier is associated with the lack of opportunities for diverse employees to get the type of work assignments that qualify them for senior management positions.

4. *An unsupportive and hostile working environment for diverse employees.* Diverse employees are frequently excluded from social events and the friendly camaraderie that takes place in most offices.

5. *Lack of political savvy on the part of diverse employees.* Diverse employees may not get promoted because they do not know how to "play the game" of getting along and getting ahead in an organization. Research reveals that employees in the designated groups are excluded from organizational networks.

6. *Difficulty in balancing career and family issues.* Women often still assume the majority of the responsibilities associated with raising children.

7. *Fears of reverse discrimination.* Some employees believe that managing diversity is a smoke screen for reverse discrimination. This belief leads to

> ### Employment equity
> Legislation intended to remove employment barriers and promote equality for the members of four designated groups—women, visible minorities, aboriginal people, and persons with disabilities.

> ### Managing diversity
> Policies, activities, and organizational changes aimed at managing individual differences in order to enable all people to perform up to their maximum potential.

One of the few Canadian women to break through the glass ceiling is Annette Verschuran, president of Home Depot Canada.

FIGURE 1–1 The Four Layers of Diversity

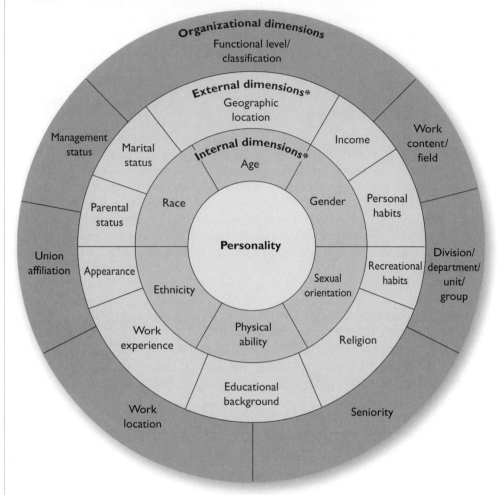

*Internal Dimensions and External Dimensions are adapted from Loden and Rosener, *Workforce America!* (Homewood, IL: Business One Irwin, 1991).

Source: L Gardenswartz and A Rowe, *Diverse Teams at Work: Capitalizing on the Power of Diversity* (New York: McGraw-Hill, 1994), p. 33. © 1994. Reproduced with permission of The McGraw-Hill Companies.

very strong resistance because people feel that one person's gain is another person's loss.

8. *Diversity is not seen as an organizational priority.* This leads to subtle resistance that shows up in the form of complaints about the time, energy, and resources devoted to diversity that could have been spent doing "real work."

9. *The need to revamp the organization's performance appraisal and reward system.* Performance appraisals and reward systems must reinforce the need to effectively manage diversity. Thus success will be based on a new set of criteria, which may be resisted if perceived to adversely affect promotions and financial rewards.

10. *Resistance to change.* Effectively managing diversity entails significant organizational and personal change. As discussed in Chapter 13, people resist change for many different reasons.

Syncrude Canada Ltd.—Committed to Diversity

After earning an electrical engineering degree from the University of Manitoba in 1991, Dan Brown jumped at the opportunity to work at Syncrude Canada Ltd.'s huge oilsands mining and upgrading operation near Fort McMurray, Alberta. The company offered very good salaries and benefits, but what really attracted Brown, who is of Cree descent, was the company's commitment to a diverse workforce. Syncrude is Canada's largest industrial employer of aboriginal people, with about 700 currently on staff, and indirectly employs many others by supporting aboriginal contractors. As well, Brown, 40, has had the opportunity to work with people from around the world. "I wouldn't even want to count the countries our engineers come from," he says.

Syncrude, which has shipped well over a billion barrels of oil and is currently in the midst of a 10-year, $8-billion expansion, also actively encourages employees to diversify their work experience. Brown, for instance, spent three years early in his career apprenticing with blue-collar technicians who maintain the massive upgrader, which gave him a better understanding of how oil-drenched sand is converted into crude oil.

Source: D Jenish and B Woodward, "Committed to Diversity," *Maclean's*, November 5, 2001, p 52.

A landmark study of the diversity practices used by 16 organizations that successfully managed diversity uncovered 52 different practices, 20 of which were used by the majority of the companies sampled. The 52 practices were classified into three main types: accountability; developmental; and recruitment.[43] The top practices associated with each type are shown in Table 1–3. They are discussed below in relative order of importance.

Accountability Practices   Accountability practices relate to managers' responsibility to treat diverse employees fairly. Table 1–3 reveals that companies predominantly accomplish this objective by creating administrative procedures aimed at integrating diverse employees into the management ranks (practices numbered 3, 4, 5, 6, 8, 9, and 10). In contrast, work and family policies (practice 7) focus on creating an environment that fosters employee commitment and productivity. Moreover, organizations increasingly are attempting to build an accountability component into their diversity programs in order to motivate managers to effectively manage diversity.

Developmental Practices   The use of developmental practices to manage diversity is relatively new compared with the historical use of accountability and recruitment practices. Developmental practices focus on preparing diverse employees for greater responsibility and advancement. Theses activities are needed because most non-traditional employees have not been exposed to the types of activities and job assignments that develop effective leadership and social networks.[44] Table 1–3 indicates that diversity training

A Friendly Game of Golf?

Consider the following: On Saturday morning, the boss invites his subordinates, Tom, David, and Hal, for a friendly game of golf. Mary and Rajiv, who don't play golf, are not invited.

You Decide...

Is this Saturday morning golf game simply a friendly social occasion, or is it a subtle form of discrimination? Explain.

Source: Adapted from L Bierman, "Regulating Reindeer Games," *Academy of Management Executive*, November 1997, p 92.

ETHICS AT WORK

TABLE 1-3   Common Diversity Practices

Accountability Practices	Development Practices	Recruitment Practices
1. Top management's personal intervention	1. Diversity training programs	1. Targeted recruitment of nonmanagers
2. Internal advocacy groups	2. Networks and support groups	2. Key outside hires
3. Emphasis on employment equity statistics, profiles	3. Development programs for all high-potential managers	3. Extensive public exposure on diversity
4. Inclusion of diversity in performance evaluation goals, ratings	4. Informal networking activities	4. Corporate image as liberal, progressive, or benevolent
5. Inclusion of diversity in promotion decisions, criteria	5. Job rotation	5. Partnerships with educational institutions
6. Inclusion of diversity in management succession planning	6. Formal mentoring program	6. Recruitment incentives such as cash supplements
7. Work and family policies	7. Informal mentoring program	7. Internships
8. Policies against racism, sexism	8. Entry development programs for all high-potential new hires	8. Publications or PR products that highlight diversity
9. Internal audit or attitude survey	9. Internal training (such as personal safety or language)	9. Targeted recruitment of managers
10. Active employment equity committee, office	10. Recognition events, awards	10. Partnership with nontraditional groups

Source: Abstracted from Tables A.10, A.11, and A.12 in A M Morrison, *The New Leaders: Guidelines on Leadership Diversity in America* (San Francisco: Jossey-Bass, 1992).

programs, networks and support groups, and mentoring programs are among the most frequently used developmental practices.

Recruitment Practices   Recruitment practices focus on attracting diverse job applicants at all levels who are willing to accept challenging work assignments. This focus is critical because people learn the leadership skills needed for advancement by successfully accomplishing increasingly responsible work assignments. As shown in Table 1-3, targeted recruitment of nonmanagers (practice 1), and managers (practice 9) are commonly used to identify and recruit workers in groups that are commonly under-represented in the workforce.

In summary, effective workforce diversity management requires a number of OB skills, including managing change (Chapter 13), dealing with conflict (Chapter 8), and political issues (Chapter 10), and most of all, exhibiting strong leadership skills (Chapter 11).

The Contingency Approach: Applying Lessons from Research and Practice

Contingency approach

Using management tools and techniques in a situationally-appropriate manner; avoiding the "one best way" mentality.

Practical lessons can be learned as OB researchers steadily push back the frontiers of knowledge. One important general research finding is that in OB, there is rarely one best way to manage people; the specific situation must also be considered. The **contingency approach** calls for using management concepts and techniques in a situationally-appropriate manner, instead of trying to rely on "one best way."

Learning from Research

Research methodologies used in OB include field studies of real-life situations; laboratory studies conducted under controlled conditions; survey questionnaires; case studies of a single individual, group or organization; and meta-analyses that pool the results of many previous studies through statistical procedures. New knowledge can be applied directly, e.g., stress reduction techniques; can have a conceptual impact, e.g., a more positive attitude to hiring older workers upon learning that their absenteeism rates are low; and can help reinforce already existing policies and procedures.[45]

Learning from Practice

Learning to manage people is like learning to ride a bicycle. You watch others do it. Sooner or later, you get up the courage to try it yourself.[46] You fall off and skin your knee. You climb back on the bike a bit smarter, and so on, until wobbly first attempts turn into a smooth ride. Your chances of becoming a successful manager can be enhanced by studying the theory, research, and practical examples in this textbook.

summary of key concepts

- *Define organizational behaviour and explain why it is so important for managers.* Organizational behaviour (OB) is a field of study dedicated to better understanding and managing people at work, both individually and in groups. OB is important for managers because of the increasing evidence that there is a strong connection between how organizations manage their people and the economic results achieved by the organization.

- *Identify at least four people-centred practices in successful companies and define the term management.* Seven people-centred practices are job security, careful hiring, power to the people, generous pay for performance, lots of training, less emphasis on status, and trust building.

- *Contrast McGregor's Theory X and Theory Y assumptions about employees.* Theory X employees, according to traditional thinking, dislike work, require close supervision, and are primarily interested in security. According to the modern Theory Y view, employees are capable of self-direction, of seeking responsibility, and of being creative.

- *Identify the four principles of total quality management (TQM).* The four principles of TQM are (a) do it right the first time to eliminate costly rework; (b) listen to and learn from customers and employees; (c) make continuous improvement an everyday matter; and (d) build teamwork, trust, and mutual respect.

- *Define the term E-business, and specify five ways the Internet is affecting the management of people at work.* E-business involves using the Internet to more effectively and efficiently manage every aspect of a business. The Internet is reshaping the management of people in the following areas: E-management (networking), E-communication (E-mail and telecommuting), goal setting and feedback, organizational structure (virtual teams and organizations), job design (desire for more challenge), decision making (greater speed and employee empowerment), conflict and stress triggered by increased speed, rapid change and inevitable conflict and resistance, and ethical problems such as overwork and privacy issues.

- *Describe the four layers of diversity in an organization's workforce. Explain three general diversity management practices.* The four layers of diversity are: (1) personality, which is unique to every individual, (2) internal dimensions such as age and race, (3) external dimensions such as religion and marital status, and (4) organizational dimensions such as job title. Three general diversity management practices are: (a) accountability practices to ensure that diverse employees are treated fairly, (b) development practices to prepare diverse employees for greater responsibility and advancement, and (c) recruitment practices to attract diverse job applicants at all levels.

key terms

contingency approach, 16	glass ceiling, 12	Theory X, 8
diversity, 12	management, 4	Theory Y, 8
E-business, 10	managing diversity, 13	total quality management, 9
employment equity, 13	organizational behaviour, 4	

discussion questions

1. How would you respond to a fellow student who says, "I have a hard time getting along with other people, but I think I could be a good manager?"

2. Based on either personal experience as a manager or on your observation of managers at work, are the 11 skills in Table 1–1 a realistic portrayal of what managers do?

3. What is your personal experience with Theory X and Theory Y managers (see Table 1–2)? Which did you prefer? Why?

4. How would you respond to a new manager who made this statement? "TQM is about statistical process control, not about people."

5. Consider a situation when you felt like a "telecommuter" while working on a group assignment for a class. How did you strike a balance between independence and feelings of isolation?

6. Using the "diversity wheel," analyze a group of people you belong to (family, sports team, study group, etc.). What are the main sources of similarities and differences amongst members of the group on each layer of diversity? Do any of the areas of diversity create strength on the team? Weaknesses? Explain.

internet exercises

www.hp.com

1. People-Centred Practices

The purpose of this exercise is to focus on one well-known company with a good general reputation (Hewlett-Packard) and look for evidence of the seven people-centred practices discussed at the beginning of this chapter (go back and review them to refresh your memory). On the Internet, go to Hewlett-Packard's home page (**www.hp.com**), and select the heading "company information." Next, in the section "about hp," select "history & facts." Be sure to read the section titled "corporate objectives," especially the parts titled "our people" and "management."

QUESTIONS

1. On a scale of 1 = low to 10 = high, how people-centred is HP?
2. What *specific* evidence of each of the seven people-centred practices did you find?
3. Which of the seven practices appears to be HP's strongest suit?
4. Do HP's culture and values give it a strategic competitive advantage? Explain.
5. Would you like to work for HP? Why or why not?

2. Exploring Employment Equity

Go to the Web site of the Alliance for Employment Equity (**www.web.net/~allforee**). Read about the Alliance and its mission to expand employment equity legislation in Canada. Then click on "Links" and select "Saskatchewan Government Human Rights Links—Great Resources!" Click on:

(a) Global Applied Disability Research and Information Network on Employment and Training (GLADNET). Click on "Projects." Look for one or two Canadian research projects and one or two projects in other countries that are summarized here.

(b) Graduate Program in Disability Management. Review the information on this University of Northern British Columbia masters degree.

(c) (Optional) Holocaust and Hope: Artists Against Racism. Check out the Web site created by students at Ryerson University.

QUESTIONS

1. Why is the Alliance for Employment Equity having trouble staying in operation? How might they increase their funding?
2. How will the results of the research projects funded by GLADNET contribute to increasing the representation of disabled workers in the workforce?
3. How will graduates of the UNBC masters program in disability management help to increase the representation of disabled workers in the workforce?

experiential exercises

1. What Are the Strategies for Breaking the Glass Ceiling?

Instructions

Read the 13 career strategies shown below that may be used to break the glass ceiling. Next, rank order each strategy in terms of its importance for contributing to the advancement of a woman to a senior management position. Rank the strategies from 1 (most important) to 13 (least important). Once this is completed, compute the gap between your rankings and those provided by the women executives who participated in this research. Their rankings are presented in Endnote 47 at the back of the book. In computing the gaps, use the absolute value of the gap. (Absolute values are always positive, so just ignore the sign of your gap.) Finally, compute your total gap score. The larger the gap, the greater the difference in opinion between you and the women executives. What does your total gap score indicate about your recommended strategies?

Strategy	My Rating	Survey Rating	Gap (Your Rating Survey Rating)
1. Develop leadership outside office	_____	_____	_____
2. Gain line management experience	_____	_____	_____
3. Network with influential colleagues	_____	_____	_____
4. Change companies	_____	_____	
5. Be able to relocate	_____	_____	
6. Seek difficult or high visibility assignments	_____	_____	
7. Upgrade educational credentials	_____	_____	
8. Consistently exceed performance expectations	_____	_____	
9. Move from one functional area to another	_____	_____	
10. Initiate discussion regarding career aspirations	_____	_____	
11. Have an influential mentor	_____	_____	
12. Develop style that men are comfortable with	_____	_____	
13. Gain international experience	_____	_____	_____

Source: Strategies and data were taken from B R Ragins, B Townsend, and M Mattis, "Gender Gap in the Executive Suite: CEOs and Female Executives Report on Breaking the Glass Ceiling," *The Academy of Management Executive*, February 1998, pp 28–42.

2. Who Comes First? Employees, Customers, or Stockholders?

Instructions

1. Drawing from your own value system and business philosophy, rank the three groups in the title of this exercise first, second, and third in terms of managerial priority. What is the rationale for your ranking?
2. Read the two brief quotes below.
3. Based on the opinions of these two respected business leaders, would you change your initial priority ranking? Why? With whom do you agree more, Iacocca or Kelleher? Why?

Consult our Web site for an interpretation of this exercise: **www.mcgrawhill.ca/college/kreitner**.

Lee Iacocca, former president of Ford and retired CEO of Chrysler:

> Just be sure to take care of your customers. You have to go eyeball to eyeball with them and say, "Do I have a deal for you!" And then stand behind your product or service. Don't worry about stockholders or employees. If you take care of your customers, everything else will fall into place.*

Herb Kelleher, cofounder and chairman of Southwest Airlines:

> In the old days, my mother told me that in business school they'd say, "This is a real conundrum: Who comes first, your employees, your shareholders, or your customers?" My mother taught me that your employees come first. If you treat them well, then they treat the customers well, and that means your customers come back and your shareholders are happy.**

Sources: *As quoted in L McCauley and C Canabou, eds., "Unit of One: The Voice of Experience," *Fast Company*, May 2001, p 82. **As quoted in J Huey, "Outlaw Flyboy CEOs," *Fortune*, November 13, 2000, p 246.

personal awareness and growth exercise

How Does Your Diversity Profile Affect Your Relationships with Other People?

Objectives

1. To identify the diversity profile of yourself and others.
2. To consider the implications of similarities and differences across diversity profiles.

Introduction

People vary along four layers of diversity: personality, internal dimensions, external dimensions, and organizational dimensions. Differences across these four layers are likely to influence interpersonal relationships and the ability or willingness to work with others. You will be asked to compare yourself with a group of other people you interact with and then to examine the quality of the relationships between yourself and these individuals. This enables you to gain a better understanding of how similarities and differences among people influence attitudes and behaviour.

Instructions

Complete the diversity profile by first selecting five current or past co-workers/work associates or fellow students. Alternatively, you can select five people you interact with in order to accomplish your personal goals (e.g., team members on a class project). Write their names on the diagonal lines at the top of the worksheet. Next, determine whether each person is similar to or different from you with respect to each diversity dimension. Mark an "S" if the person is the same or a "D" if the person is different from yourself. Finally, answer the questions for discussion.

QUESTIONS FOR DISCUSSION

1. To whom are you most similar and different?
2. Which diversity dimensions have the greatest influence with respect to whom you are drawn to and whom you like the best?
3. Which dimensions of diversity seem relatively unimportant with respect to the quality of your interpersonal relationships?
4. Consider the individual that you have the most difficult time working with or getting along with. Which dimensions are similar and different? Which dimensions seem to be the source of your difficulty?
5. If you choose co-workers for this exercise, discuss the management actions, policies, and/or programs that could be used to increase inclusiveness, reduce turnover, and increase job satisfaction.

Diversity Worksheet

Diversity Dimensions	Work Associates				
Personality					
e.g., Loyalty					
Internal Dimensions					
Age					
Gender					
Sexual orientation					
Physical ability					
Ethnicity					
Race					
External Dimensions					
Geographic location					
Income					
Personal habits					
Recreational habits					
Religion					
Educational background					
Work experience					
Appearance					
Parental status					
Marital status					
Organizational Dimensions					
Functional level/classification					
Work content/field					
Division/department/unit/group					
Seniority					
Work location					
Union affiliation					
Management status					

Source: This exercise was modified from Garden Swartz and Rowe, *Diverse Teams At Work*, (New York: McGraw-Hill 1994), pp. 60–61. © 1994 reprinted with permission of the McGraw-Hill Companies.

CBC video case

Loyalty in the Workplace

In the past, employers provided job security for their employees, who in turn remained loyal to their employer. But with the downsizing and layoffs of the 1990s, this relationship is history. Today's youth entering the workforce see their employment as an economic transaction "they pay me and I work hard," and they don't feel that they owe the company anything else. The twenty-something Nexus generation grew up, remote control in hand, changing channels as they experienced their parents' layoffs and divorces. Now they are always looking for their next job through online job banks that send E-mails whenever an opportunity arises that fits their profile.

Employers like John Honderich of the Toronto Star are disappointed with this behaviour. They would like young employees to be loyal, but is this realistic? These employees are products of the information age with the potential to become valuable employees. The Royal Bank and other companies are spending on research and consulting advice on how to attract and retain young workers. Results show that a young employee's relationship with his or her manager is very important for building organizational commitment. Other companies are trying to reach out and generate loyalty by hiring contract workers into the permanent workforce, and providing company shares. But in the end, both parties agree that there are no guarantees.

QUESTIONS FOR DISCUSSION

1. Is it realistic to expect young workers to be loyal to an organization?
2. How important is employee loyalty to company performance?
3. For companies who do want to create loyalty in their employees, what can employers do to build organizational commitment in their younger employees?

Source: Based on "Loyalty in the Workplace," *CBC Venture 777* (March 6, 2001).

chapter
two
Perception, Personality, and Emotion

LEARNING OUTCOMES

After reading the material in this chapter, you should be able to:

- Define *perception* and describe the four-stage model of social perception.
- Identify and briefly explain four managerial implications of social perception.
- Explain how external and internal causal attributions are formulated.
- Distinguish between self-esteem and self-efficacy.
- Contrast high and low self-monitoring individuals, and describe resulting problems each may have.
- Identify and describe the Big Five personality dimensions, and specify which one is correlated most strongly with job performance.
- Explain the difference between an internal and external locus of control.
- Describe the attitude called "job satisfaction" and explain its relationship to work motivation, organizational commitment, and job performance.
- Distinguish between positive and negative emotions, and describe a person with high emotional intelligence.

PERCEPTIONS ABOUT WOMEN AND THE NEW ECONOMY: EBAY'S LORNA BORENSTEIN

Perceptions about women in the workplace are slowly changing. Ask Lorna Borenstein how women are faring in the New Economy, and the general manager of eBay Canada Ltd. says:

"I can walk into a room now and no one is going to mistake me for an assistant. That hasn't always been the case. I've been asked to get the coffee more than once."

Ms. Borenstein, a lawyer who also has an MBA, started out in the legal profession, then moved to Hewlett-Packard and ran her own Internet consulting firm. In her mid-thirties, she says New Economy companies are an ideal place for women, or anyone, to prove themselves because people do not generally use stereotypes to make assumptions about your ability.

Nevertheless, the leadership of major Internet firms is still mostly male. One exception is eBay itself, with female CEO Meg Whitman and other women like Borenstein leading eBay operations in other countries. She pre-dicts that as the industry matures and recovers from its recent meltdown, the eBay example will become the norm.

Borenstein attributes her own self-esteem to the confidence of her mother, who became a superior court judge in Quebec and never doubted that women should be able to have the same success as men. That's a belief she hopes to pass on to her own three children and especially her two young daughters.

But Borenstein worries that lack of career-related self-efficacy may deter many women from promoting themselves as much as they should. Borenstein's own moves from law through industry and now to management of an Internet firm were the result of a series of careful decisions—indicating her internal locus of control—but she also acknowledges the involvement of an external force called luck!

Lorna Borenstein, general manager of eBay Canada Ltd.

Source: Adapted from E Church, "EBay executive sees level field," *Globe & Mail*, March 29, 2001, p B17.

Social Perception

If you're reading this textbook late at night and are hungry, this photo might have caught your attention before anything else on the page. It's an example of *salient* stimuli, or something that stands out from its context. The context for this example is the text on this page.

Perception is a cognitive process that enables us to interpret and understand our surroundings, including people, events and objects. A cognitive process involves a person's knowledge, opinions, or beliefs. Since OB's principal focus is on people, the following discussion emphasizes *social* perception, also known as social **cognition**.

Social perception involves a four-stage sequence, as illustrated in Figure 2–1. The first three stages in this model describe how specific social information is observed and stored in memory. The fourth stage involves turning mental representations into real-world judgments and decisions.

Stage 1: Selective Attention/ Comprehension

People are constantly bombarded by physical and social stimuli in the environment. Because they do not have the mental capacity to fully comprehend all this information, they selectively perceive subsets of environmental stimuli. This is where attention plays a role. **Attention** is the process of becoming consciously aware of something or someone. Attention can be focused on information either from the environment or from memory. Regarding the latter situation, if you sometimes find yourself thinking about totally unrelated events or people while reading a textbook, your memory is the focus of your attention.

In general, people tend to pay attention to salient stimuli. Something is *salient* when it stands out from its context. For example, a 110-kg man would certainly be salient in a women's aerobics class but not at a meeting of the Canadian Football League Players' Association. One's needs and goals often dictate which stimuli are salient. For a driver whose gas gauge is on empty, a Petro-Canada or Shell sign is more salient than a McDonald's or Burger King sign. In addition, people have a tendency to

Perception

Process of interpreting one's environment.

Cognition

A person's knowledge, opinions, or beliefs.

Attention

Being consciously aware of something or someone.

FIGURE 2–1 Social Perception Model

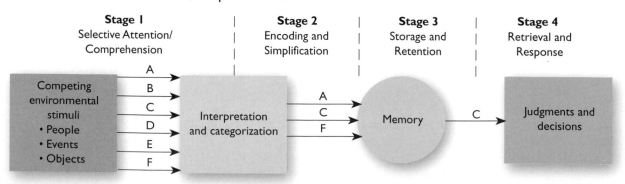

Source: Adapted in part from B J Pannett and S Withane, "Hofstede's Value Survey Module: To Embrace or Abandon?" in *Advances in International Comparative Management*, vol 5, ed S B Prasad (Greenwich, CT: JAI Press, 1990), pp 69–89.

Towards a Better Understanding of Diversity

There are a lot of myths surrounding our perception of population groups other than our own. The following summary reflects the most common stereotypes about several groups, based on a University of Chicago study of Canadian workers.

Group	Common Stereotypes
Asian Canadians	—excel only in science, math, and technical subjects
African Canadians	—incapable of excelling
People With Disabilities	—incapable —dependent —weak, ill
Younger Workers	—not credible
Older Workers	—can't learn new things, especially computer technology —weak, in poor health
Gays and Lesbians	—chose their sexual orientation
Women	—weak leaders —less competent than men —to blame for offensive sexual behaviour —career advanced by using sexuality
White Men	—racist —sexist —patronizing —hold power

Source: T Parvanova, "Toward a Better Understanding of Diversity," *Workplace Today*, June 1999, pp 24–26.

pay more attention to negative than positive information. This leads to a negativity bias.[1] This bias helps explain the gawking factor that slows traffic to a crawl following a car accident.

Stage 2: Encoding and Simplification

Observed information is not stored in memory in its original form. Raw information is encoded (interpreted or translated) into mental representations. To accomplish this, perceivers assign pieces of information to **cognitive categories**. "By *category* we mean a number of objects that are considered equivalent. Categories are generally designated by names, e.g., *dog, animal.*"[2]

People use stereotypes during encoding in order to organize and simplify social information.[3] "A **stereotype** is an individual's set of beliefs about the characteristics or attributes of a group,"[4] which may or may not be accurate. In general, stereotypic characteristics are used to differentiate a particular group of people from other groups. Unfortunately, stereotypes can lead to poor decisions; can create barriers for women, aboriginals, people of colour, and people with disabilities; and can undermine loyalty and job satisfaction.

Cognitive categories

Mental depositories for storing information.

Stereotype

Beliefs about the characteristics of a group.

We use the encoding process to interpret and evaluate our environment. Interestingly, this process can result in differing interpretations and evaluations of the same person or event. Table 2–1 describes five common perceptual errors that influence our judgments about others. Because these perceptual errors often distort the evaluation of job applicants and of employee performance, managers need to guard against them.

Stage 3: Storage and Retention

This phase involves storage of information in long-term memory. Long-term memory consists of separate but related categories, which can be connected. Overall, long-term memory is made up of three compartments containing categories of information about events, general knowledge, and people.[5]

Stage 4: Retrieval and Response

People retrieve information from memory when they make judgments and decisions. Our ultimate judgments and decisions are either based on the process of drawing on, interpreting, and integrating categorical information stored in long-term memory or on retrieving a summary judgment that was already made.[6]

TABLE 2–1   Commonly Found Perceptual Errors

Perceptual Error	Description	Example
Halo	A rater forms an overall impression about an object and then uses that impression to bias ratings about the object.	Rating a professor high on the teaching dimensions of ability to motivate students, knowledge, and communication because we like him or her.
Leniency	A personal characteristic that leads an individual to consistently evaluate other people or objects in an extremely positive fashion.	Rating a professor high on all dimensions of performance regardless of his or her actual performance. The rater who hates to say negative things about others.
Central tendency	The tendency to avoid all extreme judgments and rate people and objects as average or neutral.	Rating a professor average on all dimensions of performance regardless of his or her actual performance.
Recency effects	The tendency to remember recent information. If the recent information is negative, the person or object is evaluated negatively.	Although a professor has given good lectures for 12 to 15 weeks, he or she is evaluated negatively because lectures over the last three weeks were done poorly.
Contrast effects	The tendency to evaluate people or objects by comparing them with characteristics of recently observed people or objects.	Rating a good professor as average because you compared his or her performance with three of the best professors you have ever had in university. You are currently taking courses from the three excellent professors.

Inaccurate Perceptions Limit International Opportunities for Female Managers

One of the most significant challenges for women in international business is convincing companies to send them abroad in the first place, due to the widespread, yet erroneous, perception that it is very difficult for women to work in other countries. Specific misperceptions range from beliefs that women aren't as "internationally mobile" as men, that they encounter more work-life conflict than men when taking international assignments, and that they aren't as successful with international clients as men because these clients are more comfortable doing business with men. Stereotypes such as these make it less likely that decision makers are going to consider female managers when they build global executive teams.

These faulty perceptions are largely unfounded—women have succeeded in international postings everywhere from Kuwait to Japan. These stereotypes are not supported by the results of a recent survey by Catalyst (a research and advisory organization). The survey results showed that 80% of women working abroad have never turned down a relocation, compared to 71% of men; that both women and men experience difficulties with work-life balance; and that 71% of women report having been very effective in building business relationships with international clients.

It is true that attitudes toward women can still be different in other countries, but there is often a separate standard for foreign businesswomen. In fact, foreign businesswomen are seen as a "third sex" in some countries. As such, foreign women are treated as equals in business situations even in most male-dominated societies such as Japan, and some Islamic countries. Women gain this status through having a good position in their company, a strong educational background, or a thorough knowledge of their product or business.

Decision makers need to be mindful of the fact that failed international assignments are often due to the wrong person being sent abroad to do the job. The most important criteria for selecting expatriate managers—male or female—are adaptability, resilience, the ability to thrive in an atmosphere of ambiguity, and astute powers of perception.

Source: Adapted from A Kaminsky, "Misconceptions may limit women's opportunities for international assignments," *Canadian HR Reporter*, May 7, 2001, p 22; "Women not given international work," *Canadian HR Reporter*, January 15, 2001, p 13; D Brown, "Resilient employees needed for successful relocations," *Canadian HR Reporter*, June 5, 2000, pp 9, 14.

Managerial Implications

Social cognition is the window through which we all observe, interpret, and prepare our responses to people and events. A wide variety of managerial activities, organizational processes, and quality-of-life issues are thus affected by perception. Consider, for example, the following implications.

Hiring Interviewers make hiring decisions based on their impression of how an applicant fits the perceived requirements of a job. Inaccurate impressions in either direction produce poor hiring decisions. Moreover, interviewers with racist or sexist perceptions can undermine the accuracy and legality of hiring decisions. Those invalid perceptions need to be confronted and improved through coaching and training. A recent study demonstrated that training improved interviewers' ability to obtain high-quality, job-related information and to stay focused on the interview task. Trained interviewers provided more balanced judgments about applicants than did nontrained interviewers.[7]

Performance Appraisal   Faulty perceptions about what constitutes good versus poor performance can lead to inaccurate performance appraisals, which erode work motivation, commitment, and loyalty. Therefore, it is important for managers to accurately identify the behavioural characteristics and results indicative of good performance at the beginning of a performance review cycle. These characteristics then can serve as the benchmarks for evaluating employee performance. Managers are advised to use more objectively based measures of performance as much as possible because subjective indicators are prone to bias and inaccuracy. In those cases where the job does not possess objective measures of performance, however, managers should still use subjective evaluations. Furthermore, because memory for specific instances of employee performance deteriorates over time, managers need a mechanism for accurately recalling employee behaviour. Research reveals that individuals can be trained to be more accurate raters of performance.[8]

Communication   Managers need to remember that social perception is a screening process that can distort communication, both coming and going. Messages are interpreted and categorized according to perceptions developed through past experiences and influenced by one's age, gender, and ethnic, geographic, and cultural orientations. Effective communicators try to tailor their messages to the receiver's perceptions. This requires well-developed listening and observation skills and cross-cultural sensitivity.

Self-Perception

Self is the core of one's conscious existence. Awareness of self is referred to as self-concept, and is based on self-perception. A **self-concept** would be impossible without the capacity to think. Three topics invariably mentioned in conjunction with self-concept, are self-esteem, self-efficacy, and self-monitoring.

Self-concept

Person's self-perception as a physical, social, spiritual being.

Self-esteem

One's overall self-evaluation.

Self-Esteem

Self-esteem is a belief about one's own self-worth based on an overall self-evaluation.[9] People with high self-esteem see themselves as worthwhile, capable, and acceptable. People with low self-esteem view themselves in negative terms. They do not feel good about themselves and are hampered by self-doubts.[10]

Managers can build employee self-esteem in four ways:[11]

1. Be supportive by showing concern for personal problems, interests, status, and contributions.
2. Offer work involving variety, autonomy, and challenges that suit the individual's values, skills, and abilities.
3. Strive for management—employee cohesiveness and build trust.
4. Have faith in each employee's self-management ability. Reward successes.

Self-Efficacy ("I can do that.")

Self-efficacy

Belief in one's ability to do a task.

Self-efficacy is a person's belief about his or her chances of successfully accomplishing a specific task. Helpful assistance from parents, role models, and mentors are central to the development of high self-efficacy. Consider, for example, this recent interview exchange with Nathan Lane, the successful Broadway and Hollywood actor:

> I asked Lane if he ever considered giving up during his early years of trying to succeed as an actor, when times were tough.
>
> He seemed startled by the question. "What else would I do?" he replied. "I have no other skills. I didn't for a moment think I *wasn't* going to make it. I just thought it may take a while. Certainly, at times you lose confidence, but I always believed there was a place for me. People believing in you is what gives you the confidence to go on. After that, it's a matter of perseverance, luck, and being ready when the opportunity does arrive."[12]

Self-efficacy expectations can come into play during public speaking sessions. Prior experience is the most potent source of these beliefs.

The relationship between self-efficacy and performance is a cyclical one. Efficacy → performance cycles can spiral upward toward success or downward toward failure.[13] Researchers have documented a strong linkage between high self-efficacy expectations and success in widely varied physical and mental tasks. Those with low self-efficacy expectations tend to have low success rates. Chronically low self-efficacy is associated with a condition called **learned helplessness**, the severely debilitating belief that one has no control over one's environment.[14] Thus people program themselves for success or failure by enacting their self-efficacy expectations.

Learned helplessness

Debilitating lack of faith in one's ability to control the situation.

Managerial Implications   On-the-job research evidence encourages managers to nurture self-efficacy, both in themselves and in others. Significant positive correlation between self-efficacy and job performance have been documented by researchers.[15] Self-efficacy requires constructive action in each of the following managerial areas:

1. *Recruiting/selection/job assignments*. Interview questions can be designed to probe job applicants' general self-efficacy as a basis for determining orientation and training needs. Care needs to be taken not to hire solely on the basis of self-efficacy because studies have detected below-average self-esteem and self-efficacy among women and protected minorities.[16]

2. *Job design*. Complex, challenging, and autonomous jobs tend to enhance perceived self-efficacy.[17] Boring, tedious jobs generally do the opposite.

3. *Training and development*. Employees' self-efficacy expectations for key tasks can be improved through guided experiences, mentoring, and role modelling.[18]

4. *Self-management*. Systematic self-management training involves enhancement of self-efficacy expectations.[19]

5. *Goal setting and quality improvement*. Goal difficulty needs to match the individual's perceived self-efficacy.[20] As self-efficacy and performance improve, goals and quality standards can be made more challenging.

6. *Coaching*. Those with low self-efficacy and employees victimized by learned helplessness need lots of constructive pointers and positive feedback.[21]

7. *Leadership*. Needed leadership talent surfaces when top management gives high self-efficacy managers a chance to prove themselves under pressure.

8. *Rewards*. Small successes need to be rewarded as stepping-stones to a stronger self-image and greater achievements.

Self-Monitoring

Consider these contrasting scenarios:

1. You are rushing to an important meeting when a co-worker pulls you aside and starts to discuss a personal problem. You want to break off the conversation, so you glance at your watch. He keeps talking. You say, "I'm late for a big meeting." He continues. You turn and start to walk away. The person keeps talking as if they never received any of your verbal and nonverbal signals that the conversation was over.

2. Same situation. Only this time, when you glance at your watch, the person immediately says, "I know, you've got to go. Sorry. We'll talk later."

In the first all-too-familiar scenario, you are talking to a "low self-monitor." The second scenario involves a "high self-monitor." But more is involved here than an irritating situation. A significant and measurable individual difference in self-expression behaviour, called self-monitoring, is highlighted. **Self-monitoring** is the extent to which a person observes their own self-expressive behaviour and adapts it to the demands of the situation.[22]

Self-monitoring

Observing one's own behaviour and adapting it to the situation.

In organizational life, both high and low monitors are subject to criticism. High self-monitors are sometimes called *chameleons*, who readily adapt their self-presentation to their surroundings. Low self-monitors, on the other hand, often are criticized for being on their own planet and insensitive to others. Importantly, within an OB context, self-monitoring is like any other individual difference—not a matter of right or wrong or good versus bad, but rather a source of diversity that needs to be adequately understood by present and future managers.

Causal Attributions

Attribution theory describes a perceptual process based on the premise that people attempt to infer causes for observed behaviour. Rightly or wrongly, we constantly formulate cause-and-effect explanations for our own and others' behaviour. Attributional statements such as the following are common: "Joe drinks too much because he has no willpower; but I need a couple of drinks after work because I'm under a lot of pressure." Formally defined, **causal attributions** are suspected or inferred causes of behaviour. It is important to understand how people formulate attributions because they profoundly affect organizational behaviour. For example, a supervisor who attributes an employee's poor performance to a lack of effort might reprimand that individual. However, training might be deemed necessary if the supervisor attributes the poor performance to a lack of ability.

Causal attributions

Suspected or inferred causes of behaviour.

Generally speaking, people formulate causal attributions by considering the events preceding an observed behaviour. Attribution theory proposes that behaviour can be attributed either to *internal factors* within a person (such as ability) or to *external factors* within the environment (such as a difficult task). People make causal attributions after gathering information about three dimensions of behaviour: consensus, distinctiveness, and consistency.[23] These dimensions vary independently, thus forming various combinations and leading to differing attributions.

- *Consensus* involves a comparison of an individual's behaviour with that of his or her peers. There is high consensus when one acts like the rest of the group and low consensus when one acts differently.

- *Distinctiveness* is determined by comparing a person's behaviour on one task with his or her behaviour on other tasks. High distinctiveness means the individual has performed the task in question in a significantly different manner than he or she has performed other tasks. Low distinctiveness means stable performance or quality from one task to another.

- *Consistency* is determined by judging if the individual's performance on a given task is consistent over time. High consistency implies that a person performs a certain task the same, time after time. Unstable performance of a given task over time would mean low consistency.

It is important to remember that consensus relates to other *people*, distinctiveness relates to other *tasks*, and consistency relates to *time*. The question now is: How does information about these three dimensions of behaviour lead to internal or external attributions?

People attribute behaviour to *external* causes (environmental factors) when they perceive high consensus, high distinctiveness, and low consistency. *Internal* attributions (personal factors) tend to be made when observed behaviour is characterized by low consensus, low distinctiveness, and high consistency. So, for example, when all employees are performing poorly (high consensus), when the poor performance occurs on only one of several tasks (high distinctiveness), and the poor performance occurs during only one time period (low consistency), a supervisor will probably attribute an employee's poor performance to an external source such as peer pressure or an overly difficult task. In contrast, performance will be attributed to an employee's personal characteristics (an internal attribution) when only the individual in question is performing poorly (low consensus), when the inferior performance is found across several tasks (low distinctiveness), and when the low performance has persisted over time (high consistency). Many studies supported this predicted pattern of attributions.[24]

Attributional Tendencies

Researchers have uncovered two attributional tendencies that distort one's interpretation of observed behaviour—*fundamental attribution bias* and *self-serving bias*.

Fundamental Attribution Bias   The **fundamental attribution bias** reflects one's tendency to attribute another person's behaviour to his or her personal characteristics, as opposed to situational factors. This bias causes perceivers to ignore important environmental forces that often significantly affect behaviour.

Fundamental attribution bias

Ignoring environmental factors that affect behaviour.

Self-Serving Bias   The **self-serving bias** represents one's tendency to take more personal responsibility for success than for failure. Employees tend to attribute their successes to internal factors (high ability and/or hard work) and their failures to uncontrollable external factors (tough job, bad luck, unproductive co-workers, or an unsympathetic boss).[25] This self-serving bias is evident in how students typically analyze their performance on exams. "A" students are likely to attribute their grade to high ability or hard work. "D" students, meanwhile, tend to pin the blame on factors like an unfair test, bad luck, or unclear lectures.

Self-serving bias

Taking more personal responsibility for success than failure.

Managerial Application and Implications   These attributional tendencies have several important implications for managers. First, managers tend to disproportionately attribute behaviour to *internal* causes.[26] This can result in inaccurate evaluations of performance, leading to reduced employee motivation. No one likes to be blamed because of factors they perceive to be beyond their control. Further, because managers' responses to employee performance vary according to their attributions, attributional biases may lead to inappropriate managerial actions, including promotions, transfers, layoffs, and so forth. This can dampen motivation and performance. Attributional training sessions for managers are in order. Basic attributional processes can be explained, and managers can be taught to detect and avoid attributional biases. Finally, an employee's attributions for his or her own performance have dramatic effects on subsequent motivation, performance, and personal attitudes such as self-esteem. For instance, people tend to give up, develop lower expectations for future success, and experience decreased self-esteem when they attribute failure to a lack of ability. Fortunately, attributional retraining can improve both motivation and performance. Research shows that employees can be taught to attribute their failures to a lack of effort rather than to a lack of ability.[27] This attributional realignment paves the way for improved motivation and performance.

Personality Dynamics

Individuals have their own way of thinking and acting, their own unique style or *personality*. **Personality** is defined as the combination of stable physical and mental characteristics that give the individual his or her identity.[28] These characteristics or traits—including how one looks, thinks, acts, and feels—are the product of interacting genetic and environmental influences. In this section, we introduce the Big Five personality dimensions and discuss a key personality dynamic called locus of control.

Personality

Stable physical and mental characteristics responsible for a person's identity.

The Big Five Personality Dimensions

Long and confusing lists of personality dimensions have been distilled in recent years to the Big Five.[29] They are extraversion, agreeableness, conscientiousness, emotional stability, and openness to experience (see Table 2–2 for descriptions). Standardized personality tests determine how positively or negatively a person scores on each of the Big Five. For example, someone scoring negatively on extraversion would be an introverted person prone to shy and withdrawn behaviour.[30] Someone scoring negatively on emo-

TABLE 2–2   The Big Five Personality Dimensions

Personality Dimension	Characteristics of a Person Scoring Positively on the Dimension
1. Extraversion	Outgoing, talkative, sociable, assertive
2. Agreeableness	Trusting, good-natured, cooperative, softhearted
3. Conscientiousness	Dependable, responsible, achievement oriented, persistent
4. Emotional stability	Relaxed, secure, unworried
5. Openness to experience	Intellectual, imaginative, curious, broad-minded

Source: Adapted from M R Barrick and M K Mount, "Autonomy as a Moderator of the Relationships between the Big Five Personality Dimensions and Job Performance," *Journal of Applied Psychology*, February 1993, pp 111–18.

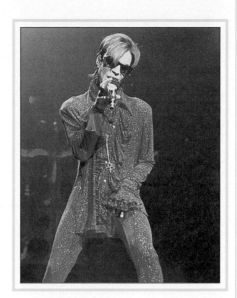

tional stability would be nervous, tense, angry, and worried. A person's scores on the Big Five reveal a personality profile as unique as his or her fingerprints. Yet one important question lingers: Are personality models unique to the culture in which they were developed? At least as far as the Big Five model goes, recent cross-cultural research evidence points in the direction of "no." Specifically, the Big Five personality structure held up very well in a study of women and men from Russia, Canada, Hong Kong, Poland, Germany, and Finland.[31]

Personality and Job Performance   Those interested in OB want to know the connection between the Big Five and job performance. Ideally, Big Five personality dimensions that correlate positively and strongly with job performance would be helpful in the selection, training, and appraisal of employees. Among the Big Five, *conscientiousness* has the strongest positive correlation with job performance and training performance. Researchers have found that individuals who exhibit traits associated with a strong sense of purpose, obligation, and persistence generally perform better than those who do not.[32] Also, extraversion (an outgoing personality) is associated with success for managers and salespeople, and is a stronger predictor of job performance than agreeableness, across all professions. Researchers have concluded that, "It appears that being courteous, trusting, straightforward, and softhearted has a smaller impact on job performance than being talkative, active, and assertive."[33]

Locus of Control: Self or Environment?

Individuals vary in terms of how much personal responsibility they take for their behaviour and its consequences. This dimension of personality is called **locus of control**.

> **Locus of control**
>
> Attributions regarding one's behaviour and its consequences to internal versus external factors.

People who believe they control the events and consequences that affect their lives are said to possess an *internal* locus of control. For example, such a person tends to attribute positive outcomes, such as getting a passing grade on an exam, to her or his own abilities. Similarly, an "internal" tends to blame negative events, such as failing an exam, on personal shortcomings— not studying hard enough, perhaps. Many entrepreneurs eventually succeed because their internal locus of control

Source: *The Arizona Republic*, May 19, 2001, p D2.

helps them overcome setbacks and disappointments. They see themselves as masters of their own fate and not simply lucky.[34]

On the other side of this personality dimension are those who believe their performance is the product of circumstances beyond their immediate control. These individuals are said to possess an *external* locus of control and tend to attribute outcomes to environmental causes, such as luck or fate. Unlike someone with an internal locus of control, an "external" would attribute a passing grade on an exam to something external (an easy test or a good day) and attribute a failing grade to an unfair test or problems at home.

Researchers have found important behavioural differences between internals and externals:

- Internals display greater work motivation.
- Internals have stronger expectations that effort leads to performance.
- Internals exhibit higher performance on tasks involving learning or problem solving, when performance leads to valued rewards.
- There is a stronger relationship between job satisfaction and performance for internals than for externals.
- Internals obtain higher salaries and greater salary increases than externals.
- Externals tend to be more anxious than internals.[35]

Managerial Implications The preceding summary of research findings on locus of control has important implications for managing people at work. First, since internals have a tendency to believe they control the work environment through their behaviour, they will attempt to exert control over the work setting. This can be done by trying to influence work procedures, working conditions, task assignments, or relationships with peers and supervisors. As these possibilities imply, internals may resist a manager's attempts to closely supervise their work. Therefore, management may want to place internals in jobs requiring high initiative and low compliance. Externals, on the other hand, might be more amenable to highly structured jobs requiring greater compliance. Direct participation also can bolster the attitudes and performance of externals.[36]

Second, locus of control has implications for reward systems. Given that internals have a greater belief that their effort leads to performance, internals likely would prefer and respond more productively to incentives such as merit pay or sales commissions.[37]

Attitudes

An **attitude** is defined as "a learned predisposition to respond in a consistently favourable or unfavourable manner with respect to a given object."[38] Attitudes relate to behaviour directed toward specific objects, persons, or situations.[39] One of the most important attitudes in organizations is job satisfaction.

Attitude

Learned predisposition toward a given object, person, or situation.

Job satisfaction

An attitude concerning one's job.

Job Satisfaction   **Job satisfaction** is an attitude concerning various facets of one's job. This definition means job satisfaction is not a unitary concept. Rather, a person can be relatively satisfied with one aspect of his or her job and dissatisfied with one or more other aspects.

Several explanations regarding the cause of job satisfaction have been suggested. One explanation is that job satisfaction is determined by the extent to which the characteristics of a job allow an individual to fulfil his or her needs.[40] Another explanation is that job satisfaction is a result of the difference between what an individual expects to receive from a job, such as good pay and promotional opportunities, and what he or she actually receives.[41] A third explanation is that satisfaction results from the perception that a job allows for fulfilment of an individual's important work values.[42] Fourth, job satisfaction has been explained as a function of how fairly an individual is treated at work.[43] Finally, it has been suggested that job satisfaction is related to personality traits such as self-esteem and locus of control.[44]

There are many consequences of job satisfaction. Table 2–3 provides a summary of the results of thousands of research studies examining the relationship between job satisfaction and motivation, job performance, organizational commitment (another work-related attitude), perceived stress, and important work behaviours including absenteeism, turnover, organizational citizenship behaviour (going above and beyond the call of duty) and job involvement (the extent to which an individual is personally involved with his or her work).

Correlates of Job Satisfaction   **TABLE 2–3**

Variables Related to Job Satisfaction	Direction of Relationship	Strength of Relationship
Motivation	Positive	Moderate
Job Involvement	Positive	Moderate
Organizational citizenship behaviour	Positive	Moderate
Organizational commitment	Positive	Strong
Absenteeism	Negative	Weak
Turnover	Negative	Weak
Perceived stress	Negative	Strong
Job performance	Positive	Weak

Emotions in the Workplace

In the ideal world of management theory, employees pursue organizational goals in a logical and rational manner, without emotion. Yet day-to-day organizational life shows us how prevalent and powerful emotions can be. Anger and jealousy, both potent emotions, often push aside logic and rationality in the workplace. Managers use fear and other emotions to both motivate and intimidate.

Positive and Negative Emotions

Emotions are "complex, patterned, organismic reactions to how we think we are doing in our lifelong efforts to survive and flourish and to achieve what we wish for ourselves."[45] Emotions involve the *whole* person—biological, psychological, and social. Emotions play roles in both causing and adapting to stress and its associated biological and psychological problems. The destructive effect of emotional behaviour on social relationships is all too obvious in daily life.

> **Emotions**
>
> Intense feelings in reaction to personal achievements and setbacks that may be felt and displayed.

Importantly, psychologists draw a distinction between felt and displayed emotions.[46] For example, someone might feel angry (felt emotion) at a rude coworker but not make a nasty remark in return (displayed emotion). Why? Because people typically want to avoid conflict and maintain harmony in the workplace. In many cases, a job specifically requires that an employee suppress a felt emotion and instead display an emotion that is desired by the organization during interpersonal transactions. This job requirement has now been formally recognized as **emotional labour**.[47] Examples include medical professionals who must remain calm when patients are in terrible pain or are dying; police officers who must not demonstrate anger when dealing with suspected child molesters and murderers; and anyone involved in serving the public (e.g., restaurant servers, flight attendants, bank tellers, retail salespeople) who must express an "appropriate" professional demeanor when dealing with unhappy, belligerent, or angry customers. This creates a situation called **emotional dissonance**, where there is a conflict between required and true emotions. This dissonance contributes to stress and job burnout.[48]

> **Emotional labour**
>
> Job requirement that employees must suppress felt emotions and display organizationally desired emotions during interpersonal transactions.

> **Emotional dissonance**
>
> Conflict between organizationally desired and true emotions.

Emotions centre on a person's goals. Accordingly, the distinction between positive and negative emotions is goal oriented. Some emotions are triggered by frustration and failure when pursuing one's goals. These are called *negative* emotions. They are said to be goal incongruent. For example, which of the six negative emotions in Figure 2–2 are you likely to experience if you fail the final exam in a required course? Failing the exam would be incongruent with your goal of graduating on time. On the other hand, which of the four *positive* emotions in Figure 2–2 would you probably experience if you graduated on time and with honours? The emotions you would experience in this situation are positive because they are congruent (or consistent) with an important lifetime goal. The individual's goals, it is important to note, may or may not be socially acceptable. Thus, a positive emotion, such as love/affection, may be undesirable if associated with sexual harassment. Oppositely, slight pangs of guilt, anxiety, and envy can motivate extra effort. On balance, the constructive or destructive nature of a particular emotion must be judged in terms of both its intensity and the person's relevant goal.

More Attention Needed

The OB research literature is sparse regarding emotions. Emotional behaviour typically is not covered as a central variable but rather as a subfactor in discussions of organizational politics, conflict, and stress. Here are some recent insights. According to a British organizational psychologist, we need to do a better job of dealing with emotions in career management programs.[49] Under the new employment contract, job-hunting skills are not enough. Emotional skills are needed to handle frequent and often difficult career transitions. A pair of laboratory studies with college/university students as subjects found no gender difference in *felt* emotions. But the women were more emotionally *expressive* than the men.[50] Two field studies with nurses and accountants as subjects found a strong

Positive and Negative Emotions | **FIGURE 2–2**

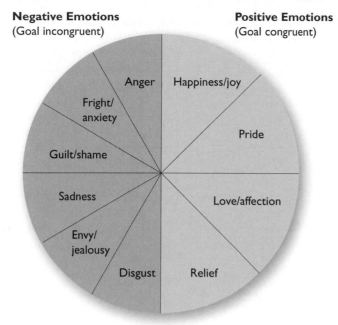

Source: Adapted from discussion in R S Lazarus, *Emotion and Adaptation* (New York: Oxford University Press, 1991), Chs 6, 7.

linkage between the work group's collective mood and the individual's mood.[51] The bad news: Foul moods are contagious. But so are good moods. Go spread the cheer!

Emotional Intelligence (EI)

In 1995, Daniel Goleman, a psychologist turned journalist, created a stir in education and management circles with the publication of his book *Emotional Intelligence*. Hence, an obscure topic among psychologists became mainstream. According to Goleman, traditional models of intelligence (IQ) are too narrow. His approach to **emotional intelligence** (EI) includes

> **Emotional intelligence**
>
> The ability to recognize emotions in one's self and others, taking advantage of helpful ones and keeping control over destructive ones.

... abilities such as being able to motivate oneself and persist in the face of frustrations; to control impulse and delay gratification; to regulate one's moods and keep distress from swamping the ability to think; to empathize and to hope. Unlike IQ, with its nearly one-hundred-year history of research with hundreds of thousands of people, emotional intelligence is a new concept. No one can yet say exactly how much of the variability from person to person in life's course it accounts for. But what data exist suggest it can be as powerful, and at times more powerful, than IQ.[52]

There are five dimensions of emotional intelligence:[53]

- self-awareness—the ability to recognize one's own emotions
- self-regulation—the ability to control one's own emotions
- self-motivation—the ability to direct one's own emotions toward personal goals
- empathy—the ability to understand and be sensitive to the feelings of others
- social skill—the ability to manage the emotions of other people.

ETHICS AT WORK

Anger Leads to Tragedy

In 1999, Pierre Lebrun, a transit worker at OC Transpo in Ottawa, complained that he was being ridiculed and harassed due to his speech impediment and facial tick. Nothing was done, and Lebrun's anger turned to rage that boiled over when he shot and killed four of his co-workers and then killed himself.

You Decide...

Was it ethical for managers who knew about the harassment to ignore it? Do you think that the fundamental attribution bias was at work here? Was Lebrun stereotyped because of his physical handicap?

Source: L Young, "On-the-job harassment precipitates co-worker violence: Inquest," *Canadian HR Reporter*, March 27, 2000, pp 1, 3.

It is difficult to measure emotional intelligence. Even Goleman concedes, "It's very tough to measure our own emotional intelligence, because most of us don't have a very clear sense of how we come across to other people. . . ."[54] Honest feedback from others is necessary. Still, the area of emotional intelligence is important to managers because, unlike IQ, social problem solving and the ability to control one's emotions can be taught and learned (see Table 2–4). Some organizations, including Western Union Insurance, American Express, and the US Air Force, are using EI tests for screening prospective employees, and others use it as a basis for identifying training and development needs.[55]

TABLE 2–4   How to Manage Anger in Yourself and Others

Reducing Chronic Anger [in Yourself]	Responding to Angry Provocation
Guides for Action • Appreciate the potentially valuable lessons from anger. • Use mistakes and slights to learn. • Recognize that you and others can do well enough without being perfect. • Trust that most people want to be caring, helpful family members and colleagues. • Forgive others and yourself. • Confront unrealistic, blame-oriented assumptions. • Adopt constructive, learning-oriented assumptions.	**Guides for Action** • Expect angry people to exaggerate. • Recognize the other's frustrations and pressures. • Use the provocation to develop your abilities. • Allow the other to let off steam. • Begin to problem solve when the anger is at moderate levels. • Congratulate yourself on turning an outburst into an opportunity to find solutions. • Share successes with partners.
Pitfalls to Avoid • Assume every slight is a painful wound. • Equate not getting what you want with catastrophe. • See every mistake and slip as a transgression that must be corrected immediately. • Attack someone for your getting angry. • Attack yourself for getting angry. • Try to be and have things perfect. • Suspect people's motives unless you have incontestable evidence that people can be trusted. • Assume any attempt to change yourself is an admission of failure. • Never forgive.	**Pitfalls to Avoid** • Take every word literally. • Denounce the most extreme statements and ignore more moderate ones. • Doubt yourself because the other does. • Attack because you have been attacked. • Forget the experience without learning from it.

Source: Reprinted with permission from D Tjosvold, *Learning to Manage Conflict: Getting People to Work Together Productively*, pp 127–29. Copyright © 1993 Dean Tjosvold. First published by Lexington Books. All rights reserved.

summary of key concepts

- *Define perception and describe the four-stage model of social perception.* Perception is a cognitive process that enables us to interpret and understand our surroundings. Social perception, also known as social cognition, is a four-stage process. The four stages are selective attention/comprehension, encoding and simplification, storage and retention, and retrieval and response. During social cognition, salient stimuli are assigned to cognitive categories, and stored in long-term memory.

- *Identify and briefly explain managerial implications of social perception.* Social perception affects hiring decisions, performance appraisals, and communication processes. Inaccurate perceptions may be used to evaluate job applicants. Similarly, faulty perceptions about what constitutes good versus poor performance can lead to inaccurate performance appraisals. Managers are advised to use objective rather than subjective measures of performance. Finally, communication is influenced by perceptions used to interpret any message. Effective communicators try to tailor their messages to the receiver's perceptions.

- *Distinguish between self-esteem and self-efficacy.* Self-esteem is an overall evaluation of oneself, one's perceived self-worth. Self-efficacy is the belief in one's ability to successfully perform a task.

- *Contrast high and low self-monitoring individuals, and describe resulting problems each may have.* A high self-monitor strives to make a good public impression by closely monitoring his or her behaviour and adapting it to the situation. Very high self-monitoring can create a "chameleon" who is seen as insincere and dishonest. Low self-monitors do the opposite by acting out their momentary feelings, regardless of their surroundings. Very low self-monitoring can lead to a one-way communicator who seems to ignore verbal and nonverbal cues from others.

- *Explain how external and internal causal attributions are formulated.* Attribution theory attempts to describe how people infer causes for observed behaviour. External attributions tend to be made when consensus and distinctiveness are high and consistency is low. Internal (personal responsibility) attributions tend to be made when consensus and distinctiveness are low and consistency is high.

- *Identify and describe the Big Five personality dimensions, and specify which one is correlated most strongly with job performance.* The Big Five personality dimensions are extraversion (social and talkative), agreeableness (trusting and cooperative), conscientiousness (responsible and persistent), emotional stability (relaxed and unworried), and openness to experience (intellectual and curious). Conscientiousness is the best predictor of job performance.

- *Explain the difference between an internal and external locus of control.* People with an *internal* locus of control, such as entrepreneurs, believe they are masters of their own fate. Those with an *external* locus of control attribute their behaviour and its results to situational forces.

- *Describe the attitude called "job satisfaction" and explain its relationship to work motivation, organizational commitment, and job performance.* Job satisfaction is an attitude concerning one's job, whereby one feels either favourably or unfavourably disposed to his or her job. Job satisfaction has a moderate positive correlation with work motivation, a strong positive correlation with organizational commitment, and a weak positive correlation with job performance.

- *Distinguish between positive and negative emotions, and describe a person with high emotional intelligence.* Positive emotions—happiness/joy, pride, love/affection, and relief—are personal reactions to circumstances congruent with one's goals. Negative emotions—anger, fright/anxiety, guilt/shame, sadness, envy/jealousy, and disgust—are personal reactions to circumstances incongruent with one's goals. Someone with high emotional intelligence has the ability to recognize and control their own emotions; to direct their own emotions toward personal goals; to understand and be sensitive to the feelings of others; and to manage the emotions of others.

key terms

discussion questions

1. Why is it important for managers to have a working knowledge of perception and attribution?

2. Which type of stereotype (sex, age, race, disability) do you believe is more pervasive in organizations? Why?

3. How is someone you know with low self-efficacy, relative to a specific task, "programming themselves for failure?" What could be done to help that individual develop higher self-efficacy?

4. What evidence of the self-serving bias have you observed lately?

5. On a scale of 1 (low) to 10 (high), how would you rate yourself on the Big Five personality dimensions? Is your profile suitable for a managerial position?

6. How would you react to the following statement? "Whenever possible, managers should hire people with an external locus of control."

internet exercises

www.haygroup.ca

1. A Free Online Interactive Emotional Intelligence (EI) Test

Go to the Hay Group's EI Internet site (**www.haygroup.ca**) and select "emotional intelligence quiz" from the resources menu. Read the instructions and complete the 10 test items. (Note: This is a very quick-and-easy test.) Follow the prompt to submit your answer to automatic scoring.

QUESTIONS
1. Do you believe that this sort of paper-and-pencil psychological testing has any merit? Explain.
2. Could self-serving bias influence the way people evaluate intelligence tests? For example, "I scored high so I think it's a good test." "I scored low so it's an unfair or invalid test."
3. Do you agree with psychologist Daniel Goleman that EI can be more important and powerful than IQ? Explain.

www.userpage.fu-berlin.de/~health

2. The General Self-Efficacy Scale (GSE)

In OB, we are most often concerned with self-efficacy in a specific sense related to a given task. However, researchers have also developed a generalized self-efficacy scale to be used for predicting coping with daily life and adaptation after experiencing stressful life experiences. The GSE can be viewed on the Web at **www.userpage.fu-berlin.de/~health**. Click to view the questionnaire in the language of your choice. Complete the 10-item questionnaire at the bottom of the page and follow the scoring instructions (in the administration section).

QUESTIONS

1. Does your GSE score match your self-perception of GSE? Explain.
2. Do you think GSE could be useful in organizational settings? Why or why not?

experiential exercises

1. Anger Control Role Play

Objectives

1. To demonstrate that emotions can be managed.
2. To develop your interpersonal skills for managing both your own and someone else's anger.

Introduction

Personal experience and research tell us that anger begets anger. People do not make their best decisions when angry. Angry outbursts often inflict unintentional interpersonal damage by triggering other emotions (e.g., disgust in observers and subsequent guilt and shame in the angry person). Effective managers know how to break the cycle of negative emotions by defusing anger in themselves and others. This is a role-playing exercise for groups of four. You will have a chance to play two different roles. All the roles are generic, so they can be played as either a woman or a man.

Instructions

Your instructor will divide the class into groups of four. Everyone should read all five roles described. Members of each foursome will decide among themselves who will play which roles. All told, you will participate in two rounds of role playing (each round lasting no longer than eight minutes). In round one, one person will play Role 1 and another will play Role 3; the remaining two group members will play Role 5. In round two, those who played Role 5 in the first round will play Roles 2 and 4. The other two will switch to Role 5.

Role 1: The Angry (Out-Of-Control) Shift Supervisor

You work for a leading electronics company that makes computer chips and other computer-related equipment. Your factory is responsible for assembling and testing the company's most profitable line of computer microprocessors. Business has been good, so your factory is working three shifts. The day shift, which you are now on, is the most desirable one. The night shift, from 11 P.M. to 7:30 A.M. is the least desirable and least productive. In fact, the night shift is such a mess that your boss, the factory manager, wants you to move to the night shift next week. Your boss just broke this bad news as the two of you are having lunch in the company cafeteria. You are shocked and angered because you are one of the most senior and highly rated shift supervisors in the factory. Thanks to your leadership, your shift has broken all production records during the past year. As the divorced single parent of a 10-year-old child, the radical schedule change would be a major lifestyle burden. Questions swirl through your head. "Why me?" "What kind of reliable child-care will be available when I sleep during the day and work at night?" "Why should I be 'punished' for being a top supervisor?" "Why don't they hire someone for the position?" Your boss asks what you think.

When playing this role, be as realistic as possible without getting so loud that you disrupt the other groups. Also, if anyone in your group would be offended by foul language, please refrain from cursing during your angry outburst.

ROLE 2: THE ANGRY (UNDER-CONTROL) SHIFT SUPERVISOR

Same situation as in Role 1. But this role will require you to read and act according to the tips for reducing chronic anger in the left side of Table 2–4. You have plenty of reason to be frustrated and angry, but you realize the importance of maintaining a good working relationship with the factory manager.

ROLE 3: THE (HARD-DRIVING) FACTORY MANAGER

You have a reputation for having a "short fuse." When someone gets angry with you, you attack. When playing this role, be as realistic as possible. Remember, you are responsible for the entire factory with its 1,200 employees and hundreds of millions of dollars of electronics products. A hiring freeze is in place, so you have to move one of your current supervisors. You have chosen your best supervisor because the night shift is your biggest threat to profitable operations. The night-shift supervisor gets a 10% pay premium. Ideally, the move will only be for six months.

ROLE 4: THE (MELLOW) FACTORY MANAGER

Same general situation as in Role 3. However, this role will require you to read and act according to the tips for responding to angry provocation in the right side of Table 2–4. You have a reputation for being results-oriented but reasonable. You are good at taking a broad, strategic view of problems and are a good negotiator.

ROLE 5: SILENT OBSERVER

Follow the exchange between the shift supervisor and the factory manager without talking or getting actively involved. Jot down some notes (for later class discussion) as you observe whether the factory manager did a good job of managing the supervisor's anger.

QUESTIONS FOR DISCUSSION
1. Why is uncontrolled anger a sure road to failure?
2. Is it possible to express anger without insulting others? Explain.
3. Which is more difficult, controlling anger in yourself or defusing someone else's anger? Why?
4. What useful lessons did you learn from this role-playing exercise?

2. Using Attribution Theory to Resolve Performance Problems

Objectives

1. To gain experience determining the causes of performance.
2. To decide on corrective action for employee performance.

Introduction

Attributions are typically made to internal and external factors. Perceivers arrive at their assessments by using various informational cues or antecedents. To determine the types of antecedents people use, we have developed a case containing various informational cues about an individual's performance. You will be asked to read the case and make attributions about the causes of performance. To assess the impact of attributions on managerial behaviour, you will also be asked to recommend corrective action.

Instructions

Presented below is a case that depicts the performance of Mary Martin, a computer programmer. Please read the case to the right and then identify the causes of her behaviour by answering the questions following the case. Then determine whether you made an internal or external attribution. After completing this task, decide on the appropriateness of various forms of corrective action. A list of potential recommendations has been developed. The list is divided into four categories. Read each action, and evaluate its appropriate-

ness by using the scale provided. Next, compute a total score for each of the four categories.

Causes of Performance

To what extent was each of the following a cause of Mary's performance? Use the following scale:

Very Little				Very Much
1 ———— 2 ———— 3 ———— 4 ———— 5				

a. High ability	1	2	3	4	5
b. Low ability	1	2	3	4	5
c. Low effort	1	2	3	4	5
d. Difficult job	1	2	3	4	5
e. Unproductive co-workers	1	2	3	4	5
f. Bad luck	1	2	3	4	5

Internal attribution (total score for causes a, b, and c) _____

External attribution (total score for causes d, e, and f) _____

THE CASE OF MARY MARTIN

Mary Martin, 30, received her bachelor's degree in computer science from a reputable university. She also graduated with above-average grades. Mary is currently working in the computer support/analysis department as a programmer for a nationally based firm. During the past year, Mary has missed 10 days of work. She seems unmotivated and rarely has her assignments completed on time. Mary is usually given the harder programs to work on.

Past records indicate Mary, on the average, completes programs classified as "routine" in about 45 hours. Her co-workers, on the other hand, complete "routine" programs in an average time of 32 hours. Further, Mary finishes programs considered "major problems," on the average, in about 115 hours. Her co-workers, however, finish these same "major problem" assignments, on the average,

in about 100 hours. When Mary has worked in programming teams, her peer performance reviews are generally average to negative. Her male peers have noted she is not creative in attacking problems and she is difficult to work with.

The computer department recently sent a questionnaire to all users of its services to evaluate the usefulness and accuracy of data received. The results indicate many departments are not using computer output because they cannot understand the reports. It was also determined that the users of output generated from Mary's programs found the output chaotic and not useful for managerial decision making.

Appropriateness of Corrective Action

Evaluate the following courses of action by using the scale below:

Very Inappropriate   **Very Appropriate**

1 ———— 2 ———— 3 ———— 4 ———— 5

Coercive Actions

		1	2	3	4	5
a.	Reprimand Mary for her performance	1	2	3	4	5
b.	Threaten to fire Mary if her performance does not improve	1	2	3	4	5

Change Job

c.	Transfer Mary to another job	1	2	3	4	5
d.	Demote Mary to a less demanding job	1	2	3	4	5

Nonpunitive Actions

e.	Work with Mary to help her do the job better	1	2	3	4	5
f.	Offer Mary encouragement to help her improve	1	2	3	4	5

No Immediate Actions

g.	Do nothing	1	2	3	4	5
h.	Promise Mary a pay raise if she improves	1	2	3	4	5

Compute a score for the four categories.

Coercive actions = a + b =

Change job = c + d =

Nonpunitive actions = e + f =

No immediate actions = g + h =

QUESTIONS FOR DISCUSSION

1. How would you evaluate Mary's performance in terms of consensus, distinctiveness, and consistency?
2. Is Mary's performance due to internal or external causes?
3. What did you identify as the top two causes of Mary's performance?
4. Which of the four types of corrective action do you think is most appropriate? Explain. Can you identify any negative consequences of this choice?

personal awareness and growth exercises

1. How Good Are You at Self-Monitoring?

Instructions

In an honest self-appraisal, mark each of the following statements as true (T) or false (F), and then consult the scoring key.

_____ 1. I guess I put on a show to impress or entertain others.

_____ 2. In a group of people I am rarely the centre of attention.

_____ 3. In different situations and with different people, I often act like very different persons.

_____ 4. I would not change my opinions (or the way I do things) in order to please someone or win their favour.

_____ 5. I have considered being an entertainer.

_____ 6. I have trouble changing my behaviour to suit different people and different situations.

_____ 7. At a party I let others keep the jokes and stories going.

_____ 8. I feel a bit awkward in public and do not show up quite as well as I should.

_____ 9. I can look anyone in the eye and tell a lie with a straight face (if for a right end).

_____ 10. I may deceive people by being friendly when I really dislike them.

Scoring Key

Score one point for each of the following answers:
1. T; 2. F; 3. T; 4. F; 5. T; 6. F; 7. F; 8. F; 9. T; 10. T
Score: _____
1–3 = Low self-monitoring
4–5 = Moderately low self-monitoring
6–7 = Moderately high self-monitoring
8–10 = High self-monitoring

Source: Excerpted and adapted from M Snyder and S Gangestad, "On the Nature of Self-Monitoring: Matters of Assessment, Matters of Validity," *Journal of Personality and Social Psychology*, July 1986, p 137.

2. Where Is Your Locus of Control?

Circle one letter for each pair of items, in accordance with your beliefs:

1. A. Many of the unhappy things in people's lives are partly due to bad luck.
   B. People's misfortunes result from the mistakes they make.
2. A. Unfortunately, an individual's worth often passes unrecognized no matter how hard he tries.
   B. In the long run, people get the respect they deserve.
3. A. Without the right breaks one cannot be an effective leader.
   B. Capable people who fail to become leaders have not taken advantage of their opportunities.
4. A. I have often found that what is going to happen will happen.
   B. Trusting to fate has never turned out as well for me as making a decision to take a definite course of action.

5. A. Most people don't realize the extent to which their lives are controlled by accidental happenings.
   B. There really is no such thing as "luck."
6. A. In the long run, the bad things that happen to us are balanced by the good ones.
   B. Most misfortunes are the result of lack of ability, ignorance, laziness, or all three.
7. A. Many times I feel I have little influence over the things that happen to me.
   B. It is impossible for me to believe that chance or luck plays an important role in my life.

Note: In determining your score, A = 0 and B = 1.

Arbitrary norms for this shortened version are: External locus of control = 1–3; Balanced internal and external locus of control = 4; Internal locus of control = 5–7.

Source: Excerpted from J B Rotter, "Generalized Expectancies for Internal versus External Control of Reinforcement," *Psychological Monographs*, vol. 80 (Whole no. 609, 1966), pp 11–12. Copyright © 1966 by the American Psychological Association. Reprinted with permission.

CBC video case

The Tragically Smart

The smartest man in America, with an IQ of 195 (and a 52-inch chest), has spent the last 30 years working as a bouncer. In his spare time he is writing a book to explain the universe. Others with high-IQs are outlaw bikers and bus drivers. Many of these high-IQ people seem to be underachievers, based on conventional expectations. In addition, they say they often feel isolated and lonely. Mensa, an organization for those with high IQs (132+) is more of a support group for lonely brilliant people than the source of solutions to the world's problems, as it was originally intended to be. These people reject the notion of conformity to society's expectations and say that they are doing what is important to them.

Thus IQ is no guarantee of traditional success, and may have been overvalued. Studies have found that only about 6% of career success is related to IQ. The concept of EQ (emotional quotient) may be the reason that the "tragically smart" don't seem to be living up to their potential. The ability to manage emotion in oneself and others has been found to be very important for success in today's world.

QUESTIONS FOR DISCUSSION
1. Why is EQ so important for success?
2. Why do high-IQ people appear to have low EQ?
3. Do you agree with the perception of the high-IQ people on the video that it is their right to live life without maximizing their potential in a more traditional fashion?

Source: Based on "The Tragically Smart," *CBC Fifth Estate* (November 22, 2000).

chapter three

Motivation

After reading the material in this chapter, you should be able to:

- Contrast Maslow's and McClelland's need theories.

- Describe how to motivate employees through job design.

- Explain the practical significance of Herzberg's distinction between motivators and hygiene factors.

- Discuss the role of perceived inequity in employee motivation.

- Describe the practical lessons derived from equity theory.

- Explain Vroom's expectancy theory.

- Describe the practical implications of expectancy theory.

- Identify five practical lessons to be learned from goal-setting research.

- Specify issues that should be addressed before implementing a motivational program.

THE NATURE OF THE WORK MOTIVATES DELOITTE CONSULTING STAFF

Kate Peacock, the new leader of Deloitte Consulting in Canada, says that when she signed on with the firm in 1981, she figured she would last for a couple of years. "I had moved every two years in my jobs before and, of course, that's what I expected to happen here," she says about her stints working in the insurance and banking industries and for a technology company.

Twenty years later, Ms. Peacock is still working in the Toronto office of the international firm, only now she is running the show. What made her stay? Ms. Peacock says it is the nature of the work more than anything else. "It was impossible to get bored." As Deloitte Consulting's new managing director for Canada, holding on to the firm's talent has now become part of her job. After all, the fortunes of a consulting practice are pretty firmly linked to the knowledge of its employees and can suffer terribly if that talent walks out the door.

In recent years, that has been a real danger, especially during the dot-com frenzy when the lure of stock options and quick for-

Kate Peacock, managing director, Deloitte Consulting, Canada.

tunes prompted many consulting firms to try to retain staff with jazzy new offices and special initiatives such as venture capital funds and E-business branches, including Deloitte's own DC.com. While that pull has subsided, at least temporarily, Ms. Peacock says keeping top talent is still a priority.

Beyond that, Peacock says, the firm has developed what it calls a "mothership-and-pod" system, which allows employees to move into smaller divisions or joint ventures if they feel a need to work in a more entrepreneurial environment—one that has a pool table and cappuccino bar. This enables employees to try something new, she says, with the understanding that they can always come back to the mothership—Deloitte's traditional consulting practice.

Keeping top talent is a top priority for Ms. Peacock, who says "We really focus on making this an environment where you can do exciting work. That's No. 1."

Source: Adapted from E Church, "Keeping top talent a top priority," *Globe and Mail*, May 17, 2001, p B14.

The Fundamentals of Employee Motivation

Effective employee motivation has long been one of management's most difficult and important duties. Success in this endeavour is becoming more challenging in light of organizational trends to downsize and reengineer and the demands associated with managing a diverse workforce. The purpose of this chapter is to provide a foundation for understanding the complexities of employee motivation.

The term *motivation* derives from the Latin word *movere*, meaning "to move." In the present context, **motivation** represents "those psychological processes that cause the arousal, direction, and persistence of voluntary actions that are goal directed."[1] Managers need to understand these psychological processes if they are to successfully guide employees toward accomplishing organizational objectives. This section thus provides a conceptual framework for understanding motivation and examines need theories of motivation.

Motivation

Psychological processes that arouse and direct goal-directed behaviour.

Need Theories of Motivation

Needs

Physiological or psychological deficiencies that arouse behaviour.

Need theories attempt to pinpoint internal factors that energize behaviour. **Needs** are physiological or psychological deficiencies that arouse behaviour. They can be strong or weak and they may vary over time and place. Two popular need theories are discussed in this section: Maslow's need hierarchy theory and McClelland's need theory.

Maslow's Need Hierarchy Theory   In 1943, psychologist Abraham Maslow published his now-famous need hierarchy theory of motivation. Maslow proposed that motivation is a function of five basic needs—physiological, safety, social, esteem, and self-actualization, as shown in Figure 3–1. Maslow believed that human needs generally emerge in a predictable stair-step fashion. Once a need is satisfied it activates the next higher need in the hierarchy. This process continues until the need for self-actualization is activated.[2]

Although research does not clearly support this theory of motivation, there is one key managerial implication of Maslow's theory worth noting. That is, a satisfied need may lose its motivational potential. Therefore, managers are advised to motivate employees by devising programs or practices aimed at satisfying emerging or unmet needs. Many companies have responded to this recommendation by offering employees flexible scheduling and benefit plans.

McClelland's Need Theory   David McClelland, a well-known psychologist, has been studying the relationship between needs and behaviour since the late 1940s. He found three specific needs—need for achievement, need for affiliation, and need for power.

Need for achievement

Desire to accomplish something difficult.

- The **need for achievement** is defined as the desire to accomplish something difficult; to master, manipulate, or organize physical objects, human beings, or ideas; to do this as rapidly and as independently as possible; to overcome obstacles; to rival and surpass others; and to increase self-regard by the successful exercise of talent.[3] Achievement-motivated people share three common characteristics: (1) a preference for working on tasks of moderate difficulty; (2) a preference for situations in which performance is due to their efforts rather than other factors, such as luck; and (3) they desire

Motivation in China

In China, money talks, and competition between foreign companies to attract and retain English-speaking Chinese staff is fierce. Some firms are offering such workers double and triple salaries to change jobs. Money is important because the low standard of living in China creates an ongoing need to meet basic physiological and safety needs.

Foreign companies can also help Chinese workers meet their esteem needs because attachment to anything foreign confers status. Thus workers are motivated to work for foreign companies because they get to practise their English and learn about life and cultures outside China. Some employees will leave if they are assigned to a local Chinese boss.

Another major motivator that retains Chinese workers is the chance to travel abroad, particularly for training. This opportunity allows them the workers to fulfil their need for self-actualization. Chinese workers want to be trained in Singapore, Australia, New Zealand, and the US. This arrangement also meets the high growth needs of some employees, and can increase skill variety and task variety in their jobs. The main advantage to the employer is that they can link this developmental assignment to an agreement for individuals to stay with the company for two to three years after they return.

Source: Adapted from M Johnson, " 'Beyond Pay': What Rewards Work Best When Doing Business in China," *Compensation and Benefits Review*, November/December 1998, pp 51–56.

Maslow's Need Hierarchy   FIGURE 3–1

Self-Actualization
Desire for self-fulfilment—to become the best one is capable of becoming.

Esteem
Need for reputation, prestige, and recognition from others. Also contains need for self-confidence and strength.

Social
The desire to spend time in social relationships and activities. Contains the needs for affection and belonging.

Safety
Consists of the need to be safe from physical and psychological harm.

Physiological
Most basic need. Entails having enough food, air, and water to survive.

Source: Adapted from descriptions provided by A H Maslow, "A Theory of Human Motivation," *Psychological Review*, July 1943, pp 370–96.

more feedback on their successes and failures than do low achievers. Need for achievement is similar to Maslow's self-actualization need.

- People with a high **need for affiliation** prefer to spend more time maintaining social relationships, joining groups, and wanting to be loved. Individuals high in this need are not the most effective managers or leaders because they have a hard time making difficult decisions without worrying about being disliked. Need for affiliation is similar to Maslow's social need.

Need for affiliation

Desire to spend time in social relationships and activities.

- The **need for power** reflects an individual's desire to influence, coach, teach, or encourage others to achieve. People with a high need for power like to work and are concerned with discipline and self-respect. There is a positive and negative side to this need. The negative face of power is characterized by an "if I win, you lose" mentality. In contrast, people with a positive orientation to power focus on accomplishing group goals and helping employees obtain the feeling of competence. Because effective managers must positively influence others, McClelland proposes that top managers should have a high need for power coupled with a low need for affiliation. He also believes that individuals with high achievement motivation are *not* best suited for top management positions. Several studies support these propositions.[4] Need for power is similar to Maslow's esteem need.

Need for power

Desire to influence, coach, teach, or encourage others to achieve.

There are three managerial implications associated with McClelland's need theory. First, given that adults can be trained to increase their achievement motivation, and achievement motivation is correlated with performance, organizations should consider the benefits of providing achievement training for employees.[5] Second, achievement, affiliation, and power needs can be considered during the selection process, for better placement. For example, a study revealed that people with a high need for achievement were more attracted to companies that had a pay-for-performance environment than were those with a low achievement motivation.[6] Finally, managers should create challenging task assignments or goals because the need for achievement is positively correlated with goal commitment, which, in turn, influences performance.[7]

Motivating Employees through Job Design

Job design "refers to any set of activities that involve the alteration of specific jobs or interdependent systems of jobs with the intent of improving the quality of employee job experience and their on-the-job productivity."[8] Job design attempts to improve employees' job satisfaction and work effectiveness as well as to lower absenteeism and turnover, and to heighten performance.[9]

Job design

Changing the content and/or process of a specific job to increase job satisfaction and performance.

Job Enlargement

This technique was first used in the late 1940s in response to complaints about tedious and overspecialized jobs. **Job enlargement** involves putting more variety into a worker's job by combining specialized tasks of comparable difficulty.

Job enlargement

Putting more variety into a job.

Job Rotation

As with job enlargement, job rotation's purpose is to give employees greater variety in their work. **Job rotation** calls for moving employees from one specialized job to another. Rather than performing only one job,

Job rotation

Moving employees from one specialized job to another.

workers are trained and given the opportunity to perform two or more separate jobs on a rotating basis. Advantages of job rotation include increased worker flexibility and easier scheduling because employees are cross-trained to perform different jobs.

Job Enrichment

Job enrichment is the practical application of Frederick Herzberg's motivator–hygiene theory of job satisfaction.[10] Herzberg found that job satisfaction was more frequently associated with achievement, recognition, characteristics of the work, responsibility, and advancement. These factors were all related to outcomes associated with the *content* of the task being performed. Herzberg labelled these factors **motivators** because each was associated with strong effort and good performance. He hypothesized that motivators cause a person to move from a state of no satisfaction to satisfaction (see Figure 3–2). Therefore, Herzberg's theory predicts managers can motivate individuals by incorporating "motivators" into an individual's job.

> **Motivators**
>
> Job characteristics associated with job satisfaction.

Herzberg found job *dissatisfaction* to be associated primarily with factors in the work *context* or environment. Specifically, company policy and administration, technical supervision, salary, interpersonal relations with one's supervisor, and working conditions were most frequently mentioned by employees expressing job dissatisfaction. Herzberg labelled this second cluster of factors **hygiene factors**. He further proposed that they were not motivational. At best, according to Herzberg's interpretation, an individual will experience no job dissatisfaction when he or she has no grievances about hygiene factors (refer to Figure 3–2).

> **Hygiene factors**
>
> Job characteristics associated with job dissatisfaction.

Herzberg's Motivator-Hygiene Model **FIGURE 3–2**

Motivators

No Satisfaction ⟶ Satisfaction

Jobs that do not offer achievement, recognition, stimulating work, responsibility, and advancement.	Jobs offering achievement, recognition, stimulating work, responsibility, and advancement.

Hygiene factors

Dissatisfaction ⟵ No Dissatisfaction

Jobs with poor company policies and administration, technical supervision, salary, interpersonal relationships with supervisors, and working conditions.	Jobs with good company policies and administration, technical supervision, salary, interpersonal relationships with supervisors, and working conditions.

Source: Adapted in part from D A Whitsett and E K Winslow, "An Analysis of Studies Critical of the Motivator–Hygiene Theory," *Personnel Psychology,* Winter 1967, pp 391–415.

Job enrichment

Building achievement, recognition, stimulating work, responsibility, and advancement into a job.

Job enrichment is based on the application of Herzberg's ideas. Specifically, **job enrichment** entails modifying a job such that an employee has the opportunity to experience achievement, recognition, stimulating work, responsibility, and advancement. In other words, employees take on tasks normally performed by their supervisors.

The Job Characteristics Model

Richard Hackman and Greg Oldham played a central role in developing the job characteristics approach. These researchers tried to determine how work can be structured so that employees are internally (or intrinsically) motivated. **Internal motivation** occurs when an individual is "turned on to one's work because of the positive internal feelings that are generated by doing well, rather than being dependent on external factors (such as incentive pay or compliments from the boss) for the motivation to work effectively."[11] These positive feelings power a self-perpetuating cycle of motivation. As shown in Figure 3–3, internal work motivation is determined by three psychological states. Managers can foster the psychological states that drive intrinsic motivation by designing jobs that possess the five core job characteristics shown in Figure 3–3. Let us examine the core job dimensions.

Internal motivation

Motivation caused by positive internal feelings.

Core job dimensions

Job characteristics found to various degrees in all jobs.

In general terms, **core job dimensions** are common characteristics found to a varying degree in all jobs. Three of the job characteristics shown in Figure 3–3 combine to determine experienced meaningfulness of work:

- *Skill variety.* The extent to which the job requires an individual to perform a variety of tasks that require him or her to use different skills and abilities.

FIGURE 3–3 The Job Characteristics Model

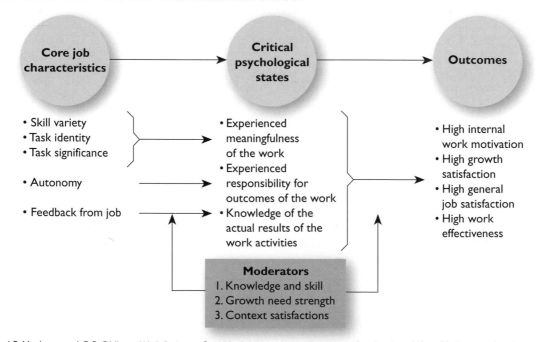

Source: J R Hackman and G R Oldham, *Work Redesign,* © 1980, Addison-Wesley Publishing Co., Reading, MA, p 90. Reprinted with permission.

Motivation Through Diversity

Mauree Stratton started working for Syncrude Canada as a file clerk in 1987, attracted by the high wages, good benefits, and generous vacations. But surveys of Canadian workers invariably show that pay and benefits alone is not enough to attract and retain the best talent. Stratton has found another motivator—the opportunity to acquire new skills. The company paid for instruction for her to become a heavy-equipment operator.

Now at the start of her workday, Stratton dons a hard hat and steel-toed work boots and climbs 18 steps to the cab of a 380-tonne dump truck that is as big as a two-story house. Seated behind the wheel, the grandmother begins her daily runs between the open-pit mines and the processing facilities at Syncrude Canada's huge oilsands operation north of Fort McMurray, Alberta. Stratton is one of 108 female operators at Syncrude, most of whom have given up nine-to-five office jobs to operate the $3-million-plus trucks. "There are openings here for anyone who wants to develop," says Stratton, "In fact, the company encourages people to change jobs."

Innovative programs that encourage diversity help keep good people—and are good for business. Companies often find that a diverse, highly motivated workforce can provide a competitive advantage.

Source: Adapted from D Jenish and B Woodward, "Canada's Top 100 Employers," *Maclean's*, November 5, 2001, pp 46–56.

- *Task identity.* The extent to which the job requires an individual to perform a whole or completely identifiable piece of work. In other words, task identity is high when a person works on a product or project from beginning to end and sees a tangible result.
- *Task significance.* The extent to which the job affects the lives of other people within or outside the organization.

Experienced responsibility is elicited by the job characteristic of autonomy, defined as follows:

- *Autonomy.* The extent to which the job enables an individual to experience freedom, independence, and discretion in both scheduling and determining the procedures used in completing the job.

Finally, knowledge of results is fostered by the job characteristic of feedback, defined as follows:

- *Feedback.* The extent to which an individual receives direct and clear information about how effectively he or she is performing the job.[12]

Hackman and Oldham recognized that everyone does not want a job containing high amounts of the five core job characteristics. They incorporated this conclusion into their model by identifying three attributes that affect how individuals respond to job enrichment (see the box labelled Moderators in Figure 3–3). These attributes are concerned with the individual's knowledge and skill, growth need strength (representing the desire to grow and develop as an individual), and context satisfaction—meaning the extent to which employees are satisfied with various aspects of their job, such as satisfaction with pay, co-workers, and supervision.

There are several practical implications associated with using the job characteristics model to enhance motivation. As a first step, diagnose the work environment to determine the level of employee motivation and job satisfaction. Job design should be used when employee motivation ranges from low to moderately high. The diagnosis can be made using employee surveys. Another important step is to determine whether job redesign is appropriate for a given group of employees. Job redesign is most likely to work in a participative environment in which employees have the necessary knowledge and skills to perform the enriched tasks and their job satisfaction is average to high. A final step is to determine how to best redesign the job. The focus of this effort is to increase those core job characteristics that are low. Employee input is essential during this step to determine the details of a redesign initiative.

Unfortunately, job redesign appears to reduce the quantity of output just as often as it has a positive effect. Caution and situational appropriateness are advised. For example, one study demonstrated that job redesign works better in less complex organizations (small plants or companies).[13] Nonetheless, managers are likely to find noticeable increases in the quality of performance after a job redesign program.

Process Theories of Motivation

Another group of motivation theories are known as process theories. They focus on cognitive/thought processes that can lead to motivation. Three of these theories will be presented here—equity theory, expectancy theory, and goal setting theory.

Equity Theory of Motivation

Equity theory

Holds that motivation is a function of fairness in social exchanges.

Defined generally, **equity theory** is a model of motivation that explains how people strive for *fairness* and *justice* in social exchanges or give-and-take relationships.[14] Psychologist J Stacy Adams pioneered application of the equity principle to the workplace. Adams points out that two primary components are involved in the employee–employer exchange, *inputs* and *outcomes*. An employee's inputs, for which he or she expects a just return, include education/training, skills, creativity, seniority, experience, effort expended, and loyalty. On the outcome side of the exchange, the organization provides such things as pay/bonuses, fringe benefits, challenging assignments, job security, promotions, status symbols, recognition, and participation in important decisions.[15] These outcomes vary widely, depending on one's organization and rank.

Negative and Positive Inequity On the job, feelings of inequity revolve around a person's evaluation of whether he or she receives adequate rewards to compensate for his or her contributive inputs. People perform these evaluations by comparing the perceived fairness of their employment exchange to that of relevant others. This comparative process, which is based on an equity norm, was found to generalize across countries.[16] People tend to compare themselves to other individuals with whom they have close interpersonal ties—such as friends—and/or to similar others—such as people performing the same job or individuals of the same gender or educational level—rather than dissimilar others.[17]

Three different equity relationships are illustrated in Figure 3–4: equity, negative inequity, and positive inequity. Assume the two people in each of the equity relation-

The highest paid **CEO** in Canada in 2000 was Nortel's John Roth, who made $70,754,000, of which $60,527,000 was in the form of long-term incentives. One year later, Nortel stock fell drastically and Roth left the company.

Negative and Positive Inequity   **FIGURE 3–4**

A. An Equitable Situation

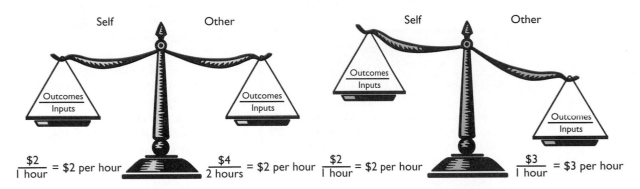

B. Negative Inequity

C. Positive inequity

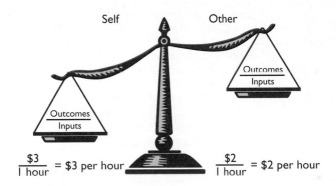

ships in Figure 3–4 have equivalent backgrounds (equal education, seniority, and so forth) and perform identical tasks. Only their hourly pay rates differ. Equity exists for an individual when his or her ratio of perceived outcomes to inputs is equal to the ratio of outcomes to inputs for a relevant co-worker (see part A in Figure 3–4). Because equity is based on comparing *ratios* of outcomes to inputs, inequity will not necessarily be perceived just because someone else receives greater rewards. If the other person's additional outcomes are due to his or her greater inputs, a sense of equity may still exist. However, if the comparison person enjoys greater outcomes for similar inputs, negative inequity will be perceived (see part B in Figure 3–4). On the other hand, a person will experience positive inequity when his or her outcome to input ratio is greater than that of a relevant co-worker (see part C in Figure 3–4).

Reducing inequity   Equity ratios can be changed by attempting to alter one's outcomes or adjusting one's inputs. For example, negative inequity might be resolved by asking for a raise or a promotion (i.e., raising outputs) or by reducing inputs (i.e., working fewer hours or exerting less effort). It also is important to note that equity can be restored by altering one's equity ratios behaviourally and/or cognitively. A cognitive strategy entails psychologically distorting perceptions of one's own or one's comparison person's outcomes and inputs (e.g., conclude that comparison other has more experience or works harder).

ETHICS AT WORK

Broken Promises at Ford Canada

In early 2000, Ford Motor Company announced that it was going to provide a computer and Internet access to all its workers worldwide for a nominal fee. Employees were thrilled, and morale soared. According to Ford, this was not just a benefit to employees, but was part of their corporate strategy to position itself on the leading edge of a move toward E-business. They believed that line workers who could not afford a computer needed to get wired given our wired world.

In November 2001, Ford Canada reneged on the promise. Citing the economic downturn, the company announced that the 17,000 Ford workers in Canada would not receive a computer, even though Ford's US workers had. Once seen as a boost to motivation, the broken corporate promise is having the opposite effect.

The Canadian Auto Workers Union, which represents Ford employees at their Oakville plant, said that employees were angry. The inequitable treatment of Canadian workers versus their counterparts in the US can be expected to unleash consequences aimed at restoring equity in the employee-employer relationship.

You Decide . . .

Were Ford's actions ethical? How might Ford's Canadian employees react to this inequity? Do you think there will be a long-term impact on employees' trust in Ford?

Sources: J Hobel, "Promises, Promises, Promises," *Canadian HR Reporter*, September 24, 2001, p 4; "Ford Reneges on Computers," *Canadian HR Reporter*, November 5, 2001, p 2; G Keenan, "Ford Scraps Plans to Give Workers Free PCs," *Globe and Mail*, October 20, 2001, p B1.

Distributive justice

The perceived fairness of how resources and rewards are distributed.

Procedural justice

The perceived fairness of the process and procedures used to make allocation decisions.

Interactional justice

The perceived fairness of the decision maker's behaviour in the process of decision making.

Expanding the Concept of Equity   Beginning in the 1980s, researchers began to expand the role of equity theory in explaining employee attitudes and behaviour. This led to a domain of research called *organizational justice*. Organizational justice reflects the extent to which people perceive that they are treated fairly at work. This, in turn, led to the identification of three different components of organizational justice: distributive, procedural, and interactional. **Distributive justice** reflects the perceived fairness of how resources and rewards are distributed or allocated.

Procedural justice is defined as the perceived fairness of the process and procedures used to make allocation decisions. Research shows that positive perceptions of distributive and procedural justice are enhanced by giving employees a "voice" in decisions that affect them. Voice represents the extent to which employees who are affected by a decision can present relevant information about the decision to others. Voice is analogous to asking employees for their input into the decision-making process.[18]

The last justice component pertains to the interpersonal side of how employees are treated at work. Specifically, **interactional justice** "refers to the interpersonal side of decision making, specifically to the fairness of the decision maker's behaviour in the process of decision making. Decision makers behave in an interactionally fair manner when they treat those affected by the decision properly and enact the decision policy or procedure properly."[19] Fair interpersonal treatment necessitates that managers communicate truthfully and treat people with courtesy and respect. Fair enactment of procedures further requires that managers suppress personal biases, consistently apply decision-making criteria, provide timely feedback, and justify decisions.

Practical Lessons from Equity Theory   Equity theory has several important practical implications. First, equity theory provides managers with yet another explanation of how beliefs and attitudes affect job performance. We are motivated to correct the situation when our ideas of fairness and justice are offended.

Second, equity theory emphasizes the need for managers to pay attention to employees' perceptions of what is fair and equitable. No matter how fair management thinks the organization's policies, procedures, and reward system are, each employee's *perception* of the equity of those factors is what counts. People respond positively when they perceive organizational and interpersonal justice. Managers thus are encouraged to make hiring and promotion decisions on merit-based, job-related information. Moreover, because justice perceptions are influenced by the extent to which managers explain their decisions, managers are encouraged to explain the rationale behind their decisions.[20]

Third, managers benefit by allowing employees to participate in making decisions about important work outcomes. Fourth, employees should be given the opportunity to appeal decisions that affect their welfare. Being able to appeal a decision promotes the belief that management treats employees fairly.

Fifth, employees are more likely to accept and support organizational change when they believe it is implemented fairly and when it produces equitable outcomes.[21]

Managers can attempt to follow these practical implications by monitoring equity and justice perceptions through informal conversations, interviews, or attitude surveys. If employees perceive their work organization as interpersonally unfair, they are probably dissatisfied and have contemplated quitting. In contrast, organizational loyalty and attachment are likely greater if they believe that they are treated fairly at work.

Expectancy Theory of Motivation

Expectancy theory holds that people are motivated to behave in ways that produce desired valued outcomes. Perception plays a central role in expectancy theory because it emphasizes cognitive ability to anticipate likely consequences of behaviour. Generally, expectancy theory can be used to predict behaviour in any situation in which a choice between two or more alternatives must be made. For example, it can be used to predict whether to quit or stay at a job; whether to exert substantial or minimal effort at a task; and whether to major in management, computer science, accounting, marketing, psychology, or communication.

> **Expectancy theory**
>
> Holds that people are motivated to behave in ways that produce valued outcomes.

Vroom's Expectancy Theory   Victor Vroom formulated a mathematical model of expectancy theory in his 1964 book *Work and Motivation*.[22] Motivation, according to Vroom, boils down to the decision of how much effort to exert in a specific task situation. As shown in Figure 3–5, this choice is based on a two-stage sequence of expectations (effort → performance and performance → outcome). First, motivation is affected by an individual's expectation that a certain level of effort will produce the intended performance goal. For example, if you do not believe increasing the amount of time you spend studying will significantly raise your grade on an exam, you probably will not study any harder than usual. Motivation also is influenced by the

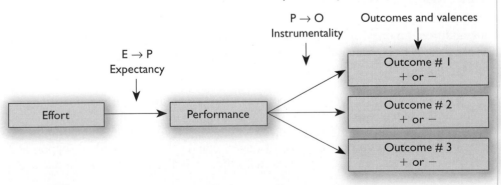

Expectancy Theory of Motivation   **FIGURE 3–5**

employee's perceived chances of getting various outcomes as a result of accomplishing his or her performance goal. Finally, individuals are motivated to the extent that they value the outcomes received.

There are three key concepts within Vroom's model—*expectancy, instrumentality,* and *valence*.

Expectancy

Belief that effort leads to a specific level of performance.

Expectancy An **expectancy** represents an individual's belief that a particular degree of effort will be followed by a particular level of performance. In other words, it is an effort → performance expectation. Expectancies take the form of subjective probabilities. As you may recall from a course in statistics, probabilities range from zero to one. An expectancy of zero indicates effort has no anticipated impact on performance, and an expectancy of one indicates that the level of effort will completely determine performance.

The following factors influence an employee's expectancy perceptions:

- Self-esteem.
- Self-efficacy.
- Previous success at the task.
- Help received from a supervisor and subordinates.
- Information necessary to complete the task.
- Good materials and equipment to work with.[23]

Instrumentality

A performance → outcome perception.

Instrumentality An **instrumentality** is a performance → outcome perception. It represents a person's belief that a particular outcome is determined by accomplishing a specific level of performance. Performance is instrumental when it leads to something else. For example, passing exams is instrumental to graduating from university.

Instrumentalities range from −1.0 to 1.0. An instrumentality of 1.0 indicates attainment of a particular outcome is totally dependent on task performance. An instrumentality of zero indicates there is no relationship between performance and outcome. For example, most companies link the number of vacation days to seniority, not job performance. Finally, an instrumentality of −1.0 reveals that high performance reduces the chance of obtaining an outcome while low performance increases the chance. For example, the more time you spend studying to get an A on an exam (high performance), the less time you will have for enjoying leisure activities. Similarly, as you lower the amount of time spent studying (low performance), you increase the amount of time that may be devoted to leisure activities.

Valence

The value of a reward or outcome.

Valence As Vroom used the term, **valence** refers to the positive or negative value people place on outcomes. Valence mirrors our personal preferences.[24] For example, most employees have a positive valence for receiving additional money or recognition. In contrast, job stress and being laid off would likely be negatively valent for most individuals. Valences can range from a large negative value to a large positive value.

Managerial Implications Expectancy theory has important practical implications for individual managers and organizations as a whole (see Table 3–1). Managers are advised to enhance effort → performance expectancies by helping employees accomplish their performance goals. Managers can do this by providing support and coaching and by increasing employees' self-efficacy. It also is important for managers

Managerial and Organizational Implications of Expectancy Theory **TABLE 3–1**

Implications for Managers	Implications for Organizations
Determine the outcomes employees value.	Reward people for desired performance, and do not keep pay decisions secret.
Identify good performance so appropriate behaviours can be rewarded.	Design challenging jobs.
Make sure employees can achieve targeted performance levels.	Tie some rewards to group accomplishments to build teamwork and encourage cooperation.
Link desired outcomes to targeted levels of performance.	Reward managers for creating, monitoring, and maintaining expectancies, instrumentalities, and outcomes that lead to high effort and goal attainment.
Make sure changes in outcomes are large enough to motivate high effort.	Monitor employee motivation through interviews or anonymous questionnaires.
Monitor the reward system for inequities.	Accommodate individual differences by building flexibility into the motivation program.

to influence employees' instrumentalities and to monitor valences for various rewards. This raises the issue of whether organizations should use monetary rewards as the primary method to reinforce performance. Although money is certainly a positively valent reward for most people, there are three issues to consider when deciding on the relative balance between monetary and nonmonetary rewards.

First, research shows that some workers value interesting work and recognition more than money.[25] Second, monetary rewards can lose their motivating properties over time and may undermine internal motivation.[26] Third, monetary rewards must be large enough to generate motivation. In summary, there is no one best type of reward. Individual differences and need theories tell us that people are motivated by different rewards. Managers should therefore focus on linking employee performance to valued rewards regardless of the type of reward used to enhance motivation.

There are four prerequisites to linking performance and rewards. First, managers need to develop and communicate performance standards to employees. Next, managers need valid and accurate performance ratings with which to compare employees. Inaccurate ratings create perceptions of inequity and thereby erode motivation. Third, managers need to determine the relative mix of individual versus team contribution to performance and then reward accordingly. Finally, managers should use the performance ratings to differentially allocate rewards among employees. That is, it is critical that managers allocate significantly different amounts of rewards for various levels of performance.

Motivation through Goal Setting

Regardless of the nature of their specific achievements, successful people tend to have one thing in common. Their lives are goal oriented. This is as true for politicians seeking votes as it is for world-class athletes. Within the context of employee motivation, this section explores the theory, research, and practice of goal setting.

Goal

What an individual is trying to accomplish.

Management by objectives

Management system incorporating participation in decision making, goal setting, and feedback.

Goals: Definition and Background   Edwin Locke, a leading authority on goal setting, and his colleagues define a **goal** as "what an individual is trying to accomplish; it is the object or aim of an action."[27] The motivational effect of performance goals and goal-based reward plans has been recognized for a long time. Recently, goal setting has been promoted through a widely used management technique called management by objectives (MBO).

    Management by objectives (MBO) is a management system that incorporates participation in decision making, goal setting, and objective feedback.[28] To further understand how MBO programs can increase both productivity and satisfaction, let us examine the process by which goal setting works.

How Does Goal Setting Work?

According to Locke's goal setting model, goal setting has four motivational mechanisms.

Goals direct attention   Goals that are personally meaningful tend to focus one's attention on what is relevant and important. If, for example, you have a term project due in a few days, your thoughts tend to revolve around completing that project.

Goals regulate effort   Not only do goals make us selectively perceptive, they also motivate us to act. The instructor's deadline for turning in your term project would prompt you to complete it, as opposed to going out with friends, watching television, or studying for another course.

Goals increase persistence   Within the context of goal setting, persistence represents the effort expended on a task over an extended period of time: It takes effort to run 100 metres; it takes persistence to run a 26-kilometre marathon. Steven Spielberg is a great example of someone who persisted at his goal to be a filmmaker:

> As the most popular and successful filmmaker ever, the 52-year-old Spielberg has directed nine of the 50 top-grossing films of all time. All totaled, films he has directed have brought in more than $5 billion worldwide, and films he's produced have brought in another $4 billion. . . . Spielberg identified his dream early in life and tenaciously pursued it. He allowed himself to imagine and trusted his imagination in his art. . . . Spielberg started making movies at age 11 when he learned how to use his father's eight-millimetre windup camera. . . . Having defined his ambition to direct movies from a young age, Spielberg suffered a setback when the prestigious UCLA and USC film schools rejected him because of low high school grades. Instead, because it was near Hollywood, he enrolled as an English major at California State University at Long Beach.
>
>   The summer before college, Spielberg took the Universal Studios Tour, and when the tour guides weren't watching, he broke away from the group to wander the giant movie-making factory.
>
>   "I went back there every day for three months," says Spielberg in Frank Sanello's *Spielberg: The Man, the Movies, the Mythology.* "I walked past the guard every day, waved at him and he waved back. I always wore a suit and carried a briefcase, and he assumed I was some kid related to some mogul."
>
>   He took over an unused office and put his name in the building directory with plastic letters: Steven Spielberg, room 23C. He immersed himself in film production at the industry's epicenter, wandering the Universal property to watch directors at work, and once got to see one of his heroes, Alfred Hitchcock, direct scenes for *Torn Curtain.*
>
>   Hanging out with directors, writers, and editors, Spielberg learned that to get the attention of studio executives he had to demonstrate his directing ability on the pro-

fessional film width of 35 millimetres. A friend who wished to become a producer fronted $15,000 for Spielberg to make the short film *Amblin,* which caught the eye of Universal executive Sid Sheinberg, who offered Spielberg a contract to direct television shows. Still several months short of graduating from college, Spielberg hesitated. In a now famous retort, Sheinberg shot back, "Kid, do you want to go to college or do you want to direct?" Spielberg dropped out and took the job.[29]

Goals foster strategies and action plans   If you are here and your goal is out there somewhere, you face the problem of getting from here to there. For example, the person who has resolved to lose 10 kilograms must develop a plan for getting from "here" (his or her present weight) to "there" (10 kilograms lighter). By virtue of setting a weight-reduction goal, the dieter may choose a strategy of exercising more, eating less, or some combination of the two.

Insights from Goal-Setting Research
Research consistently has supported goal setting as a motivational technique. Setting performance goals increases individual, group, and organizational performance. Further, goal setting works in different cultures. Reviews of the many goal-setting studies conducted over the past few decades have given managers five practical insights:

1. *Difficult goals lead to higher performance.* It is more difficult to sell nine cars a month than it is to sell three cars a month. As illustrated in Figure 3–6, however, the positive relationship between goal difficulty and performance breaks down when goals are perceived to be impossible. Figure 3–6 reveals that performance goes up when employees are given hard goals as opposed to easy or moderate goals (section A). Performance then plateaus (section B) and drops (section C) as the difficulty of a goal goes from challenging to impossible.[30]

2. *Specific, difficult goals lead to higher performance for simple rather than complex tasks.* For example, a goal of selling nine cars a month is more specific

Relationship between Goal Difficulty and Performance   FIGURE 3–6

A Performance of committed individuals with adequate ability
B Performance of committed individuals who are working at capacity
C Performance of individuals who lack commitment to high goals

Source: *A Theory of Goal Setting and Task Performance,* by Locke/Latham, © 1990. Adapted by permission of Prentice-Hall, Upper Saddle River, NJ Reprinted by permission of Prentice-Hall, Inc., Englewood Cliffs, NJ.

than telling a salesperson to do his or her best. Goal setting research found that specific, hard goals led to better performance than did easy, medium, do-your-best, or no goals.[31] At InSystems Technology in Markham, Ontario, new employees are assigned a BHAG—a big, hairy, and audacious goal.[32] However, goal-setting effects are strongest for easy tasks and weakest for complex tasks.[33]

3. *Feedback enhances the effect of specific, difficult goals.* Feedback lets people know if they are headed toward their goals or if they are off course and need to redirect their efforts. Goals plus feedback is the recommended approach.[34] Goals inform people about performance standards and expectations so that they can channel their energies accordingly. In turn, feedback provides the information needed to adjust direction, effort, and strategies for goal accomplishment.

4. *Participative goals, assigned goals, and self-set goals are equally effective.* Both managers and researchers are interested in identifying the best way to set goals. Should goals be participatively set, assigned, or set by the employee him- or herself? A summary of goal-setting research indicated that no single approach was consistently more effective than others in increasing performance.[35]

    Managers are advised to pick a method that seems best suited for the individual and situation at hand. For example, employees' preferences for participation should be considered. Some employees desire to participate in the process of setting goals, whereas others do not. Finally, a participative approach helps reduce employees' resistance to goal setting.

5. *Goal commitment and monetary incentives affect goal-setting outcomes.* In general, an individual is expected to persist in attempts to accomplish a goal when he or she is committed to it. Researchers believe that difficult goals lead to higher performance only when employees are committed to their goals. Conversely, difficult goals can lead to lower performance when people are not committed to their goals. It also is important to note that people are more likely to commit to difficult goals when they have high self-efficacy about successfully accomplishing their goals.[36] Managers thus are encouraged to consider employees' self-efficacy when setting goals.

Practical Application of Goal Setting   There are three general steps to follow when implementing a goal-setting program. Serious deficiencies in one step cannot make up for strength in the other two. The three steps need to be implemented in a systematic fashion.

Step l: Set goals   A number of sources can be used as input during this goal-setting stage. Goals may be based on the average past performance of job holders. The employee and his or her manager may set the goal participatively, through give-and-take negotiation. Goals can be set by conducting external or internal benchmarking. Benchmarking is used when an organization wants to compare its performance or internal work processes to those of other organizations (external benchmarking) or to other internal departments (internal benchmarking). For example, a company might set a goal to surpass the customer service levels or profit of a benchmarked competitor. Finally, the overall strategy of a company (e.g., become the lowest-cost producer) may affect the goals set by employees at various levels in the organization.

In accordance with available research evidence, goals should be "SMART." SMART is an acronym that stands for specific, measurable, attainable, results oriented, and time

Guidelines for Writing SMART Goals **TABLE 3-2**

Specific	Goals should be stated in precise rather than vague terms. For example, a goal that provides for 20 hours of technical training for each employee is more specific than stating that a manager should send as many people as possible to training classes. Goals should be quantified when possible.
Measurable	A measurement device is needed to assess the extent to which a goal is accomplished. Goals thus need to be measurable. It also is critical to consider the quality aspect of the goal when establishing measurement criteria. For example, if the goal is to complete a managerial study of methods to increase productivity, one must consider how to measure the quality of this effort. Goals should not be set without considering the interplay between quantity and quality of output.
Attainable	Goals should be realistic, challenging, and attainable. Impossible goals reduce motivation because people do not like to fail. Remember, people have different levels of ability and skill.
Results oriented	Corporate goals should focus on desired end-results that support the organization's vision. In turn, an individual's goals should directly support the accomplishment of corporate goals. Activities support the achievement of goals and are outlined in action plans. To focus goals on desired end-results, goals should start with the word "to," followed by verbs such as complete, acquire, produce, increase, and decrease. Verbs such as develop, conduct, implement, or monitor imply activities and should not be used in a goal statement.
Time bound	Goals specify target dates for completion.

Source: A J Kinicki, *Performance Management Systems* (Superstition Mt., AZ: Kinicki and Associates Inc., 1992), pp 2–9. Reprinted with permission; all rights reserved.

bound. Table 3–2 contains a set of guidelines for writing SMART goals. There are two additional recommendations to consider when setting goals. First, for complex tasks, managers should train employees in problem-solving techniques and encourage them to develop a performance action plan. Action plans specify the strategies or tactics to be used in order to accomplish a goal. Second, because of individual differences, it may be necessary to establish different goals for employees performing the same job.

Step 2: Promote goal commitment   Obtaining goal commitment is important because employees are more motivated to pursue goals they view as reasonable, obtainable, and fair. Goal commitment may be increased through a variety of methods. For example, managers are encouraged to conduct participative goal-setting sessions and to train employees in how to develop effective action plans. Goal commitment also can be enhanced by setting goals that are under employees control and providing them with the necessary resources.

Step 3: Provide support and feedback   Step 3 calls for providing employees with the necessary support elements or resources to get the job done. This includes ensuring that each employee has the necessary abilities and information to reach his or her goals. As a pair of goal-setting experts succinctly stated, "Motivation without knowledge is useless."[37] Training often is required to help employees achieve difficult goals. Moreover, managers should pay attention to employees' perceptions of effort → performance expectancies, self-efficacy, and valence of rewards. Finally, employees should be provided with timely, specific feedback (knowledge of results) on how they are doing.

Putting Motivational Theories to Work

Successfully designing and implementing motivational programs is not easy. Managers cannot simply take one of the theories discussed in this book and apply it word for word. Dynamics within organizations interfere with applying motivation theories in "pure" form. According to management scholar Terence Mitchell,

> There are situations and settings that make it exceptionally difficult for a motivational system to work. These circumstances may involve the kinds of jobs or people present, the technology, the presence of a union, and so on. The factors that hinder the application of motivational theory have not been articulated either frequently or systematically.[38]

Assuming a motivational program is being considered to improve productivity, quality, or customer satisfaction, the first issue revolves around the difference between motivation and performance. Motivation and performance are not one and the same. Motivation is only one of several factors that influence performance. For example, poor performance may be more a function of outdated or inefficient materials and machinery, not having goals to direct one's attention, a monotonous job, feelings of inequity, a negative work environment characterized by political behaviour and conflict, poor supervisory support and coaching, or poor work flow. Motivation cannot make up for a deficient job context. Managers, therefore, need to carefully consider the causes of poor performance and employee misbehaviour.

Individual differences are an important input that influence motivation and motivated behaviour. Managers are advised to develop employees so that they have the ability and job knowledge to effectively perform their jobs. In addition, attempts should be made to nurture positive employee characteristics, such as self-esteem, self-efficacy, positive emotions, a learning goal orientation, and need for achievement.

Because motivation is goal directed, the process of developing and setting goals is critical. Moreover, the method used to evaluate performance also needs to be considered. Without a valid performance appraisal system, it is difficult, if not impossible, to accurately distinguish good and poor performers. The problem with performance ranking systems is that they are based on subjective judgments. Motivation thus is decreased to the extent these judgments are inaccurate. Managers need to keep in mind that both equity theory and expectancy theory suggest that employee motivation is reduced by inaccurate performance ratings.

Consistent with expectancy theory, managers should relate rewards to performance.[39] In doing so, it is important that managers consider the accuracy and fairness of the reward system. As discussed under expectancy theory, the promise of increased rewards will not prompt higher effort and good performance unless those rewards are clearly tied to performance and they are large enough to gain employees' interest or attention.

Moreover, equity theory tells us that motivation is influenced by employee perceptions about the fairness of reward allocations. Motivation is decreased when employees believe rewards are inequitably allocated. Rewards also need to be integrated appropriately into the appraisal system. If performance is measured at the individual level, individual achievements need to be rewarded. On the other hand, when performance is the result of group effort, rewards should be allocated to the group.[40]

Feedback also should be linked with performance. Feedback provides the information and direction needed to keep employees focused on relevant tasks, activities, and goals. Managers should strive to provide specific, timely, and accurate feedback to employees.

Finally, an organization's culture significantly influences employee motivation and behaviour. A positive self-enhancing culture is more likely to engender higher motivation and commitment than a culture dominated by suspicion, fault finding, and blame.

summary of key concepts

- *Contrast Maslow's and McClelland's need theories.* Two well-known need theories of motivation are Maslow's need hierarchy and McClelland's need theory. Maslow's notion of a stair-step hierarchy of five levels of needs has not stood up well under research. McClelland believes that motivation and performance vary according to the strength of an individual's need for achievement. High achievers prefer moderate risks and situations where they can control their own destiny. Top managers should have a high need for power coupled with a low need for affiliation.

- *Describe how to motivate employees through job design.* Job rotation, job enlargement, job enrichment, and the job characteristics model are motivational approaches to job design, which are aimed at improving employees' job satisaction, motivation, and work effectiveness.

- *Explain the practical significance of Herzberg's distinction between motivators and hygiene factors.* Herzberg believes job satisfaction motivates better job performance. His *hygiene* factors, such as policies, supervision, and salary, erase sources of dissatisfaction. On the other hand, his *motivators,* such as achievement, responsibility, and recognition, foster job satisfaction. Herzberg's motivator–hygiene theory has practical significance for job enrichment.

- *Discuss the role of perceived inequity in employee motivation.* Equity theory is a model of motivation that explains how people strive for fairness and justice in social exchanges. On the job, feelings of inequity revolve around a person's evaluation of whether he or she receives adequate rewards to compensate for his or her contributive inputs. People perform these evaluations by comparing the perceived fairness of their employment exchange with that of relevant others. Perceived inequity creates motivation to restore equity.

- *Describe the practical lessons derived from equity theory.* Equity theory has a number of practical implications. First, because people are motivated to resolve perceptions of inequity, managers should not discount employees' feelings and perceptions when trying to motivate workers. Next, managers should pay attention to employees' *perceptions* of what is fair and equitable. It is the employee's view of reality that counts when trying to motivate someone, according to equity theory. In addition, employees should be given a voice in decisions that

affect them. Next, employees should be given the opportunity to appeal decisions that affect their welfare. Finally, employees are more likely to accept and support organizational change when they believe it is implemented fairly and when it produces equitable outcomes.

- *Explain Vroom's expectancy theory.* Expectancy theory assumes motivation is determined by one's perceived chances of achieving valued outcomes. Vroom's expectancy model of motivation reveals how effort → performance expectancies and performance → outcome instrumentalities influence the degree of effort expended to achieve desired (positively valent) outcomes.

- *Describe the practical implications of expectancy theory.* Managers are advised to enhance effort → performance expectancies by helping employees accomplish their performance goals. With respect to instrumentalities and valences, managers should attempt to link employee performance and valued rewards. There are four prerequisites to linking performance and rewards. Managers need to develop and communicate performance standards to employees, obtain valid and accurate performance ratings, determine the relative mix of individual versus team contribution to performance and then reward accordingly, and use performance ratings to differentially allocate rewards among employees.

- *Identify five practical lessons to be learned from goal-setting research.* First, difficult goals lead to higher performance than easy or moderate goals, but goals should not be impossible to achieve. Next, specific, difficult goals lead to higher performance for simple rather than complex tasks. In addition, feedback enhances the effect of specific, difficult goals. Further, participative goals, assigned goals, and self-set goals are equally effective. Finally, goal commitment and monetary incentives affect goal-setting outcomes.

- *Specify issues that should be addressed before implementing a motivational program.* Managers need to consider the variety of causes of poor performance which may be due to a host of deficient individual inputs (e.g., ability, dispositions, emotions, and beliefs) or job context factors (e.g., materials and machinery, job characteristics, reward systems, supervisory support and coaching, and social norms). Performance must be accurately evaluated and rewards should be equitably distributed.

key terms

core job dimensions, 54
distributive justice, 58
equity theory, 56
expectancy, 60
expectancy theory, 59
goal, 62
hygiene factors, 53
instrumentality, 60

interactional justice, 58
internal motivation, 54
job design, 52
job enlargement, 52
job enrichment, 54
job rotation, 52
management by objectives, 62
motivation, 50

motivators, 53
needs, 50
need for achievement, 50
need for affiliation, 52
need for power, 52
procedural justice, 58
valence, 60

discussion questions

1. From a practical standpoint, what is the major drawback of theories of motivation based on internal factors such as needs and feelings/emotions?

2. How have hygiene factors and motivators affected your job satisfaction and performance?

3. Do you know anyone who would not respond positively to an enriched job? Describe this person.

4. Have you experienced positive or negative inequity at work? Describe the circumstances in terms of the inputs and outcomes of the comparison person and yourself.

5. What work outcomes from equity theory are most important to you? Do you think different age groups value different outcomes? What are the implications for managers who seek to be equitable?

6. If someone who reported to you at work had a low expectancy that their effort would lead to successful performance, what could you do to increase this person's expectancy?

internet exercises

www.fed.org

1. Analyzing Motivation

This chapter discussed a variety of approaches for motivating employees. The purpose of this exercise is for you to identify motivational techniques or programs that are being used at different companies. Begin by visiting the Web site for the Foundation for Enterprise Development at **www.fed.org**. The Foundation is a nonprofit organization that helps managers to implement equity-based compensation and broad-based participation programs aimed at improving corporate performance. To begin your search, select the resource library and follow up by choosing to view the library by subject. You will be given a variety of categories to choose from.

Use the categories of "case studies of private companies" or "case studies of public companies," and then pick one company that you would like to analyze.

QUESTIONS
1. In what ways is this company using the theories and models discussed in this chapter?
2. To what extent is employee motivation related to this organization's culture?
3. What motivational methods is this company using that were not discussed in this chapter?

www.ge.com/canada

2. How to Motivate Employees

This chapter discussed how employee motivation is influenced by goal setting and the relationship between performance and rewards. We also reviewed the variety of issues that managers should consider when implementing motivational programs. The purpose of this exercise is for you to examine the motivational techniques used by General Electric (GE). GE is one of the most successful companies in the world. The company is well known for establishing clear corporate goals and then creating the infrastructure (e.g., rewards) to achieve them. Begin by visiting GE Canada's home page at **www.ge.com/canada**. Begin your search by locating GE's corporate values and corporate goals. Then expand your search by looking for information that discusses the different incentives GE uses to motivate its employees.

QUESTIONS
1. Based on GE's values and goals, what type of behaviour is the organization trying to motivate?
2. What rewards does GE use to reinforce desired behaviour and performance?
3. To what extent are GE's practices consistent with the material covered in this chapter?

experiential exercises

1. Measuring Perceived Fair Interpersonal Treatment

Instructions
Indicate the extent to which you agree or disagree with each of the following statements by considering what your organization is like most of the time. Then compare your overall score with the arbitrary norms that are presented.

	Strongly Disagree	Disagree	Neither	Agree	Strongly Agree
1. Employees are praised for good work.	1	2	3	4	5
2. Supervisors do not yell at employees.	1	2	3	4	5
3. Employees are trusted.	1	2	3	4	5
4. Employees' complaints are dealt with effectively.	1	2	3	4	5
5. Employees are treated with respect.	1	2	3	4	5
6. Employees' questions and problems are responded to quickly.	1	2	3	4	5
7. Employees are treated fairly.	1	2	3	4	5
8. Employees' hard work is appreciated.	1	2	3	4	5
9. Employees' suggestions are used.	1	2	3	4	5
10. Employees are told the truth.	1	2	3	4	5

Total score = _____

Arbitrary Norms
Very fair organization = 38–50
Moderately fair organization = 24–37
Unfair organization = 10–23

Source: Adapted in part from M A Donovan, F Drasgow, and L J Munson, "The Perceptions of Fair Interpersonal Treatment Scale Development and Validation of a Measure of Interpersonal Treatment in the Workplace," *Journal of Applied Psychology*, October 1998, pp 683-92.

2. What Outcomes Motivate Employees?

Objectives

1. To determine how accurately you perceive the outcomes that motivate nonmanagerial employees.
2. To examine the managerial implications of inaccurately assessing employee motivators.

Introduction

One thousand employees were given a list of 10 outcomes people want from their work. They were asked to rank these items from most important to least important.[41] We are going to have you estimate how you think these workers ranked the various outcomes. This will enable you to compare your perceptions with the average rankings documented by a researcher. The survey results are presented in endnote 42 at the end of this book. Please do not read them until indicated.

Instructions

Below is a list of 10 outcomes people want from their work. Read the list, and then rank each item according to how you think the typical nonmanagerial employee would rank them. Rank the outcomes from 1 to 10; 1 = Most important and 10 = Least important. (Please do this now before reading the rest of these instructions.) After you have completed your ranking, calculate the discrepancy between your perceptions and the actual results. Take the absolute value of the difference between your ranking and the actual ranking for each item, and then add them to get a total discrepancy score. For example, if you gave job security a ranking of 1, your discrepancy score would be 3 because the actual ranking was 4. The lower your discrepancy score, the more accurate your perception of the typical employee's needs. The actual rankings are shown in endnote 42.

How do you believe the typical nonmanagerial employee would rank these outcomes?

_____ Full appreciation of work done
_____ Job security
_____ Good working conditions
_____ Feeling of being in on things
_____ Good wages
_____ Tactful discipline
_____ Personal loyalty to employees
_____ Interesting work
_____ Sympathetic help with personal problems
_____ Promotion and growth in the organization

QUESTIONS FOR DISCUSSION

1. Were your perceptions accurate? Why or why not?
2. What would Vroom's expectancy theory suggest you should do?
3. Would you generalize the actual survey results to all non-managerial employees? Why or why not?

personal awareness and growth exercises

1. Is Your Commitment to Achieving Your Performance Goal for This Course Related to Your Behaviour?

Instructions

Begin by identifying your performance goal (desired grade) for this class. My desired grade is _____. Next, use the rating scale shown below to circle the answer that best represents how you feel about each of the following statements. After computing a total score for the goal commitment items, answer the questions related to your study habits for this course.

1 = Strongly disagree
2 = Disagree
3 = Neither agree nor disagree
4 = Agree
5 = Strongly agree

1. I am trying hard to reach my performance goal.	1	2	3	4	5
2. I am exerting my maximum effort (100%) in pursuit of my performance goal.	1	2	3	4	5

3. I am committed to my performance goal.	1	2	3	4	5
4. I am determined to reach my performance goal.	1	2	3	4	5
5. I am enthusiastic about attempting to achieve my performance goal.	1	2	3	4	5
6. I am striving to attain my performance goal.	1	2	3	4	5

Total score _____

Arbitrary Norms

Low goal commitment = 6–15
Moderate goal commitment = 15–23
High goal commitment = 24–30

Study Habits

How many hours have you spent studying for this class? _____ hours
What is your grade at this point in the course? _____
How many times have you missed class? _____ absences

Source: Items were adapted from those presented in R W Renn, C Danehower, P M Swiercz, and M L Icenogle, "Further Examination of the Measurement Properties of Leifer & McGannon's (1986) Goal Acceptance and Goal Commitment Scales," *Journal of Occupational and Organizational Psychology*, March 1999, pp 107–13.

2. Measuring Your Growth Need Strength

Purpose

This self-assessment is designed to help you estimate your level of growth need strength.

Instructions

People differ in the kinds of jobs they would most like to hold. The questions in this exercise give you a chance to say just what it is about a job that is most important to you. For each question, two different kinds of jobs are briefly described.

Please indicate which of the two jobs you personally would prefer if you had to make a choice between them. In answering each question, assume that everything else about the jobs is the same. Pay attention only to the characteristics actually listed. After circling each answer, use the scoring key in endnote 43 of this book to calculate your results for this scale. This exercise is completed alone so students can assess themselves honestly without concerns of social comparison. However, class discussion will focus on the growth need strength concept and its implications.

GROWTH NEED STRENGTH SCALE

JOB A	Circle the number indicating the degree to which you prefer Job A or Job B					JOB B
	1 Strongly Prefer A	2 Slightly Prefer A	3 Neutral	4 Slightly Prefer B	5 Strongly Prefer B	
1. A job where the pay is very good.	1	2	3	4	5	A job where there is considerable opportunity to be creative and innovative.
2. A job where you are often required to make important decisions.	1	2	3	4	5	A job with many pleasant people to work with.
3. A job in which greater responsibility is given to those who do the best work.	1	2	3	4	5	A job in which greater responsibility is given to loyal employees who have the most seniority.

GROWTH NEED STRENGTH SCALE (*continued*)

JOB A	Circle the number indicating the degree to which you prefer Job A or Job B					JOB B
	1 **Strongly** **Prefer A**	**2** **Slightly** **Prefer A**	**3** **Neutral**	**4** **Slightly** **Prefer B**	**5** **Strongly** **Prefer B**	
4. A job in a firm that is in financial trouble and might have to close down within the year.	1	2	3	4	5	A job in which you are not allowed to have any say whatever in how your work is scheduled, or in the procedures to be used in carrying it out.
5. A very routine job.	1	2	3	4	5	A job where your co-workers are not very friendly.
6. A job with a supervisor who is often very critical of you and your work in front of other people.	1	2	3	4	5	A job that prevents you from using a number of skills that you worked hard to develop.
7. A job with a supervisor who respects you and treats you fairly.	1	2	3	4	5	A job that provides constant opportunities for you to learn new and interesting things.
8. A job where there is a real chance you could be laid off.	1	2	3	4	5	A job with very little chance to do challenging work.
9. A job in which there is a real chance for you to develop new skills and advance in the organization.	1	2	3	4	5	A job that provides lots of vacation time and an excellent benefits package.
10. A job with little freedom and independence to do your work in the way you think best.	1	2	3	4	5	A job where working conditions are poor.
11. A job with very satisfying teamwork.	1	2	3	4	5	A job that allows you to use your skills and abilities to the fullest extent.
12. A job that offers little or no challenge.	1	2	3	4	5	A job that requires you to be completely isolated from co-workers.

Source: Developed by J R Hackman and G R Oldham as part of the Job Diagnostic Survey instrument. The authors have released any copyright ownership of this scale. See J R Hackman and G Oldham, *Work Redesign* (Reading, MA: Addison-Wesley, 1980), p 275.

CBC video case

The Operator

Morey Chaplick is a man in a hurry to create a video game empire. He believes that future success will come from a vertically integrated operation of video game distributors, video game arcades, an E-tailing Web site for video games, and a chain of video game retail stores. He has raised money on the stock market and persuaded former competitors in the distribution business to become his partners. He bought Microplay, an under-performing chain of 85 stores, weeded out the losers and revamped the rest as hip new state-of-the-art video game stores, based on the prototype store he established. He has also organized all the franchisees into one buying group to purchase from the distributors.

Always on the move, always on the phone, Morey is a high-energy operator who is never happier than when people say "never, never, never" and then are persuaded by him to change their minds. Once the operation is ready to commence doing business, Morey is ready to move on. He feels that he overstayed his time in his last venture. At this point, he has built the business, created shareholder value, and now needs a new challenge.

QUESTIONS FOR DISCUSSION
1. Explain how Morey is motivated by need for achievement. Give examples.
2. Explain how Morey is motivated by need for power. Give examples. Is he overly aggressive?
3. Is Morey motivated by need for affiliation?

Source: Based on "The Operator," *CBC Venture 761* (October 24, 2000).

chapter
four

Performance
Management

After reading the material in this chapter, you should be able to:

- Specify the two basic functions of feedback and three sources of feedback.

- Define upward feedback and 360-degree feedback, and summarize the general tips for giving good feedback.

- Briefly explain the four different organizational reward norms.

- Summarize the reasons rewards often fail to motivate employees.

- Explain the difference between positive reinforcement, negative reinforcement, punishment, and extinction.

- Explain the concept of behaviour shaping.

CREATING THE RIGHT ENVIRONMENT

Andrew Benedek says some of his friends and associates called him crazy back in the early 1980s when he rented a 5,400 square metre building in Burlington, Ontario for his company Zenon Environmental Inc. After all, Zenon had just 15 employees and a newly developed membrane technology used to purify and recycle water. He and his workers occupied less than a quarter of the space. But Benedek wanted a comfortable workplace where his employees could take the occasional break and have some fun.

Nobody is questioning that approach anymore. Zenon now has a global staff of nearly 600, and worldwide sales of its innovative water-treatment systems hit $85 million in 2000. The company has moved into a striking new facility in Oakville, Ontario built on a 60-hectare, partially wooded site containing trails, wildlife—deer, foxes, squirrels and birds have been spotted—and a pond. "Our employees worked with the architect to help design the building," says Benedek, who is chairman and CEO. "Coming to work at a place like this helps to motivate people."

The new building includes open concept workstations as well as traditional enclosed offices, although the latter are all the same size, reflecting Benedek's egalitarian beliefs. Employees fly economy class, and there is no space reserved for the CEO in the company parking lot.

Staff members express their views on corporate issues through a so-called value committee, referred to as the "Zenon Parliament." Such input led to the inclusion of a fitness centre in the new building as well as a subsidized cafeteria that specializes in low-fat, nutritious meals. "This is a challenging place to work because we deal with people's water supplies," says service manager Jim Imrie. "I've got my cell phone on 24 hours a day. But if you've got a good place to work, you don't mind coming in early, or taking those late night calls."

Andrew Benedek, chairman and CEO, and Jim Imrie, service manager, Zenon Environmental Inc.

Source: Adapted from D Jenish and B Woodward, "Canada's Top 100 Employers," *Maclean's*, November 5, 2001, p 50.

Providing Effective Feedback

Productivity and total quality experts tell us we need to work smarter, not harder. While it is true that a sound education and appropriate skill training are needed if one is to work smarter, the process does not end there. Today's employees need instructive and supportive feedback and desired rewards if they are to translate their knowledge into improved productivity and superior quality. This chapter discusses the effects of feedback, rewards, and positive reinforcement on behaviour and integrates those insights with perception, individual differences, and various motivational tools such as goal setting.

Numerous surveys tell us employees have a hearty appetite for feedback.[1] So also do achievement-oriented students. Following a difficult exam, for instance, students want to know two things: how they did and how their peers did. By letting students know how their work measures up to grading and competitive standards, an instructor's feedback permits the students to adjust their study habits so they can reach their goals. Likewise, managers in well-run organizations follow up goal setting with a feedback program to provide a rational basis for adjustment and improvement. For example, notice the importance Fred Smith, the founder and head of Federal Express, places on feedback when outlining his philosophy of leadership:

> When people walk in the door, they want to know: What do you expect out of me? What's in this deal for me? What do I have to do to get ahead? Where do I go in this organization to get justice if I'm not treated appropriately? They want to know how they're doing. They want some feedback. And they want to know that what they are doing is important.
>
> If you take the basic principles of leadership and answer those questions over and over again, you can be successful dealing with people.[2]

Feedback too often gets shortchanged. In fact, "poor or insufficient feedback" was the leading cause of deficient performance in a survey of US and European companies.[3]

As the term is used here, **feedback** is objective information about individual or collective performance shared with those in a position to improve the situation. Subjective assessments such as, "You're doing a poor job," "You're too lazy," or "We really appreciate your hard work" do not qualify as objective feedback. But hard data such as units sold, days absent, dollars saved, projects completed, customers satisfied, and quality rejects are all candidates for objective feedback programs. Management consultants Chip Bell and Ron Zemke offered this helpful perspective of feedback:

Feedback

Objective information about performance.

> Feedback is, quite simply, any information that answers those "How am I doing?" questions. *Good* feedback answers them truthfully and productively. It's information people can use either to confirm or correct their performance.
>
> Feedback comes in many forms and from a variety of sources. Some is easy to get and requires hardly any effort to understand. The charts and graphs tracking group and individual performance that are fixtures in many workplaces are an example of this variety. Performance feedback—the numerical type at least—is at the heart of most approaches to total quality management.
>
> Some feedback is less accessible. It's tucked away in the heads of customers and managers. But no matter how well-hidden the feedback, if people need it to keep their performance on track, we need to get it to them—preferably while it's still fresh enough to make an impact.[4]

Two Functions of Feedback

Experts say feedback serves two functions for those who receive it; one is *instructional* and the other *motivational*. Feedback instructs when it clarifies roles or teaches new behaviour. For example, an assistant accountant might be advised to handle a certain entry as a capital item rather than as an expense item. On the other hand, feedback motivates when it serves as a reward or promises a reward.[5] Having the boss tell you that a gruelling project you worked on earlier has just been completed can be a rewarding piece of news. As documented in one study, the motivational function of feedback can be significantly enhanced by pairing *specific,* challenging goals with *specific* feedback about results.[6]

Three Sources of Feedback: Others, Task, and Self

It almost goes without saying that employees receive objective feedback from *others* such as peers, supervisors, lower-level employees, and outsiders. Perhaps less obvious is the fact that the *task* itself is a ready source of objective feedback.[7] Anyone who has spent hours on a "quick" Internet search can appreciate the power of task-provided feedback. Similarly, skilled tasks such as computer programming or landing a jet airplane provide a steady stream of feedback about how well or poorly one is doing. A third source of feedback is *oneself,* but self-serving bias and other perceptual problems can contaminate this source. Those high in self-confidence tend to rely on personal feedback more than those with low self-confidence. Although circumstances vary, an employee can be bombarded by feedback from all three sources simultaneously. This is where the gatekeeping functions of perception and cognitive evaluation are needed to help sort things out.

The Recipient's Perspective of Feedback

The need for feedback varies across both individuals and situations. Feedback can be positive or negative. Generally, people tend to perceive and recall positive feedback more accurately than they do negative feedback.[8] But negative feedback (e.g., being told your performance is below average) can have a *positive* motivational effect. In fact, in one research study, those who were told they were below average on a creativity test

Regular feedback from supervisors is essential for effective performance management.

subsequently outperformed those who were led to believe their results were above average. The participants apparently took the negative feedback as a challenge and set and pursued higher goals. Those receiving positive feedback apparently were less motivated to do better.[9] Nonetheless, feedback with a negative message or threatening content needs to be administered carefully to avoid creating insecurity and defensiveness.[10] Self-efficacy also can be damaged by negative feedback. Destructive criticism by managers which attributes poor performance to internal causes reduces self-efficacy and reduces self-set goals."[11]

Upon receiving feedback, people cognitively evaluate factors such as its accuracy, the credibility of the source, the fairness of the system (e.g., performance appraisal system), their performance-reward expectancies, and the reasonableness of the standards. Any feedback that fails to clear one or more of these cognitive hurdles will be rejected or downplayed. A salesman at Ashland Canada Inc. sued the company when a performance rating of "unacceptable performance," despite the fact that he had exceeded his sales goals, led to the denial of his bonus and ultimately his dismissal. The British Columbia Supreme Court found that most of the allegations of poor performance had been fabricated and that the performance appraisal was unwarranted and undeserved. Ashland was fined $20,000 for acting in bad faith.[12]

Behavioural Outcomes of Feedback

In Chapter 3, we discussed how goal setting gives behaviour direction, increases expended effort, and fosters persistence. Because feedback is intimately related to the goal-setting process, it involves the same behavioural outcomes: direction, effort, and persistence. However, while the fourth outcome of goal setting involves formulating goal-attainment strategies, the fourth possible outcome of feedback is *resistance*. Feedback schemes that smack of manipulation or fail one or more of the perceptual and cognitive evaluation tests mentioned above breed resistance.[13]

Nontraditional Upward Feedback and 360-Degree Feedback

Traditional top-down feedback programs have given way to some interesting variations in recent years. Two newer approaches, discussed in this section, are upward feedback and 360-degree feedback. Aside from breaking away from a strict superior-to-subordinate feedback loop, these newer approaches are different because they typically involve *multiple sources* of feedback. Instead of getting feedback from one boss, often during an annual performance appraisal, more and more managers are getting structured feedback from superiors, lower-level employees, peers, and even outsiders such as customers. Nontraditional feedback is growing in popularity for at least six reasons:

1. Traditional performance appraisal systems have created widespread dissatisfaction.

2. Team-based organization structures are replacing traditional hierarchies. This trend requires managers to have good interpersonal skills that are best evaluated by team members.

3. Multiple-rater systems are said to make feedback more valid than single-source feedback.[14]

4. Advanced computer network technology (the Internet and company Intranets) greatly facilitates multiple-rater systems.[15]

5. Bottom-up feedback meshes nicely with the trend toward participative management and employee empowerment.

6. Co-workers and lower-level employees are said to know more about a manager's strengths and limitations than the boss.[16]

Together, these factors make a compelling case for looking at better ways to give and receive performance feedback.

Upward Feedback

Upward feedback stands the traditional approach on its head by having lower-level employees provide feedback on a manager's style and performance. This type of feedback is generally anonymous. Most students are familiar with upward feedback programs from years of filling out anonymous teacher evaluation surveys. Early Canadian adopters of upward evaluations include the Canadian Institute of Chartered Accountants and the Ontario Ministry of Northern Development and Mines.[17]

> **Upward feedback**
>
> Employees evaluate their boss.

Managers typically resist upward feedback programs because they believe it erodes their authority. Other critics say anonymous upward feedback can become little more than a personality contest or, worse, be manipulated by managers who make promises or threats. And researchers have found that managers who receive anonymous upward feedback receive *lower* ratings and like the process *less* than those who receive feedback from identifiable employees. This finding confirms the criticism that employees will tend to go easier on their boss when not protected by confidentiality.[18] Other studies have found that upward feedback can have a positive impact on both a leader's behaviour and on the performance of low-to-moderate performers.[19]

360-Degree Feedback

Letting individuals compare their own perceived performance with behaviourally specific (and usually anonymous) performance information from their manager, subordinates, and peers is known as **360-degree feedback.** Even outsiders may be involved in what is sometimes called full-circle feedback. The idea is to let the individual know how their behaviour affects others, with the goal of motivating change. In a 360-degree feedback program, a given manager will play different roles, including employee, superior, subordinate, and peer. Of course, the employee role is played only once. The other roles are played more than once for various other focal persons.

> **360-degree feedback**
>
> Comparison of anonymous feedback from one's superior, subordinates, and peers with self-perceptions.

Because upward feedback is a part of 360-degree feedback programs, the evidence reviewed earlier applies here as well. As with upward feedback, peer- and self-evaluations, central to 360-degree feedback programs, also are a significant affront to tradition.[20] But advocates say co-workers and managers themselves are appropriate performance evaluators because they are closest to the action.[21] Generally, research builds a stronger case for peer appraisals than for self-appraisals.[22] Self-serving bias, discussed in Chapter 2, is a problem.

Practical Recommendations

Research evidence on upward and 360-degree feedback leads us to *favour* anonymity and *discourage* the use of such results for pay and promotion decisions. Otherwise, managerial resistance and self-serving manipulation may prevail.[23] Upward and/or 360-degree feedback can be very beneficial for management development and training purposes, according to Phil Kellar, president of the Saratoga Institute in Vancouver. He cautions 360-degree feedback users not to expect immediate results, as it takes time to build a comfort level among employees.[24] The

Center for Creative Leadership reminds organizations using 360-degree feedback that the importance of training for both raters and ratees cannot be overemphasized.[25]

Why Feedback Often Fails

Experts on the subject cite the following six common trouble signs for organizational feedback systems:

1. Feedback is used to punish, embarrass, or put down employees.
2. Those receiving the feedback see it as irrelevant to their work.
3. Feedback information is provided too late to do any good.
4. People receiving feedback believe it relates to matters beyond their control.
5. Employees complain about wasting too much time collecting and recording feedback data.
6. Feedback recipients complain about feedback being too complex or difficult to understand.[26]

Managers can provide effective feedback by consciously avoiding these pitfalls and following a few practical tips:

- Relate feedback to existing performance goals and clear expectations.
- Give specific feedback tied to observable behaviour or measurable results.
- Channel feedback toward key result areas.
- Give feedback as soon as possible.
- Give positive feedback for improvement, not just final results.
- Focus feedback on performance, not personalities.
- Base feedback on accurate and credible information.

Organizational Reward Systems

Rewards are an ever-present and always controversial feature of organizational life.[27] Some employees see their job as the source of a pay cheque and little else. Others derive great pleasure from their job and association with co-workers. Even volunteers who donate their time to charitable organizations, such as the Red Cross, walk away with rewards in the form of social recognition and pride of having given unselfishly of their time. Hence, the subject of organizational rewards includes, but goes far beyond, monetary compensation.[28] This section examines key components of organizational reward systems.

Despite the fact that reward systems vary widely, it is possible to identify and interrelate some common components. The model in Figure 4–1 focuses on four important components: (1) types of rewards, (2) reward norms, (3) distribution criteria, and (4) desired outcomes. Let us examine these components.

Types of Rewards

Including the usual pay cheque, the variety and magnitude of organizational rewards boggles the mind—from subsidized day care to university tuition reimbursement to stock options.[29] An economist offered the following historical perspective of employee compensation:

One of the more striking developments . . . over the past 75 years has been the growing complexity of employee compensation. Limited at the outbreak of World War I

Key Factors in Organizational Reward Systems FIGURE 4–1

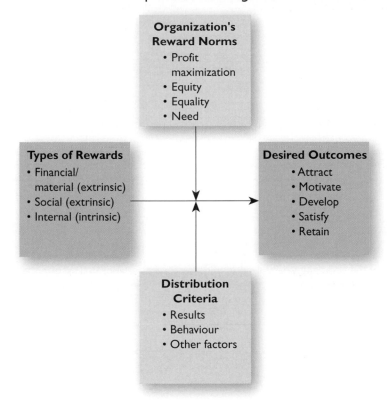

largely to straight-time pay for hours worked, compensation now includes a variety of employer-financed benefits, such as health and life insurance, retirement income, and paid time off. Although the details of each vary widely, these benefits are today standard components of the compensation package, and workers generally have come to expect them.[30]

Today, it is common for nonwage benefits to be 50% or more of total compensation.

In addition to the obvious pay and benefits, there are less obvious social and internal rewards. Social rewards include praise and recognition from others both inside and outside the organization. Internal rewards come from personal feelings of self-esteem, self-satisfaction, and accomplishment.

An alternative typology for organizational rewards is the distinction between extrinsic and intrinsic rewards. Financial, material, and social rewards qualify as **extrinsic rewards** because they come from the environment. **Intrinsic rewards** are self-granted. An employee who works to obtain extrinsic rewards, such as money or praise, is said to be extrinsically motivated. One who derives pleasure from the task itself or experiences a sense of competence or self-determination is said to be intrinsically motivated.[31] The relative importance of extrinsic and intrinsic rewards is a matter of culture and personal tastes.

Extrinsic rewards

Financial, material, or social rewards from the environment.

Intrinsic rewards

Self-granted rewards that come from within an individual.

Organizational Reward Norms

As discussed in Chapter 3 under the heading of equity theory, the employer–employee linkage can be viewed as an exchange relationship. Employees exchange their time and

Incentives in Asia

Impressions of the Asian work cultures include workers that are unwilling to express their ideas, obedient, reserved (less risk-taking), and respectful of authority. But in order to compete globally, Asian countries have begun to flatten their organizational structures and implement incentives to encourage employee empowerment.

China: Reward programs are difficult to institute in China, although officials do appraise performance and reward up to two months' extra pay. A bonus system is in place for customs officials; they receive a percentage of the value of goods recovered from smugglers.

Japan: Individual reward programs have not worked well. Workers are not willing to be conspicuous and individual pay for performance may disrupt pleasant working relationships. Therefore, Japan has opted for recognition awards; for example, awards for years of service. Team awards, however, have been effective in Japan. Team awards include incentives for outstanding performance, which take the form of special pay increases and an allowance system, usually one to two months' salary. A maximum of 15% of employees may benefit from this award.

Philippines: The public service of the Philippines has a longstanding performance appraisal system that is coupled with institutional rewards. These awards include a Presidential award given by the country's president.

Thailand: In Thailand, an employee who has performed well receives gratuities including commendations, tokens of distinguished service, and occasional salary increases.

Singapore: One-third of companies surveyed for a Watson Wyatt report offered stock options to employees. Stock options are of the most notable developments in the continuing quest to attract, retain, and motivate the Singaporean worker.

Source: "International Symposium Incentives Discussion," International Personnel Management Association, www.ipma-hr.org/public/global_template.cfm?ID=104, March 5, 2002; Rafaella Chuahy, "Stock Options and Innovative Work Structures Take Hold in Hong Kong and Singapore Companies," www.fed.org/onlinemag/aug00/international.htm, March 5, 2002.

talent for rewards. Ideally, four alternative norms dictate the nature of this exchange. In pure form, each would lead to a significantly different reward distribution system. They are as follows:

- *Profit maximization.* The objective of each party is to maximize its net gain, regardless of how the other party fares. A profit-maximizing company would attempt to pay the least amount of wages for maximum effort. Conversely, a profit-maximizing employee would seek maximum rewards, regardless of the organization's financial well-being, and leave the organization for a better deal.

- *Equity.* According to the **reward equity norm,** rewards should be allocated proportionate to contributions. Those who contribute the most should be rewarded the most. Cross-cultural studies have concluded that basic principles of fairness and justice, evident in most cultures, drive the equity norm. However, pay inequity between women and men in North America remains an unresolved issue.[32]

- *Equality.* The **reward equality norm** calls for rewarding all parties equally, regardless of their comparative contributions. Because absolute equality does not exist in today's hierarchical organizations, researchers recently explored the impact of pay *inequality.* They

Reward equity norm

Rewards should be tied to contributions.

Reward equality norm

Everyone should get the same rewards.

looked at *pay dispersion* (the pay gap between high-level and low-level employees) and found that the smaller the pay gap, the better the individual and organizational performance.[33] Thus, the huge compensation packages provided to many of today's top executives is not only a widely debated moral issue, it is a productivity issue as well.[34]

- *Need.* The **reward need norm** calls for distributing rewards according to employees' needs, rather than their contributions.[35]

> **Reward need norm**
> Rewards should be tied to needs.

These contradictory norms are typically intertwined:

> Variation occurs in the extent to which the rules for application of a norm are clear and the relative emphasis different managements will give to different norms in particular situations.[36]

Conflict and ethical debates often arise over the perceived fairness of reward allocations because of disagreement about reward norms. Stockholders might prefer a profit-maximization norm, while technical specialists would like an equity norm, and unionized hourly workers would argue for a pay system based on equality. A reward norm anchored to need might prevail in a family owned and operated business, or with regard to employee benefits.[37] Effective reward systems are based on clear and consensual exchange norms.

Distribution Criteria

According to one expert on organizational reward systems, three general criteria for the distribution of rewards are as follows:

- *Performance: results.* Tangible outcomes such as individual, group, or organization performance; quantity and quality of performance.
- *Performance: actions and behaviours.* Such as teamwork, cooperation, risk taking, creativity.
- *Nonperformance considerations.* Customary or contractual, where the type of job, nature of the work, equity, tenure, level in hierarchy, etc., are rewarded.[38]

As illustrated in the following example, the trend today is toward *performance* criteria and away from nonperformance criteria:

> At Eli Lily Canada, good work and good behaviour are recognized almost daily. Employee contributions are recognized at awards ceremonies, in the company newsletter, and on televisions mounted throughout the head office. The focus is on ensuring that employees clearly understand corporate goals, and on rewarding behaviour and work that is aligned with the goals. But according to the company's vice president of human resources, it is the spontaneous, personalized rewards that grab employees' attention. Most of all, the company listens to its employees, and that is the most important way they can be recognized and valued.[39]

Desired Outcomes

As shown in Figure 4–1, a good reward system should attract talented people and motivate and satisfy them once they have joined the organization.[40] Further, a good reward system should foster personal growth and development and keep talented people from leaving. In 2001, four of the *Report on Business Magazine*'s "50 Best Companies to Work for in Canada" had employee turnover rates below 2%. Between them, these companies offered company-wide stock options, onsite massage therapy, extended parental leaves, and an onsite fitness centre, all leading edge rewards.[41]

Mentoring—Part of Diversity Management at Rogers

Phillip Francis, Manager, Corporate Diversity at Rogers, says that commitment to diversity is "about attracting and retaining the best employees we can. It's about changing circumstances for employees and being responsible for employees' individual needs. It makes good business sense to us."

Mentoring is one way to provide feedback to employees. In 2000, Rogers successfully completed a diversity mentoring program pilot project and rolled it out nation-wide. Rather than having one-on-one mentoring, they opted for a team-based mentoring program to provide broader feedback to employees. The pilot program was made available to 25 Toronto employees with 22 participating mentors at the director or vice president level.

The mentors and employees were split into five teams, and flexibility allowed individuals to approach other teams for guidance and feedback in areas of interest that may not have been covered by their own mentors. Each team was composed of a diverse group of people, with mentors from many areas within the company, who were able to support the employees' goals. Employees receive a minimum of two hours per month with their mentors, and the teams are responsible for deciding how best to use their time.

Rogers conducted a survey of the pilot group, and found that group mentoring is a good approach to start, but some one-on-one time should be expected and encouraged, and that in order to facilitate relationship building, more time and effort is required at the beginning of the six-month period.

Another ongoing component of Rogers' diversity strategy is participation in a Goodwill program through which call centre training is provided to youths and people with disabilities, who, because of long-term unemployment, are not eligible for employment insurance.

"The reason we are involved is because we want to be seen as an employer of choice, who is open to diversity and recognized in the community," says Francis.

Since becoming participants some two and a half years ago, Roger has fully employed 20 graduates of the Goodwill program, A follow-up survey found that the former Goodwill grads-turned-Rogers employees have zero turnover—all are still with Rogers—and they all perform above average, adds Francis. That's performance management!

Source: Adapted from L Young, "Mentoring Program is One Diversity Step in a Series at Rogers," *Canadian HR Reporter*, March 27, 2000, p 8.

Why Rewards Often Fail to Motivate

Despite huge investments of time and money for organizational reward systems, the desired motivational effect often is not achieved. A management consultant recently offered these eight reasons:

1. Too much emphasis on monetary rewards.
2. Rewards lack an "appreciation effect."
3. Extensive benefits become entitlements.
4. Counterproductive behaviour is rewarded. (For example, "a pizza delivery company focused its rewards on the on-time performance of its drivers, only to discover that it was inadvertently rewarding reckless driving."[42])
5. Too long a delay between performance and rewards.
6. Too many one-size-fits-all rewards.

7. Use of one-shot rewards with a short-lived motivational impact.

8. Continued use of demotivating practices such as layoffs, across-the-board raises and cuts, and excessive executive compensation.[43]

These stubborn problems have fostered a growing interest in more effective reward and compensation practices.[44]

Positive Reinforcement

Feedback and reward programs all too often are ineffective because they are administered in haphazard ways. For example, consider these scenarios:

- A young programmer stops E-mailing creative suggestions to his boss because she never responds.

- The office politician gets a great promotion while her more skilled co-workers scratch their heads and gossip about the injustice.

In the first instance, a productive behaviour faded away for lack of encouragement. In the second situation, unproductive behaviour was unwittingly rewarded. Feedback and rewards need to be handled more precisely. Fortunately, the field of behavioural psychology can help. A behaviour modification technique called *positive reinforcement* helps managers achieve needed discipline and desired effect when providing feedback and granting rewards.[45]

Positive reinforcement is one aspect of a field known as behaviourism, which deals with **operant behaviour**, meaning learned, consequence-shaped behaviour. Operant behaviour is learned when one "operates" on the environment to produce desired consequences. For example, a salesperson continues to make sales calls until he or she sells enough to earn a bonus or a prize such as a trip to Hawaii. Another example is a student who foregoes social activities and puts in many hours of studying in order to get an "A" in a course. Behaviourism has significant implications for OB because the vast majority of organizational behaviour falls into the operant category.[46]

> **Operant behaviour**
>
> Learned, consequence-shaped behaviour.

A key concept in behaviourism is *contingent consequence*, meaning that there is a systematic linkage between a behaviour and its consequence. Contingent consequences control behaviour in four ways: positive reinforcement, negative reinforcement, punishment, and extinction.[47] These four concepts are illustrated in Figure 4-2.

Positive Reinforcement Strengthens Behaviour   **Positive reinforcement** is the process of strengthening a behaviour by contingently presenting something pleasing. (Importantly, a behaviour is strengthened when it increases in frequency and weakened when it decreases in frequency.) A design engineer who works overtime because of praise and recognition from the boss is responding to positive reinforcement.[48] Similarly, people tend to return to restaurants where they are positively reinforced with good food and friendly, high-quality service.[49]

> **Positive reinforcement**
>
> Making behaviour occur more often by contingently presenting something positive.

Negative Reinforcement Also Strengthens Behaviour
Negative reinforcement is the process of strengthening a behaviour by contingently withdrawing something displeasing. For example, an army sergeant who stops yelling when a recruit jumps out of bed has negatively reinforced that particular behaviour. Similarly, the behaviour of clamping our hands over our ears when watching a jumbo jet take off is negatively reinforced by

> **Negative reinforcement**
>
> Making behaviour occur more often by contingently withdrawing something negative.

FIGURE 4–2   Contingent Consequences in Operant Conditioning

Nature of Consequence

	Positive or Pleasing	Negative or Displeasing
Contingent Presentation	Positive Reinforcement *Behavioural outcome:* Target behaviour occurs *more* often.	Punishment *Behavioural outcome:* Target behaviour occurs *less* often.
Contingent Withdrawal	Punishment (Response Cost) *Behavioural outcome:* Target behaviour occurs *less* often.	Negative Reinforcement *Behavioural outcome:* Target behaviour occurs *more* often.

Behaviour-Consequence Relationship (vertical axis label)

(no contingent consequence)
Extinction
Behavioural outcome:
Target behaviour occurs *less* often.

An example of "response-cost" punishment is when firms require salespeople to make up any cash register shortages out of their own pocket.

You Decide ...

Do you think response-cost punishment such as this is fair? Ethical? Research indicates that observers of punishment events take two things into consideration when assessing their reactions to the event. The first consideration is characteristics of the violator such as his or her past performance and the second consideration is characteristics of the event such as level of damage from the violation. Did you take these two characteristics into consideration? Why or why not?

Source: B P Niehoff, R J Paul, and J F S Bunch, "The social effects of punishment events: The influence of violator past performance and severity of the punishment on observed justice perceptions and attitudes," *Journal of Organizational Behavior*, November 1998, pp 589–602.

relief from the noise. Negative reinforcement is often confused with punishment. But the two strategies have opposite effects on behaviour. Negative reinforcement, as the word *reinforcement* indicates, strengthens a behaviour because it provides relief from an unpleasant situation.

Punishment Weakens Behaviour

Punishment is the process of weakening behaviour through either the contingent presentation of something displeasing or the contingent withdrawal of something positive. A manager assigning a tardy employee to a dirty job exemplifies the first type of punishment. Docking a tardy employee's pay is an example of the second type of punishment, called "response cost" punishment. Sales people who must make up any cash register shortages out of their own pockets are being managed through response cost punishment.

Punishment

Making behaviour occur less often by contingently presenting something negative or withdrawing something positive.

Extinction

Making behaviour occur less often by ignoring or not reinforcing it.

Extinction Also Weakens Behaviour   **Extinction** is the weakening of a behaviour by ignoring it or making sure it is not reinforced. Getting rid of a former boyfriend or girlfriend by refusing to return their phone calls is an extinction strategy. In organizations, if feedback and management attention are only provided when things go wrong, the reliable employee who gets ignored may decide to stop working so hard. Although very different processes, both punishment and extinction have the same weakening effect on behaviour.

Schedules of Reinforcement

As just discussed, contingent consequences are an important determinant of future behaviour. The *timing* of behavioural consequences can be even more important. Based on years of tedious laboratory experiments with pigeons in highly controlled environments, Skinner and his colleagues discovered distinct patterns of responding for various schedules of reinforcement.[50] Although some of their conclusions can be generalized to negative reinforcement, punishment, and extinction, it is best to think only of positive reinforcement when discussing schedules.

Slot machines provide intermittent reinforcement as a variable ratio schedule—they pay out on a variable basis, not always after the same number of times.

Continuous Reinforcement   As indicated in Table 4–1, every instance of a target behaviour is reinforced when a **continuous reinforcement** (CRF) schedule is in effect. For instance, when your television set is operating properly, you are reinforced with a picture every time you turn it on (a CRF schedule). But, as with any CRF schedule of reinforcement, the behaviour of turning on the television will undergo rapid extinction if the set breaks. In organizations, continuous reinforcement is effective in training employees, as it provides immediate and continuous feedback when they are unsure of themselves and can benefit from constant positive reinforcement.

Intermittent Reinforcement   Unlike CRF schedules, **intermittent reinforcement** involves reinforcement of some but not all instances of a target behaviour. Four subcategories of intermittent schedules, described in Table 4–1, are fixed and variable ratio schedules and fixed and variable interval schedules. Reinforcement in *ratio* schedules is contingent on the number of responses emitted. *Interval* reinforcement is tied to the passage of time. Some common examples of the four types of intermittent reinforcement are as follows:

Continuous reinforcement

Reinforcing every instance of a behaviour.

Intermittent reinforcement

Reinforcing some but not all instances of behaviour.

- *Fixed ratio*—piece-rate pay; bonuses tied to the sale of a fixed number of units.
- *Variable ratio*—slot machines that pay off after a variable number of lever pulls; lotteries that pay off after the purchase of a variable number of tickets.
- *Fixed interval*—hourly pay; annual salary paid on a regular basis.
- *Variable interval*—random supervisory praise and pats on the back for employees who have been doing a good job.

Proper Scheduling Is Important   The schedule of reinforcement can more powerfully influence behaviour than the magnitude of reinforcement. Although this proposition grew out of experiments with pigeons, subsequent on-the-job research confirmed it. Consider, for example, a field study of 12 unionized beaver trappers employed by a lumber company to keep the large rodents from eating newly planted tree seedlings.[51]

The beaver trappers were randomly divided into two groups that alternated weekly between two different bonus plans. Under the first schedule, each trapper earned his regular $7 per hour wage plus $1 for each beaver caught. Technically, this bonus was paid on a CRF schedule. The second bonus plan involved the regular $7 per hour wage

TABLE 4–1   Schedules of Reinforcement

Schedule	Description	Probable Effects on Responding
Continuous (CRF)	Reinforcer follows every response.	Steady high rate of performance as long as reinforcement continues to follow every response.
		High frequency of reinforcement may lead to early satiation.
		Behaviour weakens rapidly (undergoes extinction) when reinforcers are withheld.
		Appropriate for newly emitted, unstable, or low-frequency responses.
Intermittent	Reinforcer does not follow every response.	Capable of producing high frequencies of responding.
		Low frequency of reinforcement precludes early satiation.
		Appropriate for stable or high-frequency responses.
Fixed ratio (FR)	A fixed number of responses must be emitted before reinforcement occurs	A fixed ratio of 1 : 1 (reinforcement occurs after every response) is the same as a continuous schedule.
		Tends to produce a high rate of response, which is vigorous and steady.
Variable ratio (VR)	A varying or random number of responses must be emitted before reinforcement occurs.	Capable of producing a high rate of response, which is vigorous, steady, and resistant to extinction.
Fixed interval (FI)	The first response after a specific period of time has elapsed is reinforced.	Produces an uneven response pattern varying from a very slow, unenergetic response immediately following reinforcement to a very fast, vigorous response immediately preceding reinforcement.
Variable interval (VI)	The first response after varying or random periods of time have elapsed is reinforced.	Tends to produce a high rate of response, which is vigorous, steady, and resistant to extinction.

Source: F Luthans and R Kreitner, *Organizational Behaviour Modification and Beyond: An Operant and Social Learning Approach* (Glenview, IL: Scott, Foresman, 1985), p 58. Used with authors' permission.

plus a one-in-four chance (as determined by rolling the dice) of receiving $4 for each beaver trapped. This second bonus plan qualified as a varable ratio (VR-4) schedule. In the long run, both incentive schemes averaged out to a $1-per-beaver bonus. Surprisingly, however, when the trappers were under the VR-4 schedule, they were 58% more productive than under the CRF schedule, despite the fact that the net amount of pay averaged out the same for the two groups during the 12-week trapping season.

Work Organizations Typically Rely on the Weakest Schedule   Generally, variable ratio and variable interval schedules of reinforcement produce the strongest behaviour that is most resistant to extinction. As gamblers will attest, variable schedules hold the promise of reinforcement after the next target response. For example, the following drama at a gambling casino is one more illustration of the potency of variable ratio reinforcement:

An elderly woman with a walker had lost her grip on the slot [machine] handle and had collapsed on the floor.

"Help," she cried weakly.

The woman at the machine next to her interrupted her play for a few seconds to try to help her to her feet, but all around her the army of slot players continued feeding coins to the machines.

A security man arrived to soothe the woman and take her away.

"Thank you," she told him appreciatively.

"But don't forget my winnings."[52]

Organizations without at least some variable reinforcement are less likely to prompt this type of dedication to task. Despite the trend toward pay-for-performance, time-based pay schemes such as hourly wages and yearly salaries that rely on the weakest schedule of reinforcement (fixed interval) are still the rule in today's workplaces.

Shaping Behaviour with Positive Reinforcement

Have you ever wondered how trainers at aquarium parks manage to get bottle-nosed dolphins to do flips, killer whales to carry people on their backs, and seals to juggle balls? The results are seemingly magical. Actually, a mundane learning process called shaping is responsible for the animals' antics.

Two-tonne killer whales, for example, have a big appetite, and they find buckets of fish very reinforcing. So if the trainer wants to ride a killer whale, he or she reinforces very basic behaviours that will eventually lead to the whale being ridden. The killer whale is contingently reinforced with a few fish for coming near the trainer, then for being touched, then for putting its nose in a harness, then for being straddled, and eventually for swimming with the trainer on its back. In effect, the trainer systematically raises the behavioural requirement for reinforcement. Thus, **shaping** is defined as the process of reinforcing closer and closer approximations to a target behaviour.

> **Shaping**
>
> Reinforcing closer and closer approximations to a target behaviour.

Shaping works very well with people, too, especially in training and quality programs involving continuous improvement. Praise, recognition, and instructive and credible feedback cost managers little more than moments of their time.[53] Yet, when used in conjunction with a behaviour-shaping program, these consequences can efficiently foster significant improvements in job performance.[54] The key to successful behaviour shaping lies in reducing a complex target behaviour to easily learned steps and then faithfully (and patiently) reinforcing any improvement.

Here are ten tips on how to effectively shape job behaviour:[55]

1. *Accommodate the process of behavioural change.* Behaviours change in gradual stages, not in broad, sweeping motions.

2. *Define new behaviour patterns specifically.* State what you wish to accomplish in explicit terms and in small amounts that can be easily grasped.

3. *Give individuals feedback on their performance.* A once-a-year performance appraisal is not sufficient.

4. *Reinforce behaviour as quickly as possible.*

5. *Use powerful reinforcement.* To be effective, rewards must be important to the employee—not to the manager.

6. *Use a continuous reinforcement schedule.* New behaviours should be reinforced every time they occur. This reinforcement should continue until these behaviours become habitual.

7. *Use a variable reinforcement schedule for maintenance.* Even after behaviour has become habitual, it still needs to be rewarded, though not necessarily every time it occurs.

8. *Reward teamwork—not competition.* Group goals and group rewards are one way to encourage cooperation in situations in which jobs and performance are interdependent.

9. *Make all rewards contingent on performance.*

10. *Never take good performance for granted.* Even superior performance, if left unrewarded, will eventually deteriorate.

summary of key concepts

- *Specify the two basic functions of feedback and three sources of feedback.* Feedback, in the form of *objective* information about performance, both instructs and motivates. Individuals receive feedback from others, the task, and from themselves.

- *Define upward feedback and 360-degree feedback, and summarize the general tips for giving good feedback.* Lower-level employees provide upward feedback (usually anonymous) to their managers. A person receives 360-degree feedback from subordinates, the manager, peers, and selected others such as customers or suppliers. Good feedback is tied to performance *goals* and clear *expectations*, linked with *specific* behaviour and/or results, reserved for *key result areas*, given as *soon* as possible, provided for *improvement* as well as for final results, focused on *performance* rather than on personalities, and based on *accurate* and *credible* information.

- *Briefly explain the four different organizational reward norms.* Maximizing individual gain is the object of the *profit maximization* reward norm. The *equity* norm calls for distributing rewards proportionate to contributions (those who contribute the most should earn the most). Everyone is rewarded equally when the *equality* reward norm is in force. The *need* reward norm involves distributing rewards based on employees' needs.

- *Summarize the reasons rewards often fail to motivate employees.* Reward systems can fail to motivate employees for these reasons: overemphasis on money, no appreciation effect, benefits become entitlements, wrong behaviour is rewarded, rewards are delayed too long, use of one-size-fits-all rewards, one-shot rewards with temporary effect, and demotivating practices such as layoffs.

- *Explain the difference between positive reinforcement, negative reinforcement, punishment, and extinction.* Positive and negative reinforcement are consequence management strategies that strengthen behaviour, whereas punishment and extinction weaken behaviour. These strategies need to be defined objectively in terms of their actual impact on behaviour frequency, not subjectively on the basis of intended impact.

- *Explain the concept of behaviour shaping.* Behaviour shaping occurs when closer and closer approximations of a target behaviour are reinforced. In effect, the standard for reinforcement is made more difficult as the individual learns. The process begins with continuous reinforcement, which gives way to intermittent reinforcement when the target behaviour becomes strong and habitual.

key terms

discussion questions

1. Relative to your school work, which of the three sources of feedback—others, task, self—has the greater impact on your performance? If you have a job, which source of feedback is most potent in that situation?

2. How would you summarize the practical benefits and drawbacks of 360-degree feedback?

3. Which of the four organizational reward norms do you prefer? Why?

4. What is your personal experience with failed organizational reward systems and practices?

5. What real-life examples of positive reinforcement, negative reinforcement, both forms of punishment, and extinction, can you draw from your recent experience? Were these strategies appropriately or inappropriately used?

6. What sort of behaviour shaping have you engaged in lately? Explain your success or failure.

internet exercises

www.panoramicfeedback.com

1. 360-Degree Feedback

As discussed in this chapter, 360-degree feedback is getting a good deal of attention these days. Our purpose here is to introduce you to a sample 360-degree evaluation from an innovative Internet-based program marketed by Panoramic Feedback. (Note: Our use of this sample is for instructional purposes only and does not constitute an endorsement of the program, which may or may not suit your needs.)

Go to the Internet home page (**www.panoramicfeedback.com**), and select "Samples: Questionnaire" from the main menu. The sample evaluation is for a hypothetical supervisor named Terry Smith. For our purposes, substitute the name of *your manager* from your present or past job. The idea is to do an *upward* evaluation of someone you actually know. Read the brief background piece, and proceed to Part One of the Questionnaire. Read and follow the instructions for the eight performance dimensions. All responses you click and any comments you type into the two boxes in Part One will show up on your printed copy, if you choose to make one. Move to Part Two and type your personal evaluations of your manager in the box provided. These comments also will be on any printed copy you may make.

QUESTIONS

1. How would you rate the eight performance dimensions in this brief sample? Relevant? Important? Good basis for constructive feedback?
2. If you were to expand this evaluation, what other performance scales would you add?
3. Is this a *fair* evaluation, as far as it goes? Explain.
4. How comfortable would you be evaluating the following people with this type of *anonymous* 360-degree instrument: Boss? Peers? Self? People reporting directly to you?
5. Would you like to be the focal person in a 360-degree review? Under what circumstances? Explain.
6. Results of anonymous 360-degree reviews should be used for which of the following purposes: Promotions? Pay raises? Job assignments? Feedback for personal growth and development? Explain.

www.joanlloyd.com

2. Manager-Employee Relationships

The Joan Lloyd at Work Web site **www.joanlloyd.com** points out that employee turnover is often a direct result of dissatisfaction with a manager. As the labour market gets tighter and tighter in the early twenty-first century, managers need to pay more attention to their management style. A quiz regarding the manager-employee relationship is included.

QUESTIONS

1. If you manage others as part of your job responsibilities, take the quiz. If you don't, then ask someone you know who is a manager to take the quiz. How did you (he or she) score?
2. Ask yourself (or the other manager) what the results mean to you (him or her). Did the questions zero in on any areas that you (he or she) find difficult? What are they?
3. Does it help you (him or her) identify areas where changes in management style might be made? What are they? How will these changes affect the manager-employee relationship?
4. Acquiring managerial skills can be difficult because behavioural change is involved. Do you (he or she) think that some supervisory training might help to strengthen managerial skill in some of the areas that were identified through the quiz that you (he or she) find difficult? What sort of training?

experiential exercises

1. Annual Pay Raises

Procedure

1. Read the job descriptions below and decide on a percentage pay increase for each of the eight employees.
2. Make salary increase recommendations for each of the eight managers that you supervise. There are no formal company restrictions on the size of raises you give, but the total for everyone should not exceed the $10,900 (a 4-percent increase in the salary pool) which has been budgeted for this purpose. You have a variety of information upon which to base the decisions, including a "productivity index" (PI), which Industrial Engineering computes as a quantitative measure of operating efficiency for each manager's work unit. This index ranges from a high of 10 to a low of 1. Indicate the percentage increase *you* would give each manager in the blank space next to each manager's name. Be prepared to explain why.

_____ *A Alvarez*   Alvarez is new this year and has a tough work group whose task is dirty and difficult. This is a hard position to fill, but you don't feel Alvarez is particularly good. The word around is that the other managers agree with you. PI = 3. Salary = $33,000.

_____ *B J Cook*   Cook is single and a "swinger" who enjoys leisure time. Everyone laughs at the problems B J has getting the work out, and you feel it certainly is lacking. Cook has been in the job two years. PI = 3. Salary = $34,500.

_____ *Z Davis*   In the position three years, Davis is one of your best people, even though some of the other managers don't agree. With a spouse who is independently wealth, Davis doesn't need money but likes to work. PI = 7. Salary = $36,600.

_____ *M Frame*   Frame has personal problems and is hurting financially. Others gossip about Frame's performance, but you are quite satisfied with this second-year employee. PI = 7. Salary = $34,700.

_____ *C M Liu*   Liu is just finishing a fine first year in a tough job. Highly respected by the others, Liu has a job offer in another company at a 15-percent increase in salary. You are impressed, and the word is that the money is important. PI = 9. Salary = $34,000.

_____ *B Ratin*   Ratin is a first-year manager whom you and the others think is doing a good job. This is a bit surprising since Ratin turned out to be a "free spirit" who doesn't seem to care much about money or status. PI = 9. Salary = $33,800.

_____ *H Smith*   A first-year manager recently divorced and with two children to support as a single parent. The others like Smith a lot, but your evaluation is not very high. Smith could certainly use extra money. PI = 5. Salary = $33,000.

_____ *G White*   White is a big spender who always has the latest clothes and a new car. In the first year on what you would call an easy job, White doesn't seem to be doing very well. For some reason, though, the others talk about White as the "cream of the new crop." PI = 5. Salary = $33,000.

3. Convene in a group of four to seven persons and share your raise decision.
4. As a group decide on a new set of raises and be prepared to report them to the rest of the class. Make sure that the group spokesperson can provide the rationale for each person's raise
5. The instructor will call on each group to report its raise decisions. After discussion, an "expert's" decision will be given.

Source: J R Schermerhorn, Jr., J G Hunt and R N Osborn *Organizational Behavior*, (7th edition) (New York: John Wiley & Sons, 2000) pp 496–497.

2. Rewards, Rewards, Rewards

Objectives

1. To tap the class's collective knowledge of organizational rewards.
2. To appreciate the vast array of potential rewards.
3. To contrast individual and group perceptions of rewards.
4. To practice your group creativity skills.

Introduction

Rewards are a centrepiece of organizational life. Both extrinsic and intrinsic rewards motivate us to join and continue contributing to organized effort. But not all rewards have the same impact on work motivation. Individuals have their own personal preferences for rewards. The best way to discover people's reward preferences is to ask them, both individually and collectively. This group brainstorming and class discussion exercise requires about 20 to 30 minutes.

Instructions

Your instructor will divide your class randomly into teams of five to eight people. Each team will go through the following four-step process:

1. Each team will have a six-minute brainstorming session, with one person acting as recorder. The objective of this brainstorming session is to list as many different organizational rewards as the group can think of. Your team might find it helpful to think of rewards by category (such as rewards from the work itself, rewards you can spend, rewards you can eat and drink, rewards you can feel, rewards you can wear, rewards you can share, rewards you cannot see, etc.). Remember, good brainstorming calls for withholding judgments about whether ideas are good or not. Quantity is wanted. Building upon other people's ideas also is encouraged.

2. Next, each individual will take four minutes to write down, in decreasing order of importance, 10 rewards they want from the job. Note: These are your *personal* preferences; your "top 10" rewards that will motivate you to do your best.

3. Each team will then take five minutes to generate a list of "today's 10 most powerful rewards." List them in decreasing order of their power to motivate job performance. Voting may be necessary.

4. A general class discussion of the questions listed below will conclude the exercise.

QUESTIONS FOR DISCUSSION

1. How did your personal "top 10" list compare with your group's "top 10" list? If there is a serious mismatch, how would it affect your motivation? (To promote discussion, the instructor may have several volunteers read their personal "top 10" lists to the class.)
2. Which team had the most productive brainstorming session? (The instructor may request each team to read its brainstormed list of potential rewards and "top 10" list to the class.)
3. Were you surprised to hear certain rewards getting so much attention? Why?
4. How can managers improve the incentive effect of the rewards most frequently mentioned in class?
5. What is the likely future of organizational reward plans? Which of today's compensation trends will probably thrive, and which are probably passing fads?

personal awareness and growth exercises

1. How Strong Is Your Desire for Performance Feedback?

Instructions

Circle one number indicating the strength of your agreement or disagreement with each statement. Total your responses, and compare your score with our arbitrary norms.

	Disagree	Agree
1. As long as I think that I have done something well, I am not too concerned about how other people think I have done.	5 — 4 — 3 — 2 — 1	

2. How other people view my work is not as important as how I view my own work.   5 — 4 — 3 — 2 — 1

3. It is usually better not to put much faith in what others say about your work, regardless of whether it is complimentary or not.   5 — 4 — 3 — 2 — 1

4. If I have done something well, I know it without other people telling me so.   5 — 4 — 3 — 2 — 1

5. I usually have a clear idea of what I am trying to do and how well I am proceeding toward my goal. $5 - 4 - 3 - 2 - 1$

6. I find that I am usually a pretty good judge of my own performance. $5 - 4 - 3 - 2 - 1$

7. It is very important to me to know what people think of my work. $1 - 2 - 3 - 4 - 5$

8. It is a good idea to get someone to check on your work before it's too late to make changes. $1 - 2 - 3 - 4 - 5$

9. Even though I may think I have done a good job, I feel a lot more confident of it after someone else tells me so. $1 - 2 - 3 - 4 - 5$

10. Since one cannot be objective about their own performance, it is best to listen to the feedback provided by others. $1 - 2 - 3 - 4 - 5$

Total score = _____

Arbitrary Norms

10–23 = Low desire for feedback
24–36 = Moderate desire for feedback
37–50 = High desire for feedback

Source: Excerpted and adapted from D M Herold, C K Parsons, and R B Rensvold, "Individual Differences in the Generation and Processing of Performance Feedback," *Educational and Psychological Measurement*, February 1996, Table 1, p 9. Copyright © 1996 by Sage Publications. Reprinted by permission of Sage Publications, Inc.

2. What Kind of Feedback Are You Getting?

Objectives

1. To provide actual examples of on-the-job feedback from three primary sources: organization/supervisor, co-workers, and self/task.
2. To provide a handy instrument for evaluating the comparative strength of positive feedback from these three sources.

Introduction

A pair of researchers from Georgia Tech developed and tested a 63-item feedback questionnaire to demonstrate the importance of both the sign and content of feedback messages.[56] Although their instrument contains both positive and negative feedback items, we have extracted 18 positive items for this self-awareness exercise.

Instructions

Thinking of your current job (or your most recent job), circle one number for each of the 18 items. Alternatively, you could ask one or more other employed individuals to complete the questionnaire. Once the questionnaire has been completed, calculate subtotal and total scores by adding the circled numbers. Then try to answer the discussion questions.

Instrument

How frequently do you experience each of the following outcomes in your present (or past) job?

ORGANIZATIONAL/SUPERVISORY FEEDBACK

	Rarely	Occasionally	Very Frequently
1. My supervisor complimenting me on something I have done.	1———2———3———4———5		
2. My supervisor increasing my responsibilities.	1———2———3———4———5		
3. The company expressing pleasure with my performance.	1———2———3———4———5		
4. The company giving me a raise.	1———2———3———4———5		
5. My supervisor recommending me for a promotion or raise.	1———2———3———4———5		
6. The company providing me with favourable data concerning my performance.	1———2———3———4———5		

Subscore = _____

CO-WORKER FEEDBACK

7. My co-workers coming to me for advice.   1———2———3———4———5

8. My co-workers expressing approval of my work. 1——2——3——4——5

9. My co-workers liking to work with me. 1——2——3——4——5

10. My co-workers telling me that I am doing a good job. 1——2——3——4——5

11. My co-workers commenting favourably on something I have done. 1——2——3——4——5

12. Receiving a compliment from my co-workers. 1——2——3——4——5

Subscore = _____

SELF/TASK FEEDBACK

13. Knowing that the way I go about my duties is superior to most others. 1——2——3——4——5

14. Feeling I am accomplishing more than I used to. 1——2——3——4——5

15. Knowing that I can now perform or do things which previously were difficult for me. 1——2——3——4——5

16. Finding that I am satisfying my own standards for "good work." 1——2——3——4——5

17. Knowing that what I am doing "feels right." 1——2——3——4——5

18. Feeling confident of being able to handle all aspects of my job. 1——2——3——4——5

Subscore = _____

Total Score = _____

QUESTIONS FOR DISCUSSION

1. Which items on this questionnaire would you rate as primarily instructional in function? Are all of the remaining items primarily motivational? Explain.

2. In terms of your own feedback profile, which of the three types is the strongest (has the highest subscore)? Which is the weakest (has the lowest subscore)? How well does your feedback profile explain your job performance and/or satisfaction?

3. How does your feedback profile measure up against those of your classmates? (Arbitrary norms, for comparative purposes, are as follows: Deficient feedback = 18–42; Moderate feedback = 43–65; Abundant feedback = 66–90.)

4. Which of the three sources of feedback is most critical to your successful job performance and/or job satisfaction? Explain.

CBC video case

Not the Retiring Kind

Many Canadians are not interested in retirement activities like golf, lawn bowling, or lying on a beach in Florida. They enjoy working and are definitely not responsive to the idea of mandatory retirement at age 65. Currently, about 6% of Canadians over the age of 65 are still working. Some have to work for financial reasons, but many make a conscious choice to continue working. They would "rather get out of bed and make things happen." Their work ranges from self-employment such as writing novels to acting as a courier to managing a chapter of the St. John's Ambulance. As the baby boomers close in on age 65, we may hear a lot more people refusing to listen to "nonsense" that they are "over the hill at

65," and more likely to believe that "life is just beginning" and that "the best is yet to come."

QUESTIONS FOR DISCUSSION

1. What motivates these people to continue working after normal retirement age?

2. What are the intrinsic rewards that people over 65 receive from their work?

3. What sources of feedback are important to those working past age 65?

Source: Based on "Not the Retiring Kind," *CBC Venture 779* (March 20, 2001).

chapter
five

Stress Management

After reading the material in this chapter, you should be able to:

- Define the term *stress*.

- Describe the model of occupational stress.

- Explain how stressful life events create stress.

- Review the model of burnout, and highlight the managerial solutions to reduce it.

- Explain the mechanisms of social support.

- Describe the coping process.

- Discuss the personality characteristic of hardiness.

- Discuss the Type A behaviour pattern and its management implications.

- Describe the holistic wellness model.

DEPRESSION FROM WORKPLACE STRESS IS PUBLIC HEALTH ENEMY NUMBER ONE

Depression brought on by workplace stress "is business and public health enemy number one," says Bill Wilkerson, a mental health advocate. "The modern workplace is the greatest source of stress in the lives of Canadians, stress is a trigger of depression, and this one disorder represents the most powerful source of worker disability in Canada and the world today," says Wilkerson, co-founder and president of the Toronto-based Business and Economic Roundtable on Addiction and Mental Health.

Depression costs North American businesses an estimated $60 billion (US) a year in lost worker productivity, and the cost to the health care system of diagnosis and treatment. Wilkerson says Canada needs to think of depression as an accident that can be prevented, and devote more resources to this invisible problem, which can cause more damage than physical ones.

Bill Wilkerson, mental health advocate, and co-founder and president of the Business and Economic Roundtable on Addiction and Mental Health.

Wilkerson advocates that workers' compensation schemes modernize their eligibility rules to more easily give benefits to depressed workers; that employers eliminate workplace behaviours leading to stress, such as "arbitrary management styles, unclear job expectations, office politics, and blame cultures;" that workplaces be equipped to detect depression and help employees get treatment as soon as possible; and that managers curb the "excessive use of email" in the workplace.

"The unyielding sensation of having too much to do—all at once, all the time—is driving workers in this country closer to diagnosable stress-related and depressive disorders," Wilkerson says.

Source: Adapted from "Depression From Workplace Stress Is #1 Enemy: Advocate," *Workplace Today*, June 2001, p 7.

Foundations of Stress

Managers need to understand the causes and consequences of stress for at least three compelling reasons. First, from a quality-of-worklife perspective, workers are more satisfied and likely to show up for work when they have a safe and comfortable work environment. Second, a moral imperative suggests that managers should reduce occupational stress because it leads to negative outcomes including depression, lost productivity, and absenteeism. Harvard University predicts that by 2020, depression will become the biggest source of workdays lost in the developed world.[1] A third reason is the staggering economic costs of stress. Stress-related illnesses cost North American businesses over $60 billion (US) annually.

We all experience stress on a daily basis. Although stress is caused by many factors, researchers conclude that stress triggers one of two basic reactions: active fighting or passive flight (running away or acceptance), the so-called **fight-or-flight response.**[2] Physiologically, this stress response is a biochemical "passing gear" involving hormonal changes that mobilize the body for extraordinary demands. Imagine how our prehistoric ancestors responded to the stress associated with a charging saber-toothed tiger. To avoid being eaten, they could stand their ground and fight the beast or run away. In either case, their bodies would have been energized by an identical hormonal change, involving the release of adrenaline into the bloodstream.

> **Fight-or-flight response**
>
> To either confront stressors or try to avoid them.

In today's hectic urbanized and industrialized society, demands include problems such as deadlines, role conflict, financial responsibilities, information overload, technology, traffic congestion, noise and air pollution, family problems, and work overload. Our response to stress may or may not trigger negative side effects, including headaches, ulcers, insomnia, heart attacks, high blood pressure, and strokes. Because stress and its consequences are manageable, it is important for managers to learn as much as they can about occupational stress.

> **Stress**
>
> Behavioural, physical, or psychological response to stressors.
>
> **Stressors**
>
> Environmental factors that produce stress.

Formally defined, **stress** is "an adaptive response, mediated by individual characteristics and/or psychological processes, that is a consequence of any external action, situation, or event that places special physical and/or psychological demands upon a person."[3] This definition is not as difficult as it seems when we reduce it to three interrelated dimensions of stress: (1) environmental demands, referred to as stressors, that produce (2) an adaptive response that is influenced by (3) individual differences.

A Model of Occupational Stress

Figure 5–1 presents an instructive model of occupational stress. The model shows that four types of stressors lead to perceived stress, which, in turn, produces a variety of outcomes. The model also specifies several individual differences that *moderate* the stressor-stress-outcome relationship. A moderator is a variable that causes the relationship between two variables—such as stress and outcomes—to be stronger for some people and weaker for others.

Stressors   **Stressors** are environmental factors that produce stress. Work is the number one cause of stress in the lives of Canadians, according to an Ipsos-Reid poll. The survey found that 45% of Cana-

A Model of Occupational Stress   FIGURE 5–1

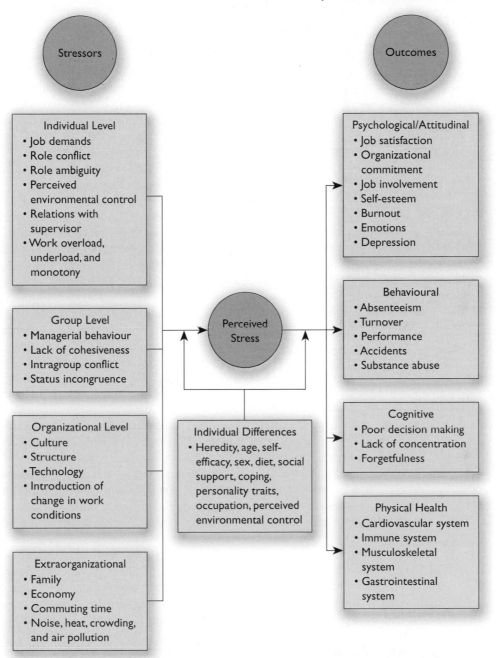

Sources: Adapted from M Koslowsky, *Modeling the Stress-Strain Relationship in Work Settings* (New York: Routledge, 1998); and M T Matteson and J M Ivancevich, "Organizational Stressors and Heart Disease: A Research Model," *Academy of Management Review*, July 1979, p 350.

dians said that their job was the biggest source of stress in their lives. Another 45% said that workplace stress is affecting their home lives.[4] Figure 5–1 shows the four major types of stressors: individual, group, organizational, and extraorganizational. *Individual-level stressors* are those directly associated with a person's job duties. The most -common examples of these stressors are job demands, work overload, role conflict, role

Managers Ignore Bullying

A woman (who asked to remain anonymous) contacted the *Toronto Star* with a story about how her life "went to hell" when a new manager took over her department at the advertising firm where she worked. He repeatedly belittled her work, made lewd comments, tried to control her whereabouts, and threatened to fire her. She complained to the human resources department and to her boss' boss. A few of her colleagues also reported ill treatment. But nothing was done, and the bullying increased. She suffered a nervous breakdown and went on medical leave. She contacted a lawyer and settled with the company for less than she wanted and with no admission of wrongdoing on the part of the company.

You Decide . . .

Did the advertising company handle this situation appropriately? What should the company have done differently to avoid legal action in this case?

Source: Adapted from N J White, "The Poisoned Workplace: Office bullies prey on co-workers and subordinates through harassment and intimidation." *Toronto Star*, December 14, 2001, p F1.

ambiguity, everyday hassles, perceived control over events occurring in the work environment, and job characteristics.[5] For instance, a study of 771 US workers and a total of 2,642 employees from Canada, the United Kingdom, and Germany revealed that the increasing amount of time people spend sending and receiving messages was a stressor at work. With respect to job demands and workload, a survey of 700 people indicated that each respondent had someone they cared about who worked too hard. More than 22% blamed a demanding supervisor for the fact that his or her spouse was a workaholic.[6] Managers can help reduce these stressors by providing direction and support and by equitably allocating work assignments within the work unit.

Finally, job security is an important individual-level stressor to manage because it is associated with increased job satisfaction, organization commitment, and performance, and it is decreasing.

Group-level stressors are caused by group dynamics and managerial behaviour. Managers create stress for employees by (1) exhibiting inconsistent behaviours, (2) failing to provide support, (3) showing lack of concern, (4) providing inadequate direction, (5) creating a high-productivity environment, and (6) focusing on negatives while ignoring good performance. Sexual harassment experiences represent another group-level stressor. Studies show that harassing experiences are negatively associated with work, supervision, and promotion satisfaction and are positively related to ambiguity, conflict, and stress.[7] Another increasingly common stressor related to group dynamics is psychological violence, including harassment, intimidation, and bullying. Bullying and other forms of psychological violence include any offensive behaviour such as cruel or humiliating words or actions intended to undermine an individual or group of employees. Psychological violence is widespread—a 2000 survey of Canadian labour unions found that 75% of workers had been harassed or bullied. For example, Timothy Lloyd of Imperial Parking in Calgary landed in a pit with the office bully, his boss. Lloyd suffered 13 months of constant threats of dismissal, constant invasion of his personal space, and constant profanity personally directed at him, before finally quitting. Glenn French, National Director of the Canadian Initiative on Workplace Violence, says:

> You have a better chance of being a workplace fatality in the United States, whereas in Canada you have a better chance of being bullied, harassed or abused.[8]

Organizational stressors affect large numbers of employees. Organizational culture is a prime example. For instance, a high-pressure environment that places chronic work demands on employees fuels the stress response.[9] In contrast, research provides preliminary support for the idea that participative management can reduce organizational

Diversity: Opportunity and Challenge

Diversity represents a major business opportunity for most companies. Having a more culturally, racially, and gender-diverse workforce will allow them to understand new and growing markets, as well as stimulating new ways of thinking and of accomplishing the job because of the additional inputs and perspective diversity creates. On the other hand, negative reactions to increased diversity in the workforce may also become a major source of workplace violence in the future. Racism and discrimination in a multicultural, multiethnic work environment can result in hostility between groups that exacerbates competition over jobs and promotions and creates a perception of bias and unfairness.

The same types of tensions that already occur among various ethnic and racial groups in society at large can be expected to enter the corporate environment as the workforce becomes more diverse. Businesses must root out the overt and the subtle forms of racism and sexism. Diversity issues are especially susceptible to being compounded severely by a lack of effective management practices, and the situations in which cultural biases are likely to surface may be especially susceptible to toxic supervisors, whose own prejudices and needs for power make existing tensions worse. Escalation toward violence is typically not one person's fault but the result of many people's interactions. There must be clear statements from senior management that discrimination is not acceptable and will not be tolerated within the company. Personnel policies should spell out the consequences of both overt and subtle prejudicial behaviour. Diversity training and education can help to deal with these issues directly in a way that de-escalates tensions.

Source: C E Labig, *Preventing Violence in the Workplace,* American Management Association, 1995, p 139.

---

stress.[10] The increased use of information technology is another source of organizational stress.

In addition to these types of stressors, some people also are technophobic. Dell Computer, for example, called 2,000 people and found out that 55% of them were anxious and fearful about using computer-related technology. On the flip side, other people are so drawn to the use of E-mail and the Internet that they developed an addiction called "Internet Addiction Disorder."[11] Finally, the office design and general office environment are important organizational-level stressors. Research demonstrates that poor lighting, loud noise, improper placement of furniture, and a dirty or smelly environment create stress.[12] Managers are advised to monitor and eliminate these stressors.

Extraorganizational stressors are those caused by factors outside the organization. For instance, conflicts associated with balancing one's career and family life are stressful. According to Canadian researcher Linda Duxbury at Carleton University:

> Many Canadians are having real difficulties balancing competing work and family demands. Our data would indicate that these difficulties have a negative impact on employees and on the organization's bottom line. For example, employees with higher levels of work-family conflict are more likely to report higher levels of job stress, overall stress, and depressed mood. They are also significantly more likely to be absent from work and less likely to be satisfied with their job or committed to their organization.[13]

A 2002 Health Canada study found that work was winning out over family in the struggle for work-life balance. Canadians are working longer hours, taking work home, and in many cases deciding not to have children because of their careers.[14] Organizations

can help employees cope with work-family balance issues by providing them with flexible schedules and cafeteria benefits.

Perceived Stress   Perceived stress represents an individual's overall perception about how various stressors are affecting his or her life. The perception of stressors is an important component within the stress process because people interpret the same stressors differently.[15] For example, some individuals perceive unemployment as a positive liberating experience, whereas others perceive it as a negative debilitating one.[16]

Outcomes   Theorists contend that stress has psychological/attitudinal, behavioural, cognitive, and physical health consequences or outcomes. A large body of research supports the negative effect of perceived stress on many aspects of our lives. Stress is negatively related to job satisfaction, organizational commitment, positive emotions, and performance and positively correlated with burnout turnover.[17] Research also provides ample evidence to support the conclusion that stress negatively affects our physical health, including lessened ability to ward off illness and infection, high blood pressure, coronary artery disease, and tension headaches.[18]

Employees who perceive that they have little or no control over stressors in their work environment tend to experience more stress than those who feel more in control on the job. In support of this finding, one study showed that employees working on an assembly line, such as the one pictured here, had more negative physiological responses to perceived stress than when they worked in a more flexible work setting.

Individual Differences   People do not experience the same level of stress or exhibit similar outcomes for a given type of stressor. For example, the type of stressors experienced at work can vary by gender—interpersonal conflict is a greater source of stress for women than men.[19] Perceived control also is a significant moderator of the stress process. People perceive lower levels of stress and experienced more favourable consequences from stress when they believe that they can exert control over the stressors affecting their lives.[20] In support of this finding, another study showed that employees had more negative physiological responses to perceived stress when they worked on an assembly line than in a more flexible work organization.[21] Assembly-line technologies allow employees much less control than other organizational arrangements.

Finally, the personality trait of chronic hostility or cynicism also moderated stress. Research demonstrated that people who were chronically angry, suspicious, or mistrustful were twice as likely to have coronary artery blockages. We all can protect our hearts by learning to avoid these tendencies.[22] In summary, even though researchers have been able to identify several important moderators, a large gap still exists in identifying relevant individual differences.

Important Stressors and Stress Outcomes

As we have seen, stressors trigger stress, which, in turn, leads to a variety of outcomes. This section explores an important category of *extraorganizational* stressors: stressful life events. Burnout, another especially troublesome stress-related outcome, is also examined.

Stressful Life Events

Events such as experiencing the death of a family member, being assaulted, moving, ending an intimate relationship, being seriously ill, or taking a big test can create stress. These events are stressful because they involve significant changes that require adaptation and often social readjustment. Accordingly, stressful life events are defined as non-work-related changes that disrupt an individual's lifestyle and social relationships. They have been the most extensively investigated extraorganizational stressors.

Numerous studies have examined the relationship between life stress and both illness and job performance. Highly stressed people have significantly more problems with chronic headaches, sudden cardiac death, and a host of minor physical ailments. Meanwhile, psychosocial problems and academic and work performance decline as stress increases.[23] *Negative* (as opposed to positive) personal life changes were associated with greater susceptibility to colds, job stress, and psychological distress, and lower levels of job satisfaction and organizational commitment.[24] Finally, recent studies revealed that women rate life events as more stressful than men. Results also showed that there were no meaningful differences in life event ratings between various age groups and income levels.[25]

The key implication is that employee illness and job performance are affected by extraorganizational stressors, particularly those that are negative and uncontrollable. Because employees do not leave their personal problems at the office door or factory gate, management needs to be aware of external sources of employee stress. Once identified, alternative work schedules, training programs, and/or counseling can be used to help employees cope with these stressors. This may not only reduce costs associated with illnesses and absenteeism but may also lead to positive work attitudes, better job performance, and reduced turnover.

In addition, by acknowledging that work outcomes are affected by extraorganizational stressors, managers may avoid the trap of automatically attributing poor performance to low motivation or lack of ability. Such awareness is likely to engender positive reactions from employees and lead to resolution of problems, not just symptoms.

Burnout

Burnout is a stress-induced problem common among members of "helping" professions such as teaching, social work, human resources, nursing, and law enforcement. It does not involve a specific feeling, attitude, or physiological outcome anchored to a specific point in time. Rather, **burnout** is a condition that occurs over time and is characterized by emotional exhaustion and a combination of negative attitudes.

> **Burnout**
> A condition of emotional exhaustion and negative attitudes.

Table 5–1 describes 10 attitudinal characteristics of burnout. Experts say a substantial number of people suffer from this problem. This result implies that burnout is not limited to people working in the helping professions. For example, burnout can be quite high among entrepreneurs who run small firms.

A Model of Burnout   A model of burnout is presented in Figure 5–2. The fundamental premise underlying the model is that burnout develops in phases. The three key phases are emotional exhaustion, depersonalization, and feeling a lack of personal accomplishment.[26]

As shown in Figure 5–2, *emotional exhaustion* is due to a combination of personal stressors and job and organizational stressors.[27] People who expect a lot from themselves and the organizations in which they work tend to create more internal stress,

TABLE 5–1 │ Attitudinal Characteristics of Burnout

Attitude	Description
Fatalism	A feeling that you lack control over your work.
Boredom	A lack of interest in doing your job.
Discontent	A sense of being unhappy with your job.
Cynicism	A tendency to undervalue the content of your job and the rewards received.
Inadequacy	A feeling of not being able to meet your objectives.
Failure	A tendency to discredit your performance and conclude that you are ineffective.
Overwork	A feeling of having too much to do and not enough time to complete it.
Nastiness	A tendency to be rude or unpleasant to your co-workers.
Dissatisfaction	A feeling that you are not being justly rewarded for your efforts.
Escape	A desire to give up and get away from it all.

Source: Adapted from D P Rogers, "Helping Employees Cope with Burnout," *Business*, October–December 1984, p 4.

which, in turn, leads to emotional exhaustion. Similarly, emotional exhaustion is fueled by having too much work to do, by role conflict, and by the type of interpersonal interactions encountered at work. Frequent, intense face-to-face interactions that are emotionally charged are associated with higher levels of emotional exhaustion.

Over time, emotional exhaustion leads to *depersonalization*, which is a state of psychologically withdrawing from one's job. This ultimately results in a *feeling of being*

FIGURE 5–1 │ A Model of Burnout

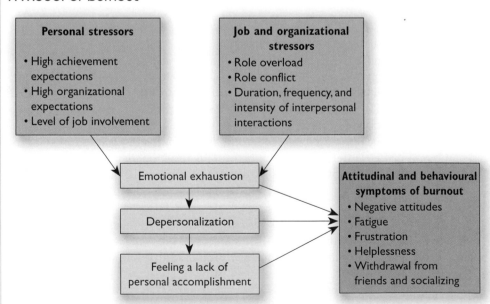

Source: Based in part on C L Cordes and T W Dougherty, "A Review and an Integration of Research on Job Burnout," *Academy of Management Review*, October 1993, p 641.

unappreciated, ineffective, or inadequate. The additive effect of these three phases is a host of negative attitudinal and behavioural outcomes.

Prevention Removing personal stressors and job and organizational stressors is the most straightforward way to prevent burnout. Managers also can reduce burnout by buffering its effects. Buffers are resources or administrative changes that alleviate the symptoms of burnout. Potential buffers include extra staff or equipment at peak work periods, support from top management, increased freedom to make decisions, recognition for accomplishments, time off for personal development or rest, and equitable rewards. Decreasing the quantity and increasing the *quality* of communications is another possible buffer. Finally, managers can change the content of an individual's job by adding or eliminating responsibilities, increasing the amount of participation in decision making, altering the pattern of interpersonal contacts, or assigning the person to a new position.[28]

> Deloitte & Touche is implementing a policy on some projects that curbs their consultants' travel time. Instead of spending five days a week at a client's offices, consultants spend three nights and four days, fly home and work a fifth day in their home cities. That means "you can plan your life and be home for a real weekend," says Malva Rabinowitz, a Deloitte managing director. Most clients "recognize it's a good thing" when they see the policy in action. . . . Similarly, Ernst & Young is involving clients on some consulting projects in setting up a "team calendar" that integrates team members' work and personal commitments, says Bob Forbes, an Ernst partner. While client needs still come first, the calendar puts people's off-the-job lives on the radar screen. . . . Ernst & Young has a committee monitoring accountants' workloads. . . . It helps burnout candidates shift clients or schedule vacations.[29]

There also are two long-term strategies for reducing burnout that are increasingly being used by companies. Apple Computer, American Express, IBM, McDonald's Corporation, and Intel, for instance, use sabbaticals to replenish employees' energy and desire to work. These programs allow employees to take a designated amount of time off from work after being employed a certain number of years. An employee retreat is the second long-term strategy. Retreats entail sending employees to an offsite location for three to five days. While there, everyone can relax, reflect, or engage in team and relationship building activities. This is precisely what Pricewaterhouse is doing to help its employees cope with work stress:

> PricewaterhouseCoopers has a two-day stress survival clinic where participants meet with a physician, nutritionist, and psychiatrist. The retreat, held in such locations as Toronto and Captiva Island, [Florida], includes Mediterranean-style cuisine served in candlelight dining rooms and time to focus on coping better with pressure.[30]

Moderators of Occupational Stress

Moderators, once again, are variables that cause the relationships between stressors, perceived stress, and outcomes to be weaker for some people and stronger for others. Managers with a working knowledge of important stress moderators can confront employee stress in the following ways:

1. Awareness of moderators helps identify those most likely to experience stress and its negative outcomes. Stress-reduction programs then can be formulated for high-risk employees.

2. Moderators, in and of themselves, suggest possible solutions for reducing negative outcomes of occupational stress.

International Employee Assistance Plans (EAPs) Help With Relocation Stress

International business assignments involving relocation are always stressful for employees and their families. Moving to a new country often means dealing with culture shock, separation anxiety, loneliness, and homesickness. This can often lead to emotional problems including sadness, anger, hostility, panic, and depression. Many employees depart for home prematurely, before their job is completed.

International EAPs have recently been devised to help expatriates manage the stressors related to living abroad. There are three stages to the assistance provided. First, a foundation for successful adaptation and productive work is provided prior to leaving through preparation activities. These activities include learning about cultural differences, anticipating culture shock, and, where applicable, developing effective coping strategies to minimize the effects of family separation, especially for children.

Second, while on assignment, ongoing assistance is provided through online counseling, liaison with English-speaking professional counselors abroad, telephone sessions with Canadian counselors for urgent requests, and support for families left behind. Third, upon return home at the completion of the foreign assignment, assistance is available for management of "reverse culture shock," preparing extended family for the return, and support during the readjustment to new job responsibilities back home.

Source: B Barker and D Schulde, "Special EAP helps expatriates face international 'culture shock'," *Canadian HR Reporter*, November 29, 1999, p 20; A Bross and G Wise, "Sustaining the relocated employee with an international EAP," *Canadian HR Reporter*, November 29, 1999, pp 18, 19, 21.

Keeping these objectives in mind, we will examine four important moderators: social support, coping, hardiness, and Type A behaviour.

Social Support

Social support

Amount of helpfulness derived from social relationships.

Talking with a friend or taking part in a bull session can be comforting during times of fear, stress, or loneliness. For a variety of reasons, meaningful social relationships help people do a better job of handling stress. **Social support** is the amount of perceived helpfulness derived from social relationships. Importantly, social support is determined by both the quantity and quality of an individual's social relationships.

Support networks evolve from five sources: cultural norms, social institutions, companies, groups, or individuals. For example, there is more cultural emphasis on caring for the elderly in Japan than in North America. Japanese culture is thus a strong source of social support for older Japanese people. Alternatively, individuals may fall back on social institutions such as the Red Cross, religious groups, or family and friends for support. In turn, these various sources provide four types of support:

- *Esteem support*. Providing information that a person is accepted and respected despite any problems or inadequacies.
- *Informational support*. Providing help in defining, understanding, and coping with problems.
- *Social companionship*. Spending time with others in leisure and recreational activities.
- *Instrumental support*. Providing financial aid, material resources, or needed services.[31]

Research Findings and Managerial Lessons   People with low social support tend to have poorer cardiovascular and immune system functioning and tend to die earlier than those with strong social support networks.[32] Negative social support, which amounts to someone undermining another person, negatively affects one's mental health.[33] We would all be well advised to avoid people who try to undermine us. It appears that social support sometimes serves as a buffer against stress, but we do not know precisely when or why. Additional research is needed to figure out this inconsistency. Finally, social support is positively related to the availability of support resources; that is, people who interact with a greater number of friends, family, or co-workers have a wider base of social support to draw upon during stressful periods.[34]

One practical recommendation is to keep employees informed about external and internal social support systems. Internally, managers can use esteem and informational support while administering daily feedback and coaching. Further, participative management programs and company-sponsored activities that make employees feel they are an important part of an "extended family" can be rich sources of social support. Employees need time and energy to adequately maintain their social relationships. If organizational demands are excessive, employees' social relationships and support networks will suffer, resulting in stress-related illness and decreased performance.

Coping

Coping is "the process of managing demands (external or internal) that are appraised as taxing or exceeding the resources of the person."[35] Because effective coping helps reduce the impact of stressors and stress, one's personal life and managerial skills can be enhanced by better understanding this process. Figure 5–3 depicts an instructive model of coping.

> **Coping**
> Process of managing stress.

The coping process has three major components: (1) situational and personal factors, (2) cognitive appraisals of the stressor, and (3) coping strategies. As shown in Figure 5–3, both situational and personal factors influence the appraisal of stressors. In turn, appraisal directly influences the choice of coping strategies. Each of the major components of this model deserves a closer look.

A Model of the Coping Process   **FIGURE 5–3**

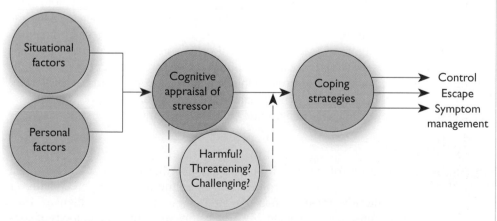

Source: Based in part on R S Lazarus and S Folkman, "Coping and Adaptation," in *Handbook of Behavioural Medicine*, ed W D Gentry (New York: The Guilford Press, 1984), pp 282–325.

Situational and Personal Factors   Situational factors such as the frequency of exposure to a stressor and personal factors such as being tired or sick can affect the appraisal of and interpretation of stressors. Traits such as locus of control, self-esteem, optimism, self-efficacy and work experience also affect the appraisal of stressors.[36]

Cognitive Appraisal of Stressors   Cognitive appraisal reflects an individual's overall perception or evaluation of a situation or stressor. Cognitive appraisal results in a categorization of the situation or stressor as either harmful, threatening, or challenging. It is important to understand the differences among these appraisals because they influence how people cope. " 'Harm' (including loss) represents damage already done; 'threat' involves the potential for harm; and 'challenge' means the potential for significant gain under difficult odds."[37] Coping with harm usually entails undoing or reinterpreting something that occurred in the past because the damage is already done. In contrast, threatening situations engage anticipatory coping. That is, people cope with threat by preparing for harm that may occur in the future. Challenge also activates anticipatory coping. In contrast with threat, an appraisal of challenge results in coping that focuses on what can be gained rather than what may be lost.

Coping Strategies   Coping strategies are characterized by the specific behaviours and cognitions used to cope with a situation. People use a combination of three approaches to cope with stressors and stress (see Figure 5–3). The first, called a **control strategy**, consists of using behaviours and cognitions to directly anticipate or solve problems. A control strategy has a take-charge tone, for example, quitting a job in order to gain flexibility in your life.

In contrast to tackling the problem head-on, an **escape strategy** amounts to avoiding the problem. Behaviours and cognitions are used to avoid or escape situations. Individuals use this strategy when they passively accept stressful situations or avoid them by failing to confront the cause of stress (an obnoxious co-worker, for instance). Finally, a **symptom management strategy** consists of using methods such as relaxation, meditation, medication, or exercise to manage the symptoms of occupational stress.

Control strategy

Coping behaviour that directly confronts or solves problems.

Escape strategy

Coping strategy that avoids or ignores stressors and problems.

Symptom management strategy

Coping strategy that focuses on reducing the symptoms of stress.

Research Findings and Managerial Recommendations   Research has not clearly identified which type of coping strategy—control, escape, or symptom management—is most effective. It appears that the best coping strategy depends on the situation at hand.[38] Escaping stress—by going on vacation, for example—is sometimes better than confronting a stressor with a control-oriented coping strategy. This result suggests that employees should be taught a contingency approach to coping with organizational stressors. This might begin by helping employees identify those stressors that they perceive as harmful or threatening. Training or managerial support can then be used to help employees manage and possibly eliminate the most serious stressors.

Hardiness

Hardiness

Personality characteristic that neutralizes stress.

A collection of personality characteristics that neutralize occupational stress, referred to as **hardiness**, involves the ability to perceptually or behaviourally transform negative stressors into positive challenges. Hardiness embraces the personality dimensions of commitment, locus of control, and challenge.[39]

Personality Characteristics of Hardiness   *Commitment* reflects the extent to which an individual is involved in whatever he or she is doing. Committed people have a sense of purpose and do not give up under pressure because they tend to invest themselves in the situation.

Individuals with an *internal locus of control* believe they can influence the events that affect their lives. People possessing this trait are more likely to foresee stressful events, thereby reducing their exposure to anxiety-producing situations. Moreover, their perception of being in control leads "internals" to use proactive coping strategies.

Challenge is represented by the belief that change is a normal part of life. Hence, change is seen as an opportunity for growth and development rather than a threat to security.

Hardiness Research and Application   Hardiness—commitment, locus of control, and challenge—reduces the probability of illness following exposure to stress.[40] Hardy individuals interpret stressors less negatively and are more likely to use control coping strategies than unhardy people.[41] Furthermore, hardy individuals display lower stress, burnout, and psychological distress and higher job satisfaction than their less hardy counterparts.[42]

One practical offshoot of this research is organizational training and development programs that strengthen the characteristics of commitment, personal control, and challenge. Because of cost limitations, it is necessary to target key employees or those most susceptible to stress (e.g., air traffic controllers). The hardiness concept also meshes nicely with job design. Enriched jobs are likely to fuel the hardiness components of commitment and challenge. A final application of the hardiness concept is as a diagnostic tool. Employees scoring low on hardiness would be good candidates for stress-reduction programs.

Type A Behaviour Pattern

Cardiovascular disease is the leading cause of death among adults in Western industrialized countries. Because Type A behaviour is linked to cardiovascular disease, researchers devote significant effort in identifying Type A characteristics and situations that elicit this behaviour pattern.

The **Type A behaviour pattern** is observed in any person who is aggressively involved in a chronic struggle to achieve more and more in less and less time, and if required to do so, against the opposing efforts of other things or persons. It is a socially acceptable—indeed often praised—form of conflict. Persons possessing this pattern often exhibit a free-floating but extraordinarily well-rationalized hostility.[43]

> **Type A behaviour pattern**
> Aggressively involved in a chronic, determined struggle to accomplish more in less time.

Type A individuals frequently tend to exhibit most of the behaviours listed in Table 5–2. In high-pressure, achievement-oriented schools and work environments, Type A behaviour is unwittingly cultivated and even admired.

Type A Research and Management Implications   Type A employees tend to be more productive than their Type B co-workers. On the other hand, Type A behaviour is associated with some negative consequences. Type A individuals have higher heart rates and blood pressure than Type B people. Type A people also show greater cardiovascular activity when they encounter the following situations:

1. Receipt of positive or negative feedback.

TABLE 5–2   Type A Characteristics

> 1. Hurried speech; explosive accentuation of key words.
> 2. Tendency to walk, move, and eat rapidly.
> 3. Constant impatience with the rate at which most events take place (e.g., irritation with slow-moving traffic and slow-talking and slow-to-act people).
> 4. Strong preference for thinking of or doing two or more things at once (e.g., reading this text and doing something else at the same time).
> 5. Tendency to turn conversations around to personally meaningful subjects or themes.
> 6. Tendency to interrupt while others are speaking to make your point or to complete their train of thought in your own words.
> 7. Guilt feelings during periods of relaxation or leisure time.
> 8. Tendency to be oblivious to surroundings during daily activities.
> 9. Greater concern for things worth *having* than with things worth being.
> 10. Tendency to schedule more and more in less and less time; a chronic sense of time urgency.
> 11. Feelings of competition rather than compassion when faced with another Type A person.
> 12. Development of nervous tics or characteristic gestures.
> 13. A firm belief that success is due to the ability to get things done faster than the other guy.
> 14. A tendency to view and evaluate personal activities and the activities of other people in terms of "numbers" (e.g., number of meetings attended, telephone calls made, visitors received).

Source: Adapted from M Friedman and R H Rosenman, *Type A Behavior and Your Heart* (Greenwich, CT: Fawcett Publications, 1974), pp 100–2.

2. Receipt of verbal harassment or criticism.

3. Tasks requiring mental as opposed to physical work.[44]

Unfortunately for Type A individuals, these situations are frequently experienced at work.

Do these results signal the need for Type A individuals to quit working so hard? Not necessarily. First, research indicates that feelings of anger, hostility, and aggression were more detrimental to our health than being Type A. We should all attempt to reduce these negative emotions. Second, stress-reduction techniques have been developed to help Type A people pace themselves more realistically and achieve better balance in their lives; they are discussed in the next section of this chapter. Management can help Type A people, however, by not overloading them with work despite their apparent eagerness to take an ever-increasing work load. Managers need to actively help rather than unthinkingly exploit Type A individuals.

Stress-Reduction Techniques

All told, it is estimated that almost 85% of all illness and injury is the result of lifestyle choices.[45] It is, therefore, not surprising that organizations are increasingly implementing a variety of stress-reduction programs to help employees cope with modern-day stress.

There are many different stress-reduction techniques available. The most frequently used approaches are muscle relaxation, time management, meditation, and cognitive restructuring. Each method involves somewhat different ways of coping with stress (see Table 5–3).

Muscle Relaxation

The common denominators of various muscle relaxation techniques are slow and deep breathing and a conscious effort to relieve muscle tension. Among the variety of techniques available, progressive relaxation is probably used most frequently. It consists of repeatedly tensing and relaxing muscles beginning at the feet and progressing to the face. Relaxation is achieved by concentrating on the warmth and calmness associated with relaxed muscles.

Time Management

Effective and efficient use of time is a necessity for employees and managers working in today's downsized organizations. There has never been so much pressure to do more and more in less and less time. Delegation is a key time management technique requiring the ability to follow up and provide feedback to others. A number of other time management techniques are available to reduce stress due to time pressures. Some basic rules to increase time *efficiency* include making a list of things to accomplish each day; prioritizing tasks; dividing up large projects, and celebrating "small wins" as each component is completed; setting deadlines; and working at something while waiting. Basic rules to increase time *effectiveness* include holding routine meetings at the end of the day; insisting that subordinates suggest solutions to problems; meeting visitors

Stress-Reduction Techniques   **TABLE 5–3**

Technique	Descriptions	Assessment
Muscle relaxation	Uses slow deep breathing and systematic muscle tension reduction.	Inexpensive and easy to use; may require a trained professional to implement.
Time Management	A variety of techniques are used to manage time more effectively and efficiently.	Can be learned through inexpensive time management seminars or books. Can be difficult to implement initially without coaching.
Meditation	The relaxation response is activated by redirecting one's thoughts away from oneself; a four-step procedure is used.	Least expensive, simple to implement, and can be practiced almost anywhere.
Cognitive restructuring	Irrational or maladaptive thoughts are identified and replaced with those that are rational or logical.	Expensive because it requires a trained psychologist or counselor.
Holistic wellness	A broad, interdisciplinary approach that goes beyond stress reduction by advocating that people strive for personal wellness in all aspects of their lives.	Involves inexpensive but often behaviourally difficult lifestyle changes.

in the doorway; not over-scheduling the day; and having someone else screen voice mail and E-mail.[46]

Meditation

Meditation activates a relaxation response by redirecting one's thoughts away from oneself. The **relaxation response** is the physiological and psychological opposite of the fight-or-flight stress response. Importantly, however, the relaxation

Relaxation response

State of peacefulness.

response must be learned and consciously activated, whereas the stress response is automatically engaged. Herbert Benson, a Harvard medical doctor, analyzed many meditation programs and derived a four-step relaxation response. The four steps are (1) find a *quiet environment,* (2) use a *mental device* such as a peaceful word or pleasant image to shift the mind from externally oriented thoughts, (3) disregard distracting thoughts by relying on a *passive attitude,* and (4) assume a *comfortable position*—preferably sitting erect—to avoid undue muscular tension or going to sleep. Benson emphasizes that the most important factor is a passive attitude.[47] Maximum benefits supposedly are obtained by following this procedure once or twice a day for 10 to 20 minutes, preferably just before breakfast and dinner. People following this advice experienced favourable reductions in blood pressure and anxiety levels and slept better.[48]

Cognitive Restructuring

A two-step procedure is followed. First, irrational or maladaptive thought processes that create stress are identified. For example, Type A individuals may believe they must be successful at everything they do. The second step consists of replacing these irrational thoughts with more rational or reasonable ones. Perceived failure would create stress for the Type A person. Cognitive restructuring would alleviate stress by encouraging the person to adopt a more reasonable belief about the outcomes associated with failure. For instance, the person might be encouraged to adopt the belief that isolated failure does not mean he or she is a bad person or a loser. Research has revealed that stress symptoms were reduced when people jointly used cognitive restructuring and meditation.[49]

A Holistic Wellness Model

Holistic wellness approach

Advocates personal responsibility in reducing stressors and stress.

A **holistic wellness approach** encompasses and goes beyond stress reduction by advocating that individuals strive for "a harmonious and productive balance of physical, mental, and social well-being brought about by the acceptance of one's personal responsibility for developing and adhering to a health promotion program."[50] Five dimensions of a holistic wellness approach are as follows:

1. *Self-responsibility.* Take personal responsibility for your wellness (e.g., quit smoking, moderate your intake of alcohol, wear your seat belt).

2. *Nutritional awareness.* Because we are what we eat, try to increase your consumption of foods high in fiber, vitamins, and nutrients—such as fresh fruits and vegetables, poultry, and fish—while decreasing those high in sugar and fat.

3. *Stress reduction and relaxation.* Use the techniques just discussed to relax and reduce the symptoms of stress.

Employees work on wellness at a fitness class. Companies who provide employees with wellness strategies often find they have less-stressed employees.

4. *Physical fitness.* Exercise to maintain strength, flexibility, endurance, and a healthy body weight. A recent review of employee fitness programs indicated that they were a cost-effective way to reduce medical costs, absenteeism, turnover, and occupational injuries. Fitness programs have also been positively linked with job performance and job satisfaction.[51] They are also used as recruitment incentives.

5. *Environmental sensitivity.* Be aware of your environment and try to identify the stressors that are causing your stress. A control coping strategy might be useful to eliminate stressors.

Only 17.5% of Canadian employers report that they are implementing a comprehensive wellness program, compared to 67% in the US. The primary reason for the lack of such programs in Canada is cost. However, workplace wellness programs like those in place at Telus, BC Hydro, and Magna International have been shown to decrease the direct costs of disability and absenteeism over three to five years. A 2001 study in Nova Scotia found that employers get $1.64 back for every dollar spent on wellness. Wellness is not a quick fix, and reversing poor lifestyle habits and improving organizational attitudes and practices relating to wellness is a process that requires patience and a lifelong commitment. According to Ed Buffet of the Wellness Council of Canada,

> The good news is a growing number of Canadian employers are beginning to recognize the value of healthy employees. The bad news is that they lag in execution.[52]

In conclusion, advocates say that both your personal and professional life can be enriched by adopting a holistic approach to wellness.

summary of key concepts

- *Define the term* stress. Stress is an adaptive reaction to environmental demands or stressors that triggers a fight-or-flight response. This response creates hormonal changes that mobilize the body for extraordinary demands.

- *Describe the model of occupational stress.* Perceived stress is caused by four sets of stressors: individual level, group level, organizational level, and extraorganizational. In turn, perceived stress has psychological/attitudinal, behavioural, cognitive, and physical health outcomes. Several individual differences moderate relationships among stressors, perceived stress, and outcomes.

- *Explain how stressful life events create stress.* Stressful life events are changes that disrupt an individual's lifestyle and social relationships. Uncontrollable events that are negative create the most stress.

- *Review the model of burnout, and highlight the managerial solutions to reduce it.* Burnout develops in phases. The three key phases are emotional exhaustion, depersonalization, and feeling a lack of personal accomplishment. Emotional exhaustion, the first phase, is due to a combination of personal stressors and job and organizational stressors. The additive effect of the burnout phases is a host of negative attitudinal and behavioural outcomes. Managers can reduce burnout by buffering its effects; potential buffers include extra staff or equipment, support from top management, increased freedom to make decisions, recognition for accomplishments, time off, equitable rewards, and increased communication from management. Managers can also change the content of an individual's job or assign the person to a new position. Sabbaticals and employee retreats also are used to reduce burnout.

- *Explain the mechanisms of social support.* Social support, an important moderator of relationships between stressors, stress, and outcomes, represents the amount of perceived helpfulness derived from social relationships. Cultural norms, social institutions, companies, groups, and individuals are sources of social support. These sources provide four types of support: esteem, informational, social companionship, and instrumental.

- *Discuss the personality characteristic of hardiness.* Hardiness is a collection of personality characteristics that neutralizes stress. It includes the characteristics of commitment, locus of control, and challenge. Research has demonstrated that hardy individuals respond less negatively to stressors and stress than unhardy people. Unhardy employees would be good candidates for stress-reduction programs.

- *Discuss the Type A behaviour pattern and its management implications.* The Type A behaviour pattern is characterized by someone who is aggressively involved in a chronic, determined struggle to accomplish more and more in less and less time. Type B is the opposite of Type A. Although there are several positive outcomes associated with being Type A, Type A behaviour is positively correlated with coronary heart disease. Management can help Type A individuals by not overloading them with work despite their apparent eagerness to take on an ever-increasing work load.

- *Describe the holistic wellness model.* Holistic wellness is an effort to achieve a balance of physical, mental, and social well-being. It involves taking personal responsibility for wellness, nutritional concerns, stress reduction and relaxation, physical fitness, and environmental sensitivity.

key terms

burnout, 103
control strategy, 108
coping, 107
escape strategy, 108
fight-or-flight response, 98

hardiness, 108
holistic wellness approach, 112
relaxation response, 112
social support, 106
stress, 98

stressors, 98
symptom management strategy, 108
Type A behaviour pattern, 109

discussion questions

1. What are the key stressors encountered by students? Which ones are under their control?

2. Describe the behavioural and physiological symptoms you have observed in others when they are under stress.

3. Why do uncontrollable events lead to more stress than controllable events?

4. Do you think your professors are likely to become burned out? Explain your rationale.

5. Which of the five sources of social support is most likely to provide individuals with social support? Explain.

6. How can someone increase their hardiness and reduce their Type A behaviour?

internet exercises

www.queendom.com

1. A Free Self-Assessment Questionnaire to Measure Your Coping Skills

The purpose of this exercise is to provide you with feedback on how well you cope with perceived stress. Go to the Internet home page for Body-Mind QueenDom (**www.queendom.com**), enter "Coping" in the search box, click and then select the Just-for-Fun Coping Test (www.queendom.com/tests/minitests/fx/coping.html). Read the instructions, complete all items, and click on the "score" button for automatic scoring. You will receive an overall coping skills score.

QUESTIONS

Possible scores for overall coping skills range from 0 (extremely poor coping skills) to 100 (extremely good coping skills).
1. How did you score? Are you surprised by the results?
2. Do you agree with the interpretation of your scores?
3. Based on the interpretation of your results, what can you do to improve your coping skills? How might you also reduce your level of perceived stress?

www.strengthtek.com

2. Wellness Programs—StrengthTek

StrengthTek is an organization that provides wellness programs to corporate clients. Go to the StrengthTek Web site at **www.strengthtek.com**. Click on "Corporate Programs and Services." Review their wellness programs and services and their fitness programs and services.

QUESTIONS
1. How do these programs promote a healthier work environment?
2. Which of the wellness and fitness programs offered through StrengthTek would you be interested in if your employer offered StrengthTek's programs? Why?
3. What are t'ai-chi and feng shui? Why are they offered as part of a wellness program?
4. What other fitness/wellness programs would you suggest be offered?

experiential exercises

1. The Revised Social Readjustment Rating Scale

Instructions

Place a check mark next to each event you experienced within the past year. Then add the life change units associated with the various events to derive your total life stress score.

Life Event	Life Change Unit
_____ Death of spouse/mate	87
_____ Death of close family member	79
_____ Major injury/illness to self	78
_____ Detention in jail or other institution	76
_____ Major injury/illness to close family member	72
_____ Foreclosure on loan/mortgage	71
_____ Divorce	71
_____ Being a victim of crime	70
_____ Being the victim of police brutality	69
_____ Infidelity	69
_____ Experiencing domestic violence/sexual abuse	69
_____ Separation or reconciliation with spouse/mate	66
_____ Being fired/laid-off/unemployed	64
_____ Experiencing financial problems/difficulties	62
_____ Death of close friend	61
_____ Surviving a disaster	59
_____ Becoming a single parent	59
_____ Assuming responsibility for sick or elderly loved one	56
_____ Loss of or major reduction in health insurance/benefits	56
_____ Self/close family member being arrested for violating the law	56
_____ Major disagreement over child support/custody/visitation	53
_____ Experiencing/involved in auto accident	53
_____ Being disciplined at work/demoted	53
_____ Dealing with unwanted pregnancy	51
_____ Adult child moving in with parent/parent moving in with adult child	50
_____ Child develops behaviour or learning problem	49
_____ Experiencing employment discrimination/sexual harassment	48
_____ Attempting to modify addictive behaviour of self	47
_____ Discovering/attempting to modify addictive behaviour of close family member	46
_____ Employer reorganization/downsizing	45
_____ Dealing with infertility/miscarriage	44
_____ Getting married/remarried	43
_____ Changing employers/careers	43
_____ Failure to obtain/qualify for a mortgage	42
_____ Pregnancy of self/spouse/mate	41
_____ Experiencing discrimination/harassment outside the workplace	39
_____ Release from jail	39
_____ Spouse/mate begins/ceases work outside the home	38
_____ Major disagreement with boss/co-worker	37
_____ Change in residence	35
_____ Finding appropriate child care/day care	34
_____ Experiencing a large unexpected monetary gain	33
_____ Changing positions (transfer, promotion)	33
_____ Gaining a new family member	33
_____ Changing work responsibilities	32
_____ Child leaving home	30
_____ Obtaining a home mortgage	30
_____ Obtaining a major loan other than home mortgage	30
_____ Retirement	28
_____ Beginning/ceasing formal education	26
_____ Receiving a ticket for violating the law	22

Total score _____

Interpretative Norms

Less than 150 = Odds are you will experience good health next year

150–300 = 50% chance of illness next year

Greater than 300 = 70% chance of illness next year

Source: C J Hobson, J Kamen, J Szostek, C M Nethercut, J W Tiedmann, and S Wojnarowicz, "Stressful Life Events: A Revision and Update of the Social Readjustment Rating Scale," *International Journal of Stress Management*, January 1998, pp 7–8.

2. Reducing the Stressors in Your Environment

Objectives

1. To identify the stressors in your environment.
2. To evaluate the extent to which each stressor is a source of stress.
3. To develop a plan for reducing the impact of stressors in your environment.

Introduction

Stressors are environmental factors that produce stress. They are prerequisites to experiencing the symptoms of stress. As previously discussed in this chapter, people do not appraise stressors in the same way. For instance, having to complete a challenging assignment may be motivational for one person and threatening to another. This exercise was designed to give you the opportunity to identify the stressors in your environment, to evaluate the extent to which these stressors create stress in your life, and to develop a plan for reducing the negative effects of these stressors.

Instructions

Your instructor will divide the class into groups of four to six. Once the group is assembled, the group should brainstorm and record a list of stressors that they believe exist in their environments. After recording all the brainstormed ideas on a piece of paper, remove redundancies and combine like items so that the group has a final list of unique stressors. Next, each group member should individually determine the extent to which each stressor is a source of stress in his or her life. For the purpose of this exercise, stress is defined as existing whenever you experience feelings of pressure, strain, or emotional upset. The stress evaluation is done by first indicating the frequency with which each stressor is a source of stress to you. Use the six-point rating scale provided. Once everyone has completed their individual ratings, combine the numerical judgments to compute an average stress score for each stressor. Next, identify the five stressors with the highest average stress ratings. Finally, the group should develop a plan for coping with each of these five stressors. Try to make your recommendations as specific as possible.

Rating Scale

Answer the following question for each stressor: To what extent is the stressor a source of stress?

1 = Never
2 = Rarely
3 = Occasionally
4 = Often
5 = Usually
6 = Always

QUESTIONS FOR DISCUSSION

1. Are you surprised by the type of stressors that were rated as creating the most stress in your lives? Explain.
2. Did group members tend to agree or disagree when evaluating the extent to which the various stressors created stress in their lives? What is the source of the different appraisals?
3. Did your coping plans include more forms of control or escape-oriented coping strategies? Explain.

personal awareness and growth exercises

1. Where Are You on the Type A–B Behaviour Continuum?

Instructions

For each question, indicate the extent to which each statement is true of you.

	Not at All True of Me	Neither Very True Nor Very Untrue of Me	Very True of Me
1. I hate giving up before I'm absolutely sure that I'm licked.	1 — 2 — 3 — 4 — 5		
2. Sometimes I feel that I shouldn't be working so hard, but something drives me on.		1 — 2 — 3 — 4 — 5	
3. I thrive on challenging situations. The more challenges I have, the better.		1 — 2 — 3 — 4 — 5	
4. In comparison to most people I know, I'm very involved in my work.		1 — 2 — 3 — 4 — 5	

5. It seems as if I need 30 hours a day to finish all the things I'm faced with. $1 — 2 — 3 — 4 — 5$

6. In general, I approach my work more seriously than most people I know. $1 — 2 — 3 — 4 — 5$

7. I guess there are some people who can be nonchalant about their work, but I'm not one of them. $1 — 2 — 3 — 4 — 5$

8. My achievements are considered to be significantly higher than those of most people I know. $1 — 2 — 3 — 4 — 5$

9. I've often been asked to be an officer of some group or groups. $1 — 2 — 3 — 4 — 5$

Total score = _____

Arbitrary Norms

Type B   = 9–22
Balanced Type A and Type B = 23–35
Type A   = 36–45

Source: Taken from R D Caplan, S Cobb, J R P French, Jr., R Van Harrison, and S R Pinneau, Jr., *Job Demands and Worker Health* (HEW Publication No. [NIOSH] 75-160), (Washington, DC: US Department of Health, Education, and Welfare, 1975), pp 253–54.

2. Are You Burned Out?

Objectives

1. To determine the extent to which you are burned out.
2. To determine if your burnout scores are predictive of burnout outcomes.
3. To identify specific stressors that affect your level of burnout.

Introduction

An OB researcher named Christina Maslach developed a self-report scale measuring burnout. This scale assesses burnout in terms of three phases: depersonalization, personal accomplishment, and emotional exhaustion. To determine if you suffer from burnout in any of these phases, we would like you to complete an abbreviated version of this scale. Moreover, because burnout has been found to influence a variety of behavioural outcomes, we also want to determine how well burnout predicts three important outcomes.

Instructions

To assess your level of burnout, complete the following 18 statements developed by Maslach.[53] Each item probes how frequently you experience a particular feeling or attitude. If you are currently working, use your job as the frame of reference for responding to each statement. If you are a full-time student, use your role as a student as your frame of reference. After you have completed the 18 items, refer to the scoring key and follow its directions. Remember, there are no right or wrong answers. Indicate your answer for each statement by circling one number from the following scale:

1 = A few times a year
2 = Monthly
3 = A few times a month
4 = Every week
5 = A few times a week
6 = Every day

Burnout Inventory

1. I've become more callous toward people since I took this job. $1 — 2 — 3 — 4 — 5 — 6$

2. I worry that this job is hardening me emotionally. $1 — 2 — 3 — 4 — 5 — 6$

3. I don't really care what happens to some of the people who need my help. $1 — 2 — 3 — 4 — 5 — 6$

4. I feel that people who need my help blame me for some of their problems. $1 — 2 — 3 — 4 — 5 — 6$

5. I deal very effectively with the problems of those people who need my help. $1 — 2 — 3 — 4 — 5 — 6$

6. I feel I'm positively influencing other people's lives through my work. $1 — 2 — 3 — 4 — 5 — 6$

7. I feel very energetic. $1 — 2 — 3 — 4 — 5 — 6$

8. I can easily create a relaxed atmosphere with those people who need my help. $1 — 2 — 3 — 4 — 5 — 6$

9. I feel exhilarated after working closely with those who need my help. $1 — 2 — 3 — 4 — 5 — 6$

10. I have accomplished many worthwhile things in this job. $1 — 2 — 3 — 4 — 5 — 6$

11. In my work, I deal with emotional problems very calmly.   1 — 2 — 3 — 4 — 5 — 6

12. I feel emotionally drained from my work.   1 — 2 — 3 — 4 — 5 — 6

13. I feel used up at the end of the workday.   1 — 2 — 3 — 4 — 5 — 6

14. I feel fatigued when I get up in the morning.   1 — 2 — 3 — 4 — 5 — 6

15. I feel frustrated by my job.   1 — 2 — 3 — 4 — 5 — 6

16. I feel I'm working too hard on my job.   1 — 2 — 3 — 4 — 5 — 6

17. Working with people directly puts too much stress on me.   1 — 2 — 3 — 4 — 5 — 6

18. I feel like I'm at the end of my rope.   1 — 2 — 3 — 4 — 5 — 6

Scoring

Compute the average of those items measuring each phase of burnout.

Depersonalization (questions 1–4)   _____

Personal accomplishment (questions 5–11)   _____

Emotional exhaustion (questions 12–18)   _____

Assessing Burnout Outcomes

1. How many times were you absent from work over the last three months (indicate the number of absences from classes last semester if using the student role)?

   _____ absences

2. How satisfied are you with your job (or role as a student)? Circle one.

   Very dissatisfied   Dissatisfied   Neutral   Satisfied   Very satisfied

3. Do you have trouble sleeping? Circle one.

   Yes   No

QUESTIONS FOR DISCUSSION

1. To what extent are you burned out in terms of depersonalization and emotional exhaustion?
   Low = 1–2.99; Moderate = 3–4.99; High = 5 or above

2. To what extent are you burned out in terms of personal accomplishment?
   Low = 5 or above; Moderate = 3–4.99; High = 1–2.99

3. How well do your burnout scores predict your burnout outcomes?

4. Do your burnout scores suggest that burnout follows a sequence going from depersonalization, to feeling a lack of personal accomplishment, to emotional exhaustion? Explain.

5. Which of the unique burnout stressors illustrated in Figure 5–2 are affecting your level of burnout?

CBC video case

Bank Battle

John Banca is facing one of the ultimate business-related stressors. He is running against the clock in his battle to save his company, Argord Industries, which has been in business for 15 years and employed 45 people. The TD Bank has called his loan, and only through a media crusade, the bank has agreed to grant him 12 more days to find alternate financing. In a desperate, last-ditch attempt to save his company, John tries to arrange deals with his landlord, his employees, other banks, his customers, and private investors. As time passes, and the Bank of Nova Scotia keeps delaying their response to his application for a loan, his lawyers manage to squeeze one more day from the TD Bank. Ultimately, the Bank of Nova Scotia declines to provide a loan, and John is forced to sell out entirely to a private investor, and give up his ownership of the company. John handles the stress of this 13-day roller coaster ride with grace and good humour, but the video images illustrate what a difficult experience this has been for him.

QUESTIONS FOR DISCUSSION

1. What stressors is John Banca subjected to during this 13-day ordeal?

2. What methods does he use to cope with these stressors effectively?

3. Does John appear to have a "hardy" personality? A Type A personality?

Source: Based on "Bank Battle," *CBC Venture 719* (September 21, 1999).

chapter

six

Decision Making
and Ethics

LEARNING OUTCOMES

After reading the material in this chapter, you should be able to:

- Compare and contrast the rational model of decision making and the bounded rationality model.

- Discuss the contingency model for selecting a solution.

- Explain the model of decision-making styles and the stages of the creative process.

- Explain how participative management affects performance.

- Review Vroom and Jago's decision-making model.

- Contrast brainstorming, the nominal group technique, the Delphi technique, and computer-aided decision making.

- Specify at least four actions managers can take to improve an organization's ethical climate.

ETHICS TIED TO PERFORMANCE: CONFERENCE BOARD

The more ethical an organization and its employees are, the better they'll perform, a 2001 Conference Board of Canada report suggests. Researchers found that employers with a written or understood ethical corporate culture are more efficient and have better bottom lines.

According to the report, organizations that make a public commitment to business ethics that is supported by senior management consistently outperform those that don't. Similarly, publicity about unethical corporate behaviour lowers stock prices for at least six months. As more organizations engage in discussions about the application of business ethics, this concept will become a practical tool that helps organizations improve their business operations as well as relations with their stockholders.

Many things are to blame for unethical employee behaviour, such as sales commissions that focus attention on money over ethics, increasing workloads that pressure people to get things done no matter what it takes, a fear that reporting problems to management is a sign of weakness, and a lack of enforcement of ethics rules. Some common breaches of ethics by employees are cutting corners on quality, lying to customers, falsifying numbers or reports, stealing company property, and paying or receiving bribes or inappropriate gifts.

Some organizations are trying to remedy unethical behaviour by giving employees training in areas such as harassment, discrimination, and business ethics. Experts also say it's important that top leaders push an ethics agenda, and that organizations adopt a written code of ethics and enforce it.

The Conference Board of Canada headquarters.

Source: Adapted from "Ethics Tied to Performance: Conference Board," *Workplace Today*, October 2001, p 6.

Models of Decision Making

Decision making is a means to an end. It entails identifying and choosing alternative solutions to problems. There are two fundamental models of decision making: (1) the rational model and (2) the bounded rationality model. Each is based on a different set of assumptions and offers unique insights into the decision-making process.

The Rational Model

Rational model

Logical four-step approach to decision making.

The **rational model** proposes that managers use a rational, four-step sequence when making decisions: (1) identifying the problem, (2) generating alternative solutions, (3) selecting a solution, and (4) implementing and evaluating the solution. According to this model, managers are completely objective and possess complete information to make a decision. Despite criticism for being unrealistic, the rational model is instructive because it analytically breaks down the decision-making process and serves as a conceptual anchor for newer models.[1] Let us now consider each of these four steps.

Identifying the Problem   A problem exists when the actual situation and the desired situation differ. For example, a problem exists when you have to pay rent at the end of the month and don't have enough money. Your problem is not that you have to pay rent. Your problem is obtaining the needed funds. Consider the situation faced by General Motors Corporation as it attempts to slash more than $1 billion from its annual warranty repair expenses.

> GM manufactures about 25,000 cars and trucks a day, which means little glitches can rapidly become epidemics. And behind every sick car is an unhappy customer. GM handles 22.5 million warranty claims a year, ranging from minor tweaks most customers barely notice to catastrophes such as engine failure. GM has made it a top priority for the entire company, from designers to dealers, to reduce warranty repairs with improved design and quality and early detection of problems. The goal is to eliminate some nine million claims. Detecting problems early also is critical to avoiding costly recalls like the one of about a million trucks that GM announced last month, in which it will foot the bill to fix a switch miswired during manufacturing.[2]

General Motors' problem is the amount of warranty expenses the company is incurring: The company is spending far too much on repairing cars that are under warranty. Potential causes of the problem include poor design, defective parts, and manufacturing glitches.

Generating Solutions   After identifying a problem, the next logical step is generating alternative solutions. For repetitive and routine decisions such as deciding when to send customers a bill, alternatives are readily available through decision rules. For example, a company might routinely bill customers three days after shipping a product. This is not the case for novel and unstructured decisions. Because there are no standard procedures for dealing with novel problems, managers must creatively generate alternative solutions. Managers can use a number of techniques to stimulate creativity.

Selecting a Solution   According to the rational model, decision makers want to optimize the outcome by choosing the alternative with the greatest value, such as highest profit or lowest cost. This is no easy task. First, assigning values to alternatives is complicated and prone to error. Not only are values subjective, but they also vary according to the preferences of the decision maker. Further, evaluating alternatives assumes they can be judged according to some standards or criteria such as quality, cost, or profit. This further assumes that (1) valid criteria exist, (2) each alternative can be compared against these criteria, and (3) the decision maker actually uses the criteria. These assumptions are frequently violated.

Implementing and Evaluating the Solution   Once a solution is chosen, it needs to be implemented. After the solution is implemented, the evaluation phase assesses its effectiveness. If the solution is effective, it should reduce the difference between the actual and desired states that created the problem. If the gap is not closed, the implementation was not successful, and one of the following is true: Either the problem was incorrectly identified, or the solution was inappropriate.

Summarizing the Rational Model   The rational model is based on the premise that managers optimize when they make decisions. **Optimizing** involves solving problems by producing the best possible solution. As noted by Herbert Simon, a decision theorist who in 1978 earned the Nobel Prize for his work on decision making, "The assumptions of perfect rationality are contrary to fact. It is not a question of approximation; they do not even remotely describe the processes that human beings use for making decisions in complex situations."[3] Thus, the rational model is at best an instructional tool. Since decision makers do not follow these rational procedures, Simon proposed a bounded rationality model of decision making.

> **Optimizing**
>
> Choosing the best possible solution.

Bounded Rationality Model

This model attempts to identify the process that managers actually use when making decisions. The process is guided by a decision maker's bounded rationality. **Bounded rationality** represents the notion that decision makers are "bounded" or restricted by a variety of constraints when making decisions. These constraints include any personal or environmental characteristics that reduce rational decision making. Examples are the limited capacity of the human mind, problem complexity and uncertainty, amount and timeliness of information at hand, criticality of the decision, and time demands.[4]

> **Bounded rationality**
>
> Constraints that restrict decision making.

As opposed to the rational model, the bounded rationality model suggests that decision making is characterized by (1) limited information processing, (2) the use of judgmental heuristics, and (3) satisficing. Each of these characteristics is now explored.

Limited Information Processing   Managers are limited by how much information they process because of bounded rationality. This results in the tendency to acquire manageable rather than optimal amounts of information. In turn, this practice makes it difficult for managers to identify all possible alternative solutions. In the long run, the constraints of bounded rationality cause decision makers to fail to evaluate all potential alternatives.

Judgmental Heuristics   **Judgmental heuristics** represent rules of thumb or shortcuts that people use to reduce information processing demands.[5] We automatically use them without conscious awareness. The use of heuristics helps decision makers to reduce the uncertainty inherent within the decision-making process. Because these shortcuts represent

> **Judgmental heuristics**
>
> Rules of thumb or shortcuts that people use to reduce information-processing demands.

This driver is satisficing with a temporary spare tire.

Availability heuristic

Tendency to base decisions on information readily available in memory.

Representativeness heuristic

Tendency to assess the likelihood of an event occurring based on impressions about similar occurrences.

knowledge gained from past experience, they can help decision makers evaluate current problems. But they also can lead to systematic errors that erode the quality of decisions. There are two common categories of heuristics that are important to consider: the availability heuristic and the representativeness heuristic.

The **availability heuristic** represents a decision maker's tendency to base decisions on information that is readily available in memory.[6] Information is more accessible in memory when it involves an event that recently occurred, when it is salient (e.g., a plane crash), and when it evokes strong emotions (e.g., innocent people being killed). This heuristic is likely to cause people to overestimate the occurrence of unlikely events such as a plane crash or a high school shooting. This bias also is partially responsible for the recency effect discussed in Chapter 2. For example, a manager is more likely to give an employee a positive performance evaluation if the employee exhibited excellent performance over the last few months.

The **representativeness heuristic** is used when people estimate the probability of an event occurring. It reflects the tendency to assess the likelihood of an event occurring based on one's impressions about similar occurrences. A manager, for example, may hire a graduate from a particular university because the past three people hired from this university turned out to be good performers. In this case, the "school attended" criterion is used to facilitate complex information processing associated with employment interviews. Unfortunately, this shortcut can result in a biased decision. Similarly, an individual may believe that he or she can master a new software package in a short period of time because he or she was able to learn how to use a different type of software. This estimate may or may not be accurate. For example, it may take the individual a much longer period of time to learn the new software because it requires learning a new programming language.

Satisficing People do not always select the optimal solution because they do not have the time, information, or ability to handle the complexity associated with following a rational process. This is not necessarily undesirable. **Satisficing** consists of choosing a solution that meets some minimum qualifications, one that is "good enough." Satisficing resolves problems by producing solutions that are satisfactory, as opposed to optimal. Finding a radio station to listen to in your car is a good example of satisficing. You cannot optimize because it is impossible to listen to all stations at the same time in order to choose the best one. You thus stop searching for a station when you find one playing a song you like or do not mind hearing.

Satisficing

Choosing a solution that meets a minimum standard of acceptance.

Dynamics of Decision Making

Decision making is part science and part art. Accordingly, this section examines four dynamics of decision making—contingency considerations, decision-making styles, escalation of commitment, and creativity—that affect the "science" component. An understanding of these dynamics can help managers make better decisions.

Selecting Solutions: A Contingency Perspective

The previous discussion of decision-making models noted that managers typically satisfice when they select solutions. However, we did not probe how managers actually

A Contingency Model for Selecting a Solution   **FIGURE 6–1**

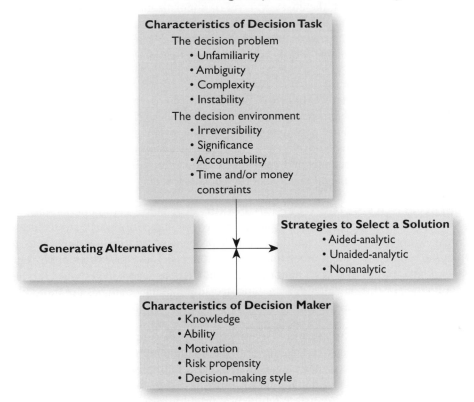

Characteristics of Decision Task
The decision problem
• Unfamiliarity
• Ambiguity
• Complexity
• Instability
The decision environment
• Irreversibility
• Significance
• Accountability
• Time and/or money
   constraints

Generating Alternatives

Strategies to Select a Solution
• Aided-analytic
• Unaided-analytic
• Nonanalytic

Characteristics of Decision Maker
• Knowledge
• Ability
• Motivation
• Risk propensity
• Decision-making style

Source: Based on L R Beach and T R Mitchell, "A Contingency Model for the Selection of Decision Strategies," *Academy of Management Review*, July 1978, pp 439–44.

evaluate and select solutions. Let us explore the model in Figure 6–1 to better understand how individuals make decisions.

Strategies for Selecting a Solution   What procedures do decision makers use to evaluate the costs and benefits of alternative solutions? One of three approaches is used: aided-analytic, unaided-analytic, and nonanalytic. Decision makers systematically use tools such as mathematical equations, calculators, or computers to analyze and evaluate alternatives within an **aided-analytic decision making** approach. Weather forecasters, astronomers, and insurance analysts are good examples of people who make their decisions by using an aided-analytic strategy. These types of professionals tend to make decisions by analyzing data with complex computer models.[7]

In contrast, decision makers rely on the confines of their minds when using an **unaided-analytic decision making** strategy. In other words, the decision maker systematically compares alternatives, but the analysis is limited to evaluating information that can be directly processed in his or her head. Decision-making tools such as a personal computer are not used. Chess masters and counselors use this strategy in the course of their work. Finally, a **nonanalytic decision making** strategy consists of using a simple preformulated rule to make a decision. Examples are flipping a coin, habit, normal convention ("we've always done it that way"), using a con-

Aided-analytic decision making

Using tools to make decisions.

Unaided-analytic decision making

Analysis is limited to processing information in one's mind.

Nonanalytic decision making

Using preformulated rules to make decisions.

servative approach ("better safe than sorry"), or following procedures offered in instruction manuals. Both the cost and level of sophistication decrease as one moves from an aided-analytic to a nonanalytic decision making strategy.

Determining which approach to use depends on two sets of contingency factors: characteristics of the decision task and characteristics of the decision maker (refer again to Figure 6–1).

Characteristics of the Decision Task
This set of contingency factors reflects the demands and constraints a decision maker faces. These characteristics are divided into two components: those pertaining to the specific problem, such as its complexity, and those related to the general decision environment, such as time constraints. In general, the greater the demands and constraints encountered by a decision maker, the higher the probability that an aided-analytic decision making approach will be used.[8]

Characteristics of the Decision Maker
Chapter 2 highlighted a variety of individual differences that affect employee behaviour and performance. In the present context, knowledge, ability, motivation, risk propensity, and decision-making style affect the type of analytical procedure used by a decision maker. For example, entrepreneurs take more risks when making decisions than managers in general.[9] Research supports the conclusion that aided-analytic decision making strategies are more likely to be used by competent and motivated individuals.[10]

Contingency Relationships
There are many ways in which characteristics of the decision task and decision maker can interact to influence the strategy used to select a solution. In choosing a strategy, decision makers compromise between their desire to make correct decisions and the amount of time and effort they put into the decision-making process. Table 6–1 lists contingency relationships that help reconcile these

TABLE 6–1   Contingency Relationships in Decision Making

1. Analytic strategies are used when the decision problem is unfamiliar, ambiguous, complex, or unstable.
2. Nonanalytic methods are employed when the problem is familiar, straightforward, or stable.
3. Assuming there are no monetary or time constraints, analytic approaches are used when the solution is irreversible and significant and when the decision maker is accountable.
4. Nonanalytic strategies are used when the decision can be reversed and is not very significant or when the decision maker is not held accountable.
5. As the probability of making a correct decision goes down, analytic strategies are used.
6. As the probability of making a correct decision goes up, nonanalytic strategies are employed.
7. Time and money constraints automatically exclude some strategies from being used.
8. Analytic strategies are more frequently used by experienced and educated decision makers.
9. Nonanalytic approaches are used when the decision maker lacks knowledge, ability, or motivation to make a good decision.

Source: Adapted from L R Beach and T R Mitchell, "A Contingency Model for the Selection of Decision Strategies," *Academy of Management Review*, July 1978, pp 439–44.

competing demands. As shown in this table, analytic strategies are more likely to be used when the problem is unfamiliar and irreversible. In contrast, nonanalytic methods are employed on familiar problems or problems in which the decision can be reversed.

Personal Decision-Making Styles

A personal decision-making style is based on the idea that styles vary along two different dimensions: value orientation and tolerance for ambiguity.[11] *Value orientation* reflects the extent to which an individual focuses on either task and technical concerns or people and social concerns when making decisions. The second dimension pertains to a person's *tolerance for ambiguity*. This individual difference indicates the extent to which a person has a high need for structure or control in his or her life. When the dimensions of value orientation and tolerance for ambiguity are combined, they form four styles of decision making (see Figure 6–2): directive, analytical, conceptual, and behavioural.

Directive   People with a directive style have a low tolerance for ambiguity and are oriented toward task and technical concerns when making decisions. They are efficient, logical, practical, and systematic in their approach to solving problems. People with this style are action oriented and decisive and like to focus on facts. In their pursuit of speed and results, however, these individuals tend to be autocratic, exercise power and control, and focus on the short run.

Analytical   This style has a much higher tolerance for ambiguity and is characterized by the tendency to overanalyze a situation. People with this style like to consider more information and alternatives than do directives. Analytic individuals are careful decision makers who take longer to make decisions but who also respond well to new or uncertain situations. They can often be autocratic.

Conceptual   People with a conceptual style have a high tolerance for ambiguity and tend to focus on the people or social aspects of a work situation. They take a broad perspective to problem solving and like to consider many options and future possibilities. Conceptual types adopt a long-term perspective and rely on intuition and discus-

Decision-Making Styles   **FIGURE 6–2**

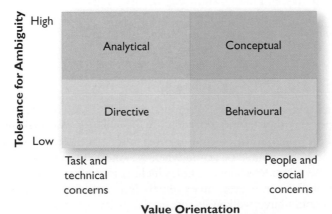

Source: Based on discussion contained in A J Rowe and R O Mason, *Managing with Style: A Guide to Understanding, Assessing, and Improving Decision Making* (San Francisco: Jossey-Bass, 1987), pp 1–17.

ETHICS AT WORK

He Likes to Watch

The decision to hire or not to hire a job applicant has taken on a new dimension in this age of violence and terror in the workplace. Employers are increasingly hiring private investigators to check out prospective new employees in order to avoid serious problems down the road. Toronto-based private investigation firm King-Reed & Associates assists employers in this task by conducting background checks, including reviewing court documents, performing media searches, rooting through people's garbage and sometimes even going so far as to follow people and videotape their activities.

But just how thorough is too thorough? Do you really want your prospective employer to know about your family, your university hijinks, perhaps even your lunch-hour sex habits?

You Decide . . .

Is it ethical for employers to use private investigators to explore the background of job applicants? How much information is too much when deciding whether to hire a prospective new employee? Would people with a directive decision-making style be more comfortable with an extensive investigation than those with other styles?

Source: R Robin, "He Likes to Watch," *Canadian Business*, September 3, 2001, pp 39–41.

sions with others to acquire information. They also are willing to take risks and are good at finding creative solutions to problems. On the downside, however, a conceptual style can foster an idealistic and indecisive approach to decision making.

Behavioural   People with this style work well with others and enjoy social interactions in which opinions are openly exchanged. Behavioural types are supportive, receptive to suggestions, show warmth, and prefer verbal to written information. Although they like to hold meetings, people with this style have a tendency to avoid conflict and to be too concerned about others. This can lead behavioural types to adopt a "wishy-washy" approach to decision making and to have a hard time saying no to others and to have difficulty making difficult decisions.

Research and Practical Implications   Research shows that very few people have only one dominant decision-making style. Rather, most managers have characteristics that fall into two or three styles. Studies also show that decision-making styles vary across occupations, job level, and countries.[12] You can use knowledge of decision-making styles in three ways. First, knowledge of styles helps you to understand yourself. Awareness of your style assists you in identifying your strengths and weaknesses as a decision maker and facilitates the potential for self-improvement. Second, you can increase your ability to influence others by being aware of styles. For example, if you are dealing with an analytical person, you should provide as much information as possible to support your ideas. This same approach is more likely to frustrate a directive type. Finally, knowledge of styles gives you an awareness of how people can take the same information and yet arrive at different decisions by using a variety of decision-making strategies. It is important to conclude with the reminder that there is no best decision-making style that applies in all situations.

Escalation of Commitment

Escalation situations involve circumstances in which things have gone wrong but where the situation can possibly be turned around by investing additional time, money, or effort. **Escalation of commitment** refers to the tendency to stick to an ineffective course of action when it is unlikely that the bad situation can be reversed. Personal examples include investing more money into an old or broken car, waiting an extremely long time for a bus to take you somewhere that you could have walked just as easily, or trying to save a disruptive interpersonal relationship that has lasted 10 years. For example, planners promised to build

Escalation of commitment

Sticking to an ineffective course of action for too long.

a high-speed subway loop under the city of Tokyo in record time and at a substantial profit. In reality, the multi-billion dollar project was several years overdue, far over budget, and is not expected to be profitable until 2040 at the earliest.[13]

Four reasons for escalation of commitment have been identified. They involve psychological and social determinants, organizational determinants, project characteristics, and contextual determinants.[14]

Psychological and Social Determinants   Ego defence and individual motivations are the key psychological contributors to escalation of commitment. Individuals "throw good money after bad" because they tend to (1) bias facts so that they support previous decisions, (2) take more risks when a decision is stated in negative terms (to recover losses) rather than positive ones (to achieve gains), and (3) get too ego-involved with the project. Because failure threatens an individual's self-esteem or ego, people tend to ignore negative signs and push forward.

Social pressures can make it difficult for a manager to reverse a course of action. For instance, peer pressure makes it difficult for an individual to drop a course of action when he or she publicly supported it in the past. Further, managers may continue to support bad decisions because they don't want their mistakes exposed to others.

Organizational Determinants   Breakdowns in communication, workplace politics, and organizational inertia cause organizations to maintain bad courses of action.

Project Characteristics   Project characteristics involve the objective features of a project. They have the greatest impact on escalation decisions. For example, because most projects do not reap benefits until some delayed time period, decision makers are motivated to stay with the project until the end.[15] Thus, there is a tendency to attribute setbacks to temporary causes that are correctable with additional expenditures. Moreover, escalation is related to whether the project has clearly defined goals and whether people receive clear feedback about performance.

Contextual Determinants   These causes of escalation are due to forces outside an organization's control. For instance, a recent study showed that a manager's national culture influenced the amount of escalation in decision making. A study of decision makers in Mexico and the United States revealed that Mexican managers exhibited more escalation than US managers.[16] External political forces also represent a contextual determinant.

Reducing Escalation of Commitment   It is important to reduce escalation of commitment because it leads to poor decision making for both individuals and groups. Recommendations to reduce escalation of commitment include:

- Set minimum targets for performance, and have decision makers compare their performance with these targets.
- Have different individuals make the initial and subsequent decisions about a project.
- Encourage decision makers to become less ego-involved with a project.
- Provide more frequent feedback about project completion and costs.
- Reduce the risk or penalties of failure.
- Make decision makers aware of the costs of persistence.

Creativity

In light of today's need for fast-paced decisions, an organization's ability to stimulate the creativity and innovation of its employees is becoming increasingly important. Although many definitions have been proposed, **creativity** is defined here as the process of using intelligence, imagination, and skill to develop a new or novel product, object, process, or thought.[17] It can be as simple as locating a new place to hang your car keys or as complex as developing a pocket-size microcomputer. There are three broad types of creativity. One can create something new (creation), one can combine or synthesize things (synthesis), or one can improve or change things (modification).

> **Creativity**
>
> Process of developing something new or unique.

Researchers are not absolutely certain how creativity takes place. Nonetheless, they do know that creativity involves "making remote associations" between unconnected events, ideas, information stored in memory, or physical objects. Consider how remote associations led to a creative idea that ultimately increased revenue for Japan Railways (JR) East, the largest rail carrier in the world:

> While JR East was building a new bullet-train line, water began to cause problems in the tunnel being dug through Mount Tanigawa. As engineers drew up plans to drain it away, some of the workers had found a use for the water—they were drinking it. A maintenance worker, whose job was to check the safety of the tunneling equipment, thought it tasted so good that he proposed that JR East should bottle and market it as premium mineral water. This past year, "Oshimizu" water generated some $60 million of sales for JR East.[18]

The maintenance worker obviously associated the tunnel water with bottled water, and this led to the idea of marketing the water as a commercial product. Researchers, however, have identified five stages underlying the creative process: preparation, concentration, incubation, illumination, and verification. Let us consider these stages.

Creativity is an active, not passive, process.

The *preparation* stage reflects the notion that creativity starts from a base of knowledge. Experts suggest that creativity involves a convergence between tacit or implied knowledge and explicit knowledge. During the *concentration* stage, an individual focuses on the problem at hand. Interestingly, Japanese companies are noted for encouraging this stage as part of a quality improvement process more than North American companies. For example, the average number of suggestions per employee for improving quality and productivity is significantly lower in the typical North American company than in comparable Japanese firms.[19]

Incubation is done unconsciously. During this stage, people engage in daily activities while their minds simultaneously mull over information and make remote associations. These associations ultimately are generated in the *illumination* stage. Finally, *verification* entails going through the entire process to verify, modify, or try out the new idea.

Creativity can be hard to elicit from today's time-challenged, stressed-out employees. A survey of Canadian marketing and advertising executives found that tight deadlines are the number one enemy of employee creativity.[20] But some organizations are taking the need for creativity seriously. In response to the ongoing need for change at mbanx, the virtual bank associated with the Bank of Montreal, the "Brainwaves" Cen-

Matsushita Electric Creates Breadmaker by Combining Tacit and Explicit Knowledge

In Japan, Matsushita Electric used to be known as *maneshita*, which means, "copycat." They were big and successful but not an innovator. That changed dramatically with the introduction of the Home Bakery, the first automatic breadmaker. A software engineer, a woman named Tanaka, recognized that with Westernization, the time had come for a breadmaker in Japan. But she knew almost nothing about baking. So she apprenticed herself to a master baker. He had all the knowledge in his fingertips, but it was very hard for him to verbalize. After watching him for two or three weeks, she went back to Matsushita to write up a set of specifications for the machine, translating his tacit knowledge into something explicit.

They made a prototype, but the bread tasted terrible. So Tanaka-san brought a group of her peers to observe the baker again. Finally, they realized what the machine lacked was the twisting motion the baker used when kneading his dough. Incorporating that understanding enabled them to develop a hugely successful product.

The breadmaker changed the corporate culture at Matsushita. People in other divisions said, "Why can't we do that?"

Source: S Sherman, "Hot Products from Hot Tubs or How Middle Managers Innovate," *Fortune*, April 29, 1996, pp 165–66. © 1996 TIME Inc. All rights reserved.

tre for Creativity and Innovation was established. The bank recognized that the management of continual change demands innovation, creativity, and continual idea generation. David Hardy, senior manager responsible for "Brainwaves" says, "All individuals have the capacity to be creative." He nurtures creativity by promoting divergent thinking, which involves suspending judgment and exploring new ideas.[21]

Group Decision Making

This section explores issues associated with group decision making. Specifically, we discuss (1) advantages and disadvantages of group-aided decision making, (2) participative management, (3) when to use groups in decision making, and (4) group problem-solving techniques.

Advantages and Disadvantages of Group-Aided Decision Making

Including groups in the decision-making process has both pros and cons (see Table 6–2). On the positive side, groups contain a greater pool of knowledge, provide more varied perspectives, create more comprehension of decisions, increase decision acceptance, and create a training ground for inexperienced employees. These advantages must be balanced, however, with the disadvantages listed in Table 6–2. In doing so, managers need to determine the extent to which the advantages and disadvantages apply to the decision situation. The following three guidelines may then be applied to help decide whether groups should be included in the decision-making process:

I. If additional information would increase the quality of the decision, managers should involve those people who can provide the needed information.

TABLE 6–2   Advantages and Disadvantages of Group-Aided Decision Making

Advantages	Disadvantages
1. *Greater pool of knowledge.* A group can bring much more information and experience to bear on a decision or problem than can an individual acting alone.	1. *Social pressure.* Unwillingness to "rock the boat" and pressure to conform may combine to stifle the creativity of individual contributors.
2. *Different perspectives.* Individuals with varied experience and interests help the group see decision situations and problems from different angles.	2. *Domination by a vocal few.* Sometimes the quality of group action is reduced when the group gives in to those who talk the loudest and longest.
3. *Greater comprehension.* Those who personally experience the give-and-take of group discussion about alternative courses of action tend to understand the rationale behind the final decision.	3. *Logrolling.* Political wheeling and dealing can displace sound thinking when an individual's pet project or vested interest is at stake.
4. *Increased acceptance.* Those who play an active role in group decision making and problem solving tend to view the outcome as "ours" rather than "theirs."	4. *Goal displacement.* Sometimes secondary considerations such as winning an argument, making a point, or getting back at a rival displace the primary task of making a sound decision or solving a problem.
5. *Training ground.* Less experienced participants in group action learn how to cope with group dynamics by actually being involved.	5. *"Groupthink."* Sometimes cohesive "in groups" let the desire for unanimity override sound judgment when generating and evaluating alternative courses of action.

Source: R Kreitner, *Management,* 7th ed (Boston: Houghton Mifflin, 1998), p 234.

2. If acceptance is important, managers need to involve those individuals whose acceptance and commitment are important.

3. If people can be developed through their participation, managers may want to involve those whose development is most important.[22]

Groupthink

A cohesive group's unwillingness to realistically view alternatives.

Groupthink occurs when members of a cohesive group strive for unanimity to the extent that it overrides their motivation to realistically appropriate alternative courses of action. It is characterized by a deterioration of mental efficiency, reality testing, and moral judgment that results from group pressures.[23] Members of groups victimized by groupthink tend to be friendly and tightly knit.

There are eight classic symptoms of groupthink. The greater the number of symptoms, the greater the probability of groupthink:

1. *Invulnerability.* An illusion that breeds excessive optimism and risk taking.

2. *Inherent morality.* A belief that encourages the group to ignore ethical implications.

3. *Rationalization.* Protects pet assumptions.

4. *Stereotyped view of opposition.* Causes group to underestimate opponents.

5. *Self-censorship.* Stifles critical debate.

6. *Illusion of unanimity.* Silence interpreted to mean consent.

7. *Peer pressure* Loyalty of dissenters is questioned.

8. *Mindguards.* Self-appointed protectors against adverse information.[24]

These symptoms thrive in the sort of climate often found inside corporate boards of directors. Many directors simply don't want to rock the boat by raising hard questions that create embarrassment or discomfort for management. They want to maintain friendly relations with others on the board.[25]

In short, policy- and decision-making groups can become so cohesive that strong-willed executives are able to gain unanimous support for poor decisions.[26] A number of suggestions on how to prevent groupthink have been proposed, as follows:[27]

1. Each member of the group should be assigned the role of critical evaluator. This role involves actively voicing objections and doubts.

2. Top-level executives should not use policy commitment to rubber-stamp decisions that have already been made.

3. Different groups with different leaders should explore the same policy questions.

4. Subgroup debates and outside experts should be used to introduce fresh perspectives.

5. Someone should be given the role of devil's advocate when discussing major alternatives. This person tries to uncover every conceivable negative factor.

6. Once a consensus has been reached, everyone should be encouraged to rethink their position to check for flaws.

Group versus Individual Performance   Before recommending that managers involve groups in decision making, it is important to examine whether groups perform better or worse than individuals. After reviewing 61 years of relevant research, a decision-making expert concluded that "Group performance was generally qualitatively and quantitatively superior to the performance of the average individual."[28] Although subsequent research of small-group decision making generally supported this conclusion, additional research suggests that managers should use a contingency approach when determining whether to include others in the decision-making process. Let us now consider these contingency recommendations.

Practical Contingency Recommendations   If the decision occurs frequently, such as deciding on promotions or who qualifies for a loan, use groups because they tend to produce more consistent decisions than do individuals. Given time constraints, let the most competent individual, rather than a group, make the decision. In the face of environmental threats such as time pressure and the potentially serious effects of a decision, groups use less information and fewer communication channels. This increases the probability of a bad decision.[29] This conclusion underscores a general recommendation that managers should keep in mind: Because the quality of communication strongly affects a group's productivity, on complex tasks it is essential to devise mechanisms to enhance communication effectiveness.

Participative Management

An organization needs to maximize its workers' potential if it wants to successfully compete in the global economy. Participative management and employee empowerment are highly touted methods for meeting this productivity challenge. Interestingly, employees also seem to desire or recognize the need for participative management.

Participative management

Involving employees in various forms of decision making.

Confusion exists about the exact meaning of participative management (PM).[30] One management expert clarified this situation by defining **participative management** as the process whereby employees play a direct role in (1) setting goals, (2) making decisions, (3) solving problems, and (4) making changes in the organization. Without question, participative management entails much more than simply asking employees for their ideas or opinions.

Advocates of PM claim employee participation increases employee satisfaction, commitment, and performance. Consistent with both Maslow's need theory and the job characteristics model of job design (see Chapter 3), participative management can increase motivation because it helps employees fulfil three basic needs: (1) autonomy, (2) meaningfulness of work, and (3) interpersonal contact. Satisfaction of these needs enhances feelings of acceptance and commitment, security, challenge, and satisfaction. In turn, these positive feelings can lead to increased innovation and performance.[31]

Participative management does not work in all situations. The design of work, the level of trust between management and employees, and the employees' competence and readiness to participate represent three factors that influence the effectiveness of PM. With respect to the design of work, individual participation is counterproductive when employees are highly interdependent on each other, as on an assembly line. The problem with individual participation in this case is that interdependent employees generally do not have a broad understanding of the entire production process. Participative management also is less likely to succeed when employees do not trust management. Finally, PM is more effective when employees are competent, prepared, and interested in participating.[32]

Research and Practical Suggestions for Managers   Participative management can significantly increase employee job involvement, organizational commitment, creativity, and perceptions of procedural justice and personal control.[33] PM has also been found to have a small but significant effect on job performance and a moderate relationship with job satisfaction.[34] This finding questions the widespread conclusion that participative management should be used to increase employee performance.

So what is a manager to do? PM is not a quick-fix solution for low productivity and motivation, as some enthusiastic supporters claim. Nonetheless, because participative management is effective in certain situations, managers can increase their chances of obtaining positive results by using a contingency approach. For example, the effectiveness of participation depends on the type of interactions between managers and employees as they jointly solve problems. Effective participation requires a constructive interaction that fosters cooperation and respect, as opposed to competition and defensiveness. Managers are advised not to use participative programs when they have destructive interpersonal interactions with their employees.

When to Have Groups Participate in Decision Making: The Vroom/Yetton/Jago Model

A model developed by Victor Vroom and Philip Yetton (later expanded by Vroom and Arthur Jago) helps managers determine the degree of group involvement in the decision-making process.[35] The model specifies decision-making styles that should be effective in different situations.

The model is represented as a decision tree. The manager's task is to move from left to right along the various branches of the tree. A specific decision-making style is prescribed at the end point of each branch. Before we apply the model, however, it is necessary to consider the different decision styles managers ultimately choose from and an approach for diagnosing the problem situation.

Five Decision-Making Styles   Five distinct decision-making styles were identified as shown in Table 6–3. The first letter indicates the basic thrust of the style. A stands for *autocratic,* C for *consultive,* and G for *group.* Style choice depends on the type of problem situation.

Matching the Situation to Decision-Making Style   Eight problem attributes are used by managers to diagnose a situation. They are shown at the top of the decision tree presented in Figure 6–3 and are expressed as questions. Answers to these questions lead managers along different branches, pointing the way to potentially effective decision-making styles.

To use the model in Figure 6–3, start at the left side and move toward the right by asking and answering the questions associated with each decision point (represented by a box in the figure) encountered. A decision-making style is prescribed at the end of each branch.

Let us track a simple example through Figure 6–3. Suppose a manager has to determine the work schedule for a group of part-time workers who report to him or her. The first question is "How important is the technical quality of this decision?" It seems rather low. This leads us to the second question: "How important is subordinate commitment to the decision?" Assuming acceptance is important, this takes us along the branch leading to the question about commitment probability (CP). If the manager were to make the decision him- or herself, is it reasonably certain that the subordinate(s) would be committed to the decision? A yes answer suggests using an AI decision-making style (see Table 6–3) and a GII style if the answer was no.

Management Decision Styles **TABLE 6–3**

AI	You solve the problem or make the decision yourself, using information available to you at that time.
AII	You obtain the necessary information from your subordinate(s), then decide on the solution to the problem yourself. You may or may not tell your subordinates what the problem is in getting the information from them. The role played by your subordinates in making the decision is clearly one of providing the necessary information to you rather than generating or evaluating solutions.
CI	You share the problem with relevant subordinates individually, getting their ideas and suggestions without bringing them together as a group. Then you make the decision that may or may not reflect your subordinates' influence.
CII	You share the problem with your subordinates as a group, collectively obtaining their ideas and suggestions. Then you make the decision that may or may not reflect your subordinates' influence.
GII	You share a problem with your subordinates as a group. Together you generate and evaluate alternatives and attempt to reach agreement (consensus) on a solution. Your role is much like that of a chairman. You do not try to influence the group to adopt "your" solution, and you are willing to accept and implement any solution that has the support of the entire group.

Source: "A New Look at Managerial Decision Making" by V H Vroom. Reprinted from *Organizational Dynamics,* Spring 1973, p 67, © 1973 American Management Association International. Reprinted by permission of American Management Association International, New York, NY. All rights reserved. www.amanet.org.

FIGURE 6–3   Vroom and Jago's Decision-Making Model

QR	Quality Requirement	How important is the technical quality of this decision?
CR	Commitment Requirement	How important is subordinate commitment to the decision?
LI	Leader's Information	Do you have sufficient information to make a high-quality decision?
ST	Problem Structure	Is the problem well structured?
CP	Commitment Probability	If you were to make the decision by yourself, is it reasonably certain that your subordinate(s) would be committed to the decision?
GC	Goal Congruence	Do subordinates share the organizational goals to be attained in solving this problem?
CO	Subordinate Conflict	Is conflict among subordinates over preferred solutions likely?
SI	Subordinate Information	Do subordinates have sufficient information to make a high-quality decision?

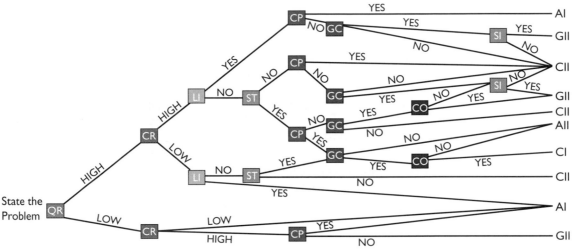

Source: Reprinted from *The New Leadership: Managing Participation in Organizations* by Victor H Vroom and Arthur G Jago, 1988, Englewood Cliffs, NJ: Prentice Hall. © 1987 by V H Vroom and A G Jago. Used with permission of the authors.

Group Problem-Solving Techniques

Consensus

Presenting opinions and gaining agreement to support a decision.

Using groups to make decisions generally requires that they reach a consensus. A **consensus** is reached when all members either agree with the decision or have expressed their opinion and were unable to convince the others of their viewpoint, and have agreed to support the outcome."[36] This definition indicates that consensus does not require unanimous agreement because group members may still disagree with the final decision but are willing to work toward its success.

Groups can experience roadblocks when trying to arrive at a consensus decision. For one, groups may not generate all relevant alternatives to a problem because an individual dominates or intimidates other group members; because of shyness on the part of other members, or because of satisficing due to time and information constraints. In order to successfully achieve consensus: Groups should use active listening skills, involve as many members as possible, seek out the reasons behind arguments, and dig for the facts. At the same time, groups should not horse trade (I'll support you on this decision because you supported me on the last one), or agree just to avoid "rocking the boat." Voting is not encouraged because it can split the group into winners and losers.[37]

Decision-making experts have developed three group problem-solving techniques—brainstorming, the nominal group technique, and the Delphi technique—to reduce the above roadblocks. Knowledge of these techniques can help current and future managers to more effectively use group-aided decision making. Further, the advent of computer-aided decision making enables managers to use these techniques to solve complex problems with large groups of people.

Brainstorming   **Brainstorming** is used to help groups generate multiple ideas and alternatives for solving problems. This technique is effective because it helps reduce interference caused by critical and judgmental reactions to one's ideas from other group members.

> **Brainstorming**
>
> Process to generate a quantity of ideas.

When brainstorming, a group is convened, and the problem at hand is reviewed. Individual members then are asked to silently generate ideas/alternatives for solving the problem. Silent idea generation is recommended over the practice of having group members randomly shout out their ideas because it leads to a greater number of unique ideas. Next, these ideas/alternatives are solicited and written on a board or flip chart. Finally, a second session is used to critique and evaluate the alternatives. Managers are advised to follow four rules for brainstorming:[38]

1. *Stress quantity over quality.* Managers should try to generate and write down as many ideas as possible. Encouraging quantity encourages people to think beyond their favourite ideas.

2. *Freewheeling should be encouraged; do not set limits.* Group members are advised to offer any and all ideas they have. The wilder and more outrageous, the better.

3. *Suspend judgment.* Don't criticize during the initial stage of idea generation. Phrases such as "we've never done it that way," "it won't work," "it's too expensive," and "the boss will never agree" should not be used.

4. *Ignore seniority.* People are reluctant to freewheel when they are trying to impress the boss or when their ideas are politically motivated. The facilitator

Successful brainstorming relies on nonjudgmental collection of as many ideas as possible to foster later discussion and evaluation.

of a brainstorming session should emphasize that everyone has the same rank. No one is given "veto power" when brainstorming.

Brainstorming is an effective technique for generating new ideas/alternatives. It is not appropriate for evaluating alternatives or selecting solutions.

Nominal group technique

Process to generate ideas and evaluate and select solutions.

The Nominal Group Technique   The **nominal group technique** (NGT) helps groups generate ideas and evaluate and select solutions. NGT is a structured group meeting that follows this format:[39] A group is convened to discuss a particular problem or issue. After the problem is understood, individuals silently generate ideas in writing. Each individual, in round-robin fashion, then offers one idea from his or her list. Ideas are recorded on a blackboard or flip chart; they are not discussed at this stage of the process. Once all ideas are elicited, the group discusses them. Anyone may criticize or defend any item. During this step, clarification is provided as well as general agreement or disagreement with the idea. Finally, group members anonymously vote for their top choices with a weighted voting procedure (e.g., 1st choice = 3 points; 2nd choice = 2 points; 3rd choice = 1 point). The group leader then adds the votes to determine the group's choice. Prior to making a final decision, the group may decide to discuss the top ranked items and conduct a second round of voting.

The nominal group technique reduces the roadblocks to group decision making by (1) separating brainstorming from evaluation, (2) promoting balanced participation among group members, and (3) incorporating mathematical voting techniques in order to reach consensus.

Delphi technique

Process to generate ideas from physically dispersed experts.

The Delphi Technique   The **Delphi technique** is a group process that anonymously generates ideas or judgments from physically dispersed experts.[40] Unlike the NGT, experts' ideas are obtained from questionnaires or via the Internet as opposed to face-to-face group discussions.

A manager begins the Delphi process by identifying the issue(s) he or she wants to investigate. For example, a manager might want to inquire about customers' future preferences, or the effect of locating a plant in a certain region of the country. Next, participants are identified and a questionnaire is developed. The questionnaire is sent to participants and returned to the manager. In today's computer-networked environments, this often means that the questionnaires are E-mailed to participants. The manager then summarizes the responses and sends feedback to the participants. At this stage, participants are asked to (1) review the feedback, (2) prioritize the issues being considered, and (3) return the survey within a specified time period. This cycle repeats until the manager obtains the necessary information.

The Delphi technique is useful when face-to-face discussions are impractical, when disagreements and conflict are likely to impair communication, when certain individuals might severely dominate group discussion, and when groupthink is a probable outcome of the group process.[41]

Computer-Aided Decision Making   The purpose of computer-aided decision making is to reduce consensus roadblocks while collecting more information in a shorter period of time. There are two types of computer-aided decision making systems: chauffeur driven and group driven.[42] Chauffeur-driven systems ask participants to answer predetermined questions on electronic keypads or dials. Live television audiences on shows such as "Who Wants to Be a Millionaire" and "Whose Line Is It Anyway?" are frequently polled with this system. The computer system tabulates participants' responses in a matter of seconds.

Group-driven electronic meetings are conducted in one of two major ways. First, managers can use E-mail or the Internet to collect information or brainstorm about a decision that must be made. The second method uses special facilities equipped with individual workstations that are networked to each other. Instead of talking, participants type their input, ideas, comments, reactions, or evaluations on their keyboards. The input simultaneously appears on a large projector screen at the front of the room, thereby enabling all participants to see all input. This computer-driven process reduces consensus roadblocks because input is anonymous, everyone gets a chance to contribute, and no one can dominate the process. Research demonstrated that computer-aided decision making produced greater quality and quantity of ideas than either traditional brainstorming or the nominal group technique for both small and large groups of people.[43]

Fostering Ethical Organizational Behaviour

The issue of ethics and ethical behaviour is receiving greater attention today, partly because of reported cases of questionable or potentially unethical behaviour and the associated costs. **Ethics** involves the study of moral issues and choices. It is concerned with right versus wrong, good versus bad, and the many shades of gray in supposedly black-and-white issues. Moral implications spring from virtually every decision, both on and off the job. Managers are challenged to have more imagination and the courage to do the right thing. Any discussion of ethics entails a consideration of the motives and goals of those involved.

Ethics

Study of moral issues and choices.

A Model of Ethical Behaviour

Ethical and unethical conduct is the product of a complex combination of influences (see Figure 6–4). At the centre of the model in Figure 6–4 is the individual decision maker. He or she has a unique combination of personality characteristics, values, and moral principles, leaning toward or away from ethical behaviour. Personal experience with being rewarded or reinforced for certain behaviours and punished for others also shapes the individual's tendency to act ethically or unethically.

Next, Figure 6–4 illustrates three major sources of influence on one's role expectations. People play many roles in life, including those of employee or manager. One's expectations for how those roles should be played are shaped by cultural, organizational, and general environmental factors.

Focusing on one troublesome source of organizational influence, many studies have found a tendency among middle- and lower-level managers to act unethically in the face of perceived pressure for results. By fostering a pressure-cooker atmosphere for results, managers can unwittingly set the stage for unethical shortcuts by employees who seek to please and be loyal to the company. In contrast, consider how the organizational culture at Timberland reinforces and encourages employees to engage in socially responsible behaviours:

> Everyone gets paid for 40 hours a year of volunteer work. On Timberland's 25th anniversary, the whole place shut down so that employees could work on community projects. One employee describes the event as a "religious experience."[44]

This example also highlights that an organization's reward system can influence ethical behaviour. Individuals are more likely to behave ethically/unethically when they are

FIGURE 6–4   A Model of Ethical Behaviour in the Workplace

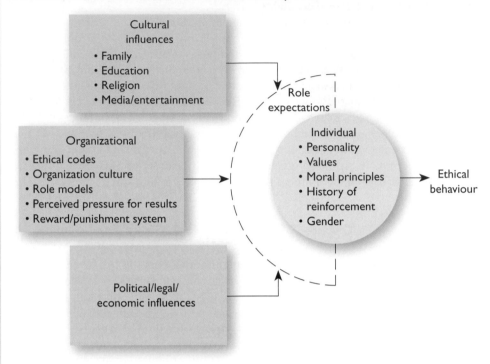

motivated to do so through incentives.[45] Managers are encouraged to examine their reward systems to ensure that the preferred types of behaviour are being reinforced.

How to Improve the Organization's Ethical Climate

A team of management researchers recommended the following actions for improving on-the-job ethics.[46]

- *Behave ethically yourself.* Managers are potent role models whose habits and actual behaviour send clear signals about the importance of ethical conduct. Ethical behaviour is a top-to-bottom proposition.

- *Screen potential employees.* Surprisingly, employers are generally lax when it comes to checking references, credentials, transcripts, and other information on applicant resumes. More diligent action in this area can screen out those given to fraud and misrepresentation. Integrity testing is fairly valid but is no panacea.[47]

- *Develop a meaningful code of ethics.* Codes of ethics can have a positive effect if they satisfy these four criteria:

  1. They are distributed to every employee.
  2. They are firmly supported by top management.
  3. They refer to specific practices and ethical dilemmas likely to be encountered by target employees (e.g., salespersons paying kickbacks, purchasing agents receiving payoffs, laboratory scientists doctoring data, or accountants "cooking the books").
  4. They are evenly enforced with rewards for compliance and strict penalties for noncompliance.

Do Moral Principles Vary by Gender?

There is considerable evidence that men and women consistently choose alternative solutions to the same moral problems or dilemmas. The reason why is not so clear. Past research has suggested that men and women differ in terms of how they conceive moral problems. Males perceived moral problems in terms of a justice perspective, while women relied on a care perspective. The male (justice) perspective draws attention to problems of inequality and oppression and holds up an ideal of reciprocal rights and equal respect for individuals. The female (care) perspective draws attention to problems of detachment or abandonment and holds up an ideal of attention and response to need. Two moral injunctions—not to treat others unfairly and not to turn away from someone in need—capture these different concerns. Thus men were expected to view moral problems in terms of rights, whereas women were predicted to conceptualize moral problems as an issue of care involving empathy and compassion.

However, the results of a recent "meta-analysis" (which combined the results of 113 prior studies) did not support the expectation that the care perspective would be used predominantly by females and the justice orientation predominantly by males. The authors concluded, "although distinct moral orientations may exist, these orientations are not strongly associated with gender." This conclusion suggests that further research is needed to identify the source of moral reasoning differences between men and women.

Sources: Adapted from L M Dawson, "Women and Men, Morality, and Ethics," *Business Horizons*, July-August 1995, pp 61–68; C Gilligan and J Attanucci, "Two Moral Orientations: Gender Differences and Similarities," *Merril-Palmer Quarterly*, July 1988, pp 223–37; and S Jaffee and J Hyde, "Gender Differences in Moral Orientation: A Meta-Analysis," *Psychological Bulletin*, September 2000, pp 703–26.

- *Provide ethics training.* Employees can be trained to identify and deal with ethical issues during orientation and through seminar and video training sessions.
- *Reinforce ethical behaviour.* Behaviour that is reinforced tends to be repeated, whereas behaviour that is not reinforced tends to disappear. Ethical conduct too often is punished while unethical behaviour is rewarded.
- *Create specific positions in the organization to deal with ethics.* Ethics need to be managed every day, not just a one-time announcement of a new ethical code that gets filed away and forgotten.

summary of key concepts

- *Compare and contrast the rational model of decision making and the bounded rationality model.* The rational decision-making model consists of identifying the problem, generating alternative solutions, evaluating and selecting a solution, and implementing and evaluating the solution. Research indicates that decision makers do not follow the series of steps outlined in the rational model.

  The bounded rationality model is guided by a decision maker's bounded rationality. Bounded rationality means that decision makers are bounded or restricted by a variety of constraints when making decisions. The normative model suggests that decision making is characterized by (a) limited information processing, (b) the use of judgmental heuristics, and (c) satisficing.

- *Discuss the contingency model for selecting a solution.* Decision makers use either an aided-analytic, unaided-analytic, or non-analytic strategy when selecting a solution. The choice of a strategy depends on the characteristics of the decision task and the characteristics of the decision maker. In general, the greater the demands and constraints faced by a decision maker, the higher the probability that an aided-analytic approach will be used. Aided-analytic strategies are more likely to be used by competent and motivated individuals. Ultimately, decision makers compromise between their desire to make correct decisions and the amount of time and effort they put into the decision-making process.

- *Explain the model of decision-making styles and the stages of the creative process.* The model of decision-making styles is based on the idea that styles vary along two different dimensions: value orientation and tolerance for ambiguity. When these two dimensions are combined, they form four styles of decision making: directive, analytical, conceptual, and behavioural. People with a directive style have a low tolerance for ambiguity and are oriented toward task and technical concerns. Analytics have a higher tolerance for ambiguity and are characterized by a tendency to overanalyze a situation. People with a conceptual style have a high threshold for ambiguity and tend to focus on people or social aspects of a work situation. This behavioural style is the most people oriented of the four styles.

  Creativity is defined as the process of using intelligence, imagination, and skill to develop a new or novel product, object, process, or thought. There are five stages of the creative process: preparation, concentration, incubation, illumination, and verification.

- *Explain how participative management affects performance.* Participative management reflects the extent to which employees participate in setting goals, making decisions, solving problems, and making changes in the organization. Participative management is expected to increase motivation because it helps employees fulfill three basic needs: (a) autonomy, (b) meaningfulness of work, and (c) interpersonal contact. Participative management does not work in all situations. The design of work and the level of trust between management and employees influence the effectiveness of participative management.

- *Review Vroom, Yetton, and Jago's decision-making model.* Vroom, Yetton, and Jago developed a model to help managers determine the extent to which they should include groups in the decision-making process. Through the use of decision trees, the model identifies appropriate decision-making styles for various types of managerial problems. The styles range from autocratic to highly participative.

- *Contrast brainstorming, the nominal group technique, the Delphi technique, and computer-aided decision making.* Group problem-solving techniques facilitate better decision making within groups. Brainstorming is used to help groups generate multiple ideas and alternatives for solving problems. The nominal group technique assists groups both to generate ideas and to evaluate and select solutions. The Delphi technique is a group process that anonymously generates ideas or judgments from physically dispersed experts. The purpose of computer-aided decision making is to reduce consensus roadblocks while collecting more information in a shorter period of time.

- *Specify at least four actions managers can take to improve an organization's ethical climate.* They can do so by (a) behaving ethically themselves, (b) screening potential employees, (c) developing a code of ethics, (d) providing ethics training, (e) reinforcing and rewarding ethical behaviour, and (f) creating specific positions within the organization to deal with ethics.

key terms

aided-analytic decision making, 125	escalation of commitment, 128	participative management, 134
availability heuristic, 124	ethics, 139	rational model, 122
bounded rationality, 123	groupthink, 132	representativeness heuristic, 124
brainstorming, 137	judgmental heuristics, 123	satisficing, 124
consensus, 136	nominal group technique, 138	unaided-analytic decision making, 125
creativity, 130	nonanalytic decision making, 125	
Delphi technique, 138	optimizing, 123	

discussion questions

1. Do you think people are, in general, rational when they make decisions? Under what circumstances would an individual tend to follow a rational process? Under what circumstances would bounded rationality likely occur?

2. Describe a situation in which you satisficed when making a decision. Why did you satisfice instead of optimize?

3. Why could decision-making styles be a source of interpersonal conflict?

4. Describe a situation in which you exhibited escalation of commitment. Why did you escalate a losing situation?

5. Given the intuitive appeal of participative management, why do you think it fails as often as it succeeds? Explain.

6. Which particular source of influence on the left hand side of Figure 6–4 do you think has had the greatest impact on your ethical behaviour? Explain.

internet exercises

www.brainstorming.co.uk

1. Creative Brainstorming

There are countless brainstorming sessions conducted by individuals and groups within organizations on a daily basis. We do not expect this trend to stop. To help you successfully facilitate and participate in a brainstorming session, this chapter provided a set of guidelines for conducting a brainstorming session. We did not, however, discuss different techniques that can be used to enhance individual and group creativity while brainstorming. The purpose of this exercise is for you to learn two techniques that can be used to enhance creative idea generation and to complete two creativity puzzles.

Begin the exercise by going to the following Internet site: **www.brainstorming.co.uk**. Then select their home page. Once at the home page, click on the option for "training on creative techniques." After a brief discussion about creativity, you will be given the option to learn more about a variety of different techniques that can be used to enhance creativity.

Choose any two techniques and then answer questions 1 and 2 below.

Now return to the home page, and select the option for creativity puzzles. Follow the instructions and attempt to complete two puzzles. Don't peek ahead to see the answers until you have tried to finish the activity. Based on your experience with these creativity puzzles, answer questions 3 and 4.

QUESTIONS

1. How might you use these techniques in a class project?
2. Should different techniques be used in different situations? Explain.
3. Why do these puzzles help people to think outside of the box?
4. How might these puzzles be used during a brainstorming session?

2. Exploring Codes of Conduct

Visit the Web site for the Canadian Centre for Ethics and Corporate Policy (**www.ethicscentre.com**) and click on "Links," then "Codes of Conduct." Choose "International Code of Ethics for Canadian Business," and review the vision, beliefs, values and principles contained in this code of ethics proposed by the Human Rights Research and Education Centre at the University of Ottawa.

QUESTIONS

1. The concept of avoiding bribery and corruption is mentioned in both the values and the principles. How realistic is this in a global economy? Why or why not?
2. Does the belief that wealth generation for stakeholders and a fair sharing of economic benefits can be achieved simultaneously seem realistic? Why or why not?
3. The vision, values, and principles all make reference to environmental protection. In what ways might this priority conflict with valuing wealth maximization for stakeholders? Is there some way to reconcile these beliefs?

experiential exercises

1. Applying the Vroom/Yetton/Jago Decision-Making Model

Introduction

Vroom and Jago extended an earlier model by Vroom and Yetton to help managers determine the extent to which they should include groups in the decision-making process. To enhance your understanding of this model, we would like you to use it to analyze a brief case. You will be asked to read the case and use the information to determine an appropriate decision-making style. This will enable you to compare your solution with that recommended by Vroom and Jago. Their analysis is presented in endnote 48 and you will be instructed when to examine it for feedback.

Instructions

Your instructor will divide the class into groups of four to six. Once the group is assembled, each member should read the case presented. It depicts a situation faced by the manufacturing manager of an electronics plant. The group should then use Vroom and Jago's model (refer to Figure 6–3 and Table 6–3) to arrive at a solution. At this point, it might be helpful for the group to reread the material that explains how to apply the model. Keep in mind that you move toward a solution by asking yourself the questions (at the top of Figure 6–3) associated with each relevant decision point. After the group completes its analysis, compare your solution with the one offered by Vroom and Jago.

LEADERSHIP CASE

You are a manufacturing manager in a large electronics plant. The company's management has recently installed new machines and put in a new simplified work system, but to the surprise of everyone, yourself included, the expected increase in productivity was not realized. In fact, production has begun to drop, quality has fallen off, and the number of employee separations has risen.

You do not believe that there is anything wrong with the machines. You have had reports from other companies that are using them, and they confirm this opinion. You have also had representatives from the firm that built the machines go over them, and they report that they are operating at peak efficiency.

You suspect that some parts of the new work system may be responsible for the change, but this view is not widely shared among your immediate subordinates, who are four first-line supervisors, each in charge of a section, and your supply manager. The drop in production has been variously attributed to poor training of the operators, lack of an adequate system of financial incentives, and poor morale. Clearly, this is an issue about which there is considerable depth of feeling within individuals and potential disagreement among your subordinates.

This morning you received a phone call from your division manager. He had just received your production figures for the last six months and was calling to express his concern. He indicated that the problem was yours to solve in any way that you think best, but that he would like to know within a week what steps you plan to take.

You share your division manager's concern with the falling productivity and know that your [people] are also concerned. The problem is to decide what steps to take to rectify the situation.

QUESTIONS FOR DISCUSSION

1. What decision-making style from Table 6–3 do you recommend?

2. Did you arrive at the same solution as Vroom and Jago (their analysis is presented in endnote 48)? If not, what do you think caused the difference?

3. Based on this experience, what problems would a manager encounter in trying to apply this model?

2. Investigating the Difference in Moral Reasoning between Men and Women

Objectives

1. To determine if men and women resolve moral/ethical problems differently.
2. To determine if males and females use a justice and care perspective, respectively, to solve moral/ethical problems.
3. To improve your understanding about the moral reasoning used by men and women.

Introduction

Men and women view moral problems and situations dissimilarly. This is one reason men and women solve identical moral or ethical problems differently. Researchers believe that men rely on a justice perspective to solve moral problems whereas women are expected to use a care perspective. This exercise presents two scenarios that possess a moral/ethical issue. You will be asked to solve each problem and to discuss the logic behind your decision. The exercise provides you with the opportunity to hear the thought processes used by men and women to solve moral/ethical problems.

Instructions

Your instructor will divide the class into groups of four to six. (An interesting option is to use gender-based groups.) Each group member should first read the scenario alone and then make a decision about what to do. Once this is done, use the space provided to outline the rationale for your decision to this scenario. Next, read the second scenario and follow the same procedure: Make a decision and explain your rationale. Once all group members have completed their analyses for both scenarios, meet as a group to discuss the results. One at a time, each group member should present his or her final decision and the associated reasoning for the first scenario. Someone should keep a running tally of the decisions so that a summary can be turned in to the professor at the end of your discussion. Follow the same procedure for the second scenario.

Scenario 1

You are the manager of a local toy store. The hottest Christmas toy of the year is the new "Peter Panda" stuffed animal. The toy is in great demand and almost impossible to find. You have received your one and only shipment of 12, and they are all promised to people who previously stopped in to place a deposit and reserve one. A woman comes by the store and pleads with you, saying that her six-year-old daughter is in the hospital very ill, and that "Peter Panda" is the one toy she has her heart set on. Would you sell her one, knowing that you will have to break your promise and refund the deposit to one of the other customers? (There is no way you will be able to get an extra toy in time.)

Your Decision: _____

	Would Sell	Would Not Sell	Unsure
Men			
Women			

Rationale for Your Decision:

Scenario 2

You sell corporate financial products, such as pension plans and group health insurance. You are currently negotiating with Paul Scott, treasurer of a *Fortune* 500 firm, for a sale that could be in the millions of dollars. You feel you are in a strong position to make the sale, but two competitors are also negotiating with Scott, and it could go either way. You have become friendly with Scott, and over lunch one day he confided in you that he has recently been under treatment for manic depression. It so happens that in your office there is a staff psychologist who does employee counseling. The thought has occurred to you that such a trained professional might be able to coach you on how to act with and relate to a personality such as Scott's, so as to persuade and influence him most effectively. Would you consult the psychologist?

Your Decision: _____

	Would Consult	Would Not Consult	Unsure
Men			
Women			

Rationale for Your Decision:

QUESTIONS FOR DISCUSSION

1. Did males and females make different decisions in response to both scenarios? (Comparative norms can be found in endnote 49.)

2. What was the moral reasoning used by women and men to solve the two scenarios?

3. To what extent did males and females use a justice and care perspective, respectively?

4. What useful lessons did you learn from this exercise?

personal awareness and growth exercises

1. What Is Your Decision-Making Style?

Instructions

This survey consists of 20 questions, each with four responses. You must consider each possible response for a question and then rank them according to how much you prefer each response. Because many of the questions are anchored to how individuals make decisions at work, you can feel free to use your student role as a frame of reference to answer the questions. For each question, use the space on the survey to rank the four responses with either a 1, 2, 4, or 8. Use the number 8 for the responses that are **most** like you, a 4 for those that are **moderately** like you, a 2 for those that are **slightly** like you, and a 1 for the responses that are **least** like you. For example, a question could be answered [8], [4], [2], [1]. Do not repeat any number when answering a question, and place the numbers in the boxes next to each of the answers. Once all of the responses for the 20 questions have been ranked, total the scores in each of the four columns. The total score for column one represents your directive style, column two your analytical style, column three your conceptual style, and column four your behavioural style.

1. My prime objective in life is to:	have a position with status	be the best in whatever I do	be recognized for my work	feel secure in my job
2. I enjoy work that:	is clear and well defined	is varied and challenging	lets me act independently	involves people
3. I expect people to be:	productive	capable	committed	responsive
4. My work lets me:	get things done	find workable approaches	apply new ideas	be truly satisfied
5. I communicate best by:	talking with others	putting things in writing	being open with others	having a group meeting
6. My planning focuses on:	current problems	how best to meet goals	future opportunities	needs of people in the organization
7. I prefer to solve problems by:	applying rules	using careful analysis	being creative	relying on my feelings
8. I prefer information:	that is simple and direct	that is complete	that is broad and informative	that is easily understood
9. When I'm not sure what to do:	I rely on my intuition	I search for alternatives	I try to find a compromise	I avoid making a decision
10. Whenever possible, I avoid:	long debates	incomplete work	technical problems	conflict with others
11. I am really good at:	remembering details	finding answers	seeing many options	working with people
12. When time is important, I:	decide and act quickly	apply proven approaches	look for what will work	refuse to be pressured
13. In social settings, I:	speak with many people	observe what others are doing	contribute to the conversation	want to be part of the discussion
14. I always remember:	people's names	places I have been	people's faces	people's personalities
15. I prefer jobs where I:	receive high rewards	have challenging assignments	can reach my personal goals	am accepted by the group
16. I work best with people who:	are energetic and ambitious	are very competent	are open minded	are polite and understanding
17. When I am under stress, I:	speak quickly	try to concentrate on the problem	become frustrated	worry about what I should do
18. Others consider me:	aggressive	disciplined	imaginative	supportive
19. My decisions are generally:	realistic and direct	systematic and logical	broad and flexible	sensitive to the other's needs
20. I dislike:	losing control	boring work	following rules	being rejected

Total score _____

Source: © Alan J. Rowe, Professor Emeritus. Revised 12/18/98. Reprinted by permission.

QUESTIONS FOR DISCUSSION

1. How do your scores compare with the following norms: directive (75), analytical (90), conceptual (80), and behavioural (55)?

2. What do the differences between your scores and the survey norms suggest about your decision-making style?

2. Measuring Your Creative Personality

Purpose

This self-assessment exercise is designed to help you measure the extent to which you have a creative personality.

Instructions

Listed below is a checklist with 30 adjectives that may or may not describe you. Put a mark in the boxes beside the words that you think accurately describe you. *Do not* mark the boxes beside words that do not describe you. When finished, you can score the test using the scoring key in endnote 50 to this chapter. This exercise is completed alone so that students can assess themselves without concerns of social comparison. However, class discussion will focus on how this scale might be applied in organizations, and the limitations of measuring creativity in work settings.

Adjective Checklist

Affected ☐	Honest ☐	Reflective ☐
Capable ☐	Humourous ☐	Resourceful ☐
Cautious ☐	Individualistic ☐	Self-confident ☐
Clever ☐	Informal ☐	Sexy ☐
Commonplace ☐	Insightful ☐	Sincere ☐
Confident ☐	Intelligent ☐	Snobbish ☐
Conservative ☐	Inventive ☐	Submissive ☐
Conventional ☐	Mannerly ☐	Suspicious ☐
Dissatisfied ☐	Narrow interests ☐	Unconventional ☐
Egotistical ☐	Original ☐	Wide interests ☐

Source: Adapted from and based on information in H G Gough and A B Heilbrun, Jr., *The Adjective Check List Manual*, Palo Alto, Calif.: Consulting Psychologists Press, 1965; and H G Gough, "A Creative Personality Scale for the Adjective Check List," *Journal of Personality and Social Psychology*, 37(8) (August 1979), pp 1398–1405.

CBC video case

Showdown on the Virtual Frontier

E-commerce and the law—it's a massive gray area. In most cases, there are no laws yet written to govern new technologies powering businesses on the Web. For example, if a company uses downloaded images from Disney on its Web site, do they need permission? One letter requesting permission was sent but no reply was received—maybe Disney isn't sure either! If a company tracks the behaviour of individual consumers online and then uses that information to create targeted ads, is that legal? When does advertising stop and invasion of privacy begin? If hackers interrupt a Web site's business activity, whom do customers sue?

So what's a budding dot-com business to do? Well, they can hire one of the few Internet lawyers around (at up to $630 per hour) who mostly advise that there is little actual law

to go on, and just a few court cases for guidance. Some say entrepreneurs just skip the legal issues entirely, deciding to "let liability fall where it may," and get on with running their business.

QUESTIONS FOR DISCUSSION

1. Is it ethical to ignore Internet law, even though there is very little of it?

2. Explain how these Internet companies exhibit bounded rationality in their decision making.

3. What would you do about legal issues if you were starting up an Internet business?

Source: Based on "Showdown On the Virtual Frontier," *CBC Venture 745* (August 15, 2000).

chapter

seven

Groups and Teamwork

LEARNING OUTCOMES

After reading the material in this chapter, you should be able to:

- Describe the five stages of Tuckman's theory of group development.

- Distinguish between role overload, role conflict, and role ambiguity.

- Contrast roles and norms, and specify four reasons norms are enforced in organizations.

- Explain how a work group becomes a team.

- List at least four things managers can do to build trust.

- Describe self-managed teams and virtual teams.

- Describe social loafing and explain how managers can prevent it.

- Describe high performance teams.

TEAMS MAKE IT HAPPEN IN ONTARIO GOVERNMENTS

Team effort is transforming the way government does work. Teams are focusing on customer needs, collaboratively looking for solutions to problems, using data to make decisions, and data to measure outcomes. The Ontario Public Service (OPS) established a service quality standard in 1998 to respond in writing to any correspondence within 15 working days from date of receipt. When initially asked to meet this standard, the Ministry of Transportation (MTO) was unable to do so. In response to this challenge, a project team was created which included a large variety of MTO staff ranging from Assistant Deputy Ministers and Directors to staff from across the organization. The team developed an automated tool that provided the ability to monitor correspondence turnaround time for the Minister, Deputy Minister, Assistant Deputy Ministers, and Directors. After only five months of implementation, average turnaround time for Ministers' correspondence had plummeted from 36.24 days to 9.45 days.

Ontario Government groups use teamwork to collaboratively solve problems and find more efficient solutions.

The Regional Municipality of Peel had a big problem: what to do with the Britannia Sanitary Landfill Site as scheduled closing dates arrived. To resolve community issues, an innovative idea of creating an executive-length golf course on closed portions of the site was initiated. The course, officially opened in 1999, exemplifies the true spirit and result of what a dedicated team can achieve. The Landfill Team was presented with the coveted CAO Teamwork Award, reinforcing the Region's core belief that, "Together We Are Better."

Source: M Strus, "Teams Make it Happen in Ontario Governments," *Excellence*, May 2002, pp 9–10.

Fundamentals of Group Behaviour

Drawing from the field of sociology, a **group** is defined as two or more freely interacting individuals who share collective norms and goals and have a common identity.[1] Organizational psychologist Edgar Schein shed additional light on this concept by drawing instructive distinctions between a group, a crowd, and an organization:

> **Group**
>
> Two or more freely interacting people with shared norms and goals and a common identity.

The size of a group is thus limited by the possibilities of mutual interaction and mutual awareness. Mere aggregates of people do not fit this definition because they do not interact and do not perceive themselves to be a group even if they are aware of each other as, for instance, a crowd on a street corner watching some event. A total department, a union, or a whole organization would not be a group in spite of thinking of themselves as "we," because they generally do not all interact and are not all aware of each other. However, work teams, committees, subparts of departments, cliques, and various other informal associations among organizational members would fit this definition of a group.[2]

Take a moment now to think of various groups of which you are a member. Does each of your "groups" satisfy the four criteria in our definition?

Formal and Informal Groups

Individuals join groups, or are assigned to groups, to accomplish various purposes. If the group is formed by a manager to help the organization accomplish its goals, then it qualifies as a formal group. Formal groups typically wear such labels as work group, team, committee, or task force. Formal groups fulfil two basic functions: *organizational* and *individual*.[3] The various functions are listed in Table 7–1. Complex combinations of these functions can be found in formal groups at any given time.

An informal group exists when the members' overriding purpose of getting together is friendship or common interest.[4] Although formal and informal groups often overlap, such as a team of corporate auditors heading for the tennis courts after work, some employees are not friends with their co-workers. The desirability of overlapping formal and informal groups is problematic. Some managers firmly believe personal friendship fosters productive teamwork on the job while others view workplace "bull sessions" as a serious threat to productivity. Both situations are common, and it is the manager's job to strike a workable balance, based on the maturity and goals of the people involved.

TABLE 7–1   Formal Groups Fulfil Organizational and Individual Functions

Organizational Functions	Individual Functions
1. Accomplish complex, interdependent tasks that are beyond the capabilities of individuals.	1. Satisfy the individual's need for affiliation.
2. Generate new or creative ideas and solutions.	2. Develop, enhance, and confirm the individual's self-esteem and sense of identity.
3. Coordinate interdepartmental efforts.	3. Give individuals an opportunity to test and share their perceptions of social reality.
4. Provide a problem-solving mechanism for complex problems requiring varied information and assessments.	4. Reduce the individual's anxieties and feelings of insecurity and powerlessness.
5. Implement complex decisions.	5. Provide a problem-solving mechanism for personal and interpersonal problems.
6. Socialize and train newcomers.	

Source: Adapted from E H Schein, *Organizational Psychology*, 3rd ed (Englewood Cliffs. NJ: Prentice-Hall, 1980), pp 149–51.

The Group Development Process

Groups and teams in the workplace go through a maturation process, such as one would find in any life-cycle situation (e.g., humans, organizations, products). While there is general agreement among theorists that the group development process occurs in identifiable stages, they disagree about the exact number, sequence, length, and nature of those stages.[5] The five-stage model in Figure 7–1 indicates how individuals give up a measure of their independence when they join and participate in a group.[6] The various stages are not necessarily of the same duration or intensity. For instance, the storming stage may be practically nonexistent or painfully long, depending on the goal clarity and the commitment and maturity of the members. This process come to life when one relates the various stages to personal experiences with work groups, committees, athletic teams, social or religious groups, or class project teams. Some group happenings that were surprising when they occurred may now make sense or seem inevitable when seen as part of a natural development process.

Stage 1: Forming   During this "ice-breaking" stage, group members tend to be uncertain and anxious about such things as their roles, who is in charge, and the group's goals. Mutual trust is low, and there is a good deal of holding back to see who takes charge and how. If the formal leader (e.g., a supervisor) does not assert his or her authority, an emergent leader will eventually step in to fulfil the group's need

Five-Stage Model of Group Development   **FIGURE 7–1**

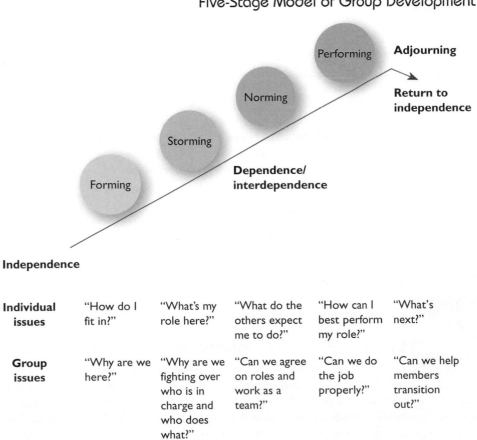

Individual issues	"How do I fit in?"	"What's my role here?"	"What do the others expect me to do?"	"How can I best perform my role?"	"What's next?"
Group issues	"Why are we here?"	"Why are we fighting over who is in charge and who does what?"	"Can we agree on roles and work as a team?"	"Can we do the job properly?"	"Can we help members transition out?"

Group cohesiveness or a "we feeling" can help groups develop through the norming stage like this group from Herman Miller who, when faced with a problem, pulled together to find a solution.

for leadership and direction. Leaders typically mistake this honeymoon period as a mandate for permanent control. But later problems may force a leadership change.

Stage 2: Storming   This is a time of testing. Individuals test the leader's policies and assumptions as they try to determine how they fit into the power structure.[7] Subgroups take shape, and subtle forms of rebellion, such as procrastination, occur. Many groups stall in stage 2 because power politics erupts into open rebellion.

Stage 3: Norming   Groups that make it through stage 2 generally do so because a respected member, other than the leader, challenges the group to resolve its power struggles so something can be accomplished. Questions about authority and power are resolved through unemotional, matter-of-fact group discussion. A feeling of team spirit is experienced because members believe they have found their proper roles.

Group cohesiveness, defined as the "we feeling" that binds members of a group together, is the principal by-product of stage 3.[8] Cohesiveness has a small but significant effect on performance, especially in small groups. Commitment to the task at hand has the most powerful impact on this link between cohesiveness and performance. Thus organizations are advised to ensure that performance standards and goals are clear and accepted, and to keep task groups small (no more than five members) unless there is a need for creativity, in which case the optimal group size would be somewhat larger.[9] Also, it must be remembered that too much cohesiveness creates the possibility of groupthink, as discussed in Chapter 6.

Group cohesiveness

A "we feeling" binding group members together.

Stage 4: Performing   Activity during this vital stage is focused on solving task problems. As members of a mature group, contributors get their work done without hampering others. There is a climate of open communication, strong cooperation, and lots of helping behaviour. Conflicts and job boundary disputes are handled constructively and efficiently. Cohesiveness and personal commitment to group goals help the group achieve more than could any one individual acting alone.

Stage 5: Adjourning   The work is done; it is time to move on to other things. Having worked so hard to get along and get something done, many members feel a compelling sense of loss. The return to independence can be eased by rituals celebrating "the end" and "new beginnings." Parties, award ceremonies, graduations, or mock funerals can provide the needed punctuation at the end of a significant group project. Leaders need to emphasize valuable lessons learned in group dynamics to prepare everyone for future group and team efforts.

Group Member Roles

Role

Expected behaviours for a given position.

Role overload

Other people's expectations of someone exceed that individual's ability.

Roles are sets of behaviours that persons expect of occupants of a position.[10] **Role overload** occurs when the total of what is expected from someone exceeds what he or she is able to do. Students who attempt to handle a full course load and maintain a social life while working 30 or more hours a week know full well the consequences of role overload. As the individual tries to do more and more in less and less time, stress mounts and personal effectiveness slips.

Sometimes people feel like they are being torn apart by the conflicting demands of those around them. **Role conflict** is experienced when different people expect different things from one person. For example, employees often face conflicting demands between work and family.[11]

Role ambiguity occurs when an individual does not know what is expected of them. New employees often complain about unclear job descriptions and vague promotion criteria. Prolonged role ambiguity can foster job dissatisfaction, erode self-confidence, and hamper job performance.

Task versus Maintenance Roles

As described in Table 7–2, both task and maintenance roles need to be performed if a work group is to accomplish anything.[12] **Task roles** enable the work group to define, clarify, and pursue a common purpose. Meanwhile, **maintenance roles** foster supportive and constructive interpersonal relationships. In short, task roles keep the group *on track* while maintenance roles keep the group *together*. A project team member is performing a task function when he or she says at an update meeting, "What is the real issue here? We don't seem to be getting anywhere." Another individual who

Role conflict
Other people have conflicting or inconsistent expectations of someone.

Role ambiguity
An individual does not know what is expected of them.

Task role
Task-oriented group behaviour.

Maintenance role
Relationship-building group behaviour.

Task and Maintenance Roles   **TABLE 7–2**

Task Roles	Description
Initiator	Suggests new goals or ideas.
Information seeker/giver	Clarifies key issues.
Opinion seeker/giver	Clarifies pertinent values.
Elaborator	Promotes greater understanding through examples or exploration of implications.
Coordinator	Pulls together ideas and suggestions.
Orienter	Keeps group headed toward its stated goal(s).
Evaluator	Tests group's accomplishments with various criteria such as logic and practicality.
Energizer	Prods group to move along or to accomplish more.
Procedural technician	Performs routine duties (e.g., handing out materials or rearranging seats).
Recorder	Performs a "group memory" function by documenting discussion and outcomes.
Maintenance Roles	**Description**
Encourager	Fosters group solidarity by accepting and praising various points of view.
Harmonizer	Mediates conflict through reconciliation or humour.
Compromiser	Helps resolve conflict by meeting others "half way."
Gatekeeper	Encourages all group members to participate.
Standard setter	Evaluates the quality of group processes.
Commentator	Records and comments on group processes/dynamics.
Follower	Serves as a passive audience.

Source: Adapted from discussion in K D Benne and P Sheats, "Functional Roles of Group Members," *Journal of Social Issues,* Spring 1948, pp 41–49.

What Determines Leadership Behaviour in Gender-Diverse Groups?

Much of the research that has examined the behaviour of people in gender-diverse work groups suggests that men are more participative and influential in task-related behaviour. However, there has also been some indication that men emerge as leaders more often when the group's task is masculine-oriented, whereas women emerge as leaders more often when the group task is feminine-oriented.

Two researchers at the University of Toronto conducted a study that examined the effects of (1) level of gender diversity in a group, and (2) gender orientation of the group's task, on leadership behaviour in the group. Student participants were randomly assigned to male-dominated, female-dominated, and balanced-gender groups. Each group analyzed two business cases. One case emphasized a stereotypically male-oriented task (business-related negotiation) and the other case involved a female-oriented task (negotiation of job responsibilities with implications of sexual harassment).

The results showed that a group member whose gender was opposite to the gender orientation of the task exhibited lower levels of leadership behaviour. Thus being in a minority position in the group does not automatically result in withdrawn behaviour, as previously thought, particularly when the individual is viewed as possessing relative expertise on the group's task. However, being in the majority reduced the adverse effects of incongruence with the task on leadership behaviour.

The authors concluded that relative numbers of men and women in a group do matter, under certain conditions. Decreases in leadership behaviour were not as pronounced for men and women who performed gender-incongruent tasks while in the majority on a group. Also, in self-managing work teams that operate without formal role status distinctions among group members, perceptions of relative competence or expertise based on gender can potentially create differences in leadership behaviour.

Source: L Karakowsky and J P Siegel, "The Effects of Proportional Representation and Gender Orientation of the Task on Emergent Leadership Behaviour in Mixed-Gender Work Groups," *Journal of Applied Psychology*, 84(4), 1999, 620–31.

says, "Let's hear from those who oppose this plan," is performing a maintenance function. Importantly, each of the various task and maintenance roles may be played in varying combinations and sequences by either the group's leader or any of its members.

International managers need to be sensitive to cultural differences regarding the relative importance of task and maintenance roles. In Japan, for example, cultural tradition calls for more emphasis on maintenance roles, especially the roles of harmonizer and compromiser:

> Courtesy requires that members not be conspicuous or disputatious in a meeting or classroom. If two or more members discover that their views differ—a fact that is tactfully taken to be unfortunate—they adjourn to find more information and to work toward a stance that all can accept. They do not press their personal opinions through strong arguments, neat logic, or rewards and threats. And they do not hesitate to shift their beliefs if doing so will preserve smooth interpersonal relations. (To lose is to win.)[13]

Norms

Norm

Shared attitudes, opinions, feelings, or actions that guide social behaviour.

Norms are more encompassing than roles. While roles involve behavioural expectations for specific positions, norms help organizational members determine right from wrong and good from bad. According to one respected team of management consultants: "A **norm** is an attitude, opinion, feeling, or action—shared by two or more people—that guides their behaviour."[14] Although norms are typically unwritten and seldom discussed openly, they have a powerful influence on group and organizational behaviour.[15] For example, groups establish performance norms—some groups push each other to work hard, others to see who can do the least; appearance norms as to what is acceptable and unacceptable; and norms regarding punctuality and loyalty to the organization.

Group members positively reinforce those who adhere to current norms with friendship and acceptance. On the other hand, nonconformists experience criticism and even **ostracism**, or rejection by group members. Anyone who has experienced the "silent treatment" from a group of friends knows what a potent social weapon ostracism can be. Norms can be put into proper perspective by understanding how they develop and why they are enforced.

Ostracism

Rejection by other group members.

How Norms Are Developed   Experts say norms evolve in an informal manner as the group or organization determines what it takes to be effective. Generally speaking, norms develop in various combinations of the following four ways:

1. *Explicit statements by supervisors or co-workers*. For instance, a group leader might explicitly set norms about not drinking alcohol at lunch.

2. *Critical events in the group's history*. At times there is a critical event in the group's history that establishes an important precedent. (For example, a key recruit may have decided to work elsewhere because a group member said too many negative things about the organization. Hence, a norm against such "sour grapes" behaviour might evolve.)

3. *Primacy*. The first behaviour pattern that emerges in a group often sets group expectations. If the first group meeting is marked by very formal interaction between supervisors and employees, then the group often expects future meetings to be conducted in the same way.

4. *Carryover behaviours from past situations*. Such carryover of individual behaviours from past situations can increase the predictability of group members' behaviours in new settings and

ETHICS AT WORK

Monkey See, Monkey Do

A study by researchers from Canada and the United Sates of 187 work group members from 20 different organizations uncovered a "monkey see, monkey do" effect relative to antisocial behaviour. Employees who observed their coworkers engaging in antisocial conduct at work tended to exhibit the same bad behaviour. Antisocial behaviour, as measured in this study, included the following acts:

—damaging company property
—saying hurtful things to coworkers
—doing poor work; working slowly
—complaining with coworkers
—bending or breaking rules
—criticizing coworkers
—doing something harmful to boss or employer
—starting an argument with a coworker
—saying rude things about the boss or organization.

According to the researchers, "The message for managers seems clear—antisocial groups encourage antisocial individual behaviour. It is crucial to nip behaviours deemed harmful in the bud so as to avoid a social influence effect. Managers who expect that isolating or ignoring antisocial groups will encourage them to change are probably mistaken."

You Decide . . .

Are these antisocial behaviours also unethical? As a manager, how would you handle these behaviours if they occurred in your work group?

Source: Quoted and adapted from S L Robinson and A M O'Leary-Kelly, "Monkey See, Monkey Do: The Influence of Work Groups on the Antisocial Behavior of Employees," *Academy of Management Journal*, December 1998, pp 658–72.

facilitate task accomplishment. For instance, students and professors carry fairly constant sets of expectations from class to class.[16]

We would like you to take a few moments and think about the norms that are currently in effect in your classroom. List the norms on a sheet of paper. Do these norms help or hinder your ability to learn? Norms can affect performance either positively or negatively.

Why Norms Are Enforced   Norms tend to be enforced by group memebers when they

- Help the group or organization survive.
- Clarify or simplify behavioural expectations.
- Help individuals avoid embarrassing situations.
- Clarify the group's or organization's central values and/or unique identity.[17]

Teams, Trust, and Teamwork

The prevalence of teams and teamwork around the world are evident in this global sampling from the business press:

- *Siemens, the $63 billion German manufacturing company:* "a new generation of managers is fostering cooperation across the company. They are setting up teams to develop products and attack new markets. They are trying hiking expeditions and weekend workshops to spur ideas and new work methods."[18]
- *Motorola's walkie-talkie plants in Penang, Malysia, and Plantation, Florida:* "The goal, pursued by Motorola worldwide, is to get employees at all levels to forget narrow job titles and work together in teams to identify and act on problems that hinder quality and productivity. . . . New applicants are screened on the basis of their attitude toward 'teamwork'."[19]
- *Fiat's new auto plant in Melfi, Italy:* "Fiat slashed the layers between plant managers and workers and spent $64 million training its 7,000 workers and engineers to work in small teams. Now, the 31 independent teams—with 15 to 100 workers apiece—oversee car-assembly tasks from start to finish."[20]
- *Ford Motor Company's product-development Web site:* "The Web brings 4,500 Ford engineers from labs in the United States, Germany, and England together in cyberspace to collaborate on projects. The idea is to break down the barriers between regional operations so basic auto components are designed once and used everywhere."[21]

All of these huge global companies have staked their future competitiveness on teams and teamwork.

The team approach to managing organizations is having diverse and substantial impacts on organizations and individuals. Teams promise to be a cornerstone of progressive management for the foreseeable future. According to management expert Peter Drucker, tomorrow's organizations will be flatter, information based, and organized around teams.[22] This means virtually all employees will need to polish their team skills. Fortunately, the trend toward teams has a receptive audience today. Both women and younger employees, according to recent studies, thrive in team-oriented organizations.[23]

In this section, we define the term *team*, discuss trust as a key to real teamwork, and explore two evolving forms of teamwork—self-managed teams and virtual teams.

A Team Is More Than Just a Group

Some experts say it is a mistake to use the terms *group* and *team* interchangeably. A **team** is "a small number of people with complementary skills who are committed to a common purpose, performance goals, and approach for which they hold themselves mutually accountable."[24] A small number of people means between 2 and 25 team members. Effective teams typically have fewer than 10 members. A survey of 400 workplace team members in the United States and Canada found that the average North American team consists of 10 members and that eight is the most common size."[25]

> **Team**
>
> Small group with complementary skills who hold themselves mutually accountable for common purpose, goals, and approach.

Thus, a group becomes a team when the following criteria are met:

1. *Leadership* becomes a shared activity.
2. *Accountability* shifts from strictly individual to both individual and collective.
3. The group develops its own *purpose* or mission.
4. *Problem solving* becomes a way of life, not a part-time activity.
5. *Effectiveness* is measured by the group's collective outcomes and products.[26]

Relative to the model of group development covered earlier—forming, storming, norming, performing, and adjourning—teams are task groups that have matured to the *performing* stage. Because of conflicts over power and authority and unstable interpersonal relations, many work groups never qualify as a real team.[27] The distinction has been described as follows: "The essence of a team is common commitment. Without it, groups perform as individuals; with it, they become a powerful unit of collective performance."[28]

Table 7–3 contains a list of characteristics of effective teams. Work teams have a much greater chance of being effective if they are nurtured and facilitated by the organization. The team's purpose needs to be consistent with the organization's strategy. Similarly, the level of participation and autonomy needed for teams to be effective requires an organizational culture that values those processes. Team members also need appropriate technological tools and training. Teamwork needs to be reinforced by the organizational reward system, which means moving away from pay and bonuses related solely to individual performance.

Trust: A Key Ingredient of Teamwork

These have not been good times for trust in the corporate world. Years of mergers, downsizings, layoffs, bloated executive bonuses, and broken promises have left many employees justly cynical about trusting management. While challenging readers of *Harvard Business Review* to do a better job of investing in what they call "social capital," experts recently offered this constructive advice:

> No one can manufacture trust or mandate it into existence. When someone says, "You can trust me," we usually don't, and rightly so. But leaders can make deliberate investments in trust. They can give people reasons to trust one another instead of reasons to watch their backs. They can refuse to reward successes that are built on untrusting behaviour. And they can display trust and trustworthiness in their own actions, both personally and on behalf of the company.[29]

Three Dimensions of Trust **Trust** is defined as reciprocal faith in others' intentions and behaviour.[30] Experts on the subject explain the reciprocal (give-and-take) aspect of trust as follows:

> **Trust**
>
> Reciprocal faith in others' intentions and behaviour.

TABLE 7–3 Characteristics of an Effective Team

1. Clear purpose	The vision, mission, goal, or task of the team has been defined and is now accepted by everyone. There is an action plan.
2. Informality	The climate tends to be informal, comfortable, and relaxed. There are no obvious tensions or signs of boredom.
3. Participation	There is much discussion, and everyone is encouraged to participate.
4. Listening	The members use effective listening techniques such as questioning, paraphrasing, and summarizing to get out ideas.
5. Civilized disagreement	There is disagreement, but the team is comfortable with this and shows no signs of avoiding, smoothing over, or suppressing conflict.
6. Consensus decisions	For important decisions, the goal is substantial but not necessarily unanimous agreement through open discussion of everyone's ideas, avoidance of formal voting, or easy compromises.
7. Open communication	Team members feel free to express their feelings on the tasks as well as on the group's operation. There are few hidden agendas. Communication takes place outside of meetings.
8. Clear roles and work assignments	There are clear expectations about the roles played by each team member. When action is taken, clear assignments are made, accepted, and carried out. Work is fairly distributed among team members.
9. Shared leadership	While the team has a formal leader, leadership functions shift from time to time depending on the circumstances, the needs of the group, and the skills of the members. The formal leader models the appropriate behaviour and helps establish positive norms.
10. External relations	The team spends time developing key outside relationships, mobilizing resources, and building credibility with important players in other parts of the organization.
11. Style diversity	The team has a broad spectrum of team-player types including members who emphasize attention to task, goal setting, focus on process, and questions about how the team is functioning.
12. Self-assessment	Periodically, the team stops to examine how well it is functioning and what may be interfering with its effectiveness.

Source: G M Parker, *Team Players and Teamwork: The New Competitive Business Strategy* (San Francisco: Jossey-Bass, 1990), Table 2, p 33. Copyright © 1990 by Jossey-Bass Inc., Publishers. Reprinted by permission of John Wiley & Sons, Inc.

When we see others acting in ways that imply that they trust us, we become more disposed to reciprocate by trusting in them more. Conversely, we come to distrust those whose actions appear to violate our trust or to distrust us.[31]

In short, we tend to give what we get: trust begets trust; distrust begets distrust.

Trust is expressed in different ways. Three dimensions of trust are *overall trust* (expecting fair play, the truth, and empathy), *emotional trust* (faith that someone will not misrepresent you to others or betray a confidence), and *reliableness* (believe that promises and appointments will be kept and commitments met).[32] These different dimensions contribute to a wide and complex range of trust, from very low to very high.

This group of people is learning the basic rule of trusting fellow colleagues: Trust must be earned, not demanded.

How to Build Trust   Trust needs to be earned; it cannot be demanded. The following six guidelines relate to building and maintaining trust:

1. *Communication.* Keep team members and employees informed by explaining policies and decisions and providing accurate feedback. Be candid about one's own problems and limitations. Tell the truth.[33]

2. *Support.* Be available and approachable. Provide help, advice, coaching, and support for team members' ideas.

3. *Respect.* Delegation, in the form of real decision-making authority, is the most important expression of managerial respect. Actively listening to the ideas of others is a close second. (Empowerment is not possible without trust.)[34]

4. *Fairness.* Be quick to give credit and recognition to those who deserve it. Make sure all performance appraisals and evaluations are objective and impartial.[35]

5. *Predictability.* Be consistent and predictable in your daily affairs. Keep both expressed and implied promises.

6. *Competence.* Enhance your credibility by demonstrating good business sense, technical ability, and professionalism.[36]

Self-Managed Teams

Entrepreneurs and artisans often boast of not having a supervisor. The same generally cannot be said for employees working in organizational offices and factories. But things are changing. In fact, an estimated half of the employees at *Fortune* 500 companies are working on teams.[37] A growing share of those teams are self-managing. Typically, managers are present to serve as trainers and facilitators. Self-managed teams come in every conceivable format today, some more autonomous than others. Honeywell

Canada implemented self-directed work teams and achieved impressive results—an 80% increase in productivity; a 90% reduction in scrap and rework; a 95% reduction in lost-time accidents; a 70% improvement in attendance; and employee satisfaction ratings in the 70 to 80% range. By linking self-directed work teams with the concept of lean manufacturing, work-in-process inventory was reduced by 80%, and cycle-time by 97%. The self-directed work team concept changed the culture of the factory workforce from one which was compelled by management to "leave their brain at the door" to the empowered, educated, thinking, committed teams which exist today.[38]

Self-managed teams are defined as groups of workers who are given administrative responsibility for their task domains. Administrative responsibility involves delegated activities such as planning, scheduling, monitoring, and staffing. These are activities normally performed by managers. In short, employees in these unique work groups act as their own supervisor.[39] Self-managed teams are variously referred to as semiautonomous work groups, autonomous work groups, and superteams.

Self-managed teams

Groups of employees granted administrative responsibility for their work.

Something much more complex is involved than this apparently simple label suggests. The term *self-managed* does not mean simply turning workers loose to do their own thing. Indeed, an organization embracing self-managed teams should be prepared to undergo revolutionary changes in management philosophy, structure, staffing and training practices, and reward systems. Moreover, the traditional notions of managerial authority and control are turned on their heads. Not surprisingly, many managers strongly resist giving up the reins of power to people they view as subordinates. They see self-managed teams as a threat to their job security.[40]

Cross-Functional Teams   A common feature of self-managed teams, particularly among those above the shop-floor or clerical level, is that they are **cross-functional teams**.[41] In other words, specialists from different areas are put on the same team. Among companies with self-managed teams, the most commonly delegated tasks are work scheduling and dealing directly with outside customers (see Table 7–4). The least common team activities are hiring and firing. Most of today's self-managed teams remain bunched at the shop-floor level in factory set-

Cross-functional teams

Teams made up of technical specialists from different areas.

TABLE 7–4 | Survey Evidence: What Self-Managing Teams Manage

Percentage of Companies Saying Their Self-Managing Teams Perform These Traditional Management Functions by Themselves	
Schedule work assignments	67%
Work with outside customers	67
Conduct training	59
Set production goals/quotas	56
Work with suppliers/vendors	44
Purchase equipment/services	43
Develop budgets	39
Do performance appraisals	36
Hire co-workers	33
Fire co-workers	14

Source: Adapted from "1996 Industry Report: What Self-Managing Teams Manage," *Training*, October 1996, p 69.

tings. Experts predict growth of the practice in the managerial ranks and in service operations.[42]

Are Self-Managed Teams Effective? The Research Evidence

Much of what we know about self-managed teams comes from testimonials and case studies, but higher quality field research is slowly developing. So far, it has been concluded that self-managed teams have:

- A positive effect on productivity.
- A positive effect on specific attitudes such as responsibility and control.
- No significant effect on general attitudes such as job satisfaction and organizational commitment.
- No significant effect on absenteeism or turnover.[43]

Although encouraging, these results do not qualify as a sweeping endorsement of self-managed teams. Nonetheless, experts say the trend toward self-managed work teams will continue upward in North America because of a strong cultural bias in favour of direct participation. Managers need to be prepared for the resulting shift in organizational administration.

In today's "wired work-places," it is possible to be a member of a virtual team while working alone.

Virtual Teams

Virtual teams are a product of modern times. Thanks to evolving information technologies such as the Internet, E-mail, videoconferencing, groupware, and fax machines, you can be a member of a work team without really being there.[44] Traditional team meetings are location specific. Team members are either physically present or absent. Virtual teams, in contrast, convene electronically with members reporting in from different locations, different organizations, and even different time zones.

Because virtual teams are so new, there is no consensual definition. Our working definition of a **virtual team** is a physically dispersed task group that conducts its business through modern information technology.[45] Advocates say virtual teams are very flexible and efficient because they are driven by information and skills, not by time and location. People with needed information and/or skills can be team members, regardless of where or when they actually do their work. On the negative side, lack of face-to-face interaction can weaken trust, communication, and accountability.

> **Virtual team**
>
> A physically dispersed task group that conducts its business through modern information technology.

Research Insights

Here is what has been learned so far from recent studies of computer-mediated groups:

- Virtual groups formed over the Internet follow a group development process similar to that for face-to-face groups.[46]
- Internet chat rooms create more work and yield poorer decisions than face-to-face meetings and telephone conferences.[47]
- Successful use of groupware (software that facilitates interaction among virtual group members) requires training and hands-on experience.[48]
- Inspirational leadership has a positive impact on creativity in electronic brainstorming groups.[49]

Technology, Protocol Keep Global Teams Going Without Face-To-Face Meetings

Technology offers global teams alternative methods of sharing information, discussing ideas and making decisions—from telephone and videoconferencing to a variety of online and Web-based options. To ensure an effective exchange of ideas and information, virtual meetings of global teams need to follow certain communication protocols. Before the meeting, the agenda and any document to be discussed during the meeting should be distributed. All team members should introduce themselves, and everyone should participate. It is important not to speak too fast and to clarify continuously. If English is the language being used, "standard" language should be used (i.e., no sports-related expressions like "covering all the bases"). All decisions and action steps should be repeated and followed up.

A German saying states: trust is not of particular importance until it is lost. Global teams need to establish and maintain trust between members to ensure that the efforts of all team members are aligned. This can be accomplished by ensuring that team members get to know one another, particularly when some come from cultures where business only takes place between people who know and like one another (e.g., Latin America); using videoconferencing from time to time; and agreeing on E-mail protocol such as who gets copied on what information.

Many global teams include members from culturally diverse countries. One of the most critical (and often least understood) differences lies in what it means to be a team. Indeed, the behaviour expected of good team players varies from country to country. In countries with collectivist cultures like Mexico and Japan, a good team player is expected to help a teammate. A team is "all for one and one for all." In countries with individualistic cultures like Canada and the United States, a good team player is expected to focus on his or her area of responsibilities. Their motto is "let everyone take care of their tasks and responsibilities and we will win." If team members do not realize they have different ideas of what a team is, they can misinterpret the actions and reactions of their colleagues, resulting in rapid erosion of trust. For example, the "jump in and help" behaviour of collectivist team members is often misinterpreted by individualist team members as an intrusion into their area of responsibility, usually with devastating consequences for the team.

When a global team is effective, it can capitalize on the cultural differences among its members: team members build on one another's ideas and significant synergy is achieved. Keeping global teams going without face-to-face meetings is a challenge that can be managed effectively by using the right remote communication protocols; following good communication practices; making an explicit effort at building and maintaining trust across distance, and taking cultural differences into account.

Source: Adapted from L Laroche and C M Bing, "Technology, protocol keep global teams going without face-to-face meetings," *Canadian HR Reporter*, October 22, 2001, pp 17, 19.

Practical Considerations Virtual teams may be in fashion, but they are not a cure-all. In fact, they may be a giant step backward for those not well versed in modern information technology. Managers who rely on virtual teams agree on one point: *Meaningful face-to-face contact, especially during early phases of the group development process, is absolutely essential.* Virtual group members need "faces" in their minds to go with names and electronic messages.[50] Additionally, virtual teams cannot succeed without some old-fashioned factors such as top-management support, hands-on training, a clear mission and specific objectives, effective leadership, and schedules and deadlines.[51]

Why Do Work Teams Fail?

Advocates of the team approach to management paint a very optimistic and bright picture. Yet there is a dark side to teams.[52] They can and often do fail. Anyone contemplating the use of teams in the workplace needs a balanced perspective of their advantages and limitations.

There are a number of reasons why work teams can be ineffective. More than half a century ago, the tendency for reduced effort as group size increases was identified, and this continues to be a problem today. In the 1970s, the devastating effect of groupthink (discussed in Chapter 6) was documented. More recently, specific problems related to self-managed teams have been identified.

Social Loafing

Is group performance less than, equal to, or greater than the sum of its parts? Can three people, for example, working together accomplish less than, the same as, or more than they would working separately? An interesting study conducted more than a half century ago found the answer to be "less than."[53] In a rope-pulling exercise, the study found that three people pulling together could achieve only two and a half times the average individual rate. Eight pullers achieved less than four times the individual rate. This tendency for individual effort to decline as group size increases has come to be called **social loafing.**[54] Let us briefly analyze this threat to group effectiveness and synergy with an eye toward avoiding it.

> **Social loafing**
>
> Decrease in individual effort as group size increases.

Social Loafing Theory and Research   Among the theoretical explanations for the social loafing effect are (1) equity of effort ("Everyone else is goofing off, so why shouldn't I?"), (2) loss of personal accountability ("I'm lost in the crowd, so who cares?"), (3) motivational loss due to the sharing of rewards ("Why should I work harder than the others when everyone gets the same reward?"), and (4) coordination loss as more people perform the task ("We're getting in each other's way.").

Research studies refined these theories by showing that social loafing occurred when

- The task was perceived to be unimportant, simple, or not interesting.[55]
- Group members thought their individual output was not identifiable.[56]
- Group members expected their co-workers to loaf.[57]

But social loafing did *not* occur when group members expected to be evaluated.[58] Also, recent research suggests that self-reliant "individualists" are more prone to social loafing than are group-oriented "collectivists." But individualists can be made more cooperative by keeping the group small and holding each member personally accountable for results.[59]

Practical Implications   These findings demonstrate that social loafing is not an inevitable part of group effort. Management can curb this threat to group effectiveness by making sure the task is challenging and perceived as important. Additionally, it is a good idea to hold group members personally accountable for identifiable portions of the group's task.[60]

Problems With Self-Managed Teams

The main threats to team effectiveness arise from unrealistic expectations on the part of both management and team members. These unrealistic expectations create frustration, which in turn leads to the abandonment of teams. Mistakes by management usually involve doing a poor job of creating a supportive environment for teams and teamwork. For example, reward plans that encourage individuals to compete with one another undermine team-work, as can inadequate training in team skills. The environment may be hostile for teams if no attempts are made to change an existing command-and-control culture. Also, teams cannot overcome weak strategies and poor business practices. This can happen if teams are adopted as a fad with no long-term commitment on the part of management.

Team members themselves can drive failure when they take on too much too quickly and drive themselves too hard for fast results. Important group dynamics and team skills get lost in the rush for results. Poor interpersonal skills and lack of trust between members often lead to conflict that can undermine team effectiveness. Also, teams need to be counselled against quitting when they run into an unanticipated obstacle. Failure is part of the learning process with teams, as it is elsewhere in life.

Team Building

Team building encompasses many activities intended to address these problems and improve the internal functioning of work groups. Team building workshops strive for greater cooperation, better communication, and less dysfunctional conflict. Experiential learning techniques such as interpersonal trust exercises, conflict-handling role-play sessions, and interactive games are common. In the mountains of British Columbia, DowElanco employees try to overcome fear and build trust as they help each other negotiate a difficult tree-top rope course.[61]

The goal of team building is to create high-performance teams with the following eight attributes:

1. *Participative leadership.* Creating interdependency by empowering, freeing up, and serving others.

2. *Shared responsibility.* Establishing an environment in which all team members feel as responsible as the manager for the performance of the work unit.

3. *Aligned on purpose.* Having a sense of common purpose about why the team exists and the function it serves.

4. *Strong communication.* Creating a climate of trust and open, honest communication.

5. *Future focused.* Seeing change as an opportunity for growth.

6. *Focused on task.* Keeping meetings focused on results.

7. *Creative talents.* Applying individual talents and creativity.

8. *Rapid response.* Identifying and acting on opportunities.[62]

These eight attributes effectively combine many of today's most progressive ideas on management, including participation, empowerment, service ethic, individual responsibility and development, self-management, trust, active listening, and envisioning. But patience and diligence are required, as it may take up to five years for a high-performance team to develop.[63]

It is unreasonable to expect employees who are accustomed to being managed and led to suddenly lead and manage themselves. Self-managed teams are likely to fail if team members are not expressly taught to engage in self-management behaviours. A key transition to self-management involves current managers engaging in self-management leadership behaviours such as encouraging others for good work; self-observation and evaluation; setting high expectations for oneself and the team; thinking about and practicing new tasks; and encouraging self-criticism.[64] Empowerment, not domination, is the goal of this type of leadership.

summary of key concepts

- *Describe the five stages of group development.* The five stages are *forming* (the group comes together), *storming* (members test the limits and each other), *norming* (questions about authority and power are resolved as the group becomes more cohesive), *performing* (effective communication and cooperation help the group get things done), and *adjourning* (group members go their own way).

- *Distinguish between role overload, role conflict, and role ambiguity.* Organizational roles are sets of behaviours persons expect of occupants of a position. One may experience role overload (too much to do in too little time), role conflict (conflicting role expectations), and role ambiguity (unclear role expectations).

- *Contrast roles and norms, and specify four reasons norms are enforced in organizations.* While roles are specific to the person's position, norms are shared attitudes that differentiate appropriate from inappropriate behaviour in a variety of situations. Norms evolve informally and are enforced because they help the group or organization survive, clarify behavioural expectations, and clarify the group's or organization's central values.

- *Explain how a work group becomes a team.* A team is a mature group where leadership is shared, accountability is both individual and collective, the members have developed their own purpose, problem solving is a way of life, and effectiveness is measured by collective outcomes.

- *List at least four things managers can do to build trust.* Six recommended ways to build trust are through communication, support, respect (especially delegation), fairness, predictability, and competence.

- *Describe self-managed teams and virtual teams.* Self-managed teams are groups of workers who are given administrative responsibility for various activities normally performed by managers—such as planning, scheduling, monitoring, and staffing. They are typically cross functional, meaning they are staffed with a mix of specialists from different areas. Self-managed teams vary widely in the autonomy or freedom they enjoy. A virtual team is a physically dispersed task group that conducts its business through modern information technology such as the Internet. Periodic and meaningful face-to-face contact seems to be crucial for virtual team members, especially during the early stages of group development.

- *Define social loafing and explain how managers can prevent it.* Social loafing involves the tendency for individual effort to decrease as group size increases. This problem can be contained if the task is challenging and important, individuals are held accountable for results, and group members expect everyone to work hard.

- *Describe high-performance teams.* Eight attributes of high-performance teams are: participative leadership; shared responsibility; aligned on purpose; strong communication; future focused for growth; focused on task; creative talents applied; and rapid response.

key terms

cross-functional teams, 160
group, 150
group cohesiveness, 152
maintenance role, 153
norm, 154
ostracism, 155

role, 152
role ambiguity, 153
role conflict, 153
role overload, 152
self-managed teams, 160
social loafing, 163

task role, 153
team, 157
trust, 157
virtual team, 161

discussion questions

1. What is your opinion about employees being friends with their co-workers (overlapping formal and informal groups)?

2. Considering your current lifestyle, how many different roles are you playing? What kind of role conflict and role ambiguity are you experiencing?

3. Why is delegation so important to building organizational trust?

4. Are virtual teams likely to be just a passing fad?

5. How would you respond to a manager who said, "Why should I teach my people to manage themselves and work myself out of a job?"

6. Have you observed any social loafing recently? What were the circumstances and what could be done to correct the problem?

internet exercises

www.queendom.com

1. Relationships and Communications Skills Testing

Managers, who are responsible for getting things accomplished with and through others, simply cannot be effective if they are unable to interact skillfully in social settings. As with any skill development program, you need to know *where you are* before constructing a learning agenda for *where you want to be*. Go to Body-Mind Queen-Dom (**www.queendom.com**), and select the category "Tests & Profiles." (Note: Our use of this site is for instructional purposes only and does not constitute an endorsement of any products that may or may not suit your needs. There is no obligation to buy anything.) Next, choose "Relationships" and select the "Communication Skills Test," read the brief instructions, complete all 34 items, and click on the "score" button for automatic scoring. It is possible, if you choose, to print a personal copy of your completed questionnaire and results.

If you have time, some of the other relationships tests are interesting and fun. We recommend trying the following ones: Arguing Style Test; Assertiveness Test; and Conflict Management Test.

QUESTIONS
1. How did you score? Are you pleasantly (or unpleasantly) surprised by your score?
2. What is your strongest social/communication skill?
3. Reviewing the questionnaire item by item, can you find obvious weak spots in your social/communication skills? For instance, are you a poor listener? Do you interrupt too often? Do you need to be more aware of others, both verbally and nonverbally? Do you have a hard time tuning into others' feelings or expressing your own feelings? How do you handle disagreement?
4. Based on the results of this questionnaire, what is your learning agenda for improving your social and communication skills?

www.akgroup.com

2. Virtual Team Readiness Testing

Virtual teams, where members attempt to complete projects despite bring geographically dispersed, will grow more common as advanced computer networks and communication technologies become even more sophisticated. Are you (and your organization) ready to work in this sort of electronically connected team environment? You can find out, thanks to the Web site of The Applied Knowledge Group, a consulting company. Go to their home page (**www.akgroup.com**) and select "Assessment Tool" from the main menu. Complete the single organizational question (for your current or past employer), complete the next 25 individual questions, and then click on the "Score Test" button. You will be given a virtual team readiness score and a brief interpretation. A personal copy of the questionnaire and results can be also printed.

1. How did you score? Are you pleasantly (or unpleasantly) surprised by your scores in Column A and Column B?
2. In what way are you ready for work on a virtual team? Review Column A and discuss your readiness with regard to communication and collaboration. Review Column B and discuss your level of comfort or discomfort with isolation.

experiential exercises

1. Is This a Mature Work Group or Team?

Objectives

1. To increase your knowledge of group processes and dynamics.
2. To give you a tool for assessing the maturity of a work group or task team as well as a diagnostic tool for pinpointing group problems.
3. To help you become a more effective group leader or contributor.

Introduction

Group action is so common today that many of us take it for granted. But are the groups and teams to which we contribute much of our valuable time mature and hence more likely to be effective? Or do they waste our time? How can they be improved? We can and should become tough critical evaluators of group processes.

Instructions

Think of a work group or task team with which you are very familiar (preferably one you worked with in the past or are currently working with). Rate the group's maturity on each of the 20 dimensions. Then add your circled responses to get your total group maturity score. The higher the score, the greater the group's maturity.

	Very False (or Never)				Very True (or Always)
1. Members are clear about group goals.	1 — 2 — 3 — 4 — 5				
2. Members agree with the group's goals.	1 — 2 — 3 — 4 — 5				
3. Members are clear about their roles.	1 — 2 — 3 — 4 — 5				

4. Members accept their roles and status.   1 — 2 — 3 — 4 — 5
5. Role assignments match member abilities.   1 — 2 — 3 — 4 — 5
6. The leadership style matches the group's developmental level.   1 — 2 — 3 — 4 — 5
7. The group has an open communication structure in which all members participate.   1 — 2 — 3 — 4 — 5
8. The group gets, gives, and uses feedback about its effectiveness and productivity.   1 — 2 — 3 — 4 — 5
9. The group spends time planning how it will solve problems and make decisions.   1 — 2 — 3 — 4 — 5
10. Voluntary conformity is high.   1 — 2 — 3 — 4 — 5
11. The group norms encourage high performance and quality.   1 — 2 — 3 — 4 — 5
12. The group expects to be successful.   1 — 2 — 3 — 4 — 5
13. The group pays attention to the details of its work.   1 — 2 — 3 — 4 — 5
14. The group accepts coalition and subgroup formation.   1 — 2 — 3 — 4 — 5
15. Subgroups are integrated into the group as a whole.   1 — 2 — 3 — 4 — 5

16. The group is highly cohesive.   1 — 2 — 3 — 4 — 5

17. Interpersonal attraction among members is high.   1 — 2 — 3 — 4 — 5

18. Members are cooperative.   1 — 2 — 3 — 4 — 5

19. Periods of conflict are frequent but brief.   1 — 2 — 3 — 4 — 5

20. The group has effective conflict-management strategies.   1 — 2 — 3 — 4 — 5

Total score = _____

Source: Excerpted from S Wheelan and J M Hochberger, "Validation Studies of the Group Development Questionnaire," *Small Group Research*, February 1996, pp 143–70.

Arbitrary Norms

20–39	"When in doubt, run in circles, scream and shout!"
40–59	A long way to go
60–79	On the right track
80–100	Ready for group dynamics graduate school

QUESTIONS FOR DISCUSSION

1. Does your evaluation help explain why the group or team was successful or not? Explain.

2. Was (or is) there anything *you* could have done (or can do) to increase the maturity of this group? Explain.

3. How will this evaluation instrument help you be a more effective group member or leader in the future?

2. How Autonomous Is Your Work Group?

Instructions

Think of your current (or past) job and work group. Characterize the group's situation by circling one number on the following scale for each statement. Add your responses for a total score:

Strongly Disagree						Strongly Agree
1	2	3	4	5	6	7

Work Method Autonomy

1. My work group decides how to get the job done.   _____

2. My work group determines what procedures to use.   _____

3. My work group is free to choose its own methods when carrying out its work.   _____

Work Scheduling Autonomy

4. My work group controls the scheduling of its work.   _____

5. My work group determines how its work is sequenced.   _____

6. My work group decides when to do certain activities.   _____

Work Criteria Autonomy

7. My work group is allowed to modify the normal way it is evaluated so some of our activities are emphasized and some deemphasized.   _____

8. My work group is able to modify its objectives (what it is supposed to accomplish).   _____

9. My work group has some control over what it is supposed to accomplish.   _____

Total score =   _____

Norms

 9–26 = Low autonomy
27–45 = Moderate autonomy
46–63 = High autonomy

Source: Adapted from an individual autonomy scale in J A Breaugh, "The Work Autonomy Scales: Additional Validity Evidence," *Human Relations*, November 1989, pp 1033–56.

personal awareness and growth exercises

1. Measuring Role Conflict and Role Ambiguity

Instructions

Step 1. While thinking of your current (or last) job, circle one response for each of the following statements. Please consider each statement carefully because some are worded positively and some negatively.

Step 2. In the space in the far right column, label each statement with either a "C" for role conflict or an "A" for role ambiguity. (See Ch. 7 endnote 65 for a correct categorization.)

Step 3. Calculate separate totals for role conflict and role ambiguity, and compare them with these arbitrary norms:

5–14 = low; 15–25 = moderate; 26–35 = high.

	Very False	**Very True**	
1. I feel certain about how much authority I have.	7 — 6 — 5 — 4 — 3 — 2 — 1		_____
2. I have to do things that should be done differently.	1 — 2 — 3 — 4 — 5 — 6 — 7		_____
3. I know that I have divided my time properly.	7 — 6 — 5 — 4 — 3 — 2 — 1		_____
4. I know what my responsibilities are.	7 — 6 — 5 — 4 — 3 — 2 — 1		_____
5. I have to buck a rule or policy in order to carry out an assignment.	1 — 2 — 3 — 4 — 5 — 6 — 7		_____
6. I feel certain how I will be evaluated for a raise or promotion.	7 — 6 — 5 — 4 — 3 — 2 — 1		_____
7. I work with two or more groups who operate quite differently.	1 — 2 — 3 — 4 — 5 — 6 — 7		_____
8. I know exactly what is expected of me.	7 — 6 — 5 — 4 — 3 — 2 — 1		_____
9. I do things that are apt to be accepted by one person and not accepted by others.	1 — 2 — 3 — 4 — 5 — 6 — 7		_____
10. I work on unnecessary things.	1 — 2 — 3 — 4 — 5 — 6 — 7		_____

Role conflict score = _____

Role ambiguity score = _____

Source: Adapted from J R Rizzo, R J House, and S I Lirtzman, "Role Conflict and Ambiguity in Complex Organizations," *Administrative Science Quarterly,* June 1970, p 156.

2. How Trusting Are You?

Objectives

1. To introduce you to different dimensions of interpersonal trust.
2. To measure your trust in another person.
3. To discuss the managerial implications of your propensity to trust.

Introduction

The trend toward more open and empowered organizations where teamwork and self-management are vital requires heightened interpersonal trust. Customers need to be able to trust organizations producing the goods and services they buy, managers need to trust nonmanagers to carry out the organization's mission, and team members need to trust each other in order to get the job done. As with any other interpersonal skill, we need to be able to measure and improve our ability to trust others. This exercise is a step in that direction.

Instructions

Think of a specific individual who currently plays an important role in your life (e.g., current or future spouse, friend, supervisor, co-worker, team member, etc.), and rate his or her trustworthiness for each statement according to the following scale. Total your responses, and compare your score with the arbitrary norms provided.

Strongly Disagree									Strongly Agree
1 — 2 —	3 —	4 —	5 —	6 —	7 —	8 —	9 —	10

Overall Trust   Score

1. I can expect this person to play fair.   _____
2. I can confide in this person and know she/he desires to listen.   _____
3. I can expect this person to tell me the truth.   _____
4. This person takes time to listen to my problems and worries.   _____

Emotional Trust

5. This person would never intentionally misrepresent my point of view to other people.   _____

6. I can confide in this person and know that he/she will not discuss it with others.   _____
7. This person responds constructively and caringly to my problems.   _____

Reliableness

8. If this person promised to do me a favour, she/he would carry out that promise.   _____
9. If I had an appointment with this person, I could count on him/her showing up.   _____
10. I could lend this person money and count on getting it back as soon as possible.   _____
11. I do not need a backup plan because I know this person will come through for me.   _____

Total score = _____

Trustworthiness Scale

77–110 = High (Trust is a precious thing.)
 45–76 = Moderate (Be careful; get a rearview mirror.)
 11–44 = Low (Lock up your valuables!)

QUESTIONS FOR DISCUSSION

1. Which particular items in this trust questionnaire are most central to your idea of trust? Why?
2. Does your score accurately depict the degree to which you trust (or distrust) the target person?
3. Why do you trust (or distrust) this individual?
4. If you trust this person to a high degree, how hard was it to build that trust? Explain. What would destroy that trust?
5. Based on your responses to this questionnaire, how would you rate your "propensity to trust"? Low? Moderate? High?
6. What are the managerial implications of your propensity to trust?

Source: Questionnaire items adapted from C Johnson-George and W C Swap, "Measurement of Specific Interpersonal Trust: Construction and Validation of a Scale to Assess Trust in Specific Other," *Journal of Personality and Social Psychology*, December 1982, pp 1306–17; and D J McAllister, "Effect- and Cognition-based Trust as Foundations for Interpersonal Cooperation in Organizations," *Academy of Management Journal*, February 1995, pp 24–59.

CBC video case

Guest-Tek

The executive team at Guest-Tek, a Calgary-based software firm, is undergoing change as the company grows and faces the need to triple its staff. The founder, Arnon Levy, and his first employee, Kris Youell, Director of Sales and Marketing, who have been there from the start three years ago, form the nucleous of the executive team. They pride themselves on being honest with one another, even though they don't always see eye-to-eye. Guest-Tek recently received $1.5 million from venture capital firm Launchworks Inc., who have placed some of their associates to work within Guest-Tek, and whose partners meet weekly with Arnon to offer advice.

Launchworks' advice has led to the hiring of older "corporate" types to help manage growth. A more difficult recommendation is that a Senior Vice President of Sales is needed, and that Kris is not the best person. This recommendation puts Arnon in a difficult position—Kris has been at his side from the start, and he doesn't want her to leave the company because of her wealth of expertise in the industry. Arnon is able to work out a plan to provide Kris with mentoring and coaching from the Launchworks consultants, and Kris is willing to accept advice on improving her management skills.

QUESTIONS FOR DISCUSSION

1. How would you describe the executive team norms at Guest-Tek?
2. How would you describe the roles played by executive team members Arnon, Kris, and the advisors from Launchworks.
3. Analyze the changes on the executive team using the model of group development.

Source: Based on "Guest-Tek," *CBC Venture 736* (January 25, 2000).

chapter
eight

Conflict and
Negotiation

After reading the material in this chapter, you should be able to:

• Define the term *conflict,* distinguish between functional and dysfunctional conflict, and identify three desired outcomes of conflict.

• Define *personality conflicts,* and explain how they should be managed.

• Discuss the role of in-group thinking in intergroup conflict, and explain what can be done to avoid cross-cultural conflict.

• Identify the five conflict-handling styles.

• Identify and describe at least four alternative dispute resolution (ADR) techniques.

• Draw a distinction between distributive and integrative negotiation, and explain the concept of added-value negotiation.

THE VERDICT IS IN

On the third floor of an office building on the edge of Toronto's financial district, lawyers in a wrongful dismissal case are discussing their case before David Griffiths, a retired Ontario Court of Appeal judge in an official-looking room that would not seem out of place in one of the country's courthouses. The details of the conflict are embarrassing to both sides, but there are no spectators in the room and no news reporters. Once Griffiths decides the case, the file will be sealed, and neither party in the dispute will be allowed to discuss it publicly. There will be no appeal to the courts.

But this isn't a regular lawsuit that has made its way through the clogged civil justice system. It's an alternative dispute resolution (ADR) option offered by a company called ADR Chambers that has a stable of retired superior court judges who operate across Canada. They provide arbitration and mediation that offers clients an opportunity to resolve conflicts in a confidential and private setting while shaving years off the time it can take in the legal system. Clients can, on consent, agree to use the retired judges for a private appeal following an arbitration or judgment in a civil action. With more than 50 retired

David Griffiths, retired Ontario Court of Appeal judge, and now arbitrator and mediator for ADR chambers.

senior appeal and trial court judges, ADR Chambers is able to offer clients the finality of a decision without having to resort to the courts.

It is the speediness and the confidentiality of ADR Chambers that has attracted the interest of companies that simply don't have time to wade through the backlogged civil courts. The Investment Dealers Association has retained the company to arbitrate disputes between brokers and clients. Automakers have hired ADR Chambers to settle differences between individual dealerships and manufacturers over such issues as franchise territory encroachment.

Griffiths says, "You can do things in mediation that you can't do on the bench as a trial judge because when you're mediating, you can find a win-win solution. Mediation, properly conducted, can be cathartic. You're suing someone. You may be mad at him. He may be mad at you. But when you come to the table, you can get it off your chest." After the two sides argue back and forth, they will often begin to compromise.

Source: M Bourrie, "The Verdict is In," *Canadian Business*, February 19, 2001, pp 60–65.

A Modern View of Conflict

Make no mistake about it. Conflict is an unavoidable aspect of modern life. These major trends conspire to make *organizational* conflict inevitable:

- Constant change.
- Greater employee diversity.
- More teams (virtual and self-managed).
- Less face-to-face communication (more electronic interaction).
- A global economy with increased cross-cultural dealings.

Dean Tjosvold, from Simon Fraser University, notes that "Change begets conflict, conflict begets change"[1] and challenges us to do better with this sobering global perspective:

> Learning to manage conflict is a critical investment in improving how we, our families, and our organizations adapt and take advantage of change. Managing conflicts well does not insulate us from change, nor does it mean that we will always come out on top or get all that we want. However, effective conflict management helps us keep in touch with new developments and create solutions appropriate for new threats and opportunities.
>
> Much evidence shows we have often failed to manage our conflicts and respond to change effectively. High divorce rates, disheartening examples of sexual and physical abuse of children, the expensive failures of international joint ventures, and bloody ethnic violence have convinced many people that we do not have the abilities to cope with our complex interpersonal, organizational, and global conflicts.[2]

But respond we must. Tools and solutions are available, if only we develop the ability and will to use them persistently.

Conflict is a process in which one party perceives that its interests are being opposed or negatively affected by another party.[3] The word *perceives* reminds us that sources of conflict and issues can be real or imagined. The resulting conflict is the same. Conflict can escalate (strengthen) or deescalate (weaken) over time. "The conflict process unfolds in a context, and whenever conflict, escalated or not, occurs the disputants or third parties can attempt to manage it in some manner."[4] Consequently, current and future managers need to understand the dynamics of conflict and know how to handle it effectively (both as disputants and as third parties).

Conflict

One party perceives its interests are being opposed or set back by another party.

A Conflict Continuum

Ideas about managing conflict underwent an interesting evolution during the 20th century. Initially, scientific management experts such as Frederick W Taylor believed all conflict ultimately threatened management's authority and thus had to be avoided or quickly resolved.[5] Later, human relationists recognized the inevitability of conflict and advised managers to learn to live with it. Emphasis remained on resolving conflict whenever possible, however. Beginning in the 1970s, OB specialists realized conflict had both positive and negative outcomes, depending on its nature and intensity. This perspective introduced the revolutionary idea that organizations could suffer from *too little* conflict.

Work groups, departments, or organizations that experience too little conflict tend to be plagued by apathy, lack of creativity, indecision, and missed deadlines. Excessive conflict, on the other hand, can erode organizational performance because of political infighting, dissatisfaction, lack of teamwork, and turnover. Workplace aggression and violence can be manifestations of excessive conflict.[6] Appropriate types and levels of conflict energize people in constructive directions.[7]

Functional versus Dysfunctional Conflict

The distinction between **functional conflict** and **dysfunctional conflict** depends on whether the organization's interests are served. According to one conflict expert,

> Some [types of conflict] support the goals of the organization and improve performance; these are functional, constructive forms of conflict. They benefit or support the main purposes of the organization. Additionally, there are those types of conflict that hinder organizational performance; these are dysfunctional or destructive forms. They are undesirable and the manager should seek their eradication.[8]

Functional conflict
Conflict that serves an organization's interests.

Dysfunctional conflict
Conflict that threatens an organization's interests.

Functional conflict is commonly referred to in management circles as constructive or cooperative conflict.[9]

For many people, conflict brings to mind visions of upset, turmoil, and anger, and they don't want to get involved. Thus, according to one expert:

> Avoiding conflict, providing perfunctory and ineffective responses or taking punitive and ill-conceived measures to resolve disputes are common but unsatisfactory attempts at resolving conflict.[10]

Dysfunctional conflict between coworkers that is avoided or ineffectively addressed by management can lead to violence, poor performance, and employee turnover. Consider the following case involving two employees at Albis Canada Inc. One employee took offence at a coworker's gesture he described as "look at those guys talking," and told the gesturing employee that he didn't like him mocking the way he spoke and then grabbed him by the neck. The gesturing employee broke free and walked away, fearful and embarrassed. The violent employee apologized the next day, and voluntarily took classes in anger management and relationship therapy. The plant manager took the incident seriously and fired the violent employee, in light of the fact that six months prior, the violent employee had received a three-day suspension for similar conduct. The fired employee grieved the dismissal and in the end, an arbitrator reinstated him without back pay, on the understanding that any further violent incidents would result in his case being immediately sent back to an arbitrator.[11]

Violent responses to this type of conflict are becoming more widespread in organizations across Canada, along with their negative consequences. According to professor Natalie Allen, an industrial and organizational psychologist at the University of Western Ontario:

> This is an important problem because organizations are going to lose good people. The consequences are lower productivity and dissatisfaction that leads to turnover.[12]

Causes of Conflict

Certain situations produce more conflict than others. By knowing the causes of conflict, managers are better able to anticipate conflict and take steps to resolve it if it becomes dysfunctional. Among the situations that tend to produce either functional or dysfunctional conflict are

- Incompatible personalities or value systems.
- Overlapping or unclear job boundaries.

This common scene of overworked survivors of layoffs illustrates a personal cause of conflict and stress.

- Competition for limited resources.
- Interdepartment/intergroup competition.
- Inadequate communication.
- Interdependent tasks (e.g., one person cannot complete his or her assignment until others have completed their work).
- Organizational complexity (conflict tends to increase as the number of hierarchical layers and specialized tasks increase).
- Unreasonable or unclear policies, standards, or rules.
- Unreasonable deadlines or extreme time pressure.
- Collective decision making (the greater the number of people participating in a decision, the greater the potential for conflict).
- Decision making by consensus.
- Unmet expectations (employees who have unrealistic expectations about job assignments, pay, or promotions are more prone to conflict).
- Unresolved or suppressed conflicts.[13]

Proactive managers carefully read these early warnings and take appropriate action. For example, group conflict sometimes can be reduced by making decisions on the basis of majority approval rather than striving for a consensus.

Desired Outcomes of Conflict

Within organizations, conflict management is more than simply a quest for agreement. If progress is to be made and dysfunctional conflict minimized, a broader agenda is in order. Three desired outcomes of conflict are:

1. *Agreement.* But at what cost? Equitable and fair agreements are best. An agreement that leaves one party feeling exploited or defeated will tend to breed resentment and subsequent conflict.

2. *Stronger relationships.* Good agreements enable conflicting parties to build bridges of goodwill and trust for future use. Moreover, conflicting parties who trust each other are more likely to keep their end of the bargain.

Source: *The Arizona Republic,* June 15, 2001, p D2.

3. *Learning*. Functional conflict can promote greater self-awareness and creative problem solving. Like the practice of management itself, successful conflict handling is learned primarily by doing. Knowledge of the concepts and techniques in this chapter is a necessary first step, but there is no substitute for hands-on practice. In a contentious world, there are plenty of opportunities to practice conflict management.[14]

Major Forms of Conflict

Certain causes of conflict deserve a closer look. This section explores the nature and organizational implications of three common forms of conflict: personality conflict, intergroup conflict, and cross-cultural conflict. Our discussion of each type of conflict includes some practical tips.

Personality Conflicts

As discussed in Chapter 2, your *personality* is the package of stable traits and characteristics creating your unique identity. According to experts on the subject:

> Each of us has a unique way of interacting with others. Whether we are seen as charming, irritating, fascinating, nondescript, approachable, or intimidating depends in part on our personality, or what others might describe as our style.[15]

Given the many possible combinations of personality traits, it is clear why personality conflicts are inevitable. We define a personality conflict as interpersonal opposition based on personal dislike and/or disagreement.

Workplace Incivility: The Seeds of Personality Conflict   Somewhat akin to physical pain, chronic personality conflicts often begin with seemingly insignificant irritations. For instance, a manager can grow to deeply dislike someone in the next cubicle who persistently whistles off-key while drumming his foot on the side of a filing cabinet. Sadly, grim little scenarios such as this are all too common today, given the steady erosion of civility in the workplace. Researchers recently noted how increased informality, pressure for results, and employee diversity have fostered an "anything goes" atmosphere in today's workplaces. They view incivility as a self-perpetuating vicious cycle that can end in violence.[16] A new study indicates the extent of workplace incivility: "71% of 1,100 workers surveyed said they'd experienced put-downs or condescending and outright rude behaviour on the job."[17]

Vicious cycles of incivility need to be avoided (or broken early) with an organizational culture that places a high value on respect for co-workers. This requires managers and leaders to act as caring and courteous role models. A positive spirit of cooperation, as opposed to one based on negativism and aggression, also helps. Some organizations have resorted to workplace etiquette training. More specifically, constructive feedback and/or skillful behaviour modification can keep a single irritating behaviour from precipitating a full-blown personality conflict (or worse).

Dealing with Personality Conflicts   Personality conflicts are a potential minefield for managers. Personality traits, by definition, are stable and resistant to change. Moreover, there are hundreds of psychological disorders that can and do show up in the workplace.[18] This brings up legal issues. Employees in Canada suffering from psychological disorders such as depression and mood-altering diseases such as alcoholism are protected from discrimination by human rights legislation. Also, sexual harassment and other forms of discrimination can grow out of apparent personality conflicts.[19] Finally, personality conflicts can spawn workplace aggression and violence.[20]

Traditionally, managers dealt with personality conflicts by either ignoring them or transferring one party. In view of the legal implications, just discussed, both of these options may be open invitations to discrimination lawsuits. Table 8–1 provides practical tips for both nonmanagers and managers who are involved in or affected by personality conflicts. Our later discussions of handling dysfunctional conflict and alternative dispute resolution techniques also apply.

Intergroup Conflict

Conflict among work groups, teams, and departments is a common threat to organizational competitiveness. Managers who understand the mechanics of intergroup conflict are better equipped to face this sort of challenge.

In-Group Thinking: The Seeds of Intergroup Conflict   As discussed in Chapter 6, *cohesiveness*—a "we feeling" binding group members together—can be a good or bad thing. A certain amount of cohesiveness can turn a group of individuals into a smooth-running team. Too much cohesiveness, however, can breed groupthink because a desire to get along pushes aside critical thinking. The study of in-groups by small group researchers has revealed a whole package of changes associated with increased group cohesiveness. Specifically,

- Members of in-groups view themselves as a collection of unique individuals, while they stereotype members of other groups as being "all alike."
- In-group members see themselves positively and as morally correct, while they view members of other groups negatively and as immoral.
- In-groups view outsiders as a threat.
- In-group members exaggerate the differences between their group and other groups. This typically involves a distorted perception of reality.[21]

TABLE 8–1   How to Deal with Personality Conflicts

Tips for Employees Having a Personality Conflict	Tips for Third Party Observers of a Personality Conflict	Tips for Managers Whose Employees Are Having a Personality Conflict
• All employees need to be familiar with and *follow* company policies for diversity, antidiscrimination, and sexual harassment.		
• Communicate directly with the other person to resolve the perceived conflict (emphasize problem solving and common objectives, not personalities). • Avoid dragging co-workers into the conflict. • If dysfunctional conflict persists, seek help from direct supervisors or human resource specialists.	• Do not take sides in someone else's personality conflict. • Suggest the parties work things out themselves in a constructive and positive way. • If dysfunctional conflict persists, refer the problem to parties' direct supervisors.	• Investigate and document conflict. • If appropriate, take corrective action (e.g., feedback or behaviour modification). • If necessary, attempt informal dispute resolution. • Refer difficult conflicts to human resource specialists or hired counselors for formal resolution attempts and other interventions.

Avid sports fans who simply can't imagine how someone would support the opposing team exemplify one form of in-group thinking. Reflect for a moment on evidence of in-group behaviour in your life. Does your circle of friends make fun of others because of their race, gender, nationality, sexual preference, or major in college/university?

In-group thinking is one more fact of organizational life that virtually guarantees conflict. Managers cannot eliminate in-group thinking, but they certainly should not ignore it when handling intergroup conflicts.

Research Lessons for Handling Intergroup Conflict   Sociologists have long recommended the contact hypothesis for reducing intergroup conflict. According to the *contact hypothesis,* the more the members of different groups interact, the less intergroup conflict they will experience. Those interested in improving race, international, and union-management relations typically encourage cross-group interaction. The hope is that *any* type of interaction, short of actual conflict, will reduce stereotyping and combat in-group thinking. But research has shown this approach to be naive and limited. Intergroup friendships are still desirable, as documented in many studies,[22] but they are readily overpowered by negative intergroup interactions.

Thus, *priority number one for managers faced with intergroup conflict is to identify and root out specific negative linkages among groups.* A single personality conflict, for instance, may contaminate the entire intergroup experience. The same goes for an employee who voices negative opinions or spreads negative rumors about another group. The updated contact model in Figure 8–1 is based on this and other recent research insights, such as the need to foster positive attitudes toward other groups.[23] Also, notice how conflict within the group and negative gossip from third parties are threats that need to be neutralized if intergroup conflict is to be minimized.

Minimizing Intergroup Conflict: An Updated Contact Model   **FIGURE 8–1**

Level of perceived intergroup conflict tends to increase when:

- Conflict within the group is high.
- There are negative interactions between groups (or between members of those groups).
- Influential third-party gossip about other group is negative.

Recommended actions:

- Work to eliminate *specific negative* interactions between groups (and members).
- Conduct team building to reduce *intra*group conflict and prepare employees for cross-functional teamwork.
- Encourage personal friendships and good working relationships across groups and departments.
- Foster positive attitudes toward members of other groups (empathy, compassion, sympathy).
- Avoid or neutralize negative gossip across groups or departments.

Source: Based on research evidence in G Labianca, D J Brass, and B Gray, "Social Networks and Perceptions of Intergroup Conflict: The Role of Negative Relationships and Third Parties," *Academy of Management Journal,* February 1998, pp 55–67; C D Batson et al., "Empathy and Attitudes: Can Feeling for a Member of a Stigmatized Group Improve Feelings toward the Group?" *Journal of Personality and Social Psychology,* January 1997, pp 105–18; and S C Wright et al., "The Extended Contact Effect: Knowledge of Cross-Group Friendships and Prejudice," *Journal of Personality and Social Psychology,* July 1997, pp 73–90.

Looking to Avoid Cross-Cultural Conflict

Katie Koehler, vice president of human resources for Marriott International's Caribbean and Latin American regions, got her foreign experience right after graduating from an executive MBA program, accepting an offer from Marriott to work in Mexico City.

Being a woman in a Latin culture posed some challenges. At a breakfast meeting, a top union leader told a crude joke in Spanish. "I was being tested," Ms. Koehler said. "Will I understand, and how will I respond?" She responded with a stern look and a lifted eyebrow, subtly signaling that, while she didn't intend to make a scene that would embarrass him and abort their budding relationship, she didn't think the joke was funny. Her approach apparently worked. "After that we had a good relationship," she says.

Source: Excerpted from H Lancaster, "To Get Shipped Abroad, Women Must Overcome Prejudice at Home," *The Wall Street Journal*, June 29, 1999, p B1.

Cross-Cultural Conflict

Doing business with people from different cultures is commonplace in our global economy where cross-border mergers, joint ventures, and alliances are the order of the day.[24] Because of differing assumptions about how to think and act, the potential for cross-cultural conflict is both immediate and huge.[25] Success or failure, when conducting business across cultures, often hinges on avoiding and minimizing actual or perceived conflict. For example, consider this cultural mismatch:

> Mexicans place great importance on saving face, so they tend to expect any conflicts that occur during negotiations to be downplayed or kept private. The prevailing attitude in [Canada], however, is that conflict should be dealt with directly and publicly to prevent hard feelings from developing on a personal level.[26]

This is a matter of accommodating cultural differences for a successful business transaction. Awareness of the cross-cultural differences is an important first step. Beyond that, cross-cultural conflict can be moderated by using international consultants and building cross-cultural relationships. The following are suggested behaviours to help build cross-cultural relationships:[27]

- Be a good listener
- Be sensitive to needs of others
- Be cooperative, rather than overly competitive
- Advocate inclusive (participative) leadership
- Compromise rather than dominate
- Build rapport through conversations
- Be compassionate and understanding
- Avoid conflict by emphasizing harmony
- Nurture others (develop and mentor)

Using International Consultants   In response to broad demand, there is a growing army of management consultants specializing in cross-cultural relations. Competency and fees vary widely, of course. But a carefully selected cross-cultural consultant can be helpful, as this illustration shows:

Workplace Conflict Resolution Around the World

For some years, researchers have been studying differences in how conflict situations are handled in workplaces throughout the world. Japanese prefer a status power model, where those with high status have the power to create and enforce their resolution. Germans prefer a regulations model, where pre-existing, independent regulations shape the nature of a conflict's resolution.

Americans prefer an integrating interests model, which focuses on resolving parties' underlying concerns, to make it more worthwhile for parties to work towards an agreement about the outcome. American norms include discussing parties' interests and synthesizing multiple issues. Chinese norms include concern for collective interests and concern for authority. Chinese are more likely to involve higher management in conflict resolution. Americans are more likely than Chinese to resolve a greater number of issues and reach more integrative outcomes.

Sources: Adapted from C Tinsley, "Models of Conflict Resolution in Japanese, German, and American Cultures," *Journal of Applied Psychology*, 83, 1998, pp 316–23; and C H Tinsley and J M Brett, "Managing Workplace Conflict in the United States and Hong Kong," *Organizational Behavior and Human Decision Processes*, 85, 2001, pp 360–81.

Last year, when electronics-maker Canon planned to set up a subsidiary in Dubai through its Netherlands division, it asked consultant Sahid Mirza of Glocom, based in Dubai, to find out how the two cultures would work together.

Mirza sent out the test questionnaires and got a sizable response. "The findings were somewhat surprising," he recalls. "We found that, at the bedrock level, there were relatively few differences. Many of the Arab businessmen came from former British colonies and viewed business in much the same way as the Dutch."

But at the level of behaviour, there was a real conflict. "The Dutch are blunt and honest in expression, and such expression is very offensive to Arab sensibilities." Mirza offers the example of a Dutch executive who says something like, "We can't meet the deadline." Such a negative expression—true or not—would be gravely offensive to an Arab. As a result of Mirza's research, Canon did start the subsidiary in Dubai, but it trained both the Dutch and the Arab executives first.[28]

Consultants also can help untangle possible personality, value, and intergroup conflicts from conflicts rooted in differing national cultures. Although the basic types of conflict have been discussed separately, they typically are encountered in complex, messy bundles.

Building Relationships Across Cultures

Canadian researcher Rosalie Tung conducted an interesting study of 409 Canadian and US managers working in multinational firms in 51 different countries around the world. She found that Canadian managers demonstrated key success factors such as listening skills, sensitivity, and cooperativeness. US managers, on the other hand, were found to be poor listeners, blunt to the point of insensitivity, and excessively competitive.[29]

Building cross-cultural relationships.

Managing Conflict

As we have seen, conflict has many faces and is a constant challenge for managers who are responsible for reaching organizational goals. Our attention now turns to the active management of both functional and dysfunctional conflict. We discuss how to stimulate functional conflict, how to handle dysfunctional conflict, and how third parties can deal effectively with conflict.

Creating Functional Conflict

Sometimes committees and decision-making groups become so bogged down in details and procedures that nothing substantive is accomplished. Carefully monitored functional conflict can help get the creative juices flowing once again. Managers basically have two options. They can fan the fires of naturally occurring conflict—although this approach can be unreliable and slow. Alternatively, managers can resort to creating conflict, preferably conflict that raises different opinions regardless of the personal feelings of the managers involved.[30] The trick is to get contributors to either defend or criticize ideas based on relevant facts rather than on the basis of personal preference or political interests. This requires disciplined role playing and effective leadership. For example, it is easy to detect the climate for conflict in these recent statements by Joseph Tucci, CEO of EMC, a leading data storage equipment maker: "Good leaders always leave room for debate and different opinions. . . . The team has to be in harmony. But before you move out, there needs to be a debate."[31]

One method of encouraging the expression of different opinions is called **devil's advocacy**. In this technique, one individual is assigned the role of devil's advocate, or critic, to uncover and air all possible objections to a proposed course of action. It is intended to generate critical thinking and reality testing.[32] It is a good idea to rotate the job of devil's advocate so that no one person or group develops a strictly negative reputation. Moreover, periodic devil's advocacy role-playing is good training for developing analytical and communication skills.

Devil's advocacy

One individual is assigned to uncover and air all possible objections to a proposed course of action.

Alternative Styles for Handling Dysfunctional Conflict

People tend to handle negative conflict in patterned ways referred to as *styles*. Several conflict styles have been categorized over the years. Five different conflict-handling styles can be plotted on a 2×2 grid. High to low cooperativeness is found on the horizontal axis of the grid while low to high assertiveness forms the vertical axis (see Figure 8–2). Various combinations of these variables produce the five different conflict-handling styles: integrating, obliging, dominating, avoiding, and compromising.[33] There is no single best style; each has strengths and limitations and is subject to situational constraints.

Collaborating   In this style (also known as integrating or problem solving), interested parties confront the issue and cooperatively identify the problem, generate and weigh alternative solutions, and select a solution. Collaborating is appropriate for complex issues plagued by misunderstanding. However, it is inappropriate for resolving conflicts rooted in opposing value systems. Its primary strength is its longer lasting impact because it deals with the underlying problem rather than merely with symptoms. The primary weakness of this style is that it is very time consuming.

Five Conflict-Handling Styles   **FIGURE 8–2**

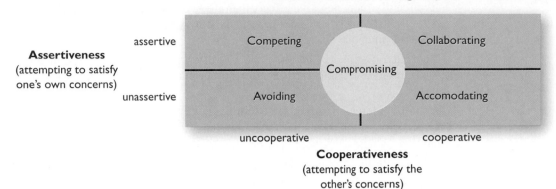

Source: K W Thomas (1992) Conflict and negotiation processes in organizations. In M D Dunnette and L M Hough (eds), *Handbook of Industrial and Organizational Psychology* (Palo Alta CA: Consulting Psychologists' Press).

Accommodating   "An obliging person neglects his or her own concern to satisfy the concern of the other party."[34] This style, often called obliging or smoothing, involves playing down differences while emphasizing commonalities. Accommodating may be an appropriate conflict-handling strategy when it is possible to eventually get something in return. But it is inappropriate for complex or worsening problems. Its primary strength is that it encourages cooperation. Its main weakness is that it's a temporary fix that fails to confront the underlying problem.

Competing   High concern for self and low concern for others encourages "I win, you lose" tactics. The other party's needs are largely ignored. Competing is appropriate when an unpopular solution must be implemented, the issue is minor, or a deadline is near. It is inappropriate in an open and participative climate. Speed is its primary strength. The primary weakness of this forcing style is that it often breeds resentment.

Avoiding   This tactic may involve either passive withdrawal from the problem or active suppression of the issue. Avoidance is appropriate for trivial issues or when the costs of confrontation outweigh the benefits of resolving the conflict. It is inappropriate for difficult and worsening problems. The main strength of this style is that it buys time in unfolding or ambiguous situations. The primary weakness is that the tactic provides a temporary fix that sidesteps the underlying problem.

Compromising   This is a give-and-take approach involving moderate concern for both self and others. Compromise is appropriate when parties have opposite goals or possess equal power. But compromise is inappropriate when overuse would lead to inconclusive action (e.g., failure to meet production deadlines). The primary strength of this tactic is that the democratic process has no losers, but it's a temporary fix that can stifle creative problem solving.

Practical Lessons from Conflict Research

Research studies have provided the following insights regarding conflict:

- people with a high need for affiliation tended to rely on a smoothing (obliging) style while avoiding a forcing (dominating) style.[35] Thus, personality traits affect how people handle conflict.

- disagreement expressed in an arrogant and demeaning manner produced significantly more negative effects than the same sort of disagreement expressed in a reasonable manner.[36] In other words, how you disagree with someone is very important in conflict situations.

- threats and punishment by one party in a disagreement tended to produce intensifying threats and punishment from the other party.[37] In short, aggression breeds aggression.

- as conflict increased, group satisfaction decreased. An integrative style of handling conflict led to higher group satisfaction than did an avoidance style.[38]

- both intradepartmental and interdepartmental conflict decreased as goal difficulty and goal clarity increased. Thus, challenging and clear goals can defuse conflict.

- higher levels of conflict tended to erode job satisfaction and internal work motivation.[39]

- men and women at the same managerial level tended to handle conflict similarly. In short, there was no gender effect.[40]

Negotiating

Formally defined, **negotiation** is a give-and-take decision-making process involving interdependent parties with different preferences.[41] Common examples include labour-management negotiations over wages, hours, and working conditions and negotiations between supply chain specialists and vendors involving price, delivery schedules, and credit terms. Self-managed work teams also need to rely on negotiated agreements with other teams. Negotiating skills are more important than ever today.[42]

Negotiation

Give-and-take process between conflicting interdependent parties.

Gender and Salaries

A statistical meta-analysis of 53 studies of gender differences in negotiation found that women receive lower monetary gains than men after a negotiation. In particular, it has been shown that when presented with the salary range for their job, women generally are not worried if they end up below the average, whereas men may often be concerned if they are not above the mean. Employers may take advantage of these findings by offering women less pay when they negotiate their compensation package.

You Decide . . .

Are the lower salary offers to women unethical? Why or why not? Should the onus be on women to change their negotiation style? Explain.

Sources: Adapted from A F Stuhlmacher and A E Walters, "Gender Differences in Negotiation Outcomes: A Meta-Analysis," *Personnel Psychology*, 52, 1992, pp 653–77; and "Women Must be Ready to Negotiate for Equal Pay," *Financial Post*, October 5–7, 1996, p 41.

Two Basic Types of Negotiation

Negotiation experts distinguish between two types of negotiation—*distributive* and *integrative*:

A *distributive* negotiation usually involves a single issue—a "fixed-pie"—in which one person gains at the expense of the other. For example, haggling over the price of a rug in a bazaar is a distributive negotiation. In most conflicts, however, more than one issue is at stake, and each party values the issues differently. The outcomes available are no longer a fixed-pie divided among all parties. An agreement can be found that is better for both parties than what they would have reached through distributive negotiation. This is an *integrative* negotiation.

However, parties in a negotiation often don't find these beneficial trade-offs because each *assumes* its interests *directly* conflict with those of the other party. "What is good for the other side must be bad for us" is a common and unfortunate perspective that most people have. This is the mind-set we call the *mythical* "fixed-pie."[43]

Distributive negotiation involves traditional win-lose thinking. Integrative negotiation calls for a progressive win-win strategy.[44] However, integrative negotiation is not equally effective across cultures. North American negotiators are generally too short-term oriented and poor relationship builders when negotiating in Asia, Latin America, and the Middle East.[45]

Added-Value Negotiation

One practical application of the integrative approach is **added-value nego-tiation** (AVN). During AVN, the negotiating parties cooperatively develop multiple deal packages while building a productive long-term relation-ship. AVN consists of these five steps:

> **Added-value negotiation**
>
> Cooperatively developing multiple-deal packages while building a long-term relationship.

1. *Clarify interests.* After each party identifies its tangible and intangible needs, the two parties meet to discuss their respective needs and find *common ground* for negotiation.

2. *Identify options.* A *marketplace of value* is created when the negotiating parties discuss desired elements of value (such as property, money, behaviour, rights, and risk reduction).

3. *Design alternative deal packages.* While aiming for *multiple deals,* each party mixes and matches elements of value from both parties in workable combinations.

4. *Select a deal.* Each party analyzes deal packages proposed by the other party. Jointly, the parties discuss and select from feasible deal packages, with a spirit of *creative agreement.*

5. *Perfect the deal.* Together the parties discuss unresolved issues, develop a written agreement, and *build relationships* for future negotiations.[46]

Ethical Pitfalls in Negotiation

The success of integrative negotiation hinges to a large extent on the quality of infor-mation exchanged.[47] Telling lies, hiding key facts, and engaging in other potentially unethical tactics listed in Table 8–2 erode trust and goodwill, both vital in win-win negotiations.[48] An awareness of these "dirty tricks" can keep good faith bargainers from being unfairly exploited.[49] Ethical negotiation practices need to be incorporated into organizational codes of ethics.

Practical Lessons from Negotiation Research

Research studies have yielded the following insights into negotiation:

- negotiators with fixed-pie expectations produced poor joint outcomes because they restricted and mismanaged information.[50]

- personality characteristics can affect negotiating success. Negotiators who scored high on the Big Five personality dimensions of extraversion and agreeableness (refer to Chapter 2) tended to do poorly with distributive, win-lose, negotiations.[51]

- good and bad moods can have positive and negative effects, respectively, on negotiators' plans and outcomes.[52]

- studies of negotiations between Japanese, between North Americans, and between Japanese and North Americans found less productive joint outcomes across

TABLE 8–2 Questionable/Unethical Tactics in Negotiation

Tactic	Description/Clarification/Range
Lies	Subject matter for lies can include limits, alternatives, the negotiator's intent, authority to bargain, other commitments, acceptability of the opponent's offers, time pressures, and available resources.
Puffery	Among the items that can be puffed up are the value of one's payoffs to the opponent, the negotiator's own alternatives, the costs of what one is giving up or is prepared to yield, importance of issues, and attributes of the products or services.
Deception	Acts and statements may include promises or threats, excessive initial demands, careless misstatements of facts, or asking for concessions not wanted.
Weakening the opponent	The negotiator here may cut off or eliminate some of the opponent's alternatives, blame the opponent for his own actions, use personally abrasive statements to or about the opponent, or undermine the opponent's alliances.
Strengthening one's own position	This tactic includes building one's own resources, including expertise, finances, and alliances. It also includes presentations of persuasive rationales to the opponent or third parties (e.g., the public, the media) or getting mandates for one's position.
Nondisclosure	Includes partial disclosure of facts, failure to disclose a hidden fact, failure to correct the opponents' misperceptions or ignorance, and concealment of the negotiator's own position or circumstances.
Information exploitation	Information provided by the opponent can be used to exploit his weaknesses, close off his alternatives, generate demands against him, or weaken his alliances.
Change of mind	Includes accepting offers one had claimed one would not accept, changing demands, withdrawing promised offers, and making threats one promised would not be made. Also includes the failure to behave as predicted.
Distraction	These acts or statements can be as simple as providing excessive information to the opponent, asking many questions, evading questions, or burying the issue. Or they can be more complex, such as feigning weakness in one area so that the opponent concentrates on it and ignores another.
Maximization	Includes demanding the opponent make concessions that result in the negotiator's gain and the opponent's equal or greater loss. Also entails converting a win-win situation into win-lose.

Source: H J Reitz, J A Wall, Jr, and M S Love, "Ethics in Negotiation: Oil and Water or Good Lubrication?" Reprinted with permission of *Business Horizons*, May–June 1998, p 6. Copyright © 1998 by the Board of Trustees at Indiana University, Kelley School of Business.

cultures than within cultures.[53] Less understanding of the other party makes cross-cultural negotiations more difficult than negotiations at home.

Third-Party Interventions: Alternative Dispute Resolution

Disputes between employees, between employees and their employer, and between companies too often end up in lengthy and costly court battles. A more constructive, less expensive approach called alternative dispute resolution has enjoyed enthusiastic growth in recent years.[54] In fact, the widely imitated "People's Court"–type television shows operating outside the formal judicial system are part of this trend toward what one writer calls "do-it-yourself justice."[55] **Alternative dispute resolution (ADR),** according to a pair of Canadian labour lawyers, "uses faster, more user-friendly methods of dispute resolution, instead of traditional, adversarial approaches (such as unilateral

Alternative dispute resolution

Avoiding costly lawsuits by resolving conflicts informally or through mediation or arbitration.

decision making or litigation)."[56] The following ADR techniques represent a progression of steps third parties can take to resolve organizational conflicts.[57] They are ranked from easiest and least expensive to most difficult and costly. A growing number of organizations have formal ADR policies involving an established sequence of various combinations of these techniques:

People's Court illustrates positive and negative aspects of Alternative Dispute Resolution (ADR)/ binding arbitration outside the formal judicial system.

- *Facilitation.* A third party, usually a manager, informally urges disputing parties to deal directly with each other in a positive and constructive manner.

- *Conciliation.* A neutral third party informally acts as a communication conduit between disputing parties. This is appropriate when conflicting parties refuse to meet face to face. The immediate goal is to establish direct communication, with the broader aim of finding common ground and a constructive solution.

- *Peer review.* A panel of trustworthy co-workers, selected for their ability to remain objective, hears both sides of a dispute in an informal and confidential meeting. Any decision by the review panel may or may not be binding, depending on the company's ADR policy. Membership on the peer review panel often is rotated among employees.

- *Ombudsperson.* Someone who works for the organization, and is widely respected and trusted by his or her co-workers, hears grievances on a confidential basis and attempts to arrange a solution. This approach, more common in Europe than North America, permits someone to get help from above without relying on the formal hierarchy chain.

- *Mediation.* "The mediator—a trained, third-party neutral—actively guides the disputing parties in exploring innovative solutions to the conflict. Although some companies have in-house mediators who have received ADR training, most also use external mediators who have no ties to the company."[58] A mediator does *not* render a decision. It is up to the disputants to reach a mutually acceptable decision.

- *Arbitration.* Disputing parties agree ahead of time to accept the decision of a neutral arbitrator in a formal courtlike setting, often complete with evidence and witnesses. Statements are confidential. Decisions are based on legal merits. Trained arbitrators, typically from provincial ministries of labour and other government agencies, are versed in relevant laws and case precedents.

summary of key concepts

- *Define the term* conflict, *distinguish between functional and dysfunctional conflict, and identify three desired outcomes of conflict.* Conflict is a process in which one party perceives that its interests are being opposed or negatively affected by another party. Too little conflict, as evidenced by apathy or lack of creativity, can be as great a problem as too much conflict. Functional conflict enhances organizational interests while dysfunctional conflict is counterproductive. Three desired conflict outcomes are agreement, stronger relationships, and learning.

- *Define* personality conflicts, *and explain how they should be managed.* Personality conflicts involve interpersonal opposition based on personal dislike and/or disagreement. Care needs to be taken with personality conflicts in the workplace because of antidiscrimination and sexual harassment laws. Managers should investigate and document personality conflicts, take corrective actions such as feedback or behaviour modification if appropriate, or attempt informal dispute resolution. Difficult or persistent personality conflicts need to be referred to human resource specialists or counselors.

- *Discuss the role of in-group thinking in intergroup conflict, and explain what can be done to avoid cross-cultural conflict.* Members of in-groups tend to see themselves as unique individuals who are more moral than outsiders, whom they view as a threat and stereotypically as all alike. Cross-cultural conflict can be minimized by being a good listener, being sensitive to others, and being more cooperative than competitive.

- *Identify the five conflict-handling styles.* The five conflict-handling styles are collaborating, accommodating, competing, avoiding, and compromising.

- *Identify and describe at least four alternative dispute resolution (ADR) techniques.* Alternative dispute resolution (ADR) involves avoiding costly court battles with more informal and user-friendly techniques such as facilitation, conciliation, peer review, ombudsperson, mediation, and arbitration.

- *Draw a distinction between distributive and integrative negotiation, and explain the concept of added-value negotiation.* Distributive negotiation involves fixed-pie and win-lose thinking. Integrative negotiation is a win-win approach to better results for both parties. The five steps in added value negotiation are as follows: clarify interests; identify options; design alternative deal packages; select a deal; and perfect the deal. Elements of value, multiple deals, and creative agreement are central to this approach.

key terms

added-value negotiation, 185
alternative dispute resolution
(ADR), 186

conflict, 174
devil's advocacy, 182
dysfunctional conflict, 175

functional conflict, 175
negotiation, 184

discussion questions

1. What examples of functional and dysfunctional conflict have you observed lately?

2. Have you ever been directly involved in a personality conflict? Explain. Was it handled well? Explain. What could have been done differently?

3. How could in-group thinking affect the performance of a manager living and working in a foreign country?

4. Which of the five conflict-handling styles is your strongest (your weakest)? How can you improve your ability to handle conflict?

5. Which of the six ADR techniques appeals the most to you? Why?

6. Has your concept of negotiation, prior to reading the chapter, been restricted to "fixed-pie" thinking? Explain.

internet exercises

www.pon.harvard.edu

1. Understanding Negotiation

Harvard Law School, in cooperation with other leading universities, hosts the Internet site "Program on Negotiation" (**www.pon.harvard.edu**). Select the heading "Publications" from the main menu. Next, click on "Negotiation Journal," scroll down and click on the hyper-link "*Negotiation Journal* homepage," select "Browse through the Table of Contents," and survey the brief article summaries from recent issues of that quarterly journal. Focus on topics and findings related to managing organizational behaviour.

QUESTIONS

1. What new insights did you pick up from the *Negotiation Journal* article summaries? Explain.
2. Do you now have a greater appreciation of the importance and complexity of the field of negotiation? Explain.
3. What do you need to do to become a better negotiator in important aspects of your life (such as relationships, family disagreements, pay raises and promotions, legal disputes, and academic assignments and grades)?

www.interculturequotient.com

2. Intercultural Quotient (IQ) Mini-Test

Enter the Web site for international cross-cultural consultant André Turcotte at **www.interculturequotient.com** and read about the "Intercultural Quotient (IQ)" which is intended to provide information about potential for cross-cultural business success. Click to take the IQ Mini-Test. Answer the questions based on your personal interest in a cross-cultural business career, complete the mini-test, and click to submit this information via E-mail. Results will be E-mailed back to you within a day or so.

QUESTIONS

1. What was the level of your (a) knowledge, (b) skills, and (c) behaviours regarding intercultural issues? What was your overall IQ?
2. What specific information was provided about your state of readiness for a cross-cultural business career? Explain.
3. Do you have some idea of areas where you need to strengthen your cross-cultural knowledge, skills, and behaviours? If so, what are they?

experiential exercises

1. Bangkok Blowup (A Role-Playing Exercise)

Objectives

1. To further your knowledge of interpersonal conflict and conflict-handling styles.
2. To give you a firsthand opportunity to try the various styles of handling conflict.

Introduction

This is a role-playing exercise intended to develop your ability to handle conflict. There is no single best way to resolve the conflict in this exercise. One style might work for one person, while another gets the job done for someone else.

Instructions

Read the following short case, "Can Larry Fit In?" Pair up with someone else and decide which of you will play the role of Larry and which will play the role of Melissa, the office manager. Pick up the action from where the case leaves off. Try to be realistic and true to the characters in the case. The manager is primarily responsible for resolving this conflict situation. Whoever plays Larry should resist any unreasonable requests or demands and cooperate with any personally workable solution. Note: To conserve time, try to resolve this situation in less than 15 minutes.

CASE: "CAN LARRY FIT IN?"

Melissa, Office Manager

You are the manager of an auditing team sent to Bangkok, Thailand, to represent a major international accounting firm headquartered in New York. You and Larry, one of your auditors, were sent to Bangkok to set up an auditing operation. Larry is about seven years older than you and has five more years seniority in the firm. Your relationship has become very strained since you were recently designated as the office manager. You feel you were given the promotion because you have established an excellent working relationship with the Thai staff as well as a broad range of international clients. In contrast, Larry has told other members of the staff that your promotion simply reflects the firm's heavy emphasis on employment equity. He has tried to isolate you from the all-male accounting staff by focusing discussions on sports, local night spots, and so forth.

You are sitting in your office reading some complicated new reporting procedures that have just arrived from the home office. Your concentration is suddenly interrupted by a loud knock on your door. Without waiting for an invitation to enter, Larry bursts into your office. He is obviously very upset, and it is not difficult for you to surmise why he is in such a nasty mood.

You recently posted the audit assignments for the coming month, and you scheduled Larry for a job you knew he wouldn't like. Larry is one of your senior auditors, and the company norm is that they get the choice assignments. This particular job will require him to spend two weeks away from Bangkok in a remote town, working with a company whose records are notoriously messy.

Unfortunately, you have had to assign several of these less-desirable audits to Larry recently because you are short of personnel. But that's not the only reason. You have received several complaints from the junior staff (all Thais) recently that Larry treats them in a condescending manner. They feel he is always looking for an opportunity to boss them around, as if he were their supervisor instead of an experienced, supportive mentor. As a result, your whole operation works more smoothly when you can send Larry out of town on a solo project for several days. It keeps him from coming into your office and telling you how to do your job, and the morale of the rest of the auditing staff is significantly higher.

Larry slams the door and proceeds to express his anger over this assignment.

Larry, Senior Auditor

You are really ticked off! Melissa is deliberately trying to undermine your status in the office. She knows that the company norm is that senior auditors get the better jobs. You've paid your dues, and now you expect to be treated with respect. And this isn't the first time this has happened. Since she was made the office manager, she has tried to keep you out of the office as much as possible. It's as if she doesn't want her rival for leadership of the office around. When you were asked to go to Bangkok, you assumed that you would be made the office manager because of your seniority in the firm. You are certain that the decision to pick Melissa is yet another indication of reverse discrimination against white males.

In staff meetings, Melissa has talked about the need to be sensitive to the feelings of the office staff as well as the clients in this multicultural setting. "Where does she come off preaching about sensitivity! What about my feelings, for heaven's sake?" you wonder. This is nothing more than a straightforward power play. She is probably feeling insecure about being the only female accountant in the office and being promoted over someone with more experience. "Sending me out of town," you decide, "is a clear case of 'out of sight, out of mind.' "

Well, it's not going to happen that easily. You are not going to roll over and let her treat you unfairly. It's time for a showdown. If she doesn't agree to change this assignment and apologize for the way she's been treating you, you're going to register a formal complaint with her boss in the New York office. You are prepared to submit your resignation if the situation doesn't improve.

QUESTIONS FOR DISCUSSION

1. What causes of conflict appear to be present in this situation? What can be done about them?
2. Having heard how others handled this conflict, did one particular style seem to work better than the others?

Source: Adapted from *Developing Management Skills* (5th edition) by D A Whetten and K S Cameron, Upper Saddle River, NJ, Prentice-Hall, 2002, pp 391–92.

2. Ugli Orange Role Play

Purpose

This exercise is designed to help you understand the dynamics of interpersonal and intergroup conflict as well as the effectiveness of negotiation strategies under specific conditions.

Materials

The instructor will distribute roles for Dr Roland, Dr Jones, and a few observers. Ideally, each negotiation should occur in a private area away from other negotiations.

Instructions

Step 1: The instructor will divide the class into an even number of teams of three people each with one participant left over for each team formed (e.g., six observers if there are six teams). One-half of the teams will take the role of Dr Roland and the other half will be Dr Jones. The instructor will distribute roles after the teams have been formed.

Step 2: Members within each team are given 10 minutes (or other time limit stated by the instructor) to learn their roles and decide on a negotiating strategy.

Step 3: After reading their roles and discussing strategy, each Dr Jones team is matched with a Dr Roland team to conduct negotiations. Two observers will be assigned to watch the paired teams during pre-negotiations and subsequent negotiations.

Step 4: At the end of the negotiations, the class will congregate for a discussion. The observers will describe the process and outcomes in their negotiating session. The instructor will then invite the negotiators to describe their experiences and the implications for conflict management.

Source: This exercise was developed by Dr Robert J House, Wharton Business School, University of Pennsylvania.

personal awareness and growth exercises

1. What Is Your Conflict-Handling Style?

Instructions

For each of the 15 items, indicate how often you rely on that tactic by circling the appropriate number.

Conflict-Handling Tactics	Rarely				Always
1. I argue my case with my co-workers to show the merits of my position.	1	2	3	4	5
2. I negotiate with my co-workers so that a compromise can be reached.	1	2	3	4	5
3. I try to satisfy the expectations of my co-workers.	1	2	3	4	5
4. I try to investigate an issue with my co-workers to find a solution acceptable to us.	1	2	3	4	5
5. I am firm in pursuing my side of the issue.	1	2	3	4	5
6. I attempt to avoid being "put on the spot" and try to keep my conflict with my co-workers to myself.	1	2	3	4	5

7. I hold on to my solution to a problem.   1   2   3   4   5

8. I use "give and take" so that a compromise can be made.   1   2   3   4   5

9. I exchange accurate information with my co-workers to solve a problem together.   1   2   3   4   5

10. I avoid open discussion of my differences with my co-workers.   1   2   3   4   5

11. I accommodate the wishes of my co-workers.   1   2   3   4   5

12. I try to bring all our concerns out in the open so that the issues can be resolved in the best possible way.   1   2   3   4   5

13. I propose a middle ground for breaking deadlocks.   1   2   3   4   5

14. I go along with the suggestions of my co-workers.   1   2   3   4   5

15. I try to keep my disagreements with my co-workers to myself in order to avoid hard feelings.   1   2   3   4   5

Integrating		Obliging		Dominating	
Item	Score	Item	Score	Item	Score
4.	_____	3.	_____	1.	_____
9.	_____	11.	_____	5.	_____
12.	_____	14.	_____	7.	_____
Total =	_____	Total =	_____	Total =	_____

Avoiding		Compromising	
Item	Score	Item	Score
6.	_____	2.	_____
10.	_____	8.	_____
15.	_____	13.	_____
Total =	_____	Total =	_____

Your primary conflict-handling style is: _____ (The category with the highest total.)

Your backup conflict-handling style is: _____ (The category with the second highest total.)

QUESTIONS FOR DISCUSSION

1. Are the results what you expected? Explain.
2. Is there a clear gap between your primary and backup styles, or did they score about the same? If they are about the same, does this suggest indecision about handling conflict on your part? Explain.
3. Will your primary conflict-handling style carry over well to many different situations? Explain.

Scoring and Interpretation

Enter your responses, item by item, in the five categories below, and then add the three scores for each of the styles. Note: There are no right or wrong answers, because individual differences are involved.

Source: Adapted from a longer instrument in M A Rahim, "A Measure of Styles of Handling Interpersonal Conflict," *Academy of Management Journal,* June 1983, pp 368–76. A validation of the original instrument can be found in E Van De Vliert and B Kabanoff, "Toward Theory-Based Measures of Conflict Management," *Academy of Management Journal,* March 1990, pp 199–209.

2. Managing Interpersonal Conflict

Respond to the following statements using the six-point rating scale that follows. Your answers should reflect your attitudes and behaviour as they are now, not as you would like them to be.

Rating Scale

1 strongly disagree
2 disagree
3 slightly disagree
4 slightly agree
5 agree
6 strongly agree

When I see something that needs correcting:

_____ 1. I avoid making personal accusations and attributing self-serving motives to the other person.

_____ 2. When stating my concerns, I present them as my problems.

_____ 3. I succinctly describe problems in terms of the behaviour that occurred, its consequences, and my feelings about it.

_____ 4. I specify the expectations and standards that have been violated.

_____ 5. I make a specific request, detailing a more acceptable option.

_____ 6. I persist in explaining my point of view until it is understood by the other person.

_____ 7. I encourage two-way interaction by inviting the respondent to express his or her perspective and to ask questions.

_____ 8. When there are several concerns, I approach the issues incrementally, starting with easy and simple issues and them progressing to those that are difficult and complex.

When someone complains about something I've done:

_____ 9. I look for our common areas of agreement.

_____ 10. I show genuine concern and interests, even when I disagree.

_____ 11. I avoid justifying my actions and becoming defensive.

_____ 12. I seek additional information by asking questions that provide specific and descriptive information.

_____ 13. I focus on one issue at a time.

_____ 14. I find some aspects of the complaint with which I can agree.

_____ 15. I ask the other person to suggest more acceptable behaviours.

_____ 16. I strive to reach agreement on a remedial plan of action.

When two other people are in conflict and I am the mediator:

_____ 17. I acknowledge that conflict exists and treat it as serious and important.

_____ 18. I help create an agenda for a problem-solving meeting by identifying the issues to be discussed, one at a time.

_____ 19. I do not take sides, but remain neutral.

_____ 20. I help focus the discussion on the impact of the conflict on work performance.

_____ 21. I keep the interaction focused on problems rather than on personalities.

_____ 22. I make certain that neither party dominates the conversation.

_____ 23. I help make the parties generate multiple alternatives.

_____ 24. I help the parties find areas on which they agree.

Compare your scores to three comparison standards:
1. compare your score with the maximum possible (144);
2. compare your scores with the scores of other students in your class;
3. compare your scores with a norm group consisting of 500 practicing managers and business school students.

In comparison to the norm group, if you scored

120 or above	you are in the top quartile
116–119	you are in the second quartile
98–115	you are in the third quartile
97 and below	you are in the bottom quartile

What do these comparisons tell you about your skill level in dealing with conflict? Explain.

Source: D A Whetton and K S Cameron, _Developing Management Skills_, 5th edition, 2002, (Upper Saddle River NJ: Prentice-Hall). Used with permission.

CBC video case

Stak-Its

Kerry Lucier, inventor of Stak-Its collectibles for kids, is in a bad financial situation, facing significant debt repayments that could lead to bankruptcy. His original group of investors has provided $500,000 over the past four years. But Kerry has found it difficult to break into the toy business, and there have still been no sales of the Stak-Its product.

In order to address the sales problem, the company hired Peter George. Kerry, Peter, and the investors all believe that Stak-Its is a great product with good sales potential. But Peter has connections to a US investor and is pursuing them for $20 million, without involving Kerry. This creates a conflict with Kerry, who is insulted at being left out. Kerry then calls a meet-

ing of the original investors and doesn't invite Peter. The next day Peter meets with both Kerry and the investors. Behind closed doors, tense negotiations ensue and eventually Kerry accepts Peter's efforts and just wants to be kept informed.

QUESTIONS FOR DISCUSSION
1. What are the sources of conflict in this situation?
2. What conflict resolution tactics were used to address the conflict between Kerry and Peter?
3. What could have been done differently to avoid or minimize the conflict before it began?

Source: Based on "Stak-Its," _CBC Venture 759_ (October 10, 2000).

chapter
nine
Communication

LEARNING OUTCOMES

After reading the material in this chapter, you should be able to:

• Describe the perceptual process model of communication.

• Demonstrate your familiarity with four causes of communication distortion between managers and employees.

• Contrast the communication styles of assertiveness, aggressiveness, and nonassertiveness.

• Discuss the primary sources of nonverbal communication and 10 keys to active listening.

• Explain the information technology of Internet/Intranet/Extranet, E-mail, video-conferencing, and collaborative computing, and explain the related use of telecommuting.

• Describe the process, personal, physical, and semantic barriers to effective communication.

TOP EMPLOYERS TAKE EMPLOYEE COMMUNICATION SERIOUSLY

Several of Canada's leading employers, as reported in Richard Yerema's book *Canada's Top 100 Employers*, are very serious about employee communication. Ottawa's AiT Corp. encourages the flow of ideas by maintaining several staff committees to deal with workplace issues. President Bernie Ashe says that the best ideas usually come from the bottom up rather than the top down. An employee committee sold him on the benefits of an exercise room, as well as a quiet room equipped with couches for software developers who may need a nap during a long day. As well, on Friday mornings, Ashe holds an open meeting to keep everyone current on new developments in the company. Such initiatives have helped keep turnover below 10 percent annually in an industry where a 20 percent change in staff is commonplace when the economy is healthy. "You feel involved and included here," says salesman Peter Sakkal. "People buy in when they feel they're contributing."

At Zenon Environmental Inc. in Burlington, Ontario, staff members can express their views on corporate issues through a special committee, referred to as the "Zenon Parliament." Such input led to the inclusion of a fit-

Bernie Ashe, President, AiT Corp.

ness centre in their new building, as well as a subsidized cafeteria that specializes in low-fat, nutritious meals.

At fast-growing high-tech firm Exfo Electro-Optical Engineering Inc., based in the Quebec City suburb of Vanier, president Germain Lamonde works at keeping his employees happy by having lunch once a month with a small group of employees. He also holds quarterly meetings for all staff.

At the accounting and professional services giant Ernst & Young LLP, the company tries to keep abreast of issues and concerns through employee surveys, and recently set up a 21-member "people's advisory forum" made up of staffers from across the Americas. The group meets quarterly in New York City with the chairman, chief executive, director of human resources, and other high-level executives. "We don't make decisions, but we do provide a reality check," says forum member Janice Rath, an audit manager in Montreal. "It's been a great opportunity to have access to leaders of the firm."

Note: In 2002, AiT Corp. merged with 3M's Security Market Centre to form 3M-AiT, Ltd.

Source: D Jenish and B Woodward, "Canada's Top 100 Employers," *Maclean's*, November 5, 2001, pp 46–56.

Basic Dimensions of the Communication Process

Every managerial function and activity involves some form of direct or indirect communication. Whether planning and organizing or directing and leading, managers find themselves communicating with and through others. Managerial decisions and organizational policies are ineffective unless they are understood by those responsible for enacting them. Moreover, effective communication is critical for employee motivation and job satisfaction. Employee satisfaction with organizational communication has been found to be positively and significantly correlated with job satisfaction and performance.[1]

Communication is defined as "the exchange of information between a sender and a receiver, and the inference (perception) of meaning between the individuals involved."[2] Analysis of this exchange reveals that communication is a two-way process consisting of consecutively linked elements (see Figure 9–1). Managers who understand this process can analyze their own communication patterns as well as design communication programs that fit organizational needs. This section reviews a perceptual process model of communication and discusses communication distortion.

> **Communication**
>
> Interpersonal exchange of information and understanding.

A Perceptual Process Model of Communication

As we all know, communicating is not that simple or clear-cut. Communication is fraught with miscommunication when receivers interpret messages by cognitively processing information. This view led to development of a perceptual model of communication that depicts communication as a process in which receivers create meaning in their own minds. Let us briefly examine the elements of the perceptual process model shown in Figure 9–1.

FIGURE 9–1   A Perceptual Model of Communication

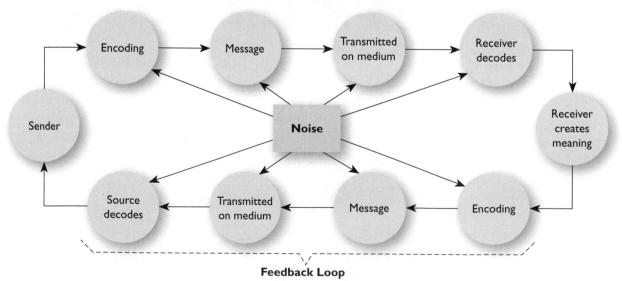

Feedback Loop

Sender   The sender is an individual, group, or organization that desires or attempts to communicate with a particular receiver. Receivers may be individuals, groups, or organizations.

Encoding   Communication begins when a sender encodes an idea or thought. Encoding translates mental thoughts into a code or language that can be understood by others. Managers typically encode using words, numbers, gestures, nonverbal cues such as facial expressions, or pictures. Moreover, different methods of encoding can be used to portray similar ideas.

The Message   The output of encoding is a message. There are two important points to keep in mind about messages. First, they contain more than meets the eye. Messages may contain hidden agendas as well as trigger emotional reactions. Second, messages need to match the medium used to transmit them. How would you evaluate the match between the message of letting someone know they have been laid off and the communication medium used in the following examples?

> A man finds out he has been let go when a restaurant won't accept his company credit card. A woman manager gets the news via a note placed on her chair during lunch. Employees at a high-tech firm learn of their fate when their security codes no longer open the front door of their office building.[3]

These horrible mismatches reveal how thoughtless managers can be when they do not carefully consider the interplay between a message and the medium used to convey it.

Selecting a Medium   Managers can communicate through a variety of media. Potential media include face-to-face conversations, telephone calls, electronic mail, voice mail, videoconferencing, written memos or letters, photographs or drawings, meetings, bulletin boards, computer output, and charts or graphs. Choosing the appropriate media depends on many factors, including the nature of the message, its intended purpose, the type of audience, proximity to the audience, time horizon for disseminating the message, personal preferences, and the complexity of the problem/situation at hand.

All media have advantages and disadvantages and should be used in different situations. Face-to-face conversations, for example, are useful for communicating about sensitive or important issues that require feedback and intensive interaction. In contrast, telephones are convenient, fast, and private, but lack nonverbal information. Although writing memos or letters is time consuming, it is a good medium when it is difficult to meet with the other person, when formality and a written record are important, and when face-to-face interaction is not necessary to enhance understanding. Electronic communication, which is discussed later in this chapter, can be used to communicate with a large number of dispersed people and is potentially a very fast medium when recipients of messages regularly check their E-mail.[4]

In order to choose an effective communication medium, its "richness" must be considered. **Media richness** is the potential information-carrying capacity of a medium. Media richness is determined by four factors: feedback (ranging from immediate to very slow); channel (ranging from a combined visual and audio to limited visual); type of communication (personal versus impersonal); and language source (body, natural, or numeric). Face-to-face is the richest form of communication because it provides immediate feedback,

Media richness

The potential information-carrying capacity of a communication medium.

FIGURE 9–2 | A Contingency Model for Selecting Communications Media

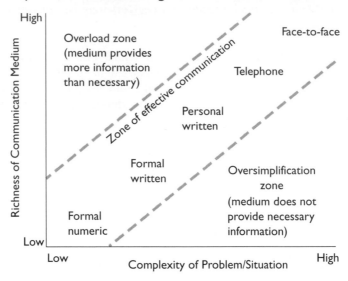

Adapted from R L Daft and R H Lengel, "Information Richness: A New Approach to Managerial Behavior and Organization Design," in *Research in Organizational Behavior,* eds B M Staw and L L Cummings (Greenwich, CT: JAI Press, 1984), p 199. Used with permission.

and it allows for the observation of multiple language clues such as body language and tone of voice, over more than one channel.

Managers choose communication media for situations that range in complexity. Low complexity situations, such as calculating a paycheque, can be managed with low-richness media such as a computer printout. Highly complex situations like a corporate reorganization are ambiguous, unpredictable, hard to analyze, and often emotionally laden. These situations need to be managed with high-richness media. A contingency model for selecting media based on the complexity of the situation is shown in Figure 9–2. Media low in richness are better suited for simple situations, while rich media are effective for complex situations. Ineffective communication results when the richness of the medium is too high or too low for the complexity of the situation.

Decoding   Decoding is the receiver's version of encoding. Decoding consists of translating verbal, oral, or visual aspects of a message into a form that can be interpreted. Decoding is a key contributor to misunderstanding in intercultural communication because decoding by the receiver is subject to social values and cultural values that may not be understood by the sender.

Creating Meaning   The perceptual model of communication is based on the belief that a receiver creates the meaning of a message in his or her head. A receiver's interpretation of a message can thus differ from that intended by the sender. In turn, receivers act according to their own interpretations, not the communicator's.

Feedback   When the receiver responds to a message, he or she becomes a sender. Specifically, the receiver encodes a response and then transmits it to the original sender. This new message is then decoded and interpreted. Thus feedback is used as a comprehension check. It gives senders an idea of how accurately their message is understood.

Noise   **Noise** represents anything that interferes with the transmission and understanding of a message. It affects all linkages of the communication process. Noise includes factors such as a speech impairment, poor telephone connections, illegible handwriting, inaccurate statistics in a memo or report, poor hearing and eyesight, and physical distance between sender and receiver. Managers can improve communication by reducing noise. For example, Chris Schneck, a Merrill Lynch financial consultant, reduces communication noise for hearing-impaired clients by discussing their investments through his typewriter or a sign interpreter.[5]

> **Noise**
> Interference with the transmission and understanding of a message.

Organizational Communication Patterns

Examining organizational communication patterns is a good way to identify factors contributing to effective and ineffective management. **Hierarchical communication** is defined as an information exchange downward from managers to employees and upward from employees to managers. Managers provide information regarding job instructions, job rationale, organizational procedures and practices, feedback about performance, and goals. Employees communicate information about themselves, coworkers and their problems, organizational practices and policies, and what needs to be done and how to do it. A recent Canadian study by Watson Wyatt found an "understanding gap" between the perceptions of managers and the perceptions of employees about critical organizational functions and activities. They pointed out that a breakdown in communication between management and employees impedes the effectiveness and productivity of people, and concluded that Canadian companies need to renew their focus on getting information to, and more importantly, from employees.[6]

> **Hierarchical communication**
> Exchange of information between managers and employees.

Employees often do not receive enough information from their immediate supervisors. It is therefore no surprise that the grapevine is such a common lateral source of information. The **grapevine** represents the unofficial communication system of the informal organization. Information from the grapevine supplements official or formal channels of communication. Although the grapevine can be a source of inaccurate rumours, it functions positively as an early warning signal for organizational changes, a medium for creating organizational culture, a mechanism for fostering group cohesiveness, and a way of informally bouncing ideas off others.[7] Evidence indicates that the grapevine is alive and well in today's organizations.

> **Grapevine**
> Unofficial communication system of the informal organization.

Research on the grapevine has found that it is faster than formal channels, it is about 75% accurate, and employees use the grapevine to acquire the majority of their on-the-job information. Further, people rely on the grapevine when they are insecure, threatened, or faced with organizational changes.[8] Managers should monitor and influence the grapevine rather than attempt to control it, by sharing relevant information with employees.

Communication distortion occurs when an employee purposely modifies the content of a message, thereby reducing the accuracy of communication between managers and employees. Employees tend to engage in this practice because of workplace politics, a desire to manage impressions, or fear of how a manager might respond to a message.[9] Communication

> **Communication distortion**
> Purposely modifying the content of a message.

ETHICS AT WORK

Résumé Fraud

A survey by Canadian reference checking firm Infocheck Ltd. found that 33 percent of short-listed job candidates lied or concealed past performance problems on their résumés. In one case, a Manitoba man applied for a school principal's job. His resume said he had 15 years' teaching experience, as well as a Bachelor of Education degree. But after investigating, Infocheck discovered that he did not have a degree. More astounding, he had died in 1996. The job applicant had assumed someone else's identity and had five criminal convictions.

It even happens with high-profile public figures. In 1996, Alberta's Deputy Minister of Health, Jane Fulton, lost her job after it was alleged that she had inflated her academic and professional credentials. In 1994, former Liberal MP Jag Bhaduria was forced to quit the Liberal caucus after it was revealed he did not have a law degree as he claimed on his résumé and campaign material.

The most serious offence is lying about education. An interesting trend is that some résumés mention "attending" various post-secondary institutions rather than listing actual educational achievements. Many others exaggerate their job titles, responsibilities, or dates of employment.

And they get away with it. Vincent Tsang, a partner in Infocheck says, "The truth is that in Canada, about 50 percent of companies put people on their payroll without conducting a proper check. . . . Why take a chance? Nightmare employees can damage a company's reputation, which turns in to a loss of productivity and a public relations nightmare. . . . These things happen more often than people realize." Tsang says that the failure to check is largely the result of widespread corporate downsizing that has left managers and human resources departments without the time or resources to carry out proper background checks.

You Decide . . .

Should companies allocate more money for reference checking? What else can they do to reduce the negative consequences of this type of fraud? Explain.

Source: Adapted from *www.infocheck.ca/news.html*, March 27, 2002.

experts point out the organizational problems caused by distortion:

Distortion is an important problem in organizations because modifications to messages cause misdirectives to be transmitted, nondirectives to be issued, incorrect information to be passed on, and a variety of other problems related to both the quantity and quality of information.[10]

Knowledge of the causes of communication distortion can help managers avoid or limit these problems.

Studies have identified four situational causes of distortion in upward communication. Distortion tends to increase when supervisors have high upward influence and/or power. Employees also tend to modify or distort information when they aspire to move upward and when they do not trust their supervisors.[11] Because managers generally do not want to reduce their upward influence or curb their direct reports' desire for upward mobility, they can reduce distortion in several ways:

1. Managers can deemphasize power differences between themselves and their direct reports.

2. They can enhance trust through a meaningful performance review process that rewards actual performance.

3. Managers can encourage staff feedback by conducting smaller, more informal meetings.

4. They can establish performance goals that encourage employees to focus on problems rather than personalities.

5. Distortion can be limited by encouraging dialogue between those with opposing viewpoints.

Interpersonal Communication

The quality of interpersonal communication within an organization is very important. People with good communication skills can help groups make better decisions and can be promoted more frequently than individuals with less developed abilities.[12] With this in mind, the goal of this section is to provide information that can help improve interpersonal communication skills. We begin by discussing the communication styles of assertiveness, aggressiveness, and nonassertiveness and then review material pertaining to nonverbal communication and active listening. We conclude this section by highlighting gender differences in communication.

Assertiveness, Aggressiveness, and Nonassertiveness

The saying,"You can attract more flies with honey than with vinegar," captures the difference between using an assertive communication style and an aggressive style. Research studies indicate that assertiveness is more effective than aggressiveness in both work-related and consumer contexts.[13] An **assertive style** is expressive and self-enhancing and is based on the "ethical notion that it is not right or good to violate our own or others' basic human rights, such as the right to self-expression or the right to be treated with dignity and respect."[14] In contrast, an **aggressive style** is expressive and self-enhancing and strives to take unfair advantage of others. A **nonassertive style** is characterized by timid and self-denying behaviour. Nonassertiveness is ineffective because it gives the other person an unfair advantage.

Assertive style

Expressive and self-enhancing, but does not take advantage of others.

Aggressive style

Expressive and self-enhancing, but takes unfair advantage of others.

Nonassertive style

Timid and self-denying behaviour.

Managers may improve their communication competence by trying to be more assertive and less aggressive or nonassertive. This can be achieved by using the appropriate nonverbal and verbal behaviours listed in Table 9–1. For instance, managers should attempt to use the nonverbal behaviours of good eye contact, a strong, steady, and audible voice, and selective interruptions. They should avoid nonverbal behaviours such as glaring or little eye contact, threatening gestures, slumped posture, and a weak or whiny voice. Appropriate verbal behaviours include direct and unambiguous language and the use of "I" messages instead of "you" statements. For example, when you say, "Mike, I was disappointed with your report because it contained typographical errors," rather than "Mike, your report was poorly done," you reduce defensiveness. "I" statements describe your feelings about someone's performance or behaviour instead of laying blame on the person.

Managers with an assertive style tend to be better communicators with their colleagues.

Sources of Nonverbal Communication

Nonverbal communication is "Any message, sent or received independent of the written or spoken word . . . [It] includes such factors as use of time and space, distance between persons when conversing, use of colour, dress, walking behaviour, standing, positioning, seating arrangement, office locations and furnishing."[15]

Experts estimate that 65% to 90% of every conversation is partially interpreted through body language.[16] Because of the prevalence of nonverbal communication and its significant effect on organizational behaviour (including, but not limited to, perceptions of others, hiring decisions, work attitudes, turnover, and the acceptance of one's ideas in a presentation),[17] it is important that managers become consciously aware of the sources of nonverbal commu-

Nonverbal communication

Messages sent outside of the written or spoken word.

TABLE 9–1   Communication Styles

Communication Style	Description	Nonverbal Behaviour Pattern	Verbal Behaviour Pattern
Assertive	Pushing hard without attacking; permits others to influence outcome; expressive and self-enhancing without intruding on others	Good eye contact Comfortable but firm posture Strong, steady, and audible voice Facial expressions matched to message Appropriately serious tone Selective interruptions to ensure understanding	Direct and unambiguous language No attributions or evaluations of other's behaviour Use of "I" statements and cooperative "we" statements
Aggressive	Taking advantage of others; expressive and self-enhancing at other's expense	Glaring eye contact Moving or leaning too close Threatening gestures (pointed finger; clenched fist) Loud voice Frequent interruptions	Swear words and abusive language Attributions and evaluations of other's behaviour Sexist or racist terms Explicit threats or put-downs
Nonassertive	Encouraging others to take advantage of us; inhibited; self-denying	Little eye contact Downward glances Slumped posture Constantly shifting weight Wringing hands Weak or whiny voice	Qualifiers ("maybe"; "kind of") Fillers ("uh," "you know," "well") Negaters ("It's not really that important"; "I'm not sure")

Source: Adapted in part from J A Waters, "Managerial Assertiveness," *Business Horizons*, September–October 1982, pp 24–29.

nication. Communications consultant Sandy French calls face-to-face communication a lost art. He says, "I have a blunt message to all supervisors, managers, and in particular executives. Stop whatever you're doing, get out of your office, and talk to your people. Many companies I work for have lost, ignore, or never cultivated this fundamental skill. . . . The great irony is that management is about working with people, it's not closed doors, voice messages, or memos."[18]

Body Movements and Gestures   Body movements, such as leaning forward or backward, and gestures, such as pointing, provide additional nonverbal information that can either enhance or detract from the communication process. Open body positions such as leaning backward, communicate *immediacy,* a term used to represent openness, warmth, closeness, and availability for communication. *Defensiveness* is communicated by gestures such as folding arms, crossing hands, and crossing one's legs. Although it is interesting to interpret body movements and gestures, it is important to remember that body-language analysis is subjective, easily misinterpreted, and highly dependent on the context and cross-cultural differences.[19] Thus, managers need to be careful when trying to interpret body movements. Inaccurate interpretations can create additional "noise" in the communication process.

Touch   Touching is another powerful nonverbal cue. People tend to touch those they like. Women do more touching during conversations than men.[20] Touching conveys an impression of warmth and caring and can be used to create a personal bond between people. Be careful about touching people from diverse cultures, however, as norms for touching vary significantly around the world.[21]

Facial Expressions   Facial expressions convey a wealth of information. Smiling, for instance, typically represents warmth, happiness, or friendship, whereas frowning conveys dissatisfaction or anger. Do you think these interpretations apply to different cross-cultural groups? A recent summary of relevant research revealed that the association between facial expressions and emotions varies across cultures.[22] A smile, for example, does not convey the same emotion in different countries. Therefore, managers need to be careful in interpreting facial expressions among diverse groups of employees.

Eye Contact   Eye contact is a strong nonverbal cue that varies across cultures. Westerners are taught at an early age to look at their parents when spoken to. In contrast, Asians are taught to avoid eye contact with a parent or superior in order to show obedience and subservience.[23] Once again, managers should be sensitive to different orientations toward maintaining eye contact with diverse employees.

Practical Tips   It is important to have good nonverbal communication skills in light of the fact that they are related to the development of positive interpersonal relationships. Consider, for example, the problems noted by Anne Warfield, a management consultant, as she worked with a manager whose department had bad morale:

> He [the manager] asked his staff what they wanted from him. They requested that he drop by their offices once in a while and also schedule regular meetings with them. The manager did both, but the morale got worse. . . . I found that the man's body language was causing all of the problems. It was domineering. When he dropped into people's offices, he'd take up the whole doorway or walk up to their desks and look them in the eye—even if they were on the phone! People found his behaviour unnerving. It sent the message that their personal space belonged to him. At

In your present employment as general manager, have you ever given someone the evil eye, hexed someone, or voodooed anyone?

Source: Harvard Business Review, April 2001.

Norms for Touching Vary Across Countries

China
—hugging or taking someone's arm is considered inappropriate
—winking or beckoning with one's index finger is considered rude

The Philippines
—handshaking and a pat on the back are common greetings

Indonesia
—handshaking and head nodding are common greetings

Japan
—business cards are exchanged before bowing or handshaking
—a weak handshake is common
—lengthy or frequent eye contact is considered impolite

Malaysia
—it is considered impolite to touch someone casually especially on the top of the head
—it is best to use your right hand to eat and to touch people and things

South Korea
—men bow slightly and shake hands, sometimes with two hands; women refrain from shaking hands
—it is considered polite to cover your mouth while laughing

Thailand
—public displays of temper or affection are frowned upon
—it is considered impolite to point at anything using your foot or to show the soles of your feet

Source: Guidelines taken from R E Axtell, *Gestures: The Do's and Taboos of Body Language Around the World* (New York: John Wiley & Sons, 1991).

meetings, the manager would place his hands behind his head, cross his legs, lean back, and look at the ceiling. That body language said that he already had all of the answers.[24]

Ms Warfield helped this manager to improve his employees' morale by pointing out and correcting the messages being sent by his body language. There are a number of specific guidelines for improving nonverbal communication skills. Positive nonverbal actions include the following:

- Maintain eye contact.
- Nod your head to convey that you are listening or that you agree.
- Smile and show interest.
- Lean forward to show the speaker you are interested.
- Use a tone of voice that matches your message.

Negative nonverbal behaviours include the following:

- Avoiding eye contact and looking away from the speaker.
- Closing your eyes or tensing your facial muscles.
- Excessive yawning.

- Using body language that conveys indecisiveness or lack of confidence (e.g., slumped shoulders, head down, flat tones, inaudible voice).
- Speaking too fast or too slow.

Active Listening

Some communication experts contend that listening is the keystone communication skill for employees involved in sales, customer service, or management. In support of this conclusion, research has found listening effectiveness to be positively associated with success in sales and obtaining managerial promotions.[25]

Listening involves much more than hearing a message. Hearing is merely the physical component of listening. **Listening** is the process of *actively* decoding and interpreting verbal messages. Listening requires cognitive attention and information processing; hearing does not. With these distinctions in mind, we examine listening styles and offer some practical advice for becoming a more effective listener.

> **Listening**
> Actively decoding and interpreting verbal messages.

Listening Styles   A pair of communication experts identified three different listening styles. Their research indicated that people prefer to hear information that is suited to their own listening style. People also tend to speak in a style that is consistent with their own listening style. Because inconsistent styles represent a barrier to effective listening, it is important for managers to understand and respond to the different listening styles. The three listening styles are called "results," "reasons," and "process." It is important to note that one style is not necessarily better than the others.[26]

Results-style listeners don't like beating around the bush. They are direct, action oriented, like to ask questions, and are interested in hearing the bottom line of the communication message first. They can be perceived as blunt or rude. **Reasons-style listeners** want to know the rationale for what someone is saying or proposing. They like to weigh and balance information and expect others to present information in a logical manner. In contrast, **process-style listeners** like to discuss issues in detail. They are more people than results oriented and have high concern for relationships, believing that people and relationships are the keys to long-term success. Process-style listeners also like to consider or receive a lot of information when making decisions, and they tend to use indirect language. The use of indirect language can frustrate results-style listeners who prefer direct communications.

> **Results-style listeners**
> Interested in hearing the bottom line or result of a message.
> **Reasons-style listeners**
> Interested in hearing the rationale behind a message.
> **Process-style listeners**
> Likes to discuss issues in detail.

Managers can gain greater acceptance of their ideas and proposals by adapting the form and content of a message to fit a receiver's listening style:

1. For a results-style listener, for instance, the sender should present the bottom line at the beginning of the discussion.
2. Explain your rationale to a reasons-style listener.
3. For a process-style listener, describe the process and the benefits.

Becoming a More Effective Listener   Listening skills can be enhanced by using the preceding recommendations, along with those presented in Table 9–2.

Women and Men Communicate Differently

Women and men have communicated differently since the dawn of time. Gender-based differences in communication are partly caused by linguistic styles commonly used by

TABLE 9–2 The Keys to Effective Listening

Keys to Effective Listening	The Bad Listener	The Good Listener
1. Capitalize on thought speed	Tends to daydream	Stays with the speaker, mentally summarizes the speaker, weighs evidence, and listens between the lines
2. Listen for ideas	Listens for facts	Listens for central or overall ideas
3. Find an area of interest	Tunes out dry speakers or subjects	Listens for any useful information
4. Judge content, not delivery	Tunes out dry or monotone speakers	Assesses content by listening to entire message before making judgments
5. Hold your fire	Gets too emotional or worked up by something said by the speaker and enters into an argument	Withholds judgment until comprehension is complete
6. Work at listening	Does not expend energy on listening	Gives the speaker full attention
7. Resist distractions	Is easily distracted	Fights distractions and concentrates on the speaker
8. Hear what is said	Shuts out or denies unfavourable information	Listens to both favourable and unfavourable information
9. Challenge yourself	Resists listening to presentations of difficult subject matter	Treats complex presentations as exercise for the mind
10. Use handouts, overheads, or other visual aids	Does not take notes or pay attention to visual aids	Takes notes as required and uses visual aids to enhance understanding of the presentation

Sources: Derived from N Skinner, "Communication Skills," *Selling Power,* July/August 1999, pp 32–34; and G Manning, K Curtis, and S McMillen, *Building the Human Side of Work Community* (Cincinnati, OH: Thomson Executive Press, 1996), pp 127–54.

Linguistic style

A person's typical speaking pattern.

women and men. Deborah Tannen, a communication expert, defines **linguistic style** as follows:

> Linguistic style refers to a person's characteristic speaking pattern. It includes such features as directness or indirectness, pacing and pausing, word choice, and the use of such elements as jokes, figures of speech, stories, questions, and apologies. In other words, linguistic style is a set of culturally learned signals by which we not only communicate what we mean but also interpret others' meaning and evaluate one another as people.[27]

Linguistic style not only helps explain communication differences between women and men, but it also influences our perceptions of others' confidence, competence, and abilities. Increased awareness of linguistic styles can thus improve communication accuracy and communication competence. This section strives to increase understanding of interpersonal communication between women and men by discussing alternative explanations for differences in linguistic styles, various communication differences between women and men, and recommendations for improving communication between the sexes.

Why Linguistic Styles Vary between Women and Men   Although researchers do not completely agree on the cause of communication differences between women and men, there are two competing explanations that involve the well-worn debate between *nature* and *nurture*. Some researchers believe that interpersonal differences between women and men are due to inherited biological differences between the sexes. More specifically, this perspective, which also is called the "Darwinian perspective" or "evolutionary psychology," attributes gender differences in communication to drives, needs, and conflicts associated with reproductive strategies used by women and men. For example, proponents would say that males communicate more aggressively, interrupt others more than women, and hide their emotions because they have an inherent desire to possess features attractive to females in order to compete with other males for purposes of mate selection. Although males are certainly not competing for mate selection during a business meeting, evolutionary psychologists propose that men cannot turn off the biologically based determinants of their behaviour.[28]

Communication between men and women differs partly because of linguistic styles.

In contrast, social role theory is based on the idea that females and males learn ways of speaking as children growing up. Research shows that girls learn conversational skills and habits that focus on rapport and relationships, whereas boys learn skills and habits that focus on status and hierarchies. Accordingly, women come to view communication as a network of connections in which conversations are negotiations for closeness. This orientation leads women to seek and give confirmation and support more so than men. Men, on the other hand, see conversations as negotiations in which people try to achieve and maintain the upper hand. It thus is important for males to protect themselves from others' attempts to put them down or push them around. This perspective increases a male's need to maintain independence and avoid failure.[29]

Gender Differences in Communication   Research demonstrates that women and men communicate differently in a number of ways.[30] Women, for example, are more likely to share credit for success, to ask questions for clarification, to tactfully give feedback by mitigating criticism with praise, and to indirectly tell others what to do. In contrast, men are more likely to boast about themselves, to bluntly give feedback, to withhold compliments, and are less likely to ask questions and to admit fault or weaknesses.

There are two important issues to keep in mind about these trends. First, the trends identified cannot be generalized to include all women and men. Some men are less likely to boast about their achievements while some women are less likely to share the credit. The point is that there are always exceptions to the rule. Second, linguistic style influences perceptions about confidence, competence, and authority. These judgments may, in turn, affect future job assignments and subsequent promotability.

Improving Communications between the Sexes   Deborah Tannen recommends that everyone needs to become aware of how linguistic styles work and how they influence our perceptions and judgments. She believes that knowledge of linguistic styles helps to ensure that people with valuable insights or ideas get heard. Consider how gender-based linguistic differences affect who gets heard at a meeting:

> Those who are comfortable speaking up in groups, who need little or no silence before raising their hands, or who speak out easily without waiting to be recognized

Cross-Gender Communication in Cyberspace

Many believe that the Internet has the potential ability to help people, no matter what their gender, race, or physical appearance, to communicate with each other with fewer prejudices and misunderstandings, than any other medium in existence. Many people have claimed that computer-mediated communication (CMC) improves communication between women and men, because it facilitates interaction as persons, without gender identity. Gladys We, a graduate student in the Department of Communication at Simon Fraser University, conducted one of the first studies of gender issues in CMC. She surveyed 25 women and men regarding how they felt about communicating online. Although very preliminary and anecdotal, her findings are fascinating.

Most of the people she surveyed felt that men and women are able to communicate far more easily online than face-to-face. The absence of physical cues such as dress, age, and voice provides women with the freedom to express ideas outside of the "prison of appearance." One woman said that she gets heard more because she can finish a thought without being interrupted. Another found that the lack of gendering of communication allowed her to make bold statements without having to worry about how her gestures or voice might falsely render them. Some found men to be more "open" and expressive online than in person. However, both men and women agreed that people can also become more obnoxious because they are hiding behind anonymity, and that both men and women feel freer to engage in "persona" creation using CMC.

Overall, these initial responses indicate that many people feel that cyberspace tends to be friendly to women. When CMC is used professionally, it is seen as relatively free of gender cues. On a more personal level, CMC, originally considered cold and alienating, has become a "cool" medium, and people can become highly emotionally involved in their personal interactions online.

Ms. We believes that CMC is a fascinating extension of the ways in which human beings already communicate. On the one hand, it has the potential to be liberating, and on the other hand, it has the potential to duplicate all the misunderstandings and confusion that currently take place in interactions between women and men in everyday life. Her eloquent conclusion was, "The choice of directions is not being made deliberately, but is being made in the thousands of daily online interactions, the choices of ways of speaking, and of subjects, which are gradually shaping, as a river slowly carves a canyon, the culture of cyberspace."

Source: G We, "Cross-Gender Communication in Cyberspace," *http://eserver.org/feminism/cross-gender-comm.txt*, March 27, 2002.

are far more likely to get heard at meetings. Those who refrain from talking until it's clear that the previous speaker is finished, who wait to be recognized, and who are inclined to link their comments to those of others will do fine at a meeting where everyone else is following the same rules but will have a hard time getting heard in a meeting with people whose styles are more like the first pattern. Given the socialization typical of boys and girls, men are more likely to have learned the first style and women the second, making meetings more congenial for men than for women.[31]

Knowledge of these linguistic differences can assist managers in devising methods to ensure that everyone's ideas are heard and given fair credit both in and out of meetings. Furthermore, it is useful to consider the organizational strengths and limitations of your linguistic style. You may want to consider modifying a linguistic characteristic that is a detriment to perceptions of your confidence, competence, and authority. In conclusion, communication between the sexes can be improved by remembering that women and men have different ways of saying the same thing.

Communication in the Computerized Information Age

Organizations are increasingly using information technology as a lever to improve productivity and customer and employee satisfaction. In turn, communication patterns at work are radically changing. Consider Chubb Insurance, which is using the latest E-commerce architecture to enable their estimated 2,000 insurance brokers across Canada to communicate with Chubb online. Chubb wanted to find a way to help these brokers issue insurance quotations and insurance policies that was less paper-intensive than the previous call-centre and mass mailing approach. Site Server technology enabled them to deliver personalized information over the Web, and do so securely.[32]

A recent poll revealed that 63% of adults used computers, and 26% used them both at home and at work. Average weekly use of computers was 15 hours, and six of them were on the Internet. For people between the ages of 30 and 39, the age range of many supervisors and managers, computer use averaged 21 hours a week, with nine of them on the Internet.[33] Interestingly, some people use the Internet with such frequency that they become dependent on it. For example, a recent study of 1,300 students revealed that nearly 10% were dependent on the Internet and that their Internet usage affected their academics, ability to meet new people, and sleep patterns.[34] This section explores five key components of information technology that influence communication patterns and management within a computerized workplace: Internet/Intranet/Extranet, electronic mail, videoconferencing, collaborative computing, and telecommuting.

Internet/Intranet/Extranet

The Internet is a global network of independently operating, but interconnected computers, linking more than 140,000 smaller networks in more than 200 countries. The Internet connects everything from supercomputers, to large mainframes contained in businesses, government, and universities, to the personal computers in our homes and offices.

An **Intranet** is nothing more than an organization's private Internet. Intranets also have *firewalls* that block outside Internet users from accessing internal information. This is done to protect the privacy and confidentiality of company documents. More than half of companies with more than 500 employees have corporate Intranets.[35]

In contrast to the internal focus of an Intranet, an **Extranet** is an extended Intranet in that it connects internal employees with selected customers, suppliers, and other strategic partners. Ford Motor Company, for instance, has an Extranet that connects its dealers worldwide. Ford's Extranet was set up to help support the sales and servicing of cars and to enhance customer satisfaction.

Intranet
An organization's private internet.

Extranet
Connects internal employees with selected customers, suppliers, and strategic partners.

The primary benefit of the Internet, Intranet, and Extranet is that they can enhance the ability of employees to find, create, manage, and distribute information. The effectiveness of these "nets," however, depends on how organizations set up and manage their Intranet/Extranet and how employees use the acquired information because information by itself cannot solve or do anything. For example, communication effectiveness actually can decrease if a corporate Intranet becomes a dumping ground of unorganized information. In this case, employees will find themselves flailing in a sea of information. Also, senior executives may feel threatened by the loss of control that occurs with greater information and communication access.[36]

To date, no rigorous research studies have been conducted that directly demonstrate productivity increases from using the Internet, Intranet, or Extranet. There are, however, case studies that reveal other organizational benefits. For example, Cisco systems uses the Internet to recruit potential employees: The company has hired 66% of its people and received 81% of its resumes from the Net. This translated into reduced costs because the company was able to employ fewer in-house recruiters as it grew from 2,000 to 8,000 people. Cisco's cost per hire in 1999 was $6,556 versus an industry average of $10,800.[37]

In contrast, other reports detail stories of people spending hours surfing the Net only to find themselves overwhelmed with information. Using the Internet can be very time consuming because the Internet is an unstructured repository of information that is becoming increasingly slow to access. Only the future will tell whether the Internet is more useful as a marketing/sales tool, a device to conduct personal transactions such as banking or ordering movies, or a management vehicle that enhances employee motivation and productivity.

Electronic Mail

Electronic mail or E-mail uses the Internet/Intranet to send computer-generated text and documents between people. The use of E-mail is on the rise throughout the world. For example, recent surveys reveal that US employees receive somewhere between 20 to 30 E-mail messages per day.[38] Further, another survey of executives by the administrative staffing firm Office Team showed that 73% of the respondents believed that E-mail would be the leading form of business communication for employees by 2005.[39] E-mail is becoming a major communication medium because of four key benefits:[40]

1. E-mail reduces the cost of distributing information to a large number of employees.

2. E-mail is a tool for increasing teamwork. It enables employees to quickly send messages to colleagues on the next floor, in another building, or in another country. In support of this benefit, a study of 375 managers indicated they used E-mail for three dominant reasons: (a) to keep others informed, (b) to follow up an earlier communication, and (c) to communicate the same thing to many people.[41]

3. E-mail reduces the costs and time associated with print duplication and paper distribution. Keep in mind, however, that the benefits of cost reduction should not override the effectiveness of electronic publications. Experts recommend that electronic publications should be carefully written in order to maximize communication effectiveness. Tips for writing electronic publications include:[42]

   - Think of each article as a personal note to the employees.
   - Address the readers as "you."
   - Keep stories short and sweet.

   (*MacWeek* suggests 300 words or less for stories on a Web site.)

   - Write in a concise, conversational tone.
   - Use simple words, short sentences, and active verbs.
   - Break copy into short, readable segments.
   - Divide stories with subheads.
   - Use bullet points and lists whenever possible.

4. E-mail fosters flexibility. This is particularly true for employees with a portable computer because they can log onto E-mail whenever and wherever they want.

In spite of these positive benefits, there are three key drawbacks to consider. First, sending and receiving E-mail can lead to a lot of wasted time and effort, or it can distract employees from completing critical job duties. Some people believe that employees waste time using E-mail instead of focusing on the important work at hand.

Information overload is the second problem associated with the increased use of E-mail. People tend to send more messages to others, and there is a lot of "spamming" going on: sending junk mail, bad jokes, or irrelevant memos (e.g., the "cc" of E-mail). Consider the situation faced by David Canham, vice president of sales and marketing for Pinacor:

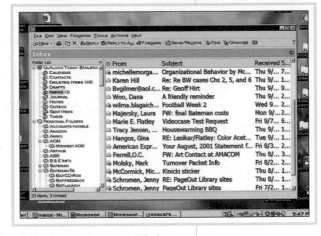

Information overload is a genuine concern for those with an increased use of E-mail, as in this Inbox.

"It used to be that the lack of information was a problem," Canham points out. "Today the reverse is true. The amount of information people are being blasted with these days is unbelievable. E-mail is just one example. You come into the office in the morning, and you have 120 messages in your box. And maybe only 10 of them include worthwhile information, but you still have to sift through the whole 120 to get to those 10. . . . To help the company's salespeople with the sifting process, Pinacor developed a Web-based tool that allows reps to pick and choose the information they want to receive. According to Canham, the program was so successful that customers soon began clamoring for a similar tool to address their own struggle with the information glut.[43]

As you can see from this example, organizations should make a concerted effort to manage the problem of information overload associated with the use of E-mail.

Finally, preliminary evidence suggests that people are using electronic mail to communicate when they should be using other media. This practice can result in reduced communication effectiveness. A four-year study of communication patterns within a university demonstrated that the increased use of electronic mail was associated with decreased face-to-face interactions and with a drop in the overall amount of organizational communication. Employees also expressed a feeling of being less connected and less cohesive as a department as the amount of E-mails increased.[44] This interpersonal "disconnection" may be caused by the trend of replacing everyday face-to-face interactions with electronic messages. Dr Jacklyn Kostner, author of *Bionic eTeamwork*, says, "Being on the same E-mail system doesn't make a team. People make a team. Communication makes a team. Trust makes a team."[45]

There are three additional issues to consider when using E-mail: (1) E-mail only works when the party you desire to communicate with also uses it. E-mail may not be a viable communication medium in all cases. (2) The speed of getting a response to an E-mail message is dependent on how frequently the receiver examines his or her messages. It is important to consider this issue when picking a communication medium. (3) Many companies do not have policies for using E-mail, which can lead to misuse and potential legal liability. Do not assume that E-mail messages are private and confidential. Organizations are advised to develop policies regarding the use of E-mail.[46]

Videoconferencing

Videoconferencing, also known as teleconferencing, uses video and audio links along with computers to enable people located at different locations to see, hear, and talk with one another. This enables people from many locations to conduct a meeting without having to travel, and thus can significantly reduce an organization's travel expenses. Many organizations set up special videoconferencing rooms or booths with specially equipped television cameras. More recent equipment enables people to attach small cameras and microphones to their desks or computer monitors. This enables employees to conduct long-distance meetings and training classes without leaving their office or cubicle.

Collaborative Computing

Collaborative computing

Using computer software and hardware to help people work better together.

Collaborative computing entails using state-of-the-art computer software and hardware to help people work better together. Collaborative systems enable people to share information without the constraints of time and space. This is accomplished by utilizing computer networks to link people across a room or across the globe. Collaborative applications include messaging and E-mail systems, calendar management, videoconferencing, computer teleconferencing, electronic whiteboards, and the type of computer-aided decision-making systems.

Organizations that use full-fledged collaborative systems have the ability to create virtual teams or to operate as a virtual organization: Virtual organizations are discussed in Chapter 12. You may recall from Chapter 7 that a virtual team represents a physically dispersed task group that conducts its business by using the types of information technology currently being discussed. Specifically, virtual teams tend to use Internet/Intranet systems, collaborative software systems, and videoconferencing systems.[47] These real-time systems enable people to communicate with anyone at anytime.

It is important to keep in mind that modern-day information technology only enables people to interact virtually; it doesn't guarantee effective communications. Interestingly, there are a whole host of unique communication problems associated with using the information technology needed to operate virtually.[48]

Telecommuting

Telecommuting

Doing work that is generally performed in the office away from the office using different information technologies.

Telecommuting involves doing work that is generally performed in the office away from the office using a variety of information technologies. Employees typically receive and send work from home via phone and fax or by using a modem to link a home computer to an office computer. Telecommuting is more common for jobs that involve computer work, writing, and phone or brain work that requires concentration and limited interruptions. Statistics Canada estimates that about 1.5 million Canadian workers were telecommuting in 2002, including employees at Bell Canada, Nortel, IBM Canada, and the British Columbia Ministry of Finance.[49] Experts predict that more than 137 million workers around the world will be involved in some type of remote work by 2003.[50] Proposed benefits of telecommuting include the following:

1. *Reduction of capital costs.* IBM reported lower costs by letting employees work at home.
2. *Increased flexibility and autonomy for workers.*
3. *Competitive edge in recruitment.* Arthur Anderson, Merrill Lynch, and Cisco used telecommuting to increase their ability to keep and attract qualified personnel.
4. *Increased job satisfaction and lower turnover.* Employees like telecommuting because it helps resolve work-family conflicts. Merrill Lynch's turnover fell significantly after it implemented a telework program.
5. *Increased productivity.* Telecommuting resulted in productivity increases of 25% and 35% for FourGen Software and Continental Traffic Services, respectively.

6. *Tapping nontraditional labour pools* (such as prison inmates and homebound disabled persons).[51]

Although telecommuting represents an attempt to accommodate employee needs and desires, it requires adjustments and is not for everybody. Many people thoroughly enjoy the social camaraderie that exists within an office setting. These individuals probably would not like to telecommute. Others lack the self-motivation needed to work at home. Finally, organizations must be careful to implement telecommuting in a nondiscriminatory manner. Organizations can easily and unknowingly violate human rights laws.[52] In many cases, a combination of telecommuting and working in the office works best.

Barriers to Effective Communication

Communication noise is a barrier to effective communication because it interferes with the accurate transmission and reception of a message. Management awareness of these barriers is a good starting point to improve the communication process. There are four key barriers to effective communication: (1) process barriers, (2) personal barriers, (3) physical barriers, and (4) semantic barriers.

Process Barriers

Every element of the perceptual model of communication shown in Figure 9–1 is a potential process barrier. Consider the following examples:

1. *Sender barrier.* A customer gets incorrect information from a customer service agent because he or she was recently hired and lacks experience.

2. *Encoding barrier.* An employee for whom English is a second language has difficulty explaining why a delivery was late.

3. *Message barrier.* An employee misses a meeting for which he or she never received a confirmation memo.

4. *Medium barrier.* A salesperson gives up trying to make a sales call when the potential customer fails to return three previous phone calls.

5. *Decoding barrier.* An employee does not know how to respond to a manager's request to stop exhibiting "passive aggressive" behaviour.

6. *Receiver barrier.* A student who is talking to his or her friend during a lecture asks the professor the same question that was just answered.

7. *Feedback barrier.* The nonverbal head nodding of an interviewer leads an interviewee to think that he or she is doing a great job answering questions.

Barriers in any of these process elements can distort the transfer of meaning. Reducing these barriers is essential but difficult given the current diversity of the workforce.

Personal Barriers

There are many personal barriers to communication. We highlight eight of the more common ones. The first is our *ability to effectively communicate*. As highlighted throughout this chapter, people possess varying levels of communication skills. The *way people process and interpret information* is a second barrier. Chapter 2 highlighted the fact that people selectively attend to various stimuli. All told, these differences affect both what we say and what we think we hear. Third, the *level of interpersonal trust between people* can either be a barrier or enabler of effective communication. Communication is more likely to be distorted when people do not trust each other. Watson Wyatt's Work-

Canada 2000 survey found that 45% of managers rated the level of trust between managers and employees as good or very good; but only 29% of employees did. This result provides clear evidence that suspicion underlies management–employee relations in many Canadian organizations (as well as providing an example of how differently employees and managers can perceive an identical situation).[53] *Stereotypes and prejudices* are a fourth barrier. They can powerfully distort what we perceive about others. Our *egos* are a fifth barrier. Egos can cause political battles, turf wars, and pursuit of power, credit, and resources. Egos influence how people treat each other as well as our receptiveness to being influenced by others. *Poor listening skills* are a sixth barrier.[54]

Carl Rogers, a renowned psychologist, identified the seventh and eighth barriers that interfere with interpersonal communication.[55] The seventh barrier is a *natural tendency to evaluate or judge a sender's message*. To highlight the natural tendency to evaluate, consider how you might respond to the statement "I like the book you are reading." What would you say? Your likely response is to approve or disapprove the statement. You may say, "I agree," or alternatively, "I disagree, the book is boring." The point is that we all tend to evaluate messages from our own point of view or frame of reference. The tendency to evaluate messages is greatest when one has strong feelings or emotions about the issue being discussed. An *inability to listen with understanding* is the eighth personal barrier to effective communication. Listening with understanding occurs when a receiver can "see the expressed idea and attitude from the other person's point of view, to sense how it feels to him, to achieve his frame of reference in regard to the thing he is talking about."[56] Listening with understanding reduces defensiveness and improves accuracy in perceiving a message.

Physical Barriers

The distance between employees can interfere with effective communication. It is hard to understand someone who is speaking to you from 20 metres away. Time zone differences between the Maritimes and Western Canada also represent physical barriers. Work and office noise are additional barriers. The quality of telephone lines or crashed computers represent physical barriers that impact our ability to communicate with information technology.

In spite of the general acceptance of physical barriers, they can be reduced. For example, employees in the Maritimes can agree to call their Western Canada peers prior to leaving for lunch. Distracting or inhibiting walls also can be torn down. It is important that managers attempt to manage this barrier by choosing a medium that optimally reduces the physical barrier at hand.

Semantic Barriers

Semantics is the study of words. Semantic barriers show up as encoding and decoding errors because these phases of communication involve transmitting and receiving words and symbols. These barriers occur very easily. Consider the following statement: Crime is ubiquitous.

Do you understand this message? Even if you do, would it not be simpler to say that "crime is all around us" or "crime is everywhere"? Choosing our words more carefully is the easiest way to reduce semantic barriers. This barrier can also be decreased by attentiveness to mixed messages and cultural diversity. Mixed messages occur when a person's words imply one message while his or her actions or nonverbal cues suggest something different. Obviously, understanding is enhanced when a person's actions and nonverbal cues match the verbal message.

summary of key concepts

- *Describe the perceptual process model of communication.* Communication is a process of consecutively linked elements. This model of communication depicts receivers as information processors who create the meaning of messages in their own mind. Because receivers' interpretations of messages often differ from those intended by senders, miscommunication is a common occurrence.

- *Demonstrate your familiarity with four causes of communication distortion between managers and employees.* Communication distortion is a common problem that consists of modifying the content of a message. Employees distort upward communication when their supervisor has high upward influence and/or power. Distortion also increases when employees aspire to move upward and when they do not trust their supervisor.

- *Contrast the communication styles of assertiveness, aggressiveness, and nonassertiveness.* An assertive style is expressive and self-enhancing but does not violate others' basic human rights. In contrast, an aggressive style is expressive and self-enhancing but takes unfair advantage of others. A nonassertive style is characterized by timid and self-denying behaviour. An assertive communication style is more effective than either an aggressive or nonassertive style.

- *Discuss the primary sources of nonverbal communication and 10 keys to active listening.* Body movements and gestures, touch, facial expressions, and eye contact are important nonverbal cues. The interpretation of these nonverbal cues significantly varies across cultures. Good listeners use the following 10 listening habits: (a) staying with the speaker and listening between the lines, (b) listen for ideas rather than facts, (c) identify areas of interest between the speaker and listener, (d) judge content and not delivery, (e) do not judge until the speaker has completed his or her message, (f) put energy and effort into listening, (g) resist distractions, (h) listen to both favourable and unfavourable information, (i) read or listen to complex material to exercise the mind, and (j) take notes when necessary and use visual aids to enhance understanding.

- *Explain the information technology of Internet/Intranet/Extranet, E-mail, videoconferencing, and collaborative computing, and explain the related use of telecommuting.* The Internet is a global network of computer networks. An Intranet is an organization's private Internet. It contains a firewall that blocks outside Internet users from accessing private internal information. An Extranet connects an organization's internal employees with selected customers, suppliers, and strategic partners. The primary benefit of these "nets" is that they can enhance the ability of employees to find, create, manage, and distribute information. E-mail uses the Internet/Intranet/Extranet to send text and documents between people. Videoconferencing uses video and audio links along with computers to enable people located at different locations to see, hear, and talk with one another. Collaborative computing entails using state-of-the-art computer software and hardware to help people work better together. Information is shared across time and space by linking people with computer networks. Telecommuting involves doing work that is generally performed in the office away from the office using a variety of information technologies.

- *Describe the process, personal, physical, and semantic barriers to effective communication.* Every element of the perceptual model of communication is a potential process barrier. There are eight personal barriers that commonly influence communication: (a) the ability to effectively communicate, (b) the way people process and interpret information, (c) the level of interpersonal trust between people, (d) the existence of stereotypes and prejudices, (e) the egos of the people communicating, (f) the ability to listen, (g) the natural tendency to evaluate or judge a sender's message, and (h) the inability to listen with understanding. Physical barriers pertain to distance, physical objects, time, and work and office noise. Semantic barriers show up as encoding and decoding errors because these phases of communication involve transmitting and receiving words and symbols. Cultural diversity is a key contributor to semantic barriers.

key terms

aggressive style, 201	hierarchical communication, 199	nonverbal communication, 201
assertive style, 201	intranet, 209	process-style listeners, 205
collaborative computing, 212	linguistic style, 206	reasons-style listeners, 205
communication, 196	listening, 205	results-style listeners, 205
communication distortion, 199	media richness, 197	telecommuting, 212
extranet, 209	noise, 199	
grapevine, 199	nonassertive style, 201	

discussion questions

1. What are some sources of noise that interfere with communication during a class lecture, an encounter with a professor in his or her office, and a movie?

2. Have you ever distorted upward communication? What was your reason? Was it related to one of the four causes of communication distortion?

3. Would you describe your prevailing communication style as assertive, aggressive, or nonassertive? How can you tell? Would your style help or hinder you as a manager?

4. Are you good at reading nonverbal communication? Give some examples.

5. Describe a miscommunication that occurred between you and someone of the opposite sex. What might have been done to improve this communication?

6. What is your personal experience with the grapevine? Do you see it as a useful factor in the workplace? Explain.

internet exercises

www.queendom.com

1. A Free Self-Assessment Questionnaire for Assertiveness

As covered in this chapter, communication styles vary from nonassertive to aggressive. We recommended that you strive to use an assertive style while avoiding the tendencies of being nonassertive or aggressive. In trying to be assertive, however, keep in mind that too much of a good thing is bad. That is, the use of an assertive style can transform to an aggressive one if it is taken too far.

The purpose of this exercise is to provide you with feedback on the extent to which you use an assertive communication style. Go to the Internet home page for Body-Mind QueenDom (**www.queendom.com**), and select the tests and profiles icon. (Note: Our use of this questionnaire is for instructional purposes only and does not constitute an endorsement of any products that may or may not suit your needs. There is no obligation to buy anything.) At the tests

and profiles page, select the career icon. Now select the "Assertiveness Test," and then read the instructions, complete all 32 items, and click on the "score" button for automatic scoring. Read the interpretation of your results.

QUESTIONS

1. Possible scores on the self-assessment questionnaire range from 0 to 100. How did you score? Are you surprised by the results? Do you agree with the interpretation of your score?

2. Reviewing the questionnaire item by item, can you find aspects of communication in which you are either nonassertive or possibly too assertive? Do you think that your communication style can be improved by making adjustments within these areas of communication?

2. Gender Games

Go to the "Gender Games" Web site of Australian business communications consultant Candy Tymson (**www.tymson .com.au**). Click on the picture of Tymson to enter. Then click on "Articles and Stories." Read the short article "Business Communication—Bridging the Gender Gap." Then if you are a male, review "10 Strategies for Men When Dealing With Women in Business," and if you are a female, review "10 Strategies for Women When Dealing With Men in Business." At the next meeting of a work or study group you are part of, look for opportunities to use these tips, and make a serious effort to adapt your communication style when dealing with group members of the opposite sex.

QUESTIONS
1. Were there any strategies that you immediately sensed would be helpful? What past experiences did you have that led to this perception?
2. Which strategy did you find most useful? What happened when you used it?
3. Which strategy or strategies seemed to be most effective in making cross-gender communication easier? Why?

experiential exercises

1. Practicing Different Styles of Communication

Objectives

1. To demonstrate the relative effectiveness of communicating assertively, aggressively, and nonassertively.
2. To give you hands-on experience with different styles of communication.

Introduction

Research shows that assertive communication is more effective than either an aggressive or nonassertive style. This *role-playing exercise* is designed to increase your ability to communicate assertively. Your task is to use different communication styles while attempting to resolve the work-related problems of a poor performer.

Instructions

Divide into groups of three, and read the "Poor Performer" and "Store Manager" roles provided here. Then decide who will play the poor performer role, who will play the managerial role, and who will be the observer. The observer will be asked to provide feedback to the manager after each role play. When playing the managerial role, you should first attempt to resolve the problem by using an aggressive communication style. Attempt to achieve your objective by using the nonverbal and verbal behaviour patterns associated with the aggressive style shown in Table 9–1. Take about four to six minutes to act out the instructions. The observer should give feedback to the manager after completing the role play. The

observer should comment on how the employee responded to the aggressive behaviours displayed by the manager.

After feedback is provided on the first role play, the person playing the manager should then try to resolve the problem with a nonassertive style. Observers once again should provide feedback. Finally, the manager should confront the problem with an assertive style. Once again, rely on the relevant nonverbal and verbal behaviour patterns presented in Table 9–1, and take four to six minutes to act out each scenario. Observers should try to provide detailed feedback on how effectively the manager exhibited nonverbal and verbal assertive behaviours. Be sure to provide positive and constructive feedback.

After completing these three role plays, switch roles: manager becomes observer, observer becomes poor performer, and poor performer becomes the manager. When these role plays are completed, switch roles once again.

ROLE: POOR PERFORMER

You sell shoes full-time for a national chain of shoe stores. During the last month you have been absent three times without giving your manager a reason. The quality of your work has been slipping. You have a lot of creative excuses when your boss tries to talk to you about your performance.

When playing this role, feel free to invent a personal problem that you may eventually want to share with your manager. However, make the manager dig for information about this problem. Otherwise, respond to your manager's comments as you normally would.

ROLE: STORE MANAGER

You manage a store for a national chain of shoe stores. In the privacy of your office, you are talking to one of your salespeople who has had three unexcused absences from work during the last month. (This is excessive, according to company guidelines, and must be corrected.) The quality of his or her work has been slipping. Customers have complained that this person is rude, and co-workers have told you this individual isn't carrying his or her fair share

of the work. You are fairly sure this person has some sort of personal problem. You want to identify that problem and get him or her back on the right track.

QUESTIONS FOR DISCUSSION

1. What drawbacks of the aggressive and nonassertive styles did you observe?
2. What were major advantages of the assertive style?
3. What were the most difficult aspects of trying to use an assertive style?
4. How important was nonverbal communication during the various role plays? Explain with examples.

2. A Not-So-Trivial Cross-Cultural Communication Game

Purpose

This exercise is designed to develop and test your knowledge of cross-cultural differences in communication and etiquette.

Instructions

Step 1: This class is divided into an even number of teams. Ideally, each team would have three students. (Two or four student teams are possible if matched with an equal-sized team.) Each team is then matched with another team and the matched teams are assigned a private space away from other matched teams.

Step 2: The instructor will hand each pair of teams a stack of cards with the multiple choice questions face down. These cards have questions and answers about cross-cultural differences in communication and etiquette. No books or other aids are allowed.

Step 3: The exercise begins with a member of Team "A" picking up one card from the top of the pile and asking the question on that card to students on Team "B." The information given to Team "B" includes the question and all alternatives listed on the card. Team "B" has 30 seconds to give an answer and earns one point if the correct answer is given. If Team "B"'s answer is incorrect, however, Team "A" earns that point. Correct answers to each question are indicated on the card and, of course, should not be revealed until the question is correctly answered or the time is up. Whether Team "B" answers correctly or not, it picks up the next card on the pile and asks the question on it to members of Team "A." In other words, cards are read alternately to each team. This procedure is repeated until all of the cards have been read or the time has elapsed. The team that receives the most points wins.

Important note

The textbook provides very little information pertaining to the questions in this exercise. Rather, you must rely on past learning, logic, and luck to win.

Source: © 2001 Steven L. McShane.

personal awareness and growth exercises

1. Assessing Your Listening Skills

Instructions

The following statements reflect various habits we use when listening to others. For each statement, indicate the extent to which you agree or disagree with it by selecting one number from the scale provided. Circle your response for each statement. Remember, there are no right or wrong answers. After completing the survey, add up your total score for the 17 items, and record it in the space provided.

Listening Skills Survey

1 = Strongly disagree
2 = Disagree
3 = Neither agree nor disagree
4 = Agree
5 = Strongly agree

1. I daydream or think about other things when listening to others.   1 2 3 4 5

2. I do not mentally summarize the ideas being communicated by a speaker.   1 2 3 4 5

3. I do not use a speaker's body language or tone of voice to help interpret what he or she is saying.   1 2 3 4 5

4. I listen more for facts than overall ideas during classroom lectures.   1 2 3 4 5

5. I tune out dry speakers.   1 2 3 4 5

6. I have a hard time paying attention to boring people.   1 2 3 4 5

7. I can tell whether someone has anything useful to say before he or she finishes communicating a message.   1 2 3 4 5

8. I quit listening to a speaker when I think he or she has nothing interesting to say.   1 2 3 4 5

9. I get emotional or upset when speakers make jokes about issues or things that are important to me.   1 2 3 4 5

10. I get angry or distracted when speakers use offensive words.   1 2 3 4 5

11. I do not expend a lot of energy when listening to others.   1 2 3 4 5

12. I pretend to pay attention to others even when I'm not really listening.   1 2 3 4 5

13. I get distracted when listening to others.   1 2 3 4 5

14. I deny or ignore information and comments that go against my thoughts and feelings.   1 2 3 4 5

15. I do not seek opportunities to challenge my listening skills.   1 2 3 4 5

16. I do not pay attention to the visual aids used during lectures.   1 2 3 4 5

17. I do not take notes on handouts when they are provided.   1 2 3 4 5

Total Score = _____

Norms

Use the following norms to evaluate your listening skills:
17–34 = Good listening skills
35–53 = Moderately good listening skills
54–85 = Poor listening skills.
How would you evaluate your listening skills?

2. Monkey Say, Monkey See, Monkey Do: A Lesson in Interpersonal Communication

In an age dominated by E-mail and voicemail, we tend to focus our attention on verbal messages. We ignore nonverbal messages (or "body language") at our own peril. Without careful attention to these emotion-laden messages, we may miss the heart of the real message. This exercise, based on work by famed family therapist Virginia Satir, encourages you to be more observant during interpersonal communication activities in your daily life.

Instructions

Choose a partner for this exercise. Sit directly facing one another. You will take turns making a statement to your partner while your partner listens silently. The first person to speak makes a statement in his or her characteristic manner. The listening partner then repeats the statement mirroring the speaker's tone of voice, rate of speech, body posture, gestures, and facial expression. Then reverse roles. The first speaker now becomes the listener and mirrors the statement and nonverbal communication of the new speaker. Repeat this exercise so that each partner is speaker twice and listener twice. Discuss briefly after each speaking activity.

QUESTIONS FOR DISCUSSION

1. Discuss the speaker's reaction to the listener's perception of his or her communication style in each case. What aspect of mirroring was most surprising for you when you were the speaker?
2. What aspects of the speaker's communication style were most striking?
3. Did you and your partner both react in a similar manner? Explain.
4. What aspects of nonverbal communication did you find most surprising in your speaker-listener activities?

Source: Adapted from C A Sales, F A Owen, and M A Lesperance, *Experiential Exercises in Organizational Behaviour*, #37 (Scarborough ON: Pearson Education Canada, 2000). Used with permission.

CBC video case

Pitching a Dream

Young Canadian high-tech entrepreneurs seeking to raise capital from Silicon Valley venture capitalists have found that the industry demands a 30-second "pitch" of the company and its product (the time limit is based roughly on the length of a 10-floor elevator ride). Based on this brief presentation, a decision is typically made as to whether the venture capitalists want to hear more.

Thus the "Great Canadian Elevator Ride Pitch Contest" is being held in San Jose, California, the heart of Silicon Valley. Contestants practice their 30-second pitches, and try to build in a hook that will leave their audience wanting to hear more. Those who are chosen to move on to the second round make a 10-minute presentation followed by a five minute question and answer session with the judging panel (composed of real live venture capitalists). It's a really important communication challenge!

QUESTIONS FOR DISCUSSION

1. What "noise" arises in the "elevator ride" communication scenario? In the contest?
2. What were the most effective nonverbal aspects of the presentations shown in the video?
3. How could the presentations been made more effective?

Source: Based on "Pitching a Dream," *CBC Venture* 774 (February 13, 2001).

chapter
ten

Power and Politics

After reading the material in this chapter, you should be able to:

- Name five "soft" and four "hard" influence tactics, and summarize the practical lessons from influence research.

- Identify and briefly describe French and Raven's five bases of power.

- Define the term *empowerment,* and explain how to make it succeed.

- Define *organizational politics,* explain what triggers it, and specify the three levels of political action in organizations.

- Distinguish between favourable and unfavourable impression management tactics.

- Explain how to manage organizational politics.

WHY SMALL IS BIG

The term "lobbyist" conjures up images of slick, well-fed men in dark suits tunnelling beneath the official corridors of power. But then there's Catherine Swift. The CEO and president of the Canadian Federation of Independent Business (CFIB) is one of the most high-profile lobbyists in Canada, and her agenda is the relentless promotion of small-business owners and their interests.

Swift says small business' muscle reflects several broad socioeconomic shifts, including market changes in attitudes and priorities. "As a society, we're less compliant than we used to be," she says. "We won't toe the line the way people used to. We ask more questions and want more control." Younger generations—especially of women, who represent 40% of small-business owners—have more entrepreneurial role models that in the past, a

Catherine Swift, CEO Canadian Federation of Independent Business.

trend helped along by the recent high-tech boom. "Small business success is lionized," notes Swift. "It's become much more accepted and respected."

Despite the strides, Swift wouldn't be a lobbyist if she didn't have issues that still require attention on behalf of her 100,000 association members. At the top of the list is a more aggressive reduction of government regulation and bureaucracy, which Swift claims is stifling productivity and innovation. Swift comes by her wariness about the power of big government—and big banks—honestly. She's a former federal civil servant who also spent four years working at the Toronto-Dominion Bank as a senior economist. She admits she chafed in such structured working environments, but as both a daughter and a wife of a small-business owner, as well as a self-described "political junkie," Swift says the CFIB job is a perfect fit. "My motto is, never give up, never go away," she explains. "But I'm quite content to take my victories in 10% increments over time. You almost never win 100% in one shot." For Catherine Swift, slow and steady just might win the race.

Source: D McMurdy, "Why Small is Big," *Canadian Business*, February 4, 2002, p 11.

Influencing Others

In a perfect world, individual and collective interests would be closely aligned and everyone would move forward as one. Instead, we typically find a rather messy situation in which self-interests often override the collective mission. Personal hidden agendas are pursued, political coalitions are formed, false impressions are made, and people end up working at cross purposes. Managers need to be able to guide diverse individuals, who are often powerfully motivated to put their own self-interests first, to pursue common objectives. At stake in this tug-of-war between individual and collective interests is no less than the ultimate survival of the organization.

How do you get others to carry out your wishes? Do you simply tell them what to do? Or do you prefer a less direct approach, such as promising to return the favour? Whatever approach you use, the crux of the issue is *social influence*. A large measure of interpersonal interaction involves attempts to influence others, including parents, bosses, co-workers, spouses, teachers, friends, and children.

Nine Generic Influence Tactics

A particularly fruitful stream of research involved asking employees how they managed to get either their bosses, co-workers, or subordinates to do what they wanted them to do.[1] Statistical refinements and replications by other researchers eventually yielded nine influence tactics. The nine tactics, ranked in diminishing order of use in the workplace are as follows:

1. *Rational persuasion*. Trying to convince someone with reason, logic, or facts.
2. *Inspirational appeals*. Trying to build enthusiasm by appealing to others' emotions, ideals, or values.
3. *Consultation*. Getting others to participate in planning, making decisions, and changes.
4. *Ingratiation*. Getting someone in a good mood prior to making a request; being friendly, helpful, and using praise or flattery.
5. *Personal appeals*. Referring to friendship and loyalty when making a request.
6. *Exchange*. Making express or implied promises and trading favours.
7. *Coalition tactics*. Getting others to support your effort to persuade someone.
8. *Pressure*. Demanding compliance or using intimidation or threats.
9. *Legitimating tactics*. Basing a request on one's authority or right, organizational rules or policies, or express or implied support from superiors.[2]

These approaches can be considered *generic* influence tactics because they characterize social influence in all directions—downward, upward, or lateral.[3] Some call the first five influence tactics—rational persuasion, inspirational appeals, consultation, ingratiation, and personal appeals—"soft" tactics because they are friendlier and not as coercive as the last four tactics. Exchange, coalition, pressure, and legitimating tactics accordingly are called "hard" tactics because they involve more overt pressure.

Three Influence Outcomes

Put yourself in this familiar situation. It's Wednesday and a big project you've been working on for your project team is due Friday. You're behind on the preparation of your computer graphics for your final report and presentation. You catch a friend who is great at computer graphics as they head out of the office at quitting time. You try this

How to Win Clients and Influence People

Brian Mulroney's habit of helping out his pals hurt him when he was prime minister, but now that he's become a private sector operator, the same schmoozy approach is making him—and his clients—very rich. Mulroney has been able to parlay his background into a global lobbying business. You're likely to find him zig-zagging the globe, lobbying foreign governments on behalf of big-name clients.

Mulroney sits on the boards of several carefully selected companies, including Barrick Gold. Soon after he took his place on the board, Mulroney had a chance to show his stuff. Barrick had bought Lac Minerals of Toronto, which operated gold mines in Chile. But one of its main deposits ran across the border into Argentina. Since relations between the two countries were quite strained, Barrick Gold didn't see how it could go about mining the deposit. So Mulroney was asked to smooth the way.

His technique was very straightforward. "I met with the two heads of state separately," he says. "Then I talked to their ministers, as well as representatives from the private sector." Result: two years later, Chile and Argentina had signed a new mining agreement. Now, everything needed to operate the mine can flow freely from one side of the Andes to the other. How do you convince two heads of state to change their legislation? "It's all in the way you present things," explains Mulroney. "Politicians have their own concerns, constraints, and agendas. I know what they are and how to satisfy them. I'm on an equal footing with these leaders. I have credibility. The solutions I propose are realistic."

Source: D Bérard, "How to Win Clients and Influence People," *Canadian Business*, April 30, 1999, pp 42–45.

exchange tactic to get your friend to help you out: "I'm way behind. I need your help. If you could come back in for two to three hours tonight and help me with these graphics, I'll complete those spreadsheets you've been complaining about." According to researchers, your friend will engage in one of three possible influence outcomes:

1. *Commitment*. Your friend enthusiastically agrees and will demonstrate initiative and persistence while completing the assignment.
2. *Compliance*. Your friend grudgingly complies and will need prodding to satisfy minimum requirements.
3. *Resistance*. Your friend will say no, make excuses, stall, or put up an argument.[4]

The best outcome is commitment because the target person's intrinsic motivation will energize good performance. However, managers often have to settle for compliance in today's hectic workplace. Resistance means a failed influence attempt.

Practical Research Insights

Research studies have taught us useful lessons about the relative effectiveness of influence tactics along with other instructive insights:

• Commitment is more likely when people rely on consultation, strong rational persuasion, and inspirational appeals and *do not* rely on pressure and coalition tactics.[5] Interestingly, in one study, managers were not very effective at *downward* influence. They relied most heavily on inspiration (an effective tactic), ingratiation (a moderately effective tactic), and pressure (an ineffective tactic).[6]

• Ingratiation (making the boss feel good) can slightly improve your performance appraisal results and make your boss like you significantly more.[7]

- Commitment is more likely when the influence attempt involves something *important* and *enjoyable* and is based on a *friendly* relationship.[8]
- Preliminary evidence indicates that employees tend to perceive their superiors' "soft" influence tactics as fair and "hard" influence tactics as unfair. *Unfair* influence tactics are associated with greater *resistance* among employees.[9]
- After reviewing relevant studies, a team of researchers concluded: "Each tactic includes a broad variety of behaviours; when planning an influence attempt, it is important to consider not only what tactic to use but also what forms of each tactic are most appropriate for the situation."[10]
- Interpersonal influence is culture bound. The foregoing research evidence on influence tactics has a bias in favour of European-North Americans. Much remains to be learned about how to effectively influence others (without unintended insult) in today's diverse labour force and cross-cultural economy.

Finally, Barbara Moses, Toronto-based consultant and author, offers this advice on influencing your boss:

> If your boss doesn't understand the need for change, this might be partly your fault. You can't make change; you have to sell it. And the key to selling anything is to understand where the other person is coming from—rather than to assume that your boss is a complete jerk. But most of us communicate from an egocentric place. We construct an idea or a project mainly in terms of what makes sense to us. Instead, ask yourself: "What's most important to my boss?" "What are his greatest concerns?" Go forward only after you've answered these questions.[11]

Strategic Alliances and Reciprocity

The concept of corporate strategic alliances has been extended to interpersonal influence.[12] Hardly a day goes by without another mention in the business press of a new strategic alliance between two global companies intent on staying competitive. These win-win relationships are based on complementary strengths. Managers need to follow suit by forming some strategic alliances of their own with anyone who has a stake in their area. This is particularly true given today's rapid change, crossfunctional work teams, and diminished reliance on traditional authority structures.

The following four strategies can be used to turn co-workers into strategic allies:[13]

1. *Mutual respect.* Assume they are competent and smart.
2. *Openness.* Talk straight to them. It isn't possible for any one person to know everything, so give them the information they need to know to help you better.
3. *Trust.* Assume that no one will take any action that is purposely intended to hurt another, so hold back no information that the other could use, even if it doesn't help your immediate position.
4. *Mutual benefit.* Plan every strategy so that both parties win. If that doesn't happen over time, the alliance will break up. When dissolving a partnership becomes necessary as a last resort, try to do it in a clean way that minimizes residual anger. Some day, you may want a new alliance with that person.

Reciprocity

Widespread belief that people should be paid back for their positive and negative acts.

It is true that these tactics involve taking some personal risks. But the effectiveness of interpersonal strategic alliances is anchored to the concept of reciprocity. "**Reciprocity** is the almost universal belief that people should be paid back for what they do—that one good (or bad) turn deserves another."[14] In short, people tend to get what they give when attempting to influence others.

In order to learn more about how today's managers can and do reconcile individual and organizational interests, a review of social power is necessary.

Social Power and Empowerment

The term *power* evokes mixed and often passionate reactions. To skeptics, Lord Acton's time-honoured declaration that "power corrupts and absolute power corrupts absolutely" is truer than ever. However, OB specialists remind us that, like it or not, power is a fact of life in modern organizations. According to one management writer:

> Power must be used because managers must influence those they depend on. Power also is crucial in the development of managers' self-confidence and willingness to support subordinates. From this perspective, power should be accepted as a natural part of any organization. Managers should recognize and develop their own power to coordinate and support the work of subordinates; it is powerlessness, not power, that undermines organizational effectiveness.[15]

| **Social power** |
| Ability to get things done with human, informational, and material resources. |
| **Socialized power** |
| Directed at helping others. |
| **Personalized power** |
| Directed at helping oneself. |

Thus, power is a necessary and generally positive force in organizations.[16] As the term is used here, **social power** is defined as "the ability to marshal the human, informational, and material resources to get something done."[17]

Importantly, the exercise of social power in organizations is not necessarily a downward proposition. Employees can and do exercise power upward and laterally.

Dimensions of Power

While power may be an elusive concept to the casual observer, social scientists view power as having reasonable clear dimensions. Two dimensions of power that deserve our attention are (1) socialized versus personalized power and (2) the five bases of power.

Two Types of Power   Behavioural scientists contend that one of the basic human needs is for power. Because this need is learned and not innate, the need for power has been extensively studied. Researchers have drawn a distinction between **socialized power** and **personalized power**.

Jim Balsillie and Mike Lazaridis, co-CEOs of Waterloo, Ontario-based Research in Motion have expert power due to their invention of the wireless E-mail technology in their handheld Black Berry product. It's so addictive that some call it Crack Berry!

Socialized power relates to the use of power out of concern for others and personalized power relates to the use of power for personal benefit. This distinction between socialized and personalized power helps explain why power has a negative connotation for many people.[18] Managers and others who pursue personalized power for their own selfish ends give power a bad name.

Five Bases of Power   Classic research by John French and Bertram Raven proposed that power arises from five different bases: reward power, coercive power, legitimate power, expert power, and referent power.[19] Each involves a different approach to influencing others. Each has advantages and drawbacks.

Women Gain "Slow and Steady" Ground in Canada's Boardrooms

Female representation in Canada's boardrooms is growing—but more than half of the country's largest companies still have no women directors, according to the Catalyst Census of Women Board Directors of Canada. In 2001, women held 9.8% of board seats on the FP 500-listed companies, up from 6.2% in 1998. Nearly 49% of companies now have at least one woman on their board, up from 36% in 1998. Canada badly lags behind the US, where women represent more than 12% of board membership of Fortune 500 firms, and 87% of companies overall have at least one woman on the board.

In the Catalyst survey, crown corporations had some of the highest representation of women. At the Canadian Broadcasting Corporation, for example, four of the 10 directors are women. Businesses that rank well include credit unions; food and drugstores; and publishing and printing. Topping the list of worst culprits for having few or no women on their boards are brewers and distillers; engineering and construction firms; and mining, metals and minerals companies.

Jocelyne Cote-O'Hara, who sits on the boards of six companies, including Manitoba Telecom and Xerox Canada, spoke at the luncheon where the report was released. "I would like to see critical mass, 30% women," she says, "and that's still a long way off."

Source: K MacNamara, "Women Gain 'Slow and Steady' Ground in Canada's Boardrooms: Corporate Canada Still Badly Lags US Boards," *National Post*, March 27, 2002, p FP7.

Reward power

Obtaining compliance with promised or actual rewards.

Coercive power

Obtaining compliance through threatened or actual punishment.

Legitimate power

Obtaining compliance through formal authority.

Expert power

Obtaining compliance through one's knowledge or information.

Referent power

Obtaining compliance through charisma or personal attraction.

Reward Power   Managers have **reward power** if they can obtain compliance by promising or granting rewards. Pay-for-performance plans and positive reinforcement programs attempt to exploit reward power.

Coercive Power   Threats of punishment and actual punishment give an individual **coercive power.** A marketing manager who threatens to fire any salesperson who uses a company car for recreational purposes is relying on coercive power.

Legitimate Power   This base of power is anchored to one's formal position or authority. Thus, managers who obtain compliance primarily because of their formal authority to make decisions have **legitimate power.** Legitimate power may be expressed either positively or negatively. Positive legitimate power focuses constructively on job performance. Negative legitimate power tends to be threatening and demeaning to those being influenced. Its main purpose is to build the power holder's ego.

Expert Power   Valued knowledge or information gives an individual **expert power** over those who need such knowledge or information. The power of supervisors is enhanced because they know about work assignments and schedules before their employees do. Knowledge *is* power in today's high-tech workplaces.

Referent Power   Also called charisma, **referent power** comes into play when one's personality becomes the reason for compliance. Role models have referent power over those who identify closely with them.[20]

In a factory situation, what types of power do you think a plant manager would have?

Practical Lessons from Research

Researchers have identified the following relationships between power bases and work outcomes such as job performance, job satisfaction, and turnover:

- Expert and referent power had a generally positive effect.
- Reward and legitimate power had a slightly positive effect.
- Coercive power had a slightly negative effect.[21]

Research investigating the relationship between influence styles and bases of power found that rational persuasion was a highly acceptable managerial influence tactic. Why? Because employees perceived it to be associated with the three bases of power they viewed positively: legitimate, expert, and referent.[22]

In summary, expert and referent power appear to get the best *combination* of results and favourable reactions from lower-level employees.[23]

Employee Empowerment

An exciting trend in today's organizations centres on giving employees a greater say in the workplace. This trend wears various labels, including "participative management" and "open-book management."[24] Regardless of the label one prefers, it is all about empowerment. One management writer defines **empowerment** in terms of serving the customer:

> Empowerment quite simply means granting supervisors or workers permission to give the customer priority over other issues in the operation. In practical terms, it relates to the resources, skill, time and support to become leaders rather than controllers or mindless robots.[25]

Empowerment

Sharing varying degrees of power with lower-level employees to better serve the customer.

General Electric's Steve Kerr, a pioneer in employee empowerment, explains: "We say empowerment is moving decision making down to the lowest level *where a competent decision can be made."*[26] Of course, it is naive and counterproductive to hand power over to unwilling and/or unprepared employees.

The concept of empowerment requires some adjustment in traditional thinking. First and foremost, power is *not* a zero-sum situation where one person's gain is another's loss. Social power is unlimited. This requires win-win thinking. According to Philip J Carroll Jr, Chairman and CEO of Fluor Corporation:

> Power is very essential, but how you distribute it is very important. Most people, given power, tend to want to hold onto it, to accumulate it and increase the amount one has. Accumulation of power has a lessening effect on the ability to use power. You have to have it, but you have to give it away skilfully in order to make it functional and useful. If you are not willing to give power away then you lose it.[27]

Authoritarian managers who view employee empowerment as a threat to their personal power are missing the point because of their win-lose thinking.[28]

The second adjustment to traditional thinking involves seeing empowerment as a matter of degree, not as an either-or proposition.[29] Figure 10–1 illustrates how power can be shifted to the hands of non-managers step by step. The overriding goal is to increase productivity and competitiveness in leaner organizations. Each step in this evolution increases the power of organizational contributors who traditionally had little or no power. The highest degree of empowerment is **delegation**, the process of granting decision-making authority to lower-level employees. This amounts to power distribution. Delegation has long been the recommended way to lighten the busy manager's load while at the same time developing employees' abilities. Importantly, delegation gives non-managerial employees more than simply a voice in decisions. It empowers them to make their own decisions.

For example, at the Xerox plant in Mississauga, Ontario, workplace reorganization has led to a significant shift in responsibility to workers on the plant floor. Many work-

> **Delegation**
>
> Granting decision-making authority to people at lower levels.

FIGURE 10–1   The Evolution of Power: From Domination to Delegation

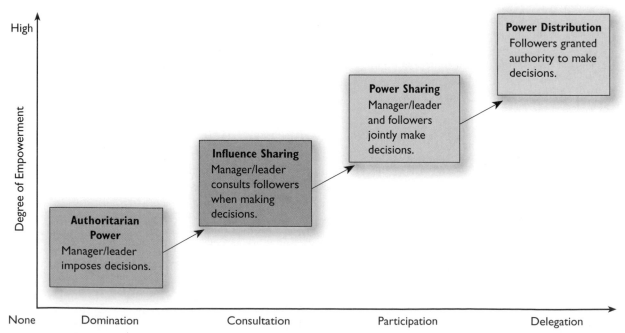

ers feel this has made their jobs more interesting and challenging, but that it has also increased stress. Xerox workers have taken over a number of supervisory functions such as production planning, time-card and vacation scheduling, tool maintenance and control, inventory-quality monitoring, safety monitoring, equipment ordering, coordinating cross-training, and conducting housekeeping audits. As one manager said,

> Ultimately we're eliminating ourselves as managers because we're non-value-added, as such. People can really manage themselves and maintain what it is they have to do.

One of the workers says,

> We have a lot more freedom in what we say and what we can do. We see our supervisor at the beginning and at the end of the shift and that's it. We basically run the line. I find it a lot more interesting. I am working a hell of a lot harder than I ever did. The supervisor and engineer work for me now. What I tell them, they'll pretty well listen now.[30]

Making Empowerment Work

Empowerment can work well if managers go about it properly. However, empowerment is a sweeping concept with many different definitions, and consequently, cause-effect relationships can be hard to identify. Managers committed to the idea of employee empowerment need to follow the path of continuous improvement, learning from their successes and failures. Eight years of research with 10 "empowered" companies led consultant W Alan Randolph to formulate the three-pronged empowerment plan in Figure 10–2. Notice how open-book management and active information sharing are needed to build the necessary foundation of trust. Beyond that, clear goals and lots of relevant training are needed. While noting that the empowerment process can take several years to unfold, Randolph offered this perspective:

> While the keys to empowerment may be easy to understand, they are hard to implement. It takes tremendous courage to start sharing sensitive information. It takes true strength to build more structure just at the point when people want more freedom of

---

ETHICS AT WORK

Empowerment or Sham?

Unions are often suspicious of empowerment, as is evident from the Web site of the Canadian Auto Workers Union:

> . . . the idea of "empowerment" is in the United States, even more than the Canadian system, a complete sham. Safety suggestion boxes are often the best that can be done to solicit worker input. Asking workers what they think in ad hoc safety crew meetings where the supervisor is in charge with no formal mechanism for them to consider their point of view and present it in a formal way to management, makes a mockery of the idea of empowerment. In fact, the power remains with management and the workers must do what they are told.

CAW Local 2301 says in an article entitled "Employee Empowerment—The Hidden Agenda":

> It looks like the company has decided to bypass the union leadership and introduce this new concept directly to the membership. It looks clear that management responsibilities are trying to be shifted over to our members, i.e., due diligence, WCB, etc. . . . According to our information, the union was a topic discussed throughout this management workshop. They talked about union resistance and how to get the union to buy into the "Employee Empowerment" concept. From what we know about this concept the union will go on record right now that—YES, there will be resistance to the "Employee Empowerment" concept and we will not buy into the Team Concept, Multi-Skilling, undermining of seniority and. . . .

You Decide . . .

Is it ethical for management to try to introduce the concept of empowerment without informing the union? Is it ethical for the union to oppose an empowerment initiative before they have information about it? How would you respond to these comments? What could management do to avoid this kind of response from being generated in the first place?

Sources: Adapted from www.caw.ca/whatwedo/health&safety/awcbc.asp.

FIGURE 10–2   Randolph's Empowerment Model

The Empowerment Plan

Share Information
- Share company performance information.
- Help people understand the business.
- Build trust through sharing sensitive information.
- Create self-monitoring possibilities.

Create Autonomy through Structure	**Let Teams Become the Hierarchy**
• Create a clear vision and clarify the little pictures. • Create new decision-making rules that support empowerment. • Clarify goals and roles collaboratively. • Establish new empowering performance management processes. • Use heavy doses of training.	• Provide direction and training for new skills. • Provide encouragement and support for change. • Gradually have managers let go of control. • Work through the leadership vacuum stage. • Acknowledge the fear factor.

**Remember: Empowerment is not magic;
it consists of a few simple steps and a lot of persistence.**

Source: "Navigating the Journey to Empowerment," by W Alan Randolph. Reprinted from *Organizational Dynamics,* Spring 1995. © 1995 American Management Association International. Reprinted by permission of the American Management Association International, New York, NY. All rights reserved. www.amanet.org

action. It takes real growth to allow teams to take over the management decision-making process. And above all, it takes perseverance to complete the empowerment process.[31]

Organizational Politics and Impression Management

Most students of OB find the study of organizational politics intriguing. Politics is an ever-present and sometimes annoying feature of modern work life. On the other hand, organizational politics is often a positive force in modern work organizations. Skilful and well-timed politics can help you get your point across, neutralize resistance to a key project, or get a choice job assignment.[32]

We explore this important and interesting area by (1) defining the term *organizational politics,* (2) identifying three levels of political action, (3) discussing eight specific political tactics, (4) considering a related area called *impression management,* and (5) discussing how to curb organizational politics.

Definition and Domain of Organizational Politics

Organizational politics

Intentional enhancement of self-interest.

"**Organizational politics** involves intentional acts of influence to enhance or protect the self-interest of individuals or groups."[33] An emphasis on *self-interest* distinguishes this form of social influence. Managers are endlessly challenged to achieve a workable balance between employees' self-interests and organizational interests. When a proper balance exists, the pursuit of self-interest may serve the organization's interests. Political behaviour becomes a negative force when self-interests erode or defeat organizational interests. For example, the political tactic of filtering and distorting information flowing up to the boss is a self-serving practice that puts the reporting employees in the best possible light.[34]

Political Behaviour Triggered by Uncertainty   Political maneuvering is triggered primarily by *uncertainty*. Five common sources of uncertainty within organizations are

1. Unclear objectives.
2. Vague performance measures.
3. Ill-defined decision processes.
4. Strong individual or group competition.[35]
5. Any type of change.

Regarding this last source of uncertainty, organization development specialist Anthony Raia noted, "Whatever we attempt to change, the political subsystem becomes active. Vested interests are almost always at stake and the distribution of power is challenged."[36]

   Thus, we would expect a field sales representative, striving to achieve an assigned quota, to be less political than a management trainee working on a variety of projects. While some management trainees stake their career success on hard work, competence, and a bit of luck, many do not. These people attempt to gain a competitive edge through some combination of the political tactics discussed below. Meanwhile, the salesperson's performance is measured in actual sales, not in terms of being friends with the boss or taking credit for others' work. Thus, the management trainee would tend to be more political than the field salesperson because of greater uncertainty about management's expectations. Because employees generally experience greater uncertainty during the earlier stages of their careers, junior employees are more political than more senior ones.

Three Levels of Political Action   Although much political maneuvering occurs at the individual level, it also can involve group or collective action. Figure 10–3 illustrates three different levels of political action: the individual level, the coalition level, and the network level.[37] Each level has its distinguishing characteristics. At the individual level, personal self-interests are pursued by the individual. The political aspects of coalitions and networks are not so obvious, however.

Levels of Political Action in Organizations   **FIGURE 10–3**

Coalition

Temporary groupings of people who actively pursue a single issue.

People with a common interest can become a political coalition by fitting the following definition. In an organizational context, a **coalition** is an informal group bound together by the *active* pursuit of a *single* issue. Coalitions may or may not coincide with formal group membership. When the target issue is resolved (a sexually harassing supervisor is fired, for example), the coalition disbands. Experts note that political coalitions have "fuzzy boundaries," meaning they are fluid in membership, flexible in structure, and temporary in duration.[38] Coalitions are a potent political force in organizations. During the 1990s, coalitions on the corporate boards of American Express, IBM, and General Motors ousted the heads of those giant companies.

A third level of political action involves networks.[39] Unlike coalitions, which pivot on specific issues, networks are loose associations of individuals seeking social support for their general self-interests. Politically, networks are people oriented, while coalitions are issue oriented. Networks have broader and longer term agendas than do coalitions. For instance, Amex Canada has numerous employee networking groups, ranging from gay to Christian.[40]

Eight Political Tactics   Anyone who has worked in an organization has firsthand knowledge of blatant politicking. Blaming someone else for your mistake is an obvious political ploy. But other political tactics are more subtle. Researchers have identified a range of political behaviour.

One study asked employees to describe organizational political tactics and personal characteristics of effective political actors based upon their accumulated experience in *all* organizations in which they had worked."[41] Listed in descending order of occurrence, the eight political tactics that emerged were

1. Attacking or blaming others.
2. Using information as a political tool.
3. Creating a favourable image. (Also known as *impression management*.)[42]
4. Developing a base of support.
5. Praising others (ingratiation).
6. Forming power coalitions with strong allies.
7. Associating with influential people.
8. Creating obligations (reciprocity).

(DILBERT reprinted by permission of United Feature Syndicate, Inc.)

The researchers distinguished between reactive and proactive political tactics. Some of the tactics, such as scapegoating, were *reactive* because the intent was to *defend* one's self-interest. Other tactics, such as developing a base of support, were *proactive* because they sought to *promote* the individual's self-interest.

Impression Management

Impression management is defined as "the process by which people attempt to control or manipulate the reactions of others to images of themselves or their ideas."[43] This encompasses how one talks, behaves, and looks. Most impression management attempts are directed at making a *good* impression on relevant others. But, as we will see, some employees strive to make a *bad* impression. For purposes of conceptual clarity, we will focus on *upward* impression management (trying to impress one's immediate supervisor) because it is most relevant for managers. Still, it is good to remember that *anyone* can be the intended target of impression management. Parents, teachers, peers, employees, and customers are all fair game when it comes to managing the impressions of others.

> **Impression management**
> Getting others to see us in a certain manner.

Good Impressions If you "dress for success," project an upbeat attitude at all times, and avoid offending others, you are engaging in favourable impression management—particularly so if your motive is to improve your chances of getting what you want in life.[44] There are questionable ways to create a good impression, as well. For instance, Stewart Friedman, director of the University of Pennsylvania's Leadership Program, recently offered this gem:

> Last year, I was doing some work with a large bank. The people there told me a story that astounded me: After 7 pm, people would open the door to their office, drape a spare jacket on the back of their chair, lay a set of glasses down on some reading material on their desk—and then go home for the night. The point of this elaborate gesture was to create the illusion that they were just out grabbing dinner and would be returning to burn the midnight oil.[45]

In an interview situation, first impressions are most important. The choice of "power suit" can make or break a job offer.

Impression management often strays into unethical territory.

Three categories of favourable upward impression management tactics are *job-focused* (manipulating information about one's job performance), *supervisor-focused* (praising and doing favours for one's supervisor), and *self-focused* (presenting oneself as a polite and nice person).[46] A moderate amount of upward impression management is a necessity for the average employee today. Too little, and busy managers are liable to overlook some of your valuable contributions when they make job assignment, pay, and promotion decisions. Too much, and you run the risk of being branded a "schmoozer," a "phony," and other unflattering things by your co-workers.[47] Excessive flattery and ingratiation can backfire by embarrassing the target person and damaging one's credibility. Also, the risk of unintended insult is very high when impression management tactics cross gender, racial, ethnic, and cultural lines.[48] International management experts warn:

The impression management tactic is only as effective as its correlation to accepted norms about behavioural presentation. In other words, slapping a Japanese subordinate on the back with a rousing "Good work, Hiro!" will not create the desired impression in Hiro's mind that the expatriate intended. In fact, the behaviour will likely create the opposite impression.[49]

Bad Impressions   At first glance, the idea of consciously trying to make a bad impression in the workplace seems absurd.[50] But an interesting new line of impression management research has uncovered both motives and tactics for making oneself look *bad*. In a survey of the work experiences of business students, more than half "reported witnessing a case of someone intentionally looking bad at work."[51] Why? Four motives came out of the study:

(1) *Avoidance:* Employee seeks to avoid additional work, stress, burnout, or an unwanted transfer or promotion. (2) *Obtain concrete rewards:* Employee seeks to obtain a pay raise or a desired transfer, promotion, or demotion. (3) *Exit:* Employee seeks to get laid off, fired, or suspended, and perhaps also to collect unemployment or workers' compensation. (4) *Power:* Employee seeks to control, manipulate, or intimidate others, get revenge, or make someone else look bad.[52]

Within the context of these motives, *unfavourable* upward impression management makes sense.

Five unfavourable upward impression management tactics identified by the researchers are as follows:

- *Decreasing performance*—restricting productivity, making more mistakes than usual, lowering quality, neglecting tasks.
- *Not working to potential*—pretending ignorance, having unused capabilities.
- *Withdrawing*—being tardy, taking excessive breaks, faking illness.
- *Displaying a bad attitude*—complaining, getting upset and angry, acting strangely, not getting along with co-workers.
- *Broadcasting limitations*—letting co-workers know about one's physical problems and mistakes (both verbally and nonverbally).[53]

Recommended ways to manage employees who try to make a bad impression can be found throughout this book. They include more challenging work, greater autonomy, better feedback, supportive leadership, clear and reasonable goals, and a less stressful work setting.[54]

Keeping Organizational Politics in Check

Organizational politics cannot be eliminated. A manager would be naive to expect such an outcome. But political maneuvering can and should be managed to keep it constructive and within reasonable bounds. Harvard's Abraham Zaleznik put the issue this way: "People can focus their attention on only so many things. The more it lands on politics, the less energy—emotional and intellectual—is available to attend to the problems that fall under the heading of real work."[55]

An individual's degree of political activity is a matter of personal values, ethics, and temperament. People who are either strictly nonpolitical or highly political generally pay a price for their behaviour. The former may experience slow promotions and feel left out, while the latter may run the risk of being called self-serving and lose their credibility. People at both ends of the political spectrum may be considered poor team players. Canada's WestJet Airlines has worked hard to build a low-politics culture, beginning with their legendary values:

- We are positive and passionate about what we do
- We take our jobs seriously, but not ourselves
- We embrace change and innovation
- We are friendly and caring towards our People and Customers and we treat everyone with respect
- We provide people with the tools and training they need to do their jobs
- We celebrate our success
- We personify the hardworking "can do" attitude
- We are honest, open, and keep our commitments
- We are TEAM WESTJET!

These values clearly indicate that self-serving political behaviour does not fit with the company's culture.[56]

A moderate amount of prudent political behaviour generally is considered a survival tool in complex organizations. Experts remind us that

. . . political behaviour has earned a bad name only because of its association with politicians. On its own, the use of power and other resources to obtain your objectives is not inherently unethical. It all depends on what the preferred objectives are.[57]

With this perspective in mind, the practical steps in Table 10–1 are recommended. Notice the importance of reducing uncertainty through standardized performance evaluations and clear performance-reward linkages. Measurable objectives are management's first line of defence against negative expressions of organizational politics.[58]

Practical Tips for Managing Organizational Politics   **TABLE 10–1**

To Reduce System Uncertainty

Make clear what are the bases and processes for evaluation.

Differentiate rewards among high and low performers.

Make sure the rewards are as immediately and directly related to performance as possible.

To Reduce Competition

Try to minimize resource competition among managers.

Replace resource competition with externally oriented goals and objectives.

To Break Existing Political Fiefdoms

Where highly cohesive political empires exist, break them apart by removing or splitting the most dysfunctional subgroups.

If you are an executive, be keenly sensitive to managers whose mode of operation is the personalization of political patronage. First, approach these persons with a directive to "stop the political maneuvering." If it continues, remove them from the positions and, preferably, the company.

To Prevent Future Fiefdoms

Make one of the most important criteria for promotion an apolitical attitude that puts organizational ends ahead of personal power ends.

Source: D R Beeman and T W Sharkey, "The Use and Abuse of Corporate Politics." Reprinted with permission of *Business Horizons*, March–April 1987, p 30. Copyright © 1987 by the Board of Trustees at Indiana University, Kelley School of Business.

summary of key concepts

- *Name five "soft" and four "hard" influence tactics, and summarize the practical lessons from influence research.* Five soft influence tactics are rational persuasion, inspirational appeals, consultation, ingratiation, and personal appeals. They are more friendly and less coercive than the four hard influence tactics: exchange, coalition tactics, pressure, and legitimating tactics. According to research, soft tactics are better for generating commitment and are perceived as more fair than hard tactics.

- *Identify and briefly describe French and Raven's five bases of power.* French and Raven's five bases of power are reward power (rewarding compliance), coercive power (punishing noncompliance), legitimate power (relying on formal authority), expert power (providing needed information), and referent power (relying on personal attraction).

- *Define the term* empowerment, *and explain how to make it succeed.* Empowerment involves sharing varying degrees of power and decision-making authority with lower-level employees to better serve the customer. Empowerment requires active sharing of key information, structure that encourages autonomy, transfer of control from managers to teams, and persistence. Trust and training also are very important.

- *Define organizational politics, explain what triggers it, and specify the three levels of political action in organizations.* Organizational politics is defined as intentional acts of influence to enhance or protect the self-interests of individuals or groups. Uncertainty triggers most politicking in organizations. Political action occurs at individual, coalition, and network levels. Coalitions are informal, temporary, and single-issue alliances.

- *Distinguish between favourable and unfavourable impression management tactics.* Favourable upward impression management can be job-focused (manipulating information about one's job performance), supervisor-focused (praising or doing favours for the boss), or self-focused (being polite and nice). Unfavourable upward impression management tactics include decreasing performance, not working to potential, withdrawing, displaying a bad attitude, and broadcasting one's limitations.

- *Explain how to manage organizational politics.* Because organizational politics cannot be eliminated, managers need to learn to deal with it. Uncertainty can be reduced by evaluating performance and linking rewards to performance. Measurable objectives are key. Participative management also helps.

key terms

coalition, 234
coercive power, 228
delegation, 230
empowerment, 229
expert power, 228

impression management, 235
legitimate power, 228
organizational politics, 232
personalized power, 227
reciprocity, 226

referent power, 228
reward power, 228
social power, 227
socialized power, 227

discussion questions

1. Of the nine generic influence tactics, which do you use the most when dealing with friends, parents, your boss, or your professors? Would other tactics be more effective?

2. Before reading this chapter, did the term *power* have a negative connotation to you? Do you view it differently now? Explain.

3. What base(s) of power do you rely on in your daily affairs? Do you handle power effectively and responsibly?

4. In your opinion, how much empowerment is too much in today's workplaces?

5. What personal experiences have you had with coalitions? Explain any positive or negative outcomes.

6. How much impression management do you see in your classroom and/or workplace today? Citing specific examples, are those tactics effective?

internet exercises

www.influenceatwork.com

1. A Free Tutorial on Social Influence

Do you get the feeling advertisers, the media, politicians, salespeople, parents and teachers, and friends sometimes are trying to "trick" you by manipulating words and images in self-serving ways? According to Professor Robert B Cialdini and his colleague, consultant Kelton Rhoads, you are right to feel a bit put upon. After all, as their research has documented, each of us is the recipient (or victim) of countless social influence attempts during every waking hour. Their fascinating Internet site (**www.influenceatwork.com**) provides an inside look at social influence so we will not be unfairly or unwittingly manipulated.

At the home page, select the "Academic" path. We recommend you start by clicking on the "What's Your Influence Quotient?" icon. The short quiz will get you thinking about the power and pervasiveness of social influence. Back at the main menu, you might want to select the heading "The Authors" for relevant background. Returning once again to the Academic page, select "Introduction to Influence" from the main menu. All of the tutorial pieces are worth exploration, but we especially recommend the first six categories, including the two on ethics. The "6 Principles" and collection of readings on "Framing" are very interesting and instructive.

QUESTIONS

1. Having read selections from the social influence tutorial, are you more aware of day-to-day influence processes and tactics? Explain.
2. What were the most valuable insights you picked up from the social influence tutorial? Generally, do you see social influence as a constructive or sinister force in society? Explain.
3. Is it possible that employees are becoming more difficult to influence because they have become hardened or numbed as a result of excessive exposure to influence attempts?
4. How can managers use social influence *ethically*?

www.cdnbizwomen.com

2. Women's Networking

Networking groups for women in business became popular in the 1970s and now, 30 years later, there are dozens to choose from—all over the world. Go to the Web site for the Canadian Women's Business Network (**www.cdn bizwomen.com**). Click on the "Provincial Databases" in the main menu and look around the different provinces for connections that might help you as you embark on your career. Then go back to the main menu and check out the "B2B Exchange," "Online Marketing" (free Web design and banner ads), and anything else you think might be of use to someone starting out on the career path you have chosen.

QUESTIONS

1. If you are a female student, what specific information on this site can you use right now as you begin your career? Explain.
2. If you are a male student, do you feel comfortable using this information? Why or why not? If not, search for and discuss with the class a networking organization that will work for you.

experiential exercises

1. How Much Do You Rely on Upward Impression Management Tactics?

Instructions

Rate yourself on each item according to how you behave on your current (or most recent) job. Add your circled responses to calculate a total score. Compare your score with our arbitrary norms.

Job-Focused Tactics	Rarely	Very Often

1. I play up the value of my positive work results and make my supervisor aware of them.   1 — 2 — 3 — 4 — 5

2. I try to make my work appear better than it is.   1 — 2 — 3 — 4 — 5

3. I try to take responsibility for positive results, even when I'm not solely responsible for achieving them.   1 — 2 — 3 — 4 — 5

4. I try to make my negative results not as severe as they initially appear to my supervisor.   1 — 2 — 3 — 4 — 5

5. I arrive at work early and/or work late to show my supervisor I am a hard worker.   1 — 2 — 3 — 4 — 5

Supervisor-Focused Tactics

6. I show an interest in my supervisor's personal life.   1 — 2 — 3 — 4 — 5

7. I praise my supervisor on his/her accomplishments.   1 — 2 — 3 — 4 — 5

8. I do personal favours for my supervisor that I'm not required to do.   1 — 2 — 3 — 4 — 5

9. I compliment my supervisor on her/his dress or appearance.   1 — 2 — 3 — 4 — 5

10. I agree with my supervisor's major suggestions and ideas.   1 — 2 — 3 — 4 — 5

Self-Focused Tactics

11. I am very friendly and polite around my supervisor.   1 — 2 — 3 — 4 — 5

12. I try to act as a model employee around my supervisor.   1 — 2 — 3 — 4 — 5

13. I work harder when I know my supervisor will see the results.   1 — 2 — 3 — 4 — 5

Total score = _____

Arbitrary Norms

13–26 Free agent
27–51 Better safe than sorry
52–65 Hello, Hollywood

Source: Adapted from S J Wayne and G R Ferris, "Influence Tactics, Affect, and Exchange Quality in Supervisor-Subordinate Interactions: A Laboratory Experiment and Field Study," *Journal of Applied Psychology*, October 1990, pp 487–99.

2. General Software Products: An In-Basket Exercise

Purpose

This exercise is designed to help you understand the dynamics and feelings of power in an organizational setting.

Materials

The instructor will distribute in-basket materials and, later, an attitude questionnaire. Teams should have a private area where they can make their decisions.

Instructions

Step 1: The instructor will briefly describe what an in-basket is, including the time constraints. Students are then put into groups (typically of four to five people) and each group receives a package with copies of E-mails and memos. (Note: instead of working in teams, your instructor may decide to assign the in-basket exercise to individuals working alone. If so, the following steps will apply, but Step 2 would refer to individuals.)

Step 2: Teams have 25 minutes to go through the in-basket, regardless of how many items they actually complete. Please respond to each item in the package.

Step 3: Immediately after completing the in-basket exercise, each student will individually complete the attitude scale provided by the instructor.

Step 4: The instructor will debrief students on the exercise.

In-Basket Setting

Students take the role of J Carter, a personal computer (PC) software department manager in General Software Products, one of the companies owned by General Holding Corp. You are requested to respond to several E-mails, letters, and memos that have been left in your in-basket. General Holding Corp. is a large company that competes in the computer industry.

General Software develops a wide variety of software products. You, J Carter, have just been promoted from the position of computer games group manager. The new promotion represents a natural progression for someone fast-tracking through management levels at General Software Products. Your new position as PC software department manager also carries with it membership in the firm's Software Steering Committee. This committee meets with the firm's CEO, David Brown, to discuss key strategic policy decisions. The previous department manager for PC software, Sam White, died suddenly of a heart attack three weeks ago and, as many predicted (including yourself), you were appointed to the position.

Source: D Eylon and S Herman, "Exploring Empowerment: One Method for the Classroom," *Journal of Management Education*, 23 (February 1999), pp 80–94. Used with permission of the authors.

personal awareness and growth exercises

1. What Is Your Self-Perceived Power?

Instructions

Score your various bases of power for your current (or former) job, using the following scale:

1 = Strongly disagree
2 = Disagree
3 = Slightly agree
4 = Agree
5 = Strongly agree

Reward Power Score = _____

1. I can reward persons at lower levels. _____

2. My review actions affect the rewards gained at lower levels. _____

3. Based on my decisions, lower level personnel may receive a bonus. _____

Coercive Power Score = _____

1. I can punish employees at lower levels. _____

2. My work is a check on lower level employees. _____

3. My diligence reduces error. _____

Legitimate Power Score = _____

1. My position gives me a great deal of authority. _____

2. The decisions made at my level are of critical importance. _____

3. Employees look to me for guidance. _____

Expert Power Score = _____

1. I am an expert in this job. _____

2. My ability gives me an advantage in this job. _____

3. Given some time, I could improve the methods used on this job. _____

Referent Power Score = _____

1. I attempt to set a good example for other employees. _____

2. My personality allows me to work well in this job. _____

3. My fellow employees look to me as their informal leader. _____

Arbitrary norms for each of the five bases of power are:
3–6 = Weak power base
7–11 = Moderate power base
12–15 = Strong power base

Source: Adapted and excerpted in part from D L Dieterly and B Schneider, "The Effect of Organizational Environment on Perceived Power and Climate: A Laboratory Study," *Organizational Behavior and Human Performance*, June 1974, pp 316–37.

2. How Political Are You?

Objectives

1. To get to know yourself a little bit better.
2. Within an organizational context, to assess your political tendencies.
3. To consider the career implications of your political tendencies.

Introduction

Organizational politics is an unavoidable feature of modern organizational life. Your career success, job performance, and job satisfaction can hinge on your political skills. But it is important to realize that some political tactics can cause ethical problems.

Instructions

For each of the 10 statements, select the response that best characterizes your behaviour. You do not have to engage in the behaviour at all times to answer true.

1. You should make others feel important through an open appreciation of their ideas and work.   _____ True   _____ False

2. Because people tend to judge you when they first meet you, always try to make a good first impression.   _____ True   _____ False

3. Try to let others do most of the talking, be sympathetic to their problems, and resist telling people that they are totally wrong.   _____ True   _____ False

4. Praise the good traits of the people you meet and always give people an opportunity to save face if they are wrong or make a mistake.   _____ True   _____ False

5. Spreading false rumours, planting misleading information, and backstabbing are necessary, if somewhat unpleasant, methods to deal with your enemies.   _____ True   _____ False

6. Sometimes it is necessary to make promises that you know you will not or cannot keep.   _____ True   _____ False

7. It is important to get along with everybody, even with those who are generally recognized as windbags, abrasive, or constant complainers.   _____ True   _____ False

8. It is vital to do favours for others so that you can call in these IOUs at times when they will do you the most good.   _____ True   _____ False

9. Be willing to compromise, particularly on issues that are minor to you, but important to others.   _____ True   _____ False

10. On controversial issues, it is important to delay or avoid your involvement if possible.   _____ True   _____ False

Scoring and Interpretation

The author of this quiz recommends the following scoring system:

A confirmed organizational politician will answer "true" to all 10 questions. Organizational politicians with fundamental ethical standards will answer "false" to Questions 5 and 6, which deal with deliberate lies and uncharitable behaviour. Individuals who regard manipulation, incomplete disclosure, and self-serving behaviour as unacceptable will answer "false" to all or almost all of the questions.

QUESTIONS FOR DISCUSSION

1. Did this instrument accurately assess your tendencies toward organizational politics? Explain.
2. Do you think a confirmed organizational politician would answer this quiz honestly? Explain.
3. Will your political tendencies help or hinder your career? Explain.
4. Are there any potential ethical problems with any of your answers? Which ones?
5. How important is political behaviour for career success today? Explain, relative to the industry or organization you have in mind.

Source: Adapted from 10 quiz items quoted from J F Byrnes, "Connecting Organizational Politics and Conflict Resolution," *Personnel Administrator*, June 1986, p 49.

CBC video case

Battling Beauty Queens

Sylvia Stark is the power behind Miss Canada International and other smaller Canadian beauty pageants. But the business of celebrating beauty is an ugly one. Numerous past winners recount how Sylvia stripped them of their title, or threatened to, if they didn't do exactly what she said or if they questioned her. They charge that Sylvia bounced cheques, took money that was collected for charity, and was manipulative, abusive, and borderline criminal. In fact Sylvia was charged with fraud, forgery, and obstructing justice at one point, but didn't serve any jail time after pleading guilty to obstructing justice.

Questions have been raised by contestants, judges, and pageant directors about how contestants are chosen (whether Sylvia takes entry fees from contestants who do not qualify and then disqualifies them later), and how winners are chosen (there is no independent auditor tabulating the judges' scores at Sylvia's pageants—she does it herself). Sylvia in turn charges that past winners have made death threats and caused her to be unable to have children. All in all, these beauty queens' dreams have become nightmares.

QUESTIONS FOR DISCUSSION
1. What are Sylvia Stark's bases of power?
2. Does Sylvia demonstrate personalized or socialized power? Explain.
3. What political tactics does Sylvia use to further her own interests?

Source: Based on "Battling Beauty Queens," *CBC Fifth Estate* (January 12, 2001).

chapter

eleven

Leadership

After reading the material in this chapter, you should be able to:

- Explain the trait theory of leadership and discuss behavioural leadership theory.

- Explain, according to Fiedler's contingency model, how leadership style interacts with situational control.

- Discuss path–goal theory.

- Describe how charismatic leadership transforms followers and work groups.

- Explain the leader–member exchange (LMX) model of leadership and the substitutes for leadership.

- Review the principles of servant-leadership and superleadership.

LAND OF THE GIANT

Plenty of business leaders dream about building a company of truly global proportions. In 1999, Gwyn Morgan, president and CEO of Calgary-based Alberta Energy Co. Ltd. started talking about the vision to create a "global super-independent"—a company that would rank in size and performance among the top independent oil and gas producers in the world. He put this bold and seemingly farfetched vision, together with a "corporate constitution," into a set of attractively bound booklets that were handed out to employees.

His peers know Morgan as a deep thinker, as the philosopher-king of the oil patch. He wrote Alberta Energy Corp.'s corporate constitution almost single-handedly over a period of three years. The document describes the company's values, and summarizes them in tidy catchphrases such as "Seize Opportunities,"

Gwyn Morgan, president and CEO, Alberta Energy Co. Ltd.

"Teamwork and Trust," and "Fear of Status Quo." It also lays out expectations the organization has for its employees and leaders. Among other things, managers are required to lead "with character, competence and humility" and accept "nothing less than the best effort." In a preamble to the constitution Morgan talks about Alberta Energy Corp. as a "living organism" that must always adapt to avoid extinction. "We will never—and must never—stop looking for ways to get better."

Turns out Morgan was serious. In April 2002, shareholders of Alberta Energy Co, Ltd. and PanCanadian Energy Corp. voted to merge their two companies into a new entity—EnCana Corp.—that is undeniably "global" and "super." With a total enterprise value of about $30 billion, EnCana will be the biggest independent oil and gas producer in the world. Morgan says he feels fortunate to see his far-reaching vision become a reality. "I feel a tremendous sense of responsibility to the people of PanCanadian and Alberta Energy Corp.," he says. "There is a real sense of pride and excitement at both companies that we are going to have this global giant headquartered here. I've received letters from people across the country saying how great this is, and we've had tremendous support from Ottawa. This is exactly the kind of flagship company people want to see in this country."

Source: P Verburg, "Land of the Giant," *Canadian Business*, April 15, 2002, pp 26–32.

Leadership

Leadership is defined as "a social influence process in which the leader seeks the voluntary participation of subordinates in an effort to reach organizational goals."[1] This definition implies that leadership involves more than wielding power and exercising authority and is exhibited on different levels. At the individual level, for example, leadership involves mentoring, coaching, inspiring, and motivating. Leaders build teams, create cohesion, and resolve conflict at the group level. Finally, leaders build culture and create change at the organizational level.[2]

> **Leadership**
>
> Influencing employees to voluntarily pursue organizational goals.

This chapter attempts to enhance understanding about leadership by focusing on the following areas: (1) trait and behavioural approaches to leadership, (2) situational theories of leadership, (3) charismatic leadership, and (4) additional perspectives on leadership.

Trait and Behavioural Theories

This section examines the two earliest approaches used to explain leadership. Trait theories focused on identifying the personal traits that differentiated leaders from followers. Behavioural theorists tried to uncover the different kinds of leader behaviours that resulted in higher work group performance.

Leadership Trait Theory

At the turn of the 20th century, the prevailing belief was that leaders were born, not made. Selected people were thought to possess inborn traits that made them successful leaders. A **leader trait** is a physical or personality characteristic that can be used to differentiate leaders from followers. Although dozens of leadership traits were initially identified, researchers simply were unable to uncover a consistent set of traits that accurately predicted which individuals became leaders in organizations.

> **Leader trait**
>
> Personal characteristics that differentiate leaders from followers.

During the 1990s, researcher Robert House conducted a cross-cultural study of leadership in 40 countries around the world in a search for favourable and unfavourable leadership traits. Universally favourable traits include: dynamism, decisiveness, honesty, capacity to motivate, capacity to negotiate with others, and focus on performance. Universally unfavourable traits include: autocratic, egocentric, and irritable. Traits found to be favourable in some but not all cultures include: ambition, formality, risk-taking, and self-effacement.[3]

Gender and Leadership   The increase of women in the workforce has generated much interest in understanding the similarities and differences in female and male leaders. Research uncovered the following differences: (1) Men and women were seen as displaying more task and social leadership, respectively;[4] (2) women used a more democratic or participative style than men, and men used a more autocratic and directive style than women;[5] (3) men and women were equally assertive;[6] and (4) women executives, when rated by their peers, managers, and direct reports, scored higher than their male counterparts on a variety of effectiveness criteria.[7]

Behavioural Leadership Theory

This phase of leadership research began during World War II as part of an effort to develop better military leaders. The thrust of early behavioural leadership theory was to focus on leader behaviour, instead of on personality traits. It was believed that leader behaviour directly affected work group effectiveness. This led researchers to identify patterns of behaviour that enabled leaders to effectively influence others.

Researchers at both Ohio State University and the University of Michigan concluded there were only two independent dimensions of leader behaviour. **Consideration** (employee-centred) behaviour involves creating mutual respect or trust and focuses on a concern for group members' needs and desires. For example, Glenn Murphy, president of Shoppers Drug Mart, goes out for drinks with clerks and store managers, and can talk to anybody from floor sweepers to a bank president.[8] **Initiating structure** (task-centred behaviour) is leader behaviour that organizes and defines what group members should be doing to maximize output. For example, William Haseltine of Human Genome Sciences is known for directing researchers toward practical and profitable products.[9]

Consideration

Creating mutual respect and trust with followers.

Initiating structure

Organizing and defining what group members should be doing.

The Leadership Grid®   The Leadership Grid,® (developed by Robert Blake and Jane Srygley Mouton) is formed by the intersection of these two dimensions of leader behaviour (see Figure 11–1). On the horizontal axis is "concern for production" and "concern for people" is on the vertical axes. By scaling each axis of the grid from 1 (Low) to 9 (High), Blake and Mouton were able to plot five leadership styles. The styles are impoverished management (1, 1) country club management (1, 9), authority-compliance (9, 1), middle-of-the-road management (5, 5), and team management (9, 9). It initially was hypothesized that team management (9, 9) would be the one best style of leadership. Through the years, the effectiveness of this "high-high" style has been tested many times. Overall, results have been mixed. Researchers thus concluded that there is no one best style of leadership. Rather, it is believed that the effectiveness of a given leadership style depends on situational factors.[10]

Behavioural Styles Theory in Perspective   By emphasizing leader *behaviour,* something that is learned, the behavioural style approach makes it clear that leaders are made, not born. This is the opposite of the trait theorists' traditional assumption. Given what we know about behaviour shaping and model-based training, leader *behaviours* can be systematically improved and developed.[11]

Behavioural styles research also revealed that there is no one best style of leadership. The effectiveness of a particular leadership style depends on the situation at hand. For instance, employees prefer structure over consideration when faced with role ambigu-

FIGURE 11–1   The Leadership Grid®

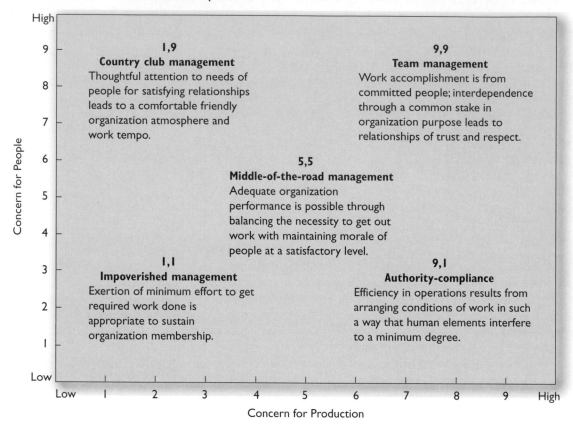

ity.[12] Finally, research also reveals that it is important to consider the difference between how frequently and how effectively managers exhibit various leader behaviours. For example, a manager might ineffectively display a lot of considerate leader behaviours. Such a style is likely to frustrate employees and possibly result in lowered job satisfaction and performance. Because the frequency of exhibiting leadership behaviours is secondary in importance to effectiveness, managers are encouraged to concentrate on improving the effective execution of their leader behaviours.[13]

Situational Theories

Situational theories

Propose that leader styles should match the situation at hand.

Situational leadership theories grew out of an attempt to explain the inconsistent findings about traits and styles. **Situational theories** propose that the effectiveness of a particular style of leader behaviour depends on the situation. As situations change, different styles become appropriate. This directly challenges the idea of one best style of leadership. For example, former New York mayor Rudy Giuliani exhibited a stunning metamorphosis in the space of a few hours on September 11, 2001, from an argumentative, hard-driving politician to a calm, focused, and inspiring leader.[14]

Fiedler's Contingency Model

Fred Fiedler, an OB scholar, developed a situational model of leadership. It is the oldest and one of the most widely known models of leadership. Fiedler's model is based on the assumption that the performance of a leader depends on two interrelated factors: (1) the degree to which the situation gives the leader control and influence, and (2) the leader's basic motivation, being either primarily on accomplishing the task or on having close supportive relations with others.[15]

With respect to a leader's basic motivation, Fiedler believes that leaders have one dominant leadership style that is resistant to change—either task motivated or relationship motivated. These basic motivations are similar to initiating structure/concern for the task and consideration/concern for people. Fiedler suggests that leaders must learn to manipulate or influence the leadership situation in order to create a "match" between their leadership style and the amount of control within the situation at hand.

New York mayor Rudy Giuliani's leadership style changed when dealing with the terrorist attacks on September 11, 2001.

Situational Control   Situational control refers to the amount of control and influence the leader has in his or her immediate work environment. Situational control ranges from high to low. Fiedler included three dimensions of situational control in his theory: leader–member relations, task structure, and position power. These dimensions vary independently, forming eight combinations of situational control (see Figure 11–2).

Representation of Fiedler's Contingency Model   FIGURE 11–2

Situational Control	High Control Situations			Moderate Control Situations			Low Control Situations	
Leader–member relations	Good	Good	Good	Good	Poor	Poor	Poor	Poor
Task structure	High	High	Low	Low	High	High	Low	Low
Position power	Strong	Weak	Strong	Weak	Strong	Weak	Strong	Weak
Situation	I	II	III	IV	V	VI	VII	VIII
Optimal Leadership Style	Task-Motivated Leadership			Relationship-Motivated Leadership			Task-Motivated Leadership	

Source: Adapted from F E Fiedler, "Situational Control and a Dynamic Theory of Leadership," in *Managerial Control and Organizational Democracy,* eds B King, S Streufert, and F E Fiedler (New York: John Wiley & Sons, 1978), p 114.

The three dimensions of situational control are defined as follows:

- *Leader-member relations* reflect the extent to which the leader has the support, loyalty, and trust of the work group.
- *Task structure* is concerned with the amount of structure contained within tasks performed by the work group.
- *Position power* refers to the degree to which the leader has formal power to reward, punish, or otherwise obtain compliance from employees.[16]

Linking Leadership Motivation and Situational Control   Fiedler's complete contingency model is presented in Figure 11–2. The last row under the Situational Control column shows that there are eight different leadership situations. Each situation represents a unique combination of leader–member relations, task structure, and position power. Situations I, II, and III represent high control situations. Figure 11–2 shows that task-motivated leaders are hypothesized to be most effective in situations of high control. Under conditions of moderate control (situations IV, V, and VI), relationship-motivated leaders are expected to be more effective. Finally, the results orientation of task-motivated leaders is predicted to be more effective under conditions of low control (situations VII and VIII).

Research and Managerial Implications   Research has provided mixed support for Fiedler's model, suggesting that the model needs theoretical refinement.[17] That said, the major contribution of Fiedler's model is that it prompted others to examine the contingency nature of leadership. This research, in turn, reinforced the notion that there is no one best style of leadership. Leaders are advised to alter their task and relationship orientation to fit the demands of the situation at hand.

Path–Goal Theory

Martin Evans and Robert House originated the path–goal theory of leadership. They proposed a model that describes how expectancy perceptions are influenced by the contingent relationships among four leadership styles and various employee attitudes and behaviours (see Figure 11–2).[18] According to the path–goal model, leader behaviour is effective when employees view it as a source of satisfaction or as paving the way to future satisfaction (see Figure 11–3). In addition, leader behaviour is motivational to the extent it (1) reduces roadblocks that interfere with goal accomplishment, (2) provides the guidance and support needed by employees, and (3) ties meaningful rewards to goal accomplishment.

Because the model deals with pathways to goals and rewards, it is called the path–goal theory of leadership. The leader's main job is seen as helping employees stay on the right paths to challenging goals and valued rewards. For example, Scott Laver, general manager of Dominion Information Services Inc. (the Telus yellow pages) says that his challenge is to create the environment that enables employees to make decisions on their own, by exhibiting trust in them and what they have done. Says Lavin, "the best leaders that I've seen established an environment where people can do their very best work. . . . You have to let people solve their problems and let them feel they matter." This view is shared by David Stroud, vice-president and general manager of Canadian operations for AT&T Global Network Services, who says, "The organization places a lot of importance on making sure that employees are happy—particularly people who

A General Representation of Path—Goal Theory | **FIGURE 11–3**

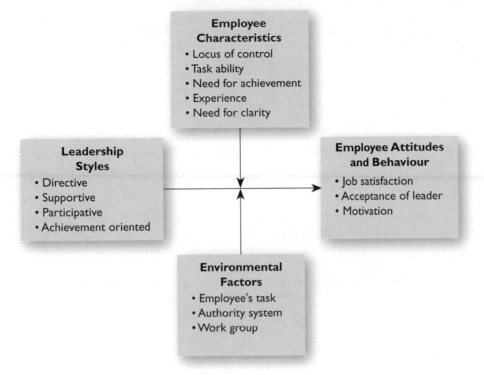

demonstrate good leadership ability. . . . People want to have a culture where they can be active in decision making and part of changing the business."[19]

Leadership Styles   This theory proposes that leaders can exhibit more than one leadership style. This contrasts with Fiedler, who proposes that leaders have one dominant style. The four leadership styles identified in path-goal theory are as follows:

- *Directive leadership.* Providing guidance to employees about what should be done and how to do it, scheduling work, and maintaining standards of performance.
- *Supportive leadership.* Showing concern for the well-being and needs of employees, being friendly and approachable, and treating workers as equals.
- *Participative leadership.* Consulting with employees and seriously considering their ideas when making decisions.
- *Achievement-oriented leadership.* Encouraging employees to perform at their highest level by setting challenging goals, emphasizing excellence, and demonstrating confidence in employee abilities.[20]

Descriptions of business leaders reinforce the belief that leaders exhibit more than one leadership style. For example, Michael Capellas, CEO of Compaq Computer Corp., uses multiple leadership styles to influence others:

> His guiding principles: make leaders personally accountable for business-unit performance and insist that they play well together. . . . Now, Capellas has hard wired accountability into the way his management team operates. Starting in January

[2000], he made customer-satisfaction goals an essential part of each executive's pay package. . . . The move already is delivering results: In the past year, the company's on-time delivery record has improved by 60%. . . . He can dispel a dark mood at a moment's notice too. On June 17, just before his first telephone conference with Wall Street analysts, Capellas noticed that people gathered in a conference room seemed nervous—and he worried that the analysts would sense it. A fan of 70s rock and roll, he had a Three Dog Night CD in his notebook PC. He turned it on, pumped up the volume, and danced with Alice McGuire, head of investor relations, to the tune "Joy to the World." By the time the conference call started, people were grinning like a bunch of kids watching an Austin Powers movie.[21]

Contingency Factors   **Contingency factors** are situational variables that cause one style of leadership to be more effective than another, because they affect expectancy or path–goal perceptions. This model has two groups of contingency variables (see Figure 11–3): employee characteristics such as ability and experience, and environmental factors such as the task itself and the work group. All of these factors have the potential to either hinder or motivate employees.

Contingency factors

Variables that influence the appropriateness of a leadership style.

Research and Managerial Implications   Although research supports the idea that leaders exhibit more than one leadership style, there is limited support for most of the moderating relationships predicted within path–goal theory.[22] This leaves us with two important managerial implications. First, leaders possess and use more than one style of leadership. Managers thus should not be hesitant to try new behaviours when the situation calls for them. Second, a small set of task and employee characteristics are relevant contingency factors. Managers are encouraged to modify their leadership style to fit these various task and employee characteristics. For example, supportive and achievement leadership are more likely to be satisfying when employees have a lot of ability and experience. Directive leadership can be effective when employees are inexperienced or when the use of incentives can increase performance.

From Transactional to Charismatic and Transformational Leadership

Most of the models and theories previously discussed in this chapter represent transactional leadership. **Transactional leadership** focuses on the interpersonal transactions between managers and employees. Leaders are seen as engaging in behaviours that maintain a quality interaction between themselves and followers. The two underlying characteristics of transactional leadership are that (1) leaders use contingent rewards to motivate employees and (2) leaders exert corrective action only when subordinates fail to obtain performance goals. Consider how Samuel Palmisano, the president of IBM, effectively uses transactional leadership to improve organizational performance:

Transactional leadership

Focuses on interpersonal interactions between managers and employees.

After several operations missed sales targets in the third quarter last year, Mr Palmisano, newly minted as president, started what he called "morning operations calls" to review performance as often as three days a week. Division general managers, sales managers, manufacturing and distribution heads participated by phone in the 7 AM meetings, which were particularly tough for managers on the West Coast, one executive says.[23]

In contrast, **charismatic leadership** emphasizes "symbolic leader behaviour, visionary and inspirational messages, nonverbal communication, appeal to ideological values, intellectual stimulation of followers by the leader, display of confidence in self and followers, and leader expectations for follower self-sacrifice and for performance beyond the call of duty."[24] Charismatic leadership is based on a strong interpersonal attraction (or "charisma") which creates respect for and trust in the leader. Charismatic leadership can produce significant organizational change and results because it motivates employees to pursue organizational goals in lieu of self-interests. While the best-known charismatic leaders, such as Winston Churchill and Martin Luther King, are often found in political life, this type of leader has appeared in the business world as well. Lee Iaccoca of Chrysler and Richard Branson of Virgin Records and Virgin Airlines are examples of charismatic business leaders.

> **Charismatic leadership**
>
> Use of interpersonal attraction, or "charisma," to motivate employees to pursue organizational goals over self-interests.

Charismatic leaders transform followers by creating changes in their goals, values, needs, beliefs, and aspirations. They accomplish this transformation by appealing to followers' self-concepts—namely, their values and personal identity. Figure 11–4 presents a model of how charismatic leadership accomplishes this transformation process.

To some, Colin Powell is an example of a powerful, and charismatic leader.

A Charismatic Model of Leadership   **FIGURE 11–4**

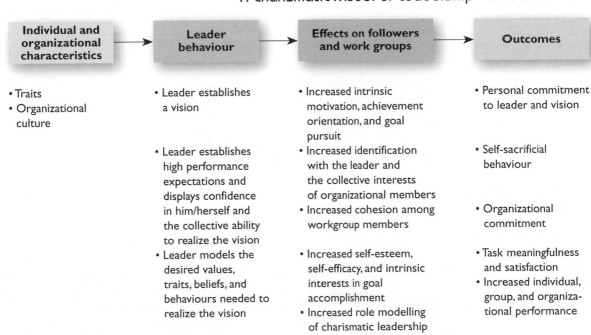

Individual and organizational characteristics	Leader behaviour	Effects on followers and work groups	Outcomes
• Traits • Organizational culture	• Leader establishes a vision • Leader establishes high performance expectations and displays confidence in him/herself and the collective ability to realize the vision • Leader models the desired values, traits, beliefs, and behaviours needed to realize the vision	• Increased intrinsic motivation, achievement orientation, and goal pursuit • Increased identification with the leader and the collective interests of organizational members • Increased cohesion among workgroup members • Increased self-esteem, self-efficacy, and intrinsic interests in goal accomplishment • Increased role modelling of charismatic leadership	• Personal commitment to leader and vision • Self-sacrificial behaviour • Organizational commitment • Task meaningfulness and satisfaction • Increased individual, group, and organizational performance

Source: Based in part on D A Waldman and F J Yammarino, "CEO Charismatic Leadership: Levels-of-Management and Levels-of-Analysis Effects," *Academy of Management Review*, April 1999, pp 266–85; and B Shamir, R J House, and M B Arthur, "The Motivational Effects of Charismatic Leadership: A Self-Concept Based Theory," *Organization Science*, November 1993, pp 577–94.

Figure 11–4 shows that charismatic leader behaviour is first influenced by various individual and organizational characteristics. For example, research reveals that charismatic leaders tend to have personalities that are more extraverted, agreeable, and proactive than noncharismatic leaders.[25] Organizational culture also influences the extent to which leaders are charismatic. Cultures that are adaptive and flexible rather than rigid and bureaucratic are more likely to create environments that foster the opportunity for charismatic leadership to be exhibited.

Charismatic leaders tend to engage in three key sets of leader behaviour (see Figure 11–4). The first set of charismatic leader behaviours involves establishing a common vision of the future. A vision is "a realistic, credible, attractive future for your organization."[26] The "right" vision unleashes human potential because it serves as a beacon of hope and common purpose. It does this by attracting commitment, energizing workers, creating meaning in employees' lives, establishing a standard of excellence, promoting high ideals, and bridging the gap between an organization's present problems and its future goals and aspirations.[27] For example, Gabriel Bouchard, vice-president and general manager of Monster.ca had a vision of how his US-based parent company could grow into a global corporation by launching it in Canada rather than going with one Web site that would be accessible all over the world. Bouchard was supported by his head office when he took the initiative to build his own vision. He in turn provides his employees with the same support for their ideas.[28]

The second set of leader behaviours involves two key components:

1. Charismatic leaders set high performance expectations and standards because they know challenging, attainable goals lead to greater productivity.

2. Charismatic leaders need to publicly express confidence in the followers' ability to meet high performance expectations. This is essential because employees are more likely to pursue difficult goals when they believe they can accomplish what is being asked of them.

The third and final set of leader behaviours involves being a role model. Through their actions, charismatic leaders model the desired values, traits, beliefs, and behaviours needed to realize the vision.

Returning to Figure 11–4, it can be seen that charismatic leadership motivates followers by increasing their motivation, identification with the leader, cohesion among workgroup members, and self-esteem and self-efficacy. In turn, these positive effects are expected to produce a host of favourable work outcomes.

A variation of charismatic leadership is known as **transformational leadership**. Transformational leaders do not necessarily have the strong interpersonal attraction, or "charisma," of charismatic leaders, but they do create, communicate, and model a vision, and exhibit behaviours aimed at building commitment to the vision on the part of their followers.[29] Transformational leaders are usually not as well-known as their charismatic counterparts, and often work in middle management where they deal with employees on an individual, day to day level. In this role, they can have a significant impact on the implementation of organizational change, specifically by building commitment to the change. It is at this operational level that acceptance of change is so crucial for its sustainability, and where resistance to change is so prevalent.

Transformational leadership

A leadership style involving the creation, communication, and modelling of a vision, and behaviours aimed at building commitment to the vision on the part of their followers.

Research and Managerial Implications

The charismatic model of leadership presented in Figure 11–4 has been partially supported by previous research. Charismatic leaders are viewed as more effective leaders

Thirtysomething Women Demonstrate Transformational Leadership Style

Recent research in the UK reveals that young women supervisors are the best bosses. A study for the Industrial Society, a UK-based think tank that campaigns to improve life at work, showed women at junior levels of management were far more likely than their older male colleagues to set a good example by their own behaviour and to complete their job successfully. The research, which looked at 9,000 employees, showed that young women were transformational in their leadership style, as they were more likely to build their working relationships on trust, and knew how to encourage and support staff. Women of all ages were perceived as better leaders than men. The study suggested that the findings indicate the changing nature of leadership, which requires a more flexible, transformational approach. The study showed that those who were younger than 35 generally had a more transformational style, and freed those closest to the job to take their own decisions, as opposed to older managers who were conditioned into a control and command style of management. It was suggested that older male managers change their ways in order to avoid being overtaken by young women.

However, in the United States and Canada, female managers are more pessimistic about their promotability. Professor Caroline Cochran of the University of Minnesota studied more than 2,800 high potential managers, and found that women received higher ratings than men with respect to managerial competence in their present positions. Men, however, received significantly higher ratings than women with respect to long-range potential. Thus gender stereotypes were found to play more of a role in evaluating future potential than in evaluating current managerial performance.

A 2000 study from the Conference Board of Canada's Centre of Excellence for Women's Management, which surveyed 100 CEOs, 400 women executives, and 130 human resource professionals, found that more than 50% of the women surveyed believe that their male counterparts perceive women managers as having less organizational commitment and professional capability. Consequently they feel under-appreciated and under-represented. The study revealed that in the private sector the percentage of women in senior management positions rests at just 20%, whereas in the public sector the ratio stands at 40%.

Sources: Adapted from www.galtglobalreview.com/business/thirtysomething_women.html, April 4, 2002; and www.womanmag.com/archive/july3_2000.html, April 4, 2002.

by both supervisors and followers and have followers who exert more effort and report higher levels of job satisfaction than noncharismatic leaders.[30] Other studies have shown that charismatic leadership is positively associated with followers' individual performance and their trust and satisfaction with their leaders.[31] At the organizational level, research has demonstrated that charismatic leadership is positively correlated with organizational measures of effectiveness.[32]

These results underscore four important managerial implications. First, the best leaders are not just charismatic, they are both transactional and charismatic. Second, charismatic leadership is not applicable in all organizational situations. According to a team of experts, charismatic leadership is most likely to be effective when the situation offers opportunities for "moral" involvement, and when exceptional effort, behaviour, sacrifices, and performance are required of both leaders and followers.[33]

Third, employees at any level in an organization can be trained to be more transactional and charismatic.[34] This reinforces the organizational value of developing and rolling out a combination of transactional and charismatic leadership training for all employees. These programs, however, should be based on an overall philosophy that

Harvard Ethics 101

In a spat that would make a compelling case study within its own pages, senior staff members at the *Harvard Business Review* have called on the magazine's editor to resign amid revelations that she got a little too close to one of her sources. Suzy Wetlaufer waited until the last minute to axe her story about former General Electric boss Jack Welch after they became romantically involved during a series of interviews for the magazine. Ms. Wetlaufer called her boss, editorial director Walter Kiechel, and they agreed to assign the project to someone else. Her colleagues agree that Ms. Wetlaufer did the right thing, but they want to know why she waited so long to do it. Mr. Kiechel agreed to review the magazine's ethical practices to try to ensure such situations do not happen again. He would not say if Ms. Wetlaufer's job was in jeopardy, but confirmed that other editors were anxious to see her go.

You Decide . . .

What should Walter Kiechel do? Should Suzy Wetlaufer be punished for waiting to reveal her conflict of interest to her boss? Should she lose her job?

Source: M Friscolanti, "Harvard Ethics 101," *National Post*, March 6, 2002, p A16.

constitutes the foundation of leadership development. At the Royal Bank Financial Group, a new leadership development program was implemented when they wanted to move away from their outdated command-and-control culture and replace it with a focus on customer satisfaction, innovation, and empowerment. Five managerial competencies were identified as necessary for the new culture: change leadership; achievement motivation; impact and influence; developing others; and teamwork and cooperation. The program included five sessions, beginning with an introduction to these competencies, and ending with a final project where theory learned in the program was applied in the workplace.[35] Fourth, charismatic leaders can be ethical or unethical. Whereas ethical charismatic leaders enable employees to enhance their self-concepts, unethical ones select or produce obedient, dependent, and compliant followers. Top management can create and maintain ethical charismatic leadership by

1. Creating and enforcing a clearly stated code of ethics.
2. Recruiting, selecting, and promoting people with high morals and standards.
3. Developing performance expectations around the treatment of employees—these expectations can then be assessed in the performance appraisal process.
4. Training employees to value diversity.
5. Identifying, rewarding, and publicly praising employees who exemplify high moral conduct.[36]

Additional Perspectives on Leadership

This section examines four additional approaches to leadership; leader–member exchange theory, substitutes for leadership, servant leadership, and superleadership. More time will be spent discussing leader–member exchange theory and substitutes for leadership because they have been more thoroughly investigated.

The Leader–Member Exchange (LMX) Model of Leadership

The leader–member exchange model of leadership revolves around the development of dyadic (two-person) relationships between managers and their direct reports. This model is quite different from those previously discussed in that it focuses on the quality of relationships between managers and subordinates as opposed to the behaviours or traits of either leaders or followers. The LMX model is based on the assumption that leaders develop unique one-to-one relationships with each of the people reporting to them. Behavioural scientists call this sort of relationship a *vertical dyad*. The forming of vertical dyads is said to be a naturally occurring process, resulting from the leader's attempt to delegate and assign work roles. As a result of this process, two distinct types of leader–member exchange relationships are expected to evolve.[37]

One type of leader–member exchange is called the **in-group exchange**. In this relationship, leaders and followers develop a partnership characterized by reciprocal influence, mutual trust, respect and liking, and a sense of common fates. In the second type of exchange, referred to as an **out-group exchange**, leaders are characterized as overseers who fail to create a sense of mutual trust, respect, or common fate.[38]

> **In-group exchange**
> A partnership characterized by mutual trust, respect, and liking.
>
> **Out-group exchange**
> A partnership characterized by a lack of mutual trust, respect, and liking.

Research Findings   Research has shown that an in-group exchange is positively associated with job satisfaction, job performance, goal commitment, trust between managers and employees, work climate, and satisfaction with leadership.[39] This type of leader–member exchange has also been found to predict career outcomes such as promotability, salary level, and receipt of bonuses.[40] Finally, studies have also found that personality similarity and demographic similarity influence the quality of an LMX.[41] Further, the quality of an LMX was positively related with the extent to which leaders and followers like each other, the leaders' positive expectations of their subordinates, and employees' impressions of management techniques.[42]

Managerial Implications   There are three important implications associated with the LMX model of leadership. First, leaders are encouraged to establish high-performance expectations for all of their direct reports because setting high-performance standards fosters high-quality LMXs. Second, because personality and demographic similarity between leaders and followers is associated with good LMXs, managers need to be careful that they avoid a heterogeneous work environment in the spirit of having positive relationships with their direct reports.

The third implication pertains to those who find themselves in a poor LMX. A poor LMX exchange means that part of the relationship with the manager may need improvement. In order to avoid a poor LMX relationship, new employees should offer their loyalty, support, and cooperativeness to their manager, and out-group members should either accept the situation, try to become an ingroup member by being cooperative and loyal, or quit. Managers need to give employees ample opportunity to prove themselves and should consciously try to expand their in-groups.[43] Finally, impression management techniques discussed in Chapter 10 may also improve a poor LMX relationship.

Substitutes for Leadership

Virtually all leadership theories assume that some sort of formal leadership is necessary, whatever the circumstances. But this basic assumption has been questioned by OB scholars who propose that there are a variety of situational variables that can substitute for, neutralize, or enhance the effects of leadership. These situational variables are referred to as *substitutes for leadership*.[44] Substitutes for leadership can thus increase or diminish a leader's ability to influence the work group. For example, leader behaviour that initiates structure would tend to be resisted by independent-minded

Nelson Mandela was a true servant-leader.

employees with high ability and vast experience. Such employees would likely be guided more by their own initiative than by managerial directives. This is often the case with self-managed teams.

Kerr and Jermier's Substitutes for Leadership Model   According to OB researchers Steven Kerr and John Jermier, the key to improving leadership effectiveness is to identify the situational characteristics that can either substitute for, neutralize, or improve the impact of a leader's behaviour. Table 11–1 lists the various substitutes for leadership. Characteristics of the subordinate, the task, and the organization can act as substitutes for traditional hierarchical leadership. Further, different characteristics are predicted to negate different types of leader behaviour. For example, tasks that provide feedback concerning accomplishment, such as taking a test, tend to negate task-oriented but not relationship-oriented leader behaviour (see Table 11–1). Although the list in Table 11–1 is not all-inclusive, it shows that there are more substitutes for task-oriented leadership than for relationship-oriented leadership.

Research and Managerial Implications   Recent research examined whether substitutes for leadership have a direct effect on employee attitudes and behaviours. The results revealed that the combination of substitute variables and leader behaviours significantly explained a variety of employee attitudes and behaviours. Interestingly, the substitutes for leadership were more important than leader behaviours in accounting for employee attitudes and behaviours.[45]

The key implication is that managers should be attentive to the substitutes listed in Table 11–1 because they directly influence employee attitudes and performance. Managers can positively influence the substitutes through employee selection, job design, work group assignments, and the design of organizational processes and systems.

Substitutes for Leadership **TABLE 11–1**

Characteristic	Relationship-Oriented or Considerate Leader Behaviour Is Unnecessary	Task-Oriented or Initiating Structure Leader Behaviour Is Unnecessary
Of the Subordinate		
1. Ability, experience, training, knowledge		X
2. Need for independence	X	X
3. "Professional" orientation	X	X
4. Indifference toward organizational rewards	X	X
Of the Task		
5. Unambiguous and routine		X
6. Methodologically invariant		X
7. Provides its own feedback concerning accomplishment		X
8. Intrinsically satisfying	X	
Of the Organization		
9. Formalization (explicit plans, goals, and areas of responsibility)		X
10. Inflexibility (rigid, unbending rules and procedures)		X
11. Highly specified and active advisory and staff functions		X
12. Closely knit, cohesive work groups	X	X
13. Organizational rewards not within the leader's control	X	X
14. Spatial distance between superior and subordinates	X	X

Source: Adapted from S Kerr and J M Jermier, "Substitutes for Leadership: Their Meaning and Measurement," *Organizational Behavior and Human Performance*, December 1978, pp 375–403.

Servant-Leadership

Servant-leadership is a philosophy of managing, a belief that great leaders act as servants, putting the needs of others, including employees, customers, and community, as their first priority. **Servant-leadership** focuses on increased service to others rather than to oneself.[46] As one expert explained, "Leadership derives naturally from a commitment to service. You know that you're practicing servant-leadership if your followers become wiser, healthier, more autonomous—and more likely to become servant-leaders themselves."[47] Servant-leadership is not a quick-fix approach to leadership. Rather, it is a long-term, transformational approach to life and work. Table 11–2 presents 10 characteristics possessed by servant-leaders. One can hardly go wrong by trying to adopt these characteristics.

Servant-leadership

Focuses on increased service to others rather than to oneself.

TABLE 11–2   Characteristics of the Servant-Leader

Servant-Leadership Characteristics	Description
1. Listening	Servant-leaders focus on listening to identify and clarify the needs and desires of a group.
2. Empathy	Servant-leaders try to empathize with others' feelings and emotions. An individual's good intentions are assumed even when he or she performs poorly.
3. Healing	Servant-leaders strive to make themselves and others whole in the face of failure or suffering.
4. Awareness	Servant-leaders are very self-aware of their strengths and limitations.
5. Persuasion	Servant-leaders rely more on persuasion than positional authority when making decisions and trying to influence others.
6. Conceptualization	Servant leaders take the time and effort to develop broader based conceptual thinking. Servant-leaders seek an appropriate balance between a short-term, day-to-day focus and a long-term, conceptual orientation.
7. Foresight	Servant-leaders have the ability to foresee future outcomes associated with a current course of action or situation.
8. Stewardship	Servant-leaders assume that they are stewards of the people and resources they manage.
9. Commitment to the growth of people	Servant-leaders are committed to people beyond their immediate work role. They commit to fostering an environment that encourages personal, professional, and spiritual growth.
10. Building community	Servant-leaders strive to create a sense of community both within and outside the work organization.

Source: These characteristics and descriptions were derived from L C Spears, "Introduction: Servant-Leadership and the Greenleaf Legacy," in *Reflections on Leadership: How Robert K Greenleaf's Theory of Servant-Leadership Influenced Today's Top Management Thinkers*, ed L C Spears (New York: John Wiley & Sons, 1995), pp 1–14.

Superleadership

A **superleader** is someone who leads others to lead themselves. Superleaders empower followers by acting as a teacher and coach rather than as a dictator and autocrat. Productive thinking is the cornerstone of superleadership, and superleaders teach followers how to engage in productive thinking.[48] This is expected to increase employees' feelings of personal control and intrinsic motivation. Superleadership has the potential to free up a manager's time because employees are encouraged to manage themselves. Future research is needed to test the validity of recommendations derived from this new approach to leadership.

Superleader

Someone who leads others to lead themselves.

summary of key concepts

- *Explain the trait theory of leadership, and discuss behavioural leadership theory.* Initially, it was believed that leaders possessed inborne traits that made them successful. However, researchers were unable to uncover a consistent set of traits that accurately predicted leadership success. Studies of leadership behaviour revealed that there were two key independent dimensions of leadership behaviour: consideration (employee-centred) and initiating structure (task-centred). The behavioural studies made it clear that leaders are made, not born, as trait theory had previously proposed. However, research did not support the premise that there is one best behavioural style of leadership.

- *Explain, according to Fiedler's contingency model, how leadership style interacts with situational control.* Fiedler believes leader effectiveness depends on an appropriate match between leadership style and situational control. Leaders are either task motivated or relationship motivated. Situation control is composed of leader–member relations, task structure, and position power. Task-motivated leaders are effective under situations of both high and low control. Relationship-motivated leaders are more effective when they have moderate situational control.

- *Discuss path–goal theory.* According to path–goal theory, leaders alternately can exhibit directive, supportive, participative, or achievement-oriented styles of leadership. The effectiveness of these styles depends on various employee characteristics and environmental factors. Path–goal theory has received limited support from research. There are two important managerial implications: (a) leaders possess and use more than one style

of leadership, and (b) managers are advised to modify their leadership style to fit a small subset of task and employee characteristics.

- *Describe how charismatic leadership transforms followers and work groups.* Individual and organizational characteristics influence whether or not managers exhibit charismatic leadership, which is composed of three sets of leader behaviour—vision, high expectations, and modelling desired behaviour. These leader behaviours, in turn, positively affect followers' and work groups' goals, values, beliefs, aspirations, and motivation. These positive effects are then associated with a host of preferred outcomes.

- *Explain the leader–member exchange model (LMX) of leadership and the substitutes for leadership.* The LMX model revolves around the development of dyadic relationships between managers and their direct reports. These leader–member exchanges qualify as either in-group or out-group relationships. Substitutes for leadership represent a variety of situational variables that can substitute for, neutralize, or enhance the effects of leadership. These substitutes contain characteristics of the subordinates, the task, and the organization.

- *Review the principles of servant-leadership and superleadership.* Servant-leadership is more a philosophy than a testable theory. It is based on the premise that great leaders act as servants, putting the needs of others, including employees, customers, and community, as their first priority. A superleader is someone who leads others to lead themselves. Superleaders empower followers by acting as a teacher and coach rather than as a dictator and autocrat.

key terms

charismatic leadership, 253
consideration, 247
contingency factors, 252
in-group exchange, 257
initiating structure, 247

leader trait, 246
leadership, 246
out-group exchange, 257
servant-leadership, 259
situational theories, 248

superleader, 260
transactional leadership, 252
transformational leadership, 254

discussion questions

1. Does it make more sense to try to change a person's leadership style, as proposed by path–goal theory, or to change the situation, as proposed by Fiedler's contingency theory? Explain.

2. Describe how a professor might use path–goal theory to clarify students' path–goal perceptions.

3. Identify three charismatic leaders, and describe their leadership traits and behavioural styles.

4. Have you ever worked for a charismatic leader? Describe how he or she transformed followers.

5. Have you ever been a member of an in-group or an out-group? For either situation describe the pattern of interaction between you and your manager.

6. In your view, which leadership theory has the greatest practical application? Why?

internet exercises

www.leader-values.com

1. Evaluating Leadership Styles

The topic of leadership has been important since the dawn of time. History is filled with examples of great leaders such as Mohandas Gandhi, Martin Luther King, and Bill Gates. These leaders likely possessed some of the leadership traits discussed in this chapter, and they probably used a situational approach to lead their followers. The purpose of this exercise is for you to evaluate the leadership styles of a historical figure.

Go to the Internet home page for Leadership Values (**www.leader-values.com**), and select the subheading "4 E's" on the left side of the screen. This section provides an overview of leadership and suggests four essential traits/behaviours that are exhibited by leaders to envision, enable, empower, and energize. After reading this material, go back to the home page, and select the subheading "Historical Leaders" from the list on the left-hand side of the page. Next, choose one of the leaders from the list of historical figures, and read the description about his or her leadership style. You may want to print all of the material you read thus far from this Web page to help you answer the following questions.

QUESTIONS
1. Describe the 4 E's of leadership.
2. Using any of the theories or models discussed in this chapter, how would you describe the leadership style of the historical figure you investigated?
3. Was this leader successful in using the 4 E's of leadership? Describe how he/she used the 4 E's.

www.ccmd-ccg.gc.ca

2. Top Seven Questions on Leadership

Go to the Web site for the Canadian Centre for Management Development at **www.ccmd-ccg.gc.ca**. Click on "English." Then click on "Leadership" in the list of themes on the left hand side of the page. Select "Top Seven Questions on Leadership" from the menu on the right hand side of the page. Go through the questions and review the answers provided for each one.

QUESTIONS
1. Do the answers provided reflect the material in this chapter?
2. Would you change or enhance any of the answers? If so, how?

experiential exercises

1. Assessing Your Leader–Member Exchange

Instructions

For each of the items shown below, use the following scale to circle the answer that best represents how you feel about the relationship between you and your current manager/supervisor. If you are not currently working, complete the survey by thinking about a previous manager. Remember, there are no right or wrong answers. After circling a response for each of the 12 items, use the scoring key to compute scores for the subdimensions within your leader–member exchange.

1 = Strongly disagree
2 = Disagree
3 = Neither agree nor disagree
4 = Agree
5 = Strongly agree

1. I like my supervisor very much as a person.   1   2   3   4   5

2. My supervisor is the kind of person one would like to have as a friend.   1   2   3   4   5

3. My supervisor is a lot of fun to work with.   1   2   3   4   5

4. My supervisor defends my work actions to a superior, even without complete knowledge of the issue in question.   1   2   3   4   5

5. My supervisor would come to my defence if I were "attacked" by others.   1   2   3   4   5

6. My supervisor would defend me to others in the organization if I made an honest mistake.   1   2   3   4   5

7. I do work for my supervisor that goes beyond what is specified in my job description.   1   2   3   4   5

8. I am willing to apply extra efforts, beyond those normally required, to meet my supervisor's work goals.   1   2   3   4   5

9. I do not mind working my hardest for my supervisor.   1   2   3   4   5

10. I am impressed with my supervisor's knowledge of his/her job.   1   2   3   4   5

11. I respect my supervisor's knowledge of and competence on the job.   1   2   3   4   5

12. I admire my supervisor's professional skills.   1   2   3   4   5

Scoring Key

Mutual affection (add items 1–3)   _____

Loyalty (add items 4–6)   _____

Contribution to work activities (add items 7–9)   _____

Professional respect (add items 10–12)   _____

Overall score (add all 12 items)   _____

Arbitrary Norms

Low mutual affection = 3–9
High mutual affection = 10–15
Low loyalty = 3–9
High loyalty = 10–15
Low contribution to work activities = 3–9
High contribution to work activities = 10–15
Low professional respect = 3–9
High professional respect = 10–15
Low overall leader–member exchange = 12–38
High overall leader–member exchange = 39–60

What is the overall quality of your LMX? Do you agree with this assessment? Which sub-dimensions are high and low? If your overall LMX and associated sub-dimensions are all high, you should be in a very good situation with respect to the relationship between you and your manager. Having a low LMX overall score or a low dimensional score, however, reveals that part of the relationship with your manager may need improvement.

Source: Survey items were taken from R C Liden and J M Maslyn, "Multidimensionality of Leader–Member Exchange: An Empirical Assessment through Scale Development," *Journal of Management*, 1998, p 56.

2. Leadership Dimensions Instrument

Purpose

This self-assessment exercise is designed to help you understand two important dimensions of leadership and to identify which of these dimensions is more prominent in your supervisor, team leader, coach, or other person to whom you are accountable.

Instructions

Reach each of the statements below and circle the response that you believe best describes your supervisor. You may substitute "supervisor" with anyone else to whom you are accountable, such as a team leader, CEO, course instructor, or sports coach. Then use the scoring key in endnote 49 of this book to calculate the results for each leadership dimensions. After completing this assessment, be prepared to discuss in class the distinctions between these leadership dimensions.

My supervisor . . .	Strongly Agree	Agree	Neutral	Disagree	Strongly Disagree
1. Focuses attention on irregularities, mistakes, exceptions, and deviations from what is expected of me.	5	4	3	2	1
2. Engages in words and deeds that enhance his/her image of competence.	5	4	3	2	1
3. Monitors performance for errors needing correction.	5	4	3	2	1
4. Serves as a role model for me.	5	4	3	2	1
5. Points out what I will receive if I do what is required.	5	4	3	2	1
6. Instills pride in being associated with him/her.	5	4	3	2	1
7. Keeps careful track of mistakes.	5	4	3	2	1
8. Can be trusted to help me overcome any obstacle.	5	4	3	2	1
9. Tells me what to do to be rewarded for my efforts.	5	4	3	2	1
10. Makes me aware of strongly held values, ideals, and aspirations that are shared.	5	4	3	2	1
11. Is alert to failure to meet standards.	5	4	3	2	1
12. Mobilizes a collective sense of mission.	5	4	3	2	1
13. Works out agreements with me on what I will receive if I do what needs to be done.	5	4	3	2	1
14. Articulates a vision of future opportunities.	5	4	3	2	1
15. Talks about special rewards for good work.	5	4	3	2	1
16. Talks optimistically about the future.	5	4	3	2	1

Source: Items and dimensions are adapted from D N Den Hartog, J J Van Muijen, and P L Koopman, "Transactional Versus Transformational Leadership: An Analysis of the MLQ," *Journal of Occupational & Organizational Psychology*, 70 (March 1997), pp 19–34. Den Hartog et al label transactional leadership as "rational–objective leadership" and label transformational leadership as "inspirational leadership." Many of their items may have originated from B M Bass and B J Avolio, *Manual for the Multifactor Leadership Questionnaire* (Palo Alto, CA: Consulting Psychologists Press, 1989).

personal awareness and growth exercises

1. How Ready Are You to Assume the Leadership Role?

Objectives

1. To assess your readiness for the leadership role.
2. To consider the implications of the gap between your career goals and your readiness to lead.

Introduction

Leaders assume multiple roles. Roles represent the expectations that others have of occupants of a position. It is important for potential leaders to consider whether they are ready for the leadership role because mismatches in expectations or skills can derail a leader's effectiveness. This exercise assesses your readiness to assume the leadership role.

Instructions

For each statement, indicate the extent to which you agree or disagree with it by selecting one number from the scale provided. Circle your response for each statement. Remember, there are no right or wrong answers. After completing the survey, add your total score for the 20 items, and record it in the space provided.

1 = Strongly disagree
2 = Disagree
3 = Neither agree nor disagree
4 = Agree
5 = Strongly agree

1. It is enjoyable having people count on me for ideas and suggestions.   1 — 2 — 3 — 4 — 5

2. It would be accurate to say that I have inspired other people.   1 — 2 — 3 — 4 — 5

3. It's a good practice to ask people provocative questions about their work.   1 — 2 — 3 — 4 — 5

4. It's easy for me to compliment others.   1 — 2 — 3 — 4 — 5

5. I like to cheer people up even when my own spirits are down.   1 — 2 — 3 — 4 — 5

6. What my team accomplishes is more important than my personal glory.   1 — 2 — 3 — 4 — 5

7. Many people imitate my ideas.   1 — 2 — 3 — 4 — 5

8. Building team spirit is important to me.   1 — 2 — 3 — 4 — 5

9. I would enjoy coaching other members of the team.   1 — 2 — 3 — 4 — 5

10. It is important to me to recognize others for their accomplishments.   1 — 2 — 3 — 4 — 5

11. I would enjoy entertaining visitors to my firm even if it interfered with my completing a report.   1 — 2 — 3 — 4 — 5

12. It would be fun for me to represent my team at gatherings outside our department.   1 — 2 — 3 — 4 — 5

13. The problems of my teammates are my problems too.   1 — 2 — 3 — 4 — 5

14. Resolving conflict is an activity I enjoy.   1 — 2 — 3 — 4 — 5

15. I would cooperate with another unit in the organization even if I disagreed with the position taken by its members.   1 — 2 — 3 — 4 — 5

16. I am an idea generator on the job.   1 — 2 — 3 — 4 — 5

17. It's fun for me to bargain whenever I have the opportunity.   1 — 2 — 3 — 4 — 5

18. Team members listen to me when I speak.   1 — 2 — 3 — 4 — 5

19. People have asked me to assume the leadership of an activity several times in my life.   1 — 2 — 3 — 4 — 5

20. I've always been a convincing person.   1 — 2 — 3 — 4 — 5

Total score: _____

Norms for Interpreting the Total Score

90–100 = High readiness for the leadership role
60–89 = Moderate readiness for the leadership role
40–59 = Some uneasiness with the leadership role
39 or less = Low readiness for the leadership role

QUESTIONS FOR DISCUSSION

1. Do you agree with the interpretation of your readiness to assume the leadership role? Explain why or why not.
2. If you scored below 60 and desire to become a leader, what might you do to increase your readiness to lead? To answer this question, we suggest that you study the statements carefully—particularly those with low responses—to determine how you might change either an attitude or a behaviour so that you can realistically answer more questions with a response of "agree" or "strongly agree."
3. How might this evaluation instrument help you to become a more effective leader?

Source: Adapted from A J DuBrin, *Leadership: Research Findings, Practice, and Skills* (Boston: Houghton Mifflin Company, 1995), pp 10–11.

2. Are You a Charismatic Leader?

Instructions

The following statements refer to the possible ways in which you might behave toward others when you are in a leadership role. Please read each statement carefully and decide to what extent it applies to you. Then circle the appropriate number.

To little or no extent   1
To a slight extent   2
To a moderate extent   3
To a considerable extent   4
To a very great extent   5

You . . .

1. Pay close attention to what others say when they are talking	1	2	3	4	5
2. Communicate clearly	1	2	3	4	5
3. Are trustworthy	1	2	3	4	5
4. Care about other people	1	2	3	4	5
5. Do not put excessive energy into avoiding failure	1	2	3	4	5
6. Make the work of others more meaningful	1	2	3	4	5
7. Seem to focus on the key issues in a situation	1	2	3	4	5
8. Get across your meaning effectively, often in unusual ways	1	2	3	4	5
9. Can be relied on to follow through on commitments	1	2	3	4	5
10. Have a great deal of self-respect	1	2	3	4	5
11. Enjoy taking carefully calculated risks	1	2	3	4	5
12. Help others feel more competent in what they do	1	2	3	4	5
13. Have a clear set of priorities	1	2	3	4	5
14. Are in touch with how others feel	1	2	3	4	5
15. Rarely change once you have taken a clear position	1	2	3	4	5
16. Focus on strengths, of yourself and others	1	2	3	4	5
17. Seem most alive when deeply involved in some project	1	2	3	4	5
18. Show others that they are all part of the same group	1	2	3	4	5
19. Get others to focus on the issues you see as important	1	2	3	4	5
20. Communicate feelings as well as ideas	1	2	3	4	5
21. Let others know where you stand	1	2	3	4	5
22. Seem to know just how you "fit" into a group	1	2	3	4	5
23. Learn from mistakes; do not treat errors as disasters, but as learning	1	2	3	4	5
24. Are fun to be around	1	2	3	4	5

Turn to endnote 50 for scoring directions and key.

Source: M Sashkin and W C Morris, *Experiencing Management* (Addison-Wesley Publishing Company, Inc., 1987).

CBC video case

Banff School of Management

Doug McNamara runs the Banff School of Management, offering a 10-day, $4,000 experience for executives that promises to change their behaviour and make them better leaders. This intensive experience is intended to bring creative thinking back to business by opening minds and by pushing participants' personal limits. This objective is accomplished through an emphasis on unorthodox activities ranging from outdoor scavenger hunts after dark, teamwork exercises, role playing, improvisation, yoga, and ceramics. The idea is that an excellent leader shows the drive and passion of artists, and that the soul and emotion are important in leadership too.

There's also more traditional classroom activity provided by management academics from across the country—business theory, managing change, turnaround strategies, and the like. By the end of the course, these participants join the ranks of 3,000 other satisfied clients, saying that their experiences have revealed a lot of things; made them better communicators; stronger leaders; keenly aware of the relationship between creativity and innovation.

QUESTIONS FOR DISCUSSION

1. Does this course primarily build task-oriented or people-oriented behaviours in leaders, or both? Explain.
2. Do you agree that the soul and emotion are important aspects of leadership? What leadership theories would support your views? Explain.
3. Would this course help to enhance a charismatic or transformational leadership style? Explain.

Source: Based on "Banff Course," *CBC Venture 656* (August 24, 1997).

chapter

twelve

Organizational Design

LEARNING OUTCOMES

After reading the material in this chapter, you should be able to:

- Describe the four characteristics common to the structure of all organizations.

- Explain the difference between closed and open systems, and contrast the biological and cognitive systems metaphors for organizations.

- Describe the four generic organizational effectiveness criteria.

- Explain what is involved in the contingency approach to organizational design.

- Discuss Burns and Stalker's findings regarding mechanistic and organic organizations.

- List at least five characteristics each for new-style and old-style organizations.

LEAVE YOUR EGO AT THE DOOR

Grant Gisel has a thing about job titles. He doesn't like them because he believes they lead to hierarchies that stifle initiative and innovation, and he has created as few as possible at Vancouver-based Sierra Systems Group Inc. Established in 1966, Sierra Systems is Canada's oldest information technology consulting firm and one of its most successful, with almost 900 employees worldwide and annual sales exceeding $120 million. Founder Gisel is president, and upon taking Sierra Systems public in 1998, he named a chief executive officer, a chief financial officer, and several vice presidents to satisfy securities regula-

Sierra Systems Group Inc., Vancouver.

tors. Beyond that there are only three job categories: partners, who manage branches across the country; principals, who are in charge of projects; and the consultants, who work under them. "I came out of a large corporate environment where everyone had defined roles," he says. "I got told what to do every step of the way. I didn't like it and I don't think most people do. I wanted to create an environment where the job is yours to do."

Sierra Systems, he says, is a flat organization, and the principle extends to more than just job titles. Every employee participates in the profit sharing plan, which is based on a percentage of salary that is the same for staff at each level of the organization. The one-size-fits-all approach also extends to professional development. All who work at Sierra Systems are encouraged to upgrade their skills annually by taking college or university courses, or shorter programs provided by suppliers such as Microsoft, and the company covers the costs. "We're in the business where everything is changing all the time," says Gisel. "We have to keep our people at the leading edge of where technology is going."

Source: D Jenish and B Woodward, "Canada's Top 100 Employers," *Maclean's*, November 5, 2001, p 50.

Organizations: Definition and Dimensions

Virtually every aspect of life is affected at least indirectly by some type of organization.[1] We look to organizations to feed, clothe, house, educate, and employ us. Organizations attend to our needs for entertainment, police and fire protection, insurance, recreation, national security, transportation, news and information, legal assistance, and health care. Many of these organizations seek a profit, others do not. Some are extremely large, others are tiny mom-and-pop operations. Despite this mind-boggling diversity, modern organizations have one basic thing in common. They are the primary context for *organizational* behaviour. In a manner of speaking, organizations are the chessboard upon which the game of organizational behaviour is played. Therefore, present and future managers need a working knowledge of modern organizations to improve their chances of making the right moves when managing people at work.

As a necessary foundation for this chapter, we need to formally define the term *organization* and clarify the meaning of organization charts.

What Is an Organization?

Organization

System of consciously coordinated activities of two or more people.

An **organization** is "a system of consciously coordinated activities or forces of two or more persons."[2] Embodied in the *conscious coordination* aspect of this definition are four common denominators of all organizations: coordination of effort, a common goal, division of labour, and a hierarchy of authority.[3] Organization theorists refer to these factors as the organization's *structure*.

Coordination of effort is achieved through formulation and enforcement of policies, rules, and regulations. Division of labour occurs when the common goal is pursued by individuals performing separate but related tasks. The hierarchy of authority, also called the chain of command, is a control mechanism dedicated to making sure the right people do the right things at the right time. Historically, managers have maintained the integrity of the hierarchy of authority by adhering to the unity of command principle. The **unity of command principle** specifies that each employee should report to only one manager. Otherwise, the argument goes, inefficiency would prevail because of conflicting orders and lack of personal accountability. (Indeed, these are problems in today's more fluid and flexible organizations based on innovations such as cross-functional and self-managed teams.) Managers in the hierarchy of authority also administer rewards and punishments. When operating in concert, the four definitional factors—coordination of effort, a common goal, division of labour, and a hierarchy of authority—enable an *organization* to exist.

Unity of command principle

Each employee should report to a single manager.

Organization Charts

An **organization chart** is a graphic representation of formal authority and division of labour relationships. To the casual observer, the term *organization chart* means the family tree-like pattern of boxes and lines posted on workplace walls. Within each box one usually finds the names and titles of current position holders. To organization theorists, however, organization charts reveal much more. The partial organization chart in Figure 12–1 reveals four basic dimensions of organizational structure: (1) hierarchy of authority (who reports to whom), (2) division of labour, (3) spans of control, and (4) line and staff positions.

Organization chart

Boxes-and-lines illustration showing chain of formal authority and division of labour.

Hierarchy of Authority   As Figure 12–1 illustrates, there is an unmistakable hierarchy of authority.[4] Working from bottom to top, the 10 directors report to the two executive directors who report to the president who reports to the chief executive officer. Ultimately, the chief executive officer answers to the board of directors. The chart in Figure 12–1 shows strict unity of command up and down the line. A formal hierarchy of authority also delineates the official communication network.

Division of Labour   In addition to showing the chain of command, the sample organization chart indicates extensive division of labour. Immediately below the hospital's president, one executive director is responsible for general administration while another is responsible for medical affairs. Each of these two specialties is further subdivided as indicated by the next layer of positions. At each successively lower level in the organization, jobs become more specialized.

Spans of Control   The **span of control** refers to the number of people reporting directly to a given manager.[5] Spans of control can range from

Span of control

The number of people reporting directly to a given manager.

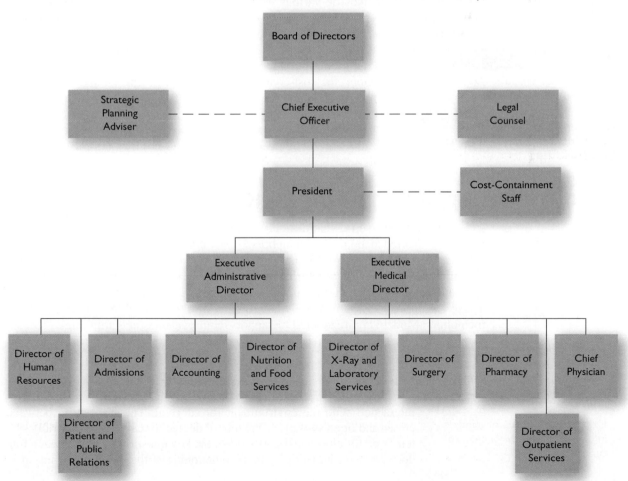

Sample Organization Chart for a Hospital   **FIGURE 12–1**
(executive and director levels only)

Organizations are human inventions to accomplish what individuals cannot do alone. Here, Jeff Bezos, founder and CEO of Amazon.com, gives a pep talk to his employees before the holiday season.

narrow to wide. For example, the president in Figure 12–1 has a narrow span of control of two. (Staff assistants usually are not included in a manager's span of control.) The executive administrative director in Figure 12–1 has a wider span of control of five. Spans of control exceeding 30 can be found in assembly-line operations where machine-paced and repetitive work substitutes for close supervision. Historically, spans of five to six were considered best. Despite years of debate, organization theorists have not arrived at a consensus regarding the ideal span of control.

Generally, the narrower the span of control, the closer the supervision and the higher the administrative costs as a result of a higher manager-to-worker ratio. Recent emphasis on leanness and administrative efficiency dictates spans of control as wide as possible but guarding against inadequate supervision and lack of coordination. Wider spans also complement the trend toward greater worker autonomy and empowerment.

Line and Staff Positions   The organization chart in Figure 12–1 also distinguishes between line and staff positions. Line managers such as the president, the two executive directors, and the various directors occupy formal decision-making positions within the chain of command. Line positions generally are connected by solid lines on organization charts. Dotted lines indicate staff relationships. **Staff managers** do background research and provide technical advice and recommendations to their **line managers,** who have the authority to make decisions. For example, the cost-containment specialists in the sample organization chart merely advise the president on relevant matters. Apart from supervising the work of their own staff assistants, they have no line authority over other organizational members. Modern trends such as cross-functional teams and reengineering are blurring the distinction between line and staff.

Staff managers

Provide research, advice, and recommendations to line managers.

Line managers

Have authority to make organizational decisions.

Modern Organizational Metaphors

The complexity of modern organizations makes them somewhat difficult to describe. Consequently, organization theorists have resorted to the use of metaphors.[6] A *metaphor* is a figure of speech that characterizes one object in terms of another object. Good metaphors help us comprehend complicated things by describing them in everyday terms. Early managers and management theorists used military units and machines as metaphors for organizations. These rigid closed-system models have given way to more dynamic and realistic metaphors. Modern organizational metaphors require *open-system* thinking.

Closed system

A relatively self-sufficient entity.

Open system

Organism that must constantly interact with its environment to survive.

Needed: Open-System Thinking

A **closed system** is said to be a self-sufficient entity. It is "closed" to the surrounding environment. In contrast, an **open system** depends on constant interaction with the environment for survival. The distinction between closed and open systems is a matter of degree. Because every worldly system is partly closed and partly open, the key question is: How great a role does the environment play in the functioning of the system? For instance, a battery-powered clock is a relatively closed system. Once the battery is inserted, the clock performs its time-keeping function hour after hour until the battery goes dead. The human body, on the other hand, is a highly open system because it requires a constant supply of life-sustaining oxygen from the environment. Nutrients also are imported from the environment. Open systems are capable of self-correction, adaptation, and growth, thanks to characteristics such as homeostasis and feedback control.

The traditional military/mechanical metaphor is a closed system model because it largely ignores environmental influences. It gives the impression that organizations are self-sufficient entities. Conversely, the biological, cognitive, and ecological metaphors discussed next emphasize interaction between organizations and their environments. These newer models are based on open-system assumptions. They reveal instructive insights about organizations and how they work. Each perspective offers something useful.

Organizations as Biological Systems

Drawing upon the field of general systems theory that emerged during the 1950s,[7] organization theorists suggested a more dynamic model for modern organizations. This metaphor likens organizations to the human body. Hence, it has been labelled the *biological model*. In his often-cited organization theory text, *Organizations in Action,* James D Thompson explained the biological model of organizations in the following terms:

> Approached as a natural system, the complex organization is a set of interdependent parts which together make up a whole because each contributes something and receives something from the whole, which in turn is interdependent with some larger environment. Survival of the system is taken to be the goal, and the parts and their relationships presumably are determined through evolutionary processes. . . .
>
> Central to the natural-system approach is the concept of homeostasis, or self-stabilization, which spontaneously, or naturally, governs the necessary relationships among parts and activities and thereby keeps the system viable in the face of disturbances stemming from the environment.[8]

Unlike the traditional military/mechanical theorists who downplayed the environment, advocates of the biological model stress organization–environment interaction. As Figure 12–2 illustrates, the biological model characterizes the organization as an open system that transforms inputs into various outputs. The outer boundary of the organization is permeable. People, information, capital, and goods and services move back and forth across this boundary. Moreover, each of the five organizational subsystems—goals and values, technical, psychosocial, structural, and managerial—is dependent on the others. Feedback about such things as sales and customer satisfaction or dissatisfaction enables the organization to self-adjust and survive despite uncertainty and change.[9] In effect, the organization is alive.

Organizations as Cognitive Systems

A more recent metaphor characterizes organizations in terms of mental functions. According to respected organization theorists Richard Daft and Karl Weick,

> This perspective represents a move away from mechanical and biological metaphors of organizations. Organizations are more than transformation processes or control systems. To survive, organizations must have mechanisms to interpret ambiguous events and to provide meaning and direction for participants. Organizations are meaning systems, and this distinguishes them from lower-level systems. . . .

FIGURE 12–2   The Organization as an Open System: The Biological Model

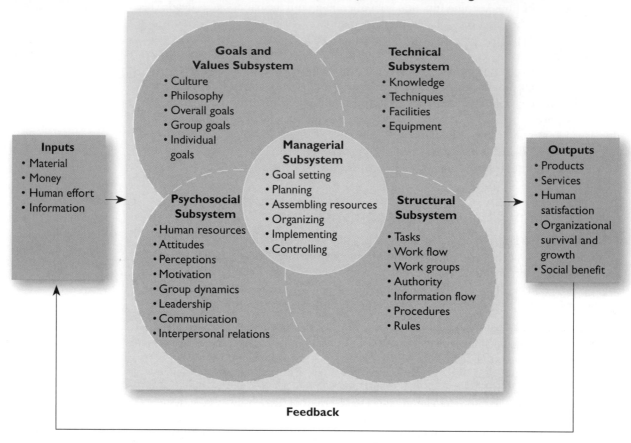

Source: This model is a combination of Figures 5–2 and 5–3 in F E Kast and J E Rosenzweig, *Organization and Management: A Systems and Contingency Approach,* 4th ed (New York: McGraw-Hill, 1986), pp 112, 114. Copyright © 1986. Reproduced with permission of the McGraw-Hill Companies.

Almost all outcomes in terms of organization structure and design, whether caused by the environment, technology, or size, depend on the interpretation of problems or opportunities by key decision makers. Once interpretation occurs, the organization can formulate a response.[10]

This interpretation process, as it migrates throughout the organization, leads to organizational *learning* and adaptation.

In fact, the concept of the *learning organization*[11] is very popular in management circles these days. It takes a cooperative culture, mutual trust, and lots of internal cross communication to fully exploit the organization as a cognitive system (or learning organization).

Some organizations even go so far as to have an executive responsible for ensuring that different parts of a company communicate and learn from each other. For example, Michael Detlefsen, Executive Vice-President, Vertical Coordination, at Maple Leaf Foods Inc., has fostered greater cooperation between independent operating companies at various stages of meat production. This has streamlined the pork and poultry "value chains"—including the genetics, feed, farming, and processing of animals—to respond to consumers' desire for more natural and better tasting products. It has also introduced greater accountability within the processing industry.[12]

Organizations as Ecosystem Participants

Managers have long joked about organizational life being a "jungle" where it is "dog eat dog." According to the newest organizational metaphor, it is indeed a jungle out there. **Organizational ecology** parallels the study of earth's natural ecosystems. Ecologists are interested in the interaction between an organism and its environment. Organizations live or die depending on the health and supportiveness of their environment, according to this metaphor. A recent review of the field produced this definition: "Organizational ecologists seek to explain how social, economic, and political conditions affect the relative abundance and diversity of organizations and attempt to account for their changing composition."[13] Organizational ecologists study organizational foundings, failures, changes, and interrelationships within the context of environmental factors. They talk in terms of *populations* (groups of similar organizations) and *communities* (networks of differing organizations).

> **Organizational ecology**
>
> The study of the effect of environmental factors on organizational success/failure and interrelationships among organizations.

Inherent in the ecological metaphor is Darwin's theory of natural selection. In the natural world, the fittest members of each species survive because their environment makes them stronger. The key to organizational survival today is learning how to selectively cooperate with ones' competitors. The joint ventures, strategic partnerships, and corporate alliances we read about today are steps in the right direction.[14] For example, consider this unusual behaviour in the global auto industry:

> Even as they compete fiercely to sell cars and trucks, the world's automakers are getting together in their quest to produce autos that run on something other than gasoline. General Motors and Toyota Motor announced a five-year partnership that will explore everything from electric cars to batteries and motors. Said GM Vice-Chairman Harry Pearce: "No single auto manufacturer can realistically expect to find all the technological answers on its own, let alone in a timely manner."[15]

Striving for Organizational Effectiveness

Assessing organizational effectiveness is an important topic for managers, stockholders, and government agencies. The purpose of this section is to introduce a widely applicable and useful model of organizational effectiveness.

Generic Effectiveness Criteria

A good way to better understand this complex subject is to consider four generic approaches to assessing an organization's effectiveness (see Figure 12–3). These effectiveness criteria apply equally well to large or small and profit or not-for-profit organizations. Moreover, as denoted by the overlapping circles in Figure 12–3, the four effectiveness criteria can be used in various combinations. The key thing to remember is "no single approach to the evaluation of effectiveness is appropriate in all circumstances or for all organization types."[16] Because a multidimensional approach is required, we need to look more closely at each of the four generic effectiveness criteria.

Goal Accomplishment   Goal accomplishment is the most widely used effectiveness criterion for organizations. Key organizational results or outputs are compared with previously stated goals or objectives. Deviations, either plus or minus, require corrective action. This is simply an organizational variation of the personal goal-setting process discussed in Chapter 3. Effectiveness, relative to the criterion of goal accomplishment, is gauged by how well the organization meets or exceeds its goals.[17]

FIGURE 12–3 | Four Dimensions of Organizational Effectiveness

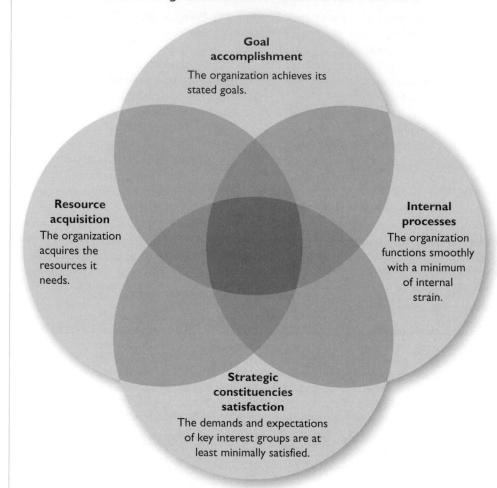

Sources: Adapted from discussion in K Cameron, "Critical Questions in Assessing Organizational Effectiveness," *Organizational Dynamics*, Autumn 1980, pp 66–80; and K S Cameron, "Effectiveness as Paradox: Consensus and Conflict in Conceptions of Organizational Effectiveness," *Management Science*, May 1986, pp 539–53.

Productivity improvement, involving the relationship between inputs and outputs, is a common organization-level goal.[18] Goals also may be set for organizational efforts such as minority recruiting, pollution prevention, and quality improvement. Given today's competitive pressures and E-commerce revolution, *innovation* and *speed* are very important organizational goals worthy of measurement and monitoring.[19] Toyota gave a powerful indicator of where things are going in this regard. The Japanese auto maker announced it could custom-build a car in just five days! A customer's new Toyota would roll off the Cambridge, Ontario, assembly line just five days after the order was placed. A 30-day lag was the industry standard at the time.[20]

Resource Acquisition This second criterion relates to inputs rather than outputs. An organization is deemed effective in this regard if it acquires necessary factors of production such as raw materials, labour, capital, and managerial and technical

Aircraft manufacturer Bombardier Inc. is effective because it is good at all four dimensions in Figure 12–3.

expertise. Charitable organizations such as the Salvation Army judge their effectiveness in terms of how much money they raise from private and corporate donations.

Internal Processes   Some refer to this third effectiveness criterion as the "healthy systems" approach. An organization is said to be a healthy system if information flows smoothly and if employee loyalty, commitment, job satisfaction, and trust prevail. Goals may be set for any of these internal processes. Healthy systems, from a behavioural standpoint, tend to have a minimum of dysfunctional conflict and destructive political maneuvering. M Scott Peck, the physician who wrote the highly regarded book, *The Road Less Traveled,* characterizes healthy organizations in ethical terms:

A healthy organization, Peck says, is one that has a genuine sense of community: It's a place where people are emotionally present with one another, and aren't afraid to talk about fears and disappointments—because that's what allows us to care for one another. It's a place where there is authentic communication, a willingness to be vulnerable, a commitment to speaking frankly and respectfully—and a commitment not to walk away when the going gets tough.[21]

ETHICS AT WORK

Family Circus

The jury is still out on Belinda Stronach—the latest Canadian rich kid to take over a family business. "Handing down a family business fails at least 50% of the time," says Richard Wolfe, an industrial psychologist based in Rochester NY. The children of Family Inc. often don't have knowledge of other industries. But according to Wolfe, those with a high level of unwarranted self-esteem—and the complementary staff of "executive yes-men" that typically surrounds them—could nevertheless decide that the family liquor business should become an entertainment company, or that dad's printing empire should acquire multimedia and cable assets, even when objective evidence suggests it might not be wise. Simply put, Wolfe says, rich kids all too often "don't know when they don't know," and that's why so many end up in difficulty.

What's at risk? Well, according to conservative estimates, Canada's family-run companies employ (directly and indirectly) around six million people, while generating about $1.4 trillion in annual revenues.

You Decide . . .

Is it ethical to hand family businesses down to family members, given that they have such a high failure rate overall? Is this fair to other stakeholders including employees, shareholders, customers, suppliers, etc.?

Source: Excerpted from T Watson, "Family Circus," *Canadian Business*, December 31, 2001, pp 105–10.

Strategic Constituencies Satisfaction   Organizations both depend on people and affect the lives of people. Consequently, many consider the satisfaction of key interested parties to be an important criterion of organizational effectiveness.

Strategic constituency

Any group of people with a stake in the organization's operation or success.

A **strategic constituency** is any group of individuals who have some stake in the organization—for example, resource providers, users of the organization's products or services, producers of the organization's output, groups whose cooperation is essential for the organization's survival, or those whose lives are significantly affected by the organization.[22]

Strategic constituencies (or *stakeholders*) generally have competing or conflicting interests.[23] For instance, after the September 11, 2001 terrorist attacks, airline passengers wanted increased security but shareholders suffered from the effect of increased security costs on corporate profits.

Mixing Effectiveness Criteria: Practical Guidelines

Experts on the subject recommend a multidimensional approach to assessing the effectiveness of modern organizations. This means no single criterion is appropriate for all stages of the organization's life cycle. Nor will a single criterion satisfy competing stakeholders. Well-managed organizations mix and match effectiveness criteria to fit the unique requirements of the situation.[24] Managers need to identify and seek input from strategic constituencies. This information, when merged with the organization's stated mission and philosophy, enables management to derive an appropriate *combination* of effectiveness criteria. The following guidelines are helpful in this regard:

* *The goal accomplishment approach* is appropriate when "goals are clear, consensual, time-bounded, measurable."[25]

* *The resource acquisition approach* is appropriate when inputs have a traceable effect on results or output. For example, the amount of money the Canadian Cancer Society receives through donations dictates the level of services provided.

* *The internal processes approach* is appropriate when organizational performance is strongly influenced by specific processes (e.g., cross-functional teamwork).

* *The strategic constituencies approach* is appropriate when powerful stakeholders can significantly benefit or harm the organization.[26]

The Contingency Approach to Designing Organizations

According to the **contingency approach** to organization design, organizations tend to be more effective when they are structured to fit the demands of the situation.[27] The purpose of this section is to introduce the contingency approach to organization design by reviewing two landmark studies, drawing a distinction between centralized and decentralized decision making, contrasting new-style and old-style organizations, and discussing today's virtual organizations.

Contingency approach

Creating an effective organization–environment fit.

Differentiation and Integration

In their classic text, *Organization and Environment*, Harvard researchers Paul Lawrence and Jay Lorsch explained how two structural forces simultaneously fragment the organization and bind it together. They cautioned that an imbalance between these

Bureaucratic Organizations and Psychological Diversity

While we usually think of diversity in terms of race, gender, or religion, the concept of diversity can also include "psychological type." If one is looking for a framework that identifies the most basic differences amongst human beings in order to explore divergent views and perspectives for the ultimate purpose of optimizing diversity and richness in an organization, one could find no better a schema than the Psychological Theory of Types put forward by noted psychologist Carl Jung. So say two researchers who, using information generated by the Myers-Briggs Type Indicator (MBTI), have argued that there is an uneven distribution of MBTI types in organizations, where the presence of the ESTJ (extroverted, sensing, thinking, judging type), who is typically concerned about usurping control, increases dramatically as one travels up the corporate ladder. The influence of ESTJ is magnified even further as power is filtered through the strict hierarchies that are the preferred organizational structure of the ESTJ.

The ESTJ's preference for "bureaucratic" forms of organization, when combined with the striking dominance of the ESTJ type in corporate decision making, translates into an overuse of these structures. The researchers believe that this is unfortunate, as bureaucratic forms of organization have been shown to inhibit creativity, collaboration, and group synergy. They are also less inclined to accommodate or even tolerate other kinds of diversity—cultural, ethnic, age, gender, etc. This built-in tendency toward a reduction of diversity of all kinds has a negative impact on the "fairness" of the typical organization in society, and its "richness."

Source: Adapted from Fudjack and P Dinkelaker, "Toward a Diversity of Psychological Type in Organization," October 1994, http://tap3x.net/ENSEMBLE/mpage1a.html, April 21, 2002.

two forces—labelled differentiation and integration—could hinder organizational effectiveness.

Differentiation occurs through the division of labour and technical specialization. A behavioural outcome of differentiation is that technical specialists such as computer analysts tend to think and act differently than specialists in, say, accounting or marketing. Excessive differentiation can cause the organization to bog down in miscommunication, conflict, and politics. Thus, differentiation needs to be offset by an opposing structural force to ensure needed coordination. This is where integration enters the picture.

> **Differentiation**
> Division of labour and specialization that cause people to think and act differently.
>
> **Integration**
> Cooperation among specialists to achieve common goals.

Integration occurs when specialists cooperate to achieve a common goal. According to Lawrence and Lorsch, integration can be achieved through various combinations of the following six mechanisms: (1) a formal hierarchy; (2) standardized policies, rules, and procedures; (3) departmentalization; (4) committees and cross-functional teams; (5) human relations training; and (6) individuals and groups acting as liaisons between specialists.

When Lawrence and Lorsch studied successful and unsuccessful companies in three industries, they concluded that as environmental complexity increased, successful organizations exhibited higher degrees of both differentiation and integration, i.e., an effective balance was achieved. Unsuccessful organizations, in contrast, tended to suffer from an imbalance of too much differentiation and not enough offsetting integration. Twenty-first century managers need to fight this tendency if their growing and increasingly differentiated organizations are to be coordinated.

Lawrence and Lorsch also discovered that "the more differentiated an organization, the more difficult it is to achieve integration."[28] Managers of today's complex organizations need to strive constantly and creatively to achieve greater integration.[29] For example, 3M Company makes sure its technical specialists frequently interact with one another so that cross-fertilization of ideas can take place. The company also has a Technology Council that regularly convenes researchers from various divisions and an annual science fair at which 3M scientists enthusiastically hawk their new ideas, not to customers, but to each other![30]

Mechanistic versus Organic Organizations

A landmark contingency design study was reported by a pair of British behavioural scientists, Tom Burns and G M Stalker. In the course of their research, they drew a very instructive distinction between what they called mechanistic and organic organizations. **Mechanistic organizations** are rigid bureaucracies with strict rules, narrowly defined tasks, and top-down communication. Ironically, it is at the cutting edge of technology that this seemingly out-of-date approach has found a home. In the highly competitive business of Web hosting—running clients' Web sites in high-security facilities humming with Internet servers—speed and reliability are everything. Enter military-style managers who require strict discipline, faithful adherence to thick rule books, and flawless execution. But, as *Business Week* observed, "The regimented atmosphere and military themes . . . may be tough to stomach for skilled workers used to a more free-spirited atmosphere."[31] Another example of a mechanistic organization is McDonald's restaurants, where fast food preparation is done in a highly regimented manner, complete with thick manuals of instruction.

Oppositely, **organic organizations** are flexible networks of multitalented individuals who perform a variety of tasks.[32] W L Gore & Associates, maker of waterproof Gore-Tex fabric, is a highly organic organization because it lacks job descriptions and a formalized hierarchy and deemphasizes titles and status.[33]

Mechanistic organizations

Rigid, command-and-control bureaucracies.

Organic organizations

Fluid and flexible network of multi-talented people.

In order to provide customers with consistent quality and fast service, McDonald's employees are required to follow defined food-preparation and customer service procedures.

Bureaucracy: The Egyptian Connection

Bureaucracy is not a modern invention; it was conceived by the Egyptians over 5,000 years ago. Many concepts in modern bureaucracies can be traced to the Egyptians. The hierarchical structure and code of ethics of the Egyptian bureaucracy are echoed in modern governments. Ancient Egyptian bureaucrats, who aspired to higher positions, were counselled to obey their superiors and keep silent in all circumstances, in other words, not to contradict or challenge the wisdom of those in charge. They were expected to have tact and good manners, be faithful in delivering messages, and display humility that verged on subservience. It is perhaps for these reasons that Egyptian officials were called civil servants, a designation that governments have adopted down through the ages.

Source: Canadian Museum of Civilization, www.civilization.ca/civil/egypt/egcgov3e.html, April 21, 2002.

A Matter of Degree   Each of the mechanistic-organic characteristics is a matter of degree. Organizations tend to be *relatively* mechanistic or *relatively* organic. Pure types are rare because divisions, departments, or units in the same organization may be more or less mechanistic or organic.

Different Approaches to Decision Making   Decision making tends to be centralized in mechanistic organizations and decentralized in organic organizations. **Centralized decision making** occurs when key decisions are made by top management. **Decentralized decision making** occurs when important decisions are made by middle- and lower-level managers. Generally, centralized organizations are more tightly controlled while decentralized organizations are more adaptive to changing situations.[34] Each has its appropriate use. For example, both Wal-Mart and General Electric are very respected and successful companies, yet the former prefers centralization while the latter pushes decentralization.

> **Centralized decision making**
>
> Top managers make all key decisions.
>
> **Decentralized decision making**
>
> Lower-level managers are empowered to make important decisions.

Experts on the subject warn against extremes of centralization or decentralization. The challenge is to achieve a workable balance between the two extremes. A management consultant put it this way:

> The modern organization in transition will recognize the pull of two polarities: a need for greater centralization to create low-cost shared resources; and, a need to improve market responsiveness with greater decentralization. Today's winning organizations are the ones that can handle the paradox and tensions of both pulls. These are the firms that analyze the optimum organizational solution in each particular circumstance, without prejudice for one type of organization over another. The result is, almost invariably, a messy mixture of decentralized units sharing cost-effective centralized resources.[35]

Centralization and decentralization are not an either-or proposition; they are a balancing act.

Practical Research Insights   When they classified a sample of actual companies as either mechanistic or organic, Burns and Stalker discovered one type was not superior to the other. Each type had its appropriate place, depending on the environment. When the environment was relatively *stable and certain,* the successful organizations tended to be *mechanistic. Organic* organizations tended to be the successful ones when the environment was *unstable and uncertain.*[36]

In a more recent study, managerial skill was found to have a greater impact on a global measure of department effectiveness in organic departments than in mechanistic departments. This led the researchers to recommend the following contingencies for management staffing and training:

> If we have two units, one organic and one mechanistic, and two potential applicants differing in overall managerial ability, we might want to assign the more competent to the organic unit since in that situation there are few structural aids available to the manager in performing required responsibilities. It is also possible that managerial training is especially needed by managers being groomed to take over units that are more organic in structure.[37]

Another interesting finding comes from a study of 42 voluntary church organizations. As the organizations became more mechanistic (more bureaucratic) the intrinsic motivation of their members decreased. Mechanistic organizations apparently undermined the volunteers' sense of freedom and self-determination. Additionally, the researchers believe their findings help explain why bureaucracy tends to feed on itself: "A mechanistic organizational structure may breed the need for a more extremely mechanistic system because of the reduction in intrinsically motivated behaviour."[38] Thus, bureaucracy begets greater bureaucracy.

Most recently, field research in two factories, one mechanistic and the other organic, found expected communication patterns. Command-and-control (downward) communication characterized the mechanistic factory. Consultative or participative (two-way) communication prevailed in the organic factory.[39]

Both Mechanistic and Organic Structures Have Their Places

Although achievement-oriented students of OB typically express a distaste for mechanistic organizations, not all organizations or subunits can or should be organic. For example, McDonald's could not achieve its admired quality and service standards without extremely mechanistic restaurant operations. Imagine the food and service you would get if McDonald's employees used their own favourite ways of doing things and worked at their own pace! On the other hand, mechanistic structure alienates some employees because it erodes their sense of self-control.

New-Style versus Old-Style Organizations

Organization theorists Jay R Galbraith and Edward E Lawler III have called for a "new logic of organizing."[40] They recommend a whole new set of adjectives to describe organizations (see Table 12–1). Traditional pyramid-shaped organizations, conforming to the old-style pattern, tend to be too slow and inflexible today. Leaner, more organic organizations increasingly are needed to accommodate today's strategic balancing act between cost, quality, and speed. These new-style organizations embrace the total quality management (TQM) principles discussed in Chapter 1. This means they are customer focused, dedicated to continuous improvement and learning, and structured around teams. These qualities, along with computerized information technology, hopefully enable big organizations to mimic the speed and flexibility of small organizations.

For example, Bell Ontario's operations, involving 10,000 employees, needed to break down barriers that had built up during the days when telephone service was a monopoly. The stable monopolistic environment meant that a giant mechanistic bureaucracy was an effective organizational structure for Bell. Deregulation meant that the competitive environment became much less stable, and included a lot of small entre-

New-Style versus Old-Style Organizations **TABLE 12–1**

New	Old
Dynamic, learning	Stable
Information rich	Information is scarce
Global	Local
Small and large	Large
Product/customer oriented	Functional
Skills oriented	Job oriented
Team oriented	Individual oriented
Involvement oriented	Command/control oriented
Lateral/networked	Hierarchical
Customer oriented	Job requirements oriented

Source: J R Galbraith and E E Lawler III, "Effective Organizations: Using the New Logic of Organizing," p 298 in *Organizing for the Future: The New Logic for Managing Complex Organizations,* eds J R Galbraith, E E Lawler III, and Associates. Copyright 1993 Jossey-Bass Inc. Publishers. Reprinted by permission of Jossey-Bass, Inc., a subsidiary of John Wiley & Sons, Inc.

preneurial companies. Bell's solution was to free up workers' natural creativity. One of its business units, the Bell Canada Mobile Computing Centre, was transformed from "a bunch of guys playing with technology" to a development group that oversaw the largest deployment of wearable computers in the telecom industry. The Walkman-sized computers with heads-up display make users look like a cyborg.[41]

Virtual Organizations

Like virtual teams, discussed in Chapter 7, modern information technology allows people in virtual organizations to get something accomplished despite being geographically dispersed.[42] Instead of relying heavily on face-to-face meetings, members of virtual organizations send E-mail and voice-mail messages, exchange project information over the Internet, and convene videoconferences among far-flung participants. In addition, cellular phones and wireless Internet service have made the dream of doing business from the beach a reality! This disconnection between work and location is causing managers to question traditional assumptions about centralized offices and factories. Why have offices for people who are never there because they are out finding and helping customers? Why have a factory when it is less expensive to contract out the work? Indeed, many so-called virtual organizations are really a *network* of several organizations hooked together contractually and electronically. A prime example is Canadian Virtual University (CVU). True to its name, CVU has no campus, no faculty building, no student union, and no football stadium. CVU provides one doorway to 13 Canadian universities offering over 175 programs available through the Internet or by distance education. Students can select courses offered by any of the participating universities. This means 2,000 courses to choose from, and the list is growing.

According to *TIME* magazine:

CVU offers its cornucopia through distance learning . . . never before has such an abundance of post-secondary education been brought together in a single institution.[43]

CVU does not grant degrees—the courses are applied toward a degree granted by one of the participating universities. Many of the programs are offered via print material through the mail, and students communicate with a tutor via phone, E-mail, or regular mail. Other courses are offered through the Internet and require the student to have access to computer equipment and an Internet browser.

People who earn a degree through virtual institutions such as CVU are usually working adults who are juggling family schedules and work commitments with the need to advance their education. But the typical 20-year-old university student is also starting to look at online courses.[44]

Gazing into the Crystal Ball   Life in the emerging virtual organizations and organizational networks promises to be very interesting and profitable for the elite core of entrepreneurs and engineers who hit on the right business formula. Turnover among the financial and information "have nots"—data entry, customer service, and production employees—will likely be high because of glaring inequities and limited opportunities for personal fulfilment and growth. Telecommuters who work from home will feel liberated and empowered (and sometimes lonely). Commitment, trust, and loyalty could erode badly if managers do not heed this caution by Charles Handy, a British management expert. According to Handy: "A shared commitment still requires personal contact to make the commitment feel real. *Paradoxically, the more virtual an organization becomes the more its people need to meet in person.*"[45] Independent contractors, both individuals and organizations, will participate in many different organizational networks and thus have diluted loyalty to any single one. Substandard working conditions and low pay at some smaller contractors will make them little more than Internet-age sweat shops.[46] Companies living from one contract to another will offer little in the way of job security and benefits. Opportunities to start new businesses will be numerous, but prolonged success could prove elusive at Internet speed.[47]

Needed: Self-Starting Team Players   The only certainty about tomorrow's organizations is they will produce a lot of surprises. Only flexible, adaptable people who see problems as opportunities, are self-starters capable of teamwork, and are committed to life-long learning will be able to handle whatever comes their way.

summary of key concepts

- *Describe the four characteristics common to the structure of all organizations.* They are coordination of effort (achieved through policies and rules), a common goal (a collective purpose), division of labour (people performing separate but related tasks), and a hierarchy of authority (the chain of command).

- *Explain the difference between closed and open systems, and contrast the biological and cognitive systems metaphors for organizations.* Closed systems, such as a battery-powered clock, are relatively self-sufficient. Open systems, such as the human body, are highly dependent on the environment for survival. Organizations are said to be open systems. The biological metaphor views the organization as a living organism striving to survive in an uncertain environment. In terms of the cognitive metaphor, an organization is like the human mind, capable of interpreting and learning from uncertain and ambiguous situations.

- *Describe the four generic organizational effectiveness criteria.* They are goal accomplishment (satisfying stated objectives), resource acquisition (gathering the necessary productive inputs), internal processes (building and maintaining healthy organizational systems), and strategic constituencies satisfaction (achieving at least minimal satisfaction for all key stakeholders).

- *Explain what is involved in the contingency approach to organizational design.* The contingency approach to organization design calls for fitting the organization to the demands of the situation.

- *Discuss Burns and Stalker's findings regarding mechanistic and organic organizations.* British researchers Burns and Stalker found that mechanistic (bureaucratic, centralized) organizations tended to be effective in stable situations. In unstable situations, organic (flexible, decentralized) organizations were more effective. These findings underscored the need for a contingency approach to organization design.

- *List at least five characteristics each for new-style and old-style organizations.* New-style organizations are characterized as dynamic and learning, information rich, global, small and large, product/customer oriented, skills oriented, team oriented, involvement oriented, lateral/networked, and customer oriented. Old-style organizations are characterized as stable, information is scarce, local, large, functional, job oriented, individual oriented, command/control oriented, hierarchical, and job requirements oriented.

key terms

centralized decision making, 281
closed system, 272
contingency approach, 278
decentralized decision making, 281
differentiation, 279
integration, 279

line managers, 272
mechanistic organizations, 280
open system, 272
organic organizations, 280
organization, 270
organization chart, 270

organizational ecology, 275
span of control, 271
staff managers, 272
strategic constituency, 278
unity of command principle, 270

discussion questions

1. How many organizations directly affect your life today? List as many as you can.

2. What would an organization chart of your current (or last) place of employment look like? Does the chart you have drawn reveal the hierarchy (chain of command), division of labour, span of control, and line-staff distinctions? Does it reveal anything else? Explain.

3. How would you respond to a manager who claimed that the only way to measure a business's effectiveness is in terms of how much profit it makes?

4. In a nutshell, what does contingency organizational design entail?

5. If organic organizations are popular with most employees, why can't all organizations be structured in an organic fashion?

6. Which of the three new organizational configurations probably will be most prevalent 10 to 15 years from now? Why?

internet exercises

www.fortune.com

1. Alternative Effectiveness Criteria

There is no single way to measure organizational effectiveness, as discussed in this chapter. Different stakeholders want organizations to do different and often conflicting things. The purpose of this exercise is to introduce alternative effectiveness criteria and to assess real companies with them.

Each year, *Fortune* magazine publishes a ranking of the World's Most Admired Companies. *Fortune* applies a set of nine attributes that arguably could be called effectiveness criteria. You can judge for yourself by going to *Fortune*'s Internet site (**www.fortune.com**) and clicking on "View all Fortune Lists." Then, select "World's Most Admired Companies."

Click on the heading "Methodology and FAQ" to find the nine criteria.

QUESTIONS

1. Do you agree that the nine attributes are really organizational effectiveness criteria? Explain. What others would you add to the list? Which would you remove from the list?
2. How did you rank each of the nine attributes?
3. Are you surprised by the top-ranked company (or companies)? Explain.
4. Do you admire the top-ranked company? Why or why not?

www.smartdraw.com

2. Organization Charting Software

Organization charting software is used by many organizations to create their organizational charts. Go to the Smartdraw.com Web site (**www.smartdraw.com**) and review their advertising material. Click on "Basic Organizational Chart Shapes."

QUESTIONS

1. What shapes are relevant to all types of organizations?
2. What shapes are relevant only for mechanistic organizations? Only for organic organizations?
3. Are there any shapes that might be required for organic or virtual organizations that are missing? Why might this be the case?

experiential exercises

1. Mechanistic or Organic?

Instructions

Think of your present (or a past) place of employment and rate it on the following eight factors. Calculate a total score and compare it to the scale.

Characteristics

1. Task definition and knowledge required	Narrow, technical	1	2	3	4	5	6	7	Broad; general
2. Linkage between individual's contribution and organization's purpose	Vague or indirect	1	2	3	4	5	6	7	Clear or direct
3. Task flexibility	Rigid; routine	1	2	3	4	5	6	7	Flexible; varied
4. Specification of techniques, obligations, and rights	Specific	1	2	3	4	5	6	7	General
5. Degree of hierarchical control	High	1	2	3	4	5	6	7	Low (self-control emphasized)
6. Primary communication pattern	Top-down	1	2	3	4	5	6	7	Lateral (between peers)
7. Primary decision-making style	Authoritarian	1	2	3	4	5	6	7	Democratic; participative
8. Emphasis on obedience and loyalty	High	1	2	3	4	5	6	7	Low

Total score = _____

Scale

 8–24 = Relatively mechanistic
25–39 = Mixed
40–56 = Relatively organic

Source: Adapted from discussion in T Burns and G M Stalker, *The Management of Innovation* (London: Tavistock, 1961), pp. 119–25.

2. Organizations Alive!

Procedure

1. Find a copy of the following items from actual organizations. These items can be obtained from the company where you now work, your parent's workplace, or from your university/college. Universities/colleges have mission statements, codes of conduct for students and faculty, organizational charts, job descriptions, performance appraisal forms, and policies/procedures. Some student organizations may also have these documents. All the items do not have to come from the same organization. Bring the following items to class:
   a. mission statement
   b. code of ethics
   c. organizational chart
   d. job description
   e. performance appraisal form
   f. policies/procedures.

2. Form groups in class as assigned by your instructor. Share your items with the group, as well as what you learned while collecting these items. For example, did you find that some firms have a mission, but it is not written down? Did you find that job descriptions existed, but they were not really used or had not been updated in years?

Source: Adapted from B L McNeely, "Make Your Principles of Management Class Come Alive," *Journal of Management Education*, 18 (2), May 1994, 246–49.

personal awareness and growth exercises

1. Bureaucratic Orientation Test

Instructions

For each statement, check the response (either mostly agree or mostly disagree) that best represents your feelings.

	Mostly Agree	Mostly Disagree
1. I value stability in my job.	_____	_____
2. I like a predictable organization.	_____	_____
3. The best job for me would be one in which the future is uncertain.	_____	_____
4. The federal government would be a nice place to work.	_____	_____
5. Rules, policies, and procedures tend to frustrate me.	_____	_____
6. I would enjoy working for a company that employed 85,000 people worldwide.	_____	_____
7. Being self-employed would involve more risk than I'm willing to take.	_____	_____
8. Before accepting a job, I would like to see an exact job description.	_____	_____
9. I would prefer a job as a freelance house painter to one as a clerk for the Department of Motor Vehicles.	_____	_____
10. Seniority should be as important as performance in determining pay increases and promotion.	_____	_____
11. It would give me a feeling of pride to work for the largest and most successful company in its field.	_____	_____
12. Given a choice, I would prefer to make $70,000 per year as a vice-president in a small company than $85,000 as a staff specialist in a large company.	_____	_____

	Mostly Agree	Mostly Disagree
13. I would regard wearing an employee badge with a number on it as a degrading experience.	_____	_____
14. Parking spaces in a company lot should be assigned on the basis of job level.	_____	_____
15. If an accountant works for a large organization, he or she cannot be a true professional.	_____	_____
16. Before accepting a job (given a choice), I would want to make sure that the company had a very fine program of employee benefits.	_____	_____
17. A company will probably not be successful unless it establishes a clear set of rules and procedures.	_____	_____
18. Regular working hours and vacations are more important to me than finding thrills on the job.	_____	_____
19. You should respect people according to their rank.	_____	_____
20. Rules are meant to be broken.	_____	_____

Turn to endnote 48 for scoring directions and key.

Source: Adapted from A J DuBrin. *Human Relations: A Job Oriented Approach*, 5th ed, 1992. Reprinted with permission of Prentice Hall, Inc., Upper Saddle River, NJ.

2. Identifying Your Preferred Organizational Structure

Purpose

This exercise is designed to help you understand how an organization's structure influences the personal needs and values of people working in that structure.

Instructions

Personal values influence how comfortable you are working in different organizational structures. You might prefer an organization with clearly defined rules or no rules at all. You might prefer a firm in which almost any employee can make important decisions, or in which senior executives screen important decisions. Read the statements below and indicate the extent to which you would like to work in an organization with that characteristic. When finished, use the scoring key in endnote 49 of this book to calculate your results. This self-assessment is completed alone so students can answer honestly without concerns of social comparison. However, class discussion will focus on the elements of organizational design and their relationship to personal needs and values.

ORGANIZATIONAL STRUCTURE PREFERENCE SCALE

I would like to work in an organization where . . .					Score
1. A person's career ladder has several steps towards higher status and responsibility.	Not at all	A little	Somewhat	Very much	_____
2. Employees perform their work with few rules to limit their discretion.	Not at all	A little	Somewhat	Very much	_____
3. Responsibility is pushed down to employees who perform the work.	Not at all	A little	Somewhat	Very much	_____
4. Supervisors have few employees, so they work closely with each person.	Not at all	A little	Somewhat	Very much	_____
5. Senior executives make most decisions to ensure that the company is consistent in its actions.	Not at all	A little	Somewhat	Very much	_____

6.	Jobs are clearly defined so there is no confusion over who is responsible for various tasks.	Not at all	A little	Somewhat	Very much	_____
7.	Employees have their say on issues, but senior executives make most of the decisions.	Not at all	A little	Somewhat	Very much	_____
8.	Job descriptions are broadly stated or nonexistent.	Not at all	A little	Somewhat	Very much	_____
9.	Everyone's work is tightly synchronized around top management's operating plans.	Not at all	A little	Somewhat	Very much	_____
10.	Most work is performed in teams without close supervision.	Not at all	A little	Somewhat	Very much	_____
11.	Work gets done through informal discussion with co-workers rather than through formal rules.	Not at all	A little	Somewhat	Very much	_____
12.	Supervisors have so many employees that they can't watch anyone very closely.	Not at all	A little	Somewhat	Very much	_____
13.	Everyone has clearly understood goals, expectations, and job duties.	Not at all	A little	Somewhat	Very much	_____
14.	Senior executives assign overall goals, but leave daily decisions to front-line teams.	Not at all	A little	Somewhat	Very much	_____
15.	Even in a large company, the CEO is only three or four levels above the person in the lowest position.	Not at all	A little	Somewhat	Very much	_____

Source: © Copyright 2000. Steven L. McShane.

CBC video case

Strange Bedfellows

Alliances with competitors—unthinkable not too long ago, but in today's fast-paced business world, "extraordinary times demand extraordinary happenings." So the *Globe and Mail* and the *Toronto Star* have joined together to create Workopolis.com, a joint, Canada-wide Internet job board to fight the juggernaut Monster.ca, as it opens up in Canada. It turns out that the Star's job site lacked the Globe's national profile, and the *Globe and Mail* job site lacked the Star's reach in Southern Ontario. The idea to join forces came from the job site managers, not senior management, and the managers were able to build trust between themselves as individuals. Both sides still compete in all other aspects of their business, such as news.

Today, competitor alliances now form approximately 50% of business alliances. These alliances are risky and complex—60 to 70% of them fail. Partners may want to steal technology, customers, and markets controlled by the other partner. As well, employees at all levels of an organization may resist the idea of cooperation with a long-time adversary. But they can be successful. To date, Workopolis has been a successful competitive alliance with great prospects for the future.

QUESTIONS FOR DISCUSSION

1. Explain how the *Globe and Mail* and the *Toronto Star* have demonstrated open-system thinking in this situation.
2. Explain how this competitive alliance illustrates characteristics of a "new style" organization.
3. Identify several strategic constituencies that have been satisfied in this case.

Source: Based on "Strange Bedfellows," *CBC Venture 739* (February 15, 2000).

chapter thirteen

Organizational Culture and Change

LEARNING OUTCOMES

After reading the material in this chapter, you should be able to:

- Discuss the layers and functions of organizational culture.

- Summarize the methods used by organizations to embed their cultures.

- Describe the three phases of organizational socialization.

- Discuss the external and internal forces that create the need for organizational change.

- Describe Lewin's change model and the systems model of change.

- Review the 10 reasons employees resist change.

- Identify alternative strategies for overcoming resistance to change.

IN THE PIT

The Toronto Symphony Orchestra (TSO), at 80 years of age, is an organization in the throes of change. External realities including an aging audience, a diminishing subscription base, and shifting urban demographics provide strong forces for change. Internal forces for change include poor morale, escalating costs, strikes by musicians, and near-bankruptcy. The symphony's former executive director, Ed Smith, declared: "The internal culture of the organization is probably beyond repair."

But out of what Bob Rae, chair of the TSO board and former premier of Ontario, calls "the orchestra's near-death experience," there has emerged a CEO who is both musician and entrepreneur, artist and marketer. Andrew Shaw is a professional cellist and a graduate of the University of Toronto's executive MBA program. He's under no illusions about what's in store. When asked about his impression of his new job, he looks ceilingward and pauses, hunting for a simile that is sufficiently extreme. "Like learning to drink water from a fire hose," he says finally.

Shaw takes the view that the worst is now behind the orchestra. A desperately needed acoustic renovation is finally underway at Roy Thomson Hall. The search for a new music director is in high gear. And Shaw speaks enthusiastically of a renewed commitment from the orchestra's musicians and of a restructured relationship between management and the board. Bob Rae concurs: "The TSO board is here to provide a framework and support—to be a sounding board, to be the orchestra's champion. . . . But we're not in the business of micro-managing. That's why we've hired a strong and dynamic CEO."

Shaw takes the advance billing guardedly, with a slightly pained smile. "Let's put it this way," he says, "I don't expect to be bored."

The Toronto Symphony Orchestra (TSO).

Source: Adapted from D Macfarlane, "In the Pit," *Report on Business Magazine*, May 2002, pp 20–22.

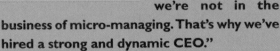

Foundation of Organizational Culture

Organizational culture is the set of shared, taken-for-granted values, beliefs, and implicit assumptions that a group holds and that determines how it perceives, thinks about, and reacts to its various environments.[1] Figure 13–1 shows the three fundamental layers of organizational culture. Each level varies in terms of outward visibility and resistance to change, and each level influences another level.[2]

Observable Artifacts   At the more visible level, culture represents observable artifacts. Artifacts consist of the physical manifestation of an organization's culture. Organizational examples include acronyms, manner of dress, awards, myths and stories told about the organization, published lists of values, observable rituals and ceremonies, special parking spaces, decorations, and so on. This level also includes visible behaviours exhibited by people and groups. Artifacts are easier to change than the less visible aspects of organizational culture.

Consider the behaviour of a supervisor at Sitel Canada in Montreal. A young woman was found lying on the ground, beaten, unconscious, and naked from the waist down in a parking lot near the company's head office. The supervisor did not call 911 and forbade his employees to call. He later claimed that he thought she was just "out of it" as he didn't see any blood. It took three hours before one employee called police from his cell phone.

The case outraged Montrealers and raises questions about corporate values and culture. Was the employee simply a "loose cannon" or was the culture of the workplace to blame? Some observers believe that the fact that employees heeded their supervisor's direction not to intervene suggests that there were larger, organizational factors at play. Others point to the fact that there was a conflict between productivity pressures and human values, and contend that the obligations of citizenship should transcend obligations to an employer. The company fired the supervisor, but refused to comment further on its investigation or the circumstances surrounding the supervisor's and employees' behaviour.[3]

FIGURE 13–1 | The Layers of Organizational Culture

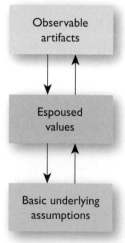

Source: Adapted from E H Schein, *Organizational Culture and Leadership,* 2nd ed (San Francisco: Jossey-Bass, 1992), p 17.

Espoused Values   Values possess five key components. "**Values** (1) are concepts or beliefs, (2) pertain to desirable end-states or behaviours, (3) transcend situations, (4) guide selection or evaluation of behaviour and events, and (5) are ordered by relative importance."[4] It is important to distinguish between values that are espoused versus those that are enacted.

Values

Enduring belief in a mode of conduct or end-state.

Espoused values represent the explicitly stated values and norms that are preferred by an organization. They are generally established by the founder of a new or small company and by the top management team in a larger organization. At Intelatech, a Mississauga, Ontario electronics supplier and service provider to the high-tech industry, the corporate values developed by its two owners are: trust, enthusiasm, creativity, courage, and honesty (TECH). Kim Barrington, human resources manager at Intelatech, says "I use them when I'm stuck with a decision and not sure how to proceed. They're a focus for how we conduct ourselves—and our business—on a personal and professional level."[5] Because espoused values constitute aspirations that are explicitly communicated to employees, managers hope that espoused values will directly influence employee behaviour. Unfortunately, aspirations do not automatically produce the desired behaviours because people do not always "walk the talk."

Espoused values

The stated values and norms that are preferred by an organization.

Enacted values, on the other hand, represent the values and norms that actually are exhibited or converted into employee behaviour. It is important to reduce gaps between espoused and enacted values because they can significantly influence employee attitudes and organizational performance. WestJet Airlines has strong espoused values, according to Siobhan Vinish, director of public relations and communications:

Enacted values

The values and norms that are exhibited by employees.

> WestJet is family. Things here are very casual. Nobody wears ties. Nobody calls each other mister. It's a very casual, family, relaxed environment.

WestJet empowers its staff at every level to think for themselves and make decisions that make sense for their clients. If a flight attendant accidentally spills a drink on someone, other airlines would offer the person a dry-cleaning certificate. The WestJet attendant is also likely to buy the customer a replacement drink. If a person misses their flight because of traffic, most airlines say the customer is out of luck. WestJet's customer service representatives are likely to simply put the customer on the next available flight.

A problem arose when the enacted values of WestJet's new CEO, Steve Smith, who had a "militaristic" leadership style, didn't match its "casual, relaxed" espoused values. Culture is not just important to WestJet—it is everything. They do whatever they need to do to protect that culture, and thus Smith and WestJet parted ways.[6]

Basic Assumptions   Basic underlying assumptions are unobservable and represent the core of organizational culture. They constitute organizational values that have become so taken for granted over time that they become assumptions that guide organizational behaviour. They thus are highly resistant to change. When basic assumptions are widely held among employees, people will find behaviour based on an inconsistent value inconceivable.

Four Functions of Organizational Culture

As illustrated in Figure 13–2, an organization's culture fulfills four functions.[7] To help bring these four functions to life, let us consider how each of them has taken shape

FIGURE 13–2 | Four Functions of Organizational Culture

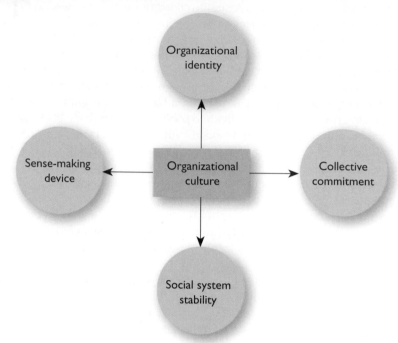

Source: Adapted from discussion in L Smircich, "Concepts of Culture and Organizational Analysis," *Administrative Science Quarterly*, September 1983, pp 339–58. Reproduced by permission of John Wiley & Sons, Ltd.

at 3M. 3M is a particularly instructive example because it has a long history of being an innovative company with a strong and distinctive culture.[8]

1. *Give members an organizational identity.* 3M is known as being an innovative company that relentlessly pursues new-product development. One way of promoting innovation is to encourage the research and development of new products and services. For example, 3M regularly sets future sales targets based on the percentage of sales that must come from new products. In one year, the senior management decreed that 30% of its sales must come from products introduced within the past four years. The old standard was 25% in five years. This identity is reinforced by creating rewards that reinforce innovation. For example, "The 3M Corporation has its version of a Nobel Prize for innovative employees. The prize is the Golden Step award, whose trophy is a winged foot. Several Golden Steps are given out each year to employees whose new products have reached significant revenue and profit levels."[9]

2. *Facilitate collective commitment.* One of 3M's corporate values is to be "a company that employees are proud to be a part of." People who like 3M's culture tend to stay employed there for long periods of time. Approximately 24,000 of its employees have more than 15 years of tenure with the company while 19,600 have stayed more than 20 years. Consider the commitment and pride expressed by Kathleen Stanislawski, a staffing manager. "I'm a 27-year 3Mer because, quite frankly, there's no reason to leave. I've had great opportunities to do different jobs and to grow a career. It's just a great company."[10]

3. *Promote social system stability.* Social system stability reflects the extent to which the work environment is perceived as positive and reinforcing, and conflict and change are managed effectively. Consider how 3M dealt with its financial problems in 1998. "Even in tough times, which have now arrived because of the upheavals in Asia, 3M hasn't become a mean, miserly, or miserable place to work. It's shedding about 4,500 jobs, but slowly, and mostly by attrition."[11] This strategy helped to maintain a positive work environment in the face of adversity. The company also attempts to promote stability through a promote-from-within culture, a strategic hiring policy that ensures that capable college graduates are hired in a timely manner, and a layoff policy that provides displaced workers six months to find another job at 3M before being terminated.

4. *Shape behaviour by helping members make sense of their surroundings.* This function of culture helps employees understand why the organization does what it does and how it intends to accomplish its long-term goals. 3M sets expectations for innovation in a variety of ways. For example, the company employs an internship and co-op program. 3M also shapes expectations and behaviour by providing detailed career feedback to its employees. New hires are measured and evaluated against a career growth standard during their first six months to three years of employment.

Outcomes Associated with Organizational Culture

Both managers and academic researchers believe that organizational culture can be a driver of employee attitudes and organizational effectiveness and performance. Several studies demonstrated that organizational culture was significantly correlated with employee behaviour and attitudes.[12] These results suggest that employees seem to prefer organizations that encourage people to interact and work with others in ways that assist them in satisfying their needs to grow and develop. Second, results from several studies revealed that the congruence between an individual's values and the organization's values was significantly associated with organizational commitment, job satisfaction, intention to quit, and turnover.[13]

You wouldn't say "The Gap" and "Brooks Brothers" in the same breath when shopping for apparel. The Gap is able to differentiate not only the culture of its customers, but also its salespeople. In fact, this culture became famous (or infamous) as a skit on *Saturday Night Live.*

Third, there is not one type of organizational culture that fuels financial performance. Finally, studies of mergers indicated that they frequently failed due to incompatible cultures. Due to the increasing number of corporate mergers around the world, and the conclusion that seven out of 10 mergers and acquisitions failed to meet their financial promise, managers within merged companies would be well advised to consider the role of organizational culture in creating a new organization.[14]

These research results underscore the significance of organizational culture. They also reinforce the need to learn more about the process of cultivating and changing an organization's culture. An organization's culture is not determined by fate. It is formed and shaped by the combination and integration of everyone who works in the organization.

How Cultures Are Embedded in Organizations

An organization's initial culture is an outgrowth of the founder's philosophy. For example, an achievement culture is likely to develop if the founder is an achievement-oriented individual driven by success. Over time, the original culture is either embedded as is or modified to fit the current environmental situation. Edgar Schein, an OB scholar, notes that embedding a culture involves a teaching process. That is, organizational members teach each other about the organization's preferred values, beliefs, expectations, and behaviours. This is accomplished by using one or more of the following mechanisms:[15]

1. *Formal statements of organizational philosophy, mission, vision, values, and materials used for recruiting, selection, and socialization.* Texas Instruments, for example, published a list of corporate values that includes integrity, innovation, and commitment.[16]

2. *The design of physical space, work environments, and buildings.*

3. *Slogans, language, acronyms, and sayings.* For example, Bank One promoted its desire to provide excellent client service through the slogan "whatever it takes." Employees are encouraged to do whatever it takes to exceed customer expectations.

4. *Deliberate role modelling, training programs, teaching, and coaching by managers and supervisors.* General Semiconductor implemented the "People Plus" program. It is an in-house leadership development and problem-solving training program that uses the company's mission and values as the springboard for creating individual development plans.[17]

5. *Explicit rewards, status symbols (e.g., titles), and promotion criteria.* Consider how Jack Welch, former CEO of General Electric, describes the reward system at General Electric: "The top 20% should be rewarded in the soul and wallet because they are the ones who make magic happen. Losing one of these people must be held up as a leadership sin," Welch says. The middle 70% should be energized to improve; the rest should be shown the door. Not getting rid of the 10% early "is not only a management failure, but false kindness as well—a form of cruelty," Welch says. They will wind up being fired eventually and "stranded" in midcareer.[18]

6. *Stories, legends, and myths about key people and events.*

7. *The organizational activities, processes, or outcomes that leaders pay attention to, measure, and control.* Dick Brown, CEO at Electronic Data Systems, believes that leaders get the behaviour they tolerate. He instituted the "performance call" to change the organization's culture from one that promoted individualism and information hoarding to one that supported teamwork and information sharing.

8. *Leader reactions to critical incidents and organizational crises.*

9. *The workflow and organizational structure.* Hierarchical structures are more likely to embed an orientation toward control and authority than a flatter organization.

10. *Organizational systems and procedures.* An organization can promote achievement and competition through the use of sales contests.

11. *Organizational goals and the associated criteria used for recruitment, selection, development, promotion, layoffs, and retirement of people.* PepsiCo

reinforces a high-performance culture by setting challenging goals. Executives strive to achieve a 15% increase in revenue per year.[19]

Embedding Organizational Culture through Socialization Processes and Mentoring

Organizational socialization is defined as "the process by which a person learns the values, norms, and required behaviours which permit him to participate as a member of the organization."[20] As previously discussed, organization socialization is a key mechanism used by organizations to embed their organizational cultures. In short, organizational socialization turns outsiders into fully functioning insiders by promoting and reinforcing the organization's core values and beliefs.

> **Organizational socialization**
>
> Process by which employees learn an organization's values, norms, and required behaviours.

Mentoring is defined as the process of forming and maintaining intensive and lasting developmental relationships between a variety of developers (i.e., people who provide career and psychosocial support) and a junior person (the protégé).[21] Mentoring can serve to embed an organization's culture through creating a sense of unity by promoting the acceptance of the organization's core values throughout the organization. The socialization aspect of mentoring also promotes a sense of membership. Mentoring will be discussed in more detail later in this chapter.

> **Mentoring**
>
> Process of forming and maintaining developmental relationships between a mentor and a junior person.

A Three-Phase Model of Organizational Socialization

One's first year in a complex organization can be confusing. There is a constant swirl of new faces, strange jargon, conflicting expectations, and apparently unrelated events. Some organizations treat new members in a rather haphazard, sink-or-swim manner. More typically, though, the socialization process is characterized by a sequence of three identifiable steps.[22]

As illustrated in Figure 13–3, the three phases of socialization are (1) anticipatory socialization, (2) encounter, and (3) change and acquisition. Each phase has its associated perceptual and social processes. The model also specifies behavioural and affective outcomes that can be used to judge how well an individual has been socialized. The entire three-phase sequence may take from a few weeks to a year to complete, depending on individual differences and the complexity of the situation.

Phase I: Anticipatory Socialization   Organizational socialization begins *before* the individual actually joins the organization. Anticipatory socialization information comes from many sources. For example, McDonald's recruiting advertisements promise flexible hours and a friendly work environment. All of this information— whether formal or informal, accurate or inaccurate—helps the individual anticipate organizational realities. Unrealistic expectations about the nature of the work, pay, and promotions are often formulated during phase 1.

Phase 2: Encounter   This second phase begins when the employment contract has been signed. It is a time for surprise and making sense as the newcomer enters unfamiliar territory. Many companies use a combination of orientation and training programs to socialize employees during the encounter phase.

FIGURE 13–3   A Model of Organizational Socialization

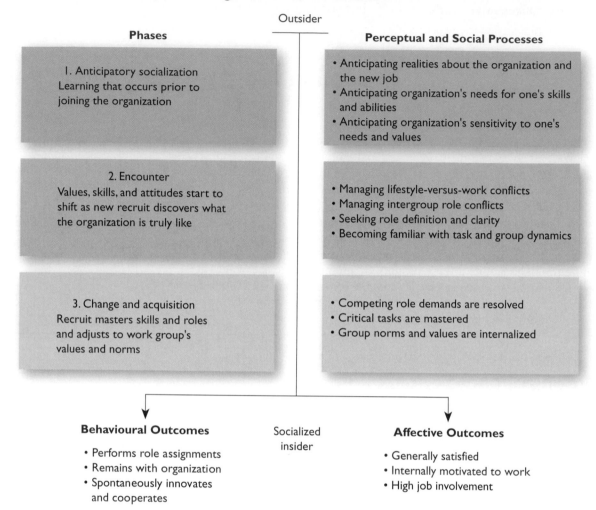

Source: Adapted from material in D C Feldman, "The Multiple Socialization of Organization Members," *Academy of Management Review*, April 1981, pp 309–18.

Phase 3: Change and Acquisition   Mastery of important tasks and resolution of role conflict signals the beginning of this final phase of the socialization process. Those who do not make the transition to phase 3 leave voluntarily or involuntarily or become isolated from social networks within the organization. Senior executives frequently play a direct role in the change and acquisition phase.

Practical Application of Socialization Research

Past research suggests four practical guidelines for managing organizational socialization:

1. Managers should avoid a haphazard, sink-or-swim approach to organizational socialization because formalized socialization tactics positively affect new hires.
2. Managers play a key role during the encounter phase. Managers need to help new hires integrate within the organizational culture.

3. The organization can benefit by training new employees to use proactive socialization behaviours.
4. Managers should pay attention to the socialization of diverse employees.

Mentoring

Research demonstrates that mentored employees perform better on the job and experience more rapid career advancement. Mentored employees also report higher job and career satisfaction and working on more challenging job assignments.[23]

Functions of Mentoring   OB researcher Kathy Kram identified two general functions—career and psychosocial—of the mentoring process. Five *career functions* that enhanced career development were sponsorship, exposure-and-visibility, coaching, protection, and challenging assignments. Four *psychosocial functions* were role modelling, acceptance-and-confirmation, counselling, and friendship. The psychosocial functions clarified the participants' identities and enhanced their feelings of competence.[24]

Getting the Most Out of Mentoring   In order to get the full benefits from a mentoring program:[25]

1. Train mentors and protégés on how to best use career and psychosocial mentoring.
2. Use both formal and informal mentoring, but do not dictate mentoring relationships.
3. Diverse employees should be informed about the benefits and drawbacks associated with establishing mentoring relationships with individuals of similar and different gender and race.
4. Women should be encouraged to mentor others. Perceived barriers need to be addressed and eliminated for this to occur.
5. Increase the number of diverse mentors in high-ranking positions.

A Model of Societal and Organizational Cultures

Societal culture involves "shared meanings" that generally remain below the threshold of conscious awareness because they involve *taken-for-granted assumptions* about how one should perceive, think, act, and feel.[26] In Canada, our national culture is based on assumptions that social justice, peace, and multiculturalism are important and desirable foundations for our country's cultural activities and legal system. We have subcultures that vary from East Coast to West Coast, and between French-speaking Canadians and English-speaking Canadians.

Societal culture
Socially derived, taken-for-granted assumptions about how to think and act.

As illustrated in Figure 13–4, culture influences organizational behaviour in two ways. Employees bring their societal culture to work with them in the form of customs and language. Organizational culture, a by-product of societal culture, in turn affects the individual's values/ethics, attitudes, assumptions, and expectations.[27] The term *societal* culture is used here instead of national culture because the boundaries of many modern nation-states were not drawn along cultural lines. The former Soviet Union, for example, included 15 republics and more than 100 ethnic nationalities, many with their

FIGURE 13–4   Cultural Influences on Organizational Behaviour

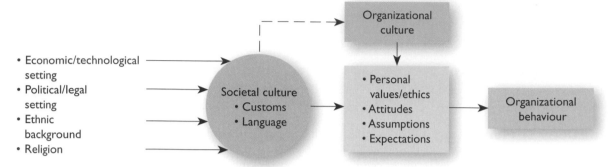

Source: Adapted in part from B J Punnett and S Withane, "Hofstede's Value Survey Module: To Embrace or Abandon?" in *Advances in International Comparative Management*, vol 5, ed S B Prasad (Greenwich, CT: JAI Press, 1990), pp 69–89.

own distinct language.[28] Meanwhile, English-speaking Canadians in Vancouver are culturally closer to Americans in Seattle than to their French-speaking compatriots in Quebec. Societal culture is shaped by the various environmental factors listed in the left-hand side of Figure 13–4.

Once inside the organization's sphere of influence, the individual is further affected by the *organization's* culture. Mixing of societal and organizational cultures can produce interesting dynamics in multinational companies. For example, with French and American employees working side by side at General Electric's medical imaging production facility in Waukesha, Wisconsin, unit head Claude Benchimol has witnessed some culture shock:

The French are surprised the American parking lots empty out as early as 5 PM; the Americans are surprised the French don't start work at 8 AM. Benchimol feels the French are more talkative and candid. Americans have more of a sense of hierarchy and are less likely to criticize. But they may be growing closer to the French. Says Benchimol: "It's taken a year to get across the idea that we are all entitled to say what we don't like to become more productive and work better."[29]

To Hire or Not to Hire?

Imagine that you manage a company located in Pakistan that has been recently purchased by a large multinational corporation (MNC). Your company has long adopted a culturally accepted Pakistani practice of guaranteeing a job to at least one of each of your employees' children. This practice reflects a deep moral concern for employees' families. However, now that your company has been purchased by the MNC, you are expected to enforce a corporate nepotism policy prohibiting hiring based solely on personal or family relationships. Both the Pakistani employment practices and the MNC's anti-nepotism policy are based on moral values that are easily justified. The Pakistani hiring practice is linked to strong family values, while the corporate policy is based on moral values of fairness and equity.

You Decide . . .

What should you do?

Same company, same company culture, yet GE's French and American co-workers have different attitudes about time, hierarchy, and communication. They are the products of different societal cultures.[30]

When managing people at work, the individual's societal culture, the organizational culture, and any interaction between the two need to be taken into consideration. For example, American workers' cultural orientation toward quality improvement differs significantly from the Japanese cultural pattern:

Japanese Firms Discontinue Jobs-for-Life Philosophy

Sony President Nobuyuki Idei must think he's in Silicon Valley. How does he rev up his staff and improve flagging profits? By tossing the whole organization chart in the air, pulling vagrant subsidiaries back into the parent company, and committing to scrapping 20% of his factories by 2003 while escorting some 17,000 workers to the door.

Idei's 1999 restructuring proposal dashed most hopes in Japan that the country's jobs-for-life policy would survive the recession. Facing hefty losses at the close of Japan's fiscal year, companies have been falling over each other to announce restructurings. NEC Corp. plans to slash 15,000 jobs worldwide over three years. Parts maker Omron Corp.'s payroll will shrink by 2,000. Japan's top 15 banks have agreed to axe almost 20,000 jobs by 2004.

Source: Excerpted from I M Kunii, E Thornton, and J Rae-Dupree, "Sony's Shake-Up," *Business Week*, March 22, 1999, p 52.

Unlike Japanese workers, Americans aren't interested in making small step-by-step improvements to increase quality. They want to achieve the breakthrough, the impossible dream. The way to motivate them: Ask for the big leap, rather than for tiny steps.[31]

Forces of Change

Organizations encounter many different forces for change. These forces come from external sources outside the organization and from internal sources. Awareness of the forces of change can help managers determine when they should consider implementing an organizational change.

External Forces

External forces for change originate outside the organization. Because these forces have global effects, they may cause an organization to question the essence of what business it is in and the process by which products and services are produced. There are four key external forces for change: demographic characteristics, technological advancements, market changes, and social and political pressures.

Demographic Characteristics   Organizations need to effectively manage diversity if they are to receive maximum contribution and commitment from employees. Consider the implications associated with hiring the 80 million people dubbed the Net or Echo-Boom Generation—people born between 1977 and 1997.

> Employers will have to face the new realities of the Net Generation's culture and values, and what it wants from work if they expect to attract and retain those talents and align them with corporate goals. . . . The new wave of 80 million young people entering the workforce during the next 20 years are technologically equipped and, therefore, armed with the most powerful tools for business. That makes their place in history unique: No previous generation has grown up understanding, using, and expanding on such a pervasive instrument as the PC.[32]

The organizational challenge will be to motivate and utilize this talented pool of employees to its maximum potential.

Technological Advancements Both manufacturing and service organizations are increasingly using technology as a means to improve productivity and market competitiveness. Development and use of information technologies is probably one of the biggest forces for change. Experts also predict that E-business will continue to create evolutionary change in organizations around the world.

Market Changes The emergence of a global economy is forcing companies to change the way they do business. For example, many Japanese companies are having to discontinue their jobs-for-life philosophy because of increased international competition.

Social and Political Pressures These forces are created by social and political events. For example, tobacco companies are experiencing a lot of pressure to alter the way they market their products. Political events can create substantial change. For instance, the collapse of the Berlin Wall and communism in Russia created many new business opportunities.

Internal Forces

Internal forces for change come from inside the organization. These forces can be subtle, such as low job satisfaction, or can manifest in outward signs, such as low productivity or high turnover and conflict. Internal forces for change come from both human resource problems and managerial behaviour/decisions. The development of Sony's Playstation illustrates this. Sony's Ken Kutaragi was playing with his daughter's Nintendo (Sony's bitter rival) in the mid-1980s. He realized it would be much better with a Sony digital audio chip. He started secret negotiations with Nintendo. When his bosses found out, they were understandably furious. But he had one far-sighted champion in the then-president (now CEO and chair) Norio Ogha, who protected him from their wrath and mandated going ahead with the project. Playstation is today a breakthrough product for Sony.[33]

Models of Planned Change

North American managers are criticized for emphasizing short-term, quick-fix solutions to organizational problems. When applied to organizational change, this approach is doomed from the start. Quick-fix solutions do not really solve underlying causes of problems and they have little staying power. Researchers and managers alike have thus tried to identify effective ways to manage the change process. This section reviews three models of planned change—Lewin's change model, a systems model of change, and Kotter's eight steps for leading organizational change—and organizational development.

Lewin's Change Model

Most theories of organizational change originated from the landmark work of social psychologist Kurt Lewin. Lewin developed a three-stage model of planned change which explained how to initiate, manage, and stabilize the change process.[34] The three stages are unfreezing, changing, and refreezing.

Unfreezing The focus of this stage is to create the motivation to change. Managers can begin the unfreezing process by disconfirming the usefulness or appropriateness of employees' present behaviours or attitudes. In other words, employees need to become

dissatisfied with the old way of doing things. Benchmarking is a technique that can be used to help unfreeze an organization. **Benchmarking** "describes the overall process by which a company compares its performance with that of other companies, then learns how the strongest-performing companies achieve their results."[35]

> **Benchmarking**
>
> Process by which a company compares its performance with that of high-performing organizations.

Changing   Because change involves learning, this stage entails providing employees with new information, new behavioural models, or new ways of looking at things. The purpose is to help employees learn new concepts or points of view. Consider, for example, the organizational changes implemented by KPMG Consulting as it transforms itself from an organization run by a partnership to one that is publicly held and focuses on meeting financial goals:

> The massive mahogany desks and expansive offices once occupied by KPMG's venerated partners have given way to cookie-cutter work spaces, pint-size offices, and managing directors. . . . KPMG Consulting has already laid off 800 of its 10,000 employees in the past 16 months, for which it will take a $15 million to $20 million charge. . . . Those who are left have had to adapt to an environment in which the focus is firmly on the numbers. Instead of measuring profitability once a year—standard operating procedure in the partnership—the company now monitors financials constantly. Every Friday, Senior Vice President Kenneth C Taormina grills his sales force on every would-be client: "I go through every single deal [asking] 'What do we need to get it done?' " Even the office kitty that partners dipped into freely for moral-building activities such as staff dinners is now under scrutiny.[36]

Directors at KPMG are clearly trying to get employees to become more customer focused and cost conscious. During the change process like that at KPMG, organizations use role models, mentors, consultants, benchmarking results, and training to facilitate change. Experts recommend that it is best to convey the idea that change is a continuous learning process rather than a one-time event.

Refreezing   Change is stabilized during refreezing by helping employees integrate the changed behaviour or attitude into their normal way of doing things. This is accomplished by first giving employees the chance to exhibit the new behaviours or attitudes. Once exhibited, positive reinforcement is used to reinforce the desired change. Additional coaching and modelling also are used at this point to reinforce the stability of the change.

Kotter's Eight Steps for Leading Organizational Change

John Kotter, an expert in leadership and change management, believes that organizational change typically fails because senior management makes a host of implementation errors. Kotter recommends that organizations should follow eight sequential steps to overcome these implementation problems (see Table 13–1).[37]

These steps also subsume Lewin's model of change. The first four steps represent Lewin's "unfreezing" stage. Steps 5, 6, and 7 represent "changing," and step 8 corresponds to "refreezing." The value of Kotter's steps is that it provides specific recommendations about behaviours that managers need to exhibit to successfully lead organizational change. It is important to remember that Kotter's research reveals that it is ineffective to skip steps and that successful organizational change is 70% to 90% leadership and only 10% to 30% management. Senior managers are thus advised to focus on leading rather than managing change.[38]

TABLE 13–1   Steps to Leading Organizational Change

Step	Description
1. Establish a sense of urgency	Unfreeze the organization by creating a compelling reason for why change is needed.
2. Create the guiding coalition	Create a cross-functional, cross-level group of people with enough power to lead the change.
3. Develop a vision and strategy	Create a vision and strategic plan to guide the change process.
4. Communicate the change vision	Create and implement a communication strategy that consistently communicates the new vision and strategic plan.
5. Empower broad-based action	Eliminate barriers to change, and use target elements of change to transform the organization. Encourage risk taking and creative problem solving.
6. Generate short-term wins	Plan for and create short-term "wins" or improvements. Recognize and reward people who contribute to the wins.
7. Consolidate gains and produce more change	The guiding coalition uses credibility from short-term wins to create more change. Additional people are brought into the change process as change cascades throughout the organization. Attempts are made to reinvigorate the change process.
8. Anchor new approaches in the culture	Reinforce the changes by highlighting connections between new behaviours and processes and organizational success. Develop methods to ensure leadership development and succession.

Source: The steps were developed by J P Kotter, *Leading Change* (Boston: Harvard Business School Press, 1996).

Organization Development

Organization development (OD) is an applied field of study and practice. A pair of OD experts defined **organization development** as follows:

> Organization development is concerned with helping managers plan change in organizing and managing people that will develop requisite commitment, coordination, and competence. Its purpose is to enhance both the effectiveness of organizations and the well-being of their members through planned interventions in the organization's human processes, structures, and systems, using knowledge of behavioural science and its intervention methods.[39]

As you can see from this definition, OD constitutes a set of techniques or interventions that are used to implement organizational change. These techniques or interventions apply to each of the change models discussed in this section. For example, OD is used during Lewin's "changing" stage. It also is used to identify and implement targeted elements of change within the systems model of change. Finally, OD might be used during Kotter's steps 1, 3, 5, 6, and 7. In this section, we briefly review the four identifying characteristics of OD and its research and practical implications.[40]

OD Involves Profound Change   Change agents using OD generally desire deep and long-lasting improvement. OD consultant Warner Burke, for example, who strives for fundamental *cultural* change, wrote: "By fundamental change, as opposed to fixing a problem or improving a procedure, I mean that some significant aspect of an organization's culture will never be the same."[41]

OD Is Value Loaded   Owing to the fact that OD is rooted partially in humanistic psychology, many OD consultants carry certain values or biases into the client organization. They prefer cooperation over conflict, self-control over institutional control, and democratic and participative management over autocratic management. In addition to OD being driven by a consultant's values, some OD practitioners now believe that there is a broader "value perspective" that should underlie any organizational change. Specifically, OD should always be customer focused. This approach implies that organizational interventions should be aimed at helping to satisfy customers' needs and thereby provide enhanced value of an organization's products and services.

OD Is a Diagnosis/Prescription Cycle   OD theorists and practitioners have long adhered to a medical model of organization. Like medical doctors, internal and external OD consultants approach the "sick" organization, "diagnose" its ills, "prescribe" and implement an intervention, and "monitor" progress.

OD Is Process Oriented   Ideally, OD consultants focus on the form and not the content of behavioural and administrative dealings. For example, product design engineers and market researchers might be coached on how to communicate more effectively with one another without the consultant knowing the technical details of their conversations. In addition to communication, OD specialists focus on other processes, including problem solving, decision making, conflict handling, trust, power sharing, and career development.

OD Research and Practical Implications   There are three practical implications derived from OD research. First, planned organization change works. However, management and change agents are advised to rely on multifaceted interventions. As indicated elsewhere in this book, goal setting, feedback, recognition and rewards, training, participation, and challenging job design have good track records relative to improving performance and satisfaction. Second, change programs are more successful when they are geared toward meeting both short-term and long-term results. Managers should not engage in organizational change for the sake of change. Change efforts should produce positive results.[42] Finally, organizational change is more likely to succeed when top management is truly committed to the change process and the desired goals of the change program. This is particularly true when organizations pursue large-scale transformation.

Understanding and Managing Resistance to Change

We are all creatures of habit. It generally is difficult for people to try new ways of doing things. It is precisely because of this basic human characteristic that most employees do not have enthusiasm for change in the workplace. Rare is the manager who does not have several stories about carefully cultivated changes that died on the vine because of resistance to change. It is important for managers to learn to manage resistance because failed change efforts are costly. Costs include decreased employee loyalty, lowered probability of achieving corporate goals, waste of money and resources, and difficulty in fixing the failed change effort. This section examines employee resistance to change and practical ways of dealing with the problem.

Why People Resist Change in the Workplace

No matter how technically or administratively perfect a proposed change may be, people make or break it. Individual and group behaviour following an organizational change can take many forms. The extremes range from acceptance to active resistance. Resistance to change is an emotional/behavioural response to real or imagined threats to an established work routine. Resistance can be as subtle as passive resignation and as overt as deliberate sabotage. Let us now consider the reasons employees resist change in the first place. Ten of the leading reasons are listed here:[43]

1. *An individual's predisposition toward change.* This predisposition is highly personal and deeply ingrained. It is an outgrowth of how one learns to handle change and ambiguity as a child. While some people are distrustful and suspicious of change, others see change as a situation requiring flexibility, patience, and understanding.[44]

2. *Surprise and fear of the unknown.* When innovative or radically different changes are introduced without warning, affected employees become fearful of the implications. Grapevine rumours fill the void created by a lack of official announcements. Harvard's Rosabeth Moss Kanter recommends appointing a transition manager charged with keeping all relevant parties adequately informed.[45]

3. *Climate of mistrust.* Trust involves reciprocal faith in others' intentions and behaviour. Mutual mistrust can doom to failure an otherwise well-conceived change. Mistrust encourages secrecy, which begets deeper mistrust. Managers who trust their employees make the change process an open, honest, and par-

Equity or Else

The movement to change the Canadian workforce by increasing its diversity has been around for a long time with no one to enforce it. The federal Employment Equity Act was introduced in 1986 as a way of requiring companies to increase the workforce representation of four designated groups—women, aboriginal people, visible minorities, and people with disabilities. The law caused a furor of resistance. Anti-equity groups sprung up across the country claiming the legislation would lead to reverse discrimination. Ontario premier Mike Harris based his 1995 election campaign in part on ditching the province's own employment equity law. Employers screamed they'd be forced to hire unqualified workers to satisfy US-style quotas. As it turned out, however, the critics didn't have much to worry about, because the federal government had neglected to put anyone in charge of enforcing the law.

That changed in 1996 when the Canadian Human Rights Commission (CHRC) was charged with enforcing employment equity legislation. The Employment Equity Branch of the CHRC has audited hundreds of organizations, looking at everything from whether the workplace is wheelchair accessible to how and where the organization advertises its job postings. Few organizations are in compliance on their first try. If a company is not in compliance, or if employees complain, the CHRC has the authority to send its case to a tribunal, which can impose strict guidelines on hiring and promotion. One of these non-compliant organizations, Health Canada, lost its case, and now whenever a job comes up, at least one candidate must be a member of a visible minority.

Changing the way organizations recruit is relatively easy. Changing attitudes isn't. "That's one of the toughest barriers to admit, and one of the biggest ones to overcome," says Nicole Chénier-Cullen, Director-General of the Employment Equity Branch of the CHRC, "because it's ingrained in the workforce." That's where consultants come in. They can offer training programs that address discrimination, diversity, and sexual harassment. "I'm sympathetic to some employers who are overwhelmed by the legislation," says consultant Renée Brazil-Jones. "We can't force people to change their beliefs, but we can force them to change their behaviour."

The Bank of Montreal decided to reduce resistance on the part of their managers by hitting them in their wallets. A portion of senior managers' bonuses is tied directly to whether they reach their hiring and retention goals for members of the four designated groups. "The message we want to send is that we are looking for top talent, and we'll look for it wherever we can find it," says Lesya Balych, vice-president of workplace equality. "And now people are really going to pay very close attention to these goals."

Source: D Calleja, "Equity or Else," *Canadian Business*, March 19, 2001, pp 29–34.

ticipative affair. Employees who, in turn, trust management are more willing to expend extra effort and take chances with something different.

4. *Fear of failure.* Intimidating changes on the job can cause employees to doubt their capabilities. Self-doubt erodes self-confidence and cripples personal growth and development.

5. *Loss of status and/or job security.* Administrative and technological changes that threaten to alter power bases or eliminate jobs generally trigger strong resistance. For example, most corporate restructuring involves the elimination of managerial jobs. One should not be surprised when middle managers

resist restructuring and participative management programs that reduce their authority and status.

6. *Peer pressure.* Someone who is not directly affected by a change may actively resist it to protect the interest of his or her friends and co-workers.

7. *Disruption of cultural traditions and/or group relationships.* Whenever individuals are transferred, promoted, or reassigned, cultural and group dynamics are thrown into disequilibrium.

8. *Personality conflicts.* Just as a friend can get away with telling us something we would resent hearing from an adversary, the personalities of change agents can breed resistance.

9. *Lack of tact and/or poor timing.* Undue resistance can occur because changes are introduced in an insensitive manner or at an awkward time.

10. *Nonreinforcing reward systems.* Individuals resist when they do not foresee positive rewards for changing. For example, an employee is unlikely to support a change effort that is perceived as requiring him or her to work longer with more pressure.

Alternative Strategies for Overcoming Resistance to Change

Before recommending specific approaches to overcome resistance, there are four key conclusions that should be kept in mind. First, an organization must be ready for change. Just as a table must be set before you can eat, so must an organization be ready for change before it can be effective.[46] Second, organizational change is less successful when top management fails to keep employees informed about the process of change.

Third, do not assume that people are consciously resisting change. Managers are encouraged to use a systems model of change to identify the obstacles that are affecting the implementation process. Fourth, employees' perceptions or interpretations of a change significantly affect resistance. Employees are less likely to resist when they perceive that the benefits of a change overshadow the personal costs. At a minimum then, managers are advised to (1) provide as much information as possible to employees about the change, (2) inform employees about the reasons/rationale for the change, (3) conduct meetings to address employees' questions regarding the change, and (4) provide employees the opportunity to discuss how the proposed change might affect them.[47] These recommendations underscore the importance of communicating with employees throughout the process of change.

In addition to communication, employee participation in the change process is another generic approach for reducing resistance. That said, however, organizational change experts have criticized the tendency to treat participation as a cure-all for resistance to change. They prefer a contingency approach because resistance can take many forms and, furthermore, because situational factors vary (see Table 13–2). As seen in Table 13–2, Participation + Involvement does have its place, but it takes time that is not always available. Each of the other five methods in Table 13–2 has its situational niche, advantages, and drawbacks. In short, there is no universal strategy for overcoming resistance to change. Managers need a complete repertoire of change strategies.

Six Strategies for Overcoming Resistance to Change   TABLE 13–2

Approach	Commonly Used in Situations	Advantages	Drawbacks
Education + Communication	Where there is a lack of information or inaccurate information and analysis.	Once persuaded, people will often help with the implementation of the change.	Can be very time consuming if lots of people are involved.
Participation + Involvement	Where the initiators do not have all the information they need to design the change and where others have considerable power to resist.	People who participate will be committed to implementing change, and any relevant information they have will be integrated into the change plan.	Can be very time consuming if participators design an inappropriate change.
Facilitation + Support	Where people are resisting because of adjustment problems.	No other approach works as well with adjustment problems.	Can be time consuming, expensive, and still fail.
Negotiation + Agreement	Where someone or some group will clearly lose out in a change and where that group has considerable power to resist.	Sometimes it is a relatively easy way to avoid major resistance.	Can be too expensive in many cases if it alerts others to negotiate for compliance.
Manipulation + Co-optation	Where other tactics will not work or are too expensive.	It can be a relatively quick and inexpensive solution to resistance problems.	Can lead to future problems if people feel manipulated.
Explicit + Implicit coercion	Where speed is essential and where the change initiators possess considerable power.	It is speedy and can overcome any kind of resistance.	Can be risky if it leaves people mad at the initiators.

Source: Reprinted by permission of the *Harvard Business Review*. An exhibit from "Choosing Strategies for Change" by J P Kotter and L A Schlesinger (March/April 1979). Copyright © 1979 by the President and Fellows of Harvard College; all rights reserved.

summary of key concepts

- *Discuss the layers and functions of organizational culture.* The three layers of organizational culture are observable artifacts, espoused values, and basic underlying assumptions. Four functions of organizational culture are organizational identity, collective commitment, social system stability, and sense-making device.

- *Summarize the methods used by organizations to embed their cultures.* Embedding a culture amounts to teaching employees about the organization's preferred values, beliefs, expectations, and behaviours. This is accomplished by using one or more of the following 11 mechanisms: (a) formal statements of organizational philosophy, mission, vision, values, and materials used for recruiting, selection, and socialization; (b) the design of physical space, work environments, and buildings; (c) slogans, language, acronyms and sayings; (d) deliberate role modelling, training programs, teaching and coaching by managers and supervisors; (e) explicit rewards, status symbols, and promotion criteria; (f) stories, legends, and myths about key people and events; (g) the organizational activities, processes or outcomes that leaders pay attention to, measure and control; (h) leader reactions to critical incidents and organizational crises; (i) the workflow and organizational structure; (j) organizational systems and procedures; and (k) organizational goals and associated criteria used for recruitment, selection, development, promotion, layoffs, and retirement of people.

- *Describe the three phases in organizational socialization.* The three phases are anticipatory socialization, encounter, and change and acquisition. Anticipatory socialization begins before an individual actually joins the organization. The encounter phase begins when the employment contract has been signed. The third phase involves the period in which employees master important tasks and resolve any role conflicts.

- *Discuss the external and internal forces that create the need for organizational change.* Organizations encounter both external and internal forces for change. There are four key external forces for change: demographic characteristics, technological advancements, market changes, and social and political pressures. Internal forces for change come from both human resource problems and managerial behaviour/decisions.

- *Describe Lewin's change model and the systems model of change.* Lewin developed a three-stage model of planned change that explained how to initiate, manage, and stabilize the change process. The three stages were *unfreezing*, which entails creating the motivation to change, *changing*, and stabilizing change through *refreezing*. A systems model of change takes a big picture perspective of change. It focuses on the interaction among the key components of change. The three main components of change are inputs, target elements of change, and outputs. The target elements of change represent the components of an organization that may be changed. They include organizing arrangements, social factors, methods, goals, and people.

- *Discuss the 10 reasons employees resist change.* Resistance to change is an emotional/behavioural response to real or imagined threats to an established work routine. Ten reasons employees resist change are (a) an individual's predisposition toward change, (b) surprise and fear of the unknown, (c) climate of mistrust, (d) fear of failure, (e) loss of status and/or job security, (f) peer pressure, (g) disruption of cultural traditions and/or group relationships, (h) personality conflicts, (i) lack of tact and/or poor timing, and (j) nonreinforcing reward systems.

- *Identify alternative strategies for overcoming resistance to change.* Organizations must be ready for change. Assuming an organization is ready for change, the alternative strategies for overcoming resistance to change are education + communication, participation + involvement, facilitation + support, negotiation + agreement, manipulation + co-operation, and explicit + implict coercion. Each has its situational appropriateness and advantages and drawbacks.

key terms

discussion questions

1. What type of organizational culture exists within your current or most recent employer? Explain.

2. Why is socialization essential to organizational success?

3. How would you describe Canadian culture to a stranger from another country?

4. Which of the external forces for change do you believe will prompt the greatest change between now and the year 2010?

5. What are some useful methods that can be used to refreeze an organizational change?

6. Have you ever resisted a change at work? Explain the circumstances and your thinking at the time.

internet exercises

www.hp.com

1. Organizational Culture

This chapter focused on the role of values and beliefs in forming an organization's culture. We also discussed how cultures are embedded and reinforced through socialization and mentoring. The topic of organizational culture is big business on the Internet. Many companies use their Web pages to describe their mission, vision, and corporate values and beliefs. There also are many consulting companies that advertise how they help organizations to change their cultures. The purpose of this exercise is for you to obtain information pertaining to the organizational culture for two different companies. You can go about this task by very simply searching on the key words "organizational culture" or "corporate vision and values." This search will identify numerous companies for you to use in answering the following questions. You may want to select a company for this exercise that you would like to work for in the future.

QUESTIONS
1. What are the organization's espoused values and beliefs?
2. What methods appear to have been used to embed culture in these organizations?

www.webhome.idirect.com/~kehamilt/ob14.html

2. How Comfortable are You With Change?

Resistance to change is a major challenge for managers. It can be helpful to assess both your own and your employees' level of resistance to (or acceptance of) change before implementing change in an organization. Go to the Web site **www.webhome.idirect.com/~kehamilt/ob14.html** for a summary of knowledge regarding organizational change. At the bottom of the page, click on the online quiz to find out how resistant you are to change (**www.webhome .idirect.com/~kehamilt/obchange.html**). Answer the 16 questions and click on "Score the Exercise" to find out your score. The higher your score, the higher your level of comfort with change.

QUESTIONS
1. What was your score? What does it tell you about your level of acceptance of change?
2. If your score was low, indicating resistance to change, what might you do to try to become more open to change? Explain.
3. If your score was high, indicating comfort with change, think about how this might make it difficult for you to deal with others who fear and resist change. How might you try to understand their point of view? Explain.

experiential exercises

1. Assessing an Organization's Readiness for Change

Instructions

Use this survey to evaluate a company that you worked for or are familiar with that undertook a change effort. Circle the number that best represents your opinions about the company being evaluated.

3 = Yes
2 = Somewhat
1 = No

1. Is the change effort being sponsored by a senior-level executive (CEO, COO)?	3	2	1
2. Are all levels of management committed to the change?	3	2	1
3. Does the organization culture encourage risk taking?	3	2	1
4. Does the organization culture encourage and reward continuous improvement?	3	2	1
5. Has senior management clearly articulated the need for change?	3	2	1
6. Has senior management presented a clear vision of a positive future?	3	2	1
7. Does the organization use specific measures to assess business performance?	3	2	1
8. Does the change effort support other major activities going on in the organization?	3	2	1
9. Has the organization benchmarked itself against world-class companies?	3	2	1
10. Do all employees understand the customers' needs?	3	2	1
11. Does the organization reward individuals and/or teams for being innovative and for looking for root causes of organizational problems?	3	2	1
12. Is the organization flexible and cooperative?	3	2	1
13. Does management effectively communicate with all levels of the organization?	3	2	1
14. Has the organization successfully implemented other change programs?	3	2	1
15. Do employees take personal responsibility for their behaviour?	3	2	1
16. Does the organization make decisions quickly?	3	2	1

Total score: _____

Arbitrary Norms

40–48 = High readiness for change
 4–39 = Moderate readiness for change
16–23 = Low readiness for change

QUESTION

1. Did the level of readiness for change relate to the success of the change effort?

Source: Based on the discussion contained in T A Stewart, "Rate Your Readiness to Change," *Fortune*, February 7, 1994, pp 106–10.

2. Cross-Cultural Awareness

Introduction

In this exercise you are asked to rank your work goals and then compare your rankings with international samples from the United States, Britain, Germany, and Japan. The objective is to understand that people from different countries and cultures want different things from their workplace.

Instructions

Below is a list of 11 goals that are potentially obtainable in the workplace. In terms of your own personal preferences, rank these goals from 1 to 11 (1 being the most important and 11 is the least important). After you have ranked all 11 work goals, compare your list with the various national samples which follow under the heading Survey Results. These national samples represent cross sections of employees from all levels and all major occupational groups. Please complete your ranking now before looking at the national samples.

Ranking

How important are the following in your work life?

Rank	Work Goals
_____	A lot of opportunity to learn new things
_____	Good interpersonal relations (supervisors, co-workers)
_____	Good opportunity for upgrading or promotion
_____	Convenient work hours
_____	A lot of variety
_____	Interesting work (work that you really like)
_____	Good job security
_____	A good match between your job requirements and your abilities and experience
_____	Good pay
_____	Good physical working conditions (such as lighting, temperature, cleanliness, low noise level, etc.)
_____	A lot of autonomy (you decide how to do your work)

Survey Results

Ranking of Work Goals By Country

1 = Most Important; 11 = Least Important

Work Goals	United States	Britain	Germany	Japan
Interesting work	1	1	3	2
Pay	2	2	1	5
Job security	3	3	2	4
Match between person and job	4	6	5	1
Opportunity to learn	5	8	9	7
Variety	6	7	6*	9
Interpersonal relations	7	4	4	6
Autonomy	8	10	8	3
Convenient work hours	9	5	6*	8
Opportunity for promotion	10	11	10	11
Working conditions	11	9	11	10

*Tie

QUESTIONS FOR DISCUSSION

1. Which national profile of work goals most closely matches your own? Is this what you expected or not?
2. Are you surprised by any of the rankings in the four national samples? Explain.
3. What types of motivational/leadership adjustments would a manager make when moving between the four countries?

Source: I Harpaz, "The Importance of Work Goals: An International Perspective," *Journal of International Business Studies*, First Quarter 1990, p 79.

personal awareness and growth exercises

1. Have You Been Adequately Socialized?

Instructions

Complete the following survey items by considering either your current job or one you held in the past. If you have never worked, identify a friend who is working and ask that individual to complete the questionnaire for his or her organization. Read each item and circle your response by using the rating scale shown below. Compute your total score by adding up your responses and compare it to the scoring norms.

	Strongly Disagree	Disagree	Neutral	Agree	Strongly Agree
1. I have been through a set of training experiences that are specifically designed to give newcomers a thorough knowledge of job-related skills.	1	2	3	4	5
2. This organization puts all newcomers through the same set of learning experiences.	1	2	3	4	5
3. I did not perform any of my normal job responsibilities until I was thoroughly familiar with departmental procedures and work methods.	1	2	3	4	5
4. There is a clear pattern in the way one role leads to another, or one job assignment leads to another, in this organization.	1	2	3	4	5
5. I can predict my future career path in this organization by observing other people's experiences.	1	2	3	4	5
6. Almost all of my colleagues have been supportive of me personally.	1	2	3	4	5
7. My colleagues have gone out of their way to help me adjust to this organization.	1	2	3	4	5
8. I received much guidance from experienced organizational members as to how I should perform my job.	1	2	3	4	5

Total Score _____

Scoring Norms

8–18 = Low socialization
19–29 = Moderate socialization
30–40 = High socialization

Source: Adapted from survey items excerpted from D Cable and C Parsons, "Socialization Tactics and Person-Organization Fit," *Personnel Psychology*, Spring 2001, pp 1–23.

2. Creating Personal Change through Force-Field Analysis

Objectives

1. To apply force-field analysis to a behaviour or situation you would like to change.
2. To receive feedback on your strategies for bringing about change.

Introduction

The theory of force-field analysis is based on the premise that people resist change because of counteracting positive and negative forces. Positive forces for change are called *thrusters*. They propel people to accept change and modify their behaviour. In contrast, *counterthrusters* or *resistors* are negative forces that motivate an individual to maintain the status quo. People frequently fail to change because they experience equal amounts of positive and negative forces to change.

Force-field analysis is a technique used to facilitate change by first identifying the thrusters and resistors that exist in a specific situation. To minimize resistance to change, it is generally recommended to first reduce or remove the negative forces to change. Removing counterthrusters should create increased pressure for an individual to change in the desired direction. Managers can also further increase motivation to change by following up the reduction of resistors with an increase in the number of positive thrusters of change.

Instructions

Your instructor will pair you up with another student. The two of you will serve as a team that evaluates the completeness of each other's force-field analysis and recommendations. Once the team is assembled, each individual should independently complete the Force-Field Analysis Form presented after these instructions. Once both of you complete this activity, one team member should present results from steps 2 through 5 from the five-step Force-Field Analysis Form. The partner should then evaluate the results by considering the following questions with his or her team member:

1. Are there any additional thrusters and counterthrusters that should be listed? Add them to the list.
2. Do you agree with the "strength" evaluations of thrusters and counterthrusters in step 4? Ask your partner to share his or her rationale for the ratings. Modify the ratings as needed.
3. Examine the specific recommendations for change listed in step 5, and evaluate whether you think they will produce the desired changes. Be sure to consider whether the focal person has the ability to eliminate, reduce, or increase each thruster and counterthruster that is the basis for a specific recommendation. Are there any alternative strategies you can think of?
4. What is your overall evaluation of your partner's intervention strategy?

Then repeat this for the other partner.

FORCE-FIELD ANALYSIS FORM

Step 1

In the space provided, please identify a number of personal problems you would like to solve or aspects of your life you would like to change. Be as imaginative as possible. You are not limited to school situations. For example, you may want to consider your work environment if you are currently employed, family situation, interpersonal relationships, club situations, and so forth. It is important that you select some aspects of your life that you would like to change but which up to now have made no effort to do.

_____

_____

_____

_____

_____

_____

_____

Step 2

Review in your mind the problems or aspects listed in step 1. Now select one that you would really like to change and which you believe lends itself easily to force-field analysis. Select one that you will feel comfortable talking about to other people.

_____

Step 3

On the form following step 4, indicate existing forces that are pushing you in the direction of change. Thrusters may be forces internal to the self (pride, regret, and fear) or they may be external to the self (friends, the boss, a professor). Also list existing forces that are preventing you from changing. Again, the counterthruster may be internal to the self (uncertainty, fear) or external to the self (poor instruction, limited resources, lack of support mechanisms).

Step 4

In the space to the right of your list of thrusters and counterthrusters indicate the relative strength. For consistency, use a scale of 1 to 10, with 1 indicating a weak force and 10 indicating a high force.

Thrusters	Strength
_____	_____
_____	_____
_____	_____
_____	_____
_____	_____
_____	_____

Counterthrusters

_____

_____

_____

_____

_____

_____

Strength

_____

_____

_____

_____

_____

_____

Step 5

Analyze your thrusters and counterthrusters, and develop a strategy for bringing about the desired change. Remember that it is possible to produce the desired results by strengthening existing thrusters, introducing new thrusters, weakening or removing counterthrusters, or some combination of these. Consider the impact of your change strategy on the system's internal stress (i.e., on yourself and others), the likelihood of success, the availability of resources, and the long-term consequences of planned

changes. Be prepared to discuss your recommendations with the partner in your group.

_____

_____

_____

_____

_____

_____

_____

_____

QUESTIONS FOR DISCUSSION

1. What was your reaction to doing a force-field analysis? Was it insightful and helpful?
2. Was it valuable to receive feedback about your force-field analysis from a partner? Explain.
3. How would you assess the probability of effectively implementing your recommendations?

Source: Based on a group exercise in L W Mealiea, _Skills for Managers in Organizations_ (Burr Ridge, IL: Irwin, 1994), pp 198–201. © 1994. Reproduced with permission of the McGraw-Hill Companies; and the force-field analysis form was quoted directly from _Skills for Managers in Organizations_, pp 199, 201.

CBC video case

Gap Adventures

Gap Adventures sells a hot holiday product—adventure travel and eco-tourism in Central and South America. The company has been very successful, growing from two employees to 70, with $12 million in sales, as well as winning awards for its ethical practices. Their corporate culture has been family-oriented, with all employees having input into decision making. At this point, owner Bruce Poon Tip sees himself as better at building businesses than at maintaining them and wants to move on to new challenges in expanding and diversifying Gap's operations.

So Bruce has hired Dave Bowen, a marketing expert from the company's largest US competitor, to shake up the Gap Adventures organization, which he sees as a bit too complacent, and in need of a shift to a more customer-focused approach. Dave works at enhancing efficiency and taking a more disciplined approach to the business, without dampening the enthusiasm of employees. One of Dave's first tasks is spearheading a major overhaul of the company's brochure. He also urges Bruce to take a tough stance when their UK partner (who handles other parts of the world) is bought by a large company and wants to change the existing relationship.

Dave's new approach to management results in a new reservation system and a new phone system, both of which have serious bugs to be worked out. He also establishes a number of new company policies, which are taking some time to get through to employees out in the field. Employees are working longer hours, and dealing with increased stress. Overall, as Bruce leaves for the Amazon to get married, he sees the culture as more serious, more controlled, more corporate and less relaxed than it was before.

QUESTIONS FOR DISCUSSION

1. What corporate values have changed at Gap Adventures since the arrival of Dave Bowen?
2. Explain how the culture change at Gap Adventures has affected the four functions of culture.
3. Do you agree with Bruce's assessment of the changes at Gap Adventures, as he expresses them at the end of the video? Explain.

Source: Based on "Gap Adventures," _CBC Venture_ 763 (November 7, 2000).

appendix

OB in Action Cases

OB in Action Case:
Steve Ballmer

(applicable to Chapter 1: Introduction to Organizational Behaviour)

Steve Ballmer, CEO, Microsoft Corp.: "I'm Trying to Let Other People Dive in Before I Do"

Steven A Ballmer's explosive temper is legendary. Back in his bad old days, before being appointed Microsoft Corp.'s president [and then CEO], Ballmer would shout himself hoarse if a lieutenant didn't do his bidding fast enough. His motivational techniques drew heavily from Attila the Hun. When he directed the company's Windows product group, he put the fear of God into engineers by bellowing at them and pounding a baseball bat into his palm.

Today, you'll find a tamer Ballmer. Since he took over running Microsoft's day-to-day operations, the 19-year veteran has worked hard to fashion a leadership style that's diplomatic rather than bullying—more Eisenhower than Patton. He still has the booming voice, but what he does with it is more constructive. "I'm trying to temper myself. I don't think I've mellowed. But I try to redirect my energy," he says, bursting into a raucous laugh. The difference is obvious to people who know Ballmer well. "He's certainly changed. He's calmer," says Microsoft board member Jon A Shirley.

The fact is, Ballmer, 43, is coming into his own as Microsoft's [new CEO]—and putting his mark on the company to boot. Since Ballmer got the job, he hasn't been content just to make the trains run on time. He's spearheading the effort to reshape Microsoft. He dreamed up a plan—which he calls Vision Version 2—for energizing employees, focusing them on customers, and broadening their outlook far beyond the narrow confines of the PC and Windows.

Wild Cheers

It's quite a different role for Ballmer. He has long played loyal sidekick to Chairman William H Gates III. The two met as undergraduates at Harvard in 1973. Both were math whizzes, but Ballmer was more outgoing. He managed the college football team, the *Harvard Crimson* newspaper, and the student literary magazine. Ballmer also was more firmly rooted in day-to-day tasks than the absent-minded Gates. Once, after Gates left his dorm door and window open to weather and burglars when he departed for Christmas vacation, a watchful Ballmer battened down the place for him.

Gates eventually dropped out of Harvard to form Microsoft. But he didn't forget Ballmer. In 1980, he coaxed

his pal to leave Stanford business school to join the fledgling company and whip into shape its chaotic business operations. The offer: A $50,000 salary and 7% of the company—a stake now worth nearly $20 billion. Later, Gates called on Ballmer to goose delivery of Microsoft's crucial Windows operating system. Then he relied on his friend to build a sales organization to compete with IBM in large corporate accounts.

Ballmer was always the passionate heart of the company. He led wild cheers at company meetings—leaping around on stage like a burly Mick Jagger. On a dare, he once dove into a pond on the company's campus in November. Charismatic as he was, Ballmer always remained in Gates's shadow. Now Gates is sharing the limelight. "Of the upper management at Microsoft, Steve's the one that gets it," says a former company executive.

Not only does Ballmer get it, but he's doing something about it. As part of Vision 2, he hopes to transform a culture where he and Gates made too many decisions themselves. Now, he's pushing authority down into the ranks. And he's more inclined to listen to subordinates before he speaks. At a review of the Consumer Windows Div.'s product plans on Apr. 30, for instance, he made polite suggestions to managers, rather than quickly telling them what they ought to do. "I see him coaching more than in the past—as opposed to pushing," says Bill Veghte, the group's general manager. Ballmer admits his biggest challenge is delegating. "I'm used to diving in deeply," he says. "Now I'm trying to let other people dive in before I do."

Ballmer's getting atta-boys for his efforts. Gates praises the way he shepherded Microsoft's new E-commerce strategy. The company hopes to get 1 million businesses to use its software to create electronic stores linked to the MSN Web portal. "I think it's a brilliant idea," says Gates. Others say Ballmer has notched up the level of teamwork in the company by forming a Business Leadership Team—14 managers who meet monthly to coordinate strategies across the operating units. "Early days, but signs are good," says Paul A Maritz, executive vice-president in charge of the Developer Group.

Ballmer appears willing to do whatever it takes to make Microsoft successful. And that includes giving up his beloved baseball bat. In late March, when marketing vice-president

Deborah N Willingham spotted him with the bat in a hallway and urged him to be careful, he handed it over to her. "He was saying you're the leaders—the bat swingers. It's a new world," Willingham says. Ballmer still unleashes his famous temper now and then—but at least he isn't swinging a bat anymore.

QUESTIONS FOR DISCUSSION

1. Which of the seven people-centred practices discussed at the beginning of Chapter 1 does Ballmer need to work on to be an effective manager? Explain your choices.

2. Which people-centred practices seem to be most evident in this brief case study of Microsoft?

3. Using Table 1–1 as a guide, how would you assess Steve Ballmer's skills as an effective manager?

4. What is the connection between TQM and Ballmer's Vision Version 2?

5. Imagine yourself as a new Microsoft manager who reports directly to Steve Ballmer. How would the fact that he owns $20 billion (that's a "B") in company stock affect the way you likely would respond to him and interact with him on a daily basis?

Source: Steve Hamm, "I'm Trying to Let Other People Dive in Before I Do," *Business Week*, May 17, 1999, pp 110–11.

OB in Action Case: Michael Milken

(applicable to Chapter 2: Perception, Personality, and Emotion)

www.cnnfn.com (search: Michael Milken)

Michael Milken: Bad Guy, Good Guy, or Both?

Having just finished up his yoga routine, Milken shows his meditation technique: He sits cross-legged, his elbows resting on his knees, hands extended, eyes closed. Yet even as he relaxes, the ultracompetitive Milken seems to be setting goals. "You know, if you are really good," he says, half-smiling, "you can stop breathing."

The miracle about Michael R Milken is that he is breathing at all. Diagnosed with terminal prostate cancer in 1993, Milken was told by his doctors that he had 12 to 18 months to live. Rather than give up, Milken counterattacked. He learned everything about his disease, took up yoga and meditation to reduce stress, and became a strict vegetarian, abandoning his diet of burgers and fries for steamed broccoli and soy shakes. So far, Milken has proven his doctors wrong: His cancer is in full remission.

Had Milken not beaten the odds, cancer would have taken one of the most storied, vilified business figures of our time. From his X-shaped trading desk, Mike Milken, as everyone knows, launched a revolution that transformed the financial system forever. But he also overreached. And when he became ensnared in a federal crackdown on insider trading, Milken's world crumbled. In the public's mind, Milken was the iconic white-collar criminal, a symbol of everything wrong with Wall Street.

It has been eight years since Milken went to jail, but the debate over who Mike Milken is and how bad his crimes were goes on. Junk-bond villain or brilliant financial innovator? There are plenty who think Milken got sandbagged with trumped up, politicized charges, and plenty more who think he simply got what he deserved. And long after many of the less reputable characters he financed have been forgotten, Milken remains controversial. . . .

All that is certain is that Mike Milken has moved on. As far as Milken is concerned, he has paid his penalties—a total of $1.1 billion—and done his time. But that doesn't mean he has faded from the scene. Far from it. For the past six years, Milken has used every waking moment to rebuild his life and his reputation. First, he became a major cancer philanthropist, raising some $75 million for research and appearing regularly on such TV programs as *Larry King Live* to push efforts to cure prostate cancer. And since 1996, he's moved back into business in a big way, founding Knowledge Universe (KU), a new venture that he hopes to build into a huge presence in the $800 billion educational-services industry. Together, his twin pursuits have given Milken a new platform from which, on his own terms, he is once again a player.

To have risen so high, to have crashed so hard, and then, to just pick up the pieces and move on. That could not have been easy. . .

Cancer doesn't seem to have slowed him. The man works—really works—15 hours a day, seven days a week. He seems almost too focused, lacking the little flaws and weaknesses that make the rest of us fallible, susceptible to distraction, and in a word, human. He doesn't touch coffee, alcohol, or even soda. He never swears. His jokes are always hopelessly wholesome and corny. Even as a kid, he never rebelled. When he married his wife, Lori, at the age of 22 in 1968, the pair had been dating since the ninth grade.

Some of his friends and those who've worked closely with Milken say his drive for perfection is both inspiring and maddening. "In so many ways, he is who you hope your kids become. He is diligent, loyal, a great listener, grounded, persistent, optimistic, generous to a fault," says Joseph Costello, who was hired by Milken in 1997 to run KU, only to quit months later after a disagreement over strategy. "But something is missing. He never seems completely relaxed. There is always a point, a purpose. If he could just lose it, let go, he would be easier to relate to.". . .

Despite all his frenetic activity, ask Milken what he wants his legacy to be and the answer will not be curing cancer or revolutionizing capital or education. Instead, his response seems to jump right out of a 1950s black-and-white TV sitcom. "I'll take 'great dad,'" he says without hesitation. "I love being a dad, a husband, a son. Relationships make life worth living. That is what got me through the legal storm.". . .

Milken, of course, isn't just making up for years lost in the past. He's also making up for the near certainty of years lost in the future. Although his cancer is in remission, he knows it could strike again at any time. Says Milken: "My hope is there will be a breakthrough." But that might take a while. And unless new treatments are found, Milken "is living with a ticking time bomb," says [his] oncologist [Dr Stuart] Holden.

QUESTIONS FOR DISCUSSION

1. How do you suppose Milken maintains his self-esteem when so many people despise him as a very wealthy white-collar criminal?
2. How would you rate Milken on self-monitoring? Explain your reasoning.
3. On scales of Low = 1 to High = 10, how would you score Milken on each of the Big Five personality dimensions in Table 2–2? How does the personality profile you have constructed for Milken explain his incredible comeback after prison and cancer?
4. Does Milken have an internal or external locus of control, and has this tendency helped or hindered him?
5. How would you rate Milken's emotional intelligence? Explain.
6. What role do *your* emotions play in your conclusion that, all things considered, Milken is a bad guy, a good guy, or both?

Source: Excerpted from K Morris, "The Reincarnation of Mike Milken," *Business Week*, May 10, 1999, pp 92–104.

OB in Action Case:
Christine Carmichael
(applicable to Chapter 3: Motivation)

Christine Carmichael

Tony Dunlop, the new president of Roselawn Manufacturing Ltd., was very concerned. He had been hired to "turn the company around" and reverse the declining customer service levels and profitability which had resulted from the disastrous implementation of new enterprise resource software, which integrated all of the company's existing systems and used one underlying data base. Roselawn Manufacturing was 30 years old, had 35 employees at its Scarborough headquarters, and just over 200 manufacturing workers at its plant in Oshawa.

The board of directors had suspected for some time that employee morale was a major problem. These suspicions had been confirmed last week when a group of employees went to the Ontario Human Rights Commission and accused Tony's predecessor, John Morgan, of creating a "poisoned environment" for employees, particularly females. Tony had just finished a long discussion with Christine Carmichael, a recently departed employee, and now was convinced that changes had to be made in the way employees were treated. He decided to review what Christine had told him about how her motivation had been destroyed during the year she worked at Roselawn Manufacturing and try to identify specific problems that needed to be addressed.

Great Expectations

Upon completing her university degree in Business Administration, Christine Carmichael applied for numerous positions she found on the Internet, in the local newspaper, and at her university's career service department. She knew it would be difficult to land her "dream job" in human resources management, as she was just starting out and had a limited network of contacts in that profession. In August, Christine applied for a management trainee position at a local company, Roselawn Manufacturing Ltd. This position appealed to her because a large component of the work was training staff on the new enterprise resource software that the company was about to implement. Also, Christine was to be groomed for a management position once one became available. Although the position had relatively low pay for a university graduate, Christine wanted to gain experience and hoped that with hard work, she would be compensated equitably.

Christine started working the first week of September, during the pilot project for the new system. Her boss, Mel, was the Accounting Supervisor. Mel was friendly and helpful, but very busy. During her first week, she was present for all training sessions on the new software, which was expected to go live on November 1. Suddenly, it was decided that the software would not be implemented until the following summer. This dramatically changed the position for which Christine was hired. Optimistically, she hoped to learn more about Roselawn Manufacturing and more about the software, and them help to train other employees before they started using it.

Christine spent the next few weeks assisting in the preparation for the new software by converting data from the old system to the new. She was given conflicting instructions by her boss (Mel), the general manager (Bill), and the Vice President of Finance (Andy). She found it difficult to complete tasks because each person acted as though they were in charge. This confusion continued through the entire duration of the project. Christine started to wonder if the delays were a result of this method of organization.

The Staff Party

Christine noticed that many of the staff seemed afraid of the new software. They seemed to have adopted the opinion that if they avoid it, they could prolong the time until they would have to start using it. Perhaps as a result of the other employees' discomfort with the idea of learning new software, Christine found it very hard to fit in at her new job. People did not welcome her because they did not welcome the purpose for which she was hired. She was ignored in the social atmosphere and looked down upon by those who feared change. Two weeks after she began her new job, the company had its annual staff party, and she was not invited. It was the talk of the office both before and after the party, which added insult to injury and made Christine feels like an outsider.

Reality Bites

After all the data conversion was completed, Christine began working for the general manager, Bill. She worked hard and frequently stayed late in order to learn the business. About three months after she started, a new manager was hired from outside to head up the accounting group that handled ordering and invoicing for large national customers. Christine was discouraged to hear that although the new manager, Phil, had just completed his business degree and was the same age as her, he was not placed in the management trainee program as she had been, but was hired as a manager immediately. One of the more experienced female staff members pointed out that all managers and executives in the company were male, and that this was not likely to change. Christine did not believe this until later when one of the managers was fired. The assistant manager, Anna, was assigned all of the former manager's duties, but received no pay increase, and had her title changed to "Department Coordinator." After a long fight with senior management, Anna ended up getting a mere $1,000 raise in annual pay.

Christine began to get discouraged when the president, John, called her into his office one morning. He said that he and the other executives had just met and decided that because Phil, the new manager, was having trouble adjusting, Christine would be moved to his group to help get him "up to speed." Christine was flattered to be a valuable member of the company that the management could depend on, but she wondered why she had to work under someone who had equal experience and education, but could not handle his own responsibilities.

Thus Christine was reduced to a member of the clerical staff. In Phil's group, she was trained for one hour on how to invoice customers, and then put to work. She had some difficulties but had little guidance as her supervisor, Phil, had no experience either. She had worked in Phil's group for three days when the company's year-end occurred.

Interrogation by the President

The previous problems with invoicing came to a halt as the entire staff had to conduct the inventory count required at year-end. Christine and the others worked as best they could on the items they were asked to inventory, but in the end, their count did not balance with the amount on the books. Christine was shocked when she, but not Phil, was asked to meet with John and Andy. They asked her questions for two hours about how she was trained and why she thought she could do the invoicing job and the inventory after only one hour of instruction. They put her in an awkward position by asking questions about the operations of the department and who gave instructions to do what. She was grilled long enough to bring tears to her eyes. John had a condescending way of asking questions, one that made Christine second guess every word she said.

After that incident, Christine noticed that every time John spoke to any member of his staff, it was to provide negative feedback. Employees cringed whenever he entered their workspace and feared speaking to him. He enjoyed this power, which was evident when he approached another new employee and asked whether she had been "warned" about him yet. As a result of this management style, every employee was more concerned with passing blame that solving problems. Departments were segregated and did not function well as a team with a common goal.

The School of Hard Knocks

One of Christine's coworkers, Mary, was responsible for ordering raw materials. Mary called in sick repeatedly. Christine was responsible for doing Mary's work when she was away, and Phil and the rest of the department did little to help her. In January, Mary went on stress leave. Christine then formally took on Mary's responsibilities for ordering without any increase in pay or any recognition.

The busy spring season rapidly approached and Christine's job responsibilities had totally changed since she was hired. She spent her days working in operations when she wanted to be in a staff function—training. John promised that she would soon be relieved of her invoicing and ordering duties, so that she could concentrate full-time on the new system. Finally, Jill was hired to take over Christine's invoicing work. She was trained by Christine to perform the invoicing function while Christine concentrated on ordering as well as acting as an assistant manager to Phil. At the beginning, Jill worked hard because of the example set by Christine. However, as time went by, Jill began to follow the other members of the group, doing as little as possible, knowing that Christine would pick up the slack. Again Christine was not promoted and never received any reward for her hard work.

Stabbed in the Back

The invoicing activities were now running much more smoothly than when Phil took over, which Christine believed was a direct result of her own hard work. It became clear that Phil wanted authority, but not accountability, when Christine had some difficulty with a supplier who overcharged on an invoice. Phil expressed his disappointment in Christine's inability to renegotiate pricing with the supplier. He called the supplier in a rage, demanded lower prices, ruined the working relationship with the supplier, and in the end, came out no further ahead than Christine had. To make matters worse, Phil took credit for the outcome Christine had obtained, in order to prove to John that the poor treatment of the supplier actually accomplished something. In addition, he had belittled her for her method of dealing with the situation, then took matters into his own hands and made the situation worse.

One day Phil received a letter from a member of the sales staff. The letter complimented Christine for her rapid service and friendly manner. Phil sent a copy of the letter to Christine through E-mail with the title "A Reverse Complaint." Again, Christine was hurt because the supervisor refused to tell her that she was doing a good job. She became increasingly depressed and lost all drive to exert effort as she felt she was being taken advantage of.

Back to the Future

In July, as the end of the busy season approached, Christine's original boss, Mel, approached Phil about Christine returning part-time to her duties on the new enterprise resource software, as it was to be implemented in six weeks. Christine was pleased about going back to the work she was initially hired for, but suspected it was too good to be true. Her workload had eased a little, but every time she tried to work on the system, Phil would give her more work. Mel criticized her for not dedicating time to the system. She was angry that the other members of the department were slacking more than ever and her hard work continued to go unappreciated.

Christine was fed up, and she started looking for a new job. Through a combination of networking and good luck, she was fortunate enough to find an entry-level job in a human resources consulting firm. She was thrilled and rejuvenated at the prospect of this new opportunity. She left Roselawn Manufacturing one week before the implementation of the new software.

Tony Dunlop realized that with Christine's departure, the company had lost a hard-working, knowledgeable employee who had been very important to the successful implementation of the new software. Others who left at the same time had told him similar stories, and it was clear that managers had to change their style in dealing with employees. He decided to try to remember some of the motivation theories he had studied in his business school days—maybe something there could help him figure out what to do.

QUESTIONS FOR DISCUSSION

1. Using Mazlow and McClelland's need theories, analyze which of Christine's needs are being met and which ones are not. What could Tony Dunlop do to try to meet the needs that are currently unmet?

2. Using Herzberg's theory, which hygiene and motivator factors are present and which are not? What could Tony Dunlop do to try to provide more hygiene and motivator factors?

3. Using the job characteristics model, which core job characteristics are involved in Christine's job, and which ones are not? What should Tony Dunlop do to improve Christine's motivation, according to the job characteristics model?

4. Does equity theory explain Christine's low motivation? Explain. How could Christine's motivation be increased, according to equity theory?

5. Does expectancy theory explain Christine's low motivation? Explain. How could Christine's motivation be increased, according to expectancy theory?

Source: © 1999 Lisa Carson and Nina D. Cole. Used with permission.

OB in Action Case:
Lincoln Electric

(applicable to Chapter 4: Performance Management)

www.lincolnelectric.com

A Model Incentive Plan Gets Caught in a Vise at Lincoln Electric

In recent years, corporations have rushed to embrace the idea of motivating employees by linking pay to performance. Nearly half of large companies have tilted their pay systems in this direction, surveys show, and many say they're eager to push the notion further. To learn more, thousands of managers flock to Cleveland-based Lincoln Electric Co. each year to look at one of the country's oldest and most radical pay-for-performance systems.

Unfortunately, the Lincoln model isn't quite the smashing success it once was. After management stumbles forced the family-controlled manufacturer of welding equipment and supplies to sell more shares to the public last year, Lincoln increasingly resembles a typical public company. With institutional shareholders and new, independent board members in place, worker bonuses are getting more of a gimlet eye. At the same time, management is readying itself for an expansion drive to remain globally competitive, putting more pressure on the balance sheet. All that has crimped bonuses, even though Lincoln is posting record sales and earnings. For workers who expect high bonuses if they deliver in output, the shift has hurt morale.

So Lincoln is taking its one-of-a-kind pay system in for an overhaul. The company is by no means ready to ditch the incentive plan, which once paid employees up to 100% of their wages in annual performance-linked bonuses. But executives are now considering ways to move toward a more traditional pay scheme and away from the flat percentage-bonus formula. "The bonus is a good program, and it has worked well, but it's got to be modified some," says Director David C Lincoln, whose father John C Lincoln founded the company in 1895. Adds Edward E Lawler, who heads the University of Southern California's Center for Effective Organizations: "One of the issues with Lincoln is how [its pay plan] can survive rapid growth and globalization."

Plans such as Lincoln's may be getting a lot of attention these days, but they date back to the 19th-century piecework system. Each of Lincoln's 3,400 employees is supposed to be a self-managing entrepreneur. There's minimal supervision. They get paid when they work—no sick or holiday pay. "How much money you make is in your own hands," says Thomas Gadomski, a painting-crew leader.

Each employee is accountable for the quality of his or her own work and is rated twice a year on quality, output, dependability, cooperation, and ideas. The ratings determine how much of the total corporate bonus pool each worker will get, which comes on top of his or her hourly wage. . . .

The average Lincoln factory hand earns $16.54 an hour, vs. the $14.25 average manufacturing wage in the surrounding area. With a 56% average bonus in 1995—the lowest in years—production employees came out ahead of workers elsewhere even after paying for health-care benefits employers typically pick up. But unlike at other companies, Lincoln has huge variations in production-worker pay: from roughly $32,000 to more than $100,000 for the most hard-driving.

There's tremendous pressure to produce, but an employee advisory board meets regularly with top management to air workers' concerns. And Lincoln guarantees work to employees with three years' experience. No one has been laid off since 1948, and turnover is less than 4% among those with at least 180 days on the job. "There isn't any other place to work like Lincoln Electric," says Kathleen Hoenigman, an 18-year veteran. "They take care of you." Indeed, Lincoln went so far as to borrow more than $100 million in 1992 and 1993 to pay bonuses, even though it lost a total of $84 million in those years, in part because of an ill-conceived foreign-acquisition spree. Says CEO Donald F Hastings: "I had to go to the board and say: 'We can't break our trust with this group because of management mistakes and recession elsewhere.'"

Still, it gets harder and harder to live up to the old deal. Even though the company has come roaring back after stumbling abroad, the red ink it spewed left Lincoln financially weakened. To make better acquisitions and expand further, Lincoln made its first public offering last July, pushing outsiders' stake to 40%. It also slashed total debt by nearly 40%, to $130 million, and paid a lower bonus per person, though the total bonus kitty was a record $64 million. . . .

The slimmer bonuses represent a sea change for employees. It didn't help that last year, Lincoln's centennial, was its first with $1 billion in sales. In November, some employees protested outside headquarters after they learned of the bonus size. "Everyone was upset," says one worker. Blue-collar workers had already been disgruntled with management when it set up a lower wage scale in 1993, at 75% of pay, for 700 new employees hired to meet demand and staff an expanded motor operation. Turnover among the new hires was high, and the disparate pay disturbed veterans. "If an individual shows he can handle the workload, he should be rewarded" with full pay, says Joseph Tuck, an inspector with 18 years at Lincoln. Because of the protests, Hastings eliminated the two-tier wage on Dec. 1.

To revamp the pay scheme without stirring up resentment, the company has set up a committee to study the bonus program. It has told employees that a new formula is in the works, and it has hired Price Waterhouse to study productivity. Although Hastings pledges that the incentive system will remain, over time, he wants employees to focus more on their overall earnings, not just the percentage bonus they receive. Already, he has started raising base pay—with a likely reduction of bonuses later—for engineering, sales, and other office staff.

Even after the changes, Lincoln's pay system is likely to remain more innovative than most. But as it tries to hire more outsiders, expand further abroad, and modernize, "we're getting to be a more normal company," says Director Frank L Steingass. That may not be quite what eager visitors expect to hear. But if Lincoln can adapt to new times without sacrificing employee goodwill, another model pay plan may yet emerge.

QUESTIONS FOR DISCUSSION

1. Relative to Figure 4–1, which organizational reward norm has long been in effect at Lincoln Electric? How can you tell?

2. Should Lincoln Electric switch to another organizational reward norm? If no, why? If yes, which one?

3. Why have Lincoln Electric's traditionally huge annual cash bonuses motivated strong effort when critics say bonuses reward *past* performance?

4. Is Lincoln Electric's organizational culture (see Chapter 13) suitable for installing team-based pay?

5. What advice would you offer the company's compensation review committee?

Source: Z Schiller, "A Model Incentive Plan Gets Caught in a Vise," *Business Week*, January 22, 1996, pp 89, 92. Reprinted from January 22, 1996 issue of *Business Week* by special permission. Copyright © 1996 by the McGraw-Hill Companies, Inc. Also see R M Hodgetts, "A Conversation with Donald F Hastings of The Lincoln Electric Company," *Organizational Dynamics*, Winter 1997, pp 68–74; and D F Hastings, "Lincoln Electric's Harsh Lessons from International Expansion," *Harvard Business Review*, May–June 1999, pp 162–78.

OB in Action Case:
Au Bon Pain

(applicable to Chapter 5: Stress Management)   **www.inc.com**

Store Managers at Au Bon Pain Have a Stressful Job

As a teenager growing up in a blue-collar family, Richard Thibeault thought of managers as people "up there on the ladder." They sat behind desks, worked 9 to 5, were pillars of the community.

What he never imagined them doing is his work these predawn hours: wheeling a rack of croissants across a nearly deserted street, past the delivery trucks and the occasional derelict. His tie flaps against his white shirt. He has been at work since 3 AM, baking muffins, preparing soups, worrying about falling sales at the Au Bon Pain bakery cafe he manages.

Inside his store, the 46-year-old Mr Thibeault sags against his desk—a converted counter in a tiny room crammed with croissant warmers and drink dispensers. Rock music from a boombox brought in by his workers pours in from the adjacent kitchen. Mr Thibeault's black briefcase sits on the lone chair. He used to bring paperwork like performance reviews home. But after seven months of 70-hour weeks he began crumpling over his desk at home and falling asleep.

Mr Thibeault earned $34,000 last year. "When I tell people what I do, they don't believe I'm a manager," he says. "Some days I think maybe I should go back to factory work. It was easier."

During the past decade, the percentage of workers classified as "managers" has increased to 14.5% from 11%; the growth has been even greater in the service sector.

But most of these jobs are far from the white-collar status positions normally associated with the term "manager." They are high-pressure, dead-end jobs with little status and low pay: the harried store manager at a fast-food restaurant; the assistant manager at a discount drug store; the manager at a travel agency; the bank-branch head.

These people carry the title manager, but they lead a blue-collar life—working long hours, often doing the same tasks as those they employ, and carrying out orders from above. Their autonomy is tightly circumscribed by corporate headquarters. They are given productivity quotas, told which products to push and which to shed, who and how many to hire. With the shrinking of middle management they have more responsibilities—dealing with personnel, meeting cost and labor targets—but less chance to move up. . . .

Dissatisfaction is mushrooming even as the number of first-line management jobs grows. A series of surveys of department store chains found that dissatisfaction among low-level managers increased to 50% in 1995 from 36% in 1986. Turnover is surging, with managers often citing little opportunity for creativity and poor prospects for promotion. A different survey of 1,300 fast-food restaurants this year found that 47% of entry-level managers "often think about quitting." . . .

Recently, Mr Thibeault calculated that he makes $7.83 cents an hour—83 cents more than he pays the part-time college students he employs.

Mr Thibeault's first stop this day, as always, is the computer that hangs over his makeshift desk. It is his constant companion, spitting out hour-by-hour projections, sent down from corporate headquarters, of how much food he should sell and how many workers he should use. This morning it tells a sad story. Last week, he was projected to make $2,100 in sales. He made $1,900. His business this year is down 28%—a drop he blames on the recent opening of a Starbucks Corp. coffee bar and a Dunkin Donuts in the neighborhood and the departure of several hundred construction workers from the area.

Because he missed corporate targets for labor and food costs, Mr Thibeault is known as an "outlyer." He was told a few weeks ago that he wouldn't get a $1,200 quarterly bonus. He appealed the decision and was given the money. But he doubts the company will let him miss targets a second time.

Mr Thibeault would like to run some discount specials to boost business. Au Bon Pain won't let him. Restaurant managers "don't have degrees in marketing," says David Peterman, the company's senior vice president of operations. All specials are determined by corporate headquarters. Mr Thibeault, who only has seven workers, would like to hire more to speed service. The computer printout says no.

Desperate to bring costs down, Mr Thibeault has trimmed staff to a handful of people and has taken on more work himself. "It's not the pressure out there from customers that gets to me," he says as he tapes a printout of the day's sales targets on the wall and runs a yellow highlighter through the key breakfast and lunch hours. "It's the pressure from higher up."

At 3:15 AM, Mr Thibeault lights the first cigarette of the pack he smokes daily, pulls on rubber gloves, and shoves 12 trays of blueberry muffins into the oven. Two years ago he was operated on successfully for stomach cancer. "My doctor keeps saying, "You're not working more than 40 or 50 hours, are you?" Mr Thibeault says, "I lie." . . .

Au Bon Pain's long hours and tight control of its managers is typical of the new breed of management jobs. Many fast-food chains track sales at their stores every 15 minutes. New computer controls allow many retail stores to track the sale of every product in every store nightly—keeping tabs on the manager's performance.

All this might be more tolerable if there was a chance to advance. In the past three months, three managers Mr Thibeault knows have quit. Kristal Doherty, a store manager who left for a state government job a few weeks ago, says, "I never got to see my two-year-old, and it was clear there was no chance to move up." (To reduce turnover, Au Bon Pain recently introduced a bonus system rewarding the top 20% of first-line managers with bonuses that can boost their annual earnings to $65,000.)

As Au Bon Pain has expanded, it has trimmed middle-management ranks, making any move upward much harder. While the ranks of its store managers has swelled to 190 from 140 in the past two years, the number of district managers—the next step up—has shrunk to 20 from 28. . . .

Mr Thibeault worries constantly about thievery and pilfering of food, which add to his costs and make him fall short of the computer-generated targets. He recently dismissed a supervisor he suspected had been stealing from him for three months. "It's not a career for them," he says. "They can go to McDonald's or Burger King."

Au Bon Pain wants managers to mingle with customers. But Mr Thibeault has no time. He greets customers when he can with a smile, exchanging pleasantries. But then a rack of croissants arrives undercooked. Mr Thibeault hurriedly pushes them into the oven. The hot oven shelf burns

a two inch mark across his forearm. He curses but keeps on loading.

Sometimes, when the pressure gets too much, Mr Thibeault walks into the store's food locker, takes a deep breath, and screams. . . .

By 1 PM the sheet on the wall with the day's hourly sales goals tells a depressing story. Mr Thibeault is already $39 behind. A packet from corporate headquarters arrives with a lengthy new form that managers will be required to fill out four times a day, monitoring the time it takes customers to be served, the quality of food, and staff morale.

Filling out the forms will take up more time, he says wearily, "but if it's the rule, I will do it." . . .

At 4:30 PM, 13½ hours after he started work, Mr Thibeault lights a final cigarette. His white shirt is splattered with coffee and pastry crumbs. "I always go home dirty," he says, "I need a shower." He will be asleep by 8:30, before his alarm goes off for a new day at 2 AM.

QUESTIONS FOR DISCUSSION

1. What are the individual-level, group-level, and extraorganizational stressors that Richard Thibeault is exposed to?
2. Which types of stress outcomes do Au Bon Pain store managers experience?
3. Use the model of burnout (see Figure 5–2) to explain how and why Au Bon Pain store managers appear to burn out.
4. How might Mr Thibeault use a control coping strategy to reduce occupational stress?
5. How would the Type A person perform as an Au Bon Pain store manager? Based on Type A research, how would this job affect the behavioural, attitudinal, and physiological outcomes of Type A individuals?
6. Would you be willing to work as a store manager at Au Bon Pain after graduating from college/university? Explain your rationale.

Source: Excerpted from J Kaufman, "In Name Only: For Richard Thibeault, Being a 'Manager' Is a Blue-Collar Life," *The Wall Street Journal*, October 1, 1996, pp A1, A4. Reprinted by permission of *The Wall Street Journal* © 1996 Dow Jones & Company, Inc. All Rights Reserved Worldwide.

OB in Action Case:
SmithKline Beecham
(applicable to Chapter 6: Decision Making and Ethics)   **www.sb.com**

SmithKline Beecham Uses a Three-Step Process to Make Resource-Allocation Decisions

In 1993, SmithKline Beecham was spending more than half a billion dollars per year on R&D, the lifeblood of any pharmaceuticals company. Ever since the 1989 merger that created the company, however, SB believed that it had been spending too much time arguing about how to value its R&D projects—and not enough time figuring out how to make them more valuable. . . .

Major resource-allocation decisions are never easy. For a company like SB, the problem is this: How do you make good decisions in a high-risk, technically complex business when the information you need to make those decisions comes largely from the project champions who are competing against one another for resources? A critical company process can become politicized when strong-willed, charismatic project leaders beat out their less competitive colleagues for resources. That in turn leads to the cynical view that your project is as good as the performance you can put on at funding time. . . .

Most organizations think of decision making as an event, not a process. They attach great importance to key decision meetings. But in most cases, and SB is no exception, the real problems occur before those meetings ever take place. And so the process that SB designed—a three-phase dialogue between the project teams and the company's decision makers—focused on the inputs to the resource-allocation decision and the role of the organization in preparing those inputs.

Phase I: Generating Alternatives

One of the major weaknesses of most resource-allocation processes is that project advocates tend to take an all-or-nothing approach to budget requests. At SB, that meant that project leaders would develop a single plan of action and present it as the *only* viable approach. Project teams rarely took the time to consider meaningful alternatives—especially if they suspected that doing so might mean a cutback in funding.

And so we insisted that each team develop at least four alternatives: the *current plan* (the team would follow the existing plan of activity), a *"buy-up" option* (the team would be given more to spend on the project), a *"buy-down" option* (the team would be given less to spend on the project), and a *minimal plan* (the team would abandon the project while preserving as much of the value earned to date as possible). Working with a facilitator, a team would begin by describing a project's objective, which usually was to develop a particular chemical entity targeted at one or more diseases. Then it would brainstorm about what it would do under each of the four funding alternatives. . . .

Near the end of this phase, the project alternatives were presented to a peer review board for guidance before any significant evaluation of the alternatives had been performed. Members of the review board, who were managers from key functions and major product groups within the pharmaceuticals organization, tested the fundamental assumptions of each alternative by asking probing questions: In the buy-down alternative, which trial should we eliminate? Should a once-a-day formulation be part of our buy-up alternative? Couldn't we do better by including Japan earlier in the current plan? The discussion session improved the overall quality of the project alternatives and helped build consensus about their feasibility and completeness.

The project teams then revised their alternatives where appropriate and submitted them again for review, this time to the group of senior managers who would, at a later point in the process, make the final investment decisions on all the projects. . . .

Phase II: Valuing Alternatives

Once we had engineered the process that took us through phase I, we needed a consistent methodology to value each one of the project alternatives. We chose to use decision analysis because of its transparency and its ability to capture the technical uncertainties and commercial risks of drug development. For each alternative, we constructed a decision tree, using the most knowledgeable experts to help structure the tree and assess the major uncertainties facing each project. . . .

We developed six requirements for achieving credibility and buy-in to the valuation of each alternative:

- First, the same information set must be provided for every project. . . .
- Second, the information must come from reliable sources. . . .

- Third, the sources of information must be clearly documented. . . .
- Fourth, the assessments must undergo peer review by experienced managers across functions and therapeutic areas. . . .
- Fifth, the valuations must be compared with those done by external industry observers and market analysts to establish that the numbers are realistic.
- Sixth, the impact of each variable on the project's expected value must be identified. . . .

We increased transparency and consistency in yet another way by having a specially designated group of analysts process the valuation information and draw preliminary insights. Having this work done by a neutral group was a relief to many project team members, who were rarely satisfied with the previous approaches to valuation, as well as to the top management group, who were tired of trying to make sense of widely disparate types of analysis. As the company's CFO for pharmaceuticals put it, "Inconsistent valuations are worse than none."

Once the alternatives had been valued, a second peer-review meeting was held to make sure that all the participants had a chance to question and understand the results. This step was designed to ensure that no surprises would emerge when the decisions were being made. And again, the peer review was followed by a senior management review that provided an opportunity to challenge, modify, and agree on the underlying assumptions driving the valuations. During the meeting, however, the senior managers were explicitly asked *not* to begin discussing which alternatives to invest in; instead, they were asked only to confirm that they understood and believed the valuations. And if they didn't, why not? What seemed out of line? . . .

Phase III: Creating a Portfolio and Allocating Resources

The goal of this phase was to create the highest-value portfolio based on all the project alternatives that had been developed. This was no easy task: with 20 major projects—each of which had four well-conceived alternatives—the number of possible configurations was enormous. We appointed a neutral analytic team, rather than the project advocates, to carry out a systematic approach to identifying the highest-value portfolio based on return on investment.

The portfolio could then be examined along a number of strategic dimensions, including stability under different scenarios, balance across therapeutic areas and stages in the development pipeline, and feasibility of success given SB's technical and commercial resources. Because the senior managers had already agreed—and vigorously debated—the underlying project descriptions (phase I) and valuations (phase II) for each alternative, they now focused their complete attention on the portfolio decisions. . . .

The first 14 project decisions, which involved increasing or maintaining funding levels, were made without controversy. However, when it came time to discuss the first project whose funding would be cut, the manager of the relevant therapeutic area challenged the decision. The meeting's chairman listened to his case for maintaining the current funding and then asked whether that case was reflected in the project valuations. The manager agreed that it was, but repeated the argument that SB would lose value by terminating the project. The chairman agreed that value would be lost but pointed out that the funds originally scheduled for the project would create more value when applied elsewhere. That ended a potentially explosive discussion.

The new process not only reduced the controversy in the resource-allocation process, it also led the company to change its investment strategy. Although top management had set out to cut back on the company's development budget, they now saw their investment decision in a new light: they believed the new portfolio to be 30% more valuable than the old one—without any additional investment. Furthermore, the marginal return on additional investment had tripled from 5:1 to 15:1. To exploit this opportunity, the company ultimately decided to increase development spending by more than 50%.

QUESTIONS FOR DISCUSSION

1. Is SmithKline Beecham's resource-allocation decision making process more characteristic of the rational model or the bounded rationality model of decision making? Discuss your rationale.
2. How does SmithKline's approach attempt to control for escalation of commitment?
3. To what extent is SmithKline's decision making process consistent with the contingency recommendations presented in Table 6–1? Explain.
4. To what extent does SmithKline Beecham promote organizational creativity and innovation?
5. Why do you think the three-step decision making process has been such a success? Discuss your rationale.

OB in Action Case: Challenger Space Shuttle

(applicable to Chapter 6: Decision Making and Ethics, and Chapter 7: Groups and Teamwork)   **www.hq.nasa.gov**

A Ten-Year Retrospective of the Challenger Space Shuttle Disaster: Was It Groupthink?

A Fateful Decision . . .

The debate over whether to launch on January 28, 1986, unfolded as follows, according to the report of the Presidential Commission on the Space Shuttle Challenger Accident:

Shortly after 1 PM ET on January 27, NASA's [the National Aeronautic and Space Administration's] booster rocket manager in Cape Canaveral, Larry Wear, asks officials of rocket maker Morton Thiokol in Utah whether cold weather on the 28th would present a problem for launch.

By 2 PM, NASA's top managers are discussing how temperatures in the 30s at the launch pad might affect the shuttle's performance. In Utah, an hour later, Thiokol engineer Roger Boisjoly learns of the forecast for the first time.

By late afternoon, midlevel NASA managers at the Cape are on the phone with Thiokol managers, who point out that the booster's rubbery O-rings, which seal in hot gases, might be affected by cold.

That concern brings in officials from NASA's Marshall Space Flight Center in Huntsville, Alabama, which buys the rockets from Thiokol and readies them for launch.

Marshall managers decide that a three-way telephone conference call is needed, linking NASA and Thiokol engineers and managers in Alabama, Florida, and Utah.

The first conference call begins about 5:45 PM, and Thiokol tells NASA it believes launch should be delayed until noon or afternoon, when the weather turns warmer. It is decided a second conference call would be needed later that evening.

Marshall deputy project manager Judson Lovingood tells shuttle projects manager Stan Reinartz at the Cape that if Thiokol persists, NASA should not launch. Top NASA managers at Marshall are told of Thiokol's concern.

At 8:45 PM, the second conference call begins, involving 34 engineers and managers from NASA and Thiokol at the three sites.

Thiokol engineers Boisjoly and Arnie Thompson present charts showing a history of leaking O-ring joints from tests and previous flights.

The data show that the O-rings perform worse at lower temperatures and that the worst leak of hot gases came in January 1985, when a shuttle launched with the temperature at 53 degrees. Thiokol managers recommend not flying Challenger at temperatures colder than that.

NASA's George Hardy says he's "appalled" at Thiokol's recommendation. Larry Mulloy, Marshall's booster rocket manager, complains that Thiokol is setting down new launch criteria and exclaims, "My God, Thiokol, when do you want me to launch, next April?"

Thiokol Vice President Joe Kilminster asks for five minutes to talk in private. The debate continues for 30 minutes. Boisjoly, Thompson, engineer Bob Ebeling, and others are overruled by Thiokol management, who decide to approve the launch.

At 11 PM, Kilminster tells NASA that Thiokol has changed its mind: Temperature is still a concern but the data are inconclusive. He recommends launch.

Thiokol's concerns that cold weather could hurt the booster joints are not passed up NASA's chain of command beyond officials at the Marshall Space Flight Center.

Challenger is launched at 11:38 AM January 28 in a temperature of 36 degrees.

Shortly after launch on January 28, 1986, Challenger was engulfed in a fiery explosion that led to the deaths of six astronauts and teacher-in-space Christa McAuliffe. As a shocked world watched great billows of smoke trail over the Atlantic, it was clear to those involved that launching Challenger in 36-degree weather was a catastrophic decision.

. . . Ten Years Later

Two who argued the longest and loudest against launch were Thiokol engineers Roger Boisjoly and Arnie Thompson. But their lives took widely differing paths after the accident.

Boisjoly remembers the prelaunch debate this way: "When NASA created the pressure, they all buckled."

He became nationally known as the primary whistleblower. Thiokol removed Boisjoly from the investigation team and sent him home after he testified before a presidential commission that the company ignored evidence that the booster rocket seals would fail in cold weather.

Boisjoly, 57, says he was blackballed by the industry and run out of town by Thiokol.

For a time, he sought psychiatric help. "It just became unbearable to function," says Boisjoly, who now lives with his wife and daughter in a small mountain town in Utah. He spoke on condition that the town not be named because he fears for his family's safety.

Boisjoly is convinced he is a marked man because some former co-workers believe his testimony contributed to resulting layoffs at Thiokol.

After the accident, he says, drivers would try to run him off the road when he was out on a walk. He got threatening phone calls. Someone tried to break into his house.

"It became so uncomfortable for me that I went out and bought a .38 revolver," he says.

Now retired, Boisjoly earns $1,500 for speeches to universities and business groups. He also runs his own engineering company and teaches Sunday school in the Mormon church, something he says he never would have dreamed of doing before the accident.

Says Thompson, the other voice against launch: "There were the two of us that didn't want to fly and we were defeated. A lot of my top managers were not happy with me."

Yet, with longer ties to Thiokol than Boisjoly, Thompson was promoted to manager and stayed on through the shuttle's redesign.

He retired three years ago at the end of a 25-year-career. Now 66, he spends his time building a small office building in Brigham City, Utah.

"My attitude was, I wanted to stay on and redesign the bird and get back into the air," says Thompson. "I had a personal goal to get flying again." . . .

Thiokol's Bob Ebeling was so sure that Challenger was doomed, he asked his daughter, Leslie, then 33, to his office to watch "a super colossal disaster" unfold on live TV.

When it exploded, "I was in the middle of a prayer for the Lord to do his will and let all these things come to a happy ending and not let this happen," says Ebeling, who managed the rocket ignition system for Thiokol. "We did our level best but it wasn't good enough."

The fact that he foresaw disaster and could not stop it has tortured him since.

Ebeling, 69, says that within a week of the accident he became impotent and suffered high stress and constant headaches, problems he still has today. After 40 years of engineering experience, Thiokol "put me out to pasture on a medical" retirement, he says.

Ebeling still feels "the decision to recommend a launch was pre-ordained by others, by NASA leaning on our upper management. The deck was stacked."

One of those who overruled Ebeling and the others was Jerry Mason, the senior Thiokol manager on the conference call. He took an early retirement from Thiokol five months after the disaster, ending a 25-year career in aerospace.

"I was basically responsible for the operation the day it happened," says Mason, 69. "It was important to the company to put that behind them and get going on the recovery and it would be hard to do that with me sitting there. So I left."

In Mason's case, that meant going abruptly from corporate chieftain to unpaid volunteer. He helped set up a local economic development board and now chairs the Utah Wildlife Federation.

"I had a pretty successful career, and would liked to have gone out with the feeling that I really had done very well all the time instead of having to go out feeling I'd made a mistake at the end."

For Judson Lovingood, the loss was more personal.

Formerly one of NASA's deputy managers for the shuttle project, he wonders still if Challenger contributed to the breakup of his marriage.

"I think (Challenger) had an effect on my personal life," says Lovingood, "a long-term effect."

After the accident, he went to work for Thiokol in Huntsville and retired as director of engineering in 1993. Now remarried, he spends his time puttering in the yard of his Gurley, Alabama, home.

"Sometimes when I think about the seven people (aboard the shuttle), it's pretty painful," says Lovingood.

Besides McAuliffe, on board Challenger were commander Dick Scobee, pilot Mike Smith, and astronauts Ron McNair, Ellison Onizuka, Judy Resnik, and Greg Jarvis.

Their families settled with the government and Thiokol for more than $1.5 billion. Still, "I think people should hold us collectively responsible as a group," Lovingood says. "Every person in that meeting the night before the launch shared in the blame." . . .

Investigations of the Challenger explosion placed much of the blame on NASA's George Hardy, a senior engineering manager.

By saying he was "appalled" by Thiokol's fears of flying in cold weather, critics charged, Hardy pressured Thiokol into approving the launch.

But Hardy refuses to shoulder the blame. "If Thiokol had stuck to their position, there wasn't any way we were going to launch," he says.

Hardy left NASA four months after the accident. Now 65, he runs a small aerospace consulting company in Athens, Alabama.

Whatever else the last decade brought, many of the recollections return to that pressure-packed conference call on the eve of launch.

QUESTIONS FOR DISCUSSION

1. Which task and maintenance roles in Table 7–2 should have been performed or performed better? By whom?
2. Which symptoms of groupthink (see Chapter 6) are evident in this case?
3. Do you think groupthink was a major contributor to the Challenger disaster? Explain.
4. All things considered, who was most to blame for the catastrophic decision to launch? Why?

Source: P Hoversten, "Thiokol Wavers, Then Decides to Launch," *USA Today*, January 22, 1996, p 2A. Copyright 1996, USA TODAY. Reprinted with permission; and from ". . . Ten Years Later" and the balance of the case are excerpted from P Hoversten, P Edmonds, and H El Nasser, "Debate Raged before Doomed Launch," *USA Today*, January 22, 1996, pp 1A–2A. Copyright 1996, USA TODAY. Reprinted with permission.

OB in Action Case:
Lucent

(applicable to Chapter 7: Groups and Teamwork)

With the Stakes High, A Lucent Duo Conquers Distance and Culture

Imagine designing the most complex product in your company's history. You need 500 engineers for the job. They will assemble the world's most delicate hardware and write more than a million lines of code. In communicating, the margin for error is minuscule.

Now, scatter those 500 engineers over 13 time zones. Over three continents. Over five states in the United States alone. The Germans schedule to perfection. The Americans work on the fly. In Massachusetts, they go to work early. In New Jersey, they stay late.

Now you have some idea of what Bill Klinger and Frank Polito have been through in the past 18 months. As top software-development managers in Lucent Technologies' Bell Labs division, they played critical roles in creating a new fiber-optic phone switch called the Bandwidth Manager, which sells for about $1 million, the kind of global product behind the company's surging earnings. The high-stakes development was Lucent's most complex undertaking by far since its spin-off from AT&T in 1996.

Managing such a far-flung staff ("distributed development," it's called) is possible only because of technology. But as the two Lucent leaders painfully learned, distance still magnifies differences, even in a high-tech age. "You lose informal interaction—going to lunch, the water cooler," Mr Klinger says. "You can never discount how many issues get solved that way."

The product grew as a hybrid of exotic, widely dispersed technologies: "light-wave" science from Lucent's Merrimack Valley plant, north of Boston, where Mr Polito works; "cross-connect" products here in New Jersey, where Mr Klinger works; timing devices from the Netherlands; and optics from Germany.

Development also demanded multiple locations because Lucent wanted a core model as a platform for special versions for foreign and other niche markets. Involving overseas engineers in the flagship product would speed the later development of spinoffs and impress foreign customers.

And rushing to market meant tapping software talent wherever it was available—ultimately at Lucent facilities in Colorado, Illinois, North Carolina, and India. "The scary thing, scary but exciting, was that no one had really pulled this off on this scale before," says Mr Polito.

Communication technology was the easy part. Lashing together big computers in different cities assured everyone was working on the same up-to-date software version. New project data from one city were instantly available on Web pages everywhere else. Test engineers in India could tweak prototypes in New Jersey. The project never went to sleep.

Technology, however, couldn't conquer cultural problems, especially acute between Messrs Klinger's and Polito's respective staffs in New Jersey and Massachusetts. Each had its own programming traditions and product histories. Such basic words as "test" could mean different things. A programming chore requiring days in one context might take weeks in another. Differing work schedules and physical distance made each location suspect the other of slacking off. "We had such clashes," says Mr Klinger.

Personality tests revealed deep geographic differences. Supervisors from the sleek, glass-covered New Jersey office, principally a research facility abounding in academics, scored as "thinking" people who used cause-and-effect analysis. Those from the old, brick facility in Massachusetts, mainly a manufacturing plant, scored as "feeling" types who based decisions on subjective, human values. Sheer awareness of the differences ("Now I know why you get on my nerves!") began to create common ground.

Amid much cynicism, the two directors hauled their technical managers into team exercises—working in small groups to scale a 14-foot wall and solve puzzles. It's corny, but such methods can accelerate trust-building when time is short and the stakes are high. At one point Mr Klinger asked managers to show up with the product manuals from their previous projects—then, in a ritualistic break from technical parochialism, instructed everyone to tear the covers to pieces.

More than anything else, it was sheer physical presence—face time—that began solidifying the group. Dozens of managers began meeting fortnightly in rotating cities, socializing as much time as their technical discussions permitted. (How better to grow familiar than over hot dogs, beer, and nine innings with the minor league Durham Bulls?) Foreign locations found the direct interaction especially valuable. "Going into the other culture is the only way to understand it," says Sigrid Hauenstein, a Lucent executive in Nuremberg,

Germany. "If you don't have a common understanding, it's much more expensive to correct it later."

Eventually the project found its pace. People began wearing beepers to eliminate time wasted on voice-mail tag. Conference calls at varying levels kept everyone in the loop. Staffers posted their photos in the project's Web directory. Many created personal pages. "It's the ultimate democracy of the Web," Mr Klinger says.

The product is now shipping—on schedule, within budget, and with more technical versatility than Lucent expected. Distributed development "paid off in spades," says Gerry Butters, Lucent optical-networking chief.

Even as it helps build the infrastructure of a digitally connected planet, Lucent is rediscovering the importance of face-to-face interaction. All the bandwidth in the world can convey only a fraction of what we are.

QUESTIONS FOR DISCUSSION

1. Could the 500 Lucent engineers who worked on the Bandwidth Manager project be called a *team?* Why or why not? Could Bill Klinger and Frank Polito be called a team? Explain.
2. What role, if any, did trust play in this case?
3. What lessons about managing virtual teams does this case teach us?
4. Based on what you have read, what was the overriding key to success in this case?

Source: T Petzinger Jr, "With the Stakes High, a Lucent Duo Conquers Distance and Culture," *The Wall Street Journal*, April 23, 1999, p B1.

OB in Action Case: Charlene Pedrolie

(applicable to Chapter 8: Conflict and Negotiation)

www.rowefurniture.com

Charlene Pedrolie Rearranged Furniture and Lifted a Business

When business picked up, the knives came out. Charlene Pedrolie had just introduced the latest management methods at the big, old flagship factory of Rowe Furniture Corp. Workers had been organized into "cells." Cross-training had been instituted. Four layers of supervision had been wiped out.

But when orders surged for the 1995 fall season, the cells couldn't keep up. Workers were pressured by stress under the new rules and frazzled by change; one had a nervous breakdown. Skeptics questioned not only the new processes but the new boss—a 34-year-old female, a complete outsider in an old-line company.

Yet today, attitudes have changed 180 degrees. Output and earnings are surging, making Rowe a hot stock in the furniture group. How Ms Pedrolie pulled it off teaches a valuable lesson not only in the management of change but also in the attainment of corporate power.

Rowe Furniture was stuck midway through a major transformation when it recruited her in April 1995 from a plant manager's job at General Electric. Rowe's research showed that people hate buying upholstered furniture. They want a much wider selection than any showroom can display, yet they refuse to wait months for a special order. So Rowe created a computer network on which customers could match fabrics and styles, promising speedy delivery and a midrange price.

The marketing solution, however, created problems upstream. Rowe's factory had to produce a much wider variety of products in much less time, all with no increase in cost. Making that happen was Ms Pedrolie's assignment.

In her mind, there was little mystery about the method. She would annihilate the inefficient old assembly line. Sewers, gluers, staplers, and stuffers would be brought together in cells of roughly 35. Through cross training, everyone in the cell could do every job related to making a sofa, instead of doing one job on every piece. When anyone had time to spare they could help someone getting backed up.

Supervisors, used to pushing for the maximum performance in a single task (more cushions! faster sewing!), would be eliminated. Perhaps most important, workers could act on their own ideas for improving productivity.

When Ms Pedrolie outlined the plan to her fellow officers during a meeting at the local Holiday Inn, "We sat there and thought, 'She's crazy,'" recalls Steve Sherlor, a company vice president.

So Ms Pedrolie resolved to pull off the plan with blinding speed, leaving no time for second-guessing. Though given to spontaneous cheers ("all right!" "way to go!"), she was stern. Some managers who resisted her changes got the axe.

The production workers, for their part, returned after the brief plant makeover agog to see their power tools dangling from the ceiling in clusters instead of in a long, straight line. Suddenly they were working alongside—and forced to communicate with—three dozen cell members. Accustomed to having the parts come to them, they were dragging raw materials to their cells and bumping into one another along the way. Productivity fell as staplers learned to glue and gluers to staple.

The success of Rowe's retailing initiative only worsened the problems at the plant. Schedules swelled to 58 hours a week; tempers grew short. "It was really touch and go," recalls General Manager John Sisson. The naysayers began their I-told-you-sos, and Ms Pedrolie began losing sleep, worrying management would call everything off.

Thankfully, the passage of a few weeks—and the regular Christmas shutdown—proved therapeutic. As workers returned from vacation to a less frenzied schedule, cells began to function as teams. Workers realized they could snuff out problems instantly when they occurred within the cell, whereas solutions were slow to come on the old assembly lines. As productivity recovered and then surpassed previous levels, incentive payments inched higher.

People also noticed that the factory was bathed in sunlight; the company had scraped the paint from the windows, the legacy of a past energy crisis. "It's important to make the environment part of the change," Ms Pedrolie says. "It prevents people from wanting to go back to the old."

Most important of all, shop-floor workers were stunned to see their ideas triggering action, which in turn triggered more ideas. One task force found a better way to stuff pillows. A loading crew made the case for larger truck trailers. Another group created a new revenue source by selling spare kiln capacity to lumber-drying operations. (Workers can leave their jobs to join task forces because of cross-training.)

Today, the plant operates at record productivity. "Everybody's a lot happier," says shop worker Sally Huffman. Ms Pedrolie is now turning her attention to the office, cross-training the credit, order, and customer-service people so that any one employee can handle all of a dealer's needs.

What is the lesson? Partly that Ms Pedrolie played the change game shrewdly. But more fundamentally, that she followed an enduring precept in the exercise of power: The more widely that true authority is dispersed, the firmer the foundations of management.

QUESTIONS FOR DISCUSSION

1. What causes of conflict can you detect in this case? Which one(s) presented the greatest obstacle to Pedrolie's new way of doing things? Explain.
2. How big a problem was in-group thinking in this case? Explain.
3. Which cross-cultural relationship building behaviours would have served Pedrolie well during the change? Explain.
4. What evidence of functional and dysfunctional conflict can you detect in this case?
5. Which conflict-handling styles did Pedrolie use effectively (or ineffectively)?

Source: Case quoted from T Petzinger, "Charlene Pedrolie Rearranged Furniture and Lifted a Business," *The Wall Street Journal*, September 13, 1996, p B1. Reprinted by permission of *The Wall Street Journal*, © 1996 Dow Jones & Company, Inc. All Rights Reserved Worldwide.

OB in Action Case:
Roberta James
(applicable to Chapter 9: Communication)

Roberta James

Roberta James was excited when she was selected for the HRI management training program. What impressed her most was HRI's emphasis on employees. As Mr. Henry Martin, President of HRI, stated in his opening remarks to her training group, "We have two bottom lines here at HRI, a profit for our shareholders and a positive working environment for our employees. The two are equally important, because neither one can exist without the other." In her six months of training Roberta had spent time in almost every division area. She had followed and learned from HRI's most effective managers.

Following completion of her training, Roberta was assigned to manage Customer Complaints, a small department in the business services division that had been plagued with problems for years. The supervisor for five years had been a nice person but ineffectual, and the department was notorious for inefficiency. Customers actually complained about the Complaint Department because of their slow response time! Six months ago, the supervisor had retired, and a new gung-ho supervisor had taken over and set up new rules, systems, and productivity quotas. The situation had gone from bad to worse. There had been 30 percent turnover in the past three months, and the other veterans were known to be looking. The department was as unproductive as ever, and customers were now complaining about rude service. Two weeks ago, the supervisor had quit to take a job with HRI's main competitor.

Details began to emerge as Roberta talked with her new employees and reviewed files. It was obvious to Roberta that the current system of handling complaints was inefficient and overly detailed. However, her bigger concern at the beginning was her employees. They were frustrated, demotivated, and even hostile. Roberta set up staff meetings every morning and asked everyone to make suggestions to improve the complaint resolution process. The most important result was a noticeable change in the behaviour of the staff. It was slow, but they were beginning to show some interest and enthusiasm. Roberta requested that the name of the department be changed to the Customer Service Department, because "complaint" sounded too negative. She wanted the staff, and other departments at HRI, to see her group as a positive part of the HRI team. Her boss, Sam Moore, agreed.

Roberta continued to work hard, and based on the changes she made, complaints about the old "Complaints Department" had slowed to a trickle. Overall, the employees were working well together, and the department was starting to develop a team attitude. Sam Moore told her that he had been hearing good comments from other employees. By the end of the year, productivity had gone up. In addition, the reports her group generated on the frequency of certain types of complaints had been instrumental in several changes in the distribution system. However, this was old news. Recently, rumours of end-of-the-year layoffs had been flying since HRI's recent acquisition of Medium Conglomerate Inc., and the general slowdown in the economy since the September 11 attacks.

Sam Moore, Roberta's boss, hadn't been down to visit her department in several months, and the junior executive grapevine was hinting that he was on his way out. If this was true, Roberta and her department were essentially in limbo until everything shook out and people were reassigned.

Recently, Francie Hill, the high-energy Vice President of Marketing, spoke to Roberta in confidence about the possibility of moving her and her department under the marketing umbrella. Roberta thought this was where her department belonged, rather than its current position in business services. In addition, Roberta got along well with Francie, and knew that she would find support with her for innovative ideas.

Roberta hoped that she would be able to keep morale and productivity up during this tough time. While she couldn't share the information she had from the junior executive grapevine and Francie, she debated just what and how much she could say to her staff.

At the Monday morning meeting, it became clear that something had to be said. The staff was restless, and focused on the issues at hand. Finally Andrea, the most outspoken member of the group, stopped in the middle of a sentence and turned to Roberta, "You know, we could all concentrate better if we knew how the layoffs will affect us. Do you have any information?"

This seemed to unleash a flood of comments. Several employees had heard the rumours about Sam Moore and were worried about where that left them. Others were more generally concerned that the slowdown in business would leave them with more employees than the department needed. "Somehow it just doesn't seem all that smart to talk about being more productive now," Sue commented. "With no new business to speak of, we could be working ourselves out of a job."

Sam Moore did leave abruptly on forced retirement, and Bob Hiberley was brought in from the main corporate office. Word on the junior executive grapevine was that he was not particularly liked at corporate, and they all breathed a sigh of relief to see the back of him. He was also rumoured to be a known hatchet man, brought in to "clean up the deadwood in business services." Hiberley had barely spoken a word to Roberta since his arrival.

Several of Roberta's key staff had privately expressed their concerns about the changes to her. It was increasingly difficult for Roberta or her staff to keep their spirits up under the changes. Several groups of consultants had been wandering around the corridors reviewing job descriptions and systems in place in other departments within business services. Roberta knew it was only a matter of time before they hit her Customer Service Department.

Although the changes Roberta and her staff had made were very positive, and she felt good about her team, Roberta was aware that there were limits to what she could accomplish given the damaging situation at HRI. As a result of the unexpected drop in revenues and the costs incurred in the acquisition of Medium Conglomerate Inc., HRI had embarked on a major austerity program, including eliminating travel, outside training, and even tuition reimbursement. This had wreaked havoc with the carefully created personal development plans each of her staff members had in place.

HRI's problems were well known by Roberta's staff. Company-wide, morale was at an all-time low. Management, from the supervisors to the vice presidents, seemed more interested in jockeying for position than moving the organization forwards, and Roberta's staff was scared that they would lose their jobs. On top of that, with Sam Moore gone, there was no one in business services that could serve as an advocate for the department. The success of the past year was gratifying, but the attitude of the company these days seemed to be, "What have you done for me lately?"

As Roberta sat in her office pondering the situation, Dolores appeared. "Roberta do you have a minute?"

"Sure, sit down Dolores. You know my door is always open to you," Roberta responded. "What's the matter? You look like you've seen a ghost."

Dolores, her voice quivering and near tears, said, "I'm scared. You know my situation, I'm a single parent and I need this job at HRI."

Roberta was startled "Dolores, what has gotten you so upset. You know that you are one of the best employees in this department. There are some layoffs happening at HRI, but our department is safe, at least at this point. Besides, with over five years of service at HRI, you're covered under the job security policy. They either have to find a new, comparable place for you or give you one year's severance at 100 percent of your current salary and benefits."

"That's just the point," Dolores said. "That's not true any more. They changed the policy. I no longer qualify for the job security program."

"I can't imagine human resources changing a policy that is so important without input or discussion with the managers," said Roberta.

"Well they did," answered Dolores. "Check your E-mail. According to my friend in HR, the decision was announced at this morning's HR staff meeting. Apparently they expect some repercussions."

"They should," responded Roberta, logging into her E-mail. "This is outrageous."

Roberta read the new job security policy. It was a simple enough change. Starting the first of next month, the minimum length of service with HRI needed to be eligible for the job security program was changed to 12 years from five. Roberta grew angry and frustrated when she realized the damage this policy change would do to morale within her department and the ability of her staff to trust HRI top management. Before, over half of her staff was eligible for the job security program. Now, none of them were. On top of this, there had been no warning to managers and no explanation. Obviously this information was already in the office pipeline, and would create a major shake-up in people already in near panic about the situation at HRI.

"Dolores, I know you're upset. So am I. I need to think about this for a minute. Then I am going to go outside and scream, followed by setting up a meeting with Bob Hiberley to get more information on this," Roberta said, "I want you to know that I will do everything in my power to keep you and all my staff in their positions. HRI needs all of you, and it needs this department. Don't forget that. Oh, and thank you for bringing this to my attention."

QUESTIONS FOR DISCUSSION

1. How should Roberta respond to the concerns of her staff about potential layoffs? How can she motivate her staff in the face of uncertainty and confusion? Is there anything she can do to reduce the fear level for her employees?

2. What medium of communication would you use to communicate a potential layoff? Explain.

3. Did HRI use the most appropriate communication medium to announce the job security policy change? What approach could HRI have taken that would have increased the likelihood of acceptance, reduced resentment, and helped maintain the employees' trust?

4. Roberta has been placed in a difficult situation by HRI. How should she approach Bob Hiberley on this and what specific questions should she ask?

5. Roberta needs to communicate to her staff about the policy change, to help clear up the confusion, and defuse anger. What is her best communication approach to this? Explain.

Source: Adapted from "the Roberta case," co-written by Edwin C. Leonard, Jr, Indiana-Purdue University at Fort Wayne and Maria Muto, Arizona State University.

OB in Action Case:
Carly Fiorina

(applicable to Chapter 10: Power and Politics,
and Chapter 11: Leadership)

www.hp.com

Will Carly Fiorina Make a Lasting Impression as Hewlett-Packard's CEO?

Carly Fiorina has a silver tongue and an iron will. When the 44-year-old was considering the CEO post at Hewlett-Packard Co., she met board member Richard A Hackborn for lunch at the Gaslight Club in Chicago's O'Hare airport. Hackborn, who had built HP's printer business into a gold mine in the 1980s, had decided to leave HP's board to devote his time to charity work. But over salads and "what felt like 10 gallons" of iced tea, Fiorina persuaded him not only to reconsider but also to step up as chairman. "You can't tell me there's a better person for the job," she told Hackborn as Gaslight's waitresses, clad in skimpy uniforms and fishnet stockings, made their rounds. Over the course of three hours, Hackborn agreed. "And no, I did not put on fishnet stockings," Fiorina says with a laugh. "Don't even go there."

It will take all of the charm and mettle Fiorina trotted out that afternoon to get her where she wants to go at HP. On July 19 [1999], the granddaddy of Silicon Valley announced that Fiorina would become its new chief executive, making her the first woman to head a Dow 30 company—and the first outsider to take the reins of the venerable computer giant. Indeed, in HP's 60-year history, this is the first time it has reached beyond its homegrown troops for any of the top jobs at the company, let alone Numero Uno.

But then, these Internet times are anything but business as usual. With rivals IBM and Sun Microsystems leading the E-business revolution, HP has seemed little more than part of the clueless Establishment. That's why the company has gone to the outside for a fresh face and a fresh approach. Fiorina's challenge is a ticklish one. In the coming months, she must strike a delicate balance between propelling HP's stodgy culture out of its moribund ways and into the high-speed Net Age while not losing the elements that have made the company an American icon—its deep engineering roots and its good, old-fashioned dependability. "Some might say we're stodgy, but no one would say this company doesn't have a shining soul," Fiorina says.

The star executive from Lucent Technologies Inc. may be just the person to bring out the best, again, at HP. Just as the computer giant needs to shed its lumbering ways, so too did Lucent—AT&T's slow-moving communications-equipment business. Fiorina managed the highly successful spin-off of Lucent in 1996. She then launched a bold, $90 million brand-building campaign that helped transform the company from a humdrum maker of phone equipment into an Internet player

supplying the gear for the New Economy. And in 1998, after being promoted to president of Lucent's $19 billion global service-provider business, she helped to turbocharge product development by the long-coddled Bell Labs engineers. "She has it all," crows Vodafone AirTouch PLC Chairman Sam Ginn, an HP director who headed the search committee.

. . . unlike her predecessors, Fiorina must recalibrate HP's vaunted culture, dubbed the "HP Way." Founders Bill Hewlett and David Packard were renowned for emphasizing teamwork and respect for co-workers. But in recent years, that has translated into a bureaucratic, consensus-style culture that is at a sharp disadvantage in the Net-speed era. "They have this ready, aim-aim-aim, fire culture," says Bain & Co. consultant Vernon E Altman, who has worked with HP. "These days, it has to be aim, fire, re-aim, re-fire." Disposing of the bad habits while retaining the good shouldn't be a problem, says Fiorina, who plans to use a scalpel and not a machete. "Our people are very proud and smart. So, first, you reinforce the things that work," she says, "and then appeal to their brains to address what doesn't." . . .

As a leader, she has a personal touch that inspires intense loyalty. She's known for giving balloons and flowers to employees who land big contracts. When Lucent was spun off from AT&T in early 1996, Fiorina stayed up all night with Comptroller Jim Lusk and other employees to make sure the prospectus for the stock offering was perfect. And it's not just business: When the wife of a senior Lucent executive fell ill recently, Fiorina helped make sure he got medical advice, doctors, and emotional support. "I think the world of Carly. She's a great leader," says Nina Aversano, president of North America for Lucent's global service-provider business.

QUESTIONS FOR DISCUSSION

1. Which of the nine generic influence tactics are evident in this case? Give specific evidence.
2. What bases of power did Fiorina rely on in this case study? Cite specific evidence.
3. Which power base do you think will serve her best during her attempts to change HP's culture? Explain.
4. As Fiorina goes about getting HP into the Internet age, is organizational politics likely to be a problem? Explain. What should she do about it?
5. Fiorina sure seems to have made a great impression on key people in this case. What is her "secret"?

Source: Excerpted from P Burrows, "The Boss," *Business Week*, August 2, 1999, pp 76–84. Also see S Zesiger, "Fortune Cover Girl Storms Valley," *Fortune*, August 16, 1999, p 29.

OB in Action Case:
Lumezzane, Italy
(applicable to Chapter 12: Organizational Design   **www.initaly.com**

Lumezzane, Italy: A Business Centre Built on Cooperation

Natives of Lumezzane, in northeastern Lombardy, often trace their intense work ethic to religion or genes. But behind the bustle of this small, grimy town, with houses perched atop workshops and factories wedged between churches and schools, lies another factor: a powerful network of ties among family, friends, and colleagues.

Time Management

Strong social capital, Harvard University political scientist Robert D Putnam argued in his studies of Italy, helps a local economy thrive—as Lumezzane's has indeed done. Today, this town of 24,000 is the world leader in silverware, faucet, and valve production, with more than 2,000 companies manufacturing these items. Residents boast one of the highest per capita incomes in Italy.

Managers and workers at Lumezzane's various companies collaborate in ways that make Lumezzane resemble one giant enterprise. Most companies have 20 or fewer employees, and each worker is a specialist. In the silverware business, for instance, the *rebbista* shapes fork tines, the *costista* sculpts the edges, and the *lucidatore* polishes. The network of craftspeople provides a reservoir of skilled labour from which to draw. When the pasta maker Barilla decided to give away silverware with its noodles a few years ago, the large order was filled by three local companies that divided the work.

Cooperation is taken to surprising extremes. When a local concern runs into financial trouble, a flurry of phone calls soon yields a group of six to eight unofficial "trustees" who steer the company to safety. Trustees are often direct competitors of the ailing business, willing to contribute money and ease competition to rescue their rival. They know implicitly that others would do the same for them. Thanks to this practice, locals aver, there has never been a bankruptcy in Lumezzane.

The town's tight industrial weave is evident after working hours, too. Workmen and bosses play cards together in the same cafés and address each other with the informal "*tu.*"

Somali, Pakistani, and other foreign workers receive extensive help with housing and job placement. As Putnam's theory of social capital predicts, involvement in city government is also high, with voter turnout in local elections at about 90%. But turnout for regional and national elections is lower.

One-Upmanship

Religion, more than politics, is a strong unifying force—as well as the pretext for business and social activities. Says Don Turla, one local parish priest: "At weddings, feast days, or funerals, after 10 minutes, every conversation turns to business." The town has no fewer than seven parishes, each of which launches projects that frequently become elaborate games of one-upmanship. When one parish funded a nursery school some years ago, others quickly followed suit. (Some of the schools have since been converted into vocational training centres.)

All is not sweetness and light. Every industrialist complains of unfair business practices by competitors, and many are locked in bitter lawsuits (though disputes are set aside when bankruptcy threatens).

Nevertheless, people are fiercely loyal to Lumezzane. They don't sell their businesses to outsiders, and they endure skyrocketing housing costs, even though they could do better in nearby Brescia. Above all, the people of Lumezzane appear to live to work, not the other way around.

QUESTIONS FOR DISCUSSION

1. Which organizational metaphor is exemplified in this case? Why?
2. What can North Americans, who culturally tend to be more competitive than cooperative, learn from the business climate in Lumezzane, Italy?
3. Do you think this particular situation is unique to Italian culture, or could it be replicated in other countries? Explain. Which countries? Why?

Source: Excerpted from T Mueller, "A Town Where Cooperation Is King," *Business Week*, December 15, 1997, p 155.

OB in Action Case:
Kingston Technology
(applicable to Chapter 13: Organizational Culture and Change)

www.kingston.com

Kingston Technology's Organizational Culture Promotes Financial Success

Nowadays Kingston Technology, the private firm the two men still own [John Tu and David Sun], is the world's second-biggest maker of add-on memory modules for personal computers. Its profits remain secret, but in 1994 its 300 workers each accounted for about $2.7 million in sales—more than oil-rich Exxon ($1.3 million) and leaving such models of high-tech efficiency as Intel ($353,400) trailing in the dust.

These numbers, the cut-throat commodity nature of the computer business, and Kingston's location in the faceless suburb, conjure up a picture of a silicon sweat shop. Not so. Mr. Sun, who was born in Taiwan, and Mr. Tu, who hails from Shanghai, decided from the outset that their employees, suppliers, and customers would be treated as members of their family. This meant instilling such Asian family values as trust, loyalty, and mutual support in an industry where screwing your customers—let alone your suppliers and employees—is second nature. Is there a method in their madness?

At first sight apparently not. The studious, bespectacled 54-year-old Mr. Tu still seems surprised at his success. The generally noisier Mr. Sun, who is 10 years younger, offers no more clues. Although some of the things they say ("we built this company to care for people") sound, on the face of it, pretty vapid, they appear to be sincere. The pair shun the trappings of office: Both sit in open cubicles in the middle of a chaotic office; neither has a secretary. Employees (two-thirds of them from ethnic minorities) are paid well above the industry average. Should the firm fail, each employee has been promised between one and two years' salary. Mr. Sun has offered to make payments on one employee's house until the end of the century.

Yet this generosity makes hard financial sense—as the sales-per-employee figure shows. Labour represents a tiny fraction of Kingston's total costs, which means it can afford to pay over the odds. And the firm's benevolence breeds extraordinary loyalty. Since Kingston was formed in 1987, only 2% of its workers have quit.

The duo bring the same family values to their relationships with outsiders—with similar tangible results. Astonishingly, most of the firm's multi-million-dollar deals are done on a handshake. Kingston never pressures suppliers on price, pays ahead of schedule if it can, and has never canceled an order. This civility (alongside the sheer size of its orders) pays off with suppliers—which include such brutes as Samsung, Hitachi, and Motorola. Not only does Kingston get the best deals on price; it also always gets its supplies—an important factor in a market that is prone to shortages.

Even more riskily, Kingston lets outsiders run a big portion of its business. Apart from design, some assembly, and final testing, it subcontracts everything to other firms. And it designs its products to be built with off-the-shelf memory chips from a variety of suppliers. Kingston usually has matching add-on memory modules ready for sale within a week of the launch of a new PC, and it fulfils customers' orders within a day. An efficient Japanese car-parts maker might turn over its stock of raw materials and work-in-progress 30 to 40 times a year; Kingston does it three times a day . . .

It is hard to argue with sales that have on average doubled every year for six years, hitting $802 million in 1994, or with a company whose overheads are the lowest in the business. For now, the basic Tu-Sun philosophy—that if you make your customers, workers, and suppliers happy, your business will prosper—is working. Sometimes Mr. Tu wraps this formula in unnecessary Confucian obfuscation. "The culture," he proclaims, "is the core competence of this company." What it really amounts to is that he and Mr. Sun have noticed earlier than others that supplying memory chips is as much a service business as it is a commodity business and that people and relationships can give you an edge in the marketplace.

Can this service culture be sustained? Not easily. As Kingston grows, job titles are already creeping in. Identity tags—those badges of corporate conformity—have been spotted. A mentoring program—"it's like brainwashing," jokes Mr. Tu—is used to indoctrinate new employees. And the firm is drafting its first mission statement. Kingston's culture may be hard to sustain as the firm continues to grow. It is also, however, a culture that is hard to copy. Imitators can mimic the firm's products or plagiarize its mission statement. The energetic paternalism of Messrs. Tu and Sun is not so easily replicated. Until Kingston's rivals find a way to clone a character, or the firm grows too big for them to control, Messrs. Tu and Sun are safe.

Since this case was written, John Tu and David Sun sold an 80% equity interest in the company to SOFTBANK Corporation in 1996. Kingston's co-founders retained the remaining 20% equity interest. SOFTBANK's leadership decided to let Kingston operate autonomously. John Tu and David Sun continue to run the company, and they were permitted to retain the company's current management and its operating philosophies. For example, Messers. Tu and Sun gave Kingston's 1,000 employees a $20 million bonus in 1998. This amounted to roughly $20,000 per employee. They had previously given a $38 million, or $69,000 per employee, bonus in 1997.

QUESTIONS FOR DISCUSSION

1. What are the shared things, sayings, doings, and feelings at Kingston Technology? Explain.
2. Explain how Kingston's organizational culture fulfils the four functions of culture.
3. How do John Tu and David Sun practice socialization and mentoring? Explain.
4. Will Kingston Technology be able to maintain its current organizational culture as the company grows? Explain.

Source: "Doing the Right Thing," *The Economist*, May 20, 1995, p 64. © 1995, The Economist Newspaper Group, Inc. Reprinted with permission. Further reproduction prohibited. www.economist.com

Chapter I

[1] J Pfeffer and J F Veiga, "Putting People First for Organizational Success," *Academy of Management Executive*, May 1999, p 37.

[2] Adapted from ibid.

[3] For alternatives to layoffs, see S Armour, "Workers Take Pay Cuts Over Pink Slips," *USA Today*, April 13, 2001, p 1B.

[4] Data from Pfeffer and Veiga, "Putting People First for Organizational Success," p 47.

[5] H Mintzberg, "The Manager's Job: Folklore and Fact," *Harvard Business Review*, July–August 1975, p 61. For an alternative perspective, see R J Samuelson, "Why I Am Not a Manager," *Newsweek*, March 22, 1999, p 47.

[6] See, for example, H Mintzberg, "Managerial Work: Analysis from Observation," *Management Science*, October 1971, pp B97–B110; and F Luthans, "Successful vs. Effective Real Managers," *Academy of Management Executive*, May 1988, pp 127–32. For an instructive critique of the structured observation method, see M J Martinko and W L Gardner, "Beyond Structured Observation: Methodological Issues and New Directions," *Academy of Management Review*, October 1985, pp 676–95. Also see N Fondas, "A Behavioral Job Description for Managers," *Organizational Dynamics*, Summer 1992, pp 47–58.

[7] Adapted from material in C Wilson, "Identify Needs with Costs in Mind," *Training and Development Journal*, July 1980, pp 58–62; and F Shopper, "A Study of the Psychometric Properties of the Managerial Skills Scales of the Survey of Management Practices," *Educational and Psychological Management*, June 1995, pp 468–479.

[8] See F Shipper, "Mastery and Frequency of Managerial Behaviors Relative to Sub-Unit Effectiveness," *Human Relations*, April 1991, pp 371–88.

[9] Data from F Shipper, "*A Study of Managerial Skills of Women and Men and Their Impact on Employees' Attitudes and Career Success in a Nontraditional Organization*," paper presented at the Academy of Management Meeting, August 1994, Dallas, Texas. The same outcome for on-the-job studies is reported in A H Eagly and B T Johnson, "Gender and Leadership Style: A Meta-Analysis," *Psychological Bulletin*, September 1990, pp 233–56.

[10] For instance, see J B Rosener, "Ways Women Lead," *Harvard Business Review*, November–December 1990, pp 119–25; and C Lee, "The Feminization of Management," *Training*, November 1994, pp 25–31.

[11] See T J Tetenbaum, "Shifting Paradigms: From Newton to Chaos," *Organizational Dynamics*, Spring 1998, pp 21–32; and R W Oliver, *The Shape of Things to Come* (New York: McGraw-Hill, 1999).

[12] Essential sources on reengineering are M Hammer and J Champy, *Reengineering the Corporation: A Manifesto for Business Revolution* (New York: HarperCollins, 1993); and J Champy, *Reengineering Management: The Mandate for New Leadership* (New York: HarperCollins, 1995). Also see "Anything Worth Doing Is Worth Doing from Scratch," *Inc.*, May 18, 1999 (20th Anniversary Issue), pp 51–52.

[13] For thoughtful discussion, see G G Dess, A M A Rasheed, K J McLaughlin, and R L Priem, "The New Corporate Architecture," *Academy of Management Executive*, August 1995, pp 7–20.

[14] See, for example, "The Dreaded 'E Word,'" *Training*, September 1998, p 19; K Dover, "Avoiding Empowerment Traps," *Management Review*, January 1999, pp 51–55; and G B Weathersby, "Management May Never Be the Same," *Management Review*, February 1999, p 5. A brief case study of empowerment in action can be found in C Dahle, "Big Learning, Fast Futures," *Fast Company*, June 1999, pp 46, 48.

[15] See M Parker Follett, *Freedom and Coordination* (London: Management Publications Trust, 1949).

[16] See D McGregor, *The Human Side of Enterprise* (New York: McGraw-Hill, 1960).

[17] See A J Slywotzky and D J Morrison, *How Digital Is Your Business?* (New York: Crown Business, 2000); and G Hamel, "Is This All You Can Build with The Net? Think Bigger," *Fortune*, April 30, 2001, pp 134–38.

[18] Data from "AMA Global Survey on Key Business Issues," *Management Review*, December 1998, p 30. Also see "1999 Annual Survey: Corporate Concerns," *Management Review*, March 1999, pp 55–56.

[19] Instructive background articles on TQM are R Zemke, "A Bluffer's Guide to TQM," *Training*, April 1993, pp 48–55; R R Gehani, "Quality Value-Chain: A Meta-Synthesis of Frontiers of Quality Movement," *Academy of Management Executive*, May 1993, pp 29–42; P Mears, "How to Stop Talking About, and Begin Progress Toward, Total Quality Management," *Business Horizons*, May–June 1993, pp 11 14; and the *Total Quality Special Issue of Academy of Management Review*, July 1994.

[20] M Sashkin and K J Kiser, *Putting Total Quality Management to Work* (San Francisco: Berrett-Koehler, 1993), p 39.

[21] See R K Reger, L T Gustafson, S M Demarie, and J V Mullane, "Reframing the Organization: Why Implementing Total Quality Is Easier Said than Done," *Academy of Management Review*, July 1994, pp 565–84.

[22] Deming's landmark work is W E Deming, *Out of the Crisis* (Cambridge, MA: MIT, 1986).

[23] See M Trumbull, "What Is Total Quality Management?" *The Christian Science Monitor*, May 3, 1993, p 12; and J Hillkirk, "World-Famous Quality Expert Dead at 93," *USA Today*, December 21, 1993, pp 1B–2B.

[24] Based on discussion in M Walton, *Deming Management at Work* (New York: Putnam/Perigee, 1990).

[25] Ibid, p 20.

[26] Adapted from D E Bowen and E E Lawler III, "Total Quality-Oriented Human Resources Management," *Organizational Dynamics*, Spring 1992, pp 29–41. Also see P B Seybold, "Get Inside the Lives of Your Customers," *Harvard Business Review*, May 2001, pp 80–89.

[27] See T F Rienzo, "Planning Deming Management for Service Organizations," *Business Horizons*, May–June 1993, pp 19–29. Also see M R Yilmaz and S Chatterjee, "Deming and the Quality of Software Development," *Business Horizons*, November–December 1997, pp 51–58.

[28] For example, see J Shea and D Gobeli, "TQM: The Experiences of Ten Small Businesses," *Business Horizons*, January–February 1995, pp 71 77; T L Zeller and D M Gillis, "Achieving Market Excellence through Quality: The Case of Ford Motor Company," *Business Horizons*, May–June 1995, pp 23–31; and P McLagan and C Nel, "A New Leadership Style for Genuine Total Quality," *Journal for Quality and Participation*, June 1996, pp 14–16.

[29] See J O'C Hamilton, "The Harder They Fall," *Business Week* E.BIZ, May 14, 2001, pp EB14, EB16.

[30] Data from G Colvin, "Shaking Hands on the Web," *Fortune*, May 14, 2001, p 54.

[31] See S E Ante, "In Search of the Net's Next Big Thing," *Business Week*, March 26, 2001, pp 140–41.

[32] Data from D Temple-Raston, "Net Economy Hale and Hearty," *USA Today*, January 12, 2001, p 6B.

[33] See Hamel, "Is This All You Can Build with the Net? Think Bigger."

[34] A Bernasek, "Buried in Tech," *Fortune*, April 16, 2001, p 52.

[35] For more, see G Meyer, "eWorkbench: Real-Time Tracking of Synchronized Goals," *HR Magazine*, April 2001, pp 115–18.

[36] Data from "Hurry Up and Decide!" *Business Week*, May 14, 2001, p 16.

[37] See B Lessard and S Baldwin, *Net Slaves: True Tales of Working the Web* (New York: McGraw-Hill, 2000); and C Wilder and J Soat, "A Question of Ethics," *Information Week.com*, February 19, 2001, pp 38–50.

[38] This discussion is based on material in R R Thomas Jr., *Redefining Diversity* (New York: AMACOM, 1996), pp 4–9.

[39] This distinction is made by M Loden, *Implementing Diversity* (Chicago: Irwin, 1996).

[40] "The 50 Best Companies to Work for in Canada," *Report on Business Magazine*, January 2002, pp 41–52.

[41] A Tomlinson, "Concrete Ceiling Harder to Break than Glass for Women of Colour," *Canadian HR Reporter*, December 17, 2001, pp 7, 13.

[42] These barriers were taken from discussions in Loden, *Implementing Diversity*; E E Spragino, "Benchmark: The Diverse Workforce," *Inc.*, January 1993, p 33; and A M Morrison, *The New Leaders: Guidelines on Leadership Diversity in Amercica* (San Francisco: Jossey-Bass, 1992)

[43] Morrison, *The New Leaders: Guidelines on Leadership Diversity in America.*

[44] Empirical support is provided by H Ibarra, "Race, Opportunity and Diversity of Social Circles in Managerial Networks, "*Academy of Management Journal*, June 1995, pp 673–703; and P J Ohlott, M N Ruderman and C D McCauley, "Gender Differences in Managers' Developmental Job Experiences," *Academy of Management Journal*, February 1994, pp 46–67.

[45] H L Tosi, Jr. and J W Slocum, Jr., "Contingency Theory: Some Suggested Directions," *Journal of Management*, Spring 1984, p 9.

[46] See J J Martocchio, "Age-Related Differences in Employee Absenteeism: A Meta-Analysis," *Psychology & Aging*, December 1989, pp 409–14.

[47] Here are the ranks for each career strategy: Strategy 1=12; Strategy 2=6; Strategy 3=5; Strategy 4=11; Strategy 5=9; Strategy 6=3; Strategy 7=10; Strategy 8=1; Strategy 9=7; Strategy 10=8; Strategy 11=4; Strategy 12=2; and Strategy 13=13.

Chapter 2

[1] The negativity bias was examined and supported by O Ybarra and W G Stephan, "Misanthropic Person Memory," *Journal of Personality and Social Psychology*, April 1996, pp 691–700; and Y Ganzach, "Negativity (and Positivity) in Performance Evaluation: Three Field Studies," *Journal of Applied Psychology*, August 1995, pp 491–99.

[2] E Rosch, C B Mervis, W D Gray, D M Johnson, and P Boyes-Braem, "Basic Objects in Natural Categories," *Cognitive Psychology*, July 1976, p 383.

[3] C M Judd and B Park, "Definition and Assessment of Accuracy in Social Stereotypes," *Psychological Review*, January 1993, p 110.

[4] For a thorough discussion of stereotype accuracy, see M C Ashton and V M Esses, "Stereotype Accuracy: Estimating the Academic Performance of Ethnic Groups," *Personality and Social Psychology Bulletin*, February 1999, pp 225–36.

[5] For a thorough discussion about the structure and organization of memory, see L R Squire, B Knowlton, and G Musen, "The Structure and Organization of Memory," in *Annual Review of Psychology*, eds L W Porter and M R Rosenzweig (Palo Alto, CA: Annual Reviews Inc., 1993), vol. 44, pp 453–95.

[6] A thorough discussion of the reasoning process used to make judgments and decisions is provided by S A Sloman, "The Empirical Case for Two Systems of Reasoning," *Psychological Bulletin*, January 1996, pp 3–22.

[7] Details of this study can be found in C K Stevens, "Antecedents of Interview Interactions, Interviewers' Ratings, and Applicants' Reactions," *Personnel Psychology*, Spring 1998, pp 55–85.

[8] The effectiveness of rater training was supported by D V Day and L M Sulsky, "Effects of Frame-of-Reference Training and Information Configuration on Memory Organization and Rating Accuracy," *Journal of Applied Psychology*, February 1995, pp 158–67.

[9] Based in part on a definition found in V Gecas, "The Self-Concept," in *Annual Review of Sociology*, eds R H Turner and J F Short Jr. (Palo Alto, CA: Annual Reveiws Inc,. 1982)." Also see N Branden, *Self-Esteem at Work: How Confident People Make Powerful Companies* (San Francisco: Jossey-Bass, 1998).

[10] For related research, see R C Liden, L Martin, and C K Parsons, "Interviewer and Applicant Behaviors in Employment Interviews," *Academy of Management Journal*, April 1993, pp 372–86; M B Setterlund and P M Niedenthal, " 'Who Am I? Why Am I Here?': Self-Esteem, Self-Clarity, and Prototype Matching," *Journal of Personality and Social Psychology*, October 1993, pp 769–80; and G J Pool, W Wood, and K Leck, "The Self-Esteem Motive in Social Influence: Agreement with Valued Majorities and Disagreement with Derogated Minorities," *Journal of Personality and Social Psychology*, October 1998, pp 967–75.

[11] Adapted from discussion in J K Matejka and R J Dunsing, "Great Expectations," *Management World*, January 1987, pp 16–17; and P Pascarella, "It All Begins With Self-Esteem," *Management Review*, February 1999, pp 60–61.

[12] D Rader, "I Always Believed There Was a Place for Me," *Parade Magazine*, May 21, 2000, p 6.

[13] Based on D H Lindsley, D A Brass, and J B Thomas, "Efficacy-Performance Spirals: A Multilevel Perspective," *Academy of Mangement Review*, July 1995, pp 645–78.

[14] For more on learned helplessness, see V Gecas, "The Social Psychology of Self-Efficacy," in *Annual Review of Sociology*, eds W R Scott and J B Lake (Palo Alto, CA: Annual Reviews Inc., 1989), vol 15, pp 291–316; M J Martinko and W L Gardner, "Learned Helplessness: An Alternative Explanation for Performance Deficits," *Academy of Management Review*, April 1982, pp 195–204; and C R Campbell and M J Martinko, "An Integrative Attributional Perspective of Empowerment and Learned Helplessness: A Multimethod Field Study," *Journal of Management*, no. 2, 1998, pp 173–200. Also see A Dickerson and M A Taylor, "Self-Limiting Behavior in Women: Self-Esteem and Self-Efficacy as Predictors," *Group & Organization Management*, June 2000, pp 191–210.

[15] Data from A D Stajkovic and F Luthans, "Self-Efficacy and Work-Related Performance: A Meta-Analysis," *Psychological Bulletin*, September 1998, pp 240–61.

[16] Based in part on discussion in Gecas, "The Social Psychology of Self-Efficacy."

[17] See S K Parker, "Enhancing Role Breadth Self-Efficacy: The Roles of Job Enrichment and Other Organizational Interventions," *Journal of Applied Psychology*, December 1998, pp 835–52.

[18] The positive relationship between self-efficacy and readiness for retraining is documented in L A Hill and J Elias, "Retraining Midcareer Managers: Career History and Self-Efficacy Beliefs," *Human Resource Management*, Summer 1990, pp 197–217. Also see A M Saks, "Longitudinal Field Investigation of the Moderating and Mediating Effects of Self-Efficacy on the Relationship between Training and Newcomer Adjustment," *Journal of Applied Psychology*, April 1995, pp 211–25.

[19] See A D Stajkovic and Fred Luthans, "Social Cognitive Theory and Self-Efficacy: Going Beyond Traditional Motivational and Behavioral Approaches," *Organizational Dynamics*, Spring 1998, pp 62–74.

[20] See P C Earley and T R Lituchy, "Delineating Goal and Efficacy Effects: A Test of Three Models," *Journal of Applied Psychology*, February 1991, pp 81–98.

[21] See W S Silver, T R Mitchell, and M E Gist, "Response to Successful and Unsuccessful Performance: The Moderating Effect of Self-Efficacy on the Relationship between Performance and Attributions," *Organizational Behavior and Human Decision Processes*, June 1995, pp 286–99; R Zemke, "The Corporate Coach," *Training*, December 1996, pp 24–28; and J P Masciarelli, "Less Lonely at the Top," *Management Review*, April 1999, pp 58–61.

[22] For a comprehensive update, see S W Gangestad and M Snyder, "Self-Monitoring: Appraisal and Reappraisal," *Psychological Bulletin*, July 2000, pp 530–55.

[23] Kelley's model is discussed in detail in H H Kelley, "The Processes of Causal Attribution," *American Psychologist*, February 1973, pp 107–28.

[24] For examples, see J Susskind, K Maurer, V Thakkar, D L Hamilton, and J W Sherman, "Perceiving Individuals and Groups: Expectancies, Dispositional Inferences, and Causal Attributions," *Journal of Personality and Social Psychology*, February 1999, pp 181–91; and J McClure, "Discounting Causes of Behavior: Are Two Reasons Better than One?" *Journal of Personality and Social Psychology*, January 1998, pp 7–20.

[25] The effect of the self-serving bias was tested and supported by P E De Michele, B Gansneder, G B Solomon, "Success and Failure Attributions of Wrestlers: Further Evidence of the Self-Serving Bias," *Journal of Sport Behavior*, August 1998, pp 242–55; and C Sedikides, W K Campbell, G D Reeder, and A J Elliot, "The Self-Serving Bias in Relational Context," *Journal of Personality and Social Psychology*, February 1998, pp 378–86.

[26] See D Konst, R Vonk, and R V D Vlist, "Inferences about Causes and Consequences of Behavior of Leaders and Subordinates," *Journal of Organizational Behavior*, March 1999, pp 261–71.

[27] See M Miserandino, "Attributional Retraining as a Method of Improving Athletic Performance," *Journal of Sport Behavior*, August 1998, pp 286–97; and F Forsterling, "Attributional Retraining: A Review," *Psychological Bulletin*, November 1985, pp 496–512.

[28] Adult personality changes are documented in L Kaufman Cartwright and P Wink, "Personality Change in Women Physicians from Medical Student to Mid-40s," *Psychology of Women Quarterly*, June 1994, pp 291–308. Also see L Pulkkinen, M Ohranen, and A Tolvanen, "Personality Antecedents of Career Orientation and Stability among Women Compared to Men," *Journal of Vocational Behavior*, February 1999, pp 37–58.

[29] The landmark report is J M Digman, "Personality Structure: Emergence of the Five-Factor Model," *Annual Review of Psychology*, vol. 41, 1990, pp 417–40. Also see C Viswesvaran and D S Ones, "Measurement Error in 'Big Five Factors' Personality Assessment: Reliability Generalization across Studies and Measures," *Educational and Psychological Measurement*, April 2000, pp 224–35.

[30] See K M DeNeve and H Cooper, "The Happy Personality: A Meta-Analysis of 137 Personality Traits and Subjective Well-Being," *Psychological Bulletin*, September 1998, pp 197–229; and D P Skarlicki, R Folger, and P Tesluk, "Personality as a Moderator in the Relationship between Fairness and Retaliation," *Academy of Management Journal*, February 1999, pp 100–108.

[31] Data from S V Paunonen et al., "The Structure of Personality in Six Cultures," *Journal of Cross-Cultural Psychology*, May 1996, pp 339–53. Also see M Dalton and M Wilson, "The Relationship of the Five-Factor Model of Personality to Job Performance for a Group of Middle Eastern Expatriate Managers," *Journal of Cross-Cultural Psychology*, March 2000, pp 250–58.

[32] M R Barrick and M K Mount, "The Big Five Personality Dimensions and Job Performance: A Meta-Analysis," *Personnel Psychology*, Spring 1991, pp 1–26. See O Behling, "Employee Selection: Will Intelligence and Conscientiousness Do the Job?" *Academy of Management Executive*, February 1998, pp 77–86; and J A Lepine and L Van Dyne, "Peer Responses to Low Performers: An Attributional Model of Helping in the Context of Groups," *Academy of Management Review*, January 2001, pp 67–84.

[33] Barrick and Mount, "The Big Five Personality Dimensions and Job Performance: A Meta-Analysis," p 21. Also see D M Tokar, A R Fischer, and L M Subich, "Personality and Vocational Behavior: A Selective Review of the Literature, 1993–1997," *Journal of Vocational Behavior*, October 1998, pp 115–53; and K C Wooten, T A Timmerman, and R Folger, "The Use of Personality and the Five-Factor Model to Predict New Business Ventures: From Outplacement to Start-up," *Journal of Vocational Behavior*, February 1999, pp 82–101.

[34] See the entire issue of "State of Small Business 2001," *Inc.*, May 29, 2001.

[35] For an overall review of research on locus of control, see P E Spector, "Behavior in Organizations as a Function of Employee's Locus of Control," *Psychological Bulletin*, May 1982, pp 482–97; the relationship between locus of control and performance and satisfaction is examined in D R Norris and R E Niebuhr, "Attributional Influences on the Job Performance–Job Satisfaction Relationship," *Academy of Management Journal*, June 1984, pp 424–31; salary differences between internals and externals were examined by P C Nystrom, "Managers' Salaries and Their Beliefs about Reinforcement Control," *Journal of Social Psychology*, August 1983, pp 291–92. Also see S S K Lam and J Schaubroeck, "The Role of Locus of Control in Reactions to Being Promoted and to Being Passed Over: A Quasi Experiment," *Academy of Management Journal*, February 2000, pp 66–78.

[36] See S R Hawk, "Locus of Control and Computer Attitude: The Effect of User Involvement," *Computers in Human Behavior*, no. 3, 1989, pp 199–206. Also see A S Phillips and A G Bedeian, "Leader-Follower Exchange Quality: The Role of Personal and Interpersonal Attributes," *Academy of Management Journal*, August 1994, pp 990–1001.

[37] These recommendations are from Spector, "Behavior in Organizations as a Function of Employee's Locus of Control."

[38] M Fishbein and I Ajzen, *Belief, Attitude, Intention and Behavior: An Introduction to Theory and Research* (Reading, MA: Addison-Wesley Publishing, 1975), p 6. For more, see D Andrich and I M Styles, "The Structural Relationship between Attitude and Behavior Statements from the Unfolding Perspective," *Psychological Methods*, December 1998, pp 454–69; A P Brief, *Attitudes In and Around Organizations* (Thousand Oaks, CA: Sage Publications, 1998); and "Tips to Pick the Best Employee," *Business Week*, March 1, 1999, p 24.

[39] For a discussion of the difference between values and attitudes, see B W Becker and P E Connor, "Changing American Values—Debunking the Myth," *Business*, January–March 1985, pp 56–59.

[40] See A R Karr, "Work Week: A Special News Report about Life on the Job—And Trends Taking Shape There," *The Wall Street Journal*, June 29, 1999, p A1.

[41] See J P Wanous, T D Poland, S L Premack, and K S Davis, "The Effects of Met Expectations on Newcomer Attitudes and Behaviors: A Review and Meta-Analysis," *Journal of Applied Psychology*, June 1992, pp 288–97.

[42] A complete description of this model is provided by E A Locke, "Job Satisfaction," in *Social Psychology and Organizational Behavior*, eds M Gruneberg and T Wall (New York: John Wiley & Sons, 1984).

[43] Results from the meta-analysis can be found in L A Witt and L G Nye, "Gender and the Relationship between Perceived Fairness of Pay or Promotion and Job Satisfaction," *Journal of Applied Psychology*, December 1992, pp 910–17.

[44] Results can be found in T A Judge and J E Bono, "Relationship of Core Self-Evaluations Traits—Self-Esteem, Generalized Self-Efficacy, Locus of Control, and Emotional Stability—with Job Satisfaction and Job Performance: A Meta-Analysis," *Journal of Applied Psychology*, February 2001, pp 80–92.

[45] R S Lazarus, *Emotion and Adaptation* (New York: Oxford University Press, 1991), p 6. Also see, Goleman, Emotional Intelligence, pp 289–90; and J A Russell and L F Barrett, "Core Affect, Prototypical Emotional Episodes, and Other Things Called Emotion: Dissecting the Elephant," *Journal of Personality and Social Psychology*, May 1999, pp 805–19.

[46] Based on discussion in R D Arvey, G L Renz, and T W Watson, "Emotionality and Job Performance: Implications for Personnel Selection," in *Research in Personnel and Human Resources Management*, vol. 16, ed G R Ferris (Stamford, CT: JAI Press, 1998), pp 103–47. Also see L A King, "Ambivalence Over Emotional Expression and Reading Emotions," *Journal of Personality and Social Psychology*, March 1998, pp 753–62.

[47] J A Morris and D C Feldman, "The Dimensions, Antecedents, and Consequences of Emotional Labor," *Academy of Management Review*, 21, 1996, pp 986–1010; B E Ashforth and R H Humphrey, "Emotional Labor in Service Roles: The Influence of Identity," *Academy of Management Review*, 18, 1993, pp 88–115.

[48] K Pugliesi, "The Consequences of Emotional Labor: Effects on Work Stress, Job Satisfaction, and Well-Being," *Motivation and Emotion*, 23, June 1999, pp 125–54; A S Wharton, "The Psychosocial Consequences of Emotional Labor," *Annals of the American Academy of Political and Social Science*, 561, January 1999, pp 158–76; J A Morris and D C Feldman, "Managing Emotions in the Workplace," *Journal of Managerial Issues*, 9, Fall 1997, pp 257–74; P K Adelmann, "Emotional Labor as a Potential Source of Job Stress," in S Sauter and L P Murphy (eds), *Organizational Risk Factors for Job Stress*, (Washington DC: American Psychological Association, 1995), Chapter 24.

[49] Based on J M Kidd, "Emotion: An Absent Presence in Career Theory," *Journal of Vocational Behavior*, June 1998, pp 275–88.

[50] Data from A M Kring and A H Gordon, "Sex Differences in Emotions: Expression, Experience, and Physiology," *Journal of Personality and Social Psychology*, March 1998, pp 686–703.

[51] Drawn from P Totterdell, S Kellett, K Teuchmann, and R B Briner, "Evidence of Mood Linkage in Work Groups," *Journal of Personality and Social Psychology*, June 1998, pp 1504–15.

[52] D Goleman, Emotional Intelligence (New York: Bantam Books, 1995), p 34. For more, see Q N Huy, "Emotional Capability, Emotional Intelligence, and Radical Change," *Academy of Management Review*, April 1999, pp 325–45; and V U Druskat and S B Wolff, "Building the Emotional Intelligence of Groups," *Harvard Business Review*, March 2001, pp 80–90.

[53] D. Goleman, "What Makes a Leader?" *Harvard Business Review*, 76, November–December 1998, pp 92–102.

[54] A Fisher, "Success Secret: A High Emotional IQ," *Fortune*, October 26, 1998, p 294.

55 B Evenson, "Americans are More Emotionally Mature: Test," *National Post*, July 15, 1999, pp A1, A11; K Vermond, "Emotional Intelligence," *HR Professional*, April-May 1999, pp 38–39; "Unconventional Smarts," *Across the Board*, 35, January 1998, pp 22–23; M N Martinez, "The Smarts That Count," *HR Magazine*, 42, November 1997, pp 72–78.

Chapter 3

1 T R Mitchell, "Motivation: New Direction for Theory, Research, and Practice," *Academy of Management Review*, January 1982, p 81.

2 For a complete description of Maslow's theory, see A H Maslow, "A Theory of Human Motivation," *Psychological Review*, July 1943, pp 370–96.

3 H A Murray, *Explorations in Personality* (New York: John Wiley & Sons, 1938), p 164.

4 See the following series of research reports: D K McNeese-Smith, "The Relationship between Managerial Motivation, Leadership, Nurse Outcomes and Patient Satisfaction," *Journal of Organizational Behavior*, March 1999, pp 243–59; A M Harrell and M J Stahl, "A Behavioral Decision Theory Approach for Measuring McClelland's Trichotomy of Needs," *Journal of Applied Psychology*, April 1981, pp 242–47; and M J Stahl, "Achievement, Power and Managerial Motivation: Selecting Managerial Talent with the Job Choice Exercise," *Personnel Psychology*, Winter 1983, pp 775–89.

5 Evidence for the validity of motivation training can be found in H Heckhausen and S Krug, "Motive Modification," in *Motivation and Society*, ed A J Stewart (San Francisco: Jossey-Bass, 1982). Also see S D Bluen, J Barling, and W Burns, "Predicting Sales Performance, Job Satisfaction, and Depression by Using the Achievement Strivings and Impatience–Irritability Dimensions of Type A Behavior," *Journal of Applied Psychology*, April 1990, pp 212–16.

6 Results can be found in D B Turban and T L Keon, "Organizational Attractiveness: An Interactionist Perspective," *Journal of Applied Psychology*, April 1993, pp 184–93.

7 See D Steele Johnson and R Perlow, "The Impact of Need for Achievement Components on Goal Commitment and Performance," *Journal of Applied Social Psychology*, November 1992, pp 1711–20.

8 J L Bowditch and A F Buono, *A Primer on Organizational Behavior* (New York: John Wiley & Sons, 1985), p 210.

9 See J D Edwards, J A Scully, and M D Brtek, "The Nature and Outcomes of Work: A Replication and Extension of Interdisciplinary Work-Design Research," *Journal of Applied Psychology*, December 2000, pp 860–68.

10 See F Herzberg, B Mausner, and B B Snyderman, *The Motivation to Work* (New York: John Wiley & Sons, 1959).

11 J R Hackman, G R Oldham, R Janson, and K Purdy, "A New Strategy for Job Enrichment," *California Management Review*, Summer 1975, p 58.

12 Definitions of the job characteristics were adapted from J R Hackman and G R Oldham, "Motivation through the Design of Work: Test of a Theory," *Organizational Behavior and Human Performance*, August 1976, pp 250–79.

13 Results can be found in M R Kelley, "New Process Technology, Job Design, and Work Organization: A Contingency Model," *American Sociological Review*, April 1990, pp 191–208.

14 See L Festinger, *A Theory of Cognitive Dissonance* (Stanford, CA: Stanford University Press, 1957).

15 Inputs and outputs are discussed by J S Adams, "Toward an Understanding of Inequity," *Journal of Abnormal and Social Psychology*, November 1963, pp 422–36.

16 The generalizability of the equity norm was examined by J K Giacobbe-Miller, D J Miller, and V I Victorov, "A Comparison of Russian and U.S. Pay Allocation Decisions, Distributive Justice Judgments, and Productivity Under Different Payment Conditions," *Personnel Psychology*, Spring 1998, pp 137–63.

17 The choice of a comparison person is discussed by P P Shah, "Who Are Employees' Social Referents? Using a Network Perspective to Determine Referent Others," *Academy of Management Journal*, June 1998, pp 249–68; and J Greenberg and C L McCarty, "Comparable Worth: A Matter of Justice," in *Research in Personnel and Human Resources Manage-*

ment, eds G R Ferris and K M Rowland (Greenwich, CT: JAI Press, 1990), vol. 8, pp 265–303.

18 See the discussion by M A Konovsky, "Understanding Procedural Justice and Its Impact on Business Organizations," *Journal of Management*, 2000, pp 489–511.

19 M A Korsgaard, L Roberson, and R D Rymph, "What Motivates Fairness? The Role of Subordinate Assertive Behavior on Manager's Interactional Fairness," *Journal of Applied Psychology*, October 1998, p 731.

20 See C R Wanberg, L W Bunce, and M B Gavin, "Perceived Fairness of Layoffs among Individuals Who Have Been Laid Off: A Longitudinal Study," *Personnel Psychology*, Spring 1999, pp 59–84.

21 The role of equity in organizational change is thoroughly discussed by A T Cobb, R Folger, and K Wooten, "The Role Justice Plays in Organizational Change," *Public Administration Quarterly*, Summer 1995, pp 135–51.

22 For a complete discussion of Vroom's theory, see V H Vroom, *Work and Motivation* (New York: John Wiley & Sons, 1964).

23 See J Chowdhury, "The Motivational Impact of Sales Quotas on Effort," *Journal of Marketing Research*, February 1993, pp 28–41; and C C Pinder, *Work Motivation* (Glenview, IL: Scott, Foresman, 1984), ch 7.

24 The measurement and importance of valence was investigated by N T Feather, "Values, Valences, and Choice: The Influence of Values on the Perceived Attractiveness and Choice of Alternatives," *Journal of Personality and Social Psychology*, June 1995, pp 1135–51.

25 Supportive results are presented in L Morris, "Employees Not Encouraged to Go Extra Mile," *Training & Development*, April 1996, pp 59–60.

26 See D R Spitzer, "Power Rewards: Rewards That Really Motivate," *Management Review*, May 1996, pp 45–50; and A Kohn, *Punished by Rewards: The Trouble with Gold Stars, Incentive Plans, A's, Praise, and Other Bribes* (Boston: Houghton Mifflin, 1993).

27 E A Locke, K N Shaw, L M Saari, and G P Latham, "Goal Setting and Task Performance: 1969–1980," *Psychological Bulletin*, July 1981, p 126.

28 A thorough discussion of MBO is provided by P F Drucker, *The Practice of Management* (New York: Harper, 1954).

29 Excerpted from M Campbell, "Dream Work: How Steven Spielberg, the Most Successful Film Director of All Time, Turned His Dreams into Reality," *Selling Power*, April 1999, pp 92–93.

30 This linear relationship was not supported by P M Wright, J R Hollenbeck, S Wolf, and G C McMahan, "The Effects of Varying Goal Difficulty Operationalizations on Goal Setting Outcomes and Processes," *Organizational Behavior and Human Decision Processes*, January 1995, pp 28–43.

31 See Locke, Shaw, Saari, and Latham, "Goal Setting and Task Performance: 1969–1980"; and A J Mento, R P Steel, and R J Karren, "A Meta-Analytic Study of the Effects of Goal Setting on Task Performance: 1966–1984," *Organizational Behavior and Human Decision Processes*, February 1987, pp 52–83.

32 D Jenish and B Woodward, "Canada's Top 100 Employers," *Maclean's*, November 5, 2001, p 54.

33 Results from the meta-analysis can be found in R E Wood, A J Mento, and E A Locke, "Task Complexity as a Moderator of Goal Effects: A Meta-Analysis," *Journal of Applied Psychology*, August 1987, pp 416–25.

34 Supportive results can be found in K L Langeland, C M Johnson, and T C Mawhinney, "Improving Staff Performance in a Community Mental Health Setting: Job Analysis, Training, Goal Setting, Feedback, and Years of Data," *Journal of Organizational Behavior Management*, 1998, pp 21–43; and L A Wilk, "The Effects of Feedback and Goal Setting on the Productivity and Satisfaction of University Admissions Staff," *Journal of Organizational Behavior Management*, 1998, pp 45–68.

35 See E A Locke and G P Latham, *A Theory of Goal Setting & Task Performance* (Englewood Cliffs, NJ: Prentice Hall, 1990).

36 Results can be found in G H Seijts and G P Latham, "The Effect of Distal Learning, Outcome, and Proximal Goals on a Moderately Complex Task," *Journal of Organizational Behavior*, May 2001, pp 291–307.

37 E A Locke and G P Latham, *Goal Setting: A Motivational Technique That Works!* (Englewood Cliffs, NJ: Prentice Hall, 1984), p 79.

38 T R Mitchell, "Motivation: New Directions for Theory, Research, and Practice," *Academy of Management Review*, January 1982, p 81.

[39] This conclusion is consistent with research summarized in F Luthans and A D Stajkovic, "Reinforce for Performance: The Need to Go Beyond Pay and Even Rewards," *Academy of Management Executive*, May 1999, pp 49–57.

[40] For a thorough discussion about the use of team rewards, see L N McClurg, "Team Rewards: How Far Have We Come?" *Human Resource Management*, Spring 2001, pp 73–86.

[41] Results from this study are reported in K A Kovach, "What Motivates Employees? Workers and Supervisors Give Different Answers," *Business Horizons*, September–October 1987, pp 58–65.

[42] Actual survey rankings are as follows: (1) interesting work, (2) full appreciation of work done, (3) feeling of being in on things, (4) personal loyalty to employees, (5) good wages, (6) promotions and growth in the organization, (7) good working conditions, (8) personal loyalty to employees, (9) tactful discipline, and (10) sympathetic help with personal problems.

[43] Scoring Key for Measuring Your Growth Need Strength:
Step 1: The Growth Need Strength Scale yields a number from 1 (strongly prefer A) to 5 (Strongly Prefer B). Write your circled numbers for the items as follows and total them: __/(#1) + __/(#5) + __/(#7) + __/(#10) + __/(#11) + __/(#12) = Subtotal A
Step 2: The remaining items in the Growth Need Strength Scale need to be reverse-scored. To calculate a reverse score, subtract the direct score from 6. For example, if you circled 4 in one of these items, the reverse score would be 2 (i.e., $6 - 4 = 2$). If you circled 1, the reverse score would be 5 (i.e., $6 - 1 = 5$). Calculate the reverse scores for each of the items listed below and write them in the space provided. Then calculate Subtotal B by totaling these reverse scores. __/(#2) + __/(#3) + __/(#4) + __/(#6) + __/(#8) + __/(#9) = Subtotal B.
Step 3: Calculate the total score by summing Subtotal A and Subtotal B.

Chapter 4

[1] For instance, see "Worker Retention Presents Challenge to U.S. Employers," *HR Magazine*, September 1998, p 22; L Wah, "An Ounce of Prevention," *Management Review*, October 1998, p 9; and S Armour, "Cash or Critiques: Which Is Best?" *USA Today*, December 16, 1998, p 6B.

[2] As quoted in C Fishman, "Fred Smith," *Fast Company*, June 2001, pp 64, 66.

[3] Data from M Hequet, "Giving Feedback," *Training*, September 1994, pp 72–77.

[4] C Bell and R Zemke, "On-Target Feedback," *Training*, June 1992, p 36.

[5] Both the definition of feedback and the functions of feedback are based on discussion in D R Ilgen, C D Fisher, and M S Taylor, "Consequences of Individual Feedback on Behavior in Organizations," *Journal of Applied Psychology*, August 1979, pp 349–71; and R E Kopelman, *Managing Productivity in Organizations: A Practical People-Oriented Perspective* (New York: McGraw-Hill, 1986), p 175.

[6] See P C Earley, G B Northcraft, C Lee, and T R Lituchy, "Impact of Process and Outcome Feedback on the Relation of Goal Setting to Task Performance," *Academy of Management Journal*, March 1990, pp 87–105.

[7] For relevant research, see J S Goodman, "The Interactive Effects of Task and External Feedback on Practice Performance and Learning," *Organizational Behavior and Human Decision Processes*, December 1998, pp 223–52.

[8] See B D Bannister, "Performance Outcome Feedback and Attributional Feedback: Interactive Effects on Recipient Responses," *Journal of Applied Psychology*, May 1986, pp 203–10.

[9] For complete details, see P M Podsakoff and J-L Farh, "Effects of Feedback Sign and Credibility on Goal Setting and Task Performance," *Organizational Behavior and Human Decision Processes*, August 1989, pp 45–67. Also see S J Ashford and A S Tsui, "Self-Regulation for Managerial Effectiveness: The Role of Active Feedback Seeking," *Academy of Management Journal*, June 1991, pp 251–80.

[10] See "How to Take the Venom Out of Vitriol," *Training*, June 2000, p 28.

[11] W S Silver, T R Mitchell, and M E Gist, "Responses to Successful and Unsuccessful Performance: The Moderating Effect of Self-Efficacy on the Relationship between Performance and Attributions," *Organizational Behavior and Human Decision Processes*, June 1995, p 297. Also see T A Louie, "Decision Makers' Hindsight Bias after Receiving Favorable and Unfavorable Feedback," *Journal of Applied Psychology*, February 1999, pp 29–41.

[12] M McDougall and L Cassiani, "HR Cited in Unfair Performance Review," *Canadian HR Reporter*, September 10, 2001, pp 1, 6.

[13] See S H Barr and E J Conlon, "Effects of Distribution of Feedback in Work Groups," *Academy of Management Journal*, June 1994, pp 641–55.

[14] See M R Edwards, A J Ewen, and W A Verdini, "Fair Performance Management and Pay Practices for Diverse Work Forces: The Promise of Multisource Assessment," *ACA Journal*, Spring 1995, pp 50–63.

[15] See G D Huet-Cox, T M Nielsen, and E Sundstrom, "Get the Most from 360-Degree Feedback: Put It on the Internet," *HR Magazine*, May 1999, pp 92–103.

[16] This list is based in part on discussion in H J Bernardin, "Subordinate Appraisal: A Valuable Source of Information about Managers," *Human Resource Management*, Fall 1986, pp 421–39.

[17] T Bentley, "Internet Addresses 360-Degree Feedback Concerns," *Canadian HR Reporter*, May 8, 2000, pp G3, G15.

[18] Data from D Antonioni, "The Effects of Feedback Accountability on Upward Appraisal Ratings," *Personnel Psychology*, Summer 1994, pp 349–56.

[19] Data from J W Smither, M London, N L Vasilopoulos, R R Reilly, R E Millsap, and N Salvemini, "An Examination of the Effects of an Upward Feedback Program Over Time," *Personnel Psychology*, Spring 1995, pp 1–34.

[20] See S Haworth, "The Dark Side of Multi-Rater Assessments," *HR Magazine*, May 1998, pp 106–14; and D A Waldman, L E Atwater, and D Antonioni, "Has 360 Degree Feedback Gone Amok?" *Academy of Management Executive*, May 1998, pp 86–94.

[21] See K E Morical, "A Product Review: 360 Assessments," *Training & Development*, April 1999, pp 43–47. Also see N E Fried, "3608 Software Shootout: Comparing Features with Needs," *HR Magazine* (Focus), December 1998, pp 8–13.

[22] See M M Harris and J Schaubroeck, "A Meta-Analysis of Self-Supervisor, Self-Peer, and Peer-Supervisor Ratings," *Personnel Psychology*, Spring 1988, pp 43–62; and J Lane and P Herriot, "Self-Ratings, Supervisor Ratings, Positions and Performance," *Journal of Occupational Psychology*, March 1990, pp 77–88.

[23] See D E Coates, "Don't Tie 360 Feedback to Pay," *Training*, September 1998, pp 68–78.

[24] D Brown, "Coming Full Circle on 360 Feedback," *Canadian HR Reporter*, March 13, 2000, pp 1, 19.

[25] W W Tornow and M London, "360-Degree Feedback: The Leadership Challenges," *Leadership in Action*, 18, 1998, pp 1, 12–13; M A Dalton, "Using 360-Degree Feedback Successfully," *Leadership in Action*, 18, 1998, pp 2, 11.

[26] Adapted from C Bell and R Zemke, "On-Target Feedback," *Training*, June 1992, pp 36–44.

[27] See B Filipczak, "Can't Buy Me Love," *Training*, January 1996, pp 29–34; and S Kerr, "Risky Business: The New Pay Game," *Fortune*, July 22, 1996, pp 94–95.

[28] See M Schrage, "Actually, I'd Rather Have That Favor Than a Raise," *Fortune*, April 16, 2001, p 412.

[29] For example, see B Nelson, *1001 Ways to Reward Employees* (New York: Workman Publishing, 1994); and "Emerging Optional Benefits," *Management Review*, December 1998, p 8. For more on stock options, see B McLean, "The Bad News about Options," *Fortune*, November 13, 2000, pp 429–30; and "Employee Stock Options Are Still Hot," *Business Week*, May 28, 2001, p 16.

[30] W J Wiatrowski, "Family-Related Benefits in the Workplace," *Monthly Labor Review*, March 1990, p 28. Also see R Kuttner, "Pensions: How Much Risk Should Workers Have to Bear?" *Business Week*, April 16, 2001, p 23.

[31] For complete discussions, see A P Brief and R J Aldag, "The Intrinsic-Extrinsic Dichotomy: Toward Conceptual Clarity," *Academy of Management Review*, July 1977, pp 496–500; E L Deci, *Intrinsic Motivation* (New York: Plenum Press, 1975), ch 2; and E L Deci, R Koestner, and R M Ryan, "A Meta-Analytic Review of Experiments Examining the

Effects of Extrinsic Rewards on Intrinsic Motivation," *Psychological Bulletin*, November 1999, pp 627–68.

[32] See "The Business World Is Still a Man's World," *USA Today*, April 11, 2001, p 1B; L Lavelle, "For Female CEOs, It's Still Stingy at the Top," *Business Week*, April 23, 2001, pp 70–71; and G Koretz, "She's a Woman, Offer Her Less," *Business Week*, May 7, 2001, p 34.

[33] Based on M Bloom, "The Performance Effects of Pay Dispersion on Individuals and Organizations," *Academy of Management Journal*, February 1999, pp 25–40.

[34] For recent data, see L Lavelle, "Executive Pay," *Business Week*, April 16, 2001, pp 76–80.

[35] List adapted from J L Pearce and R H Peters, "A Contradictory Norms View of Employer–Employee Exchange," *Journal of Management*, Spring 1985, pp 19–30.

[36] Ibid, p 25.

[37] L Cassiani, "Being a Best Employer Means Being Serious About Recognition," *Canadian HR Reporter*, March 12, 2001, pp 7, 10.

[38] M Von Glinow, "Reward Strategies for Attracting, Evaluating, and Retaining Professionals," *Human Resource Management*, Summer 1985, p 193.

[39] L Cassiani, "Being a Best Employer Means Being Serious About Recognition."

[40] Six reward system objectives are discussed in E E Lawler III, "The New Pay: A Strategic Approach," *Compensation & Benefits Review*, July–August 1995, pp 14–22.

[41] "The 50 Best Companies to Work for in Canada," *Report on Business Magazine*, January 2002, pp 41–52.

[42] D R Spitzer, "Power Rewards: Rewards That Really Motivate," *Management Review*, May 1996, p 47. Also see S Kerr, "An Academy Classic: On the Folly of Rewarding A, while Hoping for B," *Academy of Management Executive*, February 1995, pp 7–14.

[43] List adapted from discussion in Spitzer, "Power Rewards: Rewards That Really Motivate," pp 45–50. Also see R Eisenberger and J Cameron, "Detrimental Effects of Reward: Reality or Myth?" *American Psychologist*, November 1996, pp 1153–66.

[44] See, for example, T P Flannery, D A Hofrichter, and P E Platten, *People, Performance, and Pay: Dynamic Compensation for Changing Organizations* (New York: The Free Press, 1996). Also see R S Allen and R H Kilmann, "Aligning Reward Practices in Support of Total Quality Management," *Business Horizons*, May–June 2001, pp 77–84.

[45] For a recent unconventional perspective, see R J DeGrandpre, "A Science of Meaning? Can Behaviorism Bring Meaning to Psychological Science?" *American Psychologist*, July 2000, pp 721–38.

[46] For interesting discussions of Skinner and one of his students, see M B Gilbert and T F Gilbert, "What Skinner Gave Us," *Training*, September 1991, pp 42–48; and "HRD Pioneer Gilbert Leaves a Pervasive Legacy," *Training*, January 1996, p 14.

[47] See F Luthans and R Kreitner, *Organizational Behavior Modification and Beyond: An Operant and Social Learning Approach* (Glenview, IL: Scott, Foresman, 1985), pp 49–56.

[48] The effect of praise is explored in C M Mueller and C S Dweck, "Praise for Intelligence Can Undermine Children's Motivation and Performance," *Journal of Personality and Social Psychology*, July 1998, pp 33–52.

[49] See D H B Welsh, D J Bernstein, and F Luthans, "Application of the Premack Principle of Reinforcement to the Quality Performance of Service Employees," *Journal of Organizational Behavior* Management, no. 1, 1992, pp 9–32.

[50] See C B Ferster and B F Skinner, *Schedules of Reinforcement* (New York: Appleton-Century-Crofts, 1957).

[51] See L M Saari and G P Latham, "Employee Reactions to Continuous and Variable Ratio Reinforcement Schedules Involving a Monetary Incentive," *Journal of Applied Psychology*, August 1982, pp 506–8.

[52] P Brinkley-Rogers and R Collier, "Along the Colorado, the Money's Flowing," *The Arizona Republic*, March 4, 1990, p A12.

[53] The topic of managerial credibility is covered in J M Kouzes and B Z Posner, *Credibility* (San Francisco: Jossey-Bass, 1993).

[54] See, for example, J C Bruening, "Shaping Workers' Attitudes toward Safety," *Occupational Hazards*, March 1990, pp 49–51.

[55] Adapted from A T Hollingsworth and D Tanquay Hoyer, "How Supervisors Can Shape Behavior," *Personnel Journal*, May 1985, pp 86, 88.

[56] This exercise is adapted from material in D M Herold and C K Parsons, "Assessing the Feedback Environment in Work Organizations: Development of the Job Feedback Survey," *Journal of Applied Psychology*, May 1985, pp 290–305.

Chapter 5

[1] L Hyatt, "Job Stress: Have We Reached the Breaking Point?" *Workplace Today*, January 2002, pp 14–16, 37.

[2] The stress response is thoroughly discussed by H Selye, *Stress Without Distress* (New York: J B Lippincott, 1974).

[3] J M Ivancevich and M T Matteson, *Stress and Work: A Managerial Perspective* (Glenview, IL: Scott, Foresman, 1980), pp 8–9.

[4] "Work Pressure is Top Cause of Stress," *Workplace Today*, January 2001, p 6.

[5] See J D Jonge, G J P Van Breikelen, J A Landeweerd, and F J N Nijhuis, "Comparing Group and Individual Level Assessments of Job Characteristics in Testing the Job Demand-Control Model: A Multilevel Approach," *Human Relations*, January 1999, pp 95–122; and J Schaubroeck and L S Fink, "Facilitating and Inhibiting Effects of Job Control and Social Support on Stress Outcomes and Role Behavior: A Contingency Model," *Journal of Organizational Behavior*, March 1998, pp 167–95.

[6] Results from these studies are reported in C Frankie, "Americans Tops in Work Messages," *The Arizona Republic*, October 3, 1999, p A29; and A R Karr, "Work Week: A Special News Report About Life on the Job—And Trends Taking Shape There," *The Wall Street Journal*, February 9, 1999, p A1.

[7] Supportive results can be found in V J Magley, C L Hulin, L F Fitzgerald, and M DeNardo, "Outcomes of Self-Labeling Sexual Harassment," *Journal of Applied Psychology*, June 1999, pp 390–402; and L F Fitzgerald, F Drasgow, C L Hulin, M J Gelfand, and V J Magley, "Antecedents and Consequences of Sexual Harassment in Organizations: A Test of an Integrated Model," *Journal of Applied Psychology*, August 1997, pp 578–89.

[8] M Johne, "When Bullies Go to Work: Employers That Tolerate Abuse Risk Lower Productivity, Higher Staff Turnover, Costly Legal Fees—And Worse," *Globe and Mail*, April 17, 2002, p C1.

[9] The relationship between chronic work demands and stress was investigated by J Schaubroeck and D C Ganster, "Chronic Demands and Responsivity to Challenge," *Journal of Applied Psychology*, February 1993, pp 73–85.

[10] See J M Plas, *Person-Centered Leadership: An American Approach to Participatory Management* (Thousand Oaks, CA: Sage, 1996).

[11] Excerpted from R Ganzel, "Feeling Squeezed by Technology?" *Training*, April 1998, pp 62–70.

[12] See G Stern, "Take a Bite, Do Some Work, Take a Bite," *The Wall Street Journal*, January 17, 1994, pp B1, B2; R F Bettendorf, "Curing the New Ills of Technology: Proper Ergonomics Can Reduce Cumulative Trauma Disorder Among Employees," *HR Magazine*, March 1990, pp 35–36, 80; and S Overman, "Prescriptions for a Healthier Office," *HR Magazine*, February 1990, pp 30–34.

[13] L Duxbury and C Higgins, "Supportive Managers: What Are They? Why do They Matter?" *The HRM Research Quarterly*, Winter 1997, pp 1–4. See also E Church, "Work Winning Out Over Family in the Struggle for Balance," *Globe and Mail*, February 13, 2002, p B1.

[14] E Church, "Work Winning Out Over Family in the Struggle for Balance."

[15] See R Lazarus, *Stress and Emotion: A New Synthesis* (New York: Springer Publishing, 1999).

[16] Research on job loss is summarized by K A Hanisch, "Job Loss and Unemployment Research from 1994 to 1998: A Review and Recommendations for Research and Intervention," *Journal of Vocational Behavior*, October 1999, pp 188–220.

[17] Supportive results can be found in A A Grandey and R Cropanzano, "The Conservation of Resources Model Applied to Work-Family Conflict and Strain," *Journal of Vocational Behavior*, April 1999, pp 350–70; J R Edwards and N P Rothbard, "Work and Family Stress and Well-Being: An Examination of Person-Environment Fit in the Work and Family Domains," *Organizational Behavior and Human Decision Processes*, February 1999, pp 85–129; and A J Kinicki, F M McKee, and K J Wade,

"Annual Review, 1991–1995: Occupational Health," *Journal of Vocational Behavior*, October 1996, pp 190–220.

[18] Reviews of this research can be found in R S DeFrank and J M Ivancevich, "Sress on the Job: An Executive Update," *Academy of Management Executive*, August 1998, pp 55–66; and M Koslowsky, *Modeling the Stress-Strain Relationship in Work Settings*, (New York: Routledge, 1998).

[19] Results can be found in L Narayanan, S Menon, and P E Spector, "Stress in the Workplace: A Comparison of Gender and Occupations," *Journal of Organizational Behavior*, January 1999, pp 63–73.

[20] See M E Lachman and S L Weaver, "The Sense of Control as a Moderator of Social Class Differences in Health and Well-Being," *Journal of Personality and Social Psychology*, March 1998, pp 763–73.

[21] These findings are reported in B Melin, U Lundberg, J Soderlund, and M Granqvist, "Psychological and Physiological Stress Reactions of Male and Female Assembly Workers: A Comparison Between Two Different Forms of Work Organization," *Journal of Organizational Behavior*, January 1999, pp 47–61.

[22] Research on chronic hostility is discussed by "Healthy Lives: A New View of Stress." *University of California, Berkeley Wellness Letter*, June 1990, pp 4–5. Also see R S Jorgensen, B T Johnson, M E Kolodziej, and G E Schreer, "Elevated Blood Pressure and Personality: A Meta-Analytic Review," *Psychological Bulletin*, September 1996, pp 293–320.

[23] This research is discussed by K S Kendler, L M Karkowski, and C A Prescott, "Causal Relationship Between Stressful Life Events and the Onset of Major Depression," *American Journal of Psychiatry*, June 1999, pp 837–48; C Segrin, "Social Skills, Stressful Life Events, and the Development of Psychosocial Problems," *Journal of Social And Clinical Psychology*, Spring 1999, pp 14–34; and R S Bhagat, "Effects of Stressful Life Events on Individual Performance Effectiveness and Work Adjustment Processes Within Organizational Settings: A Research Model," *Academy of Management Review*, October 1983, pp 660–71.

[24] See D R Pillow, A J Zautra, and I Sandler, "Major Life Events and Minor Stressors: Identifying Mediational Links in the Stress Process," *Journal of Personality and Social Psychology*, February 1996, pp 381–94; R C Barnett, S W Raudenbush, R T Brennan, J H Pleck, and N L Marshall, "Change in Job and Marital Experiences and Change in Psychological Distress: A Longitudinal Study of Dual-Earner Couples," *Journal of Personality and Social Psychology*, November 1995, pp 839–50; and S Cohen, D A J Tyrell, and A P Smith, "Negative Life Events, Perceived Stress, Negative Affect and Susceptibility to the Common Cold," *Journal of Personality and Social Psychology*, January 1993, pp 131–40.

[25] See C J Hobson, J Kamen, V Szostek, CM Nethercut, V W Tiedmann, and S Wojnarowicz, "Stressful Life Events: A Revisions and Update of the Social Readjustment Rating Scale," *International Journal of Stress Management*, January 1998, pp 1–23; and R H Rahe, "Life Changes Scaling: Other Results; Gender Differences," *International Journal of Stress Management*, October 1998, pp 249–50.

[26] The phases are thoroughly discussed by C Maslach, *Burnout: The Cost of Caring* (Englewood Cliffs, NJ: Prentice-Hall, 1982).

[27] The discussion of the model is based on C L Cordes and T W Dougherty, "A Review and Integration of Research on Job Burnout," *Academy of Management Review*, October 1993, pp 621–56.

[28] Recommendations for reducing burnout are discussed by J E Moore, "Are You Burning Out Valuable Resources," *HR Magazine*, January 1999, pp 93–97; and L Grensing-Pophal, "Recognizing and Conquering On-the-Job Burnout: HR Heal Thyself," *HR Magazine*, March 1999, pp 82–88.

[29] S Shellenbarger, "Work and Family: Rising Before Dawn, Are You Getting Ahead or Just Getting Tired?" *The Wall Street Journal*, February 17,1999, p B1.

[30] S Armour, "Employers Urge Workers to Chill Out Before Burning Out," *USA Today*, June 22, 1999, p 5B.

[31] Types of support are discussed by S Cohen and T A Wills, "Stress, Social Support, and the Buffering Hypothesis," *Psychological Bulletin*, September 1985, pp 310–57.

[32] See B N Uchino, J T Cacioppo, and J K Kiecolt-Glaser, "The Relationship Between Social Support and Physiological Processes: A Review With Emphasis on Underlying Mechanisms and Implications for Health," *Psychological Bulletin*, May 1996, pp 488–531; and H Benson and M Staerk, *Timeless Healing: The Power and Biology of Belief* (New York: Scribner, 1996).

[33] Supporting results can be found in C J Holahan, R H Moos, C K Holohan, and R C Cronkite, "Resource Loss, Resource Gain, and Depressive Symptoms: A 10-Year Model," *Journal of Personality and Social Psychology*, September 1999, pp 620–29; D S Carlson and P L Perrewe, "The Role of Social Support in the Stressor-Strain Relationship: An Examination of Work-Family Conflict," *Journal of Management*, 1999, pp 513–540; and M H Davis, M M Morris, and L A Kraus, "Relationship-Specific and Global Perceptions of Social Support Associations with Well-Being and Attachment," *Journal of Personality and Social Psychology*, February 1998, pp 468–81.

[34] For details, see B P Buunk, B J Doosje, L G J M Jans, and L E M Hopstaken, "Perceived Reciprocity, Social Support, and Stress at Work: The Role of Exchange and Communal Orientation," *Journal of Personality and Social Psychology*, October 1993, pp 801–11; and C E Cutrona, "Objective Determinants of Perceived Social Support," *Journal of Personality and Social Psychology*, February 1986, pp 349–55.

[35] R S Lazarus and S Folkman, "Coping and Adaptation," in *Handbook of Behavioral Medicine*, ed W D Gentry (New York: The Guilford Press,1984), p 283.

[36] The antecedents of appraisal were investigated by G J Fogerty, M A Machin, M J Albion, L F Sutherland, G I Lalor, and S Revitt, "Predicting Occupational Strain and Job Satisfaction: The Role of Stress, Coping, Personality, and Affectivity Variables," *Journal of Vocational Behavior*, June 1999, pp 429–52; E C Chang, "Dispositional Optimism and Primary and Secondary Appraisal of a Stressor Controlling Influences and Relations to Coping and Psychological and Physical Adjustment," *Journal of Personality and Social Psychology*, April 1998, pp 1109–20; and J C Holder and A Vaux, "African American Professionals: Coping With Occupational Stress in Predominantly White Work Environments," *Journal of Vocational Behavior*, December 1988, pp 315–33.

[37] Lazarus and Folkman, "Coping and Adaptation," p 289.

[38] See results presented in M A Gowan, C M Riordan, and R D Gatewood, "Test of a Model of Coping with Involuntary Job Loss Following a Company Closing," *Journal of Applied Psychology*, February 1999, pp 75–86; and T M Begley, "Coping Strategies as Predictors of Employee Distress and Turnover After an Organizational Consolidation: A Longitudinal Analysis," *Journal of Occupational and Organizational Psychology*, December 1998, pp 305–29.

[39] This pioneering research is presented in S C Kobasa, "Stressful Life Events, Personality and Health: An Inquiry Into Hardiness," *Journal of Personality and Social Psychology*, January 1979, pp 1–11.

[40] See S C Kobasa, S R Maddi, and S Kahn, "Hardiness and Health: A Prospective Study," *Journal of Personality and Social Psychology*, January 1982, pp 168–77.

[41] Results can be found in V Florian, M Mikulincer, and O Taubman, "Does Hardiness Contribute to Mental Health During a Stressful Real-Life Situation? The Roles of Appraisal and Coping," *Journal of Personality and Social Psychology*, April 1995, pp 687–95; and K L Horner, "Individuality in Vulnerability: Influences on Physical Health," *Journal of Health Psychology*, January 1998, pp 71–85.

[42] See C Robitschek and S Kashubeck, "A Structural Model of Parental Alcoholism, Family Functioning, and Psychological Health: The Mediating Effects of Hardiness and Personal Growth Orientation," *Journal of Counseling Psychology*, April 1999, pp 159–72; and "Basic Behavioral Science Research for Mental Health," *American Psychologist*, January 1996, pp 22–28.

[43] M Friedman and R H Rosenman, *Type A Behavior and Your Heart* (Greenwich, CT: Fawcett Publications, 1974), p 84. (Boldface added.)

[44] Results from the meta-analysis are contained in S A Lyness, "Predictors of Differences Between Type A and B Individuals in Heart Rate and Blood Pressure Reactivity," *Psychological Bulletin*, September 1993, pp 266–95.

[45] See J Rothman, "Wellness and Fitness Programs," in *Sourcebook of Occupational Rehabilitation* ed P M King (New York: Plenum Press, 1998), pp 127–44; and S Shellenbarger, "Work and Family: Rising Before Dawn, Are You Getting Ahead or Just Getting Tired?"

[46] D A Whetten and K S Cameron, *Developing Managerial Skills* (fifth edition) (Upper Saddle River, NJ: Prentice-Hall, 2002), ch 2.

[47] See H Benson, *The Relaxation Response* (New York: William Morrow and Co., 1975).

[48] Research pertaining to meditation is discussed by A G Marlatt and JL Kristeller, "Mindfulness and Meditation," in *Integrating Spirituality Into Treatment: Resources for Practitioners*, ed W R Miller (Washington, DC: American Psychological Association, 1999), pp 67–84; and H Benson and M Stark, *Timeless Healing* (New York: Scribner, 1996).

[49] See M W Otto, "Cognitive Behavioral Therapy for Social Anxiety Disorder: Model, Methods and Outcome," *Journal of Clinical Psychiatry*, 1999, pp 14–19.

[50] R Kreitner, "Personal Wellness: It's Just Good Business," *Business Horizons*, May–June 1982, p 28.

[51] A thorough review of this research is provided by D L Gebhardt and C E Crump, "Employee Fitness and Wellness Programs in the Workplace," *American Psychologist*, February 1990, pp 262–72. Also see A J Daley and G Parfitt, "Good Health—Is it Worth It? Mood States, Physical Well-Being, Job Satisfaction and Absenteeism in Members and Non-Members of a British Corporate Health and Fitness Club," *Journal of Occupational and Organizational Psychology*, June 1996, pp 121–34.

[52] E Buffett and L Bachman, "Decreasing Disability Costs Through Worksite Wellness Programs," *HR Professional*, December 2001/January 2002, pp 44–46; L Cassiani and D Brown, "Investing in Wellness," *Canadian HR Reporter*, October 23, 2000, pp 20, 21, 24; and D Brown, "Wellness Programs Bring Healthy Bottom Line," *Canadian HR Reporter*, December 17, 2001, pp 1, 14.

[53] Adapted from C Maslach and S E Jackson, "The Measurement of Experienced Burnout," *Journal of Organizational Behavior*, April 1981, pp 99–113.

Chapter 6

[1] For a review of research on rational decision making, see K E Stanovich, *Who Is Rational?* (Mahwah, NJ: Lawrence Erlbaum, 1999), pp 1–31.

[2] Excerpted from G L White, "GM Takes Advice from Disease Sleuths to Debug Cars," *The Wall Street Journal*, April 8, 1999, p B1.

[3] H A Simon, "Rational Decision Making in Business Organizations," *American Economic Review*, September 1979, p 510.

[4] For a complete discussion of bounded rationality, see H A Simon, *Administrative Behavior*, 2nd ed (New York: Free Press, 1957).

[5] Biases associated with using shortcuts in decision making are discussed by A Tversky and D Kahneman, "Judgment under Uncertainty: Heuristics and Biases," *Science*, September 1974, pp 1124–31.

[6] For a study of the availability heuristic, see L A Vaughn, "Effects of Uncertainty on Use of the Availability of Heuristic for Self-Efficacy Judgments," *European Journal of Social Psychology*, March–May 1999, pp 407–10.

[7] See B Azar, "Why Experts Often Disagree," *APA Monitor*, May 1999, p 13.

[8] Supportive results can be found in N Harvey, "Why Are Judgments Less Consistent in Less Predictable Task Situations?" *Organizational Behavior and Human Decision Processes*, September 1995, pp 247–63; and J W Dean, Jr, and M P Sharfman, "Does Decision Process Matter? A Study of Strategic Decision-Making Effectiveness," *Academy of Management Journal*, April 1996, pp 368–96.

[9] Results can be found in W H Stewart and P L Roth, "Risk Propensity Differences between Entrepreneurs and Managers: A Meta-Analytic Review," *Journal of Applied Psychology*, February 2001, pp 145–53.

[10] See P E Johnson, S Graziolo, K Jamal, and I A Zualkernan, "Success and Failure in Expert Reasoning," *Organizational Behavior and Human Decision Processes*, November 1992, pp 173–203.

[11] The discussion of styles was based on A J Rowe and R O Mason, *Managing with Style: A Guide to Understanding, Assessing, and Improving Decision Making* (San Francisco: Jossey-Bass, 1987).

[12] See ibid.; and M J Dollinger and W Danis, "Preferred Decision-Making Styles: A Cross-Cultural Comparison," *Psychological Reports*, 1998, pp 755–61.

[13] M Fackler, "Japanese Subway Going Off Track" *Toronto Star*, July 20, 1999, p C6.

[14] The details of this case are discussed in J Ross and B M Staw, "Organizational Escalation and Exit: Lessons from the Shoreham Nuclear Power Plant," *Academy of Management Journal*, August 1993, pp 701–32.

[15] Supportive results can be found in H Moon, "Looking Forward and Looking Back: Integrating Completion and Sunk-Cost Effects within an Escalation-of-Commitment Progress Decision," *Journal of Applied Psychology*, February 2001, pp 104–13.

[16] Results can be found in C R Greer and G K Stephens, "Escalation of Commitment: A Comparison of Differences between Mexican and U.S. Decision Makers," *Journal of Management*, 2001, pp 51–78.

[17] This definition was based on R J Sternberg, "What Is the Common Thread of Creativity?" *American Psychologist*, April 2001, pp 360–62.

[18] Excerpted from S Stern, "How Companies Can Be More Creative," *HR Magazine*, April 1998, p 59.

[19] Details of this study can be found in M Basadur, "Managing Creativity: A Japanese Model," *Academy of Management Executive*, May 1992, pp 29–42.

[20] "Deadlines Stifle Creativity: Marketing Executives," *Workplace Today*, January 2002, p 38.

[21] Personal communication with David Hardy, Bank of Montreal, March 2002.

[22] These guidelines were derived from G P Huber, *Managerial Decision Making* (Glenview, IL: Scott, Foresman, 1980), p 149.

[23] I L Janis, *Groupthink*, 2nd ed, (Boston:Houghton Mifflin, 1982). For an alternative model, see R J Aldag and S Riggs Fuller, "Beyond Fiasco: A Reappraisal of the Groupthink Phenomenon and a New Model of Group Decision Processes," *Psychological Bulletin*, May 1993, pp 533–52. Also see A A Mohamed and F A Wiebe, "Toward a Process Theory of Groupthink," *Small Group Research*, August 1996, pp 416–30.

[24] Adapted from Janis, *Groupthink*, pp 174–75.

[25] L Baum, "The Job Nobody Wants," *Business Week*, September 8, 1986, p 60. Also see A Bianco and J A Byrne, " The Rush to Quality on Corporate Boards," *Business Week*, March 3, 1997, pp 34–35; B Leonard, "Workplace Diversity Should Include Boardroom," *HR Magazine*, February 1999, p 12; J D Westphal,"Collaboration in the Boardroom: Behavioural and Performance Consequences of CEO-Board Social Ties," *Academy of Management Journal*, February 1999, pp 7–24; and G Koretz, "Friendly Boards Are Not All Bad," *Business Week*, June 14, 1999, p 34.

[26] For an ethical persepctive, see R R Sims, "Linking Groupthink to Unethical Behavior in Organizations," *Journal of Business Ethics*, September 1992, pp 651–62.

[27] Adapted from discussion in I L Janis, *Groupthink*, ch 11.

[28] G W Hill, "Group versus Individual Performance: Are N + 1 Heads Better than One?" *Psychological Bulletin*, May 1982, p 535.

[29] See D L Gladstein and N P Reilly, "Group Decision Making under Threat: The Tycoon Game," *Academy of Management Journal*, September 1985, pp 613–27.

[30] This issue is thoroughly discussed by D E Drehmer, J A Belohlav, and R W Coye, "An Exploration of Employee Participation Using a Scaling Approach," *Group & Organization Management*, December 2000, pp 397–418.

[31] For an extended discussion of this model, see M Sashkin, "Participative Management Is an Ethical Imperative," *Organizational Dynamics*, Spring 1984, pp 4–22.

[32] See G Yukl and P P Fu, "Determinants of Delegation and Consultation by Managers," *Journal of Organizational Behavior*, March 1999, pp 219–32.

[33] Supporting results can be found in L A Witt, M C Andrews, and M Kacmar, "The Role of Participation in Decision-Making in the Organizational Politics-Job Satisfaction Relationship," *Human Relations*, March 2000, pp 341–58; J Hunton, T W Hall, and K H Price, "The Value of Voice in Participative Decision Making," *Journal of Applied Psychology*, October 1998, pp 788–97; and C R Leana, R S Ahlbrandt, and A J Murrell, "The Effects of Employee Involvement Programs on Unionized Workers' Attitudes, Perceptions, and Preferences in Decision Making," *Academy of Management Journal*, October 1992, pp 861–73.

[34] Results are contained in J A Wagner III, C R Leana, E A Locke, and D M Schweiger, "Cognitive and Motivational Frameworks in US Research on Participation: A Meta-Analysis of Primary Effects," *Journal of Organizational Behavior*, 1997, pp 49–65.

[35] See V H Vroom and P W Yetton, *Leadership and Decision Making* (Pittsburgh, PA: University of Pittsburgh Press, 1973); and V H Vroom and A G Jago, *The New Leadership: Managing Participation in Organizations* (Englewood Cliffs, NJ: Prentice Hall, 1988), p 184.

[36] G M Parker, *Team Players and Teamwork: The New Competitive Business Strategy* (San Francisco, CA: Jossey-Bass, 1990).

[37] These recommendations were obtained from Parker, *Team Players and Teamwork: The New Competitive Business Strategy.*

[38] These recommendations were derived from C Caggiano, "The Right Way to Brainstorm," *Inc.*, July 1999, p 94; and G McGartland, "How to Generate More Ideas in Brainstorming Sessions," *Selling Power*, July/August 1999, p 46.

[39] See J G Lloyd, S Fowell, and J G Bligh, "The Use of the Nominal Group Technique as an Evaluative Tool in Medical Undergraduate Education," *Medical Education*, January 1999, pp 8–13; and A L Delbecq, A H Van de Ven, and D H Gustafson, *Group Techniques for Program Planning: A Guide to Nominal Group and Delphi Processes* (Glenview, IL: Scott, Foresman, 1975).

[40] See N C Dalkey, D L Rourke, R Lewis, and D Snyder, *Studies in the Quality of Life: Delphi and Decision Making* (Lexington, MA: Lexington Books: D C Heath and Co., 1972).

[41] Benefits of the Delphi technique are discussed by N I Whitman, "The Committee Meeting Alternative: Using the Delphi Technique," *Journal of Nursing Administration*, July/August 1990, pp 30–36.

[42] A thorough description of computer-aided decision-making systems is provided by M C Er and A C Ng, "The Anonymity and Proximity Factors in Group Decision Support Systems," *Decision Support Systems*, May 1995, pp 75–83.

[43] Supportive results can be found in S S Lam and J Schaubroeck, "Improving Group Decisions by Better Polling Information: A Comparative Advantage of Group Decision Support Systems," *Journal of Applied Psychology*, August 2000, pp 565–73; and I Benbasat and J Lim, "Information Technology Support for Debiasing Group Judgments: An Empirical Evaluation," *Organizational Behavior and Human Decision Processes*, September 2000, pp 167–83.

[44] S Branch, "The 100 Best Companies to Work for in America," *Fortune*, January 11, 1999, pp 118–44.

[45] The role of incentives and ethical behavior was investigated by A E Tenbrunsel, "Misrepresentation and Expectations of Misrepresentation in an Ethical Dilemma: The Role of Incentives and Temptation," *Academy of Management Journal*, June 1998, pp 330–39.

[46] Adapted from W E Stead, D L Worrell, and J Garner Stead, "An Integrative Model for Understanding and Managing Ethical Behavior in Business Organizations," *Journal of Business Ethics*, March 1990, pp 233–42.

[47] For an excellent review of integrity testing, see D S Ones and C Viswesvaran, "Integrity Testing in Organizations," in *Dysfunctional Behavior in Organizations: Violent and Deviant Behavior*, eds R W Griffin et al. (Stamford, CT: JAI Press, 1998), pp 243–76.

[48] Vroom and Yago's analysis and solution: QR → critical/high importance; CR → high importance; LI → probably no; ST → no; CP → probably no; GC → probably yes; CO → not a consideration for this problem; SI → maybe (but probably not). Decision making style → CII.

[49] Comparative norms were obtained from L M Dawson, "Women and Men, Morality, and Ethics," *Business Horizons*, July–August 1995, pp 61–68. Scenario 1: would sell (28% males, 57% females); would not sell (66% males, 28% females); unsure (6% males, 15% females). Scenario 2: would consult (84% males, 32% females); would not consult (12% males, 62% females), unsure (4% males, 6% females).

[50] Assign plus one (+1) point beside the following words if you marked them: Capable, Clever, Confident, Egotistical, Humorous, Individualistic, Informal, Insightful, Intelligent, Inventive, Original, Reflective, Resourceful, Self-confident, Sexy, Snobbish, Unconventional, Wide Interest. Assign negative one (–1) point beside the following words if you marked them: Affected, Cautious, Commonplace, Conservative, Conventional, Dissatisfied, Honest, Mannerly, Narrow Interests, Sincere, Submissive, Suspicious. Add up the total score, which will range from –12 to +18.

Chapter 7

[1] This definition is based in part on one found in D Horton Smith, "A Parsimonious Definition of 'Group': Toward Conceptual Clarity and Scientific Utility," *Sociological Inquiry*, Spring 1967, pp 141–67.

[2] E H Schein, *Organizational Psychology*, 3rd ed (Englewood Cliffs, NJ: Prentice Hall, 1980), p 145. For more, see L R Weingart, "How Did They Do That? The Ways and Means of Studying Group Process," in *Research in Organizational Behavior*, vol. 19, eds L L Cummings and B M Staw (Greenwich, CT: JAI Press, 1997), pp 189–239.

[3] See Schein, *Organizational Psychology*, pp 149–53.

[4] For related research, see P P Shah, "Who Are Employees' Social Referents? Using a Network Perspective to Determine Referent Others," *Academy of Management Journal*, June 1998, pp 249–68; and A Mehra, M Kilduff, and D J Brass, "At the Margins: A Distinctiveness Approach to the Social Identity and Social Networks of Underrepresented Groups," *Academy of Management Journal*, August 1998, pp 441–52.

[5] For an instructive overview of five different theories of group development, see J P Wanous, A E Reichers, and S D Malik, "Organizational Socialization and Group Development: Toward an Integrative Perspective," *Academy of Management Review*, October 1984, pp 670–83. Also see L R Offermann and R K Spiros, "The Science and Practice of Team Development: Improving the Link," *Academy of Management Journal*, April 2001, pp 376–92.

[6] See B W Tuckman, "Developmental Sequence in Small Groups," *Psychological Bulletin*, June 1965, pp 384–99; and B W Tuckman and M A C Jensen, "Stages of Small-Group Development Revisited," *Group & Organization Studies*, December 1977, pp 419–27. An instructive adaptation of the Tuckman model can be found in L Holpp, "If Empowerment Is So Good, Why Does It Hurt?" *Training*, March 1995, p 56.

[7] Practical advice on handling a dominating group member can be found in M Finley, "Belling the Bully," *HR Magazine*, March 1992, pp 82–86.

[8] For related research, see K Aquino and A Reed II, "A Social Dilemma Perspective on Cooperative Behavior in Organizations: The Effects of Scarcity, Communication, and Unequal Access on the Use of a Shared Resource," *Group & Organization Management*, December 1998, pp 390–413; B Fehr, "Laypeople's Conceptions of Commitment," *Journal of Personality and Social Psychology*, January 1999, pp 90–103; and G L Stewart, C C Manz, and H P Sims, Jr, *Team Work and Group Dynamics* (New York: Wiley, 1999).

[9] P Yetton and P Bottger, "The Relationships Among Group Size, Member Ability, Social Decision Schemes, and Performance," *Organizational Behavior and Human Performance*, October 1983, pp 145–59.

[10] G Graen, "Role-Making Processes within Complex Organizations," in *Handbook of Industrial and Organizational Psychology*, ed M D Dunnette (Chicago: Rand McNally, 1976), p 1201. Also see L Van Dyne and J A LePine, "Helping and Voice Extra-Role Behaviors: Evidence of Construct and Predictive Validity," *Academy of Management Journal*, February 1998, pp 108–19; and B E Ashforth, G E Kreiner, and M Fugate, "All in a Day's Work: Boundaries and Micro Role Transitions," *Academy of Management Review*, July 2000, pp 472–91.

[11] A S Wharton and R J Erickson, "Managing Emotions on the Job and at Home: Understanding the Consequences of Multiple Emotional Roles," *Academy of Management Review*, July 1993, pp 457–86; and S Shellenbarger, "Feel Like You Need to be Cloned? Even That Wouldn't Work," *The Wall Street Journal*, July 10, 1996, p B1.

[12] See K D Benne and P Sheats, "Functional Roles of Group Members," *Journal of Social Issues*, Spring 1948, pp 41–49.

[13] A Zander, "The Value of Belonging to a Group in Japan," *Small Group Behavior*, February 1983, pp 7–8. Also see P R Harris and R T Moran, *Managing Cultural Differences*, 4th ed (Houston: Gulf Publishing, 1996), pp 267–76.

[14] R R Blake and J Srygley Mouton, "Don't Let Group Norms Stifle Creativity," *Personnel*, August 1985, p 28.

[15] See D Kahneman, "Reference Points, Anchors, Norms, and Mixed Feelings," *Organizational Behavior and Human Decision Processes*, March 1992, pp 296–312; and J M Marques, D Abrams, D Paez, and C Martinez-Taboada, "The Role of Categorization and In-Group Norms in Judgments of Groups and Their Members," *Journal of Personality and Social Psychology*, October 1998, pp 976–88.

[16] D C Feldman, "The Development and Enforcement of Group Norms," *Academy of Management Review*, January 1984, pp 50–52.

[17] Ibid.

[18] K Lowry Miller, "Siemens Shapes Up," *Business Week*, May 1, 1995, p 52.

[19] P Engardio and G DeGeorge, "Importing Enthusiasm," *Business Week, 1994 Special Issue: 21st Century Capitalism*, p 122.

[20] J Rossant, "The Man Who's Driving Fiat Like a Ferrari," *Business Week*, January 23, 1995, p 82.

21 S Hamm and M Stepanek, "From Reengineering to E-Engineering," *Business Week E.BIZ*, March 22, 1999, pp EB15, EB18.

22 See P F Drucker, "The Coming of the New Organization," *Harvard Business Review*, January–February 1988, pp 45–53. Also see F Mueller, S Procter, and D Buchanan, "Teamworking in Its Context(s): Antecedents, Nature and Dimensions," *Human Relations*, November 2000, pp 1387–1424.

23 See N Enbar, "What Do Women Want? Ask 'Em," *Business Week*, March 29, 1999, p 8; and M Hickins, "Duh! Gen Xers Are Cool with Teamwork," *Management Review*, March 1999, p 7.

24 J R Katzenbach and D K Smith, *The Wisdom of Teams: Creating the High-Performance Organization* (New York: HarperBusiness, 1999), p 45.

25 "A Team's-Eye View of Teams," *Training*, November 1995, p 16.

26 Condensed and adapted from Katzenbach and Smith, *The Wisdom of Teams: Creating the High-Performance Organization*, p 214.

27 See L G Bolman and T E Deal, "What Makes a Team Work?" *Organizational Dynamics*, Autumn 1992, pp 34–44.

28 J R Katzenbach and D K Smith, "The Discipline of Teams," *Harvard Business Review*, March–April 1993, p 112.

29 L Prusak and D Cohen, "How to Invest in Social Capital," *Harvard Business Review*, June 2001, p 90. Also see V U Druskat and S B Wolff, "Building the Emotional Intelligence of Groups," *Harvard Business Review*, March 2001, pp 80–90.

30 Also see D M Rousseau, S B Sitkin, R S Burt, and C Camerer, "Not So Different After All: A Cross-Discipline View of Trust," *Academy of Management Review*, July 1998, pp 393–404; and A C Wicks, S L Berman, and T M Jones, "The Structure of Optimal Trust: Moral and Strategic Implications," *Academy of Management Review*, January 1999, pp 99–116.

31 J D Lewis and A Weigert, "Trust as a Social Reality," *Social Forces*, June 1985, p 971. Trust is examined as an indirect factor in K T Dirks, "The Effects of Interpersonal Trust on Work Group Performance," *Journal of Applied Psychology*, June 1999, pp 445–55. Also see J B Cunningham and J MacGregor, "Trust and the Design of Work: Complementary Constructs in Satisfaction and Performance," *Human Relations*, December 2000, pp 1575–88.

32 Adapted from C Johnson-George and W C Swap, "Measurement of Specific Interpersonal Trust: Construction and Validation of a Scale to Assess Trust in a Specific Other," *Journal of Personality and Social Psychology*, December 1982, pp 1306–17; and D J McAllister, "Affect- and Cognition-Based Trust as Foundations for Interpersonal Cooperation in Organizations," *Academy of Management Journal*, February 1995, pp 24–59.

33 For interesting new theory and research on telling lies, see B M DePaulo, D A Kashy, S E Kirkendol, M M Wyer, and J A Epstein, "Lying in Everyday Life," *Journal of Personality and Social Psychology*, May 1996, pp 979–95; and D A Kashy and B M DePaulo, "Who Lies?" *Journal of Personality and Social Psychology*, May 1996, pp 1037–51.

34 For support, see G M Spreitzer and A K Mishra, "Giving Up Control without Losing Control: Trust and Its Substitutes' Effects on Managers' Involving Employees in Decision Making," *Group & Organization Management*, June 1999, pp 155–87.

35 For more on fairness, see K Seiders and L L Berry, "Service Fairness: What It Is and Why It Matters," *Academy of Management Executive*, May 1998, pp 8–20.

36 Adapted from F Bartolomé, "Nobody Trusts the Boss Completely— Now What?" *Harvard Business Review*, March–April 1989, pp 135–42.

37 Data from C Joinson, "Teams at Work," *HR Magazine*, May 1999, pp 30–36.

38 J MacMillan, "Best Practices From Honeywell," *Excellence*, May 2001, pp 5–8.

39 For example, see M Selz, "Testing Self-Managed Teams, Entrepreneur Hopes to Lose Job," *The Wall Street Journal*, January 11, 1994, pp B1–B2. Also see "Even in Self-Managed Teams There Has to Be a Leader," *Supervisory Management*, December 1994, pp 7–8.

40 See M Moravec, O J Johannessen, and T A Hjelmas, "The Well-Managed SMT," *Management Review*, June 1998, pp 56–58; and "Case Study in C-Sharp Minor," *Training*, October 1998, p 21.

41 See D R Denison, S L Hart, and J A Kahn, "From Chimneys to Cross-Functional Teams: Developing and Validating a Diagnostic Model," *Academy of Management Journal*, August 1996, pp 1005–23. Cross-func-

tional teams are discussed in D Lei, J W Slocum, and R A Pitts, "Designing Organizations for Competitive Advantage: The Power of Unlearning and Learning," *Organizational Dynamics*, Winter 1999, pp 24–38.

42 See L L Thompson, *Making the Team: A Guide for Managers* (Upper Saddle River, NJ: Prentice Hall, 2000).

43 See P S Goodman, R Devadas, and T L Griffith Hughson, "Groups and Productivity: Analyzing the Effectiveness of Self-Managing Teams," in *Productivity in Organizations*, eds J P Campbell, R J Campbell and Associates (San Francisco: Jossey-Bass, 1988), pp 295–327. Also see E F Rogers, W Metlay, I T Kaplan, and T Shapiro, "Self-Managing Work Teams: Do They Really Work?" *Human Resource Planning*, no. 2, 1995, pp 53–57; V U Druskat and S B Wolff, "Effects and Timing of Developmental Peer Appraisals in Self-Managing Work Groups," *Journal of Applied Psychology*, February 1999, pp 58–74; and R C Liden, S J Wayne, and M L Kraimer, "Managing Individual Performance in Work Groups," *Human Resource Management*, Spring 2001, pp 63–72.

44 For more, see W F Cascio, "Managing a Virtual Workplace," *Academy of Management Executive*, August 2000, pp 81–90.

45 See A M Townsend, S M DeMarie, and A R Hendrickson, "Virtual Teams: Technology and the Workplace of the Future," *Academy of Management Executive*, August 1998, pp 17–29.

46 Based on P Bordia, N DiFonzo, and A Chang, "Rumor as Group Problem Solving: Development Patterns in Informal Computer-Mediated Groups," *Small Group Research*, February 1999, pp 8–28.

47 See K A Graetz, E S Boyle, C E Kimble, P Thompson, and J L Garloch, "Information Sharing in Face-to-Face, Teleconferencing, and Electronic Chat Groups," *Small Group Research*, December 1998, pp 714–43.

48 Based on F Niederman and R J Volkema, "The Effects of Facilitator Characteristics on Meeting Preparation, Set Up, and Implementation," *Small Group Research*, June 1999, pp 330–60.

49 Based on J J Sosik, B J Avolio, and S S Kahai, "Inspiring Group Creativity: Comparing Anonymous and Identified Electronic Brainstorming," *Small Group Research*, February 1998, pp 3–31. For practical advice on brainstorming, see C Caggiano, "The Right Way to Brainstorm," *Inc.*, July 1999, p 94.

50 See E Kelley, "Keys to Effective Virtual Global Teams," *Academy of Management Executive*, May 2001, pp 132–33.

51 For practical tips, see K Kiser, "Building a Virtual Team," *Training*, March 1999, p 34.

52 For example, see S R Rayner, "Team Traps: What They Are, How to Avoid Them," *National Productivity Review*, Summer 1996, pp 101–15; P W Mulvey, J F Veiga, and P M Alsass, "When Teammates Raise a White Flag," *Academy of Management Executive*, February 1996, pp 40–49; L Holpp and R Phillips, "When Is a Team Its Own Worst Enemy?" *Training*, September 1995, pp 71–82; B Richardson, "Why Work Teams Flop—and What Can Be Done About It," *National Productivity Review*, Winter 1994/95, pp 9–13; and B Dumaine, "The Trouble With Teams," *Fortune*, September 5, 1994, pp 86–92.

53 Based on discussion in B Latane, K Williams, and S Harkins, "Many Hands Make Light the Work: The Causes and Consequences of Social Loafing," *Journal of Personality and Social Psychology*, June 1979, pp 822–32; and D A Kravitz and B Martin, "Ringelmann Rediscovered: The Original Article," *Journal of Personality and Social Psychology*, May 1986, pp 936–41.

54 See J A Shepperd, "Productivity Loss in Performance Groups: A Motivation Analysis," *Psychological Bulletin*, no. 1, 1993, pp 67–81; R E Kidwell, Jr, and N Bennett, "Employee Propensity to Withhold Effort: A Conceptual Model to Intersect Three Avenues of Research," *Academy of Management Review*, July 1993, pp 429–56; and S J Karau and K D Williams, "Social Loafing: Meta-Analytic Review and Theoretical Integration," *Journal of Personality and Social Psychology*, October 1993, pp 681–706.

55 See S J Zaccaro, "Social Loafing: The Role of Task Attractiveness," *Personality and Social Psychology Bulletin*, March 1984, pp 99–106; J M Jackson and K D Williams, "Social Loafing on Difficult Tasks: Working Collectively Can Improve Performance," *Journal of Personality and Social Psychology*, October 1985, pp 937–42; and J M George, "Extrinsic and Intrinsic Origins of Perceived Social Loafing in Organizations," *Academy of Management Journal*, March 1992, pp 191–202.

56 For complete details, see K Williams, S Harkins, and B Latane, "Identifiability as a Deterrent to Social Loafing: Two Cheering Experiments," *Journal of Personality and Social Psychology*, February 1981, pp 303–11.

EndNotes **355**

57 See J M Jackson and S G Harkins, "Equity in Effort: An Explanation of the Social Loafing Effect," *Journal of Personality and Social Psychology*, November 1985, pp 1199–1206.

58 Both studies are reported in S G Harkins and K Szymanski, "Social Loafing and Group Evaluation," *Journal of Personality and Social Psychology*, June 1989, pp 934–41.

59 Data from J A Wagner III, "Studies of Individualism-Collectivism: Effects on Cooperation in Groups," *Academy of Management Journal*, February 1995, pp 152–72. Also see P W Mulvey and H J Klein, "The Impact of Perceived Loafing and Collective Efficacy on Group Goal Processes and Group performance," *Organizational Behavior and Human Decision Processes*, April 1998, pp 62–87; and P W Mulvey, L Bowes-Sperry, and H J Klein, "The Effects of Perceived Loafing and Defensive Impression Management on Group Effectiveness," *Small Group Research*, June 1998, pp 394 415.

60 See S G Scott and W O Einstein, "Strategic Performance Appraisal in Team-Based Organizations: One Size Does Not Fit All," *Academy of Management Executive*, May 2001, pp 107–16.

61 See J T Buckley, "Getting Into Outdoors Builds Corporate Buddies," *USA Today*, August 19, 1996, pp 1A–2A; and J T Taylor, "Participants Learn the Ropes of Team Building," *USA Today*, August 19, 1996, p 7B. For more on outdoor experiential learning, see H Campbell, "Adventures in Teamland," *Personnel Journal*, May 1996, pp 56–62; E Brown, "War Games to Make You Better at Business," *Fortune*, September 28, 1998, pp 291–96; and M Hickins, "A Day at the Races," *Management Review*, May 1999, pp 56–61.

62 S Bucholz and T Roth, *Creating the High-Performance Team* (New York: John Wiley and Sons, 1987), p 14. Also see S A Wheelan, D Murphy, E Tsumura, and S F Kline, "Member Perceptions of Internal Group Dynamics and Productivity," *Small Group Research*, June 1998, pp 371–93; M F R Kets De Vries, "High-Performance Teams: Lessons From the Pygmies," *Organizational Dynamics*, Winter 1999, pp 66–77; G Buzaglo and S A Wheelan, "Facilitating Work Team Effectiveness: Case Studies from Central America," *Small Group Research*, February 1999, pp 108–29; K Maani and C Benton, "Rapid Team Learning: Lessons from Team New Zealand America's Cup Campaign," *Organizational Dynamics*, Spring 1999, pp 48–62; J Lipman-Bluman and H J Leavitt, "Hot Groups 'With Attitude': A New Organizational State of Mind," *Organizational Dynamics*, Spring 1999, pp 62–73; and M J Waller, "The Timing of Adaptive Group Responses to Nonroutine Events," *Academy of Management Journal*, April 1999, pp 127–37.

63 P King, "What Makes Teamwork Work?" *Psychology Today*, December 1989, p 17. A critical view of teams is presented in C Casey, " 'Come, Join Our Family': Discipline and Integration in Corporate Organizational Culture," *Human Relations*, February 1999, pp 155–78.

64 Adapted from C C Manz and H P Sims, "Leading Workers to Lead Themselves: The External Leadership of Self-Managing Work Teams," *Administrative Science Quarterly*, March 1987, pp 106–29. Also see C C Manz, "Beyond Self-Managing Work Teams: Toward Self-Leading Teams in the Workplace," In *Research in Organizational Change and Development*, vol 4, eds R W Woodman and W A Pasmore (Greenwich, CT: JAI Press, 1990), pp 273–99; C C Manz, "Self-Leading Work Teams: Moving Beyond Self-Management Myths," *Human Relations*, no. 11, 1992, pp 1119–40; C C Manz, *Mastering Self-Leadership: Empowering Yourself for Personal Excellence* (Englewood Cliffs, NJ: Prentice-Hall, 1992); M Uhl-Bien and G B Graen, "Individual Self-Management: Analysis of 'Professional' Self-Managing Activities in Functional and Cross-Functional Work Teams," *Academy of Management Journal*, June 1998, pp 340–50; G E Prussia, J S Anderson, and C C Manz, "Self-Leadership and Performance Outcomes: The Mediating Influence of Self-Efficacy," *Journal of Organizational Behavior*, September 1998, pp 523–38; and P Troiano, "Nice Guys Finish Last," *Management Review*, December 1998, p 8.

65 1=A; 2=C; 3=A; 4=A; 5=C; 6=A; 7=C; 8=A; 9=C; 10=C.

Chapter 8

1 D Tjosvold, *Learning to Manage Conflict: Getting People to Work Together Productively* (New York: Lexington Books, 1993), p xi.

2 Ibid, pp xi–xii.

3 J A Wall, Jr, and R Robert Callister, "Conflict and Its Management," *Journal of Management*, no. 3, 1995, p 517.

4 Ibid, p 544.

5 See O Jones, "Scientific Management, Culture and Control: A First-Hand Account of Taylorism in Practice," *Human Relations*, May 2000, pp 631–53.

6 See A M O'Leary-Kelly, R W Griffin, and D J Glew, "Organization-Motivated Aggression: A Research Framework," *Academy of Management Review*, January 1996, pp 225–53; and D Bencivenga, "Dealing with the Dark Side," *HR Magazine*, January 1999, pp 50–58.

7 See S Alper, D Tjosvold, and K S Law, "Interdependence and Controversy in Group Decision Making: Antecedents to Effective Self-Managing Teams," *Organizational Behavior and Human Decision Processes*, April 1998, pp 33–52.

8 S P Robbins, " 'Conflict Management' and 'Conflict Resolution' Are Not Synonymous Terms," *California Management Review*, Winter 1978, p 70.

9 Cooperative conflict is discussed in Tjosvold, *Learning to Manage Conflict: Getting People to Work Together Productively*. Also see A C Amason, "Distinguishing the Effects of Functional and Dysfunctional Conflict on Strategic Decision Making: Resolving a Paradox for Top Management Teams," *Academy of Management Journal*, February 1996, pp 123–48.

10 C Noble, "Resolving Co-worker Disputes Through 'Coaching Conflict Management,' " *Canadian HR Reporter*, September 24, 2001, pp 18, 20.

11 J Connor, "Deciding Appropriate Penalties for Workplace Violence," *Canadian HR Reporter*, January 15, 2001, p 7.

12 M. Johns, "When Bullies Go To Work," *Globe and Mail*, April 17, 2002, p C1.

13 Adapted in part from discussion in A C Filley, *Interpersonal Conflict Resolution* (Glenview, IL: Scott, Foresman, 1975), pp 9–12; and B Fortado, "The Accumulation of Grievance Conflict," *Journal of Management Inquiry*, December 1992, pp 288–303. Also see D Tjosvold and M Poon, "Dealing with Scarce Resources: Open-Minded Interaction for Resolving Budget Conflicts," *Group & Organization Management*, September 1998, pp 237–55.

14 Adapted from discussion in Tjosvold, *Learning to Manage Conflict: Getting People to Work Together Productively*, pp 12–13.

15 L Gardenswartz and A Rowe, *Diverse Teams at Work: Capitalizing on the Power of Diversity* (New York: McGraw-Hill, 1994), p 32.

16 See L M Andersson and C M Pearson, "Tit for Tat? The Spiraling Effect of Incivility in the Workplace," *Academy of Management Review*, July 1999, pp 452–71; and C Lee, "The Death of Civility," *Training*, July 1999, pp 24–30.

17 M Elias, "Study: Rudeness Is Poisoning US Workplace," *USA Today*, June 14, 2001, p 1D; and S Anderson, "Courtesy Becomes Uncommon on Job," *The Arizona Republic*, January 15, 2001, pp E1–E4.

18 Data from D Stamps, "Yes, Your Boss Is Crazy," *Training*, July 1998, pp 35–39. Also see L Huggler, "Companies on the Couch," *HR Magazine*, November 1997, pp 80–84; and J C Connor, "The Paranoid Personality at Work," *HR Magazine*, March 1999, pp 120–26.

19 See J Muller, "Keeping an Investigation on the Right Track," *Business Week*, July 5, 1999, p 84.

20 See Bencivenga, "Dealing with the Dark Side"; and C Lee, "Tips for Surviving Rude Encounters," *Training*, July 1999, p 29.

21 Based on discussion in G Labianca, D J Brass, and B Gray, "Social Networks and Perceptions of Intergroup Conflict: The Role of Negative Relationships and Third Parties," *Academy of Management Journal*, February 1998, pp 55–67. Also see C Gómez, B L Kirkman, and D L Shapiro, "The Impact of Collectivism and In-Group/Out-Group Membership on the Evaluation Generosity of Team Members," *Academy of Management Journal*, December 2000, pp 1097–1106; and K A Jehn and E A Mannix, "The Dynamic Nature of Conflict: A Longitudinal Study of Intragroup Conflict and Group Performance," *Academy of Management Journal*, April 2001, pp 238–51.

22 For example, see S C Wright, A Aron, T McLaughlin-Volpe, and S A Ropp, "The Extended Contact Effect: Knowledge of Cross-Group Friendships and Prejudice," *Journal of Personality and Social Psychology*, July 1997, pp 73–90.

23 See C D Batson, M P Polycarpou, E Harmon-Jones, H J Imhoff, E C Mitchener, L L Bednar, T R Klein, and L Highberger, "Empathy and Attitudes: Can Feeling for a Member of a Stigmatized Group Improve Feelings toward the Group?" *Journal of Personality and Social Psychology*, January 1997, pp 105–18.

[24] For more, see A K Gupta and V Govindarajan, "Converting Global Presence into Global Competitive Advantage," *Academy of Management Executive*, May 2001, pp 45–56.

[25] For an interesting case study, see W Kuemmerle, "Go Global—or No?" *Harvard Business Review*, June 2001, pp 37–49.

[26] "Negotiating South of the Border," *Harvard Management Communication Letter*, August 1999, p 12.

[27] Adapted from R L Tung, "American Expatriates Abroad: From Neophytes to Cosmopolitans," *Journal of World Business*, Summer 1998, Table 6, p 136.

[28] Reprinted from A Rosenbaum, "Testing Cultural Waters," *Management Review*, July–August 1999, p 43 © 1999 American Management Association International. Reprinted by permission of American Management Association International, New York, NY. All rights reserved. www.amanet. org.

[29] See Tung, "American Expatriates Abroad: From Neophytes to Cosmopolitans."

[30] R A Cosier and C R Schwenk, "Agreement and Thinking Alike: Ingredients for Poor Decisions," *Academy of Management Executive*, February 1990, p 71. Also see J P Kotter, "Kill Complacency," *Fortune*, August 5, 1996, pp 168–170; and S Caudron, "Keeping Team Conflict Alive," *Training and Development*, September 1998, pp 48–52.

[31] D Jones, "CEOs Need X-Ray Vision in Transition," *USA Today*, April 23, 2001, p 4B.

[32] Good background reading on devil's advocacy can be found in C R Schwenk, "Devil's Advocacy in Management Decision Making," *Journal of Management Studies*, April 1984, pp 153–68.

[33] A statistical validation for this model can be found in M A Rahim and N R Magner, "Confirmatory Factor Analysis of the Styles of Handling Interpersonal Conflict: First-Order Factor Model and Its Invariance Across Groups," *Journal of Applied Psychology*, February 1995, pp 122–32.

[34] M A Rahim, "A Strategy for Managing Conflict in Complex Organizations," *Human Relations*, January 1985, p 84.

[35] See K Davis, "Management Communication and the Grapevine," *Harvard Business Review*, September-October 1953, pp 43–49.

[36] H B Vickery III, "Tapping Into the Employee Grapevine," *Association Management*, January 1984, pp 59–60.

[37] A thorough discussion of organizational moles is provided by J G Bruhn and A P Chesney, "Organizational Moles: Information Control and the Acquisition of Power and Status," *Health Care Supervisor*, September 1995, pp 24–31.

[38] Earlier research is discussed by Davis, "Management Communication and the Grapevine"; and R Rowan, "Where Did That Rumor Come From?" *Fortune*, August 13, 1979, pp 130–131, 134, 137. The most recent research is discussed by S M Crampton, J W Hodge, and J M Mishra, "The Informal Communication Network: Factors Influencing Grapevine Activity," *Public Personnel Management*, Winter 1998; "Pruning the Company Grapevine," *Supervision*, September 1986, p 11; and R Half, "Managing Your Career: 'How Can I Stop the Gossip?'" *Management Accounting*, September 1987, p 27.

[39] For a thorough discussion of communication distortion, see E W Larson and J B King, "The Systematic Distortion of Information: An Ongoing Challenge to Management," *Organizational Dynamics*, Winter 1996, pp 49–61.

[40] J Fulk and S Mani, "Distortion of Communication in Hierarchical Relationships," in *Communication Yearbook 9*, ed M L McLaughlin (Beverly Hills, CA: Sage Publications, 1986), p 483.

[41] Based on a definition in M A Neale and M H Bazerman, "Negotiating Rationally: The Power and Impact of the Negotiator's Frame," *Academy of Management Executive*, August 1992, pp 42–51.

[42] See, for example, J K Sebenius, "Six Habits of Merely Effective Negotiators," *Harvard Business Review*, April 2001, pp 87–95; A Fisher, "Ask Annie: Being Lowballed on Salary? How to Eke Out More Bucks," *Fortune*, April 30, 2001, p 192; G Koretz, "She's a Woman, Offer Her Less," *Business Week*, May 7, 2001, p 34; and K Hannon, "Want a Family Life? Negotiate," *USA Today*, June 11, 2001, p 7B.

[43] M H Bazerman and M A Neale, *Negotiating Rationally* (New York: The Free Press, 1992), p 16. Also See J F Brett, G B Northcraft, and R L Pinkley, "Stairways to Heaven: An Interlocking Self-Regulation Model of Negotiation," *Academy of Management Review*, July 1999, pp 435–51.

[44] Good win-win negotiation strategies can be found in R R Reck and B G Long, *The Win-Win Negotiator: How to Negotiate Favorable Agreements That Last* (New York: Pocket Books, 1987); R Fisher and W Ury, *Getting to YES: Negotiating Agreement without Giving In* (Boston: Houghton Mifflin, 1981); and R Fisher and D Ertel, *Getting Ready to Negotiate: The Getting to YES Workbook* (New York: Penguin Books, 1995).

[45] For practical advice, see K Kelly Reardon and R E Spekman, "Starting Out Right: Negotiation Lessons for Domestic and Cross-Cultural Business Alliances," *Business Horizons*, January–February 1994, pp 71–79.

[46] Adapted from K Albrecht and S Albrecht, "Added Value Negotiating," *Training*, April 1993, pp 26–29.

[47] For supporting evidence, see J K Butler Jr., "Trust Expectations, Information Sharing, Climate of Trust, and Negotiation Effectiveness and Efficiency," *Group and Organization Management*, June 1999, pp 217–38.

[48] See H J Reitz, J A Wall Jr., and M S Love, "Ethics in Negotiation: Oil and Water or Good Lubrication?" *Business Horizons*, May-June 1998, pp 5–14.

[49] For related research, see A E Tenbrunsel, "Misrepresentation and Expectations of Misrepresentation in an Ethical Dilemma: The Role of Incentives and Temptation," *Academy of Management Journal*, June 1998, pp 330–39.

[50] Based on R L Pinkley, T L Griffith, and G B Northcraft, " 'Fixed Pie' a la Mode: Information Availability, Information Processing, and the Negotiation of Suboptimal Agreements," *Organizational Behavior and Human Decision Processes*, April 1995, pp 101–12.

[51] Based on B Barry and R A Friedman, "Bargainer Characteristics in Distributive and Integrative Negotiation," *Journal of Personality and Social Psychology*, February 1998, pp 345–59. Also see C K W De Dreu, E Giebels, and E Van de Vliert,"Social Motives and Trust in Integrative Negotiation: The Disruptive Effects of Punitive Capability," *Journal of Applied Psychology*, June 1998, pp 408–22.

[52] For more, see J P Forgas, "On Feeling Good and Getting Your Way: Mood Effects on Negotiator Cognition and Bargaining Strategies," *Journal of Personality and Social Psychology*, March 1998, pp 565–77.

[53] Drawn from J M Brett and T Okumura, "Inter- and Intracultural Negotiation: US and Japanese Negotiators," *Academy of Management Journal*, October 1998, pp 495–510. For more negotiation research findings, see G B Northcraft, J N Preston, M A Neale, P H Kim, and M C Thomas-Hunt, "Non-Linear Preference Functions and Negotiated Outcomes," *Organizational Behavior and Human Decision Processes*, January 1998, pp 54–75; J T Polzer, E A Mannix, and M A Neale, "Interest Alignment and Coalitions in Multiparty Negotiation," *Academy of Management Journal*, February 1998, pp 42–54; J M Brett, D L Shapiro, and A L Lytle, "Breaking the Bonds of Reciprocity in Negotiations," *Academy of Management Journal*, August 1998, pp 410–24; W P Bottom, "Negotiator Risk: Sources of Uncertainty and the Impact of Reference Points on Negotiated Agreements," *Organizational Behavior and Human Decision Processes*, November 1998, pp 89–112; and D A Moore, T R Kurtzberg, and L L Thompson, "Long and Short Routes to Success in Electronically Mediated Negotiations: Group Affiliations and Good Vibrations," *Organizational Behavior and Human Decision Processes*, January 1999, pp 24–43.

[54] For background, see D L Jacobs, "First, Fire All the Lawyers," *Inc.*, January 1999, pp 84–85; and S Higginbotham, "Next, Online Bids Over Jail Time?" *Business Week*, July 19, 1999, p 8.

[55] See M Bordwin, "Do-It-Yourself Justice," *Management Review*, January 1999, pp 56–58.

[56] B Morrow and L M Bernardi, "Resolving Workplace Disputes," *Canadian Manager*, Spring 1999, p 17.

[57] Adapted from discussion in K O Wilburn, "Employment Disputes: Solving Them Out of Court," *Management Review*, March 1998, pp 17–21; and Morrow and Bernardi, "Resolving Workplace Disputes," pp 17–19, 27. Also see L Ioannou, "Can't We Get Along?" *Fortune*, December 7, 1998, p 244[E]; and D Weimer and S A Forest, "Forced into Arbitration? Not Any More," *Business Week*, March 16, 1998, pp 66–68.

[58] Wilburn, "Employment Disputes: Solving Them Out of Court," p 19.

Chapter 9

[1] See M A Jaasma and R J Koper, "The Relationship of Student-Faculty Out-of-Class Communication to Instructor Immediacy and Trust and to Student Motivation," *Communication Education*, January 1999, pp

41–47; and P G Clampitt and C W Downs, "Employee Perceptions of the Relationship between Communication and Productivity: A Field Study," *Journal of Business Communication*, 1993, pp 5–28.

[2] J L Bowditch and A F Buono, *A Primer on Organizational Behavior*, 4th ed (New York: John Wiley & Sons, 1997), p 120.

[3] L Labich, "How to Fire People and Still Sleep at Night," *Fortune*, June 10, 1996, p 65.

[4] For a detailed discussion about a contingency approach for selecting medium, see R H Lengel and R L Daft, "The Selection of Communication Media as an Executive Skill," *Academy of Management Executive*, August 1988, pp 225–32.

[5] See B Coates, "This Financial Consultant Really Listens to His Clients," *The Arizona Republic/The Phoenix Gazette*, May 4, 1996, p 8.

[6] R O Parker, "You're Not Listening to Me," *Canadian HR Reporter*, August 14, 2000, pp 21–23.

[7] See K Davis, "Management Communication and the Grapevine," *Harvard Buusiness Review*, September-October 1953, pp 43–49.

[8] Earlier research is discussed by Davis, "Management Communication and the Grapevine," and R Rowan, "Where Did That Rumour Come From?" *Fortune*, August 13, 1979, pp 130–31, 134, 137. The most recent research is discussed by S.M. Crampton, J W Hodge, and J M Mishra, "The Informal Communication Network: Factors Influencing Grapevine Activity," *Public Personnel Management*: Winter 1998; "Pruning the Company Grapevine," *Supervision*, September 1986, p 11; and R Half, "Managing Your Career: 'How Can I Stop the Gossip?'" *Management Accounting*, September 1987, p 27.

[9] For a thorough discussion of communication distortion, see E W Larson and J B King, "The Systematic Distortion of Information: An Ongoing Challenge to Management," *Organizational Dynamics*, Winter 1996, pp 49–61.

[10] J Fulk and S Mani, "Distortion of Communication in Hierarchical Relationships," in *Communication Yearbook* 9, ed M L McLaughlin (Beverly Hills, CA: Sage Publications, 1986), p 483.

[11] For a review of this research, see ibid, pp 483–510.

[12] Results can be found in B Davenport Sypher and T E Zorn, Jr, "Communication-Related Abilities and Upward Mobility: A Longitudinal Investigation," *Human Communication Research*, Spring 1986, pp 420–31.

[13] See E Raudsepp, "Are You Properly Assertive?" *Supervision*, June 1992, pp 17–18; and D A Infante and W I Gorden, "Superiors' Argumentativeness and Verbal Aggressiveness as Predictors of Subordinates' Satisfaction," *Human Communication Research*, Fall 1985, pp 117–25.

[14] J A Waters, "Managerial Assertiveness," *Business Horizons*, September–October 1982, p 25.

[15] Ibid, p 27.

[16] This statistic was provided by A Warfield, "Do You Speak Body Language?" *Training & Development*, April 2001, pp 60–61.

[17] See N Morgan, "The Kinesthetic Speaker: Putting Action into Words," *Harvard Business Review*, April 2001, pp 113–20; and G E Wright and K D Multon, "Employer's Perceptions of Nonverbal Communication in Job Interviews for Persons with Physical Disabilities," *Journal of Vocational Behavior*, October 1995, pp 214–27.

[18] S French, "The Lost Art of Face-to-Face Communication," *Canadian HR Reporter*, September 10, 2001, p 8.

[19] A thorough discussion of cross-cultural differences is provided by R E Axtell, *Gestures: The Do's and Taboos of Body Language Around the World* (New York: John Wiley & Sons, 1991). Problems with body language analysis also are discussed by C L Karrass, "Body Language: Beware the Hype," *Traffic Management*, January 1992, p 27.

[20] Related research is summarized by J A Hall, "Male and Female Nonverbal Behavior," in *Multichannel Integrations of Nonverbal Behavior*, eds A W Siegman and S Feldstein (Hillsdale, NJ: Lawrence Erlbaum, 1985), pp 195–226.

[21] See R E Axtell, *Gestures: The Do's and Taboos of Body Language Around the World* (New York: John Wiley & Sons, 1991).

[22] See J A Russell, "Facial Expressions of Emotion: What Lies Beyond Minimal Universality?" *Psychological Bulletin*, November 1995, pp 379–91.

[23] Norms for cross-cultural eye contact are discussed by C Engholm, *When Business East Meets Business West: The Guide to Practice and Protocol in the Pacific Rim* (New York: John Wiley & Sons, 1991).

[24] Excerpted from Warfield, *"Do You Speak Body Language?"* p 60.

[25] See D Ray, "Are You Listening?" *Selling Power*, June 1999, pp 28–30; and P Meyer, "So You Want the President's Job," *Business Horizons*, January–February 1998, pp 2–6.

[26] For a thorough discussion of the different listening styles, see R T Bennett and R V Wood, "Effective Communication via Listening Styles," *Business*, April–June 1989, pp 45–48.

[27] D Tannen, "The Power of Talk: Who Gets Heard and Why," *Harvard Business Review*, September–October 1995, p 139.

[28] For a thorough review of the evolutionary explanation of sex differences in communication, see A H Eagly and W Wood, "The Origins of Sex Differences in Human Behavior," *American Psychologist*, June 1999, pp 408–23.

[29] See D Tannen, "The Power of Talk: Who Gets Heard and Why," in *Negotiation: Readings, Exercises, and Cases*, 3rd ed, eds R J Lewicki and D M Saunders (Boston, MA: Irwin/McGraw-Hill, 1999), pp 160–73; and D Tannen, *You Just Don't Understand: Women and Men in Conversation* (New York: Ballantine Books, 1990).

[30] Research on gender differences in communication can be found in A Mulac, J J Bradac, and P Gibbons, "Empirical Support for the Gender-as-Culture Hypothesis: An Intercultural Analysis of Male/Female Language Differences," *Human Communication Research*, January 2001, pp 121–52; and K Hawkins and C B Power, "Gender Differences in Questions Asked During Small Decision-Making Group Discussions," *Small Group Research*, April 1999, pp 235–56.

[31] Tannen, *"The Power of Talk: Who Gets Heard and Why,"* pp 147–48.

[32] M MacMillan, "Out With the Old," *Computing Canada*, January 5, 2001, p 22.

[33] The Harris Poll was reported in "USA Snapshots: Computer Age," *USA Today*, June 7, 1999, p 1A.

[34] Results can be found in D Smith, "One-Tenth of College Students Are Dependent on the Internet, Research Finds," *Monitor on Psychology*, May 2001, p 10.

[35] Results were reported in A Petersen, "A Fine Line: Companies Face a Delicate Task When It Comes to Deciding What to Put on Their Intranets: How Much Is Too Much?" *The Wall Street Journal*, June 21, 1999, p R8.

[36] R O Parker, "You're Not Listening to Me".

[37] See J Useem, "For Sale Online: You," *Fortune*, July 5, 1999, pp 67–78.

[38] Statistics are reported in C Tejada, "Work Week: A Special News Report About Life on the Job—and Trends Taking Shape There," *The Wall Street Journal*, May 8, 2001, p A1; and J Wallace, "The (E-Mail) Postman Rings More Than Twice," *HR Magazine*, March 2001, p 176.

[39] Results are summarized in S Armour, "Boss: It's in the E-mail," *USA Today*, August 10, 1999, p 3B.

[40] The benefits of using E-mail were derived from discussion in R F Federico and J M Bowley, "The Great E-Mail Debate," *HR Magazine*, January 1996, pp 67–72.

[41] Results can be found in M L Markus, "Electronic Mail as the Medium of Managerial Choice," *Organization Science*, November 1994, pp 502–27.

[42] Excerpted from B. Sosnin, "Digital Newsletters 'E-volutionize' Employee Communications," *HR Magazine*, May 2001, p 101.

[43] M Fleschner, "Bold Goals: How Pinacor Wraps Itself Around the Customer," *Selling Power*, June 1999, p 57.

[44] Results can be found in M S Thompson and M S Feldman, "Electronic Mail and Organizational Communication: Does Saying 'Hi' Really Matter?" *Organization Science*, November–December 1998, pp 685–98.

[45] L Greiner, "Being on an Email System Doesn't Make a Team," *Computing Canada*, November 2, 2001, p 19.

[46] See the discussion in S Prasso, "Workers, Surf at Your Own Risk," *Business Week*, June 11, 2001, p 14; and S Miller and J Weckert, "Privacy, the Workplace and the Internet," *Journal of Business Ethics*, 2000, pp 255–65.

[47] The types of information technology used by virtual teams is discussed by A M Townsend, S M DeMarie, and A R Hendrickson, "Virtual Teams: Technology and the Workplace of the Future," *Academy of Management Executive*, August 1998, pp 17–29.

[48] Challenges associated with virtual operations are discussed by S O'Mahony and S R Barley, "Do Digital Telecommunications Affect Work and Organization? The State of Our Knowledge," in *Research in Organizational Behavior*, vol. 21, eds R I Sutton and B M Staw (Stamford, CT: JAI Press, 1999), pp 125–61.

[49] N Southworth, "Informality Governs Most Telecommuters," *Globe and Mail*, April 4, 2001, p B11.

[50] Telecommuting statistics were presented in "Work Life: What is the Future of Telework?" *HRFOCUS*, March 2001, pp 5–6.

[51] Supporting evidence is presented in S Fister, "A Lure for Labor," *Training*, February 1999, pp 56–62; M Apgar IV, "The Alternative Workplace: Changing Where and How People Work," *Harvard Business Review*, May–June 1998, pp 121–36; and C Hymowitz, "Remote Managers Find Ways to Narrow the Distance Gap," *The Wall Street Journal*, April 6, 1999, p B1.

[52] The legal considerations of telecommuting are discussed by B A Hartstein and M L Schulman, "Telecommuting: The New Workplace of the 90s," *Employee Relations* L J, Spring 1996, pp 179–88.

[53] R O Parker, "You're Not Listening to Me."

[54] The preceding barriers are discussed by J P Scully, "People: The Imperfect Communicators," *Quality Progress*, April 1995, pp 37–39.

[55] For a thorough discussion of these barriers, see C R Rogers and F J Roethlisberger, "Barriers and Gateways to Communication," *Harvard Business Review*, July–August 1952, pp 46–52.

[56] Ibid, p 47.

Chapter 10

[1] See D Kipnis, S M Schmidt, and J Wilkinson, "Intraorganizational Influence Tactics: Explorations in Getting One's Way," *Journal of Applied Psychology*, August 1980, pp 440–52. Also see C A Schriesheim and T R Hinkin, "Influence Tactics Used by Subordinates: A Theoretical and Empirical Analysis and Refinement of the Kipnis, Schmidt, and Wilkinson Subscales," *Journal of Applied Psychology*, June 1990, pp 246–57; and G Yukl and C M Falbe, "Influence Tactics and Objectives in Upward, Downward, and Lateral Influence Attempts," *Journal of Applied Psychology*, April 1990, pp 132–40.

[2] Based on Table 1 in G Yukl, C M Falbe, and J Y Youn, "Patterns of Influence Behavior for Managers," *Group & Organization Management*, March 1993, pp 5–28. An additional influence tactic is presented in B P Davis and E S Knowles, "A Disrupt-then-Reframe Technique of Social Influence," *Journal of Personality and Social Psychology*, February 1999, pp 192–99.

[3] For related reading, see M Lippitt, "How to Influence Leaders," *Training & Development*, March 1999, pp 18–22; L Schlesinger, "I've Got Three Words for You: Suck It Up," *Fast Company*, April 1999, p 104; and S M Farmer and J M Maslyn, "Why Are Styles of Upward Influence Neglected? Making the Case for a Configurational Approach to Influences," *Journal of Management*, no. 5, 1999, pp 653–682.

[4] Based on discussion in G Yukl, H Kim, and C M Falbe, "Antecedents of Influence Outcomes," *Journal of Applied Psychology*, June 1996, pp 309–17.

[5] Data from ibid.

[6] Data from G Yukl and J B Tracey, "Consequences of Influence Tactics Used with Subordinates, Peers, and the Boss," *Journal of Applied Psychology*, August 1992, pp 525–35. Also see C M Falbe and G Yukl, "Consequences for Managers of Using Single Influence Tactics and Combinations of Tactics," *Academy of Management Journal*, August 1992, pp 638–52.

[7] Data from R A Gordon, "Impact of Ingratiation on Judgments and Evaluations: A Meta-Analytic Investigation," *Journal of Personality and Social Psychology*, July 1996, pp 54–70. Also see S J Wayne, R C Liden, and R T Sparrowe, "Developing Leader-Member Exchanges," *American Behavioral Scientist*, March 1994, pp 697–714; A Oldenburg, "These Days, Hostile Is Fitting for Takeovers Only," *USA Today*, July 22, 1996, pp 8B, 10B; and J H Dulebohn and G R Ferris, "The Role of Influence Tactics in Perceptions of Performance Evaluations' Fairness," *Academy of Management Journal*, June 1999, pp 288–303.

[8] Data from Yukl, Kim, and Falbe, "Antecedents of Influence Outcomes."

[9] Data from B J Tepper, R J Eisenbach, S L Kirby, and P W Potter, "Test of a Justice-Based Model of Subordinates' Resistance to Downward Influence Attempts," *Group & Organization Management*, June 1998, pp 144–60.

[10] Yukl, Falbe and Youn, "Patterns of Influence Behavior for Managers," p 27.

[11] B Moses, "You Can't Make Change, You Have to Sell It," *Fast Company*, April 1999, p 101.

[12] A R Cohen and D L Bradford, *Influence Without Authority* (New York: John Wiley & Sons, 1990), pp 23–24.

[13] Excerpted from ibid, pp 23–24.

[14] Cohen and Bradford, *Influence Without Authority*, p 28. Another excellent source on this subject is R B Cialdini, *Influence* (New York: William Morrow, 1984).

[15] D Tjosvold, "The Dynamics of Positive Power," *Training and Development Journal*, June 1984, p 72. Also see T A Stewart, "Get with the New Power Game," *Fortune*, January 13, 1997, pp 58–62.

[16] See G Koretz, "The Last Step Up Is a Big One," *Business Week*, May 14, 2001, p 38.

[17] M W McCall, Jr, *Power, Influence, and Authority: The Hazards of Carrying a Sword*, Technical Report No. 10 (Greensboro, NC: Center for Creative Leadership, 1978), p 5. For an excellent update on power, see E P Hollander and L R Offermann, "Power and Leadership in Organizations," *American Psychologist*, February 1990, pp 179–89. Also see E Lesly, "Manager See, Manager Do," *Business Week*, April 3, 1995, pp 90–91. Also see R Greene, *The 48 Laws of Power* (New York: Viking, 1998).

[18] See B Lloyd, "The Paradox of Power," *The Futurist*, May-June 1996, p 60.

[19] See J R P French and B Raven, "The Bases of Social Power," in *Studies in Social Power*, ed D Cartwright (Ann Arbor: University of Michigan Press, 1959), pp 150–67. Also see C M Fiol, E J O'Connor, and H Aguinis, "All for One and One for All? The Development and Transfer of Power across Organizational Levels," *Academy of Management Review*, April 2001, pp 224–42.

[20] See D A Morand, "Forms of Address and Status Leveling in Organizations," *Business Horizons*, November–December 1995, pp 34–39; and H Lancaster, "A Father's Character, Not His Success, Shapes Kids' Careers," *The Wall Street Journal*, February 27, 1996, p B1.

[21] P M Podsakoff and C A Schriesheim, "Field Studies of French and Raven's Bases of Power: Critique, Reanalysis, and Suggestions for Future Research," *Psychological Bulletin*, May 1985, p 388. Also see M A Rahim and G F Buntzman, "Supervisory Power Bases, Styles of Handling Conflict with Subordinates, and Subordinate Compliance and Satisfaction," *Journal of Psychology*, March 1989, pp 195–210; D Tjosvold, "Power and Social Context in Superior-Subordinate Interaction," *Organizational Behavior and Human Decision Processes*, June 1985, pp 281–93; and C A Schriesheim, T R Hinkin, and P M Podsakoff, "Can Ipsative and Single-Item Measures Produce Erroneous Results in Field Studies of French and Raven's (1950) Five Bases of Power? An Empirical Investigation," *Journal of Applied Psychology*, February 1991, pp 106–14.

[22] See T R Hinkin and C A Schriesheim, "Relationships between Subordinate Perceptions and Supervisor Influence Tactics and Attributed Bases of Supervisory Power," *Human Relations*, March 1990, pp 221–37. Also see D J Brass and M E Burkhardt, "Potential Power and Power Use: An Investigation of Structure and Behavior," *Academy of Management Journal*, June 1993, pp 441–70; and K W Mossholder, N Bennett, E R Kemery, and M A Wesolowski, "Relationships between Bases of Power and Work Reactions: The Mediational Role of Procedural Justice," *Journal of Management*, no. 4, 1998, pp 533–52.

[23] See H E Baker III, " 'Wax On—Wax Off:' French and Raven at the Movies," *Journal of Management Education*, November 1993, pp 517–19.

[24] See R Forrester, "Empowerment: Rejuvenating a Potent Idea," *Academy of Management Executive*, August 2000, pp 67–80; M Kaminski, J S Kaufman, R Graubarth, and T G Robins, "How Do People Become Empowered? A Case Study of Union Activists," *Human Relations*, October 2000, pp 1357–83; and P Haspeslagh, T Noda, and F Boulos, "It's Not Just about the Numbers," *Harvard Business Review*, July–August 2001, pp 65–73.

[25] J Macdonald, "The Dreaded 'E Word,' " *Training*, September 1998, p 19. Also see R C Liden and S Arad, "A Power Perspective of Empowerment and Work Groups: Implications for Human Resources Management Research," in *Research in Personnel and Human Resources Management*, vol. 14, ed G R Ferris (Greenwich, CT: JAI Press, 1996), pp 205–51.

[26] R M Hodgetts, "A Conversation with Steve Kerr," *Organizational Dynamics*, Spring 1996, p 71. See L Holpp, "If Empowerment Is So

Good, Why Does It Hurt?" *Training*, March 1995, pp 52–57; Liden and Arad, "A Power Perspective of Empowerment and Work Groups: Implications for Human Resources Management Research"; and G M Spreitzer, "Social Structural Characteristics of Psychological Empowerment," *Academy of Management Journal*, April 1996, pp 483–504.

[27] K A Johnson, "Quote", *Wharton Leadership Digest*, June 1999, (www.leadership.wharton.upenn.edu/digest/index.shtml).

[28] For related discussion, see M M Broadwell, "Why Command & Control Won't Go Away," *Training*, September 1995, pp 62–68; R E Quinn and G M Spreitzer, "The Road to Empowerment: Seven Questions Every Leader Should Consider," *Organizational Dynamics*, Autumn 1997, pp 37–49; and I Cunningham and L Honold, "Everyone Can Be a Coach," *HR Magazine*, June 1998, pp 63–66.

[29] See R C Ford and M D Fottler, "Empowerment: A Matter of Degree," *Academy of Management Executive*, August 1995, pp 21–31.

[30] "Empowerment at Local 14J/Xerox," (www.write-svti.org/En/WORK_REORG...t_local_14/empowerment_at_local_14.html), June 23, 2002.

[31] W A Randolph, "Navigating the Journey to Empowerment," *Organizational Dynamics*, Spring 1995, p 31.

[32] See P L Perrewé, G R Ferris, D D Frink, and W P Anthony, "Political Skill: An Antidote for Workplace Stressors," *Academy of Management Executive*, August 2000, pp 115–23; and B Rosenstein, "Author: Don't Avoid Office Politics; Become a Master," *USA Today*, February 12, 2001, p 6B.

[33] R W Allen, D L Madison, L W Porter, P A Renwick, and B T Mayes, "Organizational Politics: Tactics and Characteristics of Its Actors," *California Management Review*, Fall 1979, p 77. Also see K M Kacmar and G R Ferris, "Politics at Work: Sharpening the Focus of Political Behavior in Organizations," *Business Horizons*, July–August 1993, pp 70–74. A comprehensive update can be found in K M Kacmar and R A Baron, "Organizational Politics: The State of the Field, Links to Related Processes, and an Agenda for Future Research," in *Research in Personnel and Human Resources Management*, vol. 17, ed G R Ferris (Stamford, CT: JAI Press, 1999), pp 1–39.

[34] See P M Fandt and G R Ferris, "The Management of Information and Impressions: When Employees Behave Opportunistically," *Organizational Behavior and Human Decision Processes*, February 1990, pp 140–58.

[35] First four based on discussion in D R Beeman and T W Sharkey, "The Use and Abuse of Corporate Politics," *Business Horizons*, March–April 1987, pp 26–30.

[36] A Raia, "Power, Politics, and the Human Resource Professional," *Human Resource Planning*, no. 4, 1985, p 203.

[37] This three-level distinction comes from A T Cobb, "Political Diagnosis: Applications in Organizational Development," *Academy of Management Review*, July 1986, pp 482–96.

[38] An excellent historical and theoretical perspective of coalitions can be found in W B Stevenson, J L Pearce, and L W Porter, "The Concept of 'Coalition' in Organization Theory and Research," *Academy of Management Review*, April 1985, pp 256–68.

[39] See K G Provan and J G Sebastian, "Networks within Networks: Service Link Overlap, Organizational Cliques, and Network Effectiveness," *Academy of Management Journal*, August 1998, pp 453–63.

[40] D Jenish and B Woodward, "Canada's Top 100 Employers," *Maclean's*, November 5, 2001, p 54.

[41] Allen, Madison, Porter, Renwick, and Mayes, "Organizational Politics: Tactics and Characteristics of Its Actors," p 77.

[42] See W L Gardner III, "Lessons in Organizational Dramaturgy: The Art of Impression Management," *Organizational Dynamics*, Summer 1992, pp 33–46.

[43] A Rao, S M Schmidt, and L H Murray, "Upward Impression Management: Goals, Influence Strategies, and Consequences," *Human Relations*, February 1995, p 147. Also see M C Andrews and K M Kacmar, "Impression Management by Association: Construction and Validation of a Scale," *Journal of Vocational Behavior*, February 2001, pp 142–61.

[44] For related research, see M G Pratt and A Rafaeli, "Organizational Dress as a Symbol of Multilayered Social Identities," *Academy of Management Journal*, August 1997, pp 862–98. Also see B Leonard, "Casual Dress Policies Can Trip Up Job Applicants," *HR Magazine*, June 2001, pp 33, 35.

[45] S Friedman, "What Do You Really Care About? What Are You Most Interested In?" *Fast Company*, March 1999, p 90. Also see B M DePaulo and D A Kashy, "Everyday Lies in Close and Casual Relationships," *Journal of Personality and Social Psychology*, January 1998, pp 63–79.

[46] See S J Wayne and G R Ferris, "Influence Tactics, Affect, and Exchange Quality in Supervisor-Subordinate Interactions: A Laboratory Experiment and Field Study," *Journal of Applied Psychology*, October 1990, pp 487–99. For another version, see Table 1 (p 246) in S J Wayne and R C Liden, "Effects of Impression Management on Performance Ratings: A Longitudinal Study," *Academy of Management Journal*, February 1995, pp 232–60.

[47] See R Vonk, "The Slime Effect: Suspicion and Dislike of Likeable Behavior toward Superiors," *Journal of Personality and Social Psychology*, April 1998, pp 849–64; and M Wells, "How to Schmooze Like the Best of Them," *USA Today*, May 18, 1999, p 14E.

[48] See P Rosenfeld, R A Giacalone, and C A Riordan, "Impression Management Theory and Diversity: Lessons for Organizational Behavior," *American Behavioral Scientist*, March 1994, pp 601–04; R A Giacalone and J W Beard, "Impression Management, Diversity, and International Management," *American Behavioral Scientist*, March 1994, pp 621–36; and A Montagliani and R A Giacalone, "Impression Management and Cross-Cultural Adaptation," *Journal of Social Psychology*, October 1998, pp 598–608.

[49] M E Mendenhall and C Wiley, "Strangers in a Strange Land: The Relationship between Expatriate Adjustment and Impression Management," *American Behavioral Scientist*, March 1994, pp 605–20.

[50] For a humorous discussion of making a bad impression, see P Hellman, "Looking BAD," *Management Review*, January 2000, p 64.

[51] T E Becker and S L Martin, "Trying to Look Bad at Work: Methods and Motives for Managing Poor Impressions in Organizations," *Academy of Management Journal*, February 1995, p 191.

[52] Ibid, p 181.

[53] Adapted from ibid, pp 180–81.

[54] Based on discussion in ibid, pp 192–93.

[55] A Zaleznik, "Real Work," *Harvard Business Review*, January–February 1989, p 60.

[56] "WestJet Spirit" (www.c0dsp.westjet.com/internet/sky/about/spirit Template.jsp), June 23, 2002.

[57] C M Koen, Jr, and S M Crow, "Human Relations and Political Skills," *HR Focus*, December 1995, p 11.

[58] See L A Witt, "Enhancing Organizational Goal Congruence: A Solution to Organizational Politics," *Journal of Applied Psychology*, August 1998, pp 666–74; and F F Reichheld, "Lead for Loyalty," *Harvard Business Review*, July–August 2001, pp 76–84.

Chapter 11

[1] C A Schriesheim, J M Tolliver, and O C Behling, "Leadership Theory: Some Implications for Managers," *MSU Business Topics*, Summer 1978, p 35.

[2] The different levels of leadership are thoroughly discussed by F J Yammarino, F Dansereau, and C J Kennedy, "A Multiple-Level Multidimensional Approach to Leadership: Viewing Leadership through an Elephant's Eye," *Organizational Dynamics*, 2001, pp 149–62.

[3] R J House et al, "Culture, Leadership and Organizational Practices," in *Advances in Global Leadership,* ed W H Mobley (Stamford, CT: JAI Press, 1999). R House, N Wright and R N Aditya, "Cross-Cultural Leadership," in *Cross-Cultural Organizational Behavior and Psychology,* eds C Earley and M Erez, (New Frontier Services of the Society for Industrial and Organizational Psychology, 1997).

[4] Gender and the emergence of leaders was examined by A H Eagly and S J Karau, "Gender and the Emergence of Leaders: A Meta-Analysis," *Journal of Personality and Social Psychology,* May 1991, pp 685–710; and R K Shelly and P T Munroe, "Do Women Engage in Less Task Behavior Than Men?" *Sociological Perspectives,* Spring 1999, pp 49–67.

[5] See A H Eagly, S J Karau, and B T Johnson, "Gender and Leadership Style among School Principals: A Meta-Analysis," *Educational Administration Quarterly,* February 1992, pp 76–102.

[6] Supportive findings are contained in J M Twenge, "Changes in Women's Assertiveness in Response to Status and Roles: A Cross-Temporal Meta-Analysis, 1931–1993," *Journal of Personality and Social Psychology,* July 2001, pp 133–45.

[7] For a summary of this research, see R Sharpe, "As Leaders, Women Rule," *Business Week,* November 20, 2000, pp 74–84.

[8] J Loring, "Attention Shoppers," *Globe and Mail*, March 29, 2002, p 50.

[9] "The TIME/CNN 25 Most Influential Global Business Executives," *TIME,* December 2001, p 70.

[10] See B M Bass, *Bass and Stogdill's Handbook of Leadership: Theory, Research and Managerial Applications*, 3rd ed (New York: The Free Press, 1990), chaps 20–25; the relationships between the frequency and mastery of leader behavior and various outcomes were investigated by F Shipper and C S White, "Mastery, Frequency and Interaction of Managerial Behaviors Relative to Subunit Effectiveness," *Human Relations*, January 1999, pp 49–66.

[11] For a corporate example of how leadership can be developed, see D Goldwasser, "Reinventing the Wheel: How American Home Products Transforms Senior Managers into Leaders," *Training*, February 2001, pp 54–65.

[12] See See B M Bass, *Bass & Stogdill's Handbook of Leadership: Theory, Research, and Managerial Applications*, 3rd ed (New York: The Free Press, 1990), chs 20–25.

[13] The relationships between the frequency and mastery of leader behavior and various outcomes were investigated by F Shipper and C S White, "Mastery, Frequency, and Interaction of Managerial Behaviors Relative to Subunit Effectiveness," *Human Relations*, January 1999, pp 49–66.

[14] R Azzopardi, "Leading in Times of Crisis," *Canadian HR Reporter*, February 25, 2002, p 19.

[15] F E Fiedler, "Job Engineering for Effective Leadership: A New Approach," *Management Review*, September 1977, p 29.

[16] Additional information on situational control is contained in F E Fiedler, "The Leadership Situation and the Black Box in Contingency Theories," in *Leadership Theory and Research: Perspectives and Directions*, eds M M Chemers and R Ayman (New York: Academic Press, 1993), pp 2–28.

[17] See L H Peters, D D Hartke, and J T Pohlmann, "Fiedler's Contingency Theory of Leadership: An Application of the Meta-Analyses Procedures of Schmidt and Hunter," *Psychological Bulletin*, March 1985, pp 274–85; and C A Schriesheim, B J Tepper, and L A Tetrault, "Least Preferred Co-Worker Score, Situational Control, and Leadership Effectiveness: A Meta-Analysis of Contingency Model Performance Predictions," *Journal of Applied Psychology*, August 1994, pp 561–73.

[18] For more detail on this theory, see R J House, "A Path–Goal Theory of Leader Effectiveness," *Administrative Science Quarterly*, September 1971, pp 321–38.

[19] "CEOs Talk," *Canadian HR Reporter*, October 8, 2001, pp 15–17.

[20] Adapted from R J House and T R Mitchell, "Path–Goal Theory of Leadership," *Journal of Contemporary Business*, Autumn 1974, p 83.

[21] Excerpted from S Hamm, "Compaq's Rockin Boss," *Business Week*, September 4, 2000, pp 92, 95.

[22] Results can be found in P M Podsakoff, S B MacKenzie, M Ahearne, and W H Bommer, "Searching for a Needle in a Haystack: Trying to Identify the Illusive Moderators of Leadership Behaviors," *Journal of Management*, 1995, pp 422–70.

[23] Excerpted from W M Bulkeley, "IBM's Next CEO May be the One to Bring Change," *The Wall Street Journal*, May 21, 2001, p B1.

[24] B Shamir, R J House, and M B Arthur, "The Motivational Effects of Charismatic Leadership: A Self-Concept Based Theory," *Organization Science*, November 1993, p 578.

[25] Supportive results can be found in T A Judge and J E Bono, "Five-Factor Model of Personality and Transformational Leadership," *Journal of Applied Psychology*, October 2000, pp 751–65; and J M Crant and T Bateman, "Charismatic Leadership Viewed from Above: The Impact of Proactive Personality," *Journal of Organizational Behavior*, February 2000, pp 63–75.

[26] B Nanus, *Visionary Leadership* (San Francisco: Jossey-Bass, 1992), p 8.

[27] See ibid; and S Yearout, G Miles, and R H Koonce, "Multi-Level Visioning," *Training & Development*, March 2001, pp 31–39.

[28] "CEOs Talk."

[29] Bass N M, "From Transactional to Transformational Leadership: Learning to Share the Visison," *Organizational Dynamics*, 18, 1990, pp 19–36. See also Bass B M and Avolio B J, "The Implications of Transactional and Transformational Leadership for Individual, Team and Organizational Diversity." In eds W Pasmore and R W Woodman *Research in*

Organizational Change and Development, vol 4 (Greenwich CT: JAI Press, 1990) pp 231–72; and Bass B M *Leadership and Performance Beyond Expectations* (New York: Free Press, 1985).

[30] Results can be obtained from T G DeGroot, D S Kiker, and T C Cross, *"A Meta-Analysis to Review the Consequences of Charismatic Leadership,"* paper presented at the annual meeting of the Academy of Management, Cincinnati, Ohio, 1996.

[31] Results can be found in J A Conger, R N Kanungo, and S T Menon, "Charismatic Leadership and Follower Effects," *Journal of Organizational Behavior*, November 2000, pp 747–68; and R Pillai and J R Meindl, "Context and Charisma: A 'Meso' Level Examination of the Relationship of Organic Structure, Collectivism, and Crisis to Charismatic Leadership," *Journal of Management*, 1998, 643–71.

[32] See K B Lowe, K G Kroeck, and N Sivasubramaniam, "Effectiveness Correlates of Transformational and Transactional Leadership: A Meta-Analytic Review of the MLQ Literature," *Leadership Quarterly*, 1996, pp 385–425.

[33] See B Shankar Pawar and K K Eastman, "The Nature and Implications of Contextual Influences on Transformational Leadership: A Conceptual Examination," *Academy of Management Review*, January 1997, pp 80–109.

[34] Supporting research is summarized by Bass and Avolio, "Transformation Leadership: A Response to Critiques," pp 49–80. The effectiveness of leadership training is discussed by J Huey, "The Leadership Industry," *Fortune*, February 21, 1994, pp 54–56.

[35] D Brown, "Leadership Development That Pays for Itself," *Canadian HR Reporter*, April 9, 2001, pp 7–8.

[36] These recommendations were derived from J M Howell and B J Avolio, "The Ethics of Charismatic Leadership: Submission or Liberation," *The Executive*, May 1992, pp 43–54.

[37] See F Dansereau, Jr, G Graen, and W Haga, "A Vertical Dyad Linkage Approach to Leadership within Formal Organizations," *Organizational Behavior and Human Performance*, February 1975, pp 46–78; and R M Dienesch and R C Liden, "Leader–Member Exchange Model of Leadership: A Critique and Further Development," *Academy of Management Review*, July 1986, pp 618–34.

[38] These descriptions were taken from D Duchon, S G Green, and T D Taber, "Vertical Dyad Linkage: A Longitudinal Assessment of Antecedents, Measures, and Consequences," *Journal of Applied Psychology*, February 1986, pp 56–60.

[39] Supportive results can be found in C Gomez and B Rosen, "The Leader–Member Exchange as a Link between Managerial Trust and Employee Empowerment," *Group & Organization Management*, March 2001, pp 53–69; C A Schriesheim, S L Castro, and F J Yammarino, "Investigating Contingencies: An Examination of the Impact of Span of Supervision and Upward Controllingness on Leader–Member Exchange Using Traditional and Multivariate Within- and Between-Entities Analysis," *Journal of Applied Psychology*, October 2000, pp 659–77; and C Cogliser and C A Schriesheim, "Exploring Work Unit Context and Leader–Member Exchange: A Multi-Level Perspective," *Journal of Organizational Behavior*, August 2000, pp 487–511.

[40] A turnover study was conducted by G B Graen, R C Liden, and W Hoel, "Role of Leadership in the Employee Withdrawal Process," *Journal of Applied Psychology*, December 1982, pp 868–72. The career progress study was conducted by M Wakabayashi and G B Graen, "The Japanese Career Progress Study: A 7-Year Follow-Up," *Journal of Applied Psychology*, November 1984, pp 603–14.

[41] A review of this research can be found in R T Sparrowe and R C Liden, "Process and Structure in Leader–Member Exchange," *Academy of Management Review*, April 1997, pp 522–52.

[42] Supporting evidence can be found in S J Wayne, L M Shore, and R C Liden, "Perceived Organizational Support and Leader–Member Exchange: A Social Exchange Perspective," *Academy of Management Journal*, February 1997, pp 82–11.

[43] These recommendations are from R P Vecchio, "Are You In or Out with Your Boss?" *Business Horizons*, November–December 1986, pp 76–78.

[44] For an expanded discussion of this model, see S Kerr and J Jermier, "Substitutes for Leadership: Their Meaning and Measurement," *Organizational Behavior and Human Performance*, December 1978, pp 375–403.

[45] For details of this study, see P M Podsakoff, S B MacKenzie, and W H Bommer, "Meta-Analysis of the Relationship between Kerr and Jermier's Substitutes for Leadership and Employee Job Attitudes, Role Perceptions, and Performance," *Journal of Applied Psychology*, August 1996, pp 380–99.

[46] An overall summary of servant leadership is provided by L C Spears, *Reflections on Leadership: How Robert K Greenleaf's Theory of Servant-Leadership Influenced Today's Top Management Thinkers* (New York: John Wiley & Sons, 1995).

[47] J Stuart, *Fast Company*, September 1999, p 114.

[48] For a discussion of superleadership, see C C Manz and H P Sims, Jr, "SuperLeadership: Beyond the Myth of Heroic Leadership," in *Leadership: Understanding the Dynamics of Power and Influence in Organizations*, ed Vecchio, pp 411–28; and C C Manz and H P Sims, Jr, *Superleadership: Leading Others to Lead Themselves* (New York: Berkley Books, 1989).

[49] Scoring Key for Leadership Dimensions Instrument: For transactional leadership, add the scores circled (1 to 7) for the odd-numbered items (1, 3, 5, 7, 9, 11 ,13, 15). Maximum score is 40. Higher scores indicate that your supervisor has a strong inclination towards transactional leadership. For transformational leadership, add the scores circled for the even-numbered items (2, 4, 6, 8, 10, 12, 14, 16). Maximum score is 40. Higher scores indicate that your supervisor has a strong inclination towards transformational leadership.

[50] Scoring for "Are You a Charismatic Leader?": The questionnaire measures each of six basic leader behaviour patterns, as well as a set of emotional responses. Each question is stated as a measure of the extent to which you engage in the behaviour, or elicit the feelings. The higher the overall score, the more you demonstrate charismatic leadership behaviour. The indicies outline a variety of traits associated with charismatic behaviour. For each index, add up the scores you gave to the relevant questions. Your score on each index can range from 4 to 20. Index 1: Management of Attention (1, 7, 13, 19). You pay close attention to people with whom you are communicating. You are also focused in on the key issues under discussion and help others to see clearly these key points. They have clear ideas about the relative importance or priorities of different issues under discussion. Index 2: Management of Meaning (2, 8, 14, 20). This set of items centres on your communication skills, specifically your ability to get the meaning of a message across, even if this means devising some quite innovative approach. Index 3: Management of Trust (3, 9, 15, 21). The key factor is your perceived trustworthiness as shown by your willingness to follow through on promises, avoidance of "flip-flop" shifts in position, and willingness to take a clear position. Index 4: Management of Self (4, 10, 16, 22). This index measures your general attitudes toward yourself and others, that is, your overall concern for others and their feelings, as well as for "taking care of" feelings about yourself in a positive sense ie. self-regard. Index 5: Management of Risk (5, 11, 17, 23) Effective charismatic leaders are deeply involved in what they do, and do not spend excessive amounts of time or energy on plans to "protect" themselves against failure. These leaders are willing to take risks, not on a "hit-or-miss" basis, but after careful estimation of the odds of success or failure. Index 6: Management of Feelings (6, 12, 18, 24). Charismatic leaders seem to consistently generate a set of feelings in others. Others feel that their work becomes more meaningful and that they are the masters of their own behaviour; that is, they feel competent. They feel a sense of community, a "we-ness" with their colleagues and their coworkers.

Chapter 12

[1] See R W Oliver, *The Shape of Things to Come: Seven Imperatives for Winning in the New World of Business* (New York: McGraw-Hill, 1999).

[2] C I Barnard, *The Functions of the Executive* (Cambridge, MA: Harvard University Press, 1938), p 73. Also see M C Suchman, "Managing Legitimacy: Strategic and Institutional Approaches," *Academy of Management Review*, July 1995, pp 571–610.

[3] Drawn from E H Schein, *Organizational Psychology*, 3rd ed (Englewood Cliffs, NJ: Prentice Hall, 1980), pp 12–15.

[4] For an interesting historical perspective of hierarchy, see P Miller and T O'Leary, "Hierarchies and American Ideals, 1900–1940," *Academy of Management Review*, April 1989, pp 250–65.

[5] For an excellent overview of the span of control concept, see D D Van Fleet and A G Bedeian, "A History of the Span of Management," *Academy of Management Review*, July 1977, pp 356–72. Also see E E Lawler III and J R Galbraith, "New Roles for the Staff: Strategic Support and Service," in *Organizing for the Future: The New Logic for Managing Complex Organizations*, eds J R Galbraith, E E Lawler III, and Associates (San Francisco: Jossey-Bass, 1993), pp 65–83.

[6] See, for example, R J Marshak, "Managing the Metaphors of Change," *Organizational Dynamics*, Summer 1993, pp 44–56; R Garud and S Kotha, "Using the Brain as a Metaphor to Model Flexible Production Systems," *Academy of Management Review*, October 1994, pp 671–98; and R W Keidel, "Rethinking Organizational Design," *Academy of Management Executive*, November 1994, pp 12–30.

[7] A management-oriented discussion of general systems theory—an interdisciplinary attempt to integrate the various fragmented sciences—may be found in K E Boulding, "General Systems Theory—The Skeleton of Science," *Management Science*, April 1956, pp 197–208.

[8] J D Thompson, *Organizations in Action* (New York: McGraw-Hill, 1967), pp 6–7. Also see A C Bluedorn, "The Thompson Interdependence Demonstration," *Journal of Management Education*, November 1993, pp 505–09.

[9] For interesting updates on the biological systems metaphor, see A M Webber, "How Business Is a Lot Like Life," *Fast Company*, April 2001, pp 130–36; and E Bonabeau and C Meyer, "Swarm Intelligence: A Whole New Way to Think about Business," *Harvard Business Review*, May 2001, pp 106–14.

[10] R L Daft and K E Weick, "Toward a Model of Organizations as Interpretation Systems," *Academy of Management Review*, April 1984, p 293.

[11] For good background reading, see the entire Autumn 1998 issue of Organizational Dynamics; D Lei, J W Slocum, and R A Pitts, "Designing Organizations for Competitive Advantage: The Power of Unlearning and Learning," *Organizational Dynamics*, Winter 1999, pp 24–38; L Baird, P Holland, and S Deacon, "Learning from Action: Imbedding More Learning into the Performance Fast Enough to Make a Difference," *Organizational Dynamics*, Spring 1999, pp 19–32; "Leading-Edge Learning: Two Views," *Training & Development*, March 1999, pp 40–42; and A M Webber, "Learning for a Change," *Fast Company*, May 1999, pp 178–88.

[12] "Top Forty Under 40," *Report on Business Magazine*, May 2002, p 73.

[13] J A C Baum, "Organizational Ecology," in *Handbook of Organization Studies*, eds S R Clegg, C Hardy and W R Nord (Thousand Oaks, CA: Sage Publications, 1996), p 77. (Emphasis added.) Also see C S Hunt and H E Aldrich, "The Second Ecology: Creation and Evolution of Organizational Communities,"in *Research in Organizational Behavior* (vol 20), eds B M Staw and L L Cummings (Greenwich CT: JAI Press, 1998), pp 267–301; and W Tsai and S Ghoshal, "Social Capital and Value Creation: The Role of Intrafirm Networks," *Academy of Management Journal*, August 1998, pp 464–76.

[14] For example, see O Harari, "The Marrying Kind," *Management Review*, June 1998, pp 23–26; and P Burrows and R Grover, "Steve Jobs, Movie Mogul," *Business Week*, November 23, 1998, pp 140–54.

[15] M Maynard, "It's Not Easy Being Green, So Carmakers Unite," *USA Today*, April 20, 1999, p 1B.

[16] K Cameron, "Critical Questions in Assessing Organizational Effectiveness," *Organizational Dynamics*, Autumn 1980, p 70. Also see J Pfeffer, "When It Comes to 'Best Practices'—Why Do Smart Organizations Occasionally Do Dumb Things?" *Organizational Dynamics*, Summer 1996, pp 33–44.

[17] See B Wysocki, Jr, "Rethinking a Quaint Idea: Profits," *The Wall Street Journal*, May 19, 1999, pp B1, B6; and J Collins, "Turning Goals into Results: The Power of Catalytic Mechanisms," *Harvard Business Review*, July–August 1999, pp 71–82.

[18] See, for example, R O Brinkerhoff and D E Dressler, *Productivity Measurement: A Guide for Managers and Evaluators* (Newbury Park, CA: Sage Publications, 1990); J McCune, "The Productivity Paradox," *Management Review*, March 1998, pp 38–40; and R J Samuelson, "Cheerleaders vs. The Grumps," *Newsweek*, July 26, 1999, p 78.

[19] For example, see B Breen, "Change Is Sweet," *Fast Company*, June 2001, pp 168–77; and C Dahle, "Is the Internet Second Nature?" *Fast Company*, July 2001, pp 145–51.

[20] Data from M Maynard, "Toyota Promises Custom Order in 5 Days," *USA Today*, August 6, 1999, p 1B.

[21] "Interview: M Scott Peck," *Business Ethics*, March–April 1994, p 17.

[22] Cameron, "Critical Questions in Assessing Organizational Effectiveness," p 67. Also see W Buxton, "Growth from Top to Bottom," *Management Review*, July–August 1999, p 11.

[23] See R K Mitchell, B R Agle, and D J Wood, "Toward a Theory of Stakeholder Identification and Salience: Defining the Principle of Who and What Really Counts," *Academy of Management Review*, October 1997, pp 853–96; W Beaver, "Is the Stakeholder Model Dead?" *Business Horizons*, March–April 1999, pp 8–12; J Frooman, "Stakeholder Influence Strategies," *Academy of Management Review*, April 1999, pp 191–205; and T M Jones and A C Wicks, "Convergent Stakeholder Theory," *Academy of Management Review*, April 1999, pp 206–21.

[24] See C Ostroff and N Schmitt, "Configurations of Organizational Effectiveness and Efficiency," *Academy of Management Journal*, December 1993, pp 1345–61.

[25] K S Cameron, "Effectiveness as Paradox: Consensus and Conflict in Conceptions of Organizational Effectiveness," *Management Science*, May 1986, p 542.

[26] Alternative effectiveness criteria are discussed in ibid; A G Bedeian, "Organization Theory: Current Controversies, Issues, and Directions," in *International Review of Industrial and Organizational Psychology*, eds C L Cooper and I T Robertson (New York: John Wiley & Sons, 1987), pp 1–33; and M Keeley, "Impartiality and Participant-Interest Theories of Organizational Effectiveness," *Administrative Science Quarterly*, March 1984, pp 1–25.

[27] For updates, see J M Pennings, "Structural Contingency Theory: A Reappraisal," *Research in Organizational Behavior* (Greenwich, CT: JAI Press, 1992), vol. 14, pp 267–309; A D Meyer, A S Tsui, and C R Hinings, "Configurational Approaches to Organizational Analysis," *Academy of Management Journal*, December 1993, pp 1175–95; and D H Doty, W H Glick, and G P Huber, "Fit, Equifinality, and Organizational Effectiveness: A Test of Two Configurational Theories," *Academy of Management Journal*, December 1993, pp 1196–1250.

[28] P R Lawrence and J W Lorsch, *Organizations and Environment* (Homewood. IL: Richard D Irwin, 1967), p 157.

[29] Pooled, sequential, and reciprocal integration are discussed in J R Lorsch, "Organizational Design: A Situational Perspective," *Organizational Dynamics*, Autumn 1977, pp 2–14. Also see J E Ettlie and E M Reza, "Organizational Integration and Process Innovation," *Academy of Management Journal*, October 1992, pp 795–827; and A L Patti and J P Gilbert, "Collocating New Product Development Teams: Why, When, Where, and How?," *Business Horizons*, November-December 1997, pp 59–64.

[30] See B Dumaine, "Ability to Innovate," *Fortune*, January 29, 1990, pp 43, 46. For good reading on innovation and technology, see O Port, "Getting to 'Eureka!'" *Business Week*, November 10, 1997, pp 72–75; J W Gurley, "Got a Good Idea? Better Think Twice," *Fortune*, December 7, 1998, pp 215–16; J C McCune," The Technology Treadmill," *Management Review*, December 1998, pp 10–12; and L Yates and P Skarzynski, "How do Companies Get to the Future First?" *Management Review*, January 1999, pp 16–22.

[31] B Elgin, "Running the Tightest Ships on the Net," *Business Week*, January 29, 2001, p 126.

[32] See D A Morand, "The Role of Behavioral Formality and Informality in the Enactment of Bureaucratic versus Organic Organizations," *Academy of Management Review*, October 1995, pp 831–72.

[33] See J Huey, "The New Post-Heroic Leadership," *Fortune*, February 21, 1994, pp 42–50; and F Shipper and C C Manz, "Employee Self-Management without Formally Designated Teams: An Alternative Road to Empowerment," *Organizational Dynamics*, Winter 1992, pp 48–61.

[34] See G P Huber, C C Miller, and W H Glick, "Developing More Encompassing Theories about Organizations: The Centralization-Effectiveness Relationship as an Example," *Organization Science*, no. 1, 1990, pp 11–40; and C Handy, "Balancing Corporate Power: A New Federalist Paper," *Harvard Business Review*, November–December 1992, pp 59–72. Also see W R Pape, "Divide and Conquer," *Inc. Technology*, no. 2, 1996, pp 25–27; and J Schmidt, "Breaking Down Fiefdoms," *Management Review*, January 1997, pp 45–49.

[35] P Kaestle, "A New Rationale for Organizational Structure," *Planning Review*, July–August 1990, p 22.

[36] Details of this study can be found in T Burns and G M Stalker, *The Management of Innovation* (London: Tavistock, 1961).

[37] D J Gillen and S J Carroll, "Relationship of Managerial Ability to Unit Effectiveness in More Organic versus More Mechanistic Departments," *Journal of Management Studies*, November 1985, pp 674–75.

[38] J D Sherman and H L Smith, "The Influence of Organizational Structure on Intrinsic versus Extrinsic Motivation," *Academy of Management Journal*, December 1984, p 883.

[39] See J A Courtright, G T Fairhurst, and L E Rogers, "Interaction Patterns in Organic and Mechanistic Systems," *Academy of Management Journal*, December 1989, pp 773–802.

[40] See J R Galbraith and E E Lawler III, "Effective Organizations: using the New Logic of Organizing," in eds J R Galbraith, E E Lawler III, and Associates, *Organizing for the Future: The New Logic for Managing Complex Organizations* (San Francisco: Jossey-Bass, 1993), pp 285–99.

[41] "Top Forty Over 40," *Report on Business Magazine*, May 2002, p 69.

[42] See W F Cascio, "Managing a Virtual Workplace," *Academy of Management Executive*, August 2000, pp 81–90; C M Christensen, "Limits of the New Corporation," *Business Week*, August 28, 2000, pp 180–81; and S. Hamm, "E-Biz: Down but Hardly Out," *Business Week*, March 26, 2001, pp 126–30.

[43] "Fostering Change: Distance Education," *TIME* (Canadian edition), November 12, 2001, p 78.

[44] www.cvu-uvc.ca/english.html, June 24, 2002.

[45] C Handy, *The Hungry Spirit: Beyond Capitalism—A Quest for Purpose in the Modern World* (New York: Broadway Books, 1998), p 186. (Emphasis added.)

[46] See B Lessard and S Baldwin, *NetSlaves: True Tales of Working the Web* (New York: McGraw-Hill, 2000).

[47] See R M Kanter, "You Are Here," *Inc.*, February 2001, pp 84–90; M J Mandel and R D Hof, "Rethinking the Internet," *Business Week*, March 26, 2001, pp 116–22; and M Beer, "How to Develop an Organization Capable of Sustained High Performance: Embrace the Drive for Results-Capability Development Paradox," *Organizational Dynamics*, Spring 2001, pp 233–47.

[48] Scoring Key for Bureaucratic Orientation Test: Give yourself one point for each statement for which you responded in the bureaucratic direction: 1 mostly agree; 2 mostly agree; 3 mostly disagree; 4 mostly agree; 5 mostly disagree; 6 mostly disagree; 7 mostly disagree; 8 mostly agree; 9 mostly disagree; 10 mostly agree; 11 mostly agree; 12 mostly disagree; 13 mostly disagree; 14 mostly agree; 15 mostly disagree; 16 mostly agree; 17 mostly disagree; 18 mostly agree; 19 mostly agree; 20 mostly disagree. A very high score (15 or over) suggests that you would enjoy working in a bureaucracy. A very low score (5 or lower) suggests that you would be frustrated working in a bureaucracy, especially a large one.

[49] Scoring Key for Identifying Your Preferred Organizational Structure: Using the table and calculation key below, calculate your three scores for Tall Hierarchy (H), Formalization (F), and Centralization (C), and your total score.

Table:
Scores for statement items 2,3,8,10,11,12,14,15: not at all =3; a little =2; somewhat=1; very much=0.
Scores for statement items 1,4,5,6,7,9,13: not at all=0; a little=1; somewhat=2; very much=3.

Write the scores for each item on the appropriate line below (statement numbers are in brackets) and total each of the three items (H, F, and C) as shown below. Then calculate the overall score by summing these three scores.

Tall Hierarchy (H): ___ (1) + ___ (4) + ___ (10) + ___ (12) + ___ (15) = ___
Formalization (F): ___ (2) + ___ (6) + ___ (8) + ___ (11) + ___ (13) = ___
Centralization (C): ___ (3) + ___ (5) + ___ (7) + ___ (9) + ___ (14) = ___
Total Score: Add scores for H, F, and C = ___

A higher total score indicates preference for mechanistic organizations, whereas a lower score indicates preference for more organic organizations.

Chapter 13

[1] E H Schein, "Culture: The Missing Concept in Organization Studies," *Administrative Science Quarterly*, June 1996, p 236.

[2] This discussion is based on E H Schein, *Organizational Culture and Leadership*, 2nd ed (San Francisco: Jossey-Bass, 1992), pp 16–48.

[3] L Cassiani, "Putting Productivity Before Humanity," *Canadian HR Reporter*, June 18, 2001, pp 3, 13.

[4] S H Schwartz, "Universals in the Content and Structure of Values: Theoretical Advances and Empirical Tests in 20 Countries," in *Advances in Experimental Social Psychology*, ed M P Zanna (New York: Academic Press, 1992), p 4.

[5] K Rowlands, "More than a Pay Cheque," *HR Professional*, December 2000/January 2001, pp 42–46.

[6] J Hampton, "CEO Steps Down in Clash of Personalities," *Canadian HR Reporter*, October 9, 2000, pp 1, 14.

[7] Adapted from L Smircich, "Concepts of Culture and Organizational Analysis," *Administrative Science Quarterly*, September 1983, pp 339–58.

[8] The 3M example was based on material contained in S Branch, "The 100 Best Companies to Work for in America," *Fortune*, January 11, 1999, pp 118–44; and D Anfuso, "3M's Staffing Strategy Promotes Productivity and Pride," *Personnel Journal*, February 1995, pp 28–34.

[9] J M Higgins, "Innovate or Evaporate: Seven Secrets of Innovative Corporations," *The Futurist*, September–October 1995, p 45.

[10] D Anfuso, "3M's Staffing Strategy Promotes Productivity and Pride," *Personnel Journal*, February 1995, pp 28–34.

[11] S Branch, "The 100 Best Companies to Work for in America," *Fortune*, January 11, 1999, pp 118–44.

[12] Results can be found in R Cooke and J Szumal, "Measuring Normative Beliefs and Shared Behavioral Expectations in Organizations: The Reliability and Validity of the Organizational Culture Inventory," *Psychological Reports*, June 1993, pp 1299–1330.

[13] Supportive results can be found in A Van Vianen, "Person-Organization Fit: The Match between Newcomers' and Recruiters' Preferences for Organizational Cultures," *Personnel Psychology*, Spring 2000, pp 113–50; and C Vandenberghe, "Organizational Culture, Person-Culture Fit, and Turnover: A Replication in the Health Care Industry," *Journal of Organizational Behavior*, March 1999, pp 175–84.

[14] The success rate of mergers is discussed in R J Grossman, "Irreconcilable Differences," *HR Magazine*, April 1999, pp 42–48.

[15] The mechanisms were based on material contained in E H Schein, "The Role of the Founder in Creating Organizational Culture," *Organizational Dynamics*, Summer 1983, pp 13–28.

[16] See the description in T Begley and D Boyd, "Articulating Corporate Values through Human Resource Policies," *Business Horizons*, July–August 2000, pp 8–12.

[17] The program is described in C Cole, "Eight Values Bring Unity to a Worldwide Company," *Workforce*, March 2001, pp 44–45.

[18] Excerpted from D Jones, "Welch: Nurture Best Workers, Lose Bottom 10%," *USA Today*, February 27, 2001, p 2B.

[19] See N M Tichy and C DeRose, "The Pepsi Challenge: Building a Leader-Driven Organization," *Training & Development*, May 1996, pp 58–66.

[20] J Van Maanen, "Breaking In: Socialization to Work," in *Handbook of Work, Organization, and Society*, ed R Dubin (Chicago: Rand-McNally, 1976), p 67.

[21] This definition is based on the network perspective of mentoring proposed by M Higgins and K Kram, "Reconceptualizing Mentoring at Work: A Developmental Network Perspective," *Academy of Management Review*, April 2001, pp 264–88.

[22] For an instructive capsule summary of the five different organizational socialization models, see J P Wanous, A E Reichers, and S D Malik, "Organizational Socialization and Group Development: Toward an Integrative Perspective," *Academy of Management Review*, October 1984, pp 670–83, Table 1. Also see D C Feldman, *Managing Careers in Organizations* (Glenview, IL: Scott, Foresman, 1988), ch 5.

[23] See L Eby, S McManus, S Simon, and J Russell, "The Protégé's Perspective Regarding Negative Mentoring Experiences: The Development of a Taxonomy," *Journal of Vocational Behavior*, August 2000, pp 1–21; and D Thomas, "The Truth about Mentoring Minorities: Race Matters," *Harvard Business Review*, April 2001, pp 99–107.

[24] Career functions are discussed in detail in K Kram, *Mentoring of Work: Developmental Relationships in Organizational Life* (Glenview, IL: Scott, Foresman, 1985).

[25] For a discussion of the practical guidelines for implementing mentoring programs, see K Tyler, "Mentoring Programs Link Employees and Experienced Execs," *HR Magazine*, April 1998, pp 99–103.

[26] See Y Kashima, "Conceptions of Culture and Person for Psychology," *Journal of Cross-Cultural Psychology*, January 2000, pp 14–32.

[27] See M Mendenhall, "A Painless Approach to Integrating 'International' into OB, HRM, and Management Courses," *Organizational Behavior Teaching Review*, no. 3 (1988–89), pp 23–27.

[28] See C L Sharma, "Ethnicity, National Integration, and Education in the Union of Soviet Socialist Republics," *The Journal of East and West Studies*, October 1989, pp 75–93; and R Brady and P Galuszka, "Shattered Dreams," *Business Week*, February 11, 1991, pp 38–42.

[29] J Main, "How to Go Global—And Why," *Fortune*, August 28, 1989, p 73.

[30] An excellent contrast between French and American values can be found in C Gouttefarde, "American Values in the French Workplace," *Business Horizons*, March–April 1996, pp 60–69.

[31] W D Marbach, "Quality: What Motivates American Workers?" *Business Week*, April 12, 1993, p 93.

[32] Excerpted from M L Alch, "Get Ready for the Net Generation," *Training & Development*, February 2000, pp 32, 34.

[33] F Horibe, "You Say Troublemaker, I Say Visionary," *Canadian HR Reporter*, October 8, 2001, p 20.

[34] For a thorough discussion of the model, see K Lewin, *Field Theory in Social Science* (New York: Harper & Row, 1951).

[35] C Goldwasser, "Benchmarking: People Make the Process," *Management Review*, June 1995, p 40.

[36] Excerpted from L Lavelle, "KPMG's Brave Leap into the Cold," *Business Week*, May 21, 2001, pp 72, 73.

[37] These errors are discussed by J P Kotter, "Leading Change: The Eight Steps to Transformation," in *The Leader's Change Handbook*, eds J A Conger, G M Spreitzer, and E E Lawler III (San Francisco: 1999), pp 87–99.

[38] The type of leadership needed during organizational change is discussed by J P Kotter, *Leading Change* (Boston: Harvard Business School Press, 1996); and B Ettorre, "Making Change," *Management Review*, January 1996, pp 13–18.

[39] M Beer and E Walton, "Developing the Competitive Organization: Interventions and Strategies," *American Psychologist*, February 1990, p 154.

[40] A historical overview of the field of OD can be found in G Farias and H Johnson, "Organizational Development and Change Management," *Journal of Applied Behavioral Science*, September 2000, pp 376–79.

[41] W W Burke, *Organization Development: A Normative View* (Reading, MA: Addison-Wesley, 1987), p 9.

[42] The importance of results-oriented change efforts is discussed by R J Schaffer and H A Thomson, "Successful Change Programs Begin with Results," *Harvard Business Review*, January–February 1992, pp 80–89.

[43] Adapted in part from B W Armentrout, "Have Your Plans for Change Had a Change of Plan?" *HRFOCUS*, January 1996, p 19; and A S Judson, *Changing Behavior in Organizations: Minimizing Resistance to Change* (Cambridge, MA: Blackwell, 1991).

[44] An individual's predisposition to change was investigated by C R Wanberg and J T Banas, "Predictors and Outcomes of Openness to Changes in a Reorganizing Workplace," *Journal of Applied Psychology*, February 2000, pp 132–42.

[45] See R Moss Kanter, "Managing Traumatic Change: Avoiding the 'Unlucky 13,'" *Management Review*, May 1987, pp 23–24.

[46] Readiness for change is discussed and investigated by L T Eby, D M Adams, J E A Russell, and S H Gaby, "Perceptions of Organizational Readiness for Change: Factors Related to Employee's Reactions to the Implementation of Team-Based Selling," *Human Relations*, March 2000, pp 419–42.

[47] For a discussion of how managers can reduce resistance to change by providing different explanations for an organizational change, see D M Rousseau and S A Tijoriwala, "What's a Good Reason to Change? Motivated Reasoning and Social Accounts in Promoting Organizational Change," *Journal of Applied Psychology*, August 1999, pp 514–28.

added-value negotiation Cooperatively developing multiple-deal packages while building a long-term relationship.

aggressive style Expressive and self-enhancing, but takes unfair advantage of others.

aided-analytic decision making Using tools to make decisions.

alternative dispute resolution (ADR) Avoiding costly lawsuits by resolving conflicts informally or through mediation or arbitration.

assertive style Expressive and self-enhancing, but does not take advantage of others.

attention Being consciously aware of something or someone.

attitude Learned predisposition toward a given object, person, or situation.

availability heuristic Tendency to base decisions on information readily available in memory.

benchmarking Process by which a company compares its performance with that of high-performing organizations.

bounded rationality Constraints that restrict decision making.

brainstorming Process to generate a quantity of ideas.

burnout A condition of emotional exhaustion and negative attitudes.

causal attributions Suspected or inferred causes of behaviour.

centralized decision making Top managers make all key decisions.

charismatic leadership Use of interpersonal attraction, or "charisma," to motivate employees to pursue organizational goals over self-interests.

closed system A relatively self-sufficient entity.

coalition Temporary groupings of people who actively pursue a single issue.

coercive power Obtaining compliance through threatened or actual punishment.

cognition A person's knowledge, opinions, or beliefs.

cognitive categories Mental depositories for storing information.

collaborative computing Using computer software and hardware to help people work better together.

communication Interpersonal exchange of information and understanding.

communication distortion Purposely modifying the content of a message.

conflict One party perceives its interests are being opposed or set back by another party.

consensus Presenting opinions and gaining agreement to support a decision.

consideration Creating mutual respect and trust with followers.

contingency approach Using management tools and techniques in a situationally-appropriate manner; avoiding the "one-best-way" mentality.

contingency approach to organization design Creating an effective organization–environment fit.

contingency factors Variables that influence the appropriateness of a leadership style.

continuous reinforcement Reinforcing every instance of a behaviour.

control strategy Coping strategy that directly confronts or solves problems.

coping Process of managing stress.

core job dimensions Job characteristics found to various degrees in all jobs.

creativity Process of developing something new or unique.

cross-functional teams Teams made up of technical specialists from different areas.

decentralized decision making Lower-level managers are empowered to make important decisions.

delegation Granting decision-making authority to people at lower levels.

delphi technique Process to generate ideas from physically dispersed experts.

devil's advocacy One individual is assigned to uncover and air all possible objections to a proposed course of action.

differentiation Division of labour and specialization that cause people to think and act differently.

distributive justice The perceived fairness of how resources and rewards are distributed.

diversity The host of individual differences that make people different from and similar to each other.

dysfunctional conflict Conflict that threatens an organization's interests.

e-business Running the *entire* business via the Internet.

emotional dissonance Conflict between organizationally desired and true emotions.

emotional intelligence The ability to recognize emotions in one's self and others, taking advantage of helpful ones and keeping control over destructive ones.

emotional labour Job requirement that employees must suppress felt emotions and display organizationally desired emotions during interpersonal transactions.

emotions Intense feelings in reaction to personal achievements and setbacks that may be felt and displayed.

employment equity Legislation intended to remove employment barriers and promote equality for the members of four designated groups—women, visible minorities, aboriginal people, and persons with disabilities.

empowerment Sharing varying degrees of power with lower-level employees to better serve the customer.

enacted values The values and norms that are exhibited by employees.

equity theory Holds that motivation is a function of fairness in social exchanges.

escalation of commitment Sticking to an ineffective course of action too long.

escape strategy Coping strategy that avoids or ignores stressors and problems.

espoused values The stated values and norms that are preferred by an organization.

ethics Study of moral issues and choices.

expectancy Belief that effort leads to a specific level of performance.

expectancy theory Holds that people are motivated to behave in ways that produce valued outcomes.

expert power Obtaining compliance through one's knowledge or information.

extinction Making behaviour occur less often by ignoring or not reinforcing it.

extranet Connects internal employees with selected customers, suppliers, and strategic partners.

extrinsic rewards Financial, material, or social rewards from the environment.

feedback Objective information about performance.

fight-or-flight response To either confront stressors or try to avoid them.

functional conflict Conflict that serves an organization's interests.

fundamental attribution bias Ignoring environmental factors that affect behaviour.

glass ceiling Invisible barrier blocking women and minorities from top management positions.

goal What an individual is trying to accomplish.

grapevine Unofficial communication system of the informal organization.

group Two or more freely interacting people with shared norms and goals and a common identity.

group cohesiveness   A "we feeling" binding group members together.

groupthink   A cohesive in-group's unwillingness to realistically view alternatives.

hardiness   Personality characteristic that neutralizes stress.

hierarchical communication   Exchange of information between managers and employees.

holistic wellness approach   Advocates personal responsibility in reducing stressors and stress.

hygiene factors   Job characteristics associated with job dissatisfaction.

impression management   Getting others to see us in a certain manner.

in-group exchange   A partnership characterized by mutual trust, respect, and liking.

initiating structure   Organizing and defining what group members should be doing.

instrumentality   A performance→ outcome perception.

integration   Cooperation among specialists to achieve common goals.

interactional justice   The perceived fairness of the decision maker's behaviour in the process of decision making.

intermittent reinforcement   Reinforcing some but not all instances of behaviour.

internal motivation   Motivation caused by positive internal feelings.

intranet   An organization's private Internet.

intrinsic rewards   Self-granted, rewards that come from within an individual.

job design   Changing the content and/or process of a specific job to increase job satisfaction and performance.

job enlargement   Putting more variety into a job.

job enrichment   Building achievement, recognition, stimulating work, responsibility, and advancement into a job.

job rotation   Moving employees from one specialized job to another.

job satisfaction   An attitude concerning one's job.

judgmental heuristics   Rules of thumb or shortcuts that people use to reduce information-processing demands.

leader trait   Personal characteristics that differentiate leaders from followers.

leadership   Influencing employees to voluntarily pursue organizational goals.

learned helplessness   Debilitating lack of faith in one's ability to control the situation.

legitimate power   Obtaining compliance through formal authority.

line managers   Have authority to make organizational decisions.

linguistic style   A person's typical speaking pattern.

listening   Actively decoding and interpreting verbal messages.

locus of control   Attributions regarding one's behaviour and its consequences to internal versus external factors.

maintenance role   Relationship-building group behaviour.

management   Process of working with and through others to achieve organizational objectives efficiently and ethically.

management by objectives   Management system incorporating participation in decision making, goal setting, and feedback.

managing diversity   Policies, activities, and organizational changes aimed at managing individual differences in order to enable all people to perform up to their maximum potential.

mechanistic organizations   Rigid, command-and-control bureaucracies.

media richness   The potential information-carrying capacity of a communication medium.

mentoring   Process of forming and maintaining developmental relationships between a mentor and a junior person.

motivation   Psychological processes that arouse and direct goal-directed behaviour.

motivators   Job characteristics associated with job satisfaction.

need for achievement   Desire to accomplish something difficult.

need for affiliation   Desire to spend time in social relationships and activities.

need for power   Desire to influence, coach, teach, or encourage others to achieve.

needs   Physiological or psychological deficiencies that arouse behaviour.

negative reinforcement   Making behaviour occur more often by contingently withdrawing something negative.

negotiation   Give-and-take process between conflicting interdependent parties.

noise   Interference with the transmission and understanding of a message.

nominal group technique   Process to generate ideas and evaluate and select solutions.

nonanalytic decision making   Using preformulated rules to make decisions.

nonassertive style   Timid and self-denying behaviour.

nonverbal communication   Messages sent outside of the written or spoken word.

norm   Shared attitudes, opinions, feelings, or actions that guide social behaviour.

open system   Organism that must constantly interact with its environment to survive.

operant behaviour   Learned, consequence-shaped behaviour.

optimizing   Choosing the best possible solution.

organic organizations   Fluid and flexible network of multitalented people.

organization   System of consciously coordinated activities of two or more people.

organization chart   Boxes-and-lines illustration showing chain of formal authority and division of labour.

organization development   A set of techniques or tools that are used to implement organizational change.

organizational behaviour   A field of study dedicated to better understanding and managing people at work, both individually and in groups.

organizational culture   Shared values, beliefs, and implicit assumptions that underlie a company's identity.

organizational ecology   The study of the effect of environmental factors on organizational success/failure and interrelationships among organizations.

organizational politics   Intentional enhancement of self-interest.

organizational socialization   Process by which employees learn an organization's values, norms, and required behaviours.

ostracism   Rejection by other group members.

out-group exchange   A partnership characterized by a lack of mutual trust, respect, and liking.

participative management   Involving employees in various forms of decision making.

perception   Process of interpreting one's environment.

personality   Stable physical and mental characteristics responsible for a person's identity.

personalized power   Directed at helping oneself.

positive reinforcement   Making behaviour occur more often by contingently presenting something positive.

procedural justice   The perceived fairness of the process and procedures used to make allocation decisions.

process-style listeners   Likes to discuss issues in detail.

punishment   Making behaviour occur less often by contingently presenting something negative or withdrawing something positive.

rational model   Logical four-step approach to decision making.

reasons-style listeners   Interested in hearing the rationale behind a message.

reciprocity   Widespread belief that people should be paid back for their positive and negative acts.

referent power   Obtaining compliance through charisma or personal attraction.

relaxation response   State of peacefulness.

representativeness heuristic   Tendency to assess the likelihood of an event occurring based on impressions about similar occurrences.

results-style listeners   Interested in hearing the bottom line or result of a message.

reward equality norm   Everyone should get the same rewards.

reward equity norm   Rewards should be tied to contributions.

reward need norm   Rewards should be tied to needs.

reward power   Obtaining compliance with promised or actual rewards.

role   Expected behaviours for a given position.

role ambiguity   An individual does not know what is expected of them.

role conflict   Other people having conflicting or inconsistent expectations of someone.

role overload   Other people's expectations of someone exceed that individual's ability.

satisficing   Choosing a solution that meets a minimum standard of acceptance.

self-concept   Person's self-perception as a physical, social, spiritual being.

self-efficacy   Belief in one's ability to do a task.

self-esteem   One's overall self-evaluation.

self-managed teams   Groups of employees granted administrative responsibility for their work.

self-monitoring   Observing one's own behaviour and adapting it to the situation.

self-serving bias   Taking more personal responsibility for success than failure.

servant-leadership   Focuses on increased service to others rather than to oneself.

shaping   Reinforcing closer and closer approximations to a target behaviour.

situational theories   Propose that leader styles should match the situation at hand.

social loafing   Decrease in individual effort as group size increases.

social power   Ability to get things done with human, informational, and material resources.

social support   Amount of helpfulness derived from social relationships.

socialized power   Directed at helping others.

societal culture   Socially derived, taken-for-granted assumptions about how to think and act.

span of control   The number of people reporting directly to a given manager.

staff managers   Provide research, advice, and recommendations to line managers.

stereotype   Beliefs about the characteristics of a group.

strategic constituency   Any group of people with a stake in the organization's operation or success.

stress   Behavioural, physical, or psychological response to stressors.

stressors   Environmental factors that produce stress.

superleader   Someone who leads others to lead themselves.

symptom management strategy Coping strategy that focuses on reducing the symptoms of stress.

task role   Task-oriented group behaviour.

team   Small group with complementary skills who hold themselves mutually

accountable for common purpose, goals, and approach.

telecommuting   Doing work that is generally performed in the office away from the office using different information technologies.

theory X   Negative, pessimistic assumptions about human nature and its effect on productivity.

theory Y   Positive assumptions about employees being responsible and creative.

360-degree feedback   Comparison of anonymous feedback from one's superior, subordinates, and peers with self-perceptions.

total quality management   An organizational culture dedicated to training, continuous improvement, and customer satisfaction.

transactional leadership   Focuses on interpersonal interactions between managers and employees.

transformational leadership   A leadership style involving the creation, communication, and modelling of a vision, and behaviours aimed at building commitment to the vision on the part of their followers.

trust   Reciprocal faith in others' intentions and behaviour.

type A behaviour pattern   Aggressively involved in a chronic, determined struggle to accomplish more in less time.

unaided-analytic decision making Analysis is limited to processing information in one's mind.

unity of command principle   Each employee should report to a single manager.

upward feedback   Employees evaluate their boss.

valence   The value of a reward or outcome.

values   Enduring belief in a mode of conduct or end-state.

virtual team   A physically dispersed task group that conducts its business through modern information technology.